FACTS & DATES OF AMERICAN SPORTS

FACTS & DATES OF AMERICAN SPORTS

Gorton Carruth
and Eugene Ehrlich

Introduction by Red Barber,
dean of American sportscasters

PERENNIAL LIBRARY

Harper & Row, Publishers, New York
Cambridge, Philadelphia, San Francisco, Washington
London, Mexico City, São Paulo, Singapore, Sydney

STAFF

Executive Editor	Raymond V. Hand, Jr.
Contributing Editors	Fon W. Boardman, Jr.
	David H. Scott
Managing Editor	Hayden Carruth
Copy Editor	Bruce Emmer
Computer Keyboarders	Antje L. Munroe
	Mary Racette
Researchers	David A. Graff
	Barbara Klein
Proofreader	Bob Brainerd
Indexers	Cynthia Crippen
	Alexandra C. Koppen

FIRST EDITION

Designed by C. Linda Dingler

Library of Congress Cataloging-in-Publication Data

Carruth, Gorton.
  Facts and dates of American sports.

  Includes index.
   1. Sports—United States—History.
2. Sports—United States—Records.
I. Ehrlich, Eugene H.   II. Title.
GV583.C37   1988   796'.0973   87-46126
ISBN 0-06-055124-0   88 89 90 91 92 RRD 10 9 8 7 6 5 4 3 2 1
ISBN 0-06-096271-2 (pbk.) 88 89 90 91 92 RRD 10 9 8 7 6 5 4 3 2 1

This book is dedicated to the
millions of loyal American fans
who enthusiastically follow
one or more of the many sports
we have included in
Facts and Dates of American Sports:
angling, archery, auto racing, badminton, ballooning, baseball,
basketball, bicycle racing, birling, bobsledding, bowling, boxing,
canoeing, court tennis, crew, cricket, croquet, curling, diving,
dog shows, dogsledding, equestrian events, fencing, field
hockey, figure skating, fishing, flying, football, Gaelic football,
gliding, golf, greyhound racing, gymnastics, handball, harness
racing, hoop rolling, horse racing, horseshoes, hunting, hurling,
iceboating, ice hockey, ice skating, jai alai, judo, karate,
kayaking, lacrosse, lawn bowls, logrolling, luge, motorcycling,
mountain climbing, Olympics, Pan American Games, polo,
power boating, quoits, racquets, rodeo, roller skating, rowing,
rugby, sculling, shuffleboard, skeet shooting, skiing, sky diving,
soccer, softball, squash racquets, squash tennis, surfing,
swimming, table tennis, target shooting, tennis, track and field,
trap shooting, volleyball, water polo, water skiing, weightlifting,
wrestling, and yachting.

Tables of Records and Statistics

Ten Memorable Sports Events

Biographies of Sports Greats

Introduction

This is truly a monumental book. It is an amazing book. The research is staggering. I just wish I had had this book during my years of broadcasting day by day at Cincinnati, at Brooklyn, and at Yankee Stadium.

The baseball announcer on radio has the never-ending problem of what to say between pitches, between plays, between outs and innings. It would have been wonderful when I was doing play-by-play to have daily looked into *Facts and Dates of American Sports* before going out to the ballpark. I trust that the fellows doing all sports today will use this book for their own education and for the enrichment of their listeners. History brings proportion to time.

I have felt that an educated person was one who knew what he didn't know, but knew where to go to find the answer. This is certainly true about sports. *Who, what, when,* and *where* are vital questions about our vast athletic canvas.

There are today many record books of our games that are most necessary. Such books usually are specialized and dated for a particular season. We do need them, however, and the rapid growth of sports literature shows how much the books are needed.

What Gorton Carruth and Eugene Ehrlich have done is to give us the entire sweep of our country's sports from colonial times on, recalling the careers of hundreds of outstanding athletes and many of the great moments in sports that fans will always treasure. They have given us facts, yes, and dates, yes, but they have also given us an overall view of the phenomenal growth of sports, its economics, its racing cars, its airplanes, its stadia, and many other facets of the incredible enterprise that is contemporary American sports.

The result is that every sports fan and sports trivia fan will find this book essential. But over and above the value of the up-to-date information in the book is the exciting reading it provides about our people and our athletes in the centuries of American life. Knowing the history of sports as told here gives us insight into ourselves.

We have dictionaries. We have other reference books on many subjects. Now we have *Facts and Dates of American Sports.*

As Casey Stengel (and he is in the book) would have said, it is an "amazing" book.

Red Barber
January 1988

1500-1699

1540 The **horse was first introduced** on a large scale into what is now the U.S. by Francisco Coronado, the Spanish explorer, who traveled through Kansas with 260 horses, most escaping to the Midwest, Mexico, and Canada. These animals eventually mingled with large French Norman horses brought to Canada by French settlers, producing the wild horses later found in North America.

1564 The **earliest hunting pictures** in what is now the U.S. were in Jacques le Moyne's account of the René de Laudonniére expedition. Some drawings showed Indians stalking deer under a deerskin, capturing alligators by ramming long poles down their throats, and fishing from pirogues, tree trunks hollowed out to make crude boats.

1585 The first eyewitness picture of **American Indians at play,** a drawing by John White, showed Indians participating in lacrosse, archery, foot racing, and pitching balls at a target on top of a high tree.

1611 The **abundance of game** in seventeenth-century Virginia was chronicled by Ralph Hamor in *A True Discourse of the Present Estate of Virginia,* published in London: "Bears, Deer, Beavers, Otter, Foxes, Racounes (almost as big as a Fox, as good meat as a lamb), Hares, wild cats, musk rats, Squirrels (flying and other sorts), and apossumes of the bignesse and likenesse of a Pigge of a month old. Eagles, wild Turkeys (much larger than our English), Cranes, Herons (white and ruesset), Hawks, wild pigeons (in winter beyond number or imagination, myself have seen three or four hours together flocks in the air, so thick that even they have shadowed the sky from us), Turkey Buzzards, Partridges, Snipers, Owls, Swans, Geese, Brants, Ducks, and Mallards, Divers, Shel Drakes, Cormorants, Teale, Widgeon, Curlews, Puits, besides other small birds, as, Blackbird, hedge sparrows, oxeies, woodpeckers, and in winter about Christmas many flocks of Parakertoths. . . ."

1611 May In Jamestown, Va., a **game of bowls** was played, the first recorded instance of such an event.

1621 Dec. 25 **Game playing** on Christmas Day by newcomers to the Plymouth colony was halted by Gov. William Bradford. The governor, scandalized at the settlers' playing of such games as "pitching the barr" and "stoole-ball," confiscated the equipment needed to play the games.

1650 The **first sporting dogs in America** were apparently a pack of foxhounds imported from England by Robert Brooke, a friend of Lord Baltimore of Maryland.

1650 Descriptions of **fox hunting** on the shores of Chesapeake Bay appeared in the press.

1652 A form of **miniature golf** appeared in New Netherland and became quite popular. A small ball was putted around a green by means of a crooked club.

1657 The first reference to **golf** in America was made in a complaint issued by the sheriff of Fort Orange, now Albany, N.Y., against three men for playing kolven on Sunday. Kolven is believed to have been an early form of golf, but it was not at all the same as the Scottish game. In 1659 the Fort Orange magistrates issued an order to "forbid all persons to play kolven in the streets."

1657 **Horse racing** within the city limits of New Amsterdam was forbidden by Peter Stuyvesant, governor of New Netherland.

1659 Sept. 30 The first indication of **tennis** play in America appeared in a proclamation issued by Gov. Peter Stuyvesant of New Netherland, forbidding it and other sports from being played during divine services. The form of tennis referred to was court tennis, widely played in France and England since the thirteenth century, first by striking a ball with the palm and later, in the sixteenth century, with a racket.

1664 The **first organized sport** in America, horse racing, began when New York's first governor, Richard Nicolls, established the Newmarket Course at Hempstead Plains, Long Island, instituted rules of racing, and offered prizes to winners. His purpose was to improve the breed of horses in the colonies.

1668 America's **first sports trophy,** a silver porringer, wrought by Pieter van Inburg, was presented to the winner of a horse race at the Newmarket Course at Hempstead Plains, Long Island.

1669 **Horse racing** was firmly established in New York when Gov. Francis Lovelace personally arranged a race for the silver crown at Newmarket Course at Hempstead Plains.

1670 The following **game** was available to hunters on Long Island, N.Y., a popular hunting area: "Deer, Bear, Wolves, Foxes, Racoon, Otters, Musquashes, and Skunks; Wild Fowl . . . Turkies, Heath Hen, Quailes, Partridges, Pigeon, Cranes, Geese of several sorts, Brants, Ducks, Widges, Teal, and divers others."

1673 Early **horse racing** in Virginia was strictly for aristocrats. James Bullock, a York County tailor, ran his mare against that of Mathew Slader for 200 lbs. of tobacco. When he tried to collect, the court fined him 100 lbs. of tobacco, declaring "racing to be a sport for gentlemen only."

1673 The appearance of a **fencing school** in Boston indicated increased interest in recreation in Puritan life.

1674 A rule against **horse racing** on public thoroughfares in the Plymouth colony stated that "whatsoever person ran a race with any horse in any street or common road should forfeit five shillings or sit in the stocks for one hour."

1693 The earliest description of **buffalo or bison hunting** in America appeared in French traveler Fr. Louis Hennepin's account of Louisiana. Coming upon a large group of buffalo, the Indians would surround them with a circle of grass fire, leaving a few openings where they waited to ambush the escaping animals.

1700-1749

1704 Reporting on **target shooting** in Connecticut, a travel writer, Mme. Sarah Knight, noted: "And on Training dayes the Youth divert themselves by Shooting at the Target, as they call it (but it very much resembles a pillory), when hee that hitts neerest the white has some yards of Red Ribbin presented him, which being tied to his hattband, the two ends streaming down his back, he is led away in Triumph, with great applause, as the winners of the Olympiack Games."

1705 Methods of **hunting** in the South were described in Robert Beverley's *History and Present State of Virginia:* Horses were taught to

walk quietly at their master's side when stalking game to keep him out of sight; rabbits were hunted with fast mongrel dogs, which caught them or forced them into a hollow tree; raccoons and opossums, hunted on foot with small dogs by the light of the moon, were treed, and agile lads climbed trees after them and shook them down; wolves were trapped; turkeys were shot or trapped.

1706 A **closed season on deer hunting** was established on Long Island, where continual hunting had almost eliminated this popular game.

1708 A **closed season,** Apr. 1 to July 31, was established on turkeys, heath hens, partridges, and quail in Kings, Queens, and Suffolk counties in New York.

1713 **Sleighing and coasting** by children in winter was suppressed by a New York City edict ordering the constable "to take any slee or slees from all and every such boys and girls rydeing or offering to ryde down any hill within ye said city and breake any slee or slees in pieces."

1714 Early interest in **lawn bowls** was indicated by an advertisement that appeared this year in the Boston *News Letter:* "The Bowling Green, formerly belonging to Mr. James Ivers, Cambridge Street, now belongs to Mr. Daniel Stevens, of the British Coffee House, where all gentlemen, merchants, and others, having a mind to recreate themselves, shall be accommodated."

1722 Apr. 30 The game of **billiards** was mentioned in the *New England Courant,* which reported that a public house in Charlestown, Mass., had set up tables for customers who wished "to Recreate themselves with a Game of Billiards."

1730 In order to improve **fox hunting** in the colonies, a Mr. Smith of Maryland imported a number of English red foxes and set them loose along the banks of the Chesapeake.

1732 The **first fishing club** in the American colonies, the Schuylkill Fishing Company, was formed at Philadelphia. A direct descendant of this club is the Fish House Club of Andalusia, Pa., a suburb of Philadelphia. Club membership is limited to 30, and the only club function is that of holding an annual meeting.

1732 In order to establish a **bowling green** in New York City, "a piece of land at the lower end of Broadway fronting to the fort" was leased to three well-known New Yorkers, John Chambers, Peter Bayard, and Peter Jay. The game to be played was lawn bowls, not tenpins. Popularity of the sport ended when the Revolution began, to be revived much later.

1734 The **first jockey club** in the world was formed as the South Carolina Jockey Club. It was disbanded in 1900.

1738 The State of Virginia banned the **taking of doe deer.**

1747 Thomas Lord Fairfax of Virginia imported a pack of **foxhounds** from England. George Washington hunted with this pack and later had foxhounds of his own. Biographer James T. Flexner wrote that the first president was "naturally gifted at riding to hounds."

1750-1774

1750 The flintlock **Kentucky rifle,** with an effective range of 200 yards, made largely by gunmakers of German extraction in Lancaster County, Pa., became the standard rifle for hunting and target shooting contests.

1750 A big **horse race** on the Newmarket Course on Hempstead Plains, Long Island, brought heavy business to the Brooklyn ferry, which carried more than 70 chairs and chaises and more than 1000 horses in one day.

1750 Col. Tasker of Belair, Md., imported **Selima,** daughter of Godolphin Arabian, one of the original thoroughbred horses. Selima became dam of several good American racers.

1751 According to the first newspaper account of a **cricket match** in the U.S., a team representing New York City defeated an eleven representing London by a score of 166 to 130.

1752 Col. Tasker's **Selima** defeated Col. Bird's Tyrall in a horse race in Maryland. Col. Tasker was so successful with the offspring of Selima that Maryland-bred horses were barred from Virginia Jockey Club purses for several years. The colonel then sent his horses to Virginia to foal and soon was winning again.

1754 In New York City John Rievers advertised

that he taught both **fencing** and dancing. His successor, W. C. Hulett, added violin and flute lessons, apparently necessary in order to make a living.

1757 **American Childers,** Lewis Morris's famous horse, won a race around Beaver Pond in Jamaica, Long Island.

1765-1775 **Horse racing** in Maryland entered its greatest period of fashion and popularity under Gov. Robert Eden. The racecourse at Annapolis, Md., was one of the best in the colonies.

1766 The **Gloucester Fox Hunting Club,** the first regularly organized fox-hunting group in America, was founded in Philadelphia. Most of its hunting was done across the Delaware R. in Gloucester County, N.J.

1766 Some **popular games** in New York City were suggested by James Rivington's advertisement that he imported "battledores, shuttlecocks, cricket balls, pellets, racquets for tennis and fives, and backgammon tables."

1767 Dec. 21 An incredible **hunting story,** and one of the earliest examples of the American tall tale, appeared in the Boston *Evening-Post.* It told of Josiah Prescott of Deerfield, Mass., who spied a moose 100 yards away and shot it dead. Immediately two more appeared and his aim was perfect; then another suffered the same fate. "One of the old ones was ten feet high and ten feet long; the other eight feet high and ten feet long. . . . After this extraordinary exploit was over, he was joined by a partner, who being at a little distance, heard the guns, came up to his assistance; and in going home he got help to dress the Mooses: A wild Cat they also killed on their return. This is a fact."

1774 **Bull baiting** was scheduled for every Thursday afternoon at 3 P.M. on Tower Hill in New York City, according to an advertisement.

1774 The Continental Congress proposed a **ban on frivolous activities** by colonials, including horse racing, cockfighting, gambling, and theatrical exhibitions, as an austerity measure during the political crisis with England. Opposition to these diversions persisted well after the end of the American Revolution.

1774 The **first hunting scene** engraved and published in the colonies appeared at the head of "The Hill Tops, A New Hunting Song," in the *Royal American Magazine* in Boston. The scene depicted the death of a stag.

1775-1799

1775 James Adair wrote a description of a **lacrosse** game played by Cherokee Indians in Florida. They used a deerskin ball stuffed hard with deer's hair and bats two ft. long with deerskin thongs. The game was usually played for high stakes between two large groups, equal in number, and the ball was kept in the air for long periods of time. The Indians were evidently very good at the game.

1779 **Sprint races,** a popular diversion of the lower and middle classes around Charlottesville, Va., were quarter-mile races between two horses of great speed. This was also called quarter-racing, according to Thomas Anbury, a British officer who distinguished between sprints and the two-, three-, and four-mile races held every spring and fall in the big towns of Richmond and Williamsburg. The latter races compared favorably with the big purse races held in England.

1779 Apr. 21 The availability of **golf equipment** was announced by James Rivington in his New York City *Gazette:* "To the GOLF PLAYERS: The Season for this pleasant and healthy Exercise now advancing, Gentlemen may be furnished with excellent CLUBS and the veritable Caledonian BALLS, by enquiring at the Printer's."

1780 Nov. Three days of **horse racing** on Hempstead Plains, Long Island, included a Gentleman's Purse, a Ladies' Subscription, and a race run by women riders. Gentlemen who were fond of fox hunting met daily at dawn at Loosely's King's Head Tavern.

1784 **Nocturnal deer hunting** in the Carolinas was made a misdemeanor because of the accidental slaughter of many domestic cows and horses.

1785 **George Washington retired from active hunting,** giving away his valuable kennel of hounds, which he had renewed after the American Revolution. Washington enjoyed riding to hounds and between 1783 and 1785 went on three hunts a week during the season.

1788 May A celebrated gray stallion, **Messenger,** believed to be the original sire of a fine breed of trotting horses, arrived from England. The line established by Messenger was so successful that upon the death of the horse, it was buried with military honors on Jan. 8, 1808.

1790 Followers of **horse racing** began to take an interest in the breeding of horses. Belair, Gimcrack, and Calypso, the offspring of Medley, an earlier champion, won repeatedly at races.

1793 A reference to **golf** appeared in the *South Carolina and Georgia Almanac,* which noted: "Golf Club formed 1786." The officers were listed, but nothing was said about playing the game.

1793 **Horse racing in public thoroughfares** in Lexington, Ky., was outlawed by the town's trustees. Such races had been frightening pedestrians.

1793 Jan. 9 The **first hot-air balloon flight in the U.S.** lifted off in Philadelphia, with Jean-Pierre Blanchard of France as the balloonist. His launching site was a prison yard, to which he charged $5 admission. He took in only $405. Among the spectators were Pres. George Washington, Thomas Jefferson, James Madison, and James Monroe. Blanchard and his small black dog were in the air for 46 min. and traveled 15 mi., landing in Deptford Township, N.J.

1795 Oct. 13 An advertisement concerning a **golf club** appeared in the Charleston, S.C., *City Gazette:* "Notice—The anniversary of the Golf Club will be held on Sat. next, at the Club House, Harleston's Green, where members are requested to attend at one o'clock." Somewhat similar notices appeared in Oct. 1796 and on Oct. 12, 1797, the latter referring to the South Carolina Golf Club, but no mention was made of playing golf.

1796 The popularity of **billiards** in the South was noted by Francis Baily, the English astronomer, who began a two-year, 2000-mi. tour of the U.S. this year. Baily observed that there were a dozen billiard tables in Norfolk, Va., alone. His narrative, *Journal of a Tour in Unsettled Parts of North America in 1796 and 1797,* was published in 1856.

1796 May Reporting on **squirrel hunting,** the *Kentucky Gazette* said a group of hunters had "rendezvoused at Irvine's Lick and produced seven thousand nine hundred and forty-one Squirrels killed by them in one day."

1797 June 2 An **early American mountaineer** was Charles Broadhead, who, with a survey party, made the first ascent of Giant Mountain (4622 ft.) in the Adirondack Mts. of New York State.

1798 The **breeding of horses** in the U.S. began in earnest. This year Diomed, the great English champion that had won the Epsom Derby in 1780, was brought to the U.S. by Col. John Hoomes of Virginia. Diomed sired many famous American horses, including Eclipse and Lexington.

1798 A large **hawk shot in Yorkshire,** the *Sporting Magazine* of England reported, had attached to its leg a brass band inscribed, "Belonging to the Governor of New Halifax, America, A.D. 1762."

1800-1819

1800 **Gouging,** a popular frontier sport, reached its peak of popularity in the Ohio R. Valley. The ultimate goal was to gouge out an opponent's eye with the thumbnail. Thumbnails were grown long for this purpose. This style of fighting was imported from England into the South and spread westward.

1802 **Public horse racing** was forbidden by a New York State law. Racing was conducted by several private organizations, so-called jockey clubs.

1802 **Expectation,** a powerful horse owned by Colonel Tayloe, won a sweepstakes race at Richmond, Va., doing 2 mi. in 3:47. After the race, Expectation was sold to Colonel Alston for $4000.

1803 A sketch made this year showed a game of **tenpin bowling** in progress in Suffolk County, N.Y., attesting to its early popularity.

1803 The racehorse **Peacemaking,** by running 2 mi. in 3:54, set a record that was to stand for 30 years.

1806 The first picture of a soccer-type **football**

Golf matches are not won on the fairways or greens. They are won on the tee—the first tee.

Old golf saying

game in America showed college president Timothy Dwight watching Yale students kicking a ball. According to Yale tradition, the game of football had been played there for 45 years. The modern American game of football, however, did not begin to develop until about 1869.

1806 June 5 A new **trotting record** was established at Harlem, N.Y., when the horse Yankee trotted a mile in 2:59, becoming the first trotter to break the 3-min. mile.

1810 Dec. 10 The first unofficial **heavyweight champion** of the U.S., Tom Molineaux, a freed slave from Virginia, was beaten in the 40th round by Tom Cribb, the English champion, in a boxing match at Copthall Common, London.

1811 The first noteworthy **rowing race** in the U.S. was between two four-oared barges. *Knickerbocker* of New York City defeated *Invincible* of Long Island for a wager in a well-publicized race that attracted thousands of spectators. The boats started at Harsimus, N.J., and finished at New York City's Battery.

1811 Sept. 28 In a **heavyweight boxing rematch** between Tom Cribb and Tom Molineaux, at Wymondham, England, Cribb, the English champion, was declared the victor in the 11th round after having broken Molineaux's jaw in the tenth. About 40,000 persons watched the bout, a record at the time.

1811 Dec. The **Savannah, Ga., Golf Club** invited its members to a social affair on the 13th. A similar notice appeared on Jan. 7, 1820, but no mention was made of playing the game.

1816 A new **mile record in horse racing** was set by Timoleon. The time was 1:47.

1816 The **first recorded boxing champion** in America was Jacob Hyer. In a grudge match billed as a "pugilistic encounter," Hyer beat Tom Beasley in a bare-knuckles contest under London Prize Ring rules. Hyer then designated himself "America's first champion" and retired. The record books have accepted his self-designation.

1819 June 1 A noted European **tightrope performer,** Mme. Adolphe, made her American debut at the Anthony Street Theater, New York City.

1820-1829

1820 Early missionaries in Hawaii **banned surfing** as immodest and a waste of time. Surfing began to become popular again at Waikiki in 1895.

1820 During this decade the **first soccerlike games** appeared in American colleges. A large round ball was kicked toward a goal. The game served as a form of hazing, especially at Yale and Harvard. Sophomores and freshmen were supposed to kick the ball, but sophomores generally kicked freshmen instead. The games were banned during the 1830s because of the large number of injuries sustained by students.

1820 July 15 The summit of **Pikes Peak** in Colorado was reached for the first time. The leader of the expedition that scaled the 14,110-ft. high mountain was Edwin James. The man for whom the peak is named, Zebulon M. Pike, explorer and U.S. Army officer, tried to climb it in 1806, when he discovered it, but failed.

1821 Laws against **public horse racing** were relaxed in New York, permitting tracks to open in Queens County. This led to the building of the Union Course on Long Island.

1822 The primitive U.S. form of **football** was prohibited at Yale College by Pres. Timothy Dwight, who ordered any violations to be reported and violators to be penalized by a fine not to exceed half a dollar.

1823 May The **first major horse race** in the U.S. was between American Eclipse from the North and the challenger Sir Henry from the South for a purse of $20,000. About 100,000 spectators jammed the Union Course on Long Island to see American Eclipse take two out of three heats, doing the 4-mi. in 7:49 and 8:24. The victory of the northern horse spread gloom in the South.

1824 A **boat race** in New York harbor for a purse of $1000 attracted an estimated crowd of 50,-000. The crew of the victorious craft, *Whitehall*, became civic heroes and received a tumultuous ovation on their appearance at the Park Theater in New York City.

1825 The **New York Trotting Club** was organized. It constructed a race course on Long Island, the first specially devoted to trotting.

1825 The **first gymnastic program** in the U.S.

was established at the Round Hill School in Northampton, Mass., by Charles Beck, an ordained Lutheran clergyman, who had been forced to flee Germany, his homeland, because of his liberal political views. He was also a follower of Friedrich Ludwig Jahn, who in 1811 opened in Berlin the first *Turnplatz,* which attracted 500 or so young men to take part in gymnastic exercises. Beck translated Jahn's book *Deutsche Turnkunst* into English. At Northampton the term *gymnasium* was applied to the program of exercise, not a building, since the activities were conducted outdoors.

1825 Summer   American Star, champion racer of rowboats in New York harbor, rowed against *Sudden Death,* a gig from the British frigate *Hussar,* for a side bet of $1000. The race was from Bedloe's Island, up the Hudson R. to Hoboken, N.J., and back to the Battery at the foot of Manhattan Island. *American Star* won by 400 yards as a large crowd watched.

1826 The **first gymnastics program in an American college** was begun at Harvard under the direction of Charles Follen. Born in Germany, Follen had been a follower of Friedrich Ludwig Jahn, a German pioneer of organized gymnastics, and had fled to the U.S. because his liberal political views were unwelcome in Germany.

1827 The ***American Shooter's Manual*** was published in Philadelphia. It treated the new sport of shooting birds on the wing, offering much practical advice.

1827 July 23 The **first swimming school** in the U.S. opened in Boston. Swimming was taught by placing a belt "around the bodies, under the arms, attached to a rope and pole, by which the head and body are kept in the proper position in the water, while the pupil is learning the use of his limbs." The school was attended by many notables, including John James Audubon and John Quincy Adams. Adams is reputed to have done some diving from the 6-ft. board when he was 61 years old.

1828 America's **first archery club** was formed by a group of famous artists. The United Bowmen of Philadelphia was formally organized by Franklin Peale, Titian Ramsey Peale, Samuel P. Griffith, Jr., Thomas Sully, and others. The initiation fee was $5 and dues 50 cents a month. Members wore Lincoln green frock coats with gold trim and broad straw hats decorated with three black ostrich plumes. The club held annual tournaments and awarded silver trophies until it disbanded in 1859. It was the forerunner of the National Archery Association, founded in 1879. The National Field Archery Association was founded in 1939.

1829 The **first sports magazine in the U.S.** began publication. It was the *American Turf Register* and *Sporting Magazine.* The founder was John Stuart Skinner in Baltimore. The magazine was devoted to the improvement of thoroughbred horses, racing, hunting, shooting, fishing, and the habits of American game.

1829 Nov. 13 **Sam Patch,** a high diver, died in a 125-ft. dive into the Genesee Falls. His body was found months later at the river's mouth. Patch had earlier made a dive of 80 to 90 ft. from the Passaic River's Chasm Bridge, a Niagara Falls jump from Goat Island, and many leaps and dives from cliffs, masts, and other bridges.

1830-1839

1830 An early form of **trapshooting** was introduced into the U.S. from England by Cincinnati sportsmen. Live pigeons were used in shoots at the Sportsmen's Club.

1830 **Town ball,** based on the English game of rounders, became popular in New England. There were several teams in Boston.

1830 A **1000-mi. walk** taking 18 days was completed by Joshua Newsam of Philadelphia.

1830 Feb. 11 The continued appeal of **cock fighting** was indicated by a great series of fights held in Harrisburg, Pa., in which $100 was put up for each fight.

1830 Sept. 9 The **first professional American balloonist,** Charles Ferson Durant, made the first of his 12 ascents over a period of four years. With 30,000 spectators on hand, he took off from Castle Garden, New York City, floated over Staten Island, and landed in South Amboy, N.J., traveling 30 mi. in 1 hr., 20 min.

1830 Sept. 18 A celebrated **race between horse and steam** was won by the horse over the *Tom Thumb,* the first locomotive built in America. During the race the locomotive pulled 40 pass-

engers over a 9-mi. course from Riley's Tavern to Baltimore. Mechanical failure, ever the plague of railroads, caused *Tom Thumb*'s poor showing. The engine sprang a leak in the boiler and failed to finish the course.

1831 Dec. 10 A popular weekly **racing sheet,** *Spirit of the Times,* founded by William Trotter Porter, began publication. Its stated purpose was to raise the reputation of horse racing and other sports.

1832 The **Philadelphia Union Cricket Club** was formed.

1832 The **first sports editor** in the U.S. was William Trotter Porter. He was given that position and title after he sold his newspaper, *Spirit of the Times,* to *The Traveller.*

1832 **Calisthenics** was prescribed for urban women in *Atkinson's Casket.* The suggestion reflected a growing fear of the physical deterioration of city dwellers. Illustrated exercises stressed muscular development of the arms and shoulders and, above all, the back.

1832 Jan. 2 The **first curling club in the U.S.,** the Orchard Lake Curling Club, was organized by a group of Scottish immigrants. Having been wrecked on the shores of Lake St. Clair, they decided to settle at Orchard Lake, Mich. The first game was played on Jan. 7, with the players using hickory blocks. In the ensuing years other curling clubs were organized, all led by Scottish enthusiasts, in Milwaukee (1845), Chicago (1854), Philadelphia (1855), New York and Boston-New England (1856), and Detroit (1865).

1833 The promotion of **fly-fishing** highlighted the angler's year. Jerome Van Crowninshield Smith's *Fishes of Massachusetts* reported that the angler "enjoys the sport and exults in its success, according as it requires an exertion of his skill. . . . There are not only individuals of whom we speak, but others who availing themselves of all the information to be acquired from books and experience, are fully aware that fly-fishing is the perfection of angling."

1833 A rudimentary form of **baseball** was played in Philadelphia by the Olympic Ball Club. Home plate was situated between two bases. As in cricket, a ball hit behind the batter was considered a hit, and runners struck by the ball were out.

1834 The **Castle Garden Amateur Boat Club Association,** the first organization of its kind in

America, was founded. It had a boathouse at Castle Garden, New York City, for its nine member clubs. The association was intended for "young men of the highest respectability, who were determined to combine pleasure with the utmost propriety of conduct." The association held annual regattas until 1842.

1834 In **horse racing,** hurdles were introduced in a race at Washington, D.C., perhaps for the first time in the U.S. Six fences were placed at intervals over the 1-mi. course. The winner was awarded a plate valued at £100.

1834 Rules for a game called **baseball** appeared in *The Book of Sports* by Robin Carver. However, the rules were for a game known to Englishmen as *rounders* and were copied from an English book. Rounders bore little resemblance to American baseball.

1835 The **first British boxing champion to visit America** was James Burke, a deaf-mute. He fought Jim O'Rourke in a ring set up near New Orleans. The bout ended after three rounds, when a riot broke out. Burke later knocked out Tom O'Connell in 10 min. in a bout held near Hart's Island, N.Y.

1835 A well publicized **10-mi. foot race** at Union Course, Long Island, N.Y., was watched by nearly 30,000 spectators. The offer of $1000 to any man who could run 10 mi. in less than an hour drew nine contestants. Henry Stannard of Killingworth, Conn., won. He covered the first mile in 5:36, the last mile in 5:54, and the entire course in 59:44. At the conclusion of the race, amid great jubilation, Stannard leaped on a horse and triumphantly retraced his winning course.

1836 In **horse racing,** the South made up for its loss to the North in 1823 in a return race at the

Union Course on Long Island. The southern horse, John Bascombe, defeated Post Boy, taking both heats of a 4-mi. race in 7:49 and 7:51½.

1836 Feb. 25 **Samuel Colt** secured his first U.S. patent for his revolving barrel multishot firearm. In 1842 he lost his business and his patents but regained them in 1846, aided by a federal government order for 1000 revolvers.

1837 **Horseback riding for women** was characterized in Donald Walker's *Exercises for Ladies.* Walker held that horseback riding tended to consolidate unnaturally the bones of the lower part of the body, causing difficulties in the performance of unspecified future womanly duties.

1837 Aug. 5 The **first ascent of Mt. Marcy,** at 5344 ft. the highest mountain in the Adirondacks, New York State, was made by a party of 15 climbers, including three guides.

1838 The **oldest existing boat club** in the U.S., the Narragansett Boat Club of Providence, R.I., was founded.

1838 **Hooprolling** on the Washington Parade Ground was a new craze among the ladies of New York City.

1839 Feb. 18 The **oldest existing yacht club** in the U.S., the Detroit Boat Club, was formed. The earliest to be formed was the Knickerbocker Boat Club, New York City. It disbanded a year after its founding in 1811.

1840-1849

1840 **Birling,** or logrolling, became a popular wagering sport at the lumber camps in the northern states and Canada. In this sport, two contestants on a floating log spin the log with their feet in order to make their opponent fall into the water.

1840 The **first international cricket match** in which a U.S. team participated took place in Toronto, Canada, where an underrated New York club beat the Toronto club by one goal. Stakes for the match were $500 a side.

1841 The unofficial **boxing championship** was claimed by Tom Hyer, son of the previous

There was ease in Casey's manner as he stepped into his place;
There was pride in Casey's bearing, and a smile on Casey's face.
And when, responding to the cheers, he lightly doffed his hat,
No stranger in the crowd could doubt 'twas Casey at the bat.

Ernest Lawrence Thayer, "Casey at the Bat"

claimant, Jacob Hyer. Young Tom was challenged by John McCluster. Hyer, who weighed 205 lbs., defeated McCluster in short order.

1842 May 20 A large crowd witnessed an **intersectional horse race** at the Union Course on Long Island, N.Y. The entry from the South, Fashion, and the entry from the North, Boston, raced for a purse of $20,000, with Fashion winning in a record for the 4-mi. course of 7 min., 32 sec. In 1845 Fashion raced another southern horse, Peytona, from Alabama, on the same course. Peytona won.

1844 In Hoboken, N.J., a **10-mi. foot race** was won by John Gildersleeve, of New York, who defeated several British entrants with a time of 57 min., 1½ sec. He won $1000 and was watched by an unruly crowd of 25,000. At this time professional runners, called pedestrians, were popular because their races provided an excellent opportunity for betting.

1844 July 29 The **New York Yacht Club** was founded aboard the schooner *Gimcrack,* docked off the Battery. John C. Stevens was elected commodore. The club held its first regatta on July 16, 1845. On Oct. 10, 1846, it held its first race over an ocean course, outside New York harbor. The schooner *Coquette* defeated Stevens's sloop *Maria.*

1845 **Baseball** took a giant step toward the modern game when Alexander J. Cartwright, a New York City fireman, drew up a set of rules and organized the first baseball club, the Knickerbockers. Other clubs were formed and adopted Cartwright's rules. Cartwright fixed four as the number of bases, not two, three, or five; set them 90 ft. apart; placed the batter in a box at home plate, not at some distance from it; made the bases flat; and ruled out "plugging" a base runner with a thrown ball to put him out.

1846 The **first seasonal hunting regulation** in the U.S. was passed by the state of Rhode Island. The intent was to protect waterfowl during spring hunting.

1846 June 19 The **first recorded baseball game** resembling the modern sport was played at Elysian Field, Hoboken, N.J., between the New York Club and the Knickerbockers. The New York Club won 23-1. Davis, its pitcher, was fined 6 cents for swearing at the umpire. Alexander J. Cartwright, founder of the Knickerbockers, had written the rules under which the game was played.

1847 After **hunting buffalo** in the valley of the Yellowstone R., an English sportsman wrote: "Holding our loaded guns in rest, we started at full speed toward the herd. Away went the huge mass raising a whirl of dust over the plain, followed by us in hot pursuit. We soon overhauled them, and continued loading and firing away into the herd. . . . Buffalo hunting is a noble sport, the animal being swift enough to give a good horse enough to do to close with him. Wheeling around with such quickness as to baffle both horse and rider for several turns before there is any certainty of bringing him down. Added to which, there is the danger of being charged by one old bull while in pursuit of another." European as well as American hunters joined in the slaughter of the bison on the Great Plains; by the end of the nineteenth century the

WILLIAM MULDOON

b. Belfast, N.Y., May 25, 1845
d. Purchase, N.Y., June 3, 1933

A Civil War veteran, policeman, saloon keeper, state boxing commissioner, health farm proprietor, and wrestler, William Muldoon had a varied career but is now chiefly remembered as an outstanding athlete of the nineteenth century. Enlisting in the Army when only 16, Muldoon served throughout the Civil War. As a member of the New York City Police Department from 1876 to 1882, he helped organize the Police Athletic League.

Taking up professional wrestling, Muldoon won the Greco-Roman title in 1880. His most notable match came in 1883, in an 8-hour struggle with Clarence Whistler, the leading contender for the championship. It ended in a draw. Twice more these two wrestled to a draw.

Muldoon retired from wrestling in 1908. Earlier he had appeared on the stage in *As You Like It* and had also toured the country with John L. Sullivan, the heavyweight boxing champion. He opened a health resort on his estate in Westchester County, New York, and in 1921, when New York State legalized boxing, Muldoon became chairman of the state boxing commission, a position he held until 1923.

bison was almost extinct, with only a small proportion having been used efficiently for food. At the start of that century, there had been about 60,000,000 of them.

1848 E. W. Bushnell of Philadelphia introduced the **all-iron skate,** which was attached to the boot by clamps. His skates replaced clumsy earlier ones made usually from wood and iron or from bone.

1848 The first mention of **greyhound coursing** in the U.S. appeared in a book titled *Oregon and California in 1848,* which described a greyhound-antelope race.

1848 **Baseball rules** were altered to provide that a runner was out at first base if the ball was held by a fielder on the bag before the runner could reach first base.

1848 Nov. 21 The Cincinnati *Turngemeinde,* the **oldest turnverein** in the U.S., was founded. The New York *Turngemeinde* was founded later the same year, and the Philadelphia *Turngemeinde* on May 15, 1849. By mid-1850 there were six such societies.

1849 Feb. 7 **Tom Hyer,** unofficial American heavyweight bare-knuckle boxing champion, met Yankee Sullivan, an Englishman who was touring the country, and knocked him out in 16 rounds. This was Hyer's last fight, for no one else challenged him.

1849 May 5 The most famous standardbred horse of all, **Hambletonian,** was foaled at Chester, N.Y., and became the property of William Rysdyck. Hambletonian never raced but became the "great father" of the modern standardbred, siring 1331 foals between 1851 and 1875. More than 95% of today's standardbreds trace their ancestry to Hambletonian.

1850-1854

1850 The **first ski clubs** in the U.S. were formed in the 1850s by Scandinavian gold miners in California, but the honor of being the first club is a matter of controversy. The Alturas Ski Club of LaPorte, Calif., was active from 1858 to 1867.

1850 The **first racquets court** of record in the U.S. was built in the Broadway Racquet Club, New York City.

1850 Oct. 4-5 The **first national turner organization,** the Turnerbund, was established by six gymnastic societies at a meeting in Philadelphia.

1851 A **sculling match** that excited much popular interest in New York City took place around Bedloe's Island. The contestants were William Decker and James Lee. A crowd, betting heavily, gathered at the Battery and saw Decker win by 300 yards.

1851 June 3 The **first baseball uniforms** were worn by the New York Knickerbockers. The outfits consisted of straw hats, white shirts, and blue full-length trousers.

1852 **Croquet was introduced to the U.S.** from England, according to the United States Croquet Association. Most sources, however, find it was not brought to America before about 1870. In any event, it quickly became popular. It was the first outdoor organized athletic activity in which women participated. More important, it could be played by men and women together. As a result, it became as much a social as an athletic activity and afforded a pleasant opportunity for courting. The vogue for the game later became so great that croquet sets with sockets for candles for night playing were introduced.

1852 Aug. 3 The **first intercollegiate rowing race** was conducted by Harvard and Yale, whose crews rowed a 2-mi. course on Lake Winnipesaukee, N.H. Harvard won by four lengths.

1853 The first club to sponsor the Irish national game of **hurling** in the U.S. was formed in San Francisco. Four years later, the Irish Hurling and Football Club was organized in New York City, and in 1879 the Irish Athletic Club introduced hurling to Boston.

1853 A club in Upperville, Va., claims to have held the **first horse show** in the U.S. This claim is disputed by clubs in Lakeside, Conn., and Springfield, Mass. There is a drawing dated Nov. 12, 1853, of a horse show in progress at Springfield.

1853 The celebrated New York-Brooklyn **baseball rivalry** began when an all-New York team defeated an all-Brooklyn team two games to one in a best-of-three series.

1853 The **first newspaper story on baseball**

was published in the New York *Mercury*. The report was by Sen. William Cauldwell, the newspaper's owner and editor.

1853 Oct. 12 The **heavyweight boxing championship** was decided on a technicality. John C. Morrissey, claiming the title vacated by Tom Hyer, was losing to challenger Yankee Sullivan. But between the 36th and 37th rounds, Sullivan left the ring to slug a few Morrissey supporters who had heckled him. He failed to get back into the ring to answer the bell for the next round, and the referee awarded the decision to Morrissey.

1854 The trotting horse **Flora Temple** broke all records by running the mile at Kalamazoo, Mich., in 2:19½—the first time a horse had run a mile faster than 2:20. The news, flashed immediately throughout the nation by telegraph, made Flora Temple a national celebrity.

1854 **Baseball rules** stipulated the exact weight and size of the baseball for the first time. The ball had to weigh between 5½ and 6 oz. and have a diameter of between 2¾ in. and 3½ in.

1854 Growing **interest in baseball** in New York City was evidenced by the establishment of many clubs, including the Eagle and the Empire of New York City and the Excelsior of Brooklyn. By 1855 Morrisania, in The Bronx, had the Union Club, and Brooklyn had added the Atlantic and the Eckford.

1855-1859

1855 The vogue for **horseback riding** among American ladies was now widespread. In Boston and New York City, numerous riding academies were set up to help women adjust to side-saddle riding. A newspaper editorial commented: "A lot of cynical old fogies ... have recently been startled ... by the rushing, galloping, slashing, and dashing exploits of the lady equestrians at the agricultural fairs. This jocund spectacle like everything else that is new ... does not suit the still veins of these respectable old goats. ... But still the ladies go on riding."

1855 July 21 A **crew race** between Harvard and Yale featured two entries from each school and crews of different sizes. Harvard entered an eight-man crew, which won, and another of four oars, which came in second. Yale's two six-oared crews lost.

1856 By 1856 **baseball** was already considered a national pastime, as evidenced by the following passage from the sporting paper *Spirit of the Times*: "With the fall of the leaf and the diminution of the daylight, many of the out-of-door sports and pastimes come to a close for the season. The manly and exhilarating pastimes of Base Ball, Cricket, Foot Ball, and Racket are not playable. ... We feel a degree of old Knickerbocker pride at the continued prevalence of Base Ball as the National game in the region of the Manhattanese."

1857 A **sliding seat for a single scull** was first used by its inventor, J. C. Babcock, of the Nassau Boat Club of New York City. He abandoned the idea, as did Walter Brown, who tried the scheme in 1861. In 1870, Babcock took out a patent for a sliding seat in a six-oared shell. This seat traveled about 10 to 12 in., compared with today's 28 to 33 in.

1857 The **first baseball association** was formed. Some 25 amateur baseball clubs agreed to meet in 1858 and establish themselves as the National Association of Baseball Players. Within two years the association had doubled in size.

1857 A new **baseball rule** fixed the length of a game at nine innings and provided that an interrupted game would be regarded as completed after five innings.

1857 The **America's Cup,** won in England in 1851 by the U.S. schooner-yacht *America,* was presented to the New York Yacht Club by members who owned *America:* J. C. Stevens, Edwin A. Stevens, Hamilton Wilkes, J. Beekman Finley, and George L. Schuyler. The gift stipulated that the cup be used perpetually as a trophy in international challenge yacht races.

1857 The **first U.S. horse to race in Europe,** Prioress, owned by Richard Ten Broeck, won the English Cesarewitch Handicap. The race ended in a dead heat; Prioress won a runoff against El Hakim and Queen Bess at the end of the day's program. The time for the 2-mi., 468-yard course was 4¼ min.

1857 Oct. 6 The **American Chess Association** was organized at the first American Chess Con-

"OLD HOSS" RADBOURN

Charles Gardner Radbourn
b. Rochester, N.Y., Dec. 11, 1854
d. Bloomington, Ill., Feb. 5, 1897

In an early period of professional baseball that is now almost legendary, Old Hoss Radbourn was surely a legendary figure. In 1884, when pitching for the Providence Grays, he won 60 games, a figure no other pitcher has ever approached, while losing only 12. In that season, he pitched a total of 672 innings, the equivalent of almost 75 nine-inning games. A modern pitcher who tried to match that feat would have to pitch almost every other game during an entire season. In 1883, Radbourn won 49 games.

At the end of the 1884 season, the Grays and the New York Metropolitans played for the championship of the American Association. Radbourn pitched three times and won three games on three successive days to win the title for his team.

Radbourn played for Buffalo, Boston, and Cincinnati as well as Providence. He won 308 games in all, becoming one of only 19 pitchers ever to win 300 or more games, and lost 191 for a .617 percentage. His career earned run average was 2.67. He had 35 shutouts, 11 of them in 1884, and struck out 1830 batters while giving up only 875 bases on balls. Radbourn was chosen for the Baseball Hall of Fame in 1939.

gress, held in New York City. There Paul C. Morphy, a 20-year-old chess wizard from New Orleans, won the American championship. Morphy toured Europe in 1858 and 1859, defeating all the masters who would meet him. Although he played only sporadically thereafter, Morphy was recognized as the first American international chess master.

1858 The **Schuylkill Navy,** an association of nine rowing clubs, was organized in Philadelphia. It hailed itself as "the oldest governing body of amateur athletes in America." The first regatta for amateur oarsmen was held under its auspices on the Schuylkill R. in 1872, and for many years this was the center of rowing in the U.S.

1858 The first meeting of the **National Association of Baseball Players** was held. The association adopted, with a few changes, rules created by the New York Knickerbocker Baseball Club, including standardized measurements for the ball and bat and for the distance between bases. Many of these rules are still in force today.

1858 Apr. 12 The **first U.S. billiards championship** was held at Fireman's Hall in Detroit. Michael J. Phelan defeated John Seereiter in a match lasting 9½ hrs. The 2000-point match was played for a $15,000 stake and was four-ball carom on a six-pocket table. The match was witnessed by a "genteel" audience that included a few ladies.

1858 July 20 The **first admission charge to a baseball game,** 50 cents, was levied for the contest between Brooklyn and the New York All-Stars at Fashion Race Course on Long Island. About 1500 spectators watched New York defeat Brooklyn 22-18.

1859 The earliest newspaper report of an organized **Gaelic football** team appeared in New Orleans. A game was promoted there by Irish fire companies. In 1899 the Dunn Trophy was donated to the Greater New York Irish-American Athletic Association to encourage Gaelic football.

1859 June 30 **Niagara Falls was crossed by a tightrope walker,** Charles Blondin. In 5 min. the sensational Frenchman, watched by 25,000 spectators, passed across a cable 1100 ft. long and 160 ft. above the seething water. In later performances Blondin made the same crossing blindfolded, pushing a wheelbarrow (July 4); carrying a man on his back (Aug. 19); and walking on stilts (Sept. 14, 1860). At age 72, in 1888, Blondin was still thrilling crowds in the U.S. and abroad with his high-wire skills.

1859 July 1 A **distance record for balloon flights** was set by four men who started out

There has never been a great athlete who did not know what pain is.

Bill Bradley

JOHN L. SULLIVAN

John Lawrence Sullivan
b.   Roxbury, Mass., Oct. 15, 1858
d.   Abingdon, Mass., Feb. 2, 1918

John L. Sullivan's career marked both the beginning of organized professional boxing in the United States and the end of the bare-knuckle era. He began boxing professionally in 1878 and was successful from the start by virtue of his devastating right-hand punches. In Mississippi City, Mississippi, on February 7, 1882, he became heavyweight champion when, in a bare-knuckle fight, he knocked out Paddy Ryan. In the last bare-knuckle title bout, Sullivan retained his title in 1889 by knocking out Jake Kilrain in the 73rd round at Richburg, Mississippi.

On September 7, 1892, in New Orleans, Sullivan and James J. Corbett were matched in the first championship bout fought using padded gloves and the new Queensberry Rules. Corbett knocked out Sullivan in the 21st round.

Sullivan retired from the professional ring after this loss but toured the country, taking on all comers in exhibition matches. This did a great deal to popularize boxing in America. Sullivan opened a bar in New York City but in 1905 announced he had stopped drinking and began lecturing on temperance. He had won a great deal of money—he was the first boxer to earn a million dollars—but he had apparently spent it all. The man known as the Boston Strong Boy and the Great John L died in near poverty.

---

from St. Louis, Mo. They covered 809 mi. in 19 hrs., 50 min., and this mark lasted until the end of the century. The balloon carried John Wise, balloonist; John LaMountain, balloon builder; O. A. Gager, a Vermont businessman who financed the flight; and William Hyde, a St. Louis journalist. They were attempting to reach New York City, but a severe storm carried them over Lake Ontario and eventually dumped them in a tree near Henderson, N.Y. No one was seriously hurt.

1859 July 1   In the **first intercollegiate baseball game** in history, Amherst defeated Williams 66-32.

1859 July 26   In the **first intercollegiate regatta,** Harvard defeated Yale and Brown at Lake Quinsigamond, Worcester, Mass. The race was in six-oared shells at 3 mi. A similar regatta planned for the previous year was canceled when the Yale stroke, George E. Dunham, drowned.

1859 Oct. 3   An **international cricket match** took place in Hoboken, N.J., between an all-England eleven and an all-U.S. squad of twenty-two from Philadelphia and New York City. The English team was victorious by 64 runs and an inning, after a match that lasted three days.

1859 Oct. 11   Josh Ward, in a single scull, won a **Championship of America race** off Staten Island, N.Y. He was awarded $100 and a belt of sterling silver, which weighed 20 oz. and was designed by Tiffany & Co.

WALTER CAMP

Walter Chauncey Camp
b.   New Britain, Conn., Apr. 4, 1859
d.   New York City, Mar. 14, 1925

Rightly called the father of American football, Walter Camp had a profound influence on the game's development. An 1880 Yale graduate, he became football coach there in 1888. As the most influential member of the college football rules committee until his death, Camp brought about many innovations: the reduction from 15 to 11 in the number of players on a side, signal calling, a system of downs and yards to be gained, the scrimmage line in place of the Rugby scrum, a new scoring system, and many others.

In 1889, Camp began his annual selection of an all-American college team, which he continued until his death and which was universally accepted. During World War I, Camp chaired a committee to see to the physical fitness of Navy personnel. Out of this grew his "daily dozen" exercises, which were taken up by thousands of civilians. He wrote more than 30 books on football and physical fitness.

1860

The **New York Skating Club** was formed. Skating was looked on as a socially acceptable form of sport for men and women jointly and provided opportunities for flirtation and dalliance.

The **first department of physical education** at an American college was established at Amherst under the leadership of Edward Hitchcock, who set up a gymnasium.

The term *seventh-inning stretch* became common at baseball games. It referred to the custom of spectators standing up and stretching just before the home team came to bat in the seventh inning. The custom served two functions, one practical and one superstitious. Spectators relieved cramped muscles and brought good luck to their team as well, since the number 7 was considered lucky.

Baseball came to San Francisco in an organized game for the first time.

The **first amateur baseball club to go on the road** was a Brooklyn team called the Excelsiors. It toured cities in upstate New York and then visited Philadelphia, Wilmington, and Baltimore, winning 15 straight in all. The captain, manager, and scheduler was J. B. Leggett. The crowds sometimes reached 3000.

The **first intercollegiate billiards match** in the U.S. was held between Harvard and Yale.

Apr. 17 A **bout that lasted 42 rounds** (2 hrs., 20 min.) between the American boxer John C. Heenan and the English champion Tom Sayers at Farnborough, England, ended when a gang of toughs broke it up. The fight was recorded as a draw. Americans claimed the rioters were backers of Sayers who were afraid he was losing the bout. Among the spectators were said to be the authors Charles Dickens and William Makepeace Thackeray.

Oct. 4 **Tenpins** may have been an unscheduled activity during the Prince of Wales's visit to the U.S. Bored by a reception at the White House, the prince slipped off with Harriet Lane, niece of Pres. James Buchanan, to the gymnasium at Mrs. Smith's Institute for Young Ladies. Newspaper accounts had it that the prince and his partner played tenpins.

1861

Edward P. Weston's walking feats this year included a journey on foot from Boston to Washington, D.C., 478 mi. in 208 hrs. The Union Army studied this feat in order to determine how far troops could be made to travel on forced marches.

The **Seneca Indian foot racer Deerfoot** was a sensation in England this year. Running in breechcloth and moccasins, Deerfoot outran every available British runner. The largest crowds ever to attend a meet, which included the royal family, flocked to see him run.

The **first baseball trophy** was offered by a newspaper, the New York *Clipper.*

ISAAC MURPHY

b. Lexington, Ky., Jan. 1, 1861?
d. Lexington, Ky., Feb. 12, 1896

Isaac Murphy, a black jockey in an era when most jockeys were black, was in his time by far the most successful rider of thoroughbred racehorses. On 1412 mounts he had 628 wins for a 44.5% average, a record that still stands.

Murphy registered his first important victory when he rode the winning horse in the Travers Stakes at Saratoga in 1879. That same year, he won 35 of 75 races. Murphy won the Kentucky Derby in 1884, 1890, and 1891, becoming the first jockey to win the Derby in consecutive years and the only one up to that time to win three times. He remains the only jockey to have won the Derby, the Kentucky Oaks, and the Clark Stakes in the same Churchill Downs meeting.

In his best years, Murphy earned about $20,000, a very large amount for the time. In 1955, he became the first jockey to be elected to the National Museum of Racing Hall of Fame. Murphy died of pneumonia when he was about 35 years old.

1862

The popularity of **trotting races** was not diminished by the war. A new track was established in New York City at 144th St. between Seventh and Eighth avenues.

The **first enclosed baseball field** opened at Union Grounds, Brooklyn, N.Y.

Dec. 25 Two **baseball teams** of Union Army men played at Hilton Head, S.C., before a crowd estimated at 40,000. When the war ended in 1865, soldiers brought baseball back to their hometowns, spreading its popularity.

1863

The **first practical four-wheel roller skate** was invented by James L. Plimpton of Medfield, Mass. This design made it possible for the first time to take curves on skates. In the same year, Plimpton organized the New York Roller Skating Association and opened a rink in New York City. In 1866 he started a public rink in Newport, R.I.

In Newport, R.I., the **Roller Skating Association** leased the Atlantic House and turned the dining hall and plaza into a roller skating rink. In this same era, the Casino in Chicago could accommodate 1000 skaters and 3000 spectators, while a rink in San Francisco advertised that it had 5000 pairs of skates for rent.

A new **baseball rule** provided that both balls and strikes were to be called.

The first attempt at **base stealing** in baseball history was made by Eddie Cuthbert of Philadelphia, when his team, the Keystones, played against the Brooklyn Atlantics.

The English sport of **racquets** was greatly encouraged by the construction of excellent courts on West 13th St., New York City, and the engagement of Frederick Foulkes of England as a professional player. In 1867 an international match with England was staged, in which William Gray, the British champion, beat the American entrant.

May 5 The **U.S. heavyweight boxing championship** was won by Joe Coburn, who knocked out Mike McCoole in the 63rd round at Charleston, Md. In 1865, Coburn retired and McCoole claimed the title.

Aug. 3 The **new Saratoga racetrack** held its first meet, with 26 horses running in eight races over four days. John Morrissey, a former boxer, politician, and gambling house proprietor in New York City, who now operated a popular casino at Saratoga, was the chief sponsor of the track. Associated with him were several millionaires and sportsmen, including Leonard W. Jerome.

Dec. 23 The **tactics of a referee** decided the outcome of a boxing match in Wadhurst, England, when an American, John C. Heenan, fought the British champion, Tom King. King was unable to come out for the 18th round in time, but the referee gave him extra time to recover. King went on to beat Heenan in the 25th round. The boxers were said to have had a $10,000 side bet on the outcome.

RICHARD D. SEARS

Richard Dudley Sears
b. Boston, Mass., Oct. 26, 1861
d. Boston, Mass., Apr. 8, 1943

Richard Sears played in and won the first U.S. national amateur tennis tournament, held at Newport, Rhode Island, in 1881. He continued to win in every year through 1887, for a total of seven consecutive singles titles, a record that has never been matched. Only Bill Tilden won the title as many times, but not consecutively. Sears also won the men's doubles six times in a row, from 1882 to 1887, and then retired undefeated. He was also court tennis champion in 1892.

Sears in 1887 and 1888 was president of the U.S. Lawn Tennis Association, founded in 1881. He was one of the first seven players elected to the International Tennis Hall of Fame when it was established in 1955.

1864

An American ballet dancing master from Chicago, **Jackson Haines** (1840-1876), introduced European skaters to his free-flowing style of figure skating, which in time would supersede the cramped and formal skating methods of the era. Haines developed the first skate to be screwed to the sole of the boot, replacing the previously used clamp attachment. His influence on the development of figure skating was immense.

The **United States Figure Skating Association** was founded.

The **first American croquet club** was founded, the Park Place Croquet Club of Brooklyn, N.Y., with 25 members.

The **first curve ball** by a baseball pitcher was thrown by William A. "Candy" Cummings of the Brooklyn Stars. He was pitching against the Brooklyn Atlantics. Skeptics claimed it was an optical illusion.

Aug. 2 A **second Saratoga racetrack** replaced the original, itself only a year old. On this inaugural day of racing, the first Travers Stakes was run. It was named for William R. Travers, a New York City broker, social figure, and wit. The first Travers was won by Kentucky, a horse that scored 20 consecutive victories. The Travers, still run on the same course, is now the oldest stakes race in the U.S. and one of the year's most important events for 3-year-olds.

1865

The **first international curling match** between the U.S. and Canada took place on Lake Erie at Black Rock, near Buffalo, N.Y. Twenty-three rinks from each country participated, with the Canadians winning 658-478. After 1888, this international event was held annually except in wartime.

The virtues of **croquet** were extolled by the recently founded Newport (R.I.) Croquet Club in its handbook of rules published this year: "Whist exercises the memory and the power of calculating probabilities, chess the imagination and the faculty of abstract reasoning, but croquet, though it taxes these mental capacities less, combines them with the delights of out-of-doors exercise and social enjoyment, fresh air and friendship—two things which are of all others most effective for promoting happiness."

Interest in **baseball** had a tremendous surge after the Civil War. This year saw 91 clubs included in the

AMOS ALONZO STAGG

b. West Orange, N.J., Aug. 16, 1862
d. Stockton, Calif., Mar. 16, 1965

Amos Alonzo Stagg was the football coach with the longest career and the longest life span. His unusual qualities became apparent first at Yale, where he was chosen in 1889 for Walter Camp's first all-American football team and where he pitched so well for the baseball team, once striking out 20 Princeton batters, that he was offered a major league baseball contract.

Instead, Stagg took a football coaching job at Springfield (Massachusetts) College but left in 1892 for the University of Chicago, where he became athletic director and football coach. He remained there for 41 years, his teams winning 268 games and losing 141. They were undefeated in five seasons and won six conference championships. Forced to retire at 70, Stagg went west and coached successfully at the College of the Pacific from 1933 to 1946. Even though he was nearing 85, he was not done with football. Coming back east to Susquehanna University, he assisted his son, who was head coach, until 1952.

Stagg had tremendous influence on the development of college football, serving on the rules committee from 1904 to 1932. He was an innovator throughout his career. He came up with the tackling dummy, the man-in-motion maneuver, the huddle, and the end-around play, among others. Most of all, Stagg was a moral force. He never drank, smoked, or swore, and saw to it that his players followed his example. Elected to the College Football Hall of Fame in 1951, Amos Alonzo Stagg died just five months before his 103rd birthday.

BOB FITZSIMMONS

Robert Prometheus Fitzsimmons
b. Helston, Cornwall, England, June 4, 1862
d. Chicago, Ill., Oct. 22, 1917

Bob Fitzsimmons grew up in New Zealand, where work in his father's blacksmith shop helped develop the muscles that would propel him to stardom in the ring. Already a boxer, he went to the United States in 1890 and, on January 14, 1891, at New Orleans, won the middleweight championship from Nonpareil Jack Dempsey, not to be confused with the great heavyweight champion.

Six years later, at Carson City, Nevada, on March 17, Fitzsimmons became heavyweight champion when he knocked out James J. Corbett in the 14th round of their title bout. It was in this fight that he became famous for his so-called solar plexus punch. Fitzsimmons, small and light for a heavyweight, reigned as champion for only two years before losing the title to Jim Jeffries in an 11th-round knockout at Coney Island, New York, on June 9, 1899.

An attempted comeback in 1902 failed when he again lost to Jeffries, but on November 25, 1903, he became light heavyweight champion, taking the title from George Gardner in 20 rounds. He lost this title on December 20, 1905, when Philadelphia Jack O'Brien knocked him out. Fitzsimmons continued to box until 1914, fighting his last bout, a six-rounder, at the age of 52.

National Association of Baseball Players. In 1866, Arthur P. Gorman was named president of the organization. A year later, 237 teams were represented.

John Wesley Hyatt received a patent for a composition billiard ball and was awarded a $10,000 prize by a billiard ball manufacturer who up to this time had to use expensive ivory. Hyatt, one of the most prolific inventors of his time, later discovered the process for the production of celluloid, thus creating a revolution in American industry. His other inventions included a type of roller bearing still in use, a water filter, and a sugarcane mill.

1866

Glass balls for trapshooting were introduced by Charlie Portlock, of Boston. They were the first inanimate substitutes for live pigeons and were widely popular in the 1870s. In the early 1880s, glass balls were replaced by clay targets.

The game of **croquet** was described by a member of the Newport (R.I.) Croquet Club, writing in *Croquet*, as "not too fatiguing for a delicate girl, nor too tame for the most adventurous boy."

The unofficial U.S. **baseball championship** game was played by the Brooklyn Atlantics and the Philadelphia Athletics. An enthusiastic crowd smashed its way to the field, causing the game to be halted and finally moved to Long Island. Brooklyn defeated the Athletics 27-10.

The first intentional **bunt** in baseball was laid down by Dickey Pierce of the Brooklyn Atlantics.

Aug. 13 In an **England vs. America croquet match** the U.S. team, playing at the Hurlingham Croquet Club in Great Britain, was badly beaten. The three U.S. team members, from the Westhampton, N.Y., Mallet Club, were Homer Landon, Henri White, and Walter Margulies, who said they found the English game altogether different from the American.

Dec. 11 In the **first great transatlantic race,** three U.S. schooner yachts of approximately 100-ft. length but of diverse design took off from Sandy Hook, N.J., to the Isle of Wight, England. The race was intentionally scheduled for the period of severest weather. Wagers totaling $90,000 were at stake. The contestants were *Vesta* (owned by Pierre Lorillard), *Fleetwing* (George and Franklin Osgood), and *Henrietta* (James Gordon Bennett, Jr.). *Henrietta* won after *Vesta* dissipated its lead while piloting the islets approaching England. *Henrietta*'s time was 13 days, 21 hrs., 55 min.

1867

A long-distance **walking record** was set by Edward P. Weston, who did the distance from Portland, Maine, to Chicago in 26 days. He won $10,000 for his efforts.

June The **Grand National Curling Club of America** was formed at a meeting at the Caledonian Club in New York City. Within a year it had 12 member clubs. In 1892 the North Western Curling Association of America was founded in St. Paul, Minn. Eventually, such regional clubs were replaced by the U.S. Curling Association.

June 19 The **first annual Belmont Stakes** was won by Ruthless, with a time of 3:05. The jockey was J. Gilpatrick. The race was held at Jerome Park, N.Y., from 1867 to 1889; at Morris Park, N.Y., from 1890 to 1905; and at Belmont Park, N.Y., from 1906 to the present. In the beginning the distance was a mile and five-eighths, but it has been changed from time to time. The Belmont Stakes is the oldest of the three classic American races.

1868

The **first baseball uniforms** were introduced by the Cincinnati Red Stockings. The uniforms, featuring knickerbockers, were ridiculed at first.

The new sport of **velociped ing** (cycling) attained great vogue in America three years after it had been perfected in Paris. Schools for all ages and both sexes were set up in all the large cities. Newspapers reported on the vogue. The fact that women could participate added greatly to its rapid spread.

June 10 The second annual **Belmont Stakes** was won by General Duke, with a time of 3:02. The jockey was Robert Swim.

Nov. 11 The first **indoor amateur track and field meet** was held by the New York Athletic Club. The meet was held in the partly completed Empire City Skating Rink, and for the first time in the U.S., spiked shoes were worn by contestants. The club, which had been organized Sept. 8, later held outdoor meets, established rules for the conduct of meets, and built the first cinder track. It continues to this day to promote track and field and other sports.

Dec. 19 Of the **popularity of bicycles**, *Harper's Weekly* wrote: "Youngsters ride down Fifth Avenue with their schoolbooks strapped in front

CONNIE MACK

Cornelius Alexander McGillicuddy
b. East Brockfield, Mass., Dec. 23, 1862
d. Philadelphia, Pa., Feb. 8, 1956

Connie Mack had by far the longest career ever in professional baseball, 67 years, a tenure unlikely to be matched. After leaving a factory job, Mack in 1883 became a catcher in the minor leagues, then played with Washington, Buffalo, Pittsburgh, and Milwaukee from 1886 to 1900. He managed the last two teams from 1894 to 1900. In his playing career, Mack had a so-so batting average of .245 and hit five home runs.

In 1900, Mack played a part in

organizing the American League, took over the Philadelphia Athletics, and eventually became principal owner of the team. He remained manager of the Athletics until midcentury, always appearing at games in a business suit, complete with shirt and tie, even while sitting in the dugout.

Mack did not retire as manager until 1950, although illness had forced him to be less active for some years, and he continued as president of the club until 1954, when it moved to Kansas City. Mr. Mack, as he was usually addressed in his long span as manager, led his team to 3776 wins and 4025 losses, records that still stand.

The Athletics won nine league championships, in 1902, 1905, 1910, 1911, 1913, 1914, 1929, 1930, and 1931. In the nine World Series that Mack's teams played, they won five, in 1910, 1911, 1913, 1929, and 1930, taking 24 out of 43 series games.

In 1929, Mr. Mack was awarded the Edward W. Bok Prize for distinguished service to Philadelphia. It was the first time the award had gone to anyone other than an artist, scientist, educator, or philanthropist. In 1937, Connie Mack was in the second group elected to the Baseball Hall of Fame.

BAN JOHNSON

Byron Bancroft Johnson
b. Norwalk, Ohio, Jan. 6, 1864
d. St. Louis, Mo., Mar. 22, 1931

The American League of professional baseball owes its existence and its equality with the older National League to the efficient, strenuous, and sometimes ruthless activities of Ban Johnson. He was a sportswriter for a Cincinnati, Ohio, newspaper when in 1893 he accepted the presidency of the failing Western League. He did not hesitate to encourage league teams to raid the National League for ballplayers, and he had no scruples against setting up new teams in NL cities to force head-to-head competition for fans.

The league's name was changed to the American League in 1900, and by 1903, in just ten years, the National League was forced to accept the other league as an equal. Johnson also succeeded in arranging a World Series between the champion teams of the two leagues, a series that began in 1903 and has been played annually since 1905. In the process of his organizing work, Johnson also reduced spectator rowdyism, which had been rather common at ballparks, and so began to attract a more respectable part of the population.

Johnson was president of the American League from 1900 to 1927 and the dominant member of the three-man commission that controlled organized baseball from 1903 to 1919. In 1937, Johnson became one of the second group to be elected to the Baseball Hall of Fame.

of their velocipedes, and expert riders cause crowds of spectators to visit public squares, which offer exellent tracks for the light vehicles to move swiftly over. The Rev. Henry Ward Beecher has secured one of the American machines."

1869

Henry Chadwick (1824-1908), English-born sports writer for New York newspapers, published **baseball's first annual handbook,** later known as *Spalding's Official Baseball Guide,* which he edited until 1878 and again from 1881 to 1908. As chairman of the rules committee of the National Association of Baseball Players, organized in 1858, Chadwick had been instrumental in developing and codifying the rules of the game during and after the Civil War, to the extent that he was later known as the father of baseball.

JIM CORBETT

James John Corbett
b. San Francisco, Calif., Sept. 1, 1866
d. New York City, Feb. 18, 1933

In 1886, when Jim Corbett first took up boxing, he was employed as an assistant bank teller. His first important fight took place in 1889, when he fought Joe Choynski. The bout began on May 30 but was not finished until several weeks later, when it was resumed on a barge in San Francisco Bay after having been stopped by the police. Corbett won after 28 rounds.

Corbett's personality soon made him popular, and he became known as Gentleman Jim. He won the heavyweight championship on September 7, 1892, when he knocked out the titleholder, John L. Sullivan, at New Orleans in the 21st round of their match. This was the first championship fight fought under the Queensberry Rules and the first in which padded gloves were used. Corbett lost his title on March 17, 1897, when he was knocked out in the 14th round by Robert P. Fitzsimmons in Carson City, Nev.

In 1900 and again in 1903, Corbett attempted comebacks but both times was defeated by Jim Jeffries. An intelligent man, Corbett was noted for his agility and his skill at punching and feinting. He is considered the first so-called scientific boxer.

Denton True Young
b. Gilmore, Ohio, Mar. 29, 1867
d. near Newcomerstown, Ohio, Nov. 4, 1955

No one will dispute the claim that Cy Young was the greatest pitcher in all baseball history and, further, that it is unlikely anyone will ever surpass him. His 511 victories are 95 more than the games won by Walter Johnson, who holds second place in this category. Young won 20 or more games in 16 seasons, which no one else has ever done.

Cy Young's claim to preeminence goes on: 77 shutouts, fourth highest; three no-hitters, a record in his time, and the last one coming in 1908, when he was already 41 years old; a perfect game, for Boston against the Philadelphia Athletics on May 15, 1904. Only 11 other pitchers have ever achieved this. Young pitched 906 games in all, losing only 313 for a winning percentage of .620. He struck out 2891 batters while giving up 1217 walks. He won 28 games in 1903 and 26 in 1904.

After playing minor league ball, Young pitched for Cleveland, at that time in the National League, from 1890 to 1898; for St. Louis in 1899 and 1900; for the Red Sox from 1901 to 1908; for Cleveland, now in the American League, from 1909 to 1910; and for Cleveland and the Boston Braves in 1911. In spite of Young's prowess, the teams he played for made it to the World Series only once, in the very first series of 1903, when Boston beat Pittsburgh five games to three. Young won two and lost one for Boston and had an earned run average of 1.59.

Sportswriters and fans called Young's lively fastball the cyclone pitch. Young was elected to the Baseball Hall of Fame in 1937, its second year.

The term *battery* was first employed in baseball parlance to denote a pitcher and catcher. The term derived from telegraphy, in which the combination of a transmitter and receiver formed a battery.

The **first ice yacht club** in the U.S., the Poughkeepsie, N.Y., Ice Yacht Club, was formed. It was followed by the New Hamburg and Hudson River ice yacht clubs.

Mar. 15 The Cincinnati Red Stockings, the **first avowedly professional baseball team,** were organized by George Ellard and Harry Wright. Their star, shortstop George Wright, was paid the top salary, $1400. The Red Stockings, traveling across the country, won 57 games, lost none, were tied once. In 1870 they ran their skein to 80 games without a loss before being stopped by the Brooklyn Atlantics, 8-7, on June 14 before a crowd of 20,000.

June 5 The third annual **Belmont Stakes** was won by Fenian, with a time of 3:04¼. The jockey was C. Miller.

June 15 The **heavyweight boxing championship** was won by Mike McCoole in a bout staged near St. Louis, Mo. McCoole defeated Tom Allen of England on a questionable foul in the ninth round. Allen came to America to dispute the championship claimed by McCoole after Joe Coburn retired. Allen based his own claim on his defeats of several American boxers.

Nov. 6 The **first intercollegiate football game** was played at New Brunswick, N.J. Rutgers beat Princeton 6-4 in a game more like soccer than football. There were 25 men on each team, and no running with the ball was allowed.

1870

The light, small-bore **.22-caliber rifle** appeared and eventually stimulated interest in target shooting among civilians.

The craze for **roller skating** spread throughout the U.S. and the rest of the world. By 1863 four rollers had been added to "parlor skates," and a young skater, William H. Fuller, developed the art of figure skating, which he displayed on a tour around the world.

Walking became one of the most popular spectator sports. Gilmore's Gardens in New York City would usually sell out when famous heel-and-toers raced there. About 1900, bicycle riders replaced walkers in popularity.

Two **popular sports** were cricket and baseball. Cricket was generally favored in the press because of its gentility.

Pimlico racetrack was built in Baltimore by a group of racing enthusiasts who were encouraged by the success of the course at Saratoga Springs, N.Y., in 1864.

Early **football matches** were played by Columbia, Princeton, and Rutgers. Technically, the game played was soccer.

Yale and Harvard met in a **crew race** on a circular course at Worcester, Mass. Yale came in first but was disqualified for colliding with the Harvard crew.

May 10 The **world heavyweight boxing championship** was won by Jem Mace of England, who had claimed the title after the retirement of Tom King, also an Englishman. To defend the claim, Mace defeated Tom Allen, another claimant, in a ten-round bout near Kennersville, La.

June 4 The fourth annual **Belmont Stakes** was won by Kingfisher, with a time of 2:59½. The jockey was W. Dick.

July 26 In a **transatlantic sailing race,** the English schooner *Cambria* defeated James Gordon Bennett's 120-ft. schooner *Dauntless* by 1 hr., 43 min. The crossing westward from Cobh, Ireland, to Sandy Hook, N.J. took 24 days.

Aug. 16 Fred Goldsmith demonstrated that the **curve ball** was not an optical illusion. Before a large crowd at the Capitoline Grounds, Brooklyn, N.Y., Goldsmith set up three poles in a straight line and hurled a ball that went to one side of the first pole, to the opposite side of the second, and back to the first side of the third.

Aug. 17 The **first ascent of Mt. Rainier** in Washington State was made by Hazard Stevens and Philemon Van Trump. The mountain is 14,410 ft. high.

Sept. 7 Two Americans **died after reaching the summit of Mont Blanc,** at 15,771 ft. the highest Alp, at Chamonix, France. They were John Randall and Joseph Bean. Along with two English climbers and seven guides and porters, the Americans perished in a violent storm. Randall's body was never found, but Bean's was recovered along with notes he had written to his wife just before he died.

1871

The **National Rifle Association** (NRA) was founded by National Guard officers. It was formed in response to the revived interest in rifle shooting resulting from the Civil War. Shooting at a target replaced shooting for a game prize. The new association quickly standardized targets and distances for competition and sponsored the first national championships at Creedmoor, Long Island, N.Y. During the meet, a U.S. team defeated riflemen from Ireland representing the Ulster Rifle Club.

The **New York Canoe Club** was founded. One of its supporters was W. P. Stephens, yachting editor of *Forest and Stream,* who publicized the pleasures of

PUDGE HEFFELFINGER

William Walter Heffelfinger
b. Minneapolis, Minn., Dec. 20, 1867
d. Blessing, Tex., Apr. 2, 1954

Pudge Heffelfinger earned unique distinctions on the gridiron in two ways. He was the best college football player of the nineteenth century, and he was the first professional football player. Heffelfinger's athletic career began at Yale, where he played guard on a team that in one season scored 698 points to 0 for its opponents. He made Walter Camp's all-American team in three successive years, 1889, 1890, and 1891. At 190 pounds the largest man on the Yale team, Heffelfinger was not only powerful but agile. He more than once broke up the flying wedge employed by teams in his time by simply hurling himself upon it. More important for the future of the game, he initiated the practice of pulling out of the line to run interference for ball-carrying backs.

On November 12, 1892, Heffelfinger was paid $500 to play for the Allegheny Athletic Association against the Pittsburgh Athletic Club, and this appears to have made him the first pro football player ever. He recovered a fumble and ran for a touchdown as well as performing ably as a linesman in his team's winning effort.

In 1916, Heffelfinger returned briefly to Yale and at the age of 48 worked out with the team. In a scrimmage he knocked out five of the undergraduate players. Heffelfinger is also said to have played a creditable last game at the age of 65.

Horse Racing
BELMONT STAKES WINNERS

	HORSE	JOCKEY		HORSE	JOCKEY
1867	Ruthless	J. Gilpatrick	1917	Hourless	J. Butwell
1868	General Duke	R. Swim	1918	Johren	F. Robinson
1869	Fenian	C. Miller	1919	Sir Barton	J. Loftus
1870	Kingfisher	W. Dick	1920	Man o' War	C. Kummer
1871	Harry Bassett	W. Miller	1921	Grey Lag	E. Sande
1872	Joe Daniels	J. Rowe	1922	Pillory	C. Miller
1873	Springbok	J. Rowe	1923	Zev	E. Sande
1874	Saxon	G. Barbee	1924	Mad Play	E. Sande
1875	Calvin	R. Swim	1925	American Flag	A. Johnson
1876	Algerine	W. Donohue	1926	Crusader	A. Johnson
1877	Cloverbrook	C. Holloway	1927	Chance Shot	E. Sande
1878	Duke of Magenta	L. Hughes	1928	Vito	C. Kummer
1879	Spendthrift	Evans	1929	Blue Larkspur	M. Garner
1880	Grenada	L. Hughes	1930	Gallant Fox	E. Sande
1881	Saunterer	T. Costello	1931	Twenty Grand	C. Kurtsinger
1882	Forester	J. McLaughlin	1932	Faireno	T. Malley
1883	George Kinney	J. McLaughlin	1933	Hurryoff	M. Garner
1884	Panique	J. McLaughlin	1934	Peace Chance	W. Wright
1885	Tyrant	P. Duffy	1935	Omaha	W. Saunders
1886	Inspector B	J. McLaughlin	1936	Granville	J. Stout
1887	Hanover	J. McLaughlin	1937	War Admiral	C. Kurtsinger
1888	Sir Dixon	J. McLaughlin	1938	Pasteurized	J. Stout
1889	Eric	W. Hayward	1939	Johnstown	J. Stout
1890	Burlington	S. Barnes	1940	Bimelech	F. Smith
1891	Foxford	E. Garrison	1941	Whirlaway	E. Arcaro
1892	Patron	W. Hayward	1942	Shut Out	E. Arcaro
1893	Comanche	W. Simms	1943	Count Fleet	J. Longden
1894	Henry of Navarre	W. Simms	1944	Bounding Home	G. Smith
1895	Belmar	F. Taral	1945	Pavot	E. Arcaro
1896	Hastings	H. Griffin	1946	Assault	W. Mehrtens
1897	Scottish Chieftain	J. Scherrer	1947	Phalanx	R. Donoso
1898	Bowling Brook	F. Littlefield	1948	Citation	E. Arcaro
1899	Jean Bereaud	R. Clawson	1949	Capot	T. Atkinson
1900	Ildrim	N. Turner	1950	Middleground	W. Boland
1901	Commando	H. Spencer	1951	Counterpoint	D. Gorman
1902	Masterman	J. Bullman	1952	One Count	E. Arcaro
1903	Africander	J. Bullman	1953	Native Dancer	E. Guerin
1904	Delhi	G. Odom	1954	High Gun	E. Guerin
1905	Tanya	E. Hildebrand	1955	Nashua	E. Arcaro
1906	Burgomaster	L. Lyne	1956	Needles	D. Erb
1907	Peter Pan	G. Mountain	1957	Gallant Man	W. Shoemaker
1908	Colin	J. Notter	1958	Cavan	P. Anderson
1909	Joe Madden	E. Dugan	1959	Sword Dancer	W. Shoemaker
1910	Sweep	J. Butwell	1960	Celtic Ash	W. Hartack
1911–12	(not run)		1961	Sherluck	B. Baeza
1913	Prince Eugene	R. Troxler	1962	Jaipur	W. Shoemaker
1914	Luke McLuke	M. Buxton	1963	Chateaugay	B. Baeza
1915	The Finn	G. Byrne	1964	Quadrangle	M. Ycaza
1916	Friar Rock	E. Haynes			*(continued)*

	HORSE	JOCKEY		HORSE	JOCKEY
1965	Hail to All	J. Sellers	1977	Seattle Slew	J. Cruguet
1966	Amberoid	W. Boland	1978	Affirmed	S. Cauthen
1967	Damascus	W. Shoemaker	1979	Coastal	R. Hernandez
1968	Stage Door Johnny	H. Gustines	1980	Temperence Hill	E. Maple
1969	Arts and Letters	B. Baeza	1981	Summing	G. Martens
1970	High Echelon	J. Rotz	1982	Conquistador Cielo	L. Pincay
1971	Pass Catcher	W. Blum	1983	Caveat	L. Pincay
1972	Riva Ridge	R. Turcotte	1984	Swale	L. Pincay
1973	Secretariat	R. Turcotte	1985	Creme Fraiche	E. Maple
1974	Little Current	M. Rivera	1986	Danzig Connection	C. McCarron
1975	Avatar	W. Shoemaker	1987	Bet Twice	C. Perret
1976	Bold Forbes	A. Cordero			

canoeing and published build-it-yourself plans and directions.

A new **baseball rule** permitted the batter to call for a high or low pitched ball. This rule was re-scinded in 1887.

Jan. 25 A **championship trapshooting match** was held when A. H. Bogardus, of Illinois, chal-lenged the champion, Ira Paine. In the contest, held on Long Island, N.Y., Paine won. Several months later, Bogardus turned the tables, de-feating Paine 87 to 86 birds. Bogardus went on to hold the title for nearly a quarter of a cen-tury.

Mar. 17 The **first professional baseball associ-ation,** the National Association of Professional Baseball Players, was organized. It replaced the amateur National Association.

June 10 The fifth annual **Belmont Stakes** was won by the horse Harry Bassett, with a time of 2:56. The jockey was W. Miller.

Aug. 20 John Davidson completed **100 hrs. of walking** at Little Rock, Ark., with only 2 hrs., 28 min. of rest. His feat began on Aug. 8. Davidson walked backward part of the time and at other times carried a 111-lb. anvil.

Sept. 11 In a **race of four-man crews,** the Ward brothers (Ellis, Gilbert, Hank, and Joshua) of Cornwall-on-Hudson, N.Y., defeated five other crews on Saratoga Lake, N.Y. Racing for a $5000 prize, the Wards won by three lengths. Two of the other crews were from England. The race attracted national interest.

1872

The **National Association of Amateur Oars-men** was founded. The members formed it, they said, because they loved rowing for its own sake and were suspicious of professionals, who made a business of it. In 1981 the name was changed to the United States Rowing Association. It is the U.S. gov-erning body of rowing.

A **U.S. rifle team** traveled to Ireland and de-feated a new challenging team of Irish marksmen. The U.S. team claimed the world championship.

An English **cricket team,** headed by the almost legendary William G. Grace, toured the U.S. In 1876, in consecutive innings he scored 344 out of 546 for the Marylebone Cricket Club and 318 not out for Gloucestershire.

A new **baseball rule** permitted the pitcher to snap his delivery of the ball. However, the pitcher was still restricted to an underhand, below-the-waist motion. Present-day regulations for the size of the ball were also set this year: not less than 5 nor more than 5¼ oz., and not less than 9 in. or more than 9¼ in. in circumference.

June 1 The sixth annual **Belmont Stakes** was

Records are made to be broken.

Old baseball saying

HURRY-UP YOST

1
8
7
3

Fielding Harris Yost
b. Fairview, W.Va., Apr. 30, 1871
d. Ann Arbor, Mich., Aug. 20, 1946

One of the most successful college football coaches ever, Fielding Yost earned his nickname by emphasizing the quality known as *hustle,* which accounted for much of his success in producing winning teams. He began

his coaching career in 1897, and from 1901 to 1927 he made the University of Michigan football teams successful almost beyond belief. His 1901 to 1904 squads were known as point-a-minute teams. They won 55 games; lost only one, to the University of Chicago; and had one tie. The teams of those years ran up 2821 points against 42 for all their opponents. Yost's 1902 team crushed

Stanford 49–0 in the first Rose Bowl game.

Altogether, teams coached by Yost won 196 games, lost 36, and tied 12. At Michigan his record was 164–20–10. From 1921 to 1927, Yost was director of athletics at Michigan as well as head coach of football. He wrote a number of books about the game and is in the College Football Hall of Fame.

---

won by the horse Joe Daniels, with a time of 2:58¼. The jockey was James Rowe.

1873

A famous decision on **collegiate football** was issued by Andrew Dickson White, president of Cornell U.: "I will not permit 30 men to travel 400 miles to agitate a bag of wind." White refused Cornell football players permission to meet Michigan at Cleveland.

Bookmakers first appeared at U.S. racetracks. The first few were English, but Americans soon learned the trade. The days of informal wagering between owners or spectators were over.

The **Fair Grounds racecourse** was opened in New Orleans. It was to operate on a system of prolonged meetings patterned after John Morrissey's races begun in Saratoga Springs in 1864.

Riflemen were the top sports idols during the 1870s. More than 100,000 people attended one national rifle shooting tournament held at Creedmoor, Long Island, N.Y., in 1873. Oarsmen were the second favorite sports figures. As many as 60,000 men, women, and children lined the banks of the Harlem R. in New York City to watch and wager on the sculling contests held there.

May 27 The first annual **Preakness Stakes** was won by Survivor, with a time of 2:43. The jockey was G. Barbee. The race was run at Pimlico, Md. The Preakness Stakes is one of the three classic

races in American racing, the others being the Kentucky Derby and the Belmont Stakes. A horse that wins all three earns the Triple Crown of American racing. The Preakness Stakes has been run over varying distances.

June 7 The seventh annual **Belmont Stakes** was won by Springbok, with a time of 3:01¾. The jockey was James Rowe.

Aug. 18 **Mt. Whitney,** in California, 14,494 ft. high, was scaled for the first time. The American team consisted of Charles Begole, A. H. Johnson, and John Lucas.

Sept. 23 The **world heavyweight boxing championship** was won in seven rounds by Tom Allen of England, who fought Mike McCoole near St. Louis, Mo.

Oct. 19 The first code of **football rules** was drafted by representatives from Yale, Princeton, Columbia, and Rutgers universities; they met in a Fifth Ave. hotel in New York City. The rules chosen were more like soccer than modern football and were abandoned in a few years in favor of the "Boston game" played at Harvard, which was more like rugby.

1874

Lawn tennis came to the U.S. for the first time, brought to Staten Island, New York City, from Bermuda by Mary Ewing Outerbridge. The Staten Island Cricket and Baseball Club, of which Mary's brother

TOM JENKINS

b. Cleveland, Ohio, 1872
d. Norwalk, Conn., June 19, 1957

Tom Jenkins was the first truly great American wrestler in a period when professional wrestling was taken seriously. He did much to popularize the sport of catch-as-catch-can, or freestyle, wrestling, which was rough and sometimes nasty but honest on the whole.

Jenkins began his march to mat fame by defeating Farmer Burns in 1893 to take the U.S. title. He held the title for 12 years, until he was beaten by Frank Gotch in 1905. He had previously defeated Gotch in 1903. In all, these two great wrestlers met eight times, Gotch winning five of the matches.

Among Jenkins's other opponents were Youssoff, the Terrible Turk, and George Hackenschmidt, the Russian Lion. Hackenschmidt beat Jenkins twice, the second time in 1904, and thus kept him from becoming world champion.

After Jenkins retired, he became wrestling and boxing instructor at West Point, where one of those he coached was Cadet Dwight D. Eisenhower.

---

was a director, set aside grounds for courts. Perhaps concurrently, Dr. James Dwight laid out a court for play at Nahant, a seaside resort 9 mi. from Boston.

Rugby football was first introduced to an American campus in a match between Harvard and McGill U. of Canada. Canadian rules for the game greatly interested sports-minded Americans and were instrumental in the development of modern football.

May 14-15 In what are said to be the first two **football contests for which admission was charged,** Harvard defeated McGill U., of Montreal, three goals to none in the first game and played to a scoreless tie in the second. The rules of the game were really those of rugby.

May 26 The second annual **Preakness Stakes** was won by Culpepper, with a time of 2:56½. The jockey was W. Donohue.

June 13 The eighth annual **Belmont Stakes** was won by Saxon, with a time of 2:39½. The jockey was G. Barbee. From this year to 1889, the distance run was 1½ miles.

Sept. 26 An **American rifle team** defeated the champion Irish team in the U.S. by a score of 934-931. The Irish had challenged the Americans through the Amateur Rifle Club, which accepted the challenge with the backing of the National Rifle Association. The event was held at Creedmoor, N.Y.

POP WARNER

Glenn Scobey Warner
b. Springville, N.Y., Apr. 5, 1872
d. Palo Alto, Calif., Sept. 7, 1954

An innovative and winning football coach at seven different schools over a period of 49 years, Pop Warner had a most interesting and diversified sports career. While studying law at Cornell, he was an outstanding guard on the Cornell football team in 1892, 1893, and 1894.

His first coaching appointment was at the University of Georgia, in 1895 and 1896. He had an unbeaten and untied team in 1896. Between 1897 and 1914, Warner alternated in coaching jobs between Cornell, in 1897 and 1898, 1904, 1905, and 1906, and the Carlisle Indian School, from 1899 to 1903 and from 1907 to 1914. At Carlisle he discovered Jim Thorpe, the great all-around athlete, whom Warner coached in track as well as in football. Warner and Thorpe put Carlisle on the collegiate sports map.

Moving on to the University of Pittsburgh, Warner produced three unbeaten teams, in 1915 to 1917, during his tenure from 1915 to 1923. Warner then moved west to Stanford University, where he coached from 1924 to 1932. His elevens played in the Rose Bowl in 1925, 1927, and 1928, winning only in 1928.

He ended his career by coaching at Temple University from 1933 to 1938 and acting as advisory coach at San Jose (Calif.) State College in 1939. Warner is credited with devising the double wing formation and is in the College Football Hall of Fame.

1875

The **New York Racquet Court Club** built a court for racquets. Today, as the Racquet and Tennis Club, on Park Ave., New York City, it occupies luxurious quarters with facilities for racquets, squash racquets, and court tennis.

The **baseball glove** was introduced by Charles G. Waite, first baseman for a Boston team. The glove was unpadded.

The Vesper Boat Club was organized in Philadelphia. Its eight-oared crew won at the 1900 Olympics and again in 1964, the only noncollegiate American crew to win this event. It was banned for many years after 1905 from the Henley Royal Regatta because of alleged infringement of the amateur code. In 1965, having been reinstated some time before, the boat club almost won the Grand Challenge Cup, finishing second.

The **oldest competitive target shooting trophy,** the Leech Cup, was contested for the first time and won by Col. John Bodine. The cup is Irish silver of the Victorian era and was originally presented to the Amateur Rifle Club of New York by Maj. Arthur Blennerhassett Leech, captain of the Irish Rifle Team, on the occasion of the team's visit to the U.S. in 1874.

The growing popularity of **coaching,** brought over from England and taken up by affluent Americans, was evident in the founding of the Coaching Club in New York City. It had its last extensive drive in 1916. Each fall there was a coaching parade on Fifth Ave. Crowds watched the four-in-hand drags and the tally-hos drawn by glossy horses. The coaches were pink, blue, or green. The well-dressed women sported large picture hats and carried parasols, while the men were splendid in their silk top hats.

Football uniforms were first worn in a game between Harvard and Tufts.

May 12 The **Westminster Kennel Club** was organized in New York City. It took its name from the hotel in which the meeting was held, which was a favorite gathering place for gentlemen dog fanciers. The club has held an annual show every year since 1877. In 1907 it first chose a best-in-show, which has become the most prestigious award in the American dog world. No award was made in 1923 because of a dispute over procedures.

May 17 The **first Kentucky Derby** was run at Churchill Downs, Ky. The winner was Aristides, with a time of 2:37¼. The jockey was Oliver Lewis.

May 28 The third annual **Preakness Stakes** was won by Tom Ochiltree, with a time of 2:43½. The jockey was L. Hughes.

May 29 Two "**Champion velocipede riders,**" as the *New York Times* called them, engaged in a 1-mi. race in Brooklyn, N.Y. They were Frank Shaw of Brooklyn and William C. Smith of Philadelphia. Shaw won and claimed, as a result

JOHN J. MCGRAW

John Joseph McGraw
b.   Truxton, N.Y., Apr. 7, 1873
d.   New Rochelle, N.Y., Feb. 25, 1934

John McGraw had a 43-year career in baseball as a player and manager, ending up with 2840 total victories as a manager, second only to Connie Mack of the Philadelphia Athletics. McGraw's teams lost 1984 games, giving him a .589 winning percentage. McGraw began playing professional baseball in 1890, and from 1891 to 1900 he was the star third baseman of the Baltimore

Orioles and became the Baltimore manager in 1899.

In 1900, McGraw helped organize the American League but soon left it for what was to be his principal career, manager of the New York Giants of the National League from 1902 through 1932. The Giants won the pennant ten times, 1904, 1905, 1911, 1912, 1913, 1917, 1921, 1922, 1923, and 1924. In 1916, the Giants ran up a 26-game winning streak that finally ended on September 30, when they lost the second game of a doubleheader to the Boston Braves. The *New York*

Times called the loss "a shock great as the fall of Troy."

McGraw's Giants played in nine World Series but won only three. In 1905, the Giants beat Connie Mack's Athletics four games to one. They also defeated the New York Yankees twice, in 1921 and 1922, first 5–4 and then 4–0. They lost the Series in 1911 through 1913 and in 1917, 1923, and 1924.

McGraw's nickname, the Little Napoleon, was aptly given. He was fiery and aggressive and always in charge. He was elected to the Baseball Hall of Fame in 1937.

SUNNY JIM FITZSIMMONS

James E. Fitzsimmons
b. Brooklyn, N.Y., July 23, 1873
d. Miami, Fla., Mar. 11, 1966

One of the all-time most successful American trainers of thoroughbred racehorses, Sunny Jim Fitzsimmons began his career as a jockey in 1889 and five years later became a trainer.

Fitzsimmons's long career had many high spots. The horses he trained won 2275 races and $13,082,911 in prize money. More than 250 of the victories were in stakes races. Among his winning horses were two Triple Crown champions, Gallant Fox in 1930 and Omaha in 1935.

Many of Fitzsimmons's horses won national champion honors, including Bold Ruler, Granville, High Voltage, Misty Morn, Nashua, and Vagrancy. Nashua won both the Preakness and Belmont stakes in 1955 and was named horse of the year, and another Fitzsimons horse, Johnstown, won both the Kentucky Derby and the Belmont Stakes in 1939.

of this and other races he had won, to be the national champion bicycle racer. He offered to bet up to $500 on himself against any challenger.

June 12 The ninth annual **Belmont Stakes** was won by Calvin, with a time of 2:42¼. The jockey was Robert Swim.

June 16 Rudolph Bourman, a Swiss, completed a **walk across the U.S.** He arrived in San Francisco, having left New Jersey on Jan. 19 and completed the journey in 135 days. He had no money when he started and reported that the Chinese laborers working on the Central Pacific Railroad were kinder to him than the Caucasian laborers on the Union Pacific.

Nov. 13 In a **football game** that combined different sets of rules, Harvard defeated Yale at New Haven four goals to none. With 15 men on a side and using an oblate ball, the game was played on a field 140 yards long and 70 wide. More than 2000 people paid 50 cents each to watch the game.

Dec. 5 The **Intercollegiate Association of Amateur Athletes of America** (IC4A) was organized at a meeting in Springfield, Mass., with representatives of 12 eastern colleges present. A further organizational meeting was held in New York City on Jan. 5, 1876, and was attended by representatives of 13 colleges.

HONUS WAGNER

John Peter Wagner
b. Carnegie, Pa., Feb. 24, 1874
d. Carnegie, Pa., Dec. 6, 1955

Honus Wagner could hit, run, field, and play almost any position, which is why some insist he was the best all-around player ever to appear on a baseball diamond. His best position was shortstop, and he played there for most of his 21-year career.

Wagner entered the major leagues when he signed with Louisville in 1897. He moved to Pittsburgh in 1900, when the Kentucky franchise was transferred there. He came to bat a total of 10,427 times; only three other players have reached five figures. Wagner's 3430 hits rank sixth, and his 703 stolen bases rank fifth. He led the league in stealing five times. Wagner ended his career as a major leaguer with a .329 batting average, having headed the league eight times in batting, in 1900, 1903, 1904, 1906, 1907, 1908, 1909, and 1911. His best year was 1900, when he batted .381.

Wagner struck out only 327 times, not much more than 15 times a season, and had 963 bases on balls. His 252 triples are still a record. He appeared in the 1903 and 1909 World Series and stole nine bases. The three Wagner stole in the 1903 Series, the first one ever played, set a mark that has since been tied by only two other players.

The Flying Dutchman had a reputation as a heavy drinker, and there is no doubt that he played rough on the base paths. He was once suspended for three days for deliberately spiking a Cincinnati player. One time he crashed his auto, then a status symbol for high-living athletes, into a railroad crossing gate. This led the *Sporting News* to call for a ban on auto ownership by ball players. Wagner was in the first group of stars elected to the Baseball Hall of Fame in 1936.

1876

Court tennis, also called real tennis or royal tennis, now modernized and standardized, was introduced into the U.S. This four-centuries-old form of tennis, played in the walled-in courtyards of kings and noblemen of England and France, bears little relationship to lawn tennis except for the use of a racket and a ball. Play in the U.S. was limited to a few exclusive clubs.

The exhibition of the **bicycle** at the Centennial Exposition in Philadelphia called attention to this vehicle for the first time. The bicycles on display had front wheels that were about 5 ft. in diameter, but the rear wheels were no more than a third that size. The machines were both difficult and dangerous to ride. Bicycles were first manufactured in the U.S. in 1878.

Polo, introduced by James Gordon Bennett, publisher of the New York *Herald,* was first played in the U.S. on the indoor floor at Dickel's Riding Academy in midtown New York City. The next locale was Jerome Park in The Bronx, N.Y. The first polo club, the Westchester, was formed soon afterward.

The **first lawn tennis tournament** held in the U.S., a social event, took place on the home court of James Dwight and F. R. Sears at Nahant, Mass.

The **catcher's mask** used in baseball was invented by Fred W. Thayer of Harvard College.

Feb. 2 **Professional baseball** became entrenched in the U.S. with the formation of the National League, consisting of teams in Philadelphia, Hartford, Boston, Chicago, Cincinnati, Louisville, St. Louis, and New York. This marked the beginning of organized professional baseball in the U.S. The first president of

the league was Morgan G. Bulkley. Chicago won the pennant with a season's record of 52 wins and 14 losses.

Feb. 5 **Women pedestrians** failed to reach the 300-mi. mark in a walking contest in Chicago. Mrs. Mary Marshall of Chicago reached the 234-mi. mark before becoming exhausted. Bertha Von Hillern of Germany gave out at the 211-mi. mark. They were competing for a purse of $500.

Feb. 26 Two expert pedestrians completed a **walk of 1000 mi. in 1000 consecutive hours.** They were Peter Goulding and John DeWitt, who performed their feat in Brooklyn, N.Y. They started on Jan. 15.

Apr. 2 In the **first official National League baseball game,** Boston beat Philadelphia 6-5. Jim O'Rourke got the first hit.

Apr. 8 In San Francisco, Daniel O'Leary completed a **500-mi. walk** in the remarkable time of 139 hrs., 32 min.

May **Nathanael Herreshoff,** a boatbuilder of Bristol, R.I., launched the *Amaryllis,* a 24-ft., 10-in. catamaran. Despite its demonstrable speed and safety, the racing catamaran failed to capture yachtsmen's fancy until 1959.

May 1 The first run of an **elegant coach,** owned by Col. De Lancey Kane of New York City, was immortalized in a painting by Henry Collins Bispham, which was made into a lithograph. The coach, "The Tally-Ho," drawn by four briskly trotting horses, with the owner holding the reins, is packed with his friends, no fewer than ten persons being outside on the top.

May 15 The second annual **Kentucky Derby** was won by Vagrant, with a time of 2:38¼. The jockey was Robert Swim.

May 23 The **first no-hitter** in National League history was pitched by Joe Borden of Boston.

JOE GANS

b. Baltimore, Md., Nov. 25, 1874
d. Baltimore, Md., Aug. 16, 1910

Joe Gans is without a doubt one of the two best boxers—the other one is Benny Leonard—ever to have ruled the lightweight division. He won the title on May 12, 1902, at Fort Erie, Ontario, Canada, when he

knocked out Frank Erne in the second round of a fight scheduled for 20 rounds.

Gans held the title until July 4, 1908, when he was knocked out in the 17th round by Battling Nelson in a bout in San Francisco. In the meantime, he had fought Joe Walcott, the welterweight champion,

to a draw on September 4, 1904.

Skill, as much as hard punching, made Gans a champion. He said he owed his success to his ability "to hit straight more than to anything else." Gans was already suffering from tuberculosis when he lost his title, and he died 15 months after he retired from the ring.

JIM JEFFRIES

James Jackson Jeffries
b. Carroll, Ohio, Apr. 15, 1875
d. Burbank, Calif., Mar. 3, 1953

Jim Jeffries began his boxing career in 1896 and within three years became the heavyweight champion. The title fight took place on June 9, 1899, at Coney Island, New York, where the newcomer knocked out champion Bob Fitzsimmons in the 11th round.

Each fighter received about $25,000, plus a share in the motion picture record of the bout.

Jeffries retired undefeated in 1905 but attempted a comeback in 1910, when there was racial agitation to find a white boxer who could win the championship from Jack Johnson, the first black to hold the title. Jeffries, badly outclassed, was knocked out in the 15th round of the

fight at Reno, Nevada, on July 4. After the fight, race riots erupted in a number of cities.

Jeffries was very strong but not especially fast. He was one of the first notable fighters to use the defensive crouch, which was later widely and successfully adopted by others.

Borden lost his effectiveness soon after and ended the season as the club's groundskeeper.

May 25 The fourth annual **Preakness Stakes** was won by Shirley, with a time of 2:44¾. The jockey was G. Barbee.

June 10 The tenth annual **Belmont Stakes** was won by Algerine, with a time of 2:40½. The jockey was W. Donohue.

July 20-21 The **first track and field meet** of the IC4A (Intercollegiate Association of Amateur Athletes of America) was held at Saratoga, N.Y. Among the winners were the following: 100-yard dash, H. W. Stevens of Williams, 11 sec.; 1-mi. run, E. C. Stimson of Dartmouth, 4 min., 58½ sec.; and running high jump, J. W. Pryor of Columbia, 5 ft., 4 in. Princeton took the team championship.

Aug. The **first recorded tennis tournament in the U.S.** was held on the private grounds of

William Appleton in Nahant, Mass. The two scratch players, Richard D. Sears and Dr. James Dwight, met in the finals, Dwight winning 12-15, 15-7, 15-13.

Aug. 11-12 The **America's Cup** was successfully defended by the yacht *Madeleine,* which won two straight heats over the Canadian challenger *Countess of Dufferin.*

Sept. For **failure to finish their scheduled baseball season,** the Athletics of Philadelphia and the New Yorks of New York City were thrown out of the National League. The teams, out of the running for the league championships, had canceled their final western trips. They were not reinstated until 1888.

Sept. 7 The **world heavyweight bare-knuckle boxing championship** was won by Joe Goss of England, who beat Tom Allen in a 27-round bout at Covington, Ky.

NAP LAJOIE

Napoleon Lajoie
b. Woonsocket, R.I., Sept. 5, 1875
d. Daytona Beach, Fla., Feb. 7, 1959

Nap Lajoie was one of the popular stars of major league bseball in the early twentiethth century. His baseball career stretched over 21 years. In his years as a player, he was a standout at the plate and at second base. Lajoie played for the

Philadelphia Athletics in 1901 and part of 1902, Cleveland from 1902 through 1914, and the Athletics again in 1915 and 1916.

Lajoie's best years were 1901, 1903, and 1904, when he won the American League batting championship. In 1901, he batted .422. His career total of 3251 hits remains tenth on the all-time list, and his career batting average was .339, 15th best. In a day when home runs

were scarce, Lajoie hit 82—about four a year on average—and led the National League with ten in 1897. He stole 395 bases.

Lajoie managed the Cleveland Indians from 1905 through 1909, compiling a record of 397 games won and 330 lost. In 1937, he was in the second group of players to be elected to the Baseball Hall of Fame.

PREAKNESS STAKES WINNERS

1876

	HORSE	JOCKEY		HORSE	JOCKEY
1873	Survivor	G. Barbee	1924	Nellie Morse	J. Merimee
1874	Culpepper	M. Donohue	1925	Coventry	C. Kummer
1875	Tom Ochiltree	L. Hughes	1926	Display	J. Maiben
1876	Shirley	G. Barbee	1927	Bostonian	A. Abel
1877	Cloverbrook	C. Holloway	1928	Victorian	R. Workman
1878	Duke of Magenta	C. Holloway	1929	Dr. Freeland	L. Schaefer
1879	Harold	L. Hughes	1930	Gallant Fox	E. Sande
1880	Grenada	L. Hughes	1931	Mate	G. Ellis
1881	Saunterer	W. Costello	1932	Burgoo King	E. James
1882	Vanguard	W. Costello	1933	Head Play	C. Kurtsinger
1883	Jacobus	G. Barbee	1934	High Quest	R. Jones
1884	Knight of Ellerslie	S. Fisher	1935	Omaha	W. Saunders
1885	Tecumseh	J. McLaughlin	1936	Bold Venture	G. Woolf
1886	The Bard	S. Fisher	1937	War Admiral	C. Kurtsinger
1887	Dunbine	W. Donoghue	1938	Dauber	M. Peters
1888	Refund	F. Littlefield	1939	Challedon	G. Seabo
1889	Buddhist	H. Anderson	1940	Bimelech	F. Smith
1890	Montague	W. Martin	1941	Whirlaway	E. Arcaro
1891–93	(not run)		1942	Alsab	B. James
1894	Assignee	F. Taral	1943	Count Fleet	J. Longden
1895	Belmar	F. Taral	1944	Pensive	C. McCreary
1896	Hargrave	H. Griffin	1945	Polynesian	W. Wright
1897	Paul Karvar	T. Thorpe	1946	Assault	W. Mehrtens
1898	Sly Fox	W. Simms	1947	Faultless	D. Dodson
1899	Half Time	R. Clawson	1948	Citation	E. Arcaro
1900	Hindus	H. Spencer	1949	Capot	T. Atkinson
1901	The Parader	F. Landry	1950	Hill Prince	E. Arcaro
1902	Old England	L. Jackson	1951	Bold	E. Arcaro
1903	Flocarline	W. Gannon	1952	Blue Man	C. McCreary
1904	Bryn Mawr	E. Hildebrand	1953	Native Dancer	E. Guerin
1905	Cairngorm	W. Davis	1954	Hasty Road	J. Adams
1906	Whimsical	W. Miller	1955	Nashua	E. Arcaro
1907	Don Enrique	G. Mountain	1956	Fabius	W. Hartack
1908	Royal Tourist	E. Dugan	1957	Bold Ruler	E. Arcaro
1909	Effendi	W. Doyle	1958	Tim Tam	I. Valenzuela
1910	Layminster	R. Estep	1959	Royal Orbit	W. Harmatz
1911	Watervale	E. Dugan	1960	Bally Ache	R. Ussery
1912	Colonel Halloway	C. Turner	1961	Carry Back	J. Sellers
1913	Buskin	J. Butwell	1962	Greek Money	J. Rotz
1914	Holiday	A. Schuttinger	1963	Candy Spots	W. Shoemaker
1915	Rhine Maiden	D. Hoffman	1964	Northern Dancer	W. Hartack
1916	Damrosch	L. McAfee	1965	Tom Rolfe	R. Turcotte
1917	Kalitan	E. Haynes	1966	Kauai King	D. Brumfield
1918	War Cloud	J. Loftus	1967	Damascus	W. Shoemaker
1919	Sir Barton	J. Loftus	1968	Forward Pass	I. Valenzuela
1920	Man o' War	C. Kummer	1969	Majestic Prince	W. Hartack
1921	Broomspun	F. Coltiletti	1970	Personality	E. Belmonte
1922	Pillory	L. Morris	1971	Canonero II	G. Avila
1923	Vigil	B. Marinelli			*(continued)*

	HORSE	JOCKEY		HORSE	JOCKEY
1972	Bee Bee Bee	E. Nelson	1980	Codex	A. Cordero
1973	Secretariat	R. Turcotte	1981	Pleasant Colony	J. Velasquez
1974	Little Current	M. Rivera	1982	Aloma's Ruler	J. Kaenel
1975	Master Derby	D. McHargue	1983	Deputed Testamony	D. Miller
1976	Elocutionist	J. Lively	1984	Gate Dancer	A. Cordero
1977	Seattle Slew	J. Cruguet	1985	Tank's Prospect	P. Day
1978	Affirmed	S. Cauthen	1986	Snow Chief	A. Solis
1979	Spectacular Bid	R. Franklin	1987	Alysheba	C. McCarron

Nov. 23 **Rules for football** were discussed at the invitation of Princeton, by delegates from Yale, Harvard, Rutgers, Columbia, and Princeton meeting at Massasoit House, Springfield, Mass. Princeton had recently adopted Harvard's rules, which in turn were based chiefly on the rules of the British Rugby Union, and these were adopted by all colleges represented at the meeting. The Intercollegiate Football Association grew out of the meeting.

1877

The **first U.S. championship swimming race,** organized by the New York Athletic Club, a 1-mi. race, was won by R. Weissenboth in the time of 44:44¼.

A new **baseball rule** exempted the batter from a time at bat when he was walked. This rule affected the determination of a batter's average but did not affect play. Another new rule stipulated that a substitute player could replace a starting player only before the fourth inning. The National League pennant winner was Boston, with a record of 31 wins, 17 losses.

May 8-10 The first **Westminster Kennel Club dog show** was held at Gilmore's Garden in New York City; it was sponsored by the Westminster Kennel Club. Setters of English, Irish, and Gordon types, as well as pointers, spaniels, mastiffs, Saint Bernards, terriers, and poodles, were well represented.

May 22 The third annual **Kentucky Derby** was won by Baden Baden, with a time of 2:38. The jockey was William Walker.

May 24 The fifth annual **Preakness Stakes** was won by Cloverbrook, with a time of 2:45½. The jockey was C. Holloway.

June 9 The 11th annual **Belmont Stakes** was won by Cloverbrook, with a time of 2:46. The jockey was C. Holloway.

June 13 The new **Ladies Club for Out-of-Door Sports** held its first garden party at New Brighton, Staten Island, N.Y. Archery, lawn tennis, and croquet were enjoyed by the club members and their guests. The club was an offshoot of the men's Staten Island Cricket and Baseball Club.

Aug. The first serious **polo game** by U.S. teams was played at Newport, R.I., between a team from Buffalo and the Westchester Polo Club team. The Westchester team won.

1878

The **first state game wardens** were appointed to enforce hunting laws in New Hampshire and Califor-

Golf is not, on the whole, a game for realists. By its exactitudes of measurement it invites the attention of pefectionists.

Heywood Hale Broun

31

BARNEY OLDFIELD

Berna Eli Oldfield
b. Wauseon, Ohio, Jan. 29, 1878
d. Beverly Hills, Calif., Oct. 4, 1946

Barney Oldfield became the best known of the dusty daredevils, the early racing car drivers whose vehicles were unpredictable and who drove on dirt roads better suited to horses.

He began as a bicycle racer and became an auto racer in October 1902, when he was given a chance to drive Henry Ford's 999 in a contest with Alexander Winton's car. Oldfield in 999 won, setting a new U.S. speed record by completing the 5-mile course in 5 minutes, 28 seconds. On June 15, 1903, Oldfield became the first person to drive an automobile at the speed of a mile a minute. Seven years later he set a record of 81.734 miles per hour at Daytona Beach, Florida.

Oldfield did his best to live up to the image of the daredevil driver. He raced with a cigar in his mouth, had numerous accidents, and gave his cars such names as Green Dragon, Big Ben, and Golden Submarine. Never modest, he said of Henry Ford the car builder and himself the racing driver, "I did much the best job of it." Oldfield retired in 1918, but we still may hear a speed demon driver referred to as a Barney Oldfield.

---

nia. By the end of the century, 29 other states had followed suit.

A record for **running down antelopes with greyhounds** was set by Maj. James H. "Hound Dog" Kelly and an assistant. Their four greyhounds got six of a dozen antelopes in a 4-mi. chase. The previous record for four dogs had been five antelopes.

The **National League baseball pennant** winner was Boston, with a season record of 41 wins and 19 defeats.

The **National Archery Association** was founded at Crawfordsville, Ind., signaling the beginning of modern archery in the U.S. The first target archery tournament was held at Chicago this same year; Will Thompson became the first champion.

Tennis scoring was introduced to the sport in Nahant, Mass., replacing the method used in racquets. Under the new method, points could be won only by the server.

Feb. 6 A **curling match** was played in Albany, N.Y., between the Albany Curling Club and the St. Andrews Club of Yonkers, N.Y. Two rinks were played, with each club winning one and St. Andrews scoring more total points, 65-59.

May 21 The fourth annual **Kentucky Derby** was won by Day Star, with a time of 2:37¼. The jockey was Jimmie Carter.

May 24 A **bicycle race** was run in Boston. The winner was C. A. Parker of Harvard, who rode the 3-mi. course in 12 min., 27 sec.

May 27 The sixth annual **Preakness Stakes** was won by Duke of Magenta, with a time of 2:41¾. The jockey was C. Holloway.

June 8 The 12th annual **Belmont Stakes** was won by Duke of Magenta, with a time of 2:43½. The jockey was L. Hughes.

July 5 The **first American victory at the Henley Regatta** was won by the four-oared Columbia College crew, which defeated Hertford College in the finals at Henley-on-Thames, England, for the Visitors' Challenge Cup. When the victors returned home to New York City, their carriage was hauled up Broadway by enthusiastic fellow students.

Fall **Badminton** arrived on the American scene, brought to our shores by New Yorkers Bayard Clark and E. Langdon Wilkes, who had seen the game independently in England and India, respectively. They formed the Badminton Club of the City of New York in the winter of 1878-1879.

Oct. 10 The earliest known American **jockey record** was Jimmie McLaughlin's riding of winners in three races in Nashville, Tenn. One of the races was run in two heats, both won by McLaughlin.

Oct. 15 R. Lyman Potter completed a **walk across the continent** while pushing a wheelbarrow before him.

1879

A **revival of lawn bowling** in the U.S. began with the founding by Christian Shepplin of the Dunellen Bowling Club of New Jersey. Soon after, clubs were formed in nearby towns, such as Montclair and East Orange, and then the movement spread to New York and Connecticut. In 1894 the Dunellen Club changed its name to the New Jersey Bowling Green Club and leased property from the Central Railroad of New Jersey for a new green and a clubhouse.

A new **baseball rule** allowed a batter to reach first base after receiving nine balls. The requirement for a walk to first base was reduced to eight balls in 1880, seven in 1881, and six in 1884, was raised to seven again in 1885, and was reduced to five in 1887 and four in 1889. This last requirement for a base on balls has persisted to the present time.

May 20   The fifth annual **Kentucky Derby** was won by Lord Murphy, with a time of 2:37. The jockey was Charlie Shauer.

May 24   The seventh annual **Preakness Stakes** was won by Harold, with a time of 2:40½. The jockey was L. Hughes.

June 5   The 13th annual **Belmont Stakes** was won by Spendthrift, with a time of 2:48¾. The jockey was named Evans.

June 24   The **first crew race** for the Childs Cup was won by the Pennsylvania U. The perpetual trophy was presented by George W. Childs of Philadelphia for competition among Columbia,

Pennsylvania, and Princeton universities. Cornell and Navy occasionally participate by invitation, but if they win, they may not claim the prize. The Childs Cup is the oldest trophy in sprint racing. It was contested by four-oared crews until 1887, by eight-oared crews since 1889. There was no competition in 1888.

Sept. 24-29   The **first six-day bicycle race** in the U.S. was run in Chicago. The winner was W. Cann of Great Britain.

Fall   Providence won the **National League baseball pennant** with a season record of 55 victories, 23 defeats.

1880

An **early parachutist** was Capt. Tom Baldwin, who toured widely in the 1880s as a daredevil who jumped from balloons.

The **Pearl Archery Club** was organized by women in New Orleans. It was not the first such

GLENN CURTISS

Glenn Hammond Curtiss
b.   Hammondsport, N.Y., Mar. 21, 1878
d.   Buffalo, N.Y., July 23, 1930

Unlike the Wright brothers, who made their experimental airplane flights in secluded places and did not enter speed contests, Glenn Curtiss from the start was eager to have the public see his planes and to try for speed records. Curtiss began his business career as manager of a bicycle shop and soon had a shop of his own. All the while he was entering and winning bike races at county fairs. In 1902, he moved up to manufacturing motorcycles and racing them. He set a speed record at Ormond Beach, Florida, in 1904.

Meanwhile, Curtiss was also experimenting with airplanes and, on

July 4, 1908, at Hammondsport, his plane, the *June Bug,* made the first public airplane flight in the United States. The next year, at Mineola, New York, he flew his plane 25 miles to win the Scientific American Trophy, and in August of the same year won the Gordon Bennett Trophy at the first international aviation meet in Europe. It was on this occasion that Curtiss flew with his first passenger, Gabriele D'Annunzio, the Italian poet and soldier.

Curtiss's most spectacular feat was performed in May 1910, when he flew his plane from Albany to New York City in 2 hours, 51 minutes to win a $10,000 prize. That same year, over Atlantic City, New Jersey, he dropped oranges to show how planes could be used to deliver bombs in wartime. In 1911, he established a

flying school for U.S. Army and Navy officers in San Diego, California. About the same time, he invented the hydroplane and made the first flights from water to land.

During World War I, Curtiss expanded his manufacturing facilities and produced thousands of war planes for the Allies. Finally there came the JN-4, the Navy-Curtiss flying boat, which made the first Atlantic Ocean crossing by air in 1919.

One of Curtiss's most important inventions was the aileron, for maintaining lateral balance of a plane. This got him involved in a lawsuit with the Wright brothers, which he won in December 1911. His production of large numbers of planes made Curtiss rich, and he enjoyed spending his money.

JACK JOHNSON

John Arthur Johnson
b. Galveston, Tex., Mar. 31, 1878
d. Raleigh, N.C., June 10, 1946

Jack Johnson encountered poverty early in life and racial prejudice throughout his boxing career, but he persevered to become the first black heavyweight boxing champion of the world. He learned to box at a Galveston athletic club and was jailed in 1901 for taking part in an illegal prizefight. Between 1902 and 1908, Johnson fought all over the country, losing only three bouts.

No white boxer would fight him until the champion, Canadian Tommy Burns, agreed to meet him in Sydney, Australia, on December 26, 1908. Johnson won in the 14th round when police stopped the bout to save Burns from further punishment. Johnson actively defended his title, including a bout on July 4, 1910, with the former champion, Jim Jeffries, who came out of retirement in response to the demand of a prejudiced public that was seeking a "white hope" to dethrone Johnson. Johnson knocked Jeffries out in the 15th round.

In 1912, Johnson was convicted of violating the Mann Act, also called the White Slave Act, and fled the country, first to Canada and then to Europe. He fought in Europe and lived lavishly. His flamboyant ways and the fact that he had a white wife made him unpopular. He remained champion until April 5, 1915, when at Havana, Cuba, he was knocked out in the 16th round by Jess Willard, a white fighter. Over his career, Johnson lost only 7 of 114 fights.

Johnson returned to the United States in 1920 and made appearances in vaudeville and at carnivals after serving a year in prison. One result of his career was the banning in New York State in February 1913 of bouts between whites and blacks.

---

organization, for the Crescent City Female Archery Club had already been founded in the same city during the 1870s.

Pres. William A. Hulbert of **baseball's National League** threw Cincinnati out of the league for disregarding the league's rules against games on Sundays and the sale of liquor in the stands. One effect of the ouster was the formation of the American Association in 1881, which permitted Sunday games and included Cincinnati and teams from cities not members of the National League.

Trapshooting in a more modern mode was now enjoyed in Cincinnati. An Englishman's production of suitable targets and an efficient trap to release them made possible the standardization of equipment and rules, followed by a rapid spread of the sport. The Interstate Association of Trapshooters was soon conducting both live-bird and trapshooting tournaments on its property on Long Island, N.Y.

The **first clay target for trapshooting** was developed by George Ligowsky of Cincinnati. The first targets were made entirely of clay, but Ligowsky soon switched to limestone and pitch. The first public appearance of these targets was at the New York State live-bird championships at Coney Island in 1880. This was also the largest live-bird shoot held to that date.

The first widely contested **tennis tournament** in the U.S. was held at the Staten Island Cricket and Baseball Club, New York City.

The **participation of women in sports** increased sharply during the 1880s. Besides tennis, archery, and croquet, they engaged in riding, cycling, swimming, boat racing, fencing, and skating. Woodcuts of the period even show women bowling.

The term *hot corner* became baseball parlance for third base. The term was coined by Ren Mulford, a writer of this period who watched a game in which Cincinnati third baseman Hick Carpenter was bombarded by several balls hit sharply in his direction.

A new **baseball rule** stipulated that a base runner was out if he was hit by a batted ball.

Jan. 19 The **world wrestling championship,** Greco-Roman style, was won by William Muldoon, who defeated Thiebaud Bauer, of France, at Madison Square Garden, New York City. Muldoon, who received his early training in saloons, the Army, and the New York City Police Dept., now became a full-time professional.

May 18 The sixth annual **Kentucky Derby** was won by Fonso, with a time of 2:37½. The jockey was George Lewis.

May 28 The eighth annual **Preakness Stakes** was won by Grenada, with a time of 2:40½. The jockey was L. Hughes.

May 31 In Newport, R.I., the **League of American Wheelmen** was organized. Representatives of 40 bicycle clubs from six states were represented, and the first president was Kirk Munroe, of New York, a world traveler and journalist.

b. Humboldt, Nebr., Apr. 27, 1878
d. Humboldt, Nebr., Dec. 16, 1917

Generally regarded as the greatest American professional wrestler ever, Frank Gotch pursued his imposing career at a time when wrestling was still a sport rather than cheap entertainment. He won his first bout on April 2, 1889, and soon attracted enough attention to be matched with the U.S. champion, Tom Jenkins, on February 2, 1903. Gotch lost, but on January 28, 1904, he defeated Jenkins in a rematch for the title.

Gotch lost his title to Jenkins in May 1905 but regained it a year later. He retired as champion in 1913, having defeated such European wrestlers as Yussif Mahmout of Turkey, Emile Maupas of France, and Jim Parr of England, as well as all the leading Americans. On April 3, 1908, he defeated the Russian Lion, George Hackenschmidt, who gave up after 2 hours, 1 minute. Gotch lost only 6 of 196 matches, and three of the losses were to Jenkins, whom he met eight times in all. His trademark was the toehold, with which he was said to have broken the legs of several opponents.

Gotch retired to his hometown of Humboldt, Nebraska, where he became president of a street railway company and an electric utility. One of the best-conditioned athletes of his day, Gotch died of uremic poisoning when only 39.

June 14 The 14th annual **Belmont Stakes** was won by Grenada, with a time of 2:47. The jockey was L. Hughes.

June 21 The **world heavyweight bare-knuckle boxing championship** was won by Paddy Ryan this year. Ryan beat the defender, Joe Goss of England, in an 87-round bout near Colliers Station, W.Va.

July *Harper's Monthly* praised the benefits of **bicycling:** "There has been heretofore in our American life, crowded to excess as it has been with the harassing cares and anxieties of business, so little attention paid to the organized practice of health-giving outdoor exercises, to which bicycling is peculiarly adapted, that the organization of the League of American Wheelmen cannot fail to be recognized as an important subject for public congratulation."

Fall The **National League championship** was won by Chicago with a season record of 67 wins and 17 losses.

1881

A **new baseball league,** the American Association, was formed. It flourished for several years, formed a working agreement with the established National League in 1886, then merged into the National League in 1891.

The **Meadow Brook Club,** shrine of American polo, in Westbury, N.Y., was formed by August Belmont, Thomas Hitchcock, Sr., and others. This year the number of players on a team was reduced from five to four.

A new **baseball rule** increased the distance of the pitcher's slab from home plate from 45 ft. to 50 ft. Another new rule provided that a pitcher be fined for hitting a batter deliberately with a pitched ball. This rule was abolished in 1882.

Coney Island, which had been a deserted sandbank four years earlier, had by this time become famous as a place for sun and recreation. Manhattan, Rockaway, and Brighton beaches were all considered to constitute *Coney Island,* but it was Cable Beach, with its boardwalk, that was to become the nucleus of Coney Island. The boardwalk, built on sturdy steel girders, included a hotel shipped piece by piece from the 1876 Centennial Exposition in Philadelphia. Coney Island also boasted museums, sideshows, orchestras, amusement rides, and sandy beaches.

May 17 The seventh annual **Kentucky Derby** was won by Hindoo, with a time of 2:40. The jockey was Jimmy McLaughlin.

May 21 Leaders from **lawn tennis clubs** in Eastern cities, variously reported to number 33 to 35, met in New York City to standardize rules and to form the United States National Lawn Tennis Association. The word *National* was later dropped. August 3, 1881, was selected as the date of the first national tournament, to be held at Newport, R.I. The English rules for tennis were adopted, notably for the height of the net and the dimensions of the court. The English tennis ball was accepted as standard.

May 27 The ninth annual **Preakness Stakes** was

CHRISTY MATHEWSON

Christopher Mathewson
b. Factoryville, Pa., July 12, 1880
d. Saranac Lake, N.Y., Oct. 7, 1925

Christy Mathewson, one of the most successful right-handed pitchers in the history of baseball, had power in his fastball and baffled batters with his fadeaway pitch. Like the screwball, the vaunted fadeaway broke in a direction opposite to that of a curve. In his career from 1900 to 1918, he recorded 373 victories, fourth all-time best, and lost 188 for a percentage of .665 and an earned run average of 2.13. He pitched a total of 83 shutouts, which still is the third highest ever.

Mathewson joined the New York Giants in 1900, then went to the Cincinnati Reds in 1916, where he managed until 1918. As a pitcher, he struck out 2502 batters while giving up only 846 walks. As a manager, he won 164 and lost 176. In the 1903, 1904, and 1905 seasons, Mathewson won 30 or more games, and his best year came in 1908, when he had 37 victories.

In 1905, he led the Giants to a World Series victory over the Philadelphia Athletics by pitching three shutouts in six days. In four World Series, he had an overall record of five wins and five losses.

Mathewson joined the Army in World War I and was gassed in France. Back in civilian life, he became president of the Boston Braves in 1923 but two years later died of tuberculosis, presumably brought on by the gassing he had suffered. In 1936, Mathewson became a member of the first group elected to the Baseball Hall of Fame.

won by Saunterer, with a time of 2:40½. The jockey was T. Costello.

June 7 The 15th annual **Belmont Stakes** was won by Saunterer, with a time of 2:47. The jockey was T. Costello.

Aug. 31 The **first U.S. National Lawn Tennis Association championship** opened at Newport, R.I. It was for men only. Twenty-five players entered the singles competition, and 13 teams entered the doubles competition. Richard D. Sears won the singles title, and Clarence W. Clark and and Fred W. Taylor, of Philadelphia, won the doubles.

Fall Chicago won the **National League baseball pennant** with a season's record of 56 victories, 28 defeats.

Oct. 15 The **first American fishing journal,** *American Angler,* owned and edited by William C. Harris, was published in Philadelphia.

Nov. 9-10 The **America's Cup** was successfully defended by the yacht *Mischief,* which won two straight heats over the Canadian challenger *Atlanta.*

1882

Squash racquets was introduced into the U.S. from Canada at Saint Paul's School in Concord,

MAX HIRSCH

Maximilian Justice Hirsch
b. Fredericksburg, Tex., July 30, 1880
d. New Hyde Park, N.Y., Apr. 3, 1969

As a private person, Max Hirsch was a warmhearted and generous man who entertained hundreds of friends and associates. As a trainer of race horses, however, he was described as crafty, cunning, and wily. In any event, he was still active in training thoroughbreds until just before he died at the age of 88, and he was unquestionably the dean of American thoroughbred trainers.

Hirsch was an exercise boy by the time he was 10, a jockey at 15, and a trainer at 19. As a jockey, he rode 123 winners in 1117 races before he became too heavy for racing. As a trainer, Hirsch had his first winner in Gautana at New Orleans in 1902. The victory he cherished most was that of Sarazen in 1924 at Latonia, Kentucky. Sarazen beat the French champion thoroughbred Epinard and in so doing set a world record of 2:00⅘ for 1¼ miles.

Hirsch went on to train horses that won the Kentucky Derby in 1936, 1946, and 1950; the Preakness Stakes in 1936 and 1946; and the Belmont Stakes in 1946. In that year, Hirsch-trained Assault took the Triple Crown. In all, the horses he trained earned $12,213,020, and four of them were national champions.

b. Pottawatomie, Kans., Dec. 29, 1881
d. Los Angeles, Calif., Dec. 15, 1968

In the eyes of some boxing fans of the time, Jess Willard's chief claim to fame was that he won the heavyweight championship from a black titleholder, Jack Johnson, and in the eyes of racists, restored the prestige of the white race. The epic encounter took place in Havana, Cuba, on April 5, 1915, in 100-degree heat. Scheduled for 45 rounds, it ended in the 26th. After 1 hour and 45 minutes of hard fighting, Willard had knocked Johnson out.

Willard did not defend his title very often but held it until July 4, 1919, when he lost to Jack Dempsey in a bout at Toledo, Ohio. This time the temperature was 110 degrees. Willard was in poor shape and took a bad beating for three rounds before his handlers threw in the towel.

Although Willard by then was 37 years old, he fought some more but was knocked out again by Dempsey and also by Luis Firpo. In all, Willard had 36 fights, winning 20 of them by knockouts and losing only three.

N.H., by its headmaster, the Rev. James P. Conover.

The **Berlin, N.H., Ski Club** was formed and was the first in the East. In the Midwest, the Minneapolis and the St. Paul, Minn., ski clubs were founded in 1885. On Jan. 19, 1886, the Aurora Ski Club was founded at Red Wing, Minn.

The **bicycle rider,** according to *The Wheelman,* was "a personage of consequence and attractiveness. He becomes at once a notable feature in the landscape, drawing to himself the admiring gaze of all eyes."

Handball was an unknown sport in the U.S. until Phil Casey, one of Ireland's finest handball players, this year came to live in Brooklyn, N.Y. Casey soon built a court and opened a school. He introduced the sport in the U.S. with the help of fellow immigrants from the British Isles.

The **U.S. Intercollegiate Lacrosse Association** was founded. The original members were Harvard, Princeton, and Columbia. Yale and New York U. were admitted the following year.

The **U.S. Lawn Tennis Association singles championship** was won by Richard D. Sears.

Feb. 7 The **world heavyweight bare-knuckle boxing championship** was won by John L. Sullivan, who defeated Paddy Ryan in a nine-round bout in Mississippi City, Miss. This year Sullivan toured the country, giving boxing exhibitions under Marquis of Queensberry rules and offering $500 to anyone who could last four rounds with him. His efforts gave boxing new respectability and wider popularity.

May 16 The eighth annual **Kentucky Derby** was won by Apollo, with a time of 2:40½. The jockey was Babe Hurd.

May 27 The tenth annual **Preakness Stakes** was won by Vanguard, with a time of 2:44½. The jockey was T. Costello.

June 8 The 16th annual **Belmont Stakes** was won by Forester, with a time of 2:43. The jockey was Jimmy McLaughlin.

June 24 The only major league **baseball umpire expelled for dishonesty,** Richard Higham, left the National League.

Fall The **National League baseball championship** was won by Chicago, with a record of 55 wins and 29 losses. Chicago split a two-game interleague playoff with Cincinnati, of the American Association. It was the first such series, the forerunner of the World Series.

Sept. 25 The **first major league double header** was played between the Providence and Worcester teams.

Oct. 4 The **National American Croquet Association** was formed at a meeting of 25 local clubs from Boston; New York; Norwich, Conn.; and Philadelphia held at the New York Croquet Club, 127th St. and Fifth Ave. The new association adopted rules to be followed by all member clubs, a task taken over in 1976 by the new United States Croquet Association.

---

*For when the one Great Scorer comes
To write against your name,
He marks—not that you won or lost—
But how you played the game.*

Grantland Rice

Horse Racing
KENTUCKY DERBY WINNERS

	HORSE	JOCKEY		HORSE	JOCKEY
1875	Aristides	O. Lewis	1924	Black Gold	J. Mooney
1876	Vagrant	R. Swim	1925	Flying Ebony	E. Sande
1877	Baden Baden	W. Walker	1926	Bubbling Over	A. Johnson
1878	Day Star	J. Carter	1927	Whiskery	L. McAtee
1879	Lord Murphy	C. Schauer	1928	Reigh Count	C. Lang
			1929	Clyde Van Dusen	L. McAtee
1880	Fonso	G. Lewis			
1881	Hindoo	J. McLaughlin	1930	Gallant Fox	E. Sande
1882	Apollo	B. Hurd	1931	Twenty Grand	C. Kurtsinger
1883	Leonatus	W. Donohue	1932	Burgoo King	E. James
1884	Buchanan	I. Murphy	1933	Brokers Tip	D. Meade
1885	Joe Cotton	E. Henderson	1934	Cavalcade	M. Garner
1886	Ben Ali	P. Duffy	1935	Omaha	W. Saunders
1887	Montrose	I. Lewis	1936	Bold Venture	I. Hanford
1888	Macbeth II	G. Covington	1937	War Admiral	C. Kurtsinger
1889	Spokane	T. Kiley	1938	Lawrin	E. Arcaro
			1939	Johnstown	J. Stout
1890	Riley	I. Murphy			
1891	Kingman	I. Murphy	1940	Gallahadion	C. Bierman
1892	Azra	A. Clayton	1941	Whirlaway	E. Arcaro
1893	Lookout	E. Kunze	1942	Shut Out	W. Wright
1894	Chant	F. Goodale	1943	Count Fleet	J. Longden
1895	Halma	J. Perkins	1944	Pensive	C. McCreary
1896	Ben Brush	W. Simms	1945	Hoop Jr.	E. Arcaro
1897	Typhoon H	F. Garner	1946	Assault	W. Mehrtens
1898	Plaudit	W. Simms	1947	Jet Pilot	E. Guerin
1899	Manuel	F. Taral	1948	Citation	E. Arcaro
			1949	Ponde	S. Brooks
1900	Lieut. Gibson	J. Boland			
1901	His Eminence	J. Winkfield	1950	Middleground	W. Boland
1902	Alan-a-Dale	J. Winkfield	1951	Count Turf	C. McCreary
1903	Judge Himes	H. Booker	1952	Hill Gail	E. Arcaro
1904	Elwood	F. Prior	1953	Dark Star	H. Moreno
1905	Agile	J. Martin	1954	Determine	R. York
1906	Sir Huon	R. Troxler	1955	Swaps	W. Shoemaker
1907	Pink Star	A. Minder	1956	Needles	D. Erb
1908	Stone Street	A. Pickens	1957	Iron Liege	W. Hartack
1909	Wintergreen	V. Powers	1958	Tim Tam	I. Valenzuela
			1959	Tomy Lee	W. Shoemaker
1910	Donau	F. Herbert			
1911	Meridian	G. Archibald	1960	Venetian Way	W. Hartack
1912	Worth	C. Shilling	1961	Carry Back	J. Sellers
1913	Donerail	R. Goose	1962	Decidedly	W. Hartack
1914	Old Rosebud	J. McCabe	1963	Chateaugay	B. Baeza
1915	Regret	J. Notler	1964	Northern Dancer	W. Hartack
1916	George Smith	J. Loftus	1965	Lucky Debonair	W. Shoemaker
1917	Omar Khayyam	C. Borel	1966	Kauai King	D. Brumfield
1918	Exterminator	W. Knapp	1967	Proud Clarion	R. Ussery
1919	Sir Barton	J. Loftus	1968	Forward Pass	I. Valenzuela
			1969	Majestic Prince	W. Hartack
1920	Paul Jones	T. Rice			
1921	Behave Yourself	C. Thompson	1970	Dust Commander	M. Manganello
1922	Morvich	A. Johnson	1971	Canonero II	G. Avila
1923	Zev	E. Sande			*(continued)*

	HORSE	JOCKEY			HORSE	JOCKEY
1972	Riva Ridge	R. Turcotte		1980	Genuine Risk	J. Vasquez
1973	Secretariat	R. Turcotte		1981	Pleasant Colony	J. Velásquez
1974	Cannonade	A. Cordero		1982	Gato del Sol	E. Delàhoussaye
1975	Foolish Pleasure	J. Vasquez		1983	Sunny's Halo	E. Delahoussaye
1976	Bold Forbes	A. Cordero		1984	Swale	L. Pincay
1977	Seattle Slew	J. Cruguet		1985	Spend a Buck	A. Cordero
1978	Affirmed	S. Cauthen		1986	Ferdinand	W. Shoemaker
1979	Spectacular Bid	R. Franklin		1987	Alysheba	C. McCarron

1883

The **national swimming championships** for the first time offered more than one event. Four freestyle races were contested at distances of 100 yards, 440 yards, 800 yards, and 1 mi.

The **U.S. Intercollegiate Lacrosse Association** was founded at Washington College, Chestertown, Md. The association now has 190 college and university members.

This year the **first national college football championship** was won by Yale, with a record of eight wins, no losses, no ties. The yearly ranking of the top college football teams was begun by the Citizens Savings Athletic Foundation. In 1936 the Associated Press inaugurated an annual poll of its sportswriters to select the champion team of the year. In 1950 United Press International began its own poll of college coaches.

The **U.S. Lawn Tennis Association singles championship** was won by Richard D. Sears. In the tournament, the reigning men's national singles champion was permitted to sit on the sidelines during the all-comers tournament and then defend his title against the winner in a challenge round. This method was to prevail until the 1920s, when the rules were changed to require the reigning champion to play through the field.

May 23 The ninth annual **Kentucky Derby** was won by Leonatus, with a time of 2:43. The jockey was Billy Donohue.

May 26 The 11th annual **Preakness Stakes** was won by Jacobus, with a time of 2:42½. The jockey was G. Barbee.

June 2 The **first baseball game played under electric lights** took place in Fort Wayne, Ind. Fort Wayne beat Quincy 19-11 in seven innings.

June 9 The 17th annual **Belmont Stakes** was won by George Kinney, with a time of 2:47½. The jockey was Jimmy McLaughlin.

June 16 The **first Ladies' Day baseball game** was staged by the New York Giants. On Ladies' Day, escorted and unescorted women were admitted to the park free.

July 4 The **first rodeo for cash prizes** was held at Pecos, Tex. There were riding and roping contests, with cash awards of $25 for first place and $15 for second place. Other towns held similar affairs around this time. The term *rodeo* had not yet come into use, and the Pecos celebration was known as a Cowboy Tournament.

July 4 Featuring rodeo events among other activities, what was probably the first performance of **Buffalo Bill Cody's Wild West Show** was given in North Platte, Nebr. A year earlier he had sponsored what was billed as an Old Glory Blow-Out in North Platte, and some sources say the first performance of the Wild West Show took place in Omaha, Nebr., on May 17, 1883.

Aug. 28 The **first controlled flight in a glider** was made by John J. Montgomery from the Motay Mesa rim at Wheeler Hill, Calif. He soared 603 ft. at a height of about 15 ft. Montgomery's craft weighed 38 lbs. and had gull-like wings.

Sept. What was called the **first championship bicycle race** took place in Springfield, Mass. The winner was G. M. Hendrie, who defeated the only other contestant, W. G. Rowe. Hendrie later became a successful automobile and motorcycle builder.

Fall Boston won the **National League baseball championship** with a season's record of 63 victories, 35 defeats.

Oct. 22 The **first annual New York Horse Show** opened at Madison Square Garden, New York

City. It was organized by the National Horse Show Association of America. Represented were 165 exhibitors and 299 horses; many workhorses, including fire-engine horses, police mounts, and draught horses, were shown. The show was immediately popular and became an annual event. After 1913 the character of the show altered; working breeds were no longer allowed, and entries were limited to show horses, gaited horses, and the like.

1884

An **early claim to a golf course** is made by the Oakhurst, W.Va., club, later called the Greenbrier Club. The Dorset, Vt., Field Club claims to have laid out its course in 1886.

The **American Kennel Club** (AKC) was founded. It keeps a registry of purebred dogs and sets standards for judging the various breeds. As of the end of 1986, nearly 30,000,000 dogs had been registered with the AKC since its founding.

This year's **national college football championship** was awarded to Yale, with a record of eight wins, no losses, one tie.

The **first black major league baseball player** was Moses Fleetwood Walker, who played for Toledo in the American Association.

Greyhound racing was introduced in Philadelphia.

The **U.S. Lawn Tennis Association singles** championship was won for the fourth year in a row by Richard D. Sears.

Apr. The baseball season opened with a **new pitching rule.** The rule requiring a pitcher to pitch underhanded was abandoned. Despite being free now to pitch overhanded, the pitcher was allowed to take only one step forward before releasing the ball.

May 16 The tenth annual **Kentucky Derby** was won by Buchanan, with a time of 2:40¼. The jockey was Isaac Murphy, one of the greatest of all time.

May 23 The 12th annual **Preakness Stakes** was won by Knight of Ellerslie, with a time of 2:39½. The jockey was S. Fisher.

June 4 The 18th annual **Belmont Stakes** was won by Panique, with a time of 2:42. The jockey was Jimmy McLaughlin.

July 4 There was a widespread **celebration by cyclists.** A meet on Boston Common attracted thousands; a parade in Portsmouth, N.H., included 70 cyclists; in the South, at Columbia, Ga., there were races for the state championship; the Kishwaukee Bicycle Club of Syracuse, Ill., made its first run; and in Salt Lake City, Utah, there were races for medals.

Fall The **American Football (soccer) Association** was formed at Newark, N.J. Teams were composed chiefly of English, Welsh, Scottish, and Irish immigrants, who played their games on vacant lots. Teams in New Jersey, New York City, Philadelphia, and Fall River, Mass., were prominent early. The AFA came to govern the professional leagues and clubs.

Fall The **National League baseball championship** was won by Providence, with a record of

HARRY GREB

Edward Henry Greb
b. Pittsburgh, Pa., June 7, 1884
d. Atlantic City, N.J., Oct. 22, 1926

Harry Greb was the only boxer who ever defeated Gene Tunney, but that is by no means his only claim to fame in the boxing world. His ring career began in 1913, and he became the middleweight champion ten years later. He held the title until February 1926, when he lost the decision to Tiger Flowers in a 15-round fight in New York City.

Greb won the light heavyweight championship by beating Tunney in May 1922. However, in February 1923, Tunney took the title back from Greb. Greb's last important bout came in August 1926, when he was clearly past his peak. In all Greb fought 288 times, winning 115 and losing 9, only one by a knockout. He had an unusually large number of no-decision fights, 164.

Although it did not become known until late in Greb's career, at some point he became blind in one eye. Greb died in hospital of heart failure after an operation stemming from his involvement in an auto accident.

HAROLD S. VANDERBILT

Harold Stirling Vanderbilt
b. Oakdale, N.Y., July 6, 1884
d. Newport, R.I., July 4, 1970

Thanks to the skill, persistence, and money of Harold Vanderbilt, the America's Cup, symbol of international yachting supremacy, remained in the United States during the 1930s. A member of a prominent and wealthy New York family, Vanderbilt was an avid sportsman as well as director of railroads and other corporations.

In 1930, his yacht *Enterprise,* racing against Sir Thomas Lipton's *Shamrock V,* won in four straight races. In 1934, Vanderbilt's *Rainbow,* after losing the first two races, won four straight from *Endeavour,* owned and raced by English sportsman T. O. M. Sopwith. Sopwith tried again in 1937 with *Endeavour II,* but Vanderbilt's *Ranger* took four straight races. This was the 16th successful defense of the America's Cup by the United States since it was first awarded in 1851.

Overall, from 1922 to 1938, Vanderbilt and his yachts won 11 major races, but Vanderbilt is even better known to some as the inventor of contract bridge, which he developed in 1926 out of other bridge games. Within two years, contract bridge became the preeminent form of bridge.

---

84 wins and 28 losses. Providence went on to defeat the New York Metropolitans, of the American Association, in a three-game series at the Polo Grounds in New York City.

1885

The **U.S. Lawn Tennis Association championship** was won for the fifth successive year by Richard D. Sears.

The **first professional baseball team of black players,** the Cuban Giants, was organized on Long Island, N.Y. It barnstormed about the country, playing teams of white players.

This year's **national college football championship** was won by Princeton, with a record of nine wins, no losses, no ties.

Douglas Tilden, a gifted West Coast sculptor, created his first work on an athletic theme, *Tired Wrestler.* Among his later works in this vein were *Baseball Player, Young Acrobat,* and *Football Players.*

Feb. 11-16 The **first national championship in clay target shooting** was held in New Orleans. William Frank "Doc" Carver defeated the favorite, A. H. Bogardus. This event was sponsored by the National Gun Association.

May 14 The 11th annual **Kentucky Derby** was won by Joe Cotton, with a time of 2:37¼. The jockey was Erskine Henderson.

May 22 The 13th annual **Preakness Stakes** was won by Tecumseh, with a time of 2:49. The jockey was Jimmy McLaughlin.

June 6 The 19th annual **Belmont Stakes** was won by Tyrant, with a time of 2:43. The jockey was P. Duffy.

Fall The **National League baseball championship** was won by Chicago, with a record of 87 wins and 25 losses. The third interleague playoff series (seven games), with St. Louis of the American Association, ended in a 3-3 tie, with one game a draw.

Sept. 14-16 The **America's Cup** was successfully defended by the U.S. yacht *Puritan,* which won two straight heats over the British challenger *Genesta.*

Dec. 20 A **weightlifting feat** of incredible proportions was accomplished by William B. Curtis, who was reported to have lifted 3239 lbs "with harness."

1886

The year saw **two firsts in U.S. soccer.** The first game was played in Central Park, New York City, and the first international match for a U.S. eleven, one selected from teams in New Jersey and the other a Canadian all-star team, was played in Canada.

HOME RUN BAKER

John Franklin Baker
b. Trappe, Md., Mar. 13, 1886
d. Trappe, Md., June 28, 1963

If playing today, Home Run Baker would certainly not qualify for his nickname. In fact, it was given to him not because of his total home run output but because he hit two home runs in the 1911 World Series, and this was a rare accomplishment at the time.

Baker first played third base for the Philadelphia Athletics and then for New York of the American League. In his career he hit 96 homers in regular season play and three in the six World Series in which he participated in the years between 1910 and 1922. Baker's best year was 1913, when he hit 12 home runs, a large number for the time. In three other years, he hit ten home runs.

But Baker was more than a slugger. His career batting average was a noteworthy .307. Baker was elected to the Baseball Hall of Fame in 1955.

The International Cup, a **polo trophy** for play between nations, was financed by subscriptions from Newport, R.I., donors. The famed English Hurlingham team accepted an invitation to compete for it with the U.S. Hurlingham captured the trophy easily and kept it until 1901. The cup is popularly known as the Westchester Cup.

The sport of **iceboating** was introduced on Gull Lake, Mich., by D. C. Olin of Kalamazoo. In 1893 the Kalamazoo Ice Yacht Club was formed.

This year's **national college football championship** was won by Yale, with a record of nine wins, no losses, and one tie.

The **first international polo match** was held between England and the U.S. at Newport, R.I. It was a gala occasion. Both teams were colorfully dressed in satin and full-length leather boots. The grounds were lined with members of the social set of New England and New York. The visiting team, more practiced, swept the match 10-4 and 14-2.

The **U.S. Lawn Tennis Association singles championship** was won for the sixth year in a row by Richard D. Sears.

Jan. 1 The **first Tournament of Roses** was held in Pasadena, Calif., staged by the Valley Hunt Club, which had been founded by Charles Frederick Holder, a distinguished naturalist. Holder suggested that the members of the Valley Hunt Club decorate their horse carriages with the native flowers of California on New Year's Day and that after a parade of these carriages a program of athletic events be devised to round out the day. Holder's floral motif has remained a feature of the tournament to this day.

May 14 The 12th annual **Kentucky Derby** was won by Ben Ali, with a time of 2:36½. The jockey was Paul Duffy.

May 21 The 14th annual **Preakness Stakes** was won by The Bard, with a time of 2:45. The jockey was S. Fisher.

June 5 The 20th annual **Belmont Stakes** was won by Inspector, with a time of 2:41. The jockey was Jimmy McLaughlin.

Fall The **National League baseball championship** was won by Chicago, with a record of 90 wins, 34 losses. The interleague playoff was won by St. Louis of the American Association, beating Chicago four games to two.

Sept. 9-11 The **America's Cup** was successfully defended by the U.S. yacht *Mayflower*, which won two straight heats over the British challenger *Galatea*.

Oct. The **first major greyhound races** in the U.S. were held at Great Bend, Kans. *Harper's Weekly* reported on the event and included a sketch showing the action of the racing.

1887

This year's **national college football championship** was won by Yale, with a record of nine wins, no losses, no ties.

The **first true golf club** in the U.S. was probably the Foxburg Golf Club, founded in Foxburg, Pa., as a result of John Mickle Fox's trip to Scotland, where he learned the game. The club is still in existence.

The **U.S. Lawn Tennis Association men's singles championship** was won for the seventh time in a row by Richard D. Sears. This year the first women's singles championship was held at the

Philadelphia Cricket Club. Ellen Hansell was the winner.

Jan. 4 Thomas Stevens became the **first man to bicycle around the world** when he arrived in San Francisco. He had started from San Francisco on Apr. 22, 1884. It had taken him 2 years, 8 months, and 12 days.

Jan. 21 The **Amateur Athletic Union** of the U.S. (AAU) was formed, winning control over amateur athletics from unscrupulous promoters. The AAU's ideal was to preserve "sport for sport's sake." At first the AAU concerned itself primarily with men's track and field and swimming events. It came to supervise and conduct programs and competitions in about 20 sports and to represent the U.S. in international amateur sports federations. Its influence has been reduced since World War II by the takeover of collegiate sports by the National Collegiate Athletic Association (NCAA) and by the increasing professionalization of many sports.

Jan. 24 The **oldest active ski club** in the U.S. was founded in Ishpeming, Mich.

Feb. 8 The **first Midwest ski tournament** was held in St. Paul, Minn., between the local ski club and the Red Wing, Minn., club. The two clubs had scheduled a tournament for Jan. 1886, but the weather was so bad that no competition could be held. At the 1887 meet, the first American ski jumper of note, Mikkel Hemmestvedt, of Red Wing, was the victor in the first ski jumping competition.

Mar. 2 The **American Trotting Association** was organized at Detroit.

May 11 In London, Queen Victoria visited the **Wild West Show of Buffalo Bill Cody,** with its rodeo events. She later noted in her journal: "We saw a very extraordinary and interesting sight." The queen was accompanied by Princess Beatrice, equerries, and ladies-in-waiting, who occupied several carriages.

May 11 The 13th annual **Kentucky Derby** was won by Montrose, with a time of 2:39¼. The jockey was Isaac Lewis.

May 13 The 15th annual **Preakness Stakes** was won by Dunbine, with a time of 2:39½. The jockey was Billy Donohue.

May 26 **Racetrack betting** became legal for the first time in New York State.

June 9 The 21st annual **Belmont Stakes** was won by Hanover, with a time of 2:43½. The jockey was Jimmy McLaughlin.

Fall The **National League baseball championship** was won by Detroit, with a record of 79 wins, 45 losses. This year's interleague playoff was notable for its 15-game road trip. Detroit bested St. Louis of the American Association ten games to five.

Sept. 17-30 The **America's Cup** was successfully defended by the U.S. yacht *Volunteer,* which won two straight heats over the British challenger *Thistle.*

Sept. 24 In a **women's tennis tournament** held at the Philadelphia Cricket Club, Ellen Hansell

ROGERS HORNSBY

b. Winters, Tex., Apr. 27, 1886
d. Chicago, Ill., Jan. 5, 1963

It is generally agreed that Rogers "Rajah" Hornsby was the best right-handed batter in the history of major league baseball. His lifetime average was .358, second only to that of Ty Cobb, and Hornsby's 1924 season average was .424, unmatched in modern times. Hornsby was the National League batting champion for six consecutive years, from 1920 to 1925, and again in 1928.

Hornsby played a steady second base for 23 years, first for the St.

Louis Cardinals from 1915 to 1926, then for the New York Giants for a year and the Boston Braves for a year, and finally for the Chicago Cubs from 1929 to 1933. During his career he had 301 home runs and 679 stolen bases.

Hornsby was a playing manager for part of his career and manager of the St. Louis Browns from 1933 to 1937. As a manager, he won 680 games and lost 798. Despite his long career and his brilliant ability, Hornsby appeared in only two World Series, 1926 and 1929.

On December 20, 1926, in what

the *New York Times* called "the biggest deal in modern baseball history," Hornsby was traded to the New York Giants for Frankie Frisch and a pitcher after the Cardinals would not pay the salary Hornsby demanded, even though he had just finished managing the Cards to a 4–3 World Series victory over the New York Yankees. The Rajah was the National League's most valuable player in 1925 and 1928 and was named to the Baseball Hall of Fame in 1942.

defeated Mrs. J. Willis Martin in the finals. The tournament had been organized by Milton Work, a sportswriter who later gained fame as a bridge player.

Nov. The game that developed into **softball** was devised by George Hancock, a reporter for the Chicago Board of Trade, indoors at the Farragut Boat Club in Chicago. He and ten friends and fellow club members were the first to attempt the game. Hancock refined the equipment used in the game and on Oct. 24, 1889, a set of rules was adopted by the Mid Winter Indoor Baseball League of Chicago.

1888

The **first public birling (logrolling) match** was held at a site not recorded.

The **first national fencing championships** sponsored by the Amateur Athletic Union were held. The winners were W. S. Lawson, foil; E. Higgins, épée; and H. K. Bloodgood, sabre. All three winners represented the New York Athletic Club. The AAU sponsored this event through 1891, after which the Amateur Fencers League of America took over.

This year's **national college football championship** was won by Yale, with a record of 13 wins, no losses, no ties. Yale scored 688 points to 0 for its opponents. It was Yale's ninth unbeaten football season in ten years.

A **major league pitching record** for most consecutive games won in a season was set by Tim Keefe of New York. He won 19 straight games.

The **U.S. Lawn Tennis Association singles championships** were won by Bertha L. Townsend in the women's division and by Henry W. Slocum in the men's division.

May **"Casey at the Bat,"** by Ernest L. Thayer, was given its first public recitation by the popular actor DeWolf Hopper, at Wallack's Theater, New York City.

May 11 The 16th annual **Preakness Stakes** was won by Refund, with a time of 2:49. The jockey was F. Littlefield.

May 14 The 14th annual **Kentucky Derby** was won by MacBeth, with a time of 2:38¼. The jockey was George Covington.

June 9 The 22nd annual **Belmont Stakes** was won by Sir Dixon, with a time of 2:40¼. The jockey was Jimmy McLaughlin, who picked up his sixth Belmont Stakes win. McLaughlin was the only jockey in Belmont history twice to win the race three times in a row (1882-1884, 1886-1888).

Fall The **National League baseball champion-**

TY COBB

Tyrus Raymond Cobb
b. Narrows, Ga., Dec. 18, 1886
d. Atlanta, Ga., July 17, 1961

On the basis of Ty Cobb's statistics and the devastating effect he had on opponents, Cobb must be judged the best baseball player of all time, especially on the offensive side of the game. The Georgia Peach entered the major leagues as an outfielder in 1905, played for 22 years with the Detroit Tigers, serving also as manager for the last six of those years, and ended his career in 1928 after two years with the Philadelphia Athletics.

Cobb set more records than any

other player has set. He came to bat 11,429 times, still second highest. He made 4191 hits, also second highest and a record not broken until September 11, 1985, by Pete Rose. Cobb hit for a career batting average that is still the best, .367. He won the American League batting championship in 12 years of his career, from 1907 to 1915 and from 1917 to 1919. His best year came in 1911, when he batted for the magnificent average of .420. He also batted better than .400 in two other years.

In runs scored, Cobb remains in first place with 2244 and is second in stolen bases with 892. His best

year in this category was 1915, with 96. Cobb played in three World Series, 1907, 1908, and 1909, but the Tigers lost them all.

Cobb had a reputation for ruthlessness in his pursuit of victory, which made him unpopular with other players. He was the type of player described as willing to run over his own grandmother if necessary to steal a base. Nevertheless, when the first elections to the Baseball Hall of Fame were held in 1936, Cobb was rightfully the first chosen, with 222 votes out of a possible 226. Babe Ruth and Honus Wagner were next with 215 each.

HAZEL HOTCHKISS WIGHTMAN

Hazel Virginia Hotchkiss Wightman
b. Healdsburg, Calif., Dec. 20, 1886
d. Newton, Mass., Dec. 5, 1974

Hazel Wightman as a tennis star was both indefatigable and seemingly indestructible. She won her first national title in 1909 and her last in 1955, when she was 68. The 1909 victory gave Wightman her first U.S. women's championship. She won the title again in 1910, 1911, and 1919.

In all, Wightman won 50 national titles in singles and doubles, indoors and outdoors, and in tournaments for seniors. She won the American doubles title six times and in 1924 teamed with Helen Wills Moody, who was just about half her age, to win the doubles at Wimbledon.

Wightman is remembered also as the donor of the Wightman Cup, which she established in 1923 for an annual contest between teams of American and British women. She played doubles in the first matches and also in 1927, 1929, and 1931.

Wightman used the volley more than most women players of the time and helped popularize the stroke, which was especially useful to her in doubles competition. She was elected to the International Tennis Hall of Fame in 1957.

---

ship was won by New York, with a record of 84 wins, 47 losses. The annual interleague playoff was won by New York, defeating St. Louis of the American Association six games to four.

Oct. The first large-scale **postseason tour of baseball players** was organized by Albert G. "Al" Spalding, owner of the Chicago White Stockings. His team was accompanied by a squad selected from other National League clubs. The players went around the world, playing in several countries from late October to early April. The tour attracted some good crowds and paid off financially, but the game failed to take root overseas.

Nov. 14 The founding of the **Saint Andrews Golf Club** in Yonkers, N.Y., and its strong influence on the game marked the point at which the game became firmly rooted in the U.S. The founder was John G. Reid, a Scotsman, who earlier had obtained some clubs and balls from Scotland. The course at first was only six holes. The first mixed foursome played a round on Mar. 30, 1889.

1889

The **game of racquets** spread from New York City to Philadelphia (Racquet Club) and Boston

NAT NILES

Nathaniel William Niles
b. 1887
d. Boston, Mass., July 11, 1932

Nat Niles was one of the pioneers of figure skating in the United States, at the time when the international style was being introduced to this country. He won his first skating title in 1914 in the waltz event of the first national championships at New Haven, Connecticut. His partner was Theresa Weld Blanchard, a champion woman figure skater and his partner for many years.

Niles won the U.S. men's title in 1918, 1925, and 1927. With Blanchard he won the pairs title nine times. In 1920, these two constituted the entire U.S. figure skating team at the Olympic Games, but they did not win any medals. They placed second in the first North American championships in 1923 and first in 1925.

Niles was active in promoting figure skating as well as competing. He and Blanchard founded *Skating* magazine in 1923. He was a major contributor to the establishment of tests of proficiency in compulsory figures. He was first vice president of the U.S. Figure Skating Association (USFSA) from 1925 to 1928 and served on the executive committee from 1923 to 1932. While a student at Harvard, he won the national intercollegiate tennis singles and doubles championships in 1908 and 1909. Niles died at the age of 45 following surgery. He was elected to the USFSA Hall of Fame in 1978.

GROVER CLEVELAND ALEXANDER

b. Elba, Nebr., Feb. 26, 1887
d. St. Paul, Nebr., Nov. 4, 1950

One of the two or three greatest right-handed pitchers in baseball history, Grover Cleveland Alexander performed many noteworthy feats on the mound. The basic fact about him is that the 373 games he won in his career ranks second only to Cy Young's 511. Alexander lost 208 games in his career, for a winning percentage of .642.

Alexander began his career in 1911 and ended it in 1930, after 20 seasons. During that time he played for the Philadelphia Phillies, the Chicago Cubs, and the St. Louis Cardinals. Alexander had a career earned run average of 2.56 and pitched 90 shutouts, second only to Walter Johnson's 110. In each of three seasons, he won 30 or more games and in 1916 recorded 16 shutouts. Much of his success was due to his mastery of control. Consider his career total of 2198 strikeouts.

Alexander appeared in three World Series, 1915, 1926, and 1928, winning three games and losing two. The most notable moment of his career came in the seventh and last game of the 1926 series. Pitching for St. Louis, Alexander came on in relief in the seventh inning. The New York Yankees had three men on base with two out and the Cards leading 3–2. Alexander proceeded to strike out the ever-dangerous Tony Lazzeri and then held the Yankees scoreless for the last two innings to give the Cardinals the championship.

Alexander was elected to the Baseball Hall of Fame in 1938.

(Boston Athletic Association). Chicago; Tuxedo Park, N.Y.; and Detroit followed. Today these six are the only significant centers of racquets play.

The **baseball rule** governing a walk to a batter set the number of balls at four, where it has remained.

The so-called **safety bicycle** was manufactured for the first time on a large scale. It was generally the same as today's bicycles, having two wheels of equal size with the saddle above and between them. It replaced the dangerous high-wheelers that had one very large and one small wheel. Cycling became a popular method of transportation for workers, causing severe traffic and parking problems.

The term *Texas leaguer* became baseball parlance for a weak hit just over the heads of the infield but short of the outfield players. The term may first have been used to describe the short hits of Arthur Sunday, a player from Texas. Another version has it that the term was coined in Syracuse, N.Y., in 1886 by a pitcher who lost a game on such hits by several former Houston players on the Toledo team.

Walter Camp listed in *Collier's Weekly* the first **all-American football team,** selecting 11 college football players as best in the nation at their positions. The actual selection was made by Caspar Whitney, a prominent sports authority of New York City, who chose the all-American teams through 1896. The selections appeared in articles in *Collier's* annually until Camp's death in 1925, when Grant-

STANLEY KETCHEL

Stanislaus Kiecal
b. Grand Rapids, Mich., Sept. 14, 1887
d. Springfield, Ohio, Oct. 15, 1910

Called the Midnight Assassin, Stanley Ketchel was probably the best middleweight boxer of all time, although his career was cut short in an untimely manner. He first boxed professionally in 1903, and five years later he won the middleweight title from Mike Sullivan on February 22,

only to lose it to Billy Papke on September 7 of the same year.

Papke had knocked Ketchel out but, less than three months later, on November 26, Ketchel took revenge when he knocked out Papke to regain the title. On October 16, 1909, Ketchel made a bid for the heavyweight crown in a bout with the champion, Jack Johnson, who outweighed him by 35 pounds. In the 12th round, Ketchel amazed the crowd by knocking down the

champion, but Johnson got to his feet and within 34 seconds knocked out Ketchel. In all, Ketchel won 46 of his 61 bouts by knockouts.

On October 15, 1910, Ketchel was shot and killed in Springfield, Ohio. Arrested for the murder, Walter A. Hurtz said he had fired in self-defense after he had accused Ketchel of making insulting remarks about a woman.

WALTER JOHNSON

Walter Perry Johnson
b. Humboldt, Kans., Nov. 6, 1887
d. Washington, D.C., Dec. 10,
    1946

By any measurement Walter Johnson, the Big Train, a right-handed pitcher for the Washington Senators for 21 years from 1907 to 1927, must rank as one of the best moundsmen in baseball history. He stands second in games won with 416. He lost 279, for a percentage of .599, and had an earned run average of 2.17.

Johnson pitched 113 shutouts, more than any other pitcher has ever recorded, and his strikeout total of 3508 remains fifth best. He won 20 or more games in 12 years, his best season being 1913, when his record was 36 wins and 7 losses for an .837 percentage. In that year, Johnson also pitched 56 consecutive scoreless innings, a record not matched until 1968. In 1912, he and Smokey Joe Wood each recorded 16 consecutive victories, an American League record not tied until 1931.

Johnson pitched a no-hitter in 1920 and a number of one-hitters during his career. In the World Series of 1924 and 1925, he won three games and lost three. He managed the Senators from 1929 to 1932 and the Cleveland Indians from 1933 to 1935.

Success came to Johnson as a result of his marvelous fastball, his control, and his intensity in competition. In 1936, he was one of the first five men elected to the new Baseball Hall of Fame.

---

land Rice took over the task. Today's selections are made by various polls of sportswriters and coaches.

The **U.S. Lawn Tennis Association singles championships** were won by Bertha L. Townsend in the women's division and Henry W. Slocum in the men's division.

This year's **national college football championship** was won by Princeton, with a record of ten wins, no losses, no ties.

May 9 The 15th annual **Kentucky Derby** was won by Spokane, with a time of 2:34½, a new Derby record. The jockey was Thomas Kiley.

May 10 The 17th annual **Preakness Stakes** was won by Buddhist, with a time of 2:17½. The jockey was H. Anderson.

June 5 **James J. Corbett,** a bank teller turned amateur boxer, defeated the well-known pro boxer Joe Choynski in 27 bloody rounds. "Gentleman Jim" Corbett finished the struggle with a left hook, a punch he was said to have conceived after suffering two broken knuckles in a bout.

June 13 The 23rd annual **Belmont Stakes** was won by Eric, with a time of 2:47. The jockey was W. Hayward.

July 8 **Bare-knuckle boxing** had its last and most memorable bout when John L. Sullivan knocked out Jake Kilrain in the 75th round for the U.S. heavyweight championship at Richburg, Miss. Sullivan won a purse of $20,000 and a diamond-studded belt given by the *Police Gazette*. Sullivan then claimed the world's championship, for Kilrain had fought a draw with the

champion of England, Jem Smith. After this bout, boxing with gloves under Marquis of Queensberry rules was introduced.

Fall The **National League baseball championship** was won by New York, with a record of 83 wins, 43 losses. New York also won the annual interleague playoff, defeating Brooklyn of the American Association six games to three.

1890

The **first Gaelic Athletic Association in the U.S.** was organized in Chicago. Three years later the association had 15 clubs representing ten Gaelic football teams and five hurling teams, with a membership of 2000. In Boston, a Gaelic Athletic Union was formed in 1895, and in 1914 the Gaelic Athletic Association of New York was established and assumed the role of administrator of the city's Irish-American sports teams.

The **first girls' baseball team** made its appearance this year. The players' abbreviated uniforms—short-sleeved shirts, short pants gathered above the knee, and long stockings—attracted much comment.

The **United States Polo Association** was formed. The game was being played at over 40 private clubs and on 37 Army posts.

The term ***Baltimore chop*** entered baseball parlance to mean a batted ball that bounced so high in

CLARENCE DEMAR

b. Reading, Mass., 1888
d. Reading, Mass., June 11, 1958

Clarence DeMar and the Boston Marathon were made for each other. Over a period of 20 years, DeMar won the demanding event seven times, a record no one else seems likely to approach.

DeMar won this race in 1911, 1922, 1923, 1924, 1927, 1928, and 1930. His time of 2 hours, 29 minutes, 40 1/5 seconds in 1924 was an American record at that time. At the Olympic Games in 1924, at Colombes, France, he finished third in the marathon.

---

the infield that the batter could reach first base before the ball could be fielded and thrown. The Baltimore team, especially players John McGraw and "Wee" Willie Keeler, was especially adept at this method of getting on base.

This year's **national college football championship** was won by Harvard, with a record of 11 wins, no losses, no ties.

The **U.S. Lawn Tennis Association singles championships** were won by Ellen C. Roosevelt in the women's division and Oliver S. Campbell in the men's division.

May 14 The 16th annual **Kentucky Derby** was won by Riley, with a time of 2:45. The jockey was Isaac Murphy.

June 10 The 18th annual **Preakness Stakes** was won by Montague, with a time of 2:36¾. The jockey was W. Martin.

June 10 The 24th annual **Belmont Stakes** was won by Burlington, with a time of 2:07¾. The jockey was S. Barnes. Because the Belmont and the Preakness were run on the same day, 1890 could see no Triple Crown winner. The question, at any rate, is moot, since neither of the winning horses on June 10 had won the Kentucky Derby.

Fall The **National League baseball championship** was won by Brooklyn, with a record of 86 wins, 43 losses. The annual interleague playoff, with the American Association's Louisville team, ended in a tie, each team winning three games, with one game ending in a tie.

Oct. 11 The **first 100-yard dash under 10 sec.** by an American was run by John Owens at the AAU track and field meet in Washington, D.C. His time was 9⅘ sec.

Nov. 29 The **first Army-Navy football game** was played at West Point, N.Y. The score was Navy 24, Army 0. The contest became an annual event between the two service academies, played every year except 1909, 1917, 1918, 1928, and 1929.

KNUTE ROCKNE

Knute Kenneth Rockne
b. Voss, Norway, Mar. 4, 1888
d. Kansas, Mar. 31, 1931

Although Knute Rockne died more than half a century ago, he remains the epitome of the hard-driving, winning college football coach. He was brought to the United States by his family in 1893 and in 1910 entered the University of Notre Dame, where he became a star player and captain of the football team. His most memorable game as a player came against Army on November 1, 1913. Displaying a new open style and unprecedented use of the forward pass, Notre Dame crushed Army 35–13.

Rockne became head football coach at Notre Dame in 1918 and remained on the job until his death in an airplane crash in 1931. By that time his teams had won 105 games, lost only 12, tied 5, and had 5 unbeaten seasons. Rockne's most famous team was that of 1924, which featured the now legendary "Four Horsemen of Notre Dame" backfield.

By the time of Rockne's death, he and Notre Dame had become bywords for football excellence. As coach he emphasized speed and deception, rather than the brute force that had been his heritage from early American football. In effect he revolutionized football with his emphasis on offense and his devising of such strategies as the Notre Dame shift and the substituting of whole teams instead of single players.

Though a no-nonsense coach on the practice and playing fields, Rockne was a genial man of wit and humor. Overall, he had more influence on the game than any man since Walter Camp.

1891

Court tennis, spreading slowly from Boston and Newport, was introduced into New York City at the Racquet and Tennis Club. Two years later, the Chicago Athletic Club put a court into operation. A famous court at Tuxedo, N.Y., was built in 1900. Of perhaps 20 courts constructed in this era, only nine survive today.

A new **baseball rule** permitted player substitution at any time during a game, removing a restriction imposed in 1877 that allowed a substitute to enter the game only before the fourth inning.

The year's **national college football championship** was won by Yale, with a record of 13 wins, no losses, no ties.

The **U.S. Lawn Tennis Association singles championships** were won by Mabel Cahill in the women's division and Oliver S. Campbell in the men's division.

This year the **Preakness Stakes** was not run. The annual event resumed with the 19th running in 1894.

Apr. 22 The **Amateur Fencers League of America** was formed at a meeting at the New York Athletic Club, attended by prominent fencers representing a number of clubs and colleges. Its purpose was to encourage participation in the sport and to establish rules for conducting fencing events. The league became the governing body for amateur fencing in the U.S.

May 13 The 17th annual **Kentucky Derby** was won by Kingman, with a time of 2:52¼. The jockey was Isaac Murphy, who scored his second straight Derby win.

June 10 The 25th annual **Belmont Stakes** was won by Foxford, with a time of 2:08¾. The jockey was Ed "Snapper" Garrison.

Fall The **National League baseball championship** was won by Boston, with a record of 87 wins, 51 losses. This year the rival American Association merged into the National League to form a 12-team league.

Oct. 20-25 The **first international six-day bicycle race** in New York City was run in Madison Square Garden. Riders used high-wheelers and worked alone, pumping until exhausted, then resting and starting again, for a total of 142 hrs. The first winner was "Plugger Bill" Martin. The record under one-man rules was established in 1898 by Charlie Miller at Madison Square Garden, who rode 2093.4 mi. Most of his competitors ended up in hospitals, suffering from exhaustion.

Dec. **Basketball originated** at the YMCA Training School at Springfield, Mass. The director of the physical training course, Luther H. Gulick, had urged his students to devise an indoor

TRIS SPEAKER

Tristram E. Speaker
b. Hubbard, Tex., Apr. 4, 1888
d. Lake Whitney, Tex., Dec. 8, 1958

Asked to name the three best players in baseball history, most followers of the game will almost automatically say Ty Cobb, Babe Ruth, and Tris Speaker. There is no doubt that Speaker was one of the very top batters, and no one could play the outfield better. He was especially adept at going backward, which enabled him to play a shallow outfield and so rob batters on short fly balls.

Speaker began as a pitcher in the minor leagues but after joining the Boston Red Sox in 1907 played mostly in center field. In 1916, he went to the Cleveland Indians for a then record price of $55,000, of which he demanded and got $10,000 for himself. Speaker finished his career with Washington in 1927 and the Philadelphia Athletics in 1928.

Speaker was the American League batting champion in 1916 with a .386 average. Cobb had won this title in the nine previous years and came back to win it in the next three, but no one has a more impressive overall batting record than Speaker. He had 3515 hits, still an all-time fifth place; a batting average of .344; and 10,196 times at bat. He is one of the very few players ever to reach five figures in this category. His keen eye at the plate is shown by his total of 1381 bases on balls and only 220 strikeouts. Speaker hit only 117 home runs, scored 1881 runs, and drove in 1559 runs. With 433 stolen bases, he ranks 21st in this category.

As manager of the Cleveland Indians from 1919 to 1926, Speaker led them to their first World Series triumph in 1920, when they defeated the Brooklyn Dodgers five games to two. Speaker entered the Baseball Hall of Fame in 1937, its second year.

1892

JIM THORPE

James Francis Thorpe
b. near Prague, Okla., May 28, 1888
d. Lomita, Calif., Mar. 28, 1953

Jim Thorpe, by general agreement the greatest American all-around male athlete, was part Indian on both his mother and father's sides. His tribal name was Bright Path. Thorpe's athletic abilities were first revealed at the Carlisle Indian School in Carlisle, Pennsylvania, where he was coached by Glenn "Pop" Warner. Warner, one of America's great football coaches, called him "the greatest football player of all time." As an elusive halfback, a fierce tackler on defense, and a skilled dropkicker, Thorpe made the all-American team in 1911 and 1912. Football fans in general remember him for his team's startling upset of mighty Harvard in 1911, when Thorpe ran 70 yards for a touchdown and kicked four field goals. He also scored 22 points when the Carlisle Indians upset Army 27–6 in 1912.

Even surpassing his football record was Thorpe's achievement at the 1912 Olympics. He won both the pentathlon and the decathlon, something no other athlete has ever done. The next year, however, it was revealed that in 1909 he had briefly played professional baseball. The AAU revoked his amateur status, and the International Olympic committee took back his medals. His amateur status was restored in 1973, and his medals were returned to his family in 1982.

From 1913 to 1920, Thorpe played professional baseball in the major leagues. In 1920, he was one of the founders of what became the National Football League and was its first president. He also played for several different teams in the league between 1921 and 1926. Thorpe is a member of the College Hall of Fame and the Pro Football Hall of Fame.

game for the winter season. James Naismith, an instructor at the school, used a soccer ball and, as goals, two peach baskets that he fastened along the outer edge of an elevated running track 10 ft. above the floor of the gym. Today's baskets remain at that height.

1892

The **first known horseshoe pitching club** was formed at Meadville, Pa. Another club also appeared this year at East Liverpool, Ohio.

In harness racing, **the bicycle-wheeled sulky** was introduced, the smaller wheel leading to increased speeds. In the early nineteenth century, trotters and pacers had been ridden horseback or driven in front of regular buggies. About a decade before the Civil War, the high-wheeled sulky had come into use.

A new song, **"Daisy Bell,"** better known by the phrase "a bicycle built for two," attested to the popularity of the pastime of cycling. The words and music were by Harry Dacre.

The expression *Garrison finish* was born when jockey Ed "Snapper" Garrison, not for the first time, came from well behind and won the Suburban Handicap at Sheepshead Bay, N.Y., by a nose.

This year's **national college football championship** was won by Yale, with a record of 13 wins, no losses, no ties.

The **U.S. Lawn Tennis Association singles championships** were won by Mabel Cahill in the women's division and Oliver S. Campbell in the men's division.

Jan. 15 **Rules for basketball,** devised by James Naismith, were printed in the *Triangle,* the newspaper of the Springfield, Mass., YMCA training school. YMCA branches, especially those in New England and metropolitan New York, quickly adopted the game. Vacationing Springfield students, at Christmas time, had already taken the game as far west as California and south to North Carolina.

A race track swarms with sweaty oafs intent on getting something for nothing and sullen if they fail. A fight crowd is exciting and excited, and vaguely pathologic. But a baseball crowd, excepting the stray cranks and exhibitionists, is a neighborly lot.

John K. Hutchens

ED "STRANGLER" LEWIS

Robert H. Friedrich
b. Muskogee, Okla., 1890
d. Muskogee, Okla., Aug. 7, 1966

Strangler Lewis, who won his first professional wrestling bout in 1904, when he was only 14, took his name because he knew his family had a low opinion of the sport. In fact, there always was some question as to how legitimate wrestling titles were, and by the end of Lewis's career, wrestling was becoming more theater than athletic activity.

There was no clear-cut system for determining the heavyweight freestyle wrestling championship, but Lewis claimed it—with some justification—no less than five times in the 1920s and 1930s. He became famous for his headlock, which appeared to threaten opponents with death. It was unpopular with fans, and the Illinois Athletic Commission banned it and the New York State legislature threatened to ban it.

Joe Stecher and Lewis, who weighed 260 pounds, fought five times, usually with the championship presumably at stake. Lewis won in 1920 and first claimed the title. Earlier, on July 4, 1916, in Omaha, Nebraska, they had wrestled for 5½ hours. The result was a draw, and the bout was the longest ever in such competition. Lewis lost the title for the last time in 1932, when he was defeated by Gus Sonnenberg, former Dartmouth football star. Sonnenberg was the exponent of the flying tackle, and some said that introduction of that tactic marked the beginning of the end for professional wrestling as a genuine sport.

Although Lewis earned about $4,000,000 in his career, which ended in 1937, he died poor and blind.

Mar. 18 Under **new racing rules,** Jockeys were prohibited from using anything but a whip and a spur on a horse during a race. The ruling was prompted by discovery that a jockey named Cook used an electric spur while riding Gyda at Guttenburg, N.J. Cook was ruled off the track.

Mar. 22 The **first national fencing championships** sponsored by the Amateur Fencers League of America were held at the Berkeley Lyceum in New York City. The winners were W. Scott O'Connor, foil; B. F. O'Connor, épée; and R. O. Haubold, saber.

May 11 The 18th annual **Kentucky Derby** was won by Azra, with a time of 2:41½. The jockey was Alonzo Clayton.

June 9 The 26th annual **Belmont Stakes** was won by Patron, with a time of 2:47. The jockey was W. Hayward.

Sept. 7 James J. Corbett won the **world heavyweight boxing championship** by knocking out John L. Sullivan in the 21st round. The bout, held in New Orleans, has been considered the first heavyweight title bout fought with gloves under Marquis of Queensberry rules, including 3-min. rounds.

Fall Boston won the **National League baseball championship** with a record of 102 wins, 48 losses. Kid Nichols pitched 35 winning games, Jack Stivetts 33, and Harry Staley 24.

Nov. 12 William "Pudge" Heffelfinger, the **first professional football player,** was paid $500 in his first professional appearance, playing for the Allegheny Athletic Association against the

---

DUKE KAHANAMOKU

Duke Paoa Kahanamoku
b. Honolulu, Hawaii, Aug. 24, 1890
d. Honolulu, Hawaii, Jan. 22, 1968

Duke Kahanamoku's many swimming records have been broken, so he is remembered primarily as the man who did more than anyone else in his time to popularize surfing. He seemed in appearance and in skill to be the model surfing hero in a tropical setting.

In his time, Kahanamoku was the best swimmer the world had ever seen. From 1912 to 1928, at one time or other, he held every record in distances up to half a mile. In 1912 and again in 1920, he won the 100-meter event at the Olympics and was second to Johnny Weissmuller in 1924. As a member of the U.S. Olympic 800-meter relay team in 1920, he also won a gold medal.

In early competition, Kahanamoku was described as a raw swimmer. With coaching and his natural talent, he became a polished performer and developed the Kahanamoku kick, in which he made six narrow scissors kicks to every full stroke of his arms.

CASEY STENGEL

Charles Dillon Stengel
b. Kansas City, Mo., July 30, 1891
d. Glendale, Calif., Sept. 29, 1975

As a major league outfielder, Casey Stengel was not a star, but as a major league manager, no one was ever more successful, and no one in his position ever created such popularity for his offbeat character. He was a delight to sportswriters, who could always count on him for a quotable remark in his own impenetrable style, which came to be known as Stengelese.

Stengel played for 14 years in the majors: for the Brooklyn Dodgers from 1912 to 1917, the Pittsburgh Pirates in 1918 and 1919, the Philadelphia Phillies in 1920 and 1921, the New York Giants from 1921 to 1923, and the Boston Braves

in 1924 and 1925. His career batting average was a thoroughly respectable .284, with 1219 hits and 60 home runs. He played in three World Series with the Dodgers and the Giants.

It was not until 1934, however, that Stengel began to make any particular mark in the baseball world. He managed the Dodgers from 1934 to 1936 and the Braves from 1938 to 1943. Moving on to the New York Yankees, whom he managed from 1949 to 1960, Stengel began to set records. During his regime the Yankees won ten American League pennants, in 1949, 1950, 1951, 1952, 1953, 1955, 1956, 1957, 1958, and 1960. They also won seven of the ten World Series they played in under Stengel, an unmatched achievement. The Yankees captured five successive

series, in 1949, 1950, 1951, 1952, and 1953. They won a sixth in 1956 and another in 1958. In all, Stengel managed 63 Series games, a record, and won 37 of them, also a record. In spite of his success, the Yankee organization dismissed him after the 1960 series.

Stengel's last managerial assignment was not so successful, although it added to his reputation as a colorful character. He took on the New York Mets, newly franchised in 1962, and held the helm through 1965. On one occasion, frustrated by the lack of talent on his team, he asked: "Can't anybody here play this game?" Overall, as a manager, his teams won 1926 games and lost 1867, for a .508 percentage. Stengel was elected to the Baseball Hall of Fame in 1966.

Pittsburgh Athletic Club. A former all-American at Yale, Heffelfinger recovered a Pittsburgh fumble and ran for a touchdown, worth 4 points. His team won 4-0.

1893

The **Chicago Fly Casting Club** was formed and conducted the first U.S. national casting tournament.

The first recognized **world championship bicycle races** were held in Chicago. The sprint title was won by Arthur Zimmerman of the U.S.

The **first basketball tournament** of record was held for teams in the New York City area. It was won by the Brooklyn Central YMCA.

Ice hockey was introduced from Canada to the U.S. Games were played at Yale and Johns Hopkins universities. Canadian hockey dates at least from 1855, when teams from the military played games in Ontario. In 1875 students at McGill U. in Montreal

formulated rules for the game. A flat puck replaced the previously used rubber ball.

The **Stanley Cup,** representing the ice hockey championship of Canada, was presented by Lord Stanley of Preston, governor general of Canada. In 1917 it became the championship trophy of Canadian professional hockey, then represented by the National Hockey Association and the Pacific Coast League. In 1926 it became associated solely with the new National Hockey League, which actually was international in membership.

The **rise of bicycling** as a means of transportation and recreation in the U.S. was indicated by the increase of bicycles in use from some 20,000 in 1882 to over 1,000,000 in 1893. Pneumatic tires came into use, and the drop frame bicycle for women was developed. It was said that the popularity of bicycling had cut piano sales by half and the use of livery stables by a third.

The first recorded **intercollegiate relay race** was run at Philadelphia between teams representing the U. of Pennsylvania and Princeton U. In 1895 Penn initiated its Penn Relay Carnival with a series of 1-mi. relay races. Today the Penn Relay is considered one of the foremost annual track and field meets in the world. Relay races are an American contribution to an ancient sport.

This year's **national college football championship** was won by Princeton, with a record of 11 wins, no losses, no ties.

The **U.S. Lawn Tennis Association singles championships** were won by Aline Terry in the women's division and Robert D. Wrenn in the men's division.

The **first national fly-casting tournament** was held at the World's Columbian Exposition by the newly formed Chicago Fly Casting Club. Accuracy fly, delicacy fly, long-distance bait, and long-distance fly events were held at distances of 75, 80, and 85 ft. The club held national tournaments in 1897, 1903, and 1905. In 1906 a permanent organization, the National Association of Scientific Angling Clubs, was formed in Racine, Wis.; it held a national tournament in 1907. This organization, still strictly amateur, is now the National Association of Angling and Casting Clubs, the governing body of fly casting.

A new **baseball rule** established the distance between the pitching slab and home plate at 60 ft., 6 in. This distance has remained unchanged to the present time.

Apr. 6 In the **longest bout fought with gloves,** Andy Bowen and Jack Burke went 110 rounds at New Orleans. The referee declared the fight no contest when both boxers refused to continue.

May 10 The 19th annual **Kentucky Derby** was won by Lookout, with a time of 2:39¼. The jockey was Eddie Kunze.

June 10 The 27th **Belmont Stakes** was won by Comanche, with a time of 1:53¼. The jockey was W. Simms.

Fall The **National League baseball championship** was won by Boston, with a record of 86 wins, 44 losses. Kid Nichols pitched 33 winning games.

Oct. 7-13 The **America's Cup** was successfully defended by the U.S. yacht *Vigilant,* which won three straight heats over the British challenger *Valkyrie.*

1894

The **Intercollegiate Fencing Association** was formed with Columbia, Harvard, and Yale as the first members. The association held its first championships, in foils only, that year at the Racquet and Tennis Club in New York City. Yale withdrew because of an accident to a member of the team, and Harvard became the first intercollegiate fencing champion by defeating Columbia 5-4. Fitzhugh Townsend, a Columbia sophomore, became the first individual title holder and won the title again two years later. There are now 13 members of the association.

The **all-time winning thoroughbred race**

MOLLA BJURSTEDT MALLORY

b. Oslo, Norway, 1892?
d. Stockholm, Sweden, Nov. 22, 1959

Molla Bjurstedt began playing tennis in her native city of Christiania (now Oslo) in 1903. She was already champion of Norway and had been for some time when she came to the United States in December 1914. Within a year and a half, she had won eight American tournaments. Three of them were for what were considered national titles at the time: the grass court at Forest Hills, New York; the indoor at the Seventh

Regiment Armory in New York City; and the clay court at Pittsburgh, Pa.

In 1915, having won the tournament that now is considered the one that decides the U.S. women's title, Molla Bjurstedt Mallory (she married in 1919) went on to demonstrate her winning ways. By taking the title in 1916, 1917, 1918, 1920, 1921, 1922, and 1926, she became an eight-time champion. Her loss in 1923 was at the hands of the future star Helen Wills Moody, who then was only 17. In all, Mallory set a record of ten appearances in the women's singles

finals, from 1915 to 1918, 1920 to 1924, and 1926.

Mallory amazed spectators and experts when she took to the courts. Her style, critics said, was that of a male player. As the *New York Times* put it, she could "cover the court with the freedom and ease of a man." Mallory ushered in a new era in women's tennis with her powerful forehand drive, fighting spirit, and great endurance. Her only weakness was her service, which was considered practically nonexistent.

1894

WALTER HAGEN

Walter Charles Hagen
b. Rochester, N.Y., Dec. 21, 1892
d. Traverse City, Mich., Oct. 5, 1969

In the 1910s and into the 1920s, Walter Hagen was the top golfer on the links tour, that is, until Bobby Jones came along. In 1950, along with Jones and Ben Hogan, Walter Hagen was voted one of the three best players of the first half of the century.

In 1914, when Hagen was only 21, he won the men's U.S. Open, as he did again five years later. His record in the PGA was even better. After winning it first in 1921, he then took the title four years in succession, from 1924 to 1927. Hagen was the first American to win the British Open. He won in 1922 and won three more times, in 1924, 1928, and 1929. He also won more than 60 other tournaments and, from 1927 to 1935, captained the American Ryder Cup team in its biennial contests with British teams.

Hagen was the first professional golfer to make the game popular with the public. He did not hesitate to play to the gallery, and his personality and dashing style of play made him a favorite. Hagen was at his best in match play, which was common at the time, and there were few opponents who could stand up to Hagen's constant pressure. His place in golf history was demonstrated in 1967, when he was made an honorary member of the Royal and Ancient Golf Club of St. Andrews, Scotland, an honor granted to only two other professionals.

---

horse, Kingston, retired with 89 victories. Foaled in 1884, Kingston first raced in 1886. In 138 lifetime starts, Kingston also finished second 33 times and third 12 times. Kingston's lifetime earnings were $138,917.

A new **baseball rule** stipulated that a wooden slab, called the rubber, 12 in. by 4 in., be sunk into the pitcher's mound 60 ft., 6 in. from the front edge of home plate and that a pitcher be required to place both feet on it at the start of his delivery. Other new rules stipulated that a foul bunt with two strikes on the batter be called strike three and that a player who sacrificed was not to be charged with a time at bat.

The **highest batting average** for a season ever compiled by a major league baseball player was Hugh Duffy's .438 this year. Duffy was an outfielder for the Boston Nationals who hit 18 home runs and batted in 145 runs. His slugging percentage was .679.

This year's **national college football championship** was won by Yale, with a record of 16 wins, no losses, no ties.

The **U.S. Lawn Tennis Association singles championships** were won by Helen Helwig in the women's division and Robert D. Wrenn in the men's division.

Feb. 9 A corporate charter was received by the **Jockey Club,** which became the governing body of thoroughbred breeding and racing.

THERESA WELD BLANCHARD

b. 1893
d. Brookline, Mass., Mar. 12, 1978

Theresa Blanchard became the *grande dame* of U.S. competitive figure skating in the early days of the sport by virtue of her prowess on the ice and her activities in organizing and promoting figure skating. As a competitor, she won the U.S. women's first national championship in 1914 and took the title from 1920 through 1924. With her longtime skating partner, Nathaniel W. Niles, she won the U.S. pairs championship nine times, in 1918 and from 1920 through 1927.

Blanchard was also the first North American women's champion in 1923 and the first U.S. waltz champion in 1914. As the first woman competitor for the U.S. in the Olympics, she won the bronze medal at the 1920 Games. Blanchard and Niles were the North American pairs champions in 1925.

Blanchard promoted figure skating while she was competing. With Niles in 1923 she founded *Skating* magazine, which became the official publication of the U.S. Figure Skating Association (USFSA). She was a member of the executive committee of the USFSA for 13 years and was a world judge of the sport. The First Lady of Figure Skating, as she became known, was elected to the USFSA Hall of Fame in 1976.

The organization was an outgrowth of a meeting of prominent owners and breeders in New York City in late Dec. 1893. A previous board of control had proved unsuccessful in regulating racing. The new club's stated purpose was to "encourage the development of the thoroughbred horse" and "establish racing on such a footing that it may command the interest as well as the confidence and favorable opinion of the public."

May 15 The 20th annual **Kentucky Derby** was won by Chant, with a time of 2:41. The jockey was Frank Goodale.

May 17 The **Preakness Stakes** was resumed after a lapse of three years, with the 19th running, under the auspices of the Brooklyn Jockey Club at its Gravesend course. The winner was Assignee, with a time of 1:49¼. The jockey was Fred Taral. The Preakness was run in Brooklyn through 1908. In 1909 it returned to Pimlico Race Course in Maryland.

June 16 The **squeeze play** was first employed in baseball by George Case and Dutch Carter, players on the Yale team, in a game against Princeton. The squeeze play is a batting maneuver in which, with a runner at third base and with less than two out, the batter bunts the ball slowly to the infield, enabling the runner on third to come home safely. It was introduced in the major leagues in 1904 by Clark Griffith, pitcher-manager of the New York Highlanders in the American League. Two types of squeeze play are now in use. One is called the delayed squeeze; in it the runner on third base does not run until the ball has been bunted. The other, more dramatic type is called the suicide squeeze, in which the runner on third base breaks toward home plate as the pitcher begins his delivery.

June 19 The 28th annual **Belmont Stakes** was won by Henry of Navarre, with a time of 1:56½. The jockey was W. Simms.

Fall The **National League baseball championship** was won by Baltimore, with a record of 89 wins, 39 losses. The New York Highlanders finished a close second.

Dec. 22 The **United States Golf Association** was founded. It became the governing body of the game in the U.S. and sponsor of the national amateur and open championships.

1895

The game of **volleyball** was invented by William G. Morgan, a physical fitness instructor at the YMCA in Holyoke, Mass. In devising the game, Morgan had middle-aged men in mind, for whom basketball was too strenuous. A basketball was used at first but proved too big and heavy. At Morgan's request, the A. G. Spalding Co. made a new type of ball. There were nine players on a side at first, but after World War I the number was reduced to six. For reasons unknown, Morgan first called the game *mignonette.*

STANISLAUS ZBYSZKO

b. Krakow, Poland, 1893
d. Savannah, Mo., June 10, 1968

Imagine a wrestler with a background like that of Stanislaus Zbyszko. He was the godson of Ignace Jan Paderewski, the Polish pianist, and was a talented pianist in his own right. He knew 13 languages, acted as an interpreter for American forces in the Pacific theater during World War II, and held a law degree from the University of Vienna.

Notwithstanding these educational qualifications, Zbyszko chose to make wrestling his profession and appeared in bouts in Europe, North America, and South America in the 1920s and 1930s. During one of his tours, in 1936, he was reported killed in action in the Spanish Civil War. He claimed the world catch-as-catch-can wrestling title at a time when there were no clear procedures for determining this. Zbyszko's chief opponents were Strangler Lewis and Joe Stecher.

Perhaps his most notable bout was that with Lewis on March 21, 1919, at Madison Square Garden, New York City. After the pair had tortured one another for about an hour and a half with their favorite holds, according to a newspaper account, Zbyszko lifted Lewis high in the air, slammed him to the mat, and brought the bout to an abrupt end.

Resident **hunting licenses** were first required by Michigan and North Dakota.

Women's skirts were made more appropriate for bicycling. They were shortened an inch or two from the ankle, and the hems were weighted with lead.

A new **baseball rule** established the infield fly rule: When runners are on first and second or on first, second, and third with less than two out, any batter hitting a fly ball that in an umpire's judgment can be caught by an infielder is automatically out. This rule was intended to protect base runners from force plays made possible by a fielder who would intentionally drop a fly ball. Other rules classified foul tips as strikes (up to a total of two strikes), restricted the length of a bat to no more than 42 in., and increased the size of the pitcher's slab from 12 in. by 4 in. to 24 in. by 6 in.

This year's **national college football championship** was won by Pennsylvania, with a record of 14 wins, no losses, no ties.

The **U.S. Lawn Tennis Association singles championships** were won by Juliette P. Atkinson in the women's division and Fred H. Hovey in the men's division.

May 6 The 21st annual **Kentucky Derby** was won by Halma, with a time of 2:37½. The jockey was James "Soup" Perkins.

May 25 The 20th annual **Preakness Stakes** was won by Belmar, with a time of 1:50½. The jockey was Fred Taral.

June 24 The **first Intercollegiate Rowing Association Regatta** was held on the Hudson R. at Poughkeepsie, N.Y. The Columbia crew won, and Cornell came in second. This foremost event in eight-man crew racing was held here until June 25, 1949. From then on, the regatta was held at various places, including Saratoga, Syracuse, and Ithaca, N.Y.; and Marietta, Ohio.

Aug. 31 The **first professional football game** was played in Latrobe, Pa., when Latrobe's team of profit-sharing players met the Jeannette, Pa., team. Latrobe hired a substitute quarterback, John Brallier, for $10 in expense money.

Sept. 7-12 The **America's Cup** was successfully defended by the U.S. yacht *Defender,* which won three straight races from the British challenger, *Valkyrie II.*

Sept. 9 The **American Bowling Congress** (ABC) was formed in Beethoven Hall, New York City, to revive waning interest in a once popular sport. Bowling alleys and matches had been taken over by gamblers and ruffians. Teams of businessmen or workers were often physically beaten in revenge after they had won their matches. The ABC became the ruling body of bowling. It standardized rules and equipment and planned national tournaments. The modern ten-pin game became standard.

Fall The **National League baseball championship** was won by Baltimore, with a record of 87 wins, 43 losses. Five Oriole players batted over .360. They were Willie Keeler, Hugh Jennings, John McGraw, Joe Kelley, and Steve Brodie.

Oct. 4 The **first U.S. Open golf tournament,**

FRANCIS D. OUIMET

b. 1893
d. Newton, Mass., Sept. 2, 1967

In the annals of American golf, Francis Ouimet is the poor boy and the amateur who proved you didn't have to be rich or a professional to excel at the game. As a gardener's son who lived across the road from the golf course at Brookline, Massachusetts, it was quite natural for Ouimet to become a caddy, which also gave him a chance to learn the game that he might otherwise never have had.

As a result, he pulled off what to this day is the most spectacular triumph in American golf. The scene was the U.S. Open tournament of 1913 at Brookline. At the end of regulation play, the 20-year-old amateur was tied with the two leading British professionals, Harry Vardon and Edward Ray. In an 18-hole playoff on September 20, Ouimet beat Vardon by five strokes and Ray by six.

He first played in the U.S. Amateur in 1910, won it in 1914 and again 17 years later. From the inception of the U.S. Walker Cup team in 1922 until 1949, Ouimet was a player or the nonplaying captain of the team. In 1955, Ouimet was awarded the first Bobby Jones Trophy for distinguished sportsmanship, but his greatest honor came in 1951, when he was named the first non-British captain of the Royal and Ancient Golf Club of St. Andrews, Scotland.

William Tatem Tilden II
b. Philadelphia, Pa., Feb. 10, 1893
d. Hollywood, Calif., June 5, 1953

If not the best tennis player ever, and many believe he deserves that rating, Bill Tilden was certainly the most dramatic. He was a showman whose every movement on the court expressed the very essence of the game. After hard training and practice, he began his record-making career in 1920 by winning the U.S. singles championship. He repeated for five more years, through 1925, and won once more in 1929 for a total of seven titles.

At the same time, in 1920, he was the first American to win the British championship, which he also won in 1921 and 1930. Tilden dominated tennis in the 1920s as no other player has since done for a similar period. Between 1918 and 1929, he was a finalist in the U.S. singles ten times. Besides these victories, he won five men's doubles and four mixed doubles titles for a record total of 16.

Tilden also helped the United States dominate Davis Cup play, then more prestigious than it is in the 1980s. He and William M. Johnston won the Davis Cup from Australia in 1920, and it was largely by their efforts that the cup remained in the United States through 1926. In those years, Tilden lost only one match in the final round of cup play, and between 1920 and 1930 he won 17 of 22 cup matches.

In 1950, an Associated Press poll rated him the greatest tennis player of the first half of the century. Tilden received 310 of the possible 391 votes. He was rangy and graceful, striding about the court like the master he was. His service was a thing of terror to opponents, and his skill was matched by his concentration and determination. Tilden was elected to the International Tennis Hall of Fame in 1958.

---

held at Newport Golf Club in Newport, R.I., under the auspices of the U.S. Golf Association, was won by Horace Rawlins. Rawlins, 19, had come from England earlier in the year to work at the Newport club. An amateur tournament was also held and was won by Charles B. Macdonald against 31 opponents.

Nov. 2 The 29th annual **Belmont Stakes** was won by Belmar, with a time of 2:11½. The jockey was Fred Taral.

Nov. 2 The **first organized auto race in the U.S.** took place in Chicago and was sponsored by the *Times-Herald* newspaper. The course of 52 mi. was laid out along the shore of Lake Michigan. Six cars were entered, but at least in part because of a heavy snowstorm only two completed the race. The winner drove a Duryea at an average speed of 6.66 mph.

Nov. 9 The **first U.S. women's amateur golf championship** was played at the Meadow Brook Club, Hempstead, N.Y. Mrs Charles B. Brown was the winner, playing the 18 holes in 132 strokes.

Nov. 28 The **first gasoline-powered automobile race** in the U.S., the Chicago-to-Evanston Thanksgiving Day Race, was won by the brothers Charles E. and J. Frank Duryea. They achieved an average speed of 7.5 mph over the 54.36-mi. course.

1896

Nathanael Herreshoff, of Bristol, R.I., built the *Alfreda* for a Minneapolis yachtsman. It was the prototype of what later became known as the Inland Lake Scow. It was so named because of its long, narrow, and almost rectangular shape and its shallow hull, well adapted to inland waters where racers seldom encountered heavy seas. The design principles have been adapted to several classes ranging in length from 16 to 38 ft.

The **Canadian sloop *Canada*** won a trophy at Toledo, Ohio. The Royal Canadian Yacht Club of Toronto then offered it as a Challenge Cup, similar to the America's Cup.

The **first women's intercollegiate basketball game** was played, under modified rules, by teams representing Stanford U. and the U. of California.

This year's **national college football championship** was won by Princeton, with a record of ten wins, no losses, one tie.

The **U.S. Lawn Tennis Association singles championships** were won by Elizabeth H. Moore in the women's division and Robert D. Wrenn in the men's division.

Jan. 6-11 The **first women's six-day bicycle race** took place in Madison Square Garden,

New York City. The winner was Frankie Nelson, who rode 418 mi.

Apr. 6 The **first modern Olympic Games** began in Athens, Greece. The games were dominated by a small team of Americans who arrived just as athletes for the first events were being called. The U.S. team, out of condition from the long ocean trip and with no time to limber up, won nine of the 12 events. James B. Connolly, who won the first event—the hop, step, and jump—was the first Olympic champion to be crowned in 15 centuries. The revival of the games was brought about by the efforts of a young French baron, Pierre de Coubertin of Paris. His plan to hold international contests every four years has been carried out for the most part.

May 6 The 22nd annual **Kentucky Derby** was won by Ben Brush, with a time of 2:07¾. The jockey was Willie Simms. This year the course distance was set at a mile and a quarter.

June 2 The 30th annual **Belmont Stakes** was won by Hastings, with a time of 2:24½. The jockey was Henry Griffin. From this year to 1925 (1904 and 1905 excepted) the distance was one and three-eighths miles.

June 6 The 21st annual **Preakness Stakes** was won by Margrave, with a time of 1:51. The jockey was Henry Griffin.

June 22 A **pioneer glider designer,** Gustave Chanute, French-born engineer, began a summer of experiments with new glider designs, assisted by Augustus M. Herring, who did the actual gliding. Their tests took place on the

sand dunes of Dune Park near Lake Michigan in Indiana. They made their longest flights in September, 253 ft. on the 4th, 256 ft. on the 11th, and 359 ft. on the 12th. Chanute and Herring built a fixed-wing biplane with a cruciform tail, a distinct advance over previous designs. Chanute also produced a five-plane craft with a rudder in the rear. Its wings could move forward and backward.

July 18 The **U.S. Open golf tournament** was won by James Foulis, with a 152 score at Shinnecock Hills, Southampton, N.Y.

Fall The **National League baseball championship** was won by Baltimore, with a record of 90 wins, 39 losses. Hugh Jennings hit .398, Willie Keeler .392, and Joe Kelley .370.

Nov. The **first amateur ice hockey league** in the U.S., the Amateur Hockey League, was formed by athletic clubs in New York City and vicinity. The championship for the 1896-1897 season was won by the New York Athletic Club. The league disbanded during World War I.

1897

A select Philadelphia **cricket team** defeated a visiting all-star Australian team by one inning and a score of 282 to 222. Until World War I, Philadelphia's great cricket clubs, notably Germantown, Merion,

GEORGE SISLER

George Harold Sisler
b. Manchester, Ohio, Mar. 24, 1893
d. Richmond Heights, Mo., Mar. 26, 1973

George Sisler ranks as one of the four best first basemen ever to play the game, his peers being Hal Chase, Lou Gehrig, and Bill Terry. Sisler played college ball for the University of Michigan and joined the St. Louis Browns in 1915. He remained there until 1928, when he played part of a

season with Washington, and then was with the Boston Braves in 1929 and 1930. He also managed St. Louis from 1924 to 1936, winning 218 games and losing 241.

Sisler was noted for his consistency as a fielder and a hitter. He made very few errors afield, and his career batting average was .314, putting him in a 14th-place tie with Gehrig. He won the American League batting title in 1920 with an average of .407 and a total of 257 hits, a season record that still holds. In 1922, Sisler

again won the batting championship, this time with a .420 average and including a hitting streak of 41 consecutive games, the third longest since 1900. He ended his career with 2812 hits, 1175 runs batted in, and 100 home runs.

His son Dick played for the St. Louis Cardinals and the Cincinnati Reds for eight years and managed the Reds in 1964 and 1965. George Sisler was elected to the Baseball Hall of Fame in 1939.

and Philadelphia, with the Belmont Club, produced players of international standing and made the city preeminent in U.S. cricket.

This year's **national college football championship** was won by Pennsylvania, with a record of 15 wins, no losses, no ties.

The **U.S. Lawn Tennis Association singles championships** were won by Juliette P. Atkinson in the women's division and Robert D. Wrenn in the men's division.

Mar. 17 The **world heavyweight boxing championship** was won by Bob Fitzsimmons, who defeated James J. "Gentleman Jim" Corbett in a 14-round bout at Carson City, Nev. This was the first boxing match photographed by a motion picture camera.

Mar. 20 The **first men's intercollegiate basketball game** was played at New Haven, Conn., between Yale and the U. of Pennsylvania. Yale won 32-10.

Apr. 19 The **first Boston Marathon** was won by John J. McDermott of New York City, with a time of 2 hrs., 55 min., 10 sec.

May 4 The 23rd annual **Kentucky Derby** was won by Typhoon II, with a time of 2:12½. The jockey was F. "Buttons" Garner.

May 9 The **first national AAU gymnastic championships** ended in St. Louis, Mo. The all-around title went to Earl Linderman, of Camden, N.J.

May 29 The 31st annual **Belmont Stakes** was won by Scottish Chieftain, with a time of 2:32¼. The jockey was J. Scherrer.

June 8 The 22nd annual **Preakness Stakes** was

won by Paul Kauvar, with a time of 1:51¼. The jockey was T. Thorpe.

Aug. 28 The **first mile in under 2 min. by a standardbred** was achieved by the pacer Star Pointer at 1:59.25 in a race at Readville, Mass. The driver was Dave McClary.

Sept. 17 The **U.S. Open golf tournament** was won by Joe Lloyd of England, with a 36-hole total of 162 at Chicago Golf Club, Wheaton, Ill.

Sept. 23 The **first Frontier Days rodeo** was held in Cheyenne, Wyo. Wild horses that had never been roped or even herded were rounded up for the event. The local newspaper, the *Sun Leader,* wrote: "The appearance of the city indicated a grand holiday. The stars and stripes and bunting adorned business houses, and on all sides were seen Frontier badges, and everyone seemed out for a celebration with seeming inspiration." Cheyenne's Frontier Days is now a nine-day rodeo, the largest such outdoor affair in the world. Purses for the competitors total over $100,000.

Fall The **National League baseball championship** was won by Boston, with a record of 93 wins, 39 losses. Kid Nichols won 30 games.

1898

The **first national birling (logrolling) championship,** sponsored by the Lumbermen's Associa-

JIM LONDOS

Christopher Theophilus
b. Argos, Greece, 1895?
d. Escondido, Calif., Aug. 19, 1975

Christopher Theophilus, who did not know the date of his birth, emigrated to the United States when he was about 13 and became Jim Londos, the Golden Greek, a popular champion wrestler in a period when the sport was partly authentic but on the way to becoming cheap entertainment. His most important

bout came on June 25, 1934, when he defeated Jim Browning for the world championship of catch-as-catch-can wrestling.

When Londos first came to the United States, he worked at several trades until one night in Los Angeles when he was asked to substitute in a wrestling bout. He won and went on between 1930 and 1946 to take part in about 2500 bouts, winning almost all of them. Strangler Lewis beat him seven times, but Londos turned the

tables on Lewis in a bruising bout and claimed the title. Some states recognized wrestling only as an exhibition so, in the absence of a regulatory body for the sport, various wrestlers claimed the championship.

Londos was known for the Japanese arm-lock and the airplane spin. He did well financially and was said to be worth $2,000,000 when he retired.

JACK DEMPSEY

William Harrison Dempsey
b. Manassa, Colo., Jan. 24, 1895
d. New York City, May 31, 1983

One of the best and most popular heavyweight boxing champions ever, Jack Dempsey, the Manassa Mauler, learned to fight in the rough-and-tumble of saloons and dance halls. He fought his first professional bout in 1914. Five years later, on July 4, 1919, at Toledo, Ohio, he won the heavyweight title from champion Jess Willard, knocking him down six times. Willard was unable to come out for the fourth round.

Dempsey's fights as champion always had an extra touch of excitement about them. In Jersey City, New Jersey, on July 2, 1921, he virtually demolished Georges Carpentier, the French champion, in four rounds. On September 14, 1923, at the Polo Grounds in New York City, he met Luis Angel Firpo, the Wild Bull of the Pampas, before a crowd of 90,000 people. Dempsey knocked Firpo down seven times in the first round, but the Argentinian got up and knocked Dempsey out of the ring. With the assistance of sportswriters at ringside, Dempsey got back in the ring in time to go on and knock Firpo out in the second round.

Dempsey lost his championship in Philadelphia on September 23, 1926, when Gene Tunney outboxed him to take the ten-round decision. The two met again in Chicago on September 22, 1927, before a crowd that paid a record $2,658,660 to see the fight at Soldier Field. Again Tunney won, although Dempsey was the victim of a long count that gave Tunney extra time after being knocked down in the seventh round because Dempsey had failed to go to a neutral corner.

Dempsey retired but made a brief attempt at a comeback in 1931 and 1932. In all, he lost only 5 of 69 fights and was noted for his savage attacks and powerful punches. Unpopular for a while during World War I because he did not join the Army, the Manassa Mauler was one of the truly great prizefighters. An Associated Press poll of sportswriters and broadcasters voted Dempsey the greatest fighter of the first half of the twentieth century. He received 251 votes; Joe Louis was second with 104.

---

tion of America, was held at Omaha, Nebr., in conjunction with the Trans-Mississippi Exposition. The first champion was Thomas Fleming of Eau Claire, Wis.

Croquet, according to a magazine editorial, "is the gaping jaw of Hades. It would be well if the enthusiasm of the clergy and laity were enlisted for suppressing the immoral practice of croquet." At this time it was charged that many players drank alcoholic beverages while playing and bet on the outcome. Others felt it was unladylike for Christian females to play such a game. Boston banned croquet, and other municipalities followed suit. At this same time, tennis was just becoming popular, and so the croquet boom ended.

Professional basketball was launched by two leagues, the National and the New England. Players in the latter were paid $150 to $225 a month. Both leagues disappeared after two seasons.

This year's **national college football championship** was won by Harvard, with a record of 11 wins, no losses, no ties.

The **U.S. Lawn Tennis Association singles championships** were won by Juliette P. Atkinson in the women's division and Malcolm D. Whitman in the men's division.

Apr. 19 The second **Boston Marathon** was won by Ronald J. McDonald of Cambridge, Mass., with a time of 2 hrs., 42 min.

Apr. 30 A **championship wrestling match,** contested on the stage of the Metropolitan Opera House in New York City, turned into a brawl, and the police had to be called in to restore order. The contestants were champion Ernest Roeber and challenger Ismael Yousoff, known as the Terrible Turk. After 20 min. of wrestling, the match became a prize fight, and supporters of both men soon joined in. Many women were present, and their shrieks added to the confusion.

May 4 The 24th annual **Kentucky Derby** was won by Plaudit, with a time of 2:09. The jockey was Willie Simms.

May 26 The 32nd annual **Belmont Stakes** was won by Bowling Brook, with a time of 2:32. The jockey was F. Littlefield.

June 11 The 23rd annual **Preakness Stakes** was won by Sly Fox, with a time of 1:49¾. The jockey was Willie Simms.

June 18 The **U.S. Open golf tournament** was won by Fred Herd. His 72-hole score at Myopia Hunt Club, South Hamilton, Mass., was 328.

GEORGE "PAPA BEAR" HALAS

George Stanley Halas
b. Chicago, Ill., Feb. 2, 1895
d. Chicago, Ill., Oct. 31, 1983

As player, coach, entrepreneur, and promoter, George Halas is usually considered the father of professional football. He began his football career at the University of Illinois, where he starred as an end in 1918. He then served briefly in the Navy in World War I.

After playing baseball for the New York Yankees, Halas in 1920 was one of the founders of what became the National Football League. He paid $100 for a franchise for the Decatur (Ill.) Staleys. He moved the team to Chicago and, in 1922, renamed them the Bears. He was coach, player, and general manager. In 1923, Halas ran a recovered fumble 98 yards for a touchdown, setting a record that still stands.

Halas made the Bears the most successful pro team for nearly 30 years. One of his coups was in 1923 to hire Red Grange, the college star, who attracted larger crowds than ever before. He also had such stars as Bronco Nagurski and Sid Luckman. The Bears reached their peak in 1940, when the Monsters of the Midway routed the Washington Redskins 73–0 to win the NFL championship.

Halas retired as coach in 1968 but remained active in the management of the team. By then, the Bears had won 321 games, lost 147, and tied 31, a record unmatched by any other pro coach. In 1963, Papa Bear became one of the charter members of the Pro Football Hall of Fame.

Fall The **National League baseball championship** was won by Boston, with a record of 102 wins, 47 losses. Kid Nichols pitched 29 winning games, Ted Lewis 25, and Vic Willis 23.

1899

The **rubber golf ball** was patented by Coburn Haskell, a golfer of Cleveland, Ohio, and Bertram G. Work of the B. F. Goodrich Co.

Official **rules for women's basketball** were issued for the first time at Springfield, Mass. At the close of the century, basketball was more popular with women than with men.

A new **baseball rule** required a pitcher to complete a throw to first base if he motions in that direction to drive a base runner back to the bag.

This year's **national college football championship** was won by Harvard, with a record of ten wins, no losses, one tie.

The **U.S. Lawn Tennis Association singles championships** were won by Marion Jones in the women's division and Malcolm D. Whitman in the men's division.

Apr. 19 The third **Boston Marathon** was won by Lawrence J. Brignolla of Cambridge, Mass., with a time of 2 hrs., 54 min., 38 sec.

May 4 The 25th annual **Kentucky Derby** was won by Manuel, with a time of 2:12. The jockey was Fred Taral. This year only three horses were entered in the race.

May 25 The 33rd annual **Belmont Stakes** was won by Jean Bereaud, with a time of 2:23. The jockey was R. Clawson.

May 30 The 24th annual **Preakness Stakes** was won by Half Time, with a time of 1:47. The jockey was R. Clawson.

June 9 The **world heavyweight boxing championship** was won by James J. Jeffries, who knocked out Bob Fitzsimmons in the 11th round of a bout at Coney Island, N.Y.

July 29 The **Championship Single Sculls,** previously known as the Senior Single Sculls, was won by Edward Hanlan Ten Eyck, who defeated Joseph Maguire and Joseph Whitehead on the Charles R. at Boston. Ten Eyck represented the Wachusett Boat Club of Worcester, Mass.

Sept. 15 The **U.S. Open golf tournament** was won by Willie Smith, who with his brother Alex and fellow Scots dominated the U.S. golf scene for two decades.

Fall The **National League baseball championship** was won by Brooklyn, with a record of 88 wins, 42 losses. Jay Hughes, with 28 wins, helped Brooklyn end Boston and Baltimore's domination of the 12-team National League.

Oct. 16-20 The **America's Cup** was successfully defended by the U.S. yacht *Columbia,* which won three straight heats over the British challenger, *Shamrock I.*

1900

Congress passed the **Lacey Act,** which prohibited interstate transportation of game killed in violation of state law at either end.

The **National Rifle Association** (NRA) added pistol shooting for the first time to the program of events at the national championships, conducted at Sea Girt, N.J. Three events in target pistol shooting had been included in the 1896 Olympic Games.

The Interstate Association of Trapshooters was succeeded by a larger **American Trapshooting Association,** which became the national governing body and conducted, on Interstate's grounds, an event called the Grand American Handicap, in reality the national championship. The first winner was R. O. Heikes. Membership for women began in 1918.

As the old century drew to a close, **shuffleboard** became a popular shipboard pastime, especially on British ocean liners.

This year's **national college football cham-**pionship was won by Yale, with a record of 12 wins, no losses, no ties.

A new **baseball rule** introduced the five-sided home plate, which is still used.

The **U.S. Lawn Tennis Association singles championships** were won by Myrtle McAteer in the women's division and Malcolm D. Whitman in the men's division.

Jan. 29 Bancroft B. "Ban" Johnson formed the **American League** in Chicago by expanding the Western League and including teams of some major eastern cities. The new baseball league demanded recognition as a major league but was refused by the National League until 1903, when the National, American, and minor leagues joined forces and set up a ruling body known as the National Commission.

Apr. 15 An early **automobile race** held at Springfield, Long Island, N.Y., was won by A. L. Riker in an electric car. He covered 50 mi. in 2 hrs., 3 min.

Apr. 19 The fourth **Boston Marathon** was won by

BABE RUTH

George Herman Ruth
b. Baltimore, Md., Feb. 6, 1895
d. New York City, Aug. 16, 1948

Babe Ruth and the glory days of major league baseball are synonymous. It is difficult to dispute his designation by some as the greatest player of all time. It also is impossible to disagree with the label of most colorful and most representative player of the American national game.

Ruth began his major league career as a left-handed pitcher with the Boston Red Sox and showed that he could have gone on to become an all-time star on the mound. However, his hitting ability was also so great that he was turned into an outfielder. Ruth was traded to the New York Yankees in 1920 for $125,000, the largest amount paid for a player up to that time. His salary was equally high for the era, $10,000. Ruth remained with the Yankees through 1934, then played for a year with the Boston Braves before retiring.

As a pitcher for Boston and New York, Ruth won 94 games and lost 46 for a winning percentage of .617, but his fame rests on his ability to hit home runs. On September 30, 1927, in the next to last game of the season, he hit homer number 60 of the season, a record that stood until 1961. In three other seasons, he had 50 or more home runs, getting 59 in 1921. Ruth hit 714 homers in all, still second best and a record not broken until 1974.

But Ruth was not just a slugger. He had a career batting average of .342, tenth on the all-time list. Ruth also had 2873 hits and 2211 runs batted in. He struck out 1330 times but drew 2056 bases on balls. Ruth appeared in ten World Series, seven of them with the Yankees. As a pitcher, he won three Series games for Boston while losing none. In Series play he also hit a total of 15 home runs and batted .326.

Ruth was easily baseball's biggest attraction ever, passing Ty Cobb in this respect. Known as the Bambino and as the Sultan of Swat, at first glance he did not look capable of his feats as an athlete. His body was too big for his spindly legs, but he was a fine outfielder as well as a great batter. He always seemed to be just a big boy who loved to play the game, and occasionally he was too flamboyant off the field. Nevertheless, he did a great deal to advance the prosperity of baseball. The new Yankee Stadium, built in 1923, was at once dubbed "the house that Ruth built." Ruth loved children, and in the year before he died, remembering his own years as a poor orphan child, he established a foundation to aid underprivileged youth. In 1936, the Babe became the second player elected to the Baseball Hall of Fame, preceded only by Ty Cobb.

TOMMY ARMOUR

Thomas Dickson Armour
b. Edinburgh, Scotland, Sept. 24,
    1895
d. Larchmont, N.Y., Sept. 11, 1968

As an amateur golfer, Tommy
Armour played for Great Britain
against an American team. After
moving to the United States, he
became a U.S. citizen and later
played on the Ryder Cup Team
against the British team.

Armour turned professional in
1924 and won three major victories:
the men's U.S. Open in 1927, the
PGA in 1930, and the British Open
in 1931. After he retired, Armour for
many years was a successful teacher
of golf.

James J. Caffrey of Hamilton, Ontario, Canada,
with a time of 2 hrs., 39 min., 44 sec.

May 3 The 26th annual **Kentucky Derby** was won
by Lieutenant Gibson, with a time of 2:06¼.
The jockey was Jimmy Boland.

May 20-Oct. 28 At the **Olympic Games** in Paris,
the U.S. finished with 20 gold medals. France
was first with 29 gold medals. John Flanagan
won the gold medal in the hammer throw and
repeated his victory in the 1904 and 1908
games.

May 24 The 34th annual **Belmont Stakes** was
won by Ildrim, with a time of 2:21½. The jockey
was Nash Turner.

May 29 The 25th annual **Preakness Stakes** was
won by Hindus, with a time of 1:48⅖. The
jockey was H. Spencer.

June 12-15 The **first Grand American,** a national event for shooting at clay targets, was
held at the Interstate Park, Queens, New York
City. The winning trapshooter was Rollo O.
"Pop" Heikes of Dayton, Ohio.

Aug. The **first known national competition in
lawn bowls** was held, with the McAusland
Medal as the trophy. It was won by the team of
W. J. Elliott, J. W. Greig, W. H. Lee, and James
Thaw of the New Jersey Bowling Green Club.

Aug. 8-10 **Davis Cup play** was inaugurated in a
match between Great Britain and the U.S. at

Take me out to the ball game,
Take me out with the crowd.
Buy me some peanuts and Cracker Jack—
I don't care if I never get back.

Jack Norworth, "Take Me Out to the Ball
Game"

Boston, won by the U.S. 3-0, with one match
unfinished and another canceled. The trophy
for international play had been donated earlier
in the year by Dwight F. Davis, a student at
Harvard College, who also played for the U.S.
team. He and Holcombe Ward won the doubles
match in straight sets. Davis and Malcolm D.
Whitman won their singles matches. There was
no competition in 1901, 1910, or in wartime, but
in other years the trophy has been fiercely contested by an increasing number of nations.

Fall The **National League baseball championship** was won by Brooklyn, with a record of 82
wins, 54 defeats. Joe "Iron Man" McGinnity
won 29 games and, in the next season, jumped
to the Baltimore Orioles.

Oct. 5 The **U.S. Open golf tournament,** played
at the Chicago Golf Club, was won by Harry
Vardon of England, the greatest golfer of the
early twentieth century.

1901

Napoleon "Nap" Lajoie, second baseman for
the Philadelphia Athletics, was credited in the official yearbook with a league-leading .405 average.
Not until 1955, after several disinterested reviews of
all the 1901 scoring books, was it discovered that a
typographical error had credited him with 220 hits
instead of 229. The correction raised Lajoie's average to .422, tops ever in the American League's modern era, superseding the .420 of Ty Cobb and
George Sisler.

This year's **national college football championship** was won by Michigan, with a record of 11
wins, no losses, no ties.

The **U.S. Lawn Tennis Association singles championships** were won by Elizabeth H. Moore in the women's division and William A. Larned in the men's division.

Jan. 8-11 The first **National Bowling Championships** were conducted in Chicago by the American Bowling Congress. Forty-one teams from 17 cities in nine states competed for a prize fund that totaled $1592.

Apr. 19 The fifth **Boston Marathon** was won by James J. Caffrey of Hamilton, Ontario, Canada, with a time of 2 hrs., 29 min., 23.6 sec.

Apr. 29 The 27th annual **Kentucky Derby** was won by His Eminence, with a time of 2:07¾. The jockey was Jimmy Winkfield.

May 23 The 35th annual **Belmont Stakes** was won by Commando, with a time of 2:21. The jockey was H. Spencer.

May 28 The 26th annual **Preakness Stakes** was won by The Parader, with a time of 1:47⅕. The jockey was Fred Landry.

June 15 The **U.S. Open golf tournament** was won by Willie Anderson at the Myopia Hunt Club in South Hamilton, Mass. His 85 in a play-off with Alex Smith was good enough to win by one stroke.

Aug. 21 **Joe "Iron Man" McGinnity,** of the Baltimore Orioles, was expelled from the National League for stepping on umpire Tom Connolly's toes, spitting in his face, and punching him. McGinnity was reinstated later because of baseball fans' pleas. He received a stiff fine and an official rebuke.

Fall The **National League baseball championship** was won by Pittsburgh, with a season record of 90 victories and 49 defeats. Honus Wagner established himself as a baseball great, at bat and in the infield.

Fall The **first American League baseball championship** was won by Chicago, with a season record of 83 victories and 53 defeats. Clark Griffith won 24 games and also managed the team to its title.

Sept. 28-Oct. 4 The **America's Cup** was successfully defended by the U.S. yacht *Columbia,* which won three straight heats over the British challenger, *Shamrock II.*

Nov. 25 The **San Francisco Scottish Bowling Club** was formally organized, a committee announced, and a green for lawn bowls was laid out in Golden Gate Park by John McLaren. Now known as the San Francisco Lawn Bowling Club, it is the oldest such club still active in its original location. After the San Francisco earthquake in Apr., 1906, the club green was rebuilt by the end of the year.

1902

The huge **ice yacht *Wolverine,*** carrying 850 sq. ft. of sail, was built. For two decades *Wolverine* dominated American large ice yacht racing, once completing a 20-mi. course at an average speed of 132 mph.

BENNY LEONARD

Benjamin Leiner
b. New York City, Apr. 7, 1896
d. New York City, Apr. 18, 1947

Benny Leonard began his boxing career in 1912, when he was still in his teens. Within five years, on May 28, 1917, he became the lightweight champion, when in New York City he knocked out the defending titleholder, Freddy Welsh of Great Britain, in the ninth round. Leonard successfully defended his title for eight years and during that period fought Johnnie Dundee eight times. Those bouts are remembered as classic ring events.

Leonard suffered a serious defeat when he fought welterweight champion Jack Britton on June 26, 1922. In the 13th round, the referee disqualified Leonard for allegedly fouling his opponent and then hitting Britton while he was on his knees in pain. Leonard retired from the ring in 1925.

The stock market debacle of 1929 cost Leonard his fortune, so in 1931–1932 he tried a comeback in an effort to restore his finances. Fighting by then as a welterweight, he was knocked out by Jimmy McLarnin, the champion. In all, Leonard had 209 bouts and won all but five of them. A hard puncher, he was especially brilliant when the odds were against him. Leonard became a fight referee and died suddenly of a heart attack while officiating at a bout in New York City.

JOE McCARTHY

Joseph Vincent McCarthy
b. Philadelphia, Pa., Apr. 21, 1897
d. Buffalo, N.Y., Jan. 3, 1978

One of the all-time greatest and most successful major league baseball managers, Joe McCarthy did not start his baseball career as a player but as a manager in the American Association, one of the top minor leagues. In 1926, he moved up to the Chicago Cubs and led them to the league title in 1929 but lost the World Series to the Philadelphia Athletics, four games to one.

McCarthy then began his 16-year tenure with the New York Yankees of the American League, and during his regime the Yankees were league champions eight times and won seven World Series. Most remarkable was the four-year reign of the Yankees between 1936 and 1939, when they won four series in a row. They beat the New York Giants twice and the Cubs and Cincinnati Reds once each, winning 16 games and losing only three in the process.

Under McCarthy, the Yanks also beat the Cubs in 1932, the Brooklyn Dodgers in 1941, and the St. Louis Cardinals in 1943 and lost a Series only to the Cardinals, in 1942.

McCarthy also managed the Boston Red Sox, in 1948, 1949, and 1950. Overall, he managed 3489 big league games, winning 2126 and losing 1335, for a winning percentage of .614, good enough to win a pennant in many seasons. In World Series competition, his teams won 30 games while losing only 13. It is true that McCarthy, especially when with the Yankees, had some of the best players available playing for him, but he also made the most of that talent and was always the boss, the man who made the decisions. Joe McCarthy was elected to the Baseball Hall of Fame in 1957.

This year's **national college football championship** was won by Michigan, with a record of 11 wins, no losses, no ties.

The **U.S. Lawn Tennis Association singles championships** were won by Marion Jones in the women's division and William A. Larned in the men's division.

Jan. 1 The **first Tournament of Roses association football game,** and the first postseason football game, was held at Pasadena, Calif. Michigan defeated Stanford 49-0. The event came to be known as the Rose Bowl game in 1923.

Apr. 19 The sixth **Boston Marathon** was won by Samuel A. Mellor of Yonkers, N.Y., with a time of 2 hrs., 43 min., 12 sec.

May 3 The 28th annual **Kentucky Derby** was won by Alan-a-Dale, with a time of 2:08¾. The jockey was Jimmy Winkfield, scoring his second straight Derby win.

May 22 The 36th annual **Belmont Stakes** was won by Masterman, with a time of 2:22½. The jockey was John Bullman.

May 27 The 27th annual **Preakness Stakes** was won by Old England, with a time of 1:45⅘. The jockey was L. Jackson.

July 17 The target of a **National League raiding party,** the American League's Baltimore club was unable to field a team for a scheduled game in St. Louis. Its stars, including John McGraw, Joe McGinnity, and Roger Bresnahan, played the rest of the season in the National League. Ban Johnson, the American League president, restocked the Baltimore team and saved the new league's life.

Aug. 8 In the **Davis Cup,** the U.S. team, led by William A. Larned, defeated the British team three matches to two. Hugh and Reginald Doherty played for the British for the first time in Davis Cup competition.

Aug. 31 An innovation in **women's riding clothes** was introduced by Mrs. Adolph Ladenburg at Saratoga, N.Y. Wearing a split skirt, she rode astride her horse and created a considerable stir in the press. She declared the fashion much more comfortable and no more immodest than costumes for sidesaddle riding.

Fall The **National League baseball championship** was won by Pittsburgh, with a season record of 103 victories and 36 defeats.

Fall The **American League baseball championship** was won by Philadelphia, with a season record of 83 victories and 53 defeats. Rube Waddell was manager Connie Mack's ace pitcher, winning 24 with an earned run average of 2.05.

Oct. 11 At the Garden City Golf Club on Long Island, N.Y., the **U.S. Open golf tournament** was won by Laurie Auchterlonie, with a 307 total.

1903

The **Australian crawl,** developed down under a decade earlier, was popularized among U.S. swimmers by visiting Australian champions Syd and Charles Cavill.

A new **baseball rule** stated that a foul tip caught after two strikes constituted a third strike and therefore resulted in an out. Baseball has since remained substantially unchanged except for scoring rules and the American League's use of the designated hitter.

The **first professional ice hockey team** in the U.S., composed largely of Canadians, was formed at Houghton, on the Upper Peninsula of Michigan.

This year's **national college football championship** was won by Princeton, with a record of 11 wins, no losses, no ties.

The **U.S. Lawn Tennis Association singles championships** were won by Elizabeth H. Moore in the women's division and Hugh L. Doherty of England in the men's division. Doherty was the first foreigner to win the title. He defeated the defending champion, William A. Larned, in straight sets.

Apr. 20   The seventh **Boston Marathon** was won by John C. Lorden of Cambridge, Mass., with a time of 2 hrs., 41 min., 29.8 sec.

Apr. 22   The **American Power Boat Association** (APBA) was formed.

Apr. 27   The opening of the **Jamaica Race Track** on Long Island, N.Y., was attended by many notable figures from the world of entertainment and gambling, including Lillian Russell, a reigning glamour queen of the time; James Buchanan "Diamond Jim" Brady; and John Warne "Bet-a-million" Gates. On Memorial Day in 1945 the track drew the largest crowd in the history of New York racing, 64,670.

May 2   The 29th annual **Kentucky Derby** was won by Judge Himes, with a time of 2:09. The jockey was Hal Booker.

May 27   The 37th annual **Belmont Stakes** was won by Africander, with a time of 2:23⅕. The jockey was John Bullman.

May 30   The 28th annual **Preakness Stakes** was won by Flocarline, with a time of 1:44⅘. The jockey was W. Gannon.

June 27   At Baltusrol Golf Club, Springfield, N.J., the **U.S. Open golf tournament** was won by Willie Anderson by a two-stroke margin in a playoff with David Brown.

Aug. 8   The U.S. lost the **Davis Cup** international tennis challenge round to Great Britain, four

GENE TUNNEY

James Joseph Tunney
b.   New York City, May 25, 1898
d.   Greenwich, Conn., Nov. 7, 1978

While on active duty with the U.S. Marines in World War I, Gene Tunney won his first boxing championship in Paris, where he fought his way to the top to become light heavyweight champion of the American Expeditionary Forces in Europe. He turned professional after the war and won the light heavyweight title on January 13, 1922, from Battling Levinsky, only to lose it later that year to Harry Greb, the only fighter ever to defeat Tunney. Tunney took the title back from Greb in 1923.

In 1924, fighting as a heavyweight, Tunney knocked out Georges Carpentier of France. Finally, on September 23, 1926, at Philadelphia, where the nation's sesquicentennial was being celebrated, Tunney got his chance at the heavyweight championship in a much heralded bout with Jack Dempsey. In ten rounds Tunney was the master, completely outboxing the champion. A crowd of 135,000 watched the fight and paid more than $2,000,000, by far the largest gate ever for a prizefight.

The two antagonists met again in Chicago on September 22, 1927, and again Tunney prevailed in ten rounds. It was a controversial decision. In the seventh round, Tunney was knocked down, but when Dempsey went to the wrong corner, the referee delayed starting the count, and Tunney recovered. Tunney fought only once more, defeating Tom Heeney in a 12th-round TKO on July 26, 1928. He then retired from the ring.

Tunney has been somewhat underrated because he was not the big puncher the fans preferred. He was, however, a most skillful boxer and an excellent analyst of his opponents' weaknesses. He fought in an upright stance, unlike most boxers of the time. Tunney, who said he liked to read Shakespeare, married a society heiress, entered business, and became a director of several corporations.

FRANKIE FRISCH

Frank Francis Frisch
b. New York City, Sept. 8, 1898
d. Wilmington, Del., Mar. 12, 1973

In a 19-year career with the St. Louis Cardinals and the New York Giants, Frankie Frisch, the Fordham Flash—he was a graduate of Fordham University—established himself as one of the best second basemen the game has known. He also ranks high as a batter and as a manager.

Frisch played for the Giants from 1919 to 1926 and for the Cardinals from 1927 to 1937. He was player-manager with the Cardinals from 1933 to 1937, then managed one more year but did not play. Frisch went on to manage Pittsburgh from 1940 to 1946 and the Chicago Cubs in 1949 and 1950. With a lifetime batting average of .316, Frisch had 105 home runs and stole 419 bases, an indication of his speed on the base paths.

Playing in eight World Series between 1921 and 1934, Frisch appeared in 50 series games and batted .294. As a manager he won 1137 games and lost 1078. Under his leadership, the Cardinals beat the Detroit Tigers in the 1934 series, four games to three.

Frisch was the National League's most valuable player in 1931 and was elected to the Baseball Hall of Fame in 1947.

---

matches to one. The Doherty brothers, Hugh and Reginald, proved too much for William A. Larned and Robert D. Wrenn.

Aug. 22-Sept. 2 The **America's Cup** was successfully defended by the U.S. yacht *Reliance,* which won three heats over the British challenger, *Shamrock III.*

Sept. **Joe "Iron Man" McGinnity** of the New York National League club pitched and won both games of a doubleheader for the third time in this baseball season. Philadelphia fell by scores of 4-1 and 9-2. Playing time of the two games totaled 3 hrs., 3 min.

Oct. 1-13 This year was born an American sports institution, the **World Series.** For the first time, the champions of the National and American

leagues met for a postseason playoff. It was a best-of-nine series. The Pittsburgh Pirates, the National League champs, took three of the first four games from the Boston Red Sox, originally called the Red Stockings. On Oct. 7 the American League champs rebounded with an 11-2 romp over the Pirates, then won the next three games to take the series five games to three and prove to the world that the American League had arrived. Boston's win no doubt ruffled a few feathers in the National camp.

Oct. 24 The **first trotting mile in under 2 min.** was achieved by Lou Dillon at Memphis, Tenn. The time was 1:58.1. On Aug. 24 at Readville, Mass., Lou Dillon had become the first trotter to do the mile in 2:00 flat.

BILL TERRY

William Harold Terry
b. Atlanta, Ga., Oct. 30, 1898

Always reliable and consistent, Bill Terry as first baseman and manager was a major asset of the New York Giants in the 1920s and 1930s. He made his entire major league career with them as a player from 1923 to 1931, as player-manager from 1932 to 1936, and as manager from 1937 to 1941.

Besides being one of the best

all-time fielding first basemen, Terry brought strength to the offense with a career batting average of .341, still 12th best. He was the National League batting champion in 1930 with a .401 average. That year he had 254 hits, a tie for the league record that still stands. Terry was not always thought of as a slugger, but in 1932 he hit 28 home runs and had a career total of 154. Before Terry became team manager, he appeared in two World Series, in

1923 and 1924, and batted .295.

Over his ten-year span as manager, Bill Terry guided the Giants to three National League pennants. They won the World Series in 1933 against the Washington Senators, four games to one. In 1936 and 1937, the Giants lost the Series to the New York Yankees, 4–2 and 4–1. Overall as a manager, Terry won 827 games and lost 661, a percentage of .555. He became a member of the Baseball Hall of Fame in 1954.

EARLE SANDE

b.   Groton, S.Dak., Nov. 13, 1898
d.   Jacksonville, Fla., Aug. 18, 1968

Earl Sande was the leading American jockey of the 1920s, winning 917 races from the time he began riding thoroughbreds in 1917. His earnings totaled almost $3,000,000 in a day when purses were much smaller than they are today.

In 1930, Sande rode Gallant Fox to victory in the Triple Crown to mark the high point of his career. He also rode the winners in the Kentucky Derby in 1923 and 1925. In the Belmont Stakes he rode to victory five times, in 1921, 1923, 1924, 1927, and 1930. At Belmont Park, New York, on October 20, 1923, Sande was the jockey on Zev, the horse that had won the Derby earlier that year, in an international race against Papyrus, the winner of the English Derby. Zev won by five lengths.

An embarrassing moment in Sande's career came just before a match race was to be run on October 12, 1920, at Windsor Park, Ontario. The great Man o' War was matched with the Canadian champion, Sir Barton. An hour before the race, Sir Barton's owner, Commander J. K. L. Ross, announced he was changing jockeys, displacing Sande, who had been scheduled for the ride. Ross thought that in a race a few days before, Sande had ridden timidly. "My boy is not in good form," he said. Sir Barton lost the race by seven lengths.

Nov. 4   **Harvard Stadium** was dedicated. It was the first stadium built especially for football. At the time, it was also the largest reinforced steel structure in the world.

Winter   The **baseball war ended** when the National and American leagues buried the hatchet, recognizing each other as equals. They established rules pertaining to shifting franchises and players from one league to the other. A National Commission was created to govern professional baseball.

1904

Platform diving and springboard diving were recognized as championship events by the *Fédération de natation amateur* (Amateur Swimming Federation). A table of dives, each assigned a value reflecting its relative difficulty, was issued, with accompanying scoring instructions. The original table listed 20 springboard dives and 14 platform dives. Seventy years later, four times as many dives were listed and performed.

The **Gold Cup,** premier event of the American Power Boat Association, was held for the first time. On the Hudson R., C. C. Riotte's *Standard* won by running one heat at 23.6 mph. The event is now a race for unlimited hydroplanes over a 2- or 2½-mi. circular course.

Jai alai (pelota) was introduced to the U.S. public at the World's Fair in St. Louis, Mo. Twenty years later it was a tourist attraction in Miami, Fla. A new Biscayne Jai Alai Fronton was completed in 1926 but was destroyed by a hurricane that same year. The game has been popular as a spectator sport where gambling is permitted, as in Florida beginning in 1935, and in Connecticut later.

The **National Rifle Association** (NRA) this year, for the first time, conducted rifle and pistol competitions both indoors and outdoors as separate events.

The game of **basketball was demonstrated** during the Olympic Games, which were held in St. Louis, Mo.

This year's **national college football championship** was won by Pennsylvania, with a record of 12 wins, no losses, no ties.

The **jujitsu** vogue was started by Pres. Theodore Roosevelt, who had a Japanese instructor call regularly at the White House.

A new **baseball rule** limited the height of the pitcher's mound to 15 in. higher than home plate.

The **U.S. Lawn Tennis Association singles championships** were won by May G. Sutton in the

---

Football is, after all, a wonderful way to get rid of aggressions without going to jail for it.

Heywood Hale Broun

ANNE TOWNSEND

Anne Barton Townsend
b. Philadelphia, Pa., 1900
d. Bryn Mawr, Pa., Feb. 3, 1984

Anne Townsend was a first-rate athlete at lacrosse, tennis, squash, golf, and bowling, but field hockey was her best and favorite sport. For practical purposes, she was all there was in American field hockey for about a quarter of a century.

Between 1923 and 1946, Townsend was selected for the all-American team 15 times, and in all but one of those years she was named captain, which in effect meant she was judged to be the best player in the country. She played at forward, center halfback, and left halfback. Townsend led the first U.S. field hockey team to England in 1924 and was captain during the first international tournament, held in Copenhagen, Denmark, in 1923.

In 1934, Townsend was selected for the U.S. lacrosse team, and she also won local championships in tennis and squash. She was president of the U.S. Field Hockey Association between 1928 and 1932, having served previously as treasurer. Townsend was inducted into the Pennsylvania Sports Hall of Fame in 1964.

women's division and Holcombe Ward in the men's division.

The **World Series** was called off this year by John McGraw, manager of the New York Giants, the National League champions. Incensed by the abuse Ban Johnson, president of the American League, had heaped on him when he switched from the Baltimore Americans in 1903, McGraw got even by refusing to let the Giants meet Boston, the American League leaders, for the postseason series. It took the persuasion of owners, managers, players, and fans to smooth the incident over. By that time it was too late for the games to be played. The bitterness between the two leagues was only temporary. In 1905 the World Series resumed and has been played every year since.

Jan. **Henry Ford** set a new world record of 91.37 mph when he drove Hi Arrow, with a large 16.7-liter engine, over an ice straightaway on Lake St. Clair, near Detroit. Of his venture, Ford wrote: "When I wasn't in the air, I was skidding; but somehow I stayed topside up . . . making a record that went all over the world." With others, Ford had organized the Ford Motor Co. in the previous year.

Jan. 28 The catch-as-catch-can **heavyweight wrestling championship** was won by Frank Gotch, who defeated Tom Jenkins at Bellingham, Wash. Gotch won the first fall and was then awarded the match by the referee after Jenkins fouled Gotch a number of times. Jenkins had held the title since the turn of the century and had beaten Gotch in Cleveland, Ohio, on Feb. 22, 1903.

TOMMY HITCHCOCK

Thomas Hitchcock, Jr.
b. Aiken, S.C., Feb. 11, 1900
d. Salisbury, England, Apr. 19, 1944

The best polo player of all time, Tommy Hitchcock seemed to have inherited his skill from his mother and father, both of whom played polo. His father achieved a ten-goal rating, the highest possible, but the younger Hitchcock outdid him with a ten-goal rating for every year from 1922 through 1940, except in 1935, when he was dropped to nine.

Hitchcock's skill and dashing personality made polo something of a popular spectator sport for a time, instead of a pastime for a few rich men. The change began in 1921, when he led an American team to victory over a British team to win the Westchester Cup. Hitchcock and the Americans repeated this victory in 1924, 1927, 1930, and 1939. On October 6, 1928, in the third and deciding game for the championship of the Americas, Hitchcock starred in the U.S. win over Argentina 13–7.

During World War I, while still in his teens, Hitchcock joined the Lafayette Escadrille, a group of American pilots fighting for the French. Shot down behind German lines, he made a daring and much publicized escape to Switzerland. After graduating from Harvard, Hitchcock worked in banking until World War II, when he joined the U.S. Air Force. While commanding a fighter group in England, Hitchcock went down with his plane and was killed.

LEFTY GROVE

Robert Moses Grove
b.   Lonaconing, Md., Mar. 6, 1900
d.   Norwalk, Ohio, May 23, 1975

The Philadelphia Athletics paid Baltimore of the International League $100,000, a very high price in 1925, to secure the services of Lefty Grove. It was money well spent. The brilliant left-hander made contenders of the Athletics from then until 1933, when he went to the Boston Red Sox. He pitched for the Sox until

the end of his career in 1941.

In Grove's years with Connie Mack's team and afterward, he won 300 games—only 18 other major league pitchers have won more—and lost 141, for a percentage of .680 and an earned run average of 3.06. In the three World Series in which Grove pitched, he won four games and lost two. His series ERA was 1.75. In 1931, he tied the American League record for consecutive victories with 16, a string that ended

on August 23, 1931, when he lost to the St. Louis Browns 1–0. Only Smokey Joe Wood and Walter Johnson had accomplished this feat, both in 1912.

In 1931, with a record of 31 wins and 4 losses, a percentage of .886, Grove was named the American League's most valuable player. Grove had 2266 strikeouts in his career. He was elected to the Baseball Hall of Fame in 1947.

Feb. 22   The **National Ski Association** of America was founded at Ishpeming, Mich. It was there that the first national ski championship was held. Conrad Thompson won the jumping competition, the only form of competition recognized at the time. In 1962 the group changed its name to the United States Ski Association. The organization sets standards and holds national competitions.

Apr. 19   The eighth **Boston Marathon** was won by Michael Spring of New York City, with a time of 2 hrs., 38 min., 4.4 sec.

May 2   The 30th annual **Kentucky Derby** was won by Elwood, with a time of 2:08½. The jockey was Frankie Prior.

May 5   The **first perfect baseball game** under

modern pitching rules, in which the pitcher did not allow any opposing player to reach first base, was pitched by Denton T. "Cy" Young of Boston (AL), in a 3-0 victory over Philadelphia.

May 14   The first **Olympic Games** to be held in the U.S. opened as part of the St. Louis Exposition in St. Louis, Mo. The U.S. won 21 events and the unofficial team championship in the third Olympiad of the modern era. Charles Daniels won three gold, one silver, and one bronze medal in swimming events. U.S. cyclists won all the cycling events for a total of 21 medals. Thomas J. Hicks became the first American to win the Olympic marathon with a time of 3 hrs., 28 min. 53 sec.

May 25   The 38th annual **Belmont Stakes** was

SHERWIN CAMPBELL BADGER

b.   1901
d.   Apr. 1972

Besides being a champion figure skater of the 1920s, Sherwin Badger influenced the future of the sport by showing a dynamic style that was well ahead of its time. He first skated on the outdoor ice of the Cambridge (Mass.) Skating Club and in 1920 won the U.S. men's championship, holding the title for five years, through 1924.

Badger captured the first North American championship in 1923 and, with Beatrix Loughran, won the U.S. pairs championship in 1930, 1931, and 1932. He competed in both the 1928 and 1932 Olympics, finishing second in 1932 in the pairs, again with Loughran.

His first triumphs on ice had come while he was a student at Harvard, where he was also coxswain of the crew in 1922 and 1923. Badger was an editor of the *Wall Street Journal*

and later an executive of a New England insurance company. He did much for the sport of figure skating, off the ice as well as on, being president of the U.S. Figure Skating Association (USFSA) twice, 1930–1932 and 1934–1935. Badger was a member of the executive committee of the USFSA for 22 years and in 1976 was elected to its hall of fame.

GENE SARAZEN

Eugene Saraceni
b. Harrison, N.Y., Feb. 27, 1901

Gene Sarazen learned to play golf as a caddy at Rye, New York, and first played in the U.S. Open in 1920. Two years later, he won this event and repeated in 1932. On the latter occasion, he carded a 286, a total that had been achieved only once before in the 26 years of this championship event.

In 1932, Sarazen also won the British Open and in the process lowered the record set by Bobby Jones by two strokes. In 1922, 1923, and 1933 he was the PGA champion. Sarazen's most spectacular triumph came in 1935 at the Masters, which he won on the 12th hole of a playoff with a double eagle. This was perhaps the greatest single hole of tournament golf ever played in the U.S. After retiring from

tournament play, Sarazen returned to win the PGA Seniors championship in 1954 and 1958.

About 1930, Sarazen invented the sand wedge, a golf club that would revolutionize the way shots are played out of bunkers. Unlike some players, he liked to use woods on the fairways. One of the best golfers ever to play the game, Sarazen and his unique skills helped increase the popularity of golf.

---

won by Delhi, with a time of 2:06⅗. The jockey was George Odom.

May 28 The 29th annual **Preakness Stakes** was won by Bryn Mawr, with a time of 1:44⅕. The jockey was Eugene Hildebrand.

July 9 The **U.S. Open golf tournament** was won by Willie Anderson, at the Glen View Club, Golf, Ill., with a 303 total.

Oct. 8 The first auto race for the **Vanderbilt Cup,** sponsored by William K. Vanderbilt, Jr., was held on Long Island, N.Y. The race, ten laps over a 28.4-mi. course, was won by George Heath, driving a 90-hp French Panhard. Heath completed the 284-mi. race in 5 hrs., 26 min., 45 sec. There were 16 starters, representing the U.S., France, Germany, and Italy.

1905

Motorcycle racing was now an established sport in the U.S. Many of the races were contested on banked board tracks.

The **first horseshoe pitching tournament** of significance was staged at Kansas State College (now U.), in Manhattan, Kans. The singles championship was won by Frank Jackson of Kellerton, Iowa, the dominant horseshoe pitcher for two decades.

A **surf club,** the Hui Nalu, was started on an unofficial basis in Hawaii by champion swimmer Duke Kahanamoku and friends. It was officially chartered in 1911 and was intended for Hawaiian surfers and paddlers.

ROGER F. TURNER

b. Milton, Mass., Mar. 3, 1901

Roger Turner has been an all-around athlete of high quality in tennis, riding, golf, gymnastics, and swimming, but it was in figure skating that he achieved his greatest success. He began ice skating on a local pond when he was about 10 and played hockey in school. By 1926, Turner had won the U.S. junior men's championship.

The U.S. men's championship

came to Turner in 1928, and he did not relinquish it until 1935. He competed for the United States in both the 1928 and the 1932 Olympics. At Madison Square Garden in New York City on February 5, 1930, he lost to Karl Schafer of Austria in competition for the world figure skating title. The *New York Times* praised Turner but found he "was far from being as spectacular as the Austrian." Turner won the silver medal in this event

again in 1931 and in 1937 won the silver in the North American championships.

During World War II, Turner served with the Red Cross. A lawyer by profession, he has remained active in figure skating affairs, serving for more than 20 years as a member of the governing council of the U.S. Figure Skating Association. He is a past vice president of the organization and has judged skating events nationally and internationally.

1 MICKEY WALKER

Edward Patrick Walker
b. Elizabeth, N.J., July 13, 1901
d. Freehold, N.J., Apr. 28, 1981

Mickey Walker, who never weighed more than 170 pounds, earned his sobriquet Toy Bulldog by his willingness to take on any boxer regardless of weight. He held titles in two weight divisions and tried for two more.

His first title came on November 1, 1922, when he defeated the champion, Jack Britton, for the welterweight crown. Walker knocked Britton down three times. He held this title until 1926, when he stepped up to the middleweight championship by defeating Tiger Flowers. Not everyone agreed with the officials.

In 1931, Walker gave up the middleweight title and fought Jack Sharkey, soon to be the heavyweight champion, to a draw. Walker weighed 162 pounds to Sharkey's 198. He also took on, and lost to, light heavyweights Tommy Loughran and Maxie Rosenbloom. Max Schmeling, another heavyweight, knocked him out in eight rounds.

Aggressive and fearless, Walker had a successful career, winning 91 of 140 fights, including 51 by knockouts. In 1955, Walker took up painting and had a one-man show in New York City.

This year's **national college football championship** was won by Chicago, with a record of 11 wins, no losses, no ties.

Football rules were revised this season by the Rules Committee of Football as a result of Pres. Theodore Roosevelt's threat to abolish football after seeing a newspaper picture of a badly mangled player. The changes included legalization of the forward pass and elimination of certain dangerous scrimmage plays. Although only a small number of schools and colleges had teams at this time, 18 players were killed and 159 were seriously injured in 1905.

The **U.S. Lawn Tennis Association singles championships** were won by Elizabeth H. Moore, for the fourth time, in the women's division and Beals C. Wright in the men's division.

At the **Wimbledon tennis championships** in England, May G. Sutton won the women's singles championship, becoming the first foreigner to win the women's singles and the first U.S. player to win a Wimbledon singles title.

Spring Five eastern colleges formed the **Intercollegiate Association Football League**: Harvard, Haverford, Columbia, Cornell, and Pennsylvania. The first league competition in 1906 was won by Haverford. In May 1907, Yale joined the group. Games were played in both spring and fall until 1914, thereafter in the fall only.

BOBBY JONES

Robert Tyre Jones
b. Atlanta, Ga., Mar. 17, 1902
d. Atlanta, Ga., Dec. 18, 1971

Bobby Jones, the quintessential amateur athlete, is arguably the greatest golfer of all time. He won his first major golf title, the U.S. Open, in 1923, at the age of 21. By the time of his retirement from competitive golf in 1930, Jones had won the U.S. Open four times, the British Open three times, the USGA Amateur title five times, and the British Amateur title once. Between 1922 and 1930, Jones missed finishing first or second in the U.S. Open only once. In 1930, he achieved the grand slam of golf, winning the U.S. Open, USGA Amateur, British Open, and British Amateur titles in the same year. He then retired from competitive golf, acknowledged by all as master of the game.

In later years, Bobby Jones helped design the Augusta National Golf Course, site of the Masters golf tournament, and for many years he played in the tournament. In the late 1940s, Jones contracted a spinal disorder that eventually confined him to a wheelchair. He died in 1971 at the age of 69.

To Bobby Jones belongs much of the credit for the sharp increase in the popularity of golf in the 1920s. Of average height and sturdy build, sporting blond hair parted nearly in the middle and a warm, broad grin, Jones became the idol of millions around the world. As Paul Gallico put it, he was "the best sportsman, the greatest gentleman, the champion of champions."

WILBUR SHAW

Warren Wilbur Shaw
b. Shelbyville, Ind., Oct. 31, 1902
d. near Peterson, Ind., Oct. 20, 1954

Wilbur Shaw did his first auto racing on dirt tracks in Indiana. Driving in his initial Indianapolis 500 in 1927, he finished fourth. Shaw came in second in 1933 and 1935 before winning the Indy in 1937. He won again in 1939 and 1940.

Trying to become the first driver to win the Indy four times, Shaw was badly injured on May 30, 1941, when his car crashed into a wall. He was leading the race at the time.

Shaw was named U.S. Auto Club national champion in 1937. In 1954, he was chosen president of the Indianapolis Motor Speedway, having retired from racing after his injury. Shaw died in the crash of a light plane that was returning from tests conducted at an auto proving ground.

Apr. 19 The ninth **Boston Marathon** was won by Frederick Lorz of Yonkers, N.Y., with a time of 2 hrs., 38 min., 25 sec.

May 10 The 31st annual **Kentucky Derby** was won by Agile, with a time of 2:10¾. The jockey was Jack Martin. For the second time in Derby history, only three horses ran in the race.

May 19 The **heavyweight wrestling championship** was regained by Tom Jenkins in a match with Frank Gotch at Madison Square Garden in New York City. Jenkins took two of three falls, and Gotch was so badly injured that it was said he could not leave his hotel room for a week.

May 24 The 39th annual **Belmont Stakes** was won by Tanya, with a time of 2:08. The jockey was Eugene Hildebrand.

May 27 The 30th annual **Preakness Stakes** was won by Cairgorn, with a time of 1:45⅘. The jockey was W. Davis.

July 3 The **world heavyweight boxing championship** was won by Marvin Hart, who knocked out Jack Root in 12 rounds in the final bout of an elimination tourney. He filled the title vacated by the retirement of James J. Jeffries in March. Jeffries refereed the bout, which was held in Reno, Nev., and declared Hart the new champion.

Sept. 22 The **U.S. Open golf tournament** was won by Willie Anderson, for the fourth time in five years. His score at Myopia Hunt Club was 314.

Oct. 9-14 The second annual **World Series** was won by the New York Giants (NL), defeating the Philadelphia Athletics (AL) four games to one. Christy Mathewson pitched three shutouts in a seven-day period for McGraw's Giants. He was to do this twice more in his career. Mathewson allowed 14 hits in 27 innings.

Oct. 21 **Soccer gained recognition** when the touring English Pilgrim Association's football (soccer) team defeated an all-New York eleven by 7-1 at the Polo Grounds, in New York City. About 2000 people attended. The Pilgrims had previously displayed the British game in Can-

MICKEY COCHRANE

Gordon Stanley Cochrane
b. Bridgewater, Mass., Apr. 6, 1903
d. Lake Forest, Ill., June 28, 1962

Durable and steady in crisis situations, Mickey Cochrane was an ideal major league baseball catcher. Behind the plate for 13 seasons, he was with the Philadelphia Athletics from 1925 to 1933 and with the Detroit Tigers from 1934 to 1937.

His work at bat and behind the plate won him the most valuable player award of the American League in 1928 and 1934. Cochrane participated in five World Series, 1929, 1930, and 1931 with the Athletics, and 1934 and 1935 with the Tigers. In the last two he was also team manager. Detroit lost the 1934 series to the St. Louis Cardinals four games to three, but won the 1935 series from the Chicago Cubs four games to two.

Cochrane's lifetime batting average was .320, and he hit 119 home runs. He was elected to the Baseball Hall of Fame in 1947.

1906

LOU GEHRIG

Henry Louis Gehrig
b. New York City, June 19, 1903
d. New York City, June 2, 1941

It was the fate of Lou Gehrig, baseball's Iron Man, the most durable star in major league baseball history, to lose that distinction while he was seemingly still going strong. His abrupt downfall was caused by a rare and fatal disease.

After leaving Columbia College, where Gehrig had set records for home run hitting, he played for two seasons with Hartford, Connecticut, in the Eastern League before being brought up to the New York Yankees in 1923.

On June 1, 1925, Gehrig was put in the lineup at first base in place of the formidable Wally Pipp and never gave up the position until May 2, 1939, when he realized he was

unable to continue. During that span, he played in 2130 consecutive games, a record that still stands. In all he appeared in 2164 regular-season major league games and 34 World Series games, all for the Yankees.

At the end of his career, he had a .340 batting average, having led the American League in 1934 with a .363 mark. His other career records include 493 home runs, having led both major leagues in 1931 with 46 (tied with Babe Ruth), and in 1934 and 1936 with 49; 2721 hits; 1888 runs scored, still seventh highest; and 1464 bases on balls, still tenth best.

In 1932, Gehrig became only the third player to hit four home runs in one game, and from 1927 to 1929 he poled 23 grand slammers, still the record. Gehrig was named the American League's most valuable

player four times, the last time in 1936. He played in seven World Series, batting .361, and had ten home runs, four of them in the four-game series of 1928.

Toward the end of Gehrig's life, the great athlete was diagnosed as having amyotrophic lateral sclerosis, a disease that since then has been known as Lou Gehrig's disease. He died within two years after he had to stop playing. At a wrenchingly sad farewell tribute that was paid him at Yankee Stadium on July 4, 1939, he said goodbye to his fans as he stood surrounded by friends and fellow players. With him, with an arm around Gehrig's shoulder, was his flamboyant teammate Babe Ruth. Gehrig had long played in Ruth's shadow, but he was too much of a man to be overshadowed by anyone.

---

ada and elsewhere in the U.S., compiling 21 wins and two losses.

Dec. 28 The **Intercollegiate Athletic Association of the United States** (IAAUS) was founded in New York City with 62 institutions as members. It was formed to establish sound requirements for intercollegiate athletics. In 1910 it changed its name to the National Collegiate Athletic Association (NCAA). A set of Standards for the Conduct of Intercollegiate Athletics was issued in 1931, and all colleges and universities were required to comply as a condition of membership. In 1986 there were 995 members of the NCAA.

1906

Jay Gould, grandson of the railroad speculator, began his remarkable 20-year reign as amateur court tennis champion. In this 20-year period, Gould also won 14 of 15 amateur doubles championships

he entered, first with W. T. H. Huhn as his partner and later with Joseph W. Wear.

Several local **angling and casting clubs** formed the National Association of Scientific Angling Clubs, now named the American Casting Association.

The **Corinthian Football (soccer) Club** of London visited the U.S., winning 13 matches, tying two, and losing one. It toured the U.S. again in 1911, winning 18, tying one, and losing one.

This year's **national college football championship** was won by Princeton, with a record of nine wins, no losses, one tie.

The **U.S. Lawn Tennis Association singles championships** were won by Helen Homans in the women's division and William J. Clothier in the men's division.

Feb. 23 The **world heavyweight boxing championship** was won by Tommy Burns, who defeated Marvin Hart in 20 rounds at Los Angeles, Calif.

Apr. 19 The tenth **Boston Marathon** was won by Timothy Ford of Cambridge, Mass., with a time of 2 hrs., 45 min., 45 sec.

Apr. 22-May 2 **Olympic Games** were held in Athens, Greece, but they were not accepted as of-

GLENNA COLLETT VARE

Mrs. Edwin H. Vare, Jr.
b.   Providence, R.I., June 20, 1903

The leading woman golfer of the 1920s and into the 1930s, Glenna Vare by her example also improved the quality of golf played by women. Somewhat of a tomboy, she drove a car and played baseball when she was 10 years old. By age 18, Vare was competing at the top of amateur tennis. In her days as an amateur,

she won 49 titles and set a U.S. Golf Association record of 19 consecutive tournament wins. Among her achievements were an unprecedented six triumphs in the National Amateur in 1922, 1925, 1928, 1929, 1930, and 1935.

During 1924, Vare won 59 of 60 events she played in, including her second Canadian Open. The one surprising defeat in her career occurred in 1930 at Sandwich,

England, when she was upset by a 19-year-old, Diana Fishwick, in the British women's championship.

Vare's drives were powerful, and she played rounds about ten strokes below what women on average had achieved before World War I. In the early 1980s, she was still playing golf. The Vare Trophy, given each year to the Ladies Professional Golf Association player with the lowest average, is named for her.

---

ficial by the International Olympic Committee. The U.S. won 12 gold medals, behind France with 15.

May 2 The 32nd annual **Kentucky Derby** was won by Sir Huon, with a time of 2:08⅘. The jockey was Roscoe Troxler.

May 22 The 31st annual **Preakness Stakes** was won by Whimsical, with a time of 1:45. The jockey was Walter Miller.

May 23 The **heavyweight wrestling title** was regained by Frank Gotch in a match with Tom Jenkins in Kansas City, Mo. Gotch took two straight falls. In all, Gotch and Jenkins wrestled each other eight times. Gotch won five bouts and scored 12 falls to eight for Jenkins.

May 25 The three entrants in the **first Bermuda Race** sailed out of Gravesend Bay, Brooklyn, N.Y. The winner was the 38-ft. yawl *Tamerlane*.

Thomas Fleming Day, editor of *Rudder*, organized the race.

May 30 The 40th annual **Belmont Stakes** was won by Burgomaster, with a time of 2:20. The jockey was L. Lyne.

June 11-24 The **first Transpacific Race,** from Los Angeles to Diamond Head, Honolulu, Hawaii, was won by the schooner *Lurline,* owned by H. H. Sinclair, commodore of the South Coast Yacht Club (now the Los Angeles Yacht Club). This yacht race is now held every odd-numbered year.

June 29 The **U.S. Open golf tournament** was won for the first time by Alex Smith over his brother Willie. Alex had a total of 295 strokes. The course was the Onwentsia Club, Lake Forest, Ill.

Sept. The **first Gordon Bennett International**

CARL HUBBELL

Carl Owen Hubbell
b.   Carthage, Mo., June 22, 1903

A rundown of Carl Hubbell's pitching record as a left-hander who could throw the screwball shows clearly why, to the New York Giants, he was known as the Meal Ticket. In his 18 years with the Giants, from 1928 to 1943, he won 253 games and lost 154, for a percentage of .621, and had an earned run average of 2.97.

In three World Series, 1933, 1936, and 1937, he won four games and lost two. Hubbell's career strikeout total was 1678.

He also has to his credit some individual exploits unmatched by other pitchers. On July 2, 1933, he pitched 18 innings against the St. Louis Cardinals, shutting them out on six hits. In the 1934 all-star game, he fanned in succession five of the best batters the American League could

offer: Babe Ruth, Lou Gehrig, Jimmy Foxx, Al Simmons, and Joe Cronin. Over the 1936 and 1937 seasons, Hubbell had a consecutive winning streak of 24 games, which finally ended after he was defeated in a game with the Cincinnati Reds on May 27, 1937.

Hubbell was elected to the Baseball Hall of Fame in 1947.

Good shot, bad luck and hell are the five basic words to be used in a game of tennis, though these, of course, can be slightly amplified.

Virginia Graham

1907

Balloon Race was won by an American, Army Lt. Frank P. Lahm. Taking off from Paris, Lahm landed in a Yorkshire, England, pasture, having flown 402 mi. in 22 hrs., 15 min. The American balloonist defeated the Italian entrant by 31 mi. Lahm and his flight companion, an Army major, shared the 12,500-franc first prize.

Oct. 9 At Friend, Nebr., the **National Coursing Association** was organized as the governing body of greyhound racing. It established its present headquarters in Abilene, Kans., in 1945 and changed its name to the National Greyhound Association in 1972.

Oct. 9-14 The third annual **World Series** was won by the Chicago White Sox (AL), who defeated the Chicago Cubs (NL) four games to two. The weak-hitting White Sox, with the worst team batting average in the league, blasted Mordecai "Three Finger" Brown and Ed Reubach in the final two games.

Nov. 28 "Philadelphia Jack" O'Brien, a light heavyweight, fought heavyweight champion Tommy Burns to a 20-round draw in Los Angeles.

The **American Masters of Foxhounds Association** was founded in Boston to govern the sport in the U.S. By the 1970s, there were hunt clubs in 25 states.

The **first mechanical lure for greyhounds** was devised by Owen Patrick Smith, secretary of the Chamber of Commerce of Hot Springs, S.Dak. At Salt Lake City, Utah, he attached a stuffed rabbit to a motorcycle to lure the racing dogs. In 1919 Smith built the first operating greyhound racetrack at Emeryville, Calif., under the name of the Blue Star Amusement Co., but it did not do very well.

George Douglas Freeth **introduced surfing** to the mainland U.S. at Redondo Beach, Calif. He had been brought from Hawaii to help promote the Redondo-Los Angeles Railway, and surfing became one of his activities.

This year's **national college football championship** was won by Yale, with a record of nine wins, no losses, one tie.

At the **Wimbledon tennis championships,** American May G. Sutton won the women's singles title for the second time in a row.

The **U.S. Lawn Tennis Association singles championships** were won by Evelyn Sears in the women's division and William A. Larned in the men's division.

Feb. 7 The **first national cross country ski race** was won by Asario Autio over a course 9 mi. long.

Feb. 14 At the **Westminster Kennel Club** dog

JOHNNY WEISSMULLER

Peter John Weissmuller
b. Windber, Pa., June 2, 1904
d. Acapulco, Mexico, Jan. 20, 1984

Although an Associated Press poll in 1950 voted Johnny Weissmuller the greatest swimmer of the first half of the century, today he is remembered first of all as the man who starred in the movies as Tarzan of the Apes.

   Weissmuller certainly was the dominant swimmer of the 1920s. Weissmuller's swimming style,

described as "a high-riding front crawl stroke," was revolutionary at the time. Between 1921 and 1928, he won 20 American championships in distances from 100 to 440 yards. On June 23, 1922, for example, he broke four world's records in one meet—in the 300- and 400-meter and the 440- and 500-yard races.

   In the 1924 Olympics in France, Weissmuller won the 100-meter freestyle in what was then a record time of 59 seconds and the

400-meter in 5 minutes, 4.2 seconds, also a record. At the 1928 Olympics, he again won the 100-meter, in a new best time of 58.6 seconds. Weissmuller retired from competitive swimming after that. In all, he had won 52 American championships and set 67 world records.

   Between 1932 and 1948, he played Tarzan in 19 movies and created the famous yodeling call that generations of small boys learned to imitate.

Harold Edward Grange
b.   Forksville, Pa., June 13, 1904

The Galloping Ghost of the Gridiron, Red Grange, was the perfect football player for the Jazz Age. In 1923, his first collegiate season at the University of Illinois, as a halfback he scored 12 touchdowns and was selected, as he was in the next two years as well, for the all-American team. In 1924, against Michigan, he ran for touchdowns the first four times he handled the ball, later scored another, and passed for a sixth.

Turning professional in 1925, Grange played first for the Chicago Bears and, in his debut on December 6, led them to victory over the New York Giants. He received $30,000 for his appearance, which was well earned. He drew 70,000 spectators to the Polo Grounds that day, the largest crowd to that date to watch a pro football game. Grange played for the New York Yankees in 1926 and 1927, then returned to the Bears from 1929 to 1935. He scored a total of 1058 points in his pro career.

In 1963 Grange was one of the first group of players to be elected to the Pro Football Hall of Fame. He is also in the College Football Hall of Fame.

---

show, Ch. Warren Remedy, a fox terrier owned by Winthrop Rutherfurd, took best-in-show.

Apr. 19   The 11th **Boston Marathon** was won by Thomas Longboat of Hamilton, Ontario, Canada, with a time of 2 hrs., 24 min., 24 sec.

May 6   The 33rd annual **Kentucky Derby** was won by Pink Star, with a time of 2:12⅗. The jockey was Andy Minder.

May 21   The 32nd annual **Preakness Stakes** was won by Don Enrique, with a time of 1:45⅖. The jockey was G. Mountain.

May 30   The 41st **Belmont Stakes** was won by Peter Pan, with a time of 2:15⅗. The jockey was G. Mountain.

June 21   The **U.S. Open golf tournament** was won by Alex Ross at the Philadelphia Cricket Club with a 302 total.

Oct. 8-12   The fourth annual **World Series** was won by the Chicago Cubs (NL), who swept the Detroit Tigers (AL) in four games after the first game ended in a tie. Cub base runners ran wild with 18 steals, led by Jimmy Slagle with six. In this series, the celebrated Tinker-to-Evers-to-Chance double-play combination made six errors but did manage to steal eight bases.

Nov.   At the National Horse Show in New York, a **woman rode astride a horse** in competition for the first time. She was Mrs. J. Marion Edmunds, said to be the "wife of the captain of a transatlantic liner." According to the *New York Times,* she wore "a long grey cloak covering her breeched knees and on her head a rough-rider hat turned up in front instead of on the side. She got no prize."

Dec. 2   The **world heavyweight boxing championship** was successfully defended by Tommy Burns, who knocked out Gunner Moir in ten rounds at London, England.

1908

Alexander Herne Ford founded the **Outrigger Canoe Club** in Waikiki, Hawaii. It was primarily for Caucasians (haoles), not Hawaiians, and was the first official surfing-oriented group.

The **National Collegiate Athletic Association** (NCAA) assumed charge of college basketball rules. The Springfield YMCA College had been the authority from 1891 to 1893 and thereafter had shared the role with the Amateur Athletic Union (AAU). In 1915 the NCAA and AAU formed a joint rules committee.

This year's **national college football championship** was won by Pennsylvania, with a record of 11 wins, no losses, one tie.

Irving Brokaw, who had studied **figure skating** in Europe, returned to the U.S. and popularized the new sport. Through his efforts the first national figure skating tournament was held in 1914 in New Haven, Conn. In this same year, figure skating became an Olympic sport for men and women.

A new **baseball rule** prohibited pitchers from deliberately soiling new baseballs.

The **U.S. Lawn Tennis Association singles championships** were won by Maud Barger-Wallach in the women's division and William A. Larned, for the fourth time, in the men's division.

Feb. 14   At the **Westminster Kennel Club** dog

Helen Newington Wills Moody
b.   Centerville, Calif., Oct. 6, 1905

Helen Wills Moody was the best woman tennis player of her time, pressed closely for superiority first by Molla Bjurstedt Mallory and then by Helen Hull Jacobs. She won her first national title, the girls', at age 15. At 17, in 1923, she replaced Mallory as U.S. champion. Mallory had reigned for seven of the previous eight years.

Moody continued to hold the U.S. title through 1925 and won again in 1927, 1928, 1929, and 1931. In the 1933 U.S. finals, because of a back and leg injury, Moody defaulted to

Jacobs in the final set, with Jacobs leading 3–0. It was Moody's first loss of a match since 1926.

Moody's record in the British championships was even more remarkable. She won a total of eight times, in 1927, 1928, 1929, 1930, 1932, 1933, 1935, and 1938. Her victory at Wimbledon in 1935 was over Jacobs. This record of eight triumphs was not matched until 1987, when Martina Navratilova won her eighth victory. Moody was also French champion in 1928, 1929, 1930, and 1932. In 1928 and 1929, she won what then were the three major titles, the U.S., British, and

French. In all, Moody was victorious in more than 30 national and international tournaments, including the singles and doubles at the 1924 Olympic Games.

Moody was known as Miss Poker Face for the determined and expressionless way she looked at opponents as she demolished them. She was a hard hitter, but it was her shrewd and methodical play that gave her the edge. Moody was also an artist whose paintings and etchings were exhibited publicly. She was elected to the International Tennis Hall of Fame in 1959.

---

show, Ch. Warren Remedy, a fox terrier owned by Winthrop Rutherfurd, took best-in-show for the second consecutive year.

Apr. 3   The **world heavyweight wrestling championship** was won by Frank Gotch when his opponent, George Hackenschmidt, quit. After 2 hrs., 1 min. of the match, Hackenschmidt, known as the Russian Bear, was exhausted and badly beaten. The two met again in Chicago on Sept. 14, 1911, with Gotch pinning his opponent twice in less than 20 min.

Apr. 20   The 12th **Boston Marathon** was won by Thomas P. Morrissey of Yonkers, N.Y., with a time of 2 hrs., 25 min., 43.2 sec.

Apr. 27-Oct. 31   At the **Summer Olympics** in London, England, the U.S. won the unofficial team championship by taking 15 of 28 events, with 23 gold medals. Ray Ewry won the standing high jump for the fourth consecutive time, while John J. Hayes won the marathon with a time of 2 hrs., 55 min., 18.4 sec. The team was honored in New York City on Aug. 29 on its return from the games. This year the men's backstroke was added to the Olympic Games. The women's backstroke was added in 1924.

May 5   The 34th annual **Kentucky Derby** was won by Stone Street, with a time of 2:15⅕. The jockey was Arthur Pickens.

May 30   The 42nd annual **Belmont Stakes** was won by Colin. No official time was recorded. The jockey was Joe Notter.

June 2   The 33rd annual **Preakness Stakes** was won by Royal Tourist, with a time of 1:46⅖. The jockey was Eddie Dugan.

July 4   The **first public flight of an airplane in the U.S.** took place at Hammondsport, N.Y., when Glenn H. Curtiss flew his *June Bug* in demonstration flights. In one flight he flew 2800 ft. in 54 sec. On another attempt he covered a little more than a mile in 1 min., 42 sec. For his achievements Curtiss was awarded the Scientific American Cup.

July 30   At the end of an **automobile race around the world,** a U.S. team was declared the winner. The race, sponsored by the *New York Times* and *Le Matin,* began on Feb. 12 when six autos and their crews left New York City and traveled north toward Albany, N.Y. The cars drove west across the U.S., Russia (via Siberia), and Eastern Europe, encountering muddy roads, snow, ice, timber wolves, and gasoline shortages. The race was led by the huge German Protos, driven by Lt. Hans Koeppen, and the U.S. Thomas Flyer with George Schuster at the wheel. The Germans arrived in Paris on July 26 but were penalized 30 days for having shipped their car by rail to Seattle, Wash., so the U.S. team was declared the winner. The only other entrant to finish was the Italian Zust, which arrived two weeks later. When the U.S. team returned home, New Yorkers turned out in large numbers to greet them.

Leroy Robert Paige
b. Mobile, Ala., July 7, 1906?
d. Kansas City, Mo., June 8, 1982

Even if Satchel Paige were only half as good a pitcher as legend and the record books have it, he was the best moundsman ever. Unfortunately, most of his playing days came before major league baseball admitted blacks to its ranks. In 1928, Paige joined the Chattanooga Black Lookouts of the Negro Southern League with a salary of $50 a month and later advanced to the Pittsburgh Crawfords, a team that some observers claimed was better than any white major league team of its day. Black teams played all over the Caribbean and Central America, and it is claimed that Paige in 1934 won 104 of 105 games he pitched. It is also reported that he had 55 career no-hit games.

Finally, in 1948, after Jackie Robinson had broken the color barrier, Paige joined the Cleveland Indians and helped them win a pennant. He was also with the St. Louis Browns, from 1951 to 1953. Twelve years later, when he was at least 49 years old—his birth date is a matter of dispute—he pitched for the Kansas City Athletics. In all, Paige won 28 major league games and lost 31. His best year was 1952, when he had a 12–10 record. Paige appeared in one World Series game in 1947 and had a career earned run average of 3.29 in the major leagues. While with St. Louis in 1952, when Paige was officially 47 years old, he became the oldest pitcher in major league history to pitch a complete game and a shutout when he beat the Detroit Tigers 1–0 in 12 innings.

In 1971, Paige became the first black to be elected to the Baseball Hall of Fame in the separate category for Negro League players who did not qualify under the regular rule of a minimum of ten years of service in the majors. His favorite saying was good advice for all of us: "Don't look back; something might be gaining on you."

On Aug. 20 Pres. Theodore Roosevelt received the winners at the White House.

Aug. 25 The American Trotting Derby, the **first $50,000 harness race** in the U.S., was run at Readville, Mass. Some 20,000 people watched 33 horses race in two elimination heats and the final. The winner of the $30,000 first prize was Allen Winter, driven by Lon McDonald.

Aug. 28 The **U.S. Open golf tournament** was won by Fred McLeod after a one-stroke victory over Willie Smith in a playoff at the Myopia Hunt Club, South Hamilton, Mass.

Sept. 7 **Walter Johnson,** 20 years old, of the Washington Senators (AL), shut out the New York Highlanders (AL) for the third time in a four-game series played in New York. In each of his games he pitched the full nine innings.

Sept. 23 Perhaps the all-time **greatest dispute in baseball** resulted from a call made at New York City's Polo Grounds in what was supposed to be the decisive game of the Chicago Cubs-New York Giants National League pennant race. In the bottom of the ninth inning, with two men out and the score tied at 1-1, New York was at bat with two men on. The batter hit safely to center field, scoring the winning run. The Chicago players correctly claimed, however, that when Fred Merkle, the man on first, saw the winning run score, he began to walk toward the clubhouse without advancing to second base, thus invalidating the play. Johnny Evers, the Chicago second baseman, tried to get the ball and step on second to put Merkle out, but the fans streamed onto the field and bedlam reigned. Days later, Harry C. Pulliam, head of the National Commission of Organized Baseball, decided to call the game a tie. The teams were forced to play a postseason playoff game, which the Cubs took 4-2. Modern fans cite Merkle's play as the classic baseball boner.

Oct. 2 Addie Joss, Cleveland pitcher, hurled a **perfect game** against the Chicago White Sox, with no batter reaching first base.

Oct. 10-14 The fifth annual **World Series** was won by the Chicago Cubs (NL), who beat the Detroit Tigers (AL) four games to one. Superb pitching by Three Finger Brown and Orval Overall overpowered Tiger bats.

Nov. 21 The **first ICAA cross-country run** was held in Princeton, N.J. Nine college teams were entered. Cornell won, with Syracuse second and Harvard third.

Dec. 26 The **world heavyweight boxing championship** was won by Jack Johnson, who defeated Tommy Burns in 14 rounds at Sydney, Australia. Johnson was the first black man to hold the title.

GERTRUDE EDERLE

Gertrude Caroline Ederle
b.   New York City, Oct. 23, 1906

Gertrude Ederle made the front pages of the world's newspapers on August 7, 1926. The day before, she had become the first woman to swim the English Channel, and in a time nearly 2 hours better than the previous record. Swimming from France to England, she had accomplished the feat in 14 hours, 31 minutes. Her record stood until 1964, when it was broken by another woman, Greta Andersen of Denmark.

Ederle in 1925 had tried and failed to swim the Channel, but that same year she swam from the Battery in New York harbor to Sandy Hook, New Jersey. On her return from her Channel triumph, Ederle was honored by a large and noisy tickertape parade in New York City.

Long before the Channel swim, Ederle had been breaking records. On September 4, 1922, when Ederle was only 15, she set six world records in one day, from 300 to 500 yards and 400 meters. Again in one day, September 3, 1923, she set U.S.

records for seven distances, from 100 to 500 yards and 300 meters. At the 1924 Olympics in Paris, Ederle won two bronze medals, in the 100- and 400-meter freestyle, and a gold medal as a member of the 400-meter relay.

Swimming made Ederle deaf, and she suffered a back injury in 1933 that kept her in a cast for four years. Nevertheless, she made a comeback and appeared in Billy Rose's *Aquacade* at the New York World's Fair in 1939. She later taught swimming to deaf children.

1909

A **platform diving championship** was added to the list of contests at men's national swimming contests. This year and the next two, George Gaidzik was the winner.

A **horseshoe pitching contest** "open to anyone in the world" was promoted at Bronson, Kans. Frank Jackson of Kellerton, Iowa, was the individual winner of this now-recognized first world championship. The sport's popularity centered in Kansas, Missouri, and Iowa.

The U.S. regained **polo's most prestigious trophy,** the Westchester Cup, by defeating Great Britain at Hurlingham 9-5 and 8-2. Larry and Monte Waterbury, Harry Payne Whitney, and Devereux

Milburn made up the U.S. team. The U.S. successfully defended the trophy against Great Britain in 1911 and 1913. Thirty thousand spectators watched the final game in 1913.

This year's **national college football championship** was won by Yale, with a record of ten wins, no losses, no ties.

Feb. 12   At the **Westminster Kennel Club** dog show, Ch. Warren Remedy, a fox terrier owned by Winthrop Rutherfurd, took best-in-show for the third straight year.

Mar. 15   At age 70, Edward P. Weston began a **walk from New York to San Francisco.** He made it in 104 days, 7 hrs. over a 3795-mi. route. The next year Weston walked from Los Angeles to New York, covering 3600 mi. in 76 days, 23 hrs.

Apr. 19   The 13th **Boston Marathon** was won by

BILL DICKEY

William Malcolm Dickey
b.   Bastrop, La., June 6, 1907

The steady man behind the plate for 17 years for the New York Yankees, Bill Dickey was the skillful handler of some of major league baseball's best pitchers, such as Lefty Gomez and Red Ruffing. Dickey may have looked slow and awkward, but he

was valuable on defense as well as offense, ending his career with a .313 batting average and 202 home runs.

Dickey's durability is shown by the fact that in his playing years, from 1928 to 1944, he caught 100 or more games in 13 consecutive years, no small accomplishment for a catcher. In all, Dickey was behind

the plate in 1789 games.

His batting average of .379 in World Series play was even better than in regular seasons. He was in eight series between 1932 and 1943, and the Yankees won seven of them. Dickey was named to the Baseball Hall of Fame in 1954.

JIMMY FOXX

James Emory Foxx
b. Sudlersville, Md., Oct. 22, 1907
d. Miami, Fla., July 21, 1967

Jimmy "Double X" Foxx, one of the most able hitters of his time, contributed greatly to the run production of the baseball teams he played for. Foxx began his long career as a catcher but for the most part played first base. He was with the Philadelphia Athletics from 1925 to 1935, then with the Boston Red Sox from 1936 to mid-season of

1942, and finally with the Chicago Cubs and Philadelphia Phillies from that year to 1945.

In his 20-year career, Foxx hit 534 home runs, still eighth on the all-time list. His best year for homers was 1932, when he hit 58, three below the present record. He led the American League in home runs that year and also in 1933, 1935 (tied), and 1939. His batting average was also impressive. Foxx won the league championship in 1933 with .356 and in 1938 with .349 and ended his

career with a .325 average. He played in three World Series, 1929, 1930, and 1931, and his team, the Athletics, won two out of three.

In runs scored, Foxx ranks 15th with 1751, and in bases on balls, 12th with 1452. These were among the accomplishments that made him the American League's most valuable player three times, in 1932, 1933, and 1938. Foxx was elected to the Baseball Hall of Fame in 1951.

Henri Renaud of Nashua, N.H., with a time of 2 hrs., 53 min., 36.8 sec.

May 3 The 35th annual **Kentucky Derby** was won by Wintergreen, with a time of 2:08⅕. The jockey was Vincent Powers.

May 12 The 34th annual **Preakness Stakes** was won by Effendi, with a time of 1:39⅘. The jockey was Willie Doyle.

June 2 The 43rd annual **Belmont Stakes** was won by Joe Madden, with a time of 2:21⅗. The jockey was Eddie Dugan.

June 5 An **endurance race for hot-air balloons** began at Indianapolis, Ind., sponsored by the Aero Club of America. Four of the nine starting balloons were still aloft the next day, and on June 7 the *Indiana* broke the endurance record of 44 hrs. in the air. One of the balloons, the *New York*, was fired on when 80 mi. north of Birmingham, Ala.; one of the three rifle shots passed through the balloon's basket.

June 24 The **U.S. Open golf tournament** was won by George Sargent with a score of 290, the lowest for 72 holes to date.

June 25 The *New York Times* reported a **boom in golf,** because it had become known that Pres. William Howard Taft played golf to keep up his health. The number of players at some public links was reported to have doubled.

June 27 The **U.S. Lawn Tennis Association singles championships** were won by Hazel Hotchkiss in the women's division and William A. Larned in the men's division (Aug. 27). Hotchkiss's aggressive forecourt play added a new dimension to women's tennis. She also

won the women's and mixed doubles championships, losing only five games in all three finals.

June 29 The **first transcontinental auto race** ended in Seattle, Wash., with Ford Car 2 the winner. The Shawmut Motor Co. car, which had protested the Ford victory, was awarded second place. Six autos had started from New York City on June 1, sent off by Pres. William Howard Taft and Mayor George B. McClellan, the former pressing a telegraph key in Washington while the latter fired a pistol in New York. The winner received $2000 and the Guggenheim Trophy, and second place won $1500.

Aug. 19 What became the site of the **Indianapolis 500** auto race at Indianapolis, Ind., opened as a dirt track for testing automobiles. It was sponsored by a group of manufacturers headed by Carl G. Fisher.

Aug. 23 At the **first International Aviation Meet** at Rheims, France, the Bennett Cup and the *Prix*

Ruthlessly pricking our gonfalon bubble,
Making a Giant hit into a double—
Words that are heavy with nothing but
*   trouble:*
"Tinker to Evers to Chance."

Franklin P. Adams (F.P.A.), describing the
Chicago Cubs' vaunted double-play
combination

HELEN HULL JACOBS

b. Globe, Ariz., Aug. 6, 1908

Helen Hull Jacobs was the first woman tennis player to win the U.S. title four times, from 1932 to 1935. She was ranked number one in all those years and number two ten times. Jacobs was also runner-up for the U.S. title five times between 1928 and 1939. She was runner-up at Wimbledon five times between

1928 and 1938 and won the English tournament in 1936. For 13 successive years, she played on the U.S. Wightman Cup team.

Jacobs's great rivalry was with Helen Wills Moody, to whom she lost four times at Wimbledon and once at Forest Hills in the U.S. championship. Her only tournament victory over Moody came in the 1933 U.S. championship, when

Moody defaulted in the final set due to a back injury.

Jacobs was noted for her sportsmanship and was always popular. She had an accurate serve, a steady volley, and a useful backhand. From 1943 to 1945, in World War II, she served as an officer in the Navy. Jacobs was elected to the International Tennis Hall of Fame in 1972.

---

de la vitesse were won by Glenn H. Curtiss. During the races he set a new speed record of 43.34 mph.

Oct. 8-16   The sixth annual **World Series** was won by the Pittsburgh Pirates (NL), who defeated the Detroit Tigers (AL) four games to three. Rookie pitcher Babe Adams won three games, and Honus Wagner outstole Ty Cobb 6-2.

Dec. 4   The great pacer **Dan Patch** was retired after an appearance at Phoenix, Ariz. Foaled in 1896, the horse had 30 times done the mile in less than 2 min. and at retirement held nine world records. Dan Patch last raced in 1905, then traveled in exhibitions, and died in 1916.

1910

Skeet shooting, a variety of trapshooting first called shooting around the clock, began its slow development on the property of Glen Rock Kennels in Andover, Mass. The owner, C. E. Davies, his son Henry W., and William H. Foster, using the standard clay targets and throwing traps, devised a form of competitive shooting in which each contestant was given the same series of shots, two from each of the 12 stations of the clocklike shooting area, and one from the center of the circle of 25 yards radius. As a form of off-season field shooting, its popularity remained localized.

The **growing popularity of flying** and the feeling that it might become a form of sport and recrea-

---

BRONCO NAGURSKI

Bronislaw Nagurski
b.   Rainy River, Ont., Canada, Nov. 3, 1908

Bronco Nagurski is not the biggest man ever to play football, but he may well be the strongest. It has been said of the great fullback that he ran his own interference, and sportswriter Grantland Rice thought he was probably the finest college player ever. When Nagurski was active, he stood 6 feet, 2 inches tall

and weighed about 235 pounds.

He played college football at the University of Minnesota, where, on his first day of practice, he is said to have knocked the tackling dummy loose. He played both tackle and fullback and made all-American. Nagurski joined the Chicago Bears in 1930, played until 1937, retired because of arthritis, but attempted a comeback briefly in 1943.

In Nagurski's pro career, he rushed for more than 4000 yards in 872

carries. A typical game for him was that of December 17, 1933, in which the Bears defeated the New York Giants for the National Football League title. Nagurski gained 65 yards in 14 attempts and started a forward-lateral pass that resulted in the winning touchdown.

Nagurski was also a professional wrestler and won more than 300 matches.

TONY CANZONERI

b. Slidel, La., Nov. 6, 1908
d. New York City, Dec. 12, 1959

A fast, aggressive boxer with punching power, Tony Canzoneri held the title in three different weight divisions during his career and between 1927 and 1937 fought 23 bouts in which world titles were at stake. The first of these was a draw in a bout for the bantamweight championship when he was only 18.

Canzoneri won the featherweight title in 1928 and held the unofficial junior welterweight title twice. It was in the lightweight division, however, that he was most active. He won this title in 1930, held it until 1933, lost it, then regained it in 1935. Canzoneri was the first boxer to regain this title after having lost it. He first won the lightweight crown on November 4, 1930, when he knocked out Al Singer in 66 seconds of the first round of a scheduled 15-round fight. He lost the title on June 23, 1933, when he dropped a ten-round decision to Barney Ross.

In all Canzoneri won 138 fights, 40 of them by knockouts, and lost only 24. He was knocked out only once.

---

tion were shown by the publication this year of the popular song hit "Come, Josephine in My Flying Machine," by Alfred Bryan and Fred Fisher.

This year's **national college football championship** was won by Harvard, with a record of eight wins, no losses, one tie.

In an early **baseball publicity stunt,** Hugh Chalmers offered a Chalmers car as first prize for the leading batter in the major leagues. He was rather hurt when the winner, Ty Cobb, sold his prize immediately.

A new **fishing record** was set when F. R. Steel caught an 83-lb. Chinook salmon in the Umpqua R. in Oregon. Until 1949 this was the largest freshwater fish ever snared by rod and reel. On May 22, 1949, Roy A. Groves fishing in the James R., S.Dak., snared a blue catfish weighing 94 lbs., 8 oz., and on Dec. 2, 1951, in the Rio Grande in Texas,

G. Valverde caught an alligator gar weighing 279 lbs.

The **first American aviation meet** was held in Los Angeles. Audiences ranging each day from 20,000 to 50,000 watched air pioneers Louis Paulhan of France and Glenn H. Curtiss, an American, break most air speed records. In spite of the popularity of the show and a great desire among many to fly, in three years only five airplanes had been sold to private persons.

Feb. 11 At the **Westminster Kennel Club** dog show, Ch. Sabine Rarebit, a fox terrier owned by Sabine Kennels of Orange, Tex., took best-in-show.

Mar. 16 A new **land speed record** of 131.7 mph was set by Barney Oldfield, who ran a timed mile in a Benz auto at Daytona Beach, Fla.

Apr. Pres. William Howard Taft **threw out the first ball** of the baseball season in Washington,

---

MAX BAER

Maximilian Adelbert Baer
b. Omaha, Nebr., Feb. 11, 1909
d. Hollywood, Calif., Nov. 21, 1959

Max Baer had one of the shortest reigns in history as heavyweight boxing champion, one day less than a year. On June 14, 1934, Baer knocked out the champion, Primo Carnera, in the 11th round of a fight in Long Island City, New York, after having floored the titleholder 12 times. In reporting the fight, the *New York Times* hailed Baer as "the new Jack Dempsey in every respect save seriousness."

On June 13, 1935, Baer lost the title to James J. Braddock in a 15-round decision. Baer lost the title at the same site where he had won it. On this occasion the *Times* called Baer "the playboy of the ring, who could not be serious even while a fortune was slipping through his fingers" and said the fight was "one of the worst heavyweight championship contests in all the long history of the ring."

Baer had one more important fight, on September 24, 1935, at Yankee Stadium, in New York City, when Joe Louis, on his way to the championship, knocked Baer out in the fourth round. On the plus side of Baer's career record was his knockout of Max Schmeling of Germany in 1933. In all, Baer had 80 fights between 1929 and 1941 and won 61 of them.

MEL OTT

Melvin Thomas Ott
b. Gretna, La., Mar. 2, 1909
d. New Orleans, La., Nov. 21, 1958

Mel Ott, the dependable outfielder for the New York Giants, who also played at third base when required from 1926 to 1947 and served as the Giants' manager from 1942 to 1948, was a consistent batter and the first National League player to hit 500 home runs in his career. He ended with a total of 511, which is 14th on the all-time list. In right field at the old Polo Grounds, Ott played caroms off the fence so adeptly that he could throw slow runners out at first base on occasion. He was only 16 when he began to play with the Giants, and this accounts for his nickname, Master Melvin.

In six seasons, Ott led or tied for the lead in home runs in the National League—in 1932, 1934, 1936, 1937, 1938, and 1942. His home run high came in 1929, when he hit 42. His lifetime batting average was an impressive .304. He ranks ninth in runs scored with 1859 and sixth in bases on balls with 1708. Ott played in three World Series, 1933, 1936, and 1937, and hit four home runs.

Mel Ott was less successful as a manager. His Giants won 464 games but lost 530 and did not win a pennant. Ott became a member of the Baseball Hall of Fame in 1951.

thus becoming the first president to do so. In the game, Walter Johnson of the Washington Senators shut out the Philadelphia Athletics 1-0, allowing but one hit.

Apr. 19 The 14th **Boston Marathon** was won by Fred L. Cameron of Amherst, Nova Scotia, Canada, with a time of 2 hrs., 28 min., 52.6 sec.

May 7 The 35th annual **Preakness Stakes** was won by Layminster, with a time of 1:40⅗. The jockey was R. Estep.

May 10 The 36th annual **Kentucky Derby** was won by Donau, with a time of 2:06⅖. The jockey was Fred Herbert.

May 29 A pioneer aviator, **Glenn H. Curtiss,** won a $10,000 prize offered by the *New York World* when he flew from Albany, N.Y. to Governors Island, New York City, in 2 hrs., 46 min. at an average speed of 54.18 mph. He made two stops on the way.

May 30 The 44th annual **Belmont Stakes** was won by Sweep, with a time of 2:22. The jockey was Jimmy Butwell.

June 18 The **U.S. Open golf tournament** was won by Alex Smith. He finished in a three-way tie with John J. McDermott and Macdonald Smith and won in an 18-hole playoff.

June 26 The **U.S. Lawn Tennis Association singles championships** were won by Hazel Hotchkiss in the women's division and William A. Larned in the men's division (Aug. 25).

July 4 The **world heavyweight boxing championship** was successfully defended by Jack Johnson, who outclassed former champ Jim Jeffries in 15 rounds. After the match, Johnson's

GLENN CUNNINGHAM

Glenn Clarence Cunningham
b. Atlanta, Kans., Aug. 4, 1909

Although Glenn Cunningham's track records have long since been broken, the Kansas Flyer was the best and most sensational miler of the 1930s. Cunningham broke the mile record several times, and he accomplished this despite the severe leg burns he suffered in a schoolhouse fire when he was a child.

Cunningham's best time for the mile was run indoors in 4 minutes, 4.4 seconds. During his career various athletes ran the mile a total of 31 times in under 4 minutes, 10 seconds, and on 12 of those occasions it was Cunningham who did so.

Cunningham also ran the 1500 meters and, on February 23, 1935, set a new mark of 3 minutes, 50.5 seconds at the national AAU meet in Madison Square Garden, New York City. He won the race by 30 yards. At the 1936 Olympics in Germany, he was not successful, losing the 1500-meter race to Jack Lovelock of New Zealand, who also bettered Cunningham's record by going the distance in 3 minutes, 47.8 seconds.

Barnet David Rosofsky
b. New York City, Dec. 23, 1909
d. Chicago, Ill., Jan. 18, 1967

Barney Ross, at the high point of his boxing career, faced an unusual problem. He held both the lightweight and the welterweight boxing titles, but the New York State Athletic Commission ruled he could defend only one of them at a time. He had won the lightweight championship from Tony Canzoneri in June 1933 and the welterweight title from Jimmy McLarnin in May 1934. This made him the first fighter in modern boxing to hold two titles at the same time.

In September 1934, however, McLarnin turned the tables and regained the welterweight title in a split decision. Then, once again, in May 1935, Ross won the title back from McLarnin. That same year, Ross surrendered his lightweight championship. On May 31, 1938, by a unanimous decision, he lost the welterweight crown for the last time, to Henry Armstrong. In his career, Ross had 82 fights and won 74 of them, 24 by knockouts. He fought four draws and lost four.

Ross took part in the invasion of Guadalcanal in World War II and won the Silver Cross for rescuing three wounded fellow Marines. Unfortunately, he was wounded and caught malaria. The drugs given him caused addiction, but he voluntarily entered a federal institution and was cured.

---

mother is reported to have said, "He said he'd bring home the bacon, and the honey boy has gone and done it." No earlier citation is known for this expression.

July 5 **Fear of race riots** led several cities to forbid showing of movies of the Johnson-Jeffries fight of July 4. There had been some disturbances after the black champion won, and as a result there had been ten deaths in seven cities. Atlanta, Baltimore, Cincinnati, St. Louis, and Washington had already banned the film.

Sept. 10 The **first Pendleton, Oreg., Round-Up** began. Side Seale won the wild horse race, and Bert Kelly was the saddle bronc champion. The Round-Up was an outgrowth of a two-day bronc-busting competition that had been held Oct. 1, 1909, as part of the Eastern Oregon District Fair in Pendleton. The second oldest rodeo in the U.S., the Pendleton Round-Up now attracts about 500 contestants and offers prizes totaling about $54,000.

Oct. 17-23 The seventh annual **World Series** was won by the Philadelphia Athletics (AL), who defeated the Chicago Cubs (NL) four games to one. Jack Coombs won three games for Connie Mack's Athletics, and Eddie Collins, the Philadelphia second baseman, starred at bat, hitting for a .428 series average.

Oct. 29 The **first international air races** in the U.S. were held over a nine-day period. Headquarters for the races were at Belmont Park, Long Island, N.Y. On this day Claude Grahame-White of Great Britain won the Gordon Bennett Trophy by setting a new speed record of 62.14 mph over a 3.11-mi. course in his 100-hp Bleriot monoplane. In addition to the cup, Grahame-White won a $5000 prize.

1911

The **Belmont Stakes** was not run in 1911 or 1912.

This year's **national college football championship** was won by Princeton, with a record of eight wins, no losses, two ties.

Cy Young retired from major league baseball this year after compiling an outstanding list of records over his 21-year career as a pitcher. He set a record for the most games pitched (906, with 516 in the National League and 390 in the American League) and also set the record for most games won by a pitcher (511).

Feb. 16 At the **Westminster Kennel Club** dog show, Ch. Tickle Em Jock, a Scottish terrier owned by A. Albright, Jr., of Newark, N.J., took best-in-show.

Apr. 19 The 15th **Boston Marathon** was won by Clarence H. DeMar of Melrose, Mass., with a time of 2 hrs., 21 min., 39.6 sec.

May 13 The 37th annual **Kentucky Derby** was won by Meridian, with a time of 2:05. The jockey was George Archibald.

May 17 The 36th annual **Preakness Stakes** was won by Watervale, with a time of 1:51. The jockey was Eddie Dugan.

JOHNNY LONGDEN

John Eric Longden
b. Wakefield, England, Feb. 14, 1910

It was while Johnny Longden was working as a miner, at the age of 15, half starved and weighing only 88 pounds, that he decided to try something else, so more or less by accident, he took advantage of his diminutive stature and became a jockey. He emigrated to the United States, but in 1927, his first year on the track, Longden rode only one winner.

As time went on, Longden became one of the most successful jockeys of his era. In 1943, he rode Count Fleet to the Triple Crown, calling the horse the greatest he had ever ridden.

Longden became the winningest jockey of all time in 1956, when he rode to his 4871st victory. This record stood until 1970.

By the time Longden retired in 1966, he had also set a record for the longest career for a jockey in the twentieth century. During that 40-year career, Johnny Longden had won 6032 races.

May 30 The **first annual Indianapolis 500** auto race was won by Ray Harroun, completing the 500-mi. course in 6 hrs., 42 min., 8 sec., at an average speed of 74.59 mph.

June 17 The **U.S. Lawn Tennis Association singles championships** were won by Hazel Hotchkiss, for the third straight time, in the women's division and William A. Larned, for the fifth straight time and the seventh in all in the men's division (Sept. 3).

June 24 The **U.S. Open golf tournament** was won by John J. McDermott in a playoff round, in which he defeated Michael Brady and George Simpson. McDermott was the first native-born U.S. winner.

Oct. 14-26 The eighth annual **World Series** was won by the Philadelphia Athletics (AL), who beat the New York Giants (NL) four games to two. Chief Bender and Jack Coombs both beat Christy Mathewson in excellent pitching duels, Bender by 2-1 and Coombs by 3-1. Home Run Baker hit two out of the park.

Oct. 24 A **record-breaking glider flight** was made at Kitty Hawk, N.C., by Orville Wright, coinventor of the airplane. His craft, a biplane that looked much like his first airplane, remained in the air for 9 min. 45 sec.

Nov. 5 The **first transcontinental airplane flight** ended in Pasadena, Calif., after 49 days en route. Calbraith P. Rodgers, the pilot, took off from New York City on Sept. 17 in a Wright biplane. He made 15 crash landings in the course of his long trip.

Nov. 11 In **one of college football's greatest**

MARIBEL VINSON

Maribel Y. Vinson Owen
b. Winchester, Mass., 1911?
d. near Brussels, Belgium, Feb. 15, 1961

As a figure skater, Maribel Vinson was of championship caliber both in singles and in pairs. In 1924, she won her first national title, the junior championship. Vinson won her first senior U.S. title in 1928, held it through 1933, and then took it from 1935 to 1937, for a total of nine times.

She won the North American championship in 1937 but never won the top prize in other international competitions. Vinson was fourth in the 1928 Olympics, won the bronze medal in 1932, and was fifth in 1936. In world championship competition, she was second in 1928 and third in 1930.

Vinson won the U.S. pairs competition as early as 1927, when she was first in the junior championship with Thornton L. Coolidge. They won the U.S. senior title in the next two years. With George E. B. Hill, Vinson was U.S. pairs champion in 1933, 1935, 1936, and 1937. She and Hill were North American champions in 1935.

Vinson became a skating coach and a journalist and was the first woman to become a member of the *New York Times* sports department. She and her two daughters, Laurence and Maribel, also star skaters, were killed in the crash of a Sabena Airlines Boeing 707 near Brussels in 1961, along with the 15 other members of the U.S. skating team on their way to the world championships in Prague. Four days before, Laurence had won the North American championship and earlier that year had also won the U.S. title.

Jay Hanna Dean (also known as Jerome Herman Dean)
b. Lucas, Ark., Jan. 16, 1911
d. Reno, Nev., July 17, 1974

Dizzy Dean always tried to live up to his nickname, but opposing batters found nothing amusing in the mound performance of this brilliant right-handed pitcher. In 12 years of major league baseball, from 1930 to 1937 with the St. Louis Cardinals and 1938 to 1941 with the Chicago Cubs, Dean won 163 games and lost 101. His lifetime earned run average was 3.03.

On July 30, 1933, Dean struck out 17 Chicago Cub batters, a modern record then but since exceeded.

Dean pitched in the 1934 and 1938 World Series. In the 1934 series, he won two games and lost one. His brother Daffy won the other two games. Dizzy's ERA was 1.73, and Daffy's was 1.00. The brothers pitched a total of 44 innings. It was Dizzy's shutout against the Detroit Tigers that won the seventh and deciding game. Dean was named the National League's most valuable player that year. He led the league in strikeouts from 1932 to 1936 and won 30 games in 1934, a feat few pitchers ever accomplish.

After Dizzy Dean retired in 1941, he became a sportscaster on radio and television, where his colorful, country-style language was picturesque, to say the least. He was voted into the Baseball Hall of Fame in 1953.

Dizzy's younger brother, Paul Lee "Daffy" Dean (born in Lucas, Ark., Aug. 14, 1913, died in Springfield, Ark., Mar. 17, 1981), pitched with the St. Louis Cardinals from 1933 to 1940, with the New York Giants from 1941 to 1943, and with the St. Louis Browns in 1943. He won 19 games in his first season and pitched a no-hitter on September 21, 1934, against the Brooklyn Dodgers. The game was the second half of a doubleheader. Dizzy pitched a three-hit shutout in the opener.

---

upsets, little-known Carlisle Indian School, of Carlisle, Pa., defeated a nationally rated Harvard team 18-15. The Carlisle Indians were led by Jim Thorpe, who was part Indian and a sensational all-around athlete. In 1912 Thorpe powered his team to an upset of Army, scoring 22 points in the 27-6 victory.

1912

U.S. Olympic champion Harry Hebner revolutionized the backstroke, which now became known as the back crawl. Previously, the backstroke had essentially been an inverted breaststroke, with simultaneous arm action. Hebner was almost disqualified by the judges, but U.S. officials pointed to the sole governing rule: Swimmers must remain on their backs throughout.

Soccer was recognized by the National Collegiate Athletic Association as an approved collegiate sport under its umbrella.

The first women's national fencing championship was held under the sponsorship of the Amateur Fencers League of America. There was competition in the foils only, won by A. Baylis of the Fencers Club.

This year's national college football championship was won by Harvard, with a record of nine wins, no losses, no ties.

Feb. 9 The U.S. Lawn Tennis Association amended the rules for men's singles championship play. The reigning champion could no longer stand by while a tournament was producing a challenger but was instead required to play through the tournament.

Feb. 22 At the Westminster Kennel Club dog show, Ch. Kenmore Sorceress, an Airedale terrier owned by William P. Wolcott, took best-in-show.

Apr. 19 The 16th Boston Marathon was won by Michael J. Ryan of New York City with a time of 2 hrs., 21 min., 18.2 sec.

Apr. 20 Fenway Park in Boston, one of the most hallowed baseball stadiums extant, opened. Before a full house of 27,000 fans, the Boston Red Sox defeated the New York Highlanders (renamed the Yankees the next year) 7-6 in 11 innings. This year Fenway Park was the home park for Joe Wood, who compiled his marvelous 31-5 season's pitching record, and was the scene of Boston's World Series victory over the New York Giants.

May 5-July 22 At the Olympic Games in Stock-

ELLSWORTH VINES

Henry Ellsworth Vines
b. Los Angeles, Calif., Sept. 28,
    1911

Ellsworth Vines had a tennis career
that was comparatively short but
highly successful while it lasted. He
won the U.S. men's singles in 1931
and 1932 and the British

championship at Wimbledon in
1932. Vines lost the next year at
Wimbledon to Jack Crawford of
Australia in what is still remembered
as a classic match between two
masters of the game.

Vines played regularly on the U.S.
Davis Cup team and won 13 of his
16 matches. In 1932, he twice

defeated Henri Cochet of France,
who was a dominant figure on the
courts at that time. In 1934, Vines
turned professional, toured with Bill
Tilden, and in 1939 won what was
then the national pro title. Vines was
named to the International Tennis
Hall of Fame in 1962.

---

holm, Sweden, the U.S. won 23 gold medals and took first place in the unofficial team championships. Jim Thorpe of the U.S. won both the decathlon and the pentathlon. This year the first women's swimming events were held: one freestyle race, one relay, and one diving event.

May 11   The 38th annual **Kentucky Derby** was won by Worth, with a time of 2:09⅖. The jockey was Carol Shilling.

May 15   The 37th annual **Preakness Stakes** was won by Colonel Holloway, with a time of 1:56⅖. The jockey was Clarence Turner.

May 30   The second **Indianapolis 500** auto race was won by Joe Dawson. He completed the course in 6 hrs., 21 min., 6 sec., at an average speed of 78.72 mph.

June 20   A silver trophy, emblematic of the **national amateur championship in soccer**, was donated to the American Amateur Football Association by Sir Thomas Dewar, a British sportsman. After the AAFA merged into the United States Football Association in 1913, play

for the trophy was opened in 1914 to professional teams, and the trophy became known as the National Challenge Cup. The first winner was the Brooklyn Field Club.

Summer   The **Power Squadron** of the Boston Yacht Club was organized by Roger Upton to provide group activities for powerboat owners.

July 20   **Duke Kahanamoku,** the great Hawaiian swimmer, set a world's record of 61.6 sec. in the 100-m. freestyle on a straight course. He had recently won the event at the Olympic Games. World War I caused cancellation of the 1916 games, but in 1920 Duke won his event again in a record 60.4 sec. In 1924 he placed second to Johnny Weissmuller, who was timed at 59.0. In 1938, at age 38, Duke again made the U.S. team but won no medals.

Aug. 2   The **U.S. Open golf tournament** was won for the second year in a row by John J. McDermott with a 294 total at the Country Club of Buffalo, N.Y.

Aug. 26   The **U.S. Lawn Tennis Association sin-**

BYRON NELSON

John Byron Nelson, Jr.
b. Fort Worth, Tex., Feb. 4, 1912

Like many other golfers, Byron
Nelson, still looked on as a master of
the game, got his start as a caddy.
He turned pro in 1932 and finished
third in his first tournament, for
which he won all of $75. Nelson's
first major tournament victory came
in 1937, when he won the Masters,

a success he repeated in 1942. In
1939, Nelson took the U.S. Open in
a playoff and the next year won the
PGA.

In 1945, when Nelson again won
the PGA, he enjoyed one of the
greatest years of any golfer ever. He
won 18 tournaments, a record for a
single year that still stands, and 11 of
the wins were consecutive. Playing
30 tournaments in that year, he

never finished lower than ninth, and
his season's average score for 18
holes was a remarkable 68.33.

Nelson might well have won a
number of other tournaments had the
peak of his playing days not come
during World War II, when most
major tournaments were canceled.
Since his retirement, Nelson has been
a teacher of golf.

gles championships were won by Mary K. Browne in the women's division and Maurice E. McLoughlin in the men's division. This was the first year in which the defending champion was required to play through the entire tournament instead of merely waiting for the end of tournament play and then playing the emerging winner in a challenge match.

Oct. 8-16 The ninth annual **World Series** was won by the Boston Red Sox (AL), who beat the New York Giants (NL) four games to three in an eight-game series. The second game was a tie, called in the 11th inning on account of darkness. Smokey Joe Wood won three for the Red Sox. It was in this series that Fred Snodgrass, the Giants center fielder, failed to catch a fly ball that cost his team the last game and the series.

1913

Shuffleboard was introduced into Florida at Daytona Beach by Mr. and Mrs. Robert Ball, who offered it to guests at their hotel.

Amateur ice hockey teams in Minnesota and Michigan formed a league named the American Amateur Hockey Association.

A new **baseball record** for the most consecutive shutout innings pitched in one season was set by Walter Johnson, of the Washington Senators (AL). This year Johnson pitched 56 consecutive innings without allowing a run to score.

This year's **national college football championship** was won by Harvard, with a record of nine wins, no losses, no ties.

Feb. 5 Mixed bouts, fights between black and Caucasian boxers, were banned by the New York State Athletic Commission. All three members of the body were said to have voted for the ban.

Feb. 14 An attempt to **prohibit amateur tennis players** from accepting expense money for transportation, board, and lodging was defeated by delegates to the annual meeting of the U.S. Lawn Tennis Association.

Feb. 21 At the **Westminster Kennel Club** dog show, Ch. Strathway Prince Albert, a bulldog owned by Alex H. Stewart, took best-in-show.

Mar. 8-10 The **NHL Stanley Cup** was won by the Quebec Bulldogs in two games over Sydney.

Apr. 19 The 17th **Boston Marathon** was won by Fritz Carlson of Minneapolis, Minn., with a time of 2 hrs., 25 min., 14.8 sec.

May 10 The 39th annual **Kentucky Derby** was won by the 91-1 long shot, Donerail, with a time of 2:04⅘. The jockey was Roscoe Goose.

May 20 The 38th annual **Preakness Stakes** was won by Buskin, with a time of 1:53⅖. The jockey was Jimmy Butwell.

May 30 The third annual **Indianapolis 500** auto race was won by Jules Goux of France, complet-

SAM SNEAD

Samuel Jackson Snead
b. Hot Springs, Va., May 27, 1912

Two things made Slamming Sammy Snead popular with golf fans: his smiling personality and his powerful drives off the tee. A high school star in football, baseball, basketball, and track, Snead soon after took up golf and became an assistant pro at White Sulphur Springs, Virginia. He was attracting favorable attention in pro tournaments by 1937, but it was not until 1942 that he won his first major victory, the PGA title. After U.S.

Navy service in World War II, he won this event again in 1949 and 1951.

Meanwhile, in 1946 he had won the British Open and in 1949 the Masters. He repeated his Masters victory in 1952 and 1954. The one major championship that escaped Snead was the U.S. Open, although he was runner-up several times. The Vardon Trophy, awarded for the lowest average score in a season, was his four times, in 1938, 1949, 1950, and 1955.

Snead won more than 100

tournaments of various kinds during his career, including five World Seniors titles. He retired officially from tournament play in the 1960s, but as recently as June 1987 he entered the U.S. Open, only to be forced to withdraw for medical reasons.

Sportswriter Grantland Rice once said of Snead that he "was a genius from the start and had the finest swing golf has ever known." Snead was named to the PGA Hall of Fame in 1963.

THE GREATEST ATHLETE IN THE WORLD

The decathlon, a grueling combination of ten track and field events, is the most demanding of individual sports events yet devised. The pentathlon, comprising five events, is merely somewhat less demanding. For an athlete to win both the decathlon and the pentathlon at the same Olympic Games in less than a week would seem unlikely, but this is what happened at Stockholm, Sweden, in 1912.

Jim Thorpe, a star football player at Carlisle Indian School, Carlisle, Pennsylvania, who excelled at every sport he ever tried, accomplished this feat. No one else has won both events at the same Olympics, either before or since.

The men's pentathlon, which dates back to the Olympic Games of ancient Greece, in its modern form consists of a 300-meter freestyle swim, 4000-meter cross-country run, 5000-meter 30-jump equestrian steeplechase, épée fencing, and target shooting at 25 meters. In Thorpe's time, the individual events in the pentathlon were different, and Thorpe won four of the five events. He won the 200-meter dash in 22.9 seconds and the 1500-meter run in 4 minutes, 44.8 seconds. He won the broad jump with a leap of 23 feet, 2¼ inches. He won the discus with a throw of 116 feet, 8¼ inches. And he placed third in the javelin

with a throw of 153 feet, 2¾ inches.

In the pentathlon at Stockholm on July 7, a reverse system of scoring was used, and Thorpe had the lowest, therefore the winning, score of 6 points. Second place was won with a score of 15, far behind Thorpe's mark.

On the next day, instead of resting for the decathlon, Thorpe entered the broad jump and the high jump and finished seventh and fourth, respectively. His opponents in those events specialized in the jumping events, so Thorpe's failure to win medals in these events can scarcely be held against him.

The decathlon in the 1912 Olympics was spread over a period of three days because of the large number of competitors, so Thorpe's stamina was not put to the fullest test, yet it must be understood that Thorpe had never competed in a decathlon before and had not even thrown a javelin until two months earlier. In light of these facts, his winning score of 8413 must be seen as a remarkable achievement. He beat his closest rival by almost 700 points. Thorpe took firsts in the 1500-meter run, the 110-meter hurdles, the high jump, and the shot put.

King Gustav V of Sweden, in addition to presenting gold medals to Thorpe for his decathlon and

pentathlon victories, made the extraordinary gesture of giving Thorpe a bronze royal bust in recognition of the athlete's achievement in winning the pentathlon. In making the presentations, the king said to Thorpe, "Sir, you are the greatest athlete in the world," to which Thorpe replied, "Thanks, King." As an additional award for Thorpe's victory in the decathlon, Czar Nicholas II of Russia presented him with a jewel-encrusted chalice.

On Thorpe's return to the United States, New York City welcomed the American sports hero with a ticker tape parade up Broadway.

But the story did not end there. On January 27, 1913, Thorpe admitted that he had played professional baseball in 1909 and 1910. As a result, he was stripped of his amateur status. The International Olympic Committee took his gold medals away from him and removed his Olympic achievements from the official records. The Swedish athlete, Hugo Wieslander, who had finished second to Thorpe in the decathlon with a score of 7724, refused to accept the gold medal.

At last, on January 18, 1983, Jim Thorpe's gold medals were returned to his family, thirty years after the great athlete's death.

---

ing the 500-mi. course in 5 hrs., 35 min., 5 sec., at an average speed of 75.93 mph.

June 7 The **first ascent of Mt. McKinley** in Alaska, at 20,320 ft. the highest mountain in North America, was accomplished by Hudson Stuck, an Episcopalian clergyman, who led a party consisting of Walter Harper, Harry P. Karstens, and R. C. Tatum. The explorer Frederick Cook stated that he had scaled Mt. McKinley in 1906, but his claim is disputed.

June 13 The 45th annual **Belmont Stakes** was

won by Prince Eugene, with a time of 2:18. The jockey was Roscoe Troxler.

June 14 The **U.S. Lawn Tennis Association singles championships** were won by Mary K. Browne in the women's division and Maurice E. McLoughlin in the men's division (Aug. 26).

June 21 The **United States Soccer Football Association** was formed by a merger of the professional American Football Association and the American Amateur Football Association. The new organization was recognized in August as the national representative for the sport by the Federation of International Football Associations. The term *soccer* was not added to the original name until 1945.

July The **first trapshooting club for women** was organized by Harriet D. Hammond of Wilmington, Del. By 1916 it had more than 60 members.

July 25-28 The **Davis Cup** international tennis challenge round was won for the first time since 1902 by the U.S., beating the British team three matches to two.

Sept. 20 The **U.S. Open golf tournament** was won in a major upset by a 20-year-old amateur named Francis Ouimet after a three-way playoff. His opponents were the two leading British professionals, Harry Vardon and Ted Ray. In the 18-hole playoff, Ouimet bested them by five and six strokes, respectively.

Oct. 7-11 The tenth annual **World Series** was won by the Philadelphia Athletics (AL), who beat the New York Giants (NL) four games to one. Chief Bender won two close ones for the Athletics. Home Run Baker hit .450, and Eddie Collins hit .421.

Nov. 1 The **first Army-Notre Dame football game** was a memorable one. The Notre Dame team was almost unknown in Eastern football circles, so its victory over Army, 35 to 13, stunned the losers. Though legend tends to focus on the passing combination of Gus Dorais and Knute Rockne, the team from South Bend, Ind., was in fact bigger than Army and was fa-

vored to win. Its all-American fullback is said to have "torn the Army line to shreds." Notre Dame demonstrated that forward passes could be devastating. Dorais completed 14 of 17 passes for 243 yards.

1914

By an amendment of its constitution, the Amateur Athletic Union (AAU) permitted the **registration of women swimmers.** In 1915 the AAU began considering and establishing women's swimming marks.

E. G. "Cannonball" Baker set a **transcontinental motorcycle record,** traveling from Los Angeles to New York City in 11 days, 12 hrs., 10 min. Over the next 30 years, he periodically lowered the record, ultimately setting a mark of 6 days, 6 hrs., 25 min.

The **Federal League,** brainchild of James A. Gilmore, Chicago businessman, proclaimed itself a third major league. Gilmore had lined up industrialists as franchise owners and began to raid the established major leagues with offers of higher salaries. Joe Tinker and Mordecai "Three Finger" Brown of the Chicago Cubs were among the scores of fading veterans and underpaid younger players who were enticed to the new league.

Ty Cobb was offered $15,000 a year for five years

BEN HOGAN

William Benjamin Hogan
b. near Stephenville, Tex., Aug. 13, 1912

Ben Hogan's selection in 1973 as one of America's five greatest golfers came as no surprise to followers of the game. (The others selected by the Golf Writers Association of America were Walter Hagen, Bobby Jones, Jack Nicklaus, and Arnold Palmer.) Hogan not only had an outstanding record of victories but was also recognized by his peers as having almost perfect form.

Hogan began his golf career as a caddy and went on to become the pro at the Oakhurst (Texas) Golf Club in 1932. For three consecutive years, 1940 to 1942, he was the leading money winner on the pro tour. After service in the U.S. Air Force from 1943 to 1945, he returned to civilian life and won the PGA championship in 1946, a win he repeated in 1948.

On February 2, 1949, Hogan was badly injured in a collision of his car with a bus, and it appeared he would never play again. Yet, making a remarkable recovery, Hogan was

playing tournament golf by January 1950 and on June 11 won the men's U.S. Open in an 18-hole playoff. He had won the Open in 1948 and did so again in 1951 and 1953 for a total of four wins in this event. In 1951 and 1953, Hogan triumphed in the Masters. His 1953 victories also included the British Open, giving him three of the four major titles in that year.

BETTY RICHEY

Frances Elizabeth Richey
b. Brookline, Mass., Oct. 20, 1912

Probably no other American woman athlete has won national honors in a greater variety of sports than Betty Richey, who had a long and successful career in lacrosse, field hockey, and squash, not to mention golf, which she now plays for pleasure without seeking competitive victories.

Richey began participating in sports in high school and continued to perform while studying at Radcliffe College and then teaching physical education at Vassar College for forty years. As early as 1933 she was named to the first national women's

lacrosse team and continued to play on the team for twenty-one more years before becoming a member of the reserve team for three more years. Richey served as president of the U.S. Women's Lacrosse Association in 1945, 1946, 1947, and 1956 and now is an honorary member of the USWLA.

While Richey was in college, she initiated a string of eighteen years on the all-American field hockey team. She played in an international tournament in Copenhagen, Denmark, in 1933 and then toured, playing the game in Germany, the Netherlands, and Great Britain. She served as first vice-president of the U.S. Field Hockey Association from

1957 to 1964. She now is an honorary member of the association and, in January 1988, was inducted as one of the first members of the USFHA Hall of Fame.

Although Richey professes not to be a great squash player, the Women's Intercollegiate Squash Association has named its sportsmanship award for her. The award is given each year at the time the national team championships are announced. In retirement now, Richey lives in Maine, where she spends a good deal of time on the links, supporting her claim that "the joy of my life is golf."

---

if he would jump from Detroit to the newly formed Federal League. He turned down the offer. Cobb, the highest paid outfielder in baseball, was making $12,000 a year with the Tigers.

The **polo team** of Great Britain regained the Westchester Cup by defeating the U.S. team by 8½ to 3 and 4 to 2¾ at Westbury, N.Y.

This year's **national college football championship** was won by Army, with a record of nine wins, no losses, no ties.

The **first great football stadium,** the Yale Bowl, seating almost 80,000, opened. After World War I, attendance at games increased, and many large stadiums were erected throughout the U.S.

The **NHL Stanley Cup** was won by the Toronto Blueshirts over Victoria, 13 goals to 8.

Feb. 2 The **U.S. Power Squadrons were formed** by several yacht clubs and boating organizations in the Northeast. Assistant Secretary of the Navy Franklin D. Roosevelt gave the squadrons active encouragement in promotion of water safety, navigational skills, and boat handling. By the mid-1960s the squadrons had more than 450 local clubs and 60,000 members.

Feb. 25 At the **Westminster Kennel Club** dog show, Ch. Brentwood Hero, an Old English sheepdog owned by Mrs. Tyler Morse, took best-in-show.

VINCE LOMBARDI

Vincent Thomas Lombardi
b. Brooklyn, N.Y., June 11, 1913
d. Washington, D.C., Sept. 3, 1970

One of the most successful football coaches of all time, Vince Lombardi played football at Fordham University and, after his graduation in 1937, played for a professional team in Brooklyn. In 1947, Lombardi became freshman coach at Fordham and two

years later assistant coach at West Point. In 1954, Lombardi joined the New York Giants' staff. In 1959, he became head coach and general manager of the Green Bay Packers and turned a losing club into a great success. Lombardi led the Packers to six conference titles and five NFL championships before retiring as head coach in 1968.

Lombardi in 1969 coached the

Washington Redskins to their first winning season in 14 years. In the next year, he died at age 57 from abdominal cancer. But Lombardi's memory will always be associated with the Packers. He was known for his dedication to the game of football and his drive to win. In Lombardi's often quoted words, "Winning isn't everything—it's the only thing."

BEAR BRYANT

Paul Bryant
b. Kingsland, Ark., Sept. 11, 1913
d. Tuscaloosa, Ala., Jan. 26, 1983

A farm boy and one of 12 children, Bear Bryant got his nickname for taking up an offer of $1 to wrestle a bear. He first turned to football in high school, where he was a tackle, and then played at the University of Alabama. He said he was not a very good player, but the three Alabama teams he played on won 23 games, lost only three, tied two, and beat Stanford in the 1935 Rose Bowl game.

Taking up coaching, Bryant served at Navy, Maryland, Kentucky, and Texas A&M before going back to Alabama. Meanwhile, he had also served in the Navy in World War II. His only really bad year to this time was 1954, when his Texas A&M team lost nine of ten games.

As head coach at Alabama from 1958 to 1982, Bryant never had a losing season. His teams were voted national champions five times. The Crimson Tide went to the Orange Bowl four times, winning two and losing two; to the Sugar Bowl seven times and winning all seven; the Cotton Bowl three times, losing all three; and the Gator Bowl, losing once.

Bryant coached such future pro stars as Joe Namath, Ken Stabler, and Richard Todd. In 1971, he recruited the first black student to play for Alabama. When Bryant retired on December 29, 1982, he was the winningest coach in college football history, with 323 wins, 85 losses, and 17 ties. An imposing figure at 6 feet, 3 inches, Bryant prowled the sidelines during games, always wearing his trademark, a checked porkpie hat. Less than a month after Bryant retired, he died of a heart attack. Bryant is in the College Football Hall of Fame.

Mar. 21 The first **U.S. figure skating championships** were held. Norman N. Scott of Montreal, Canada, won the men's singles, and Theresa Weld of Boston, Mass., won the women's singles. The pairs' event was won by Jeanne Chevalier and Norman N. Scott.

Apr. 20 The 18th **Boston Marathon** was won by James Duffy of Hamilton, Ontario, Canada, with a time of 2 hrs., 25 min., 1 sec.

May 9 The 40th annual **Kentucky Derby** was won by Old Rosebud, with a record time of 2:03⅗. The jockey was John McCabe.

May 16 The **Grand League of American Horseshoe Players** was organized by players from six states at Kansas City, Kans. Rules, equipment, and procedures were standardized.

May 21 The 39th annual **Preakness Stakes** was won by Holiday, with a time of 1:53⅘. The jockey was Andy Schuttinger.

May 30 The fourth annual **Indianapolis 500** auto race was won by René Thomas, who completed the 500-mi. course in 6 hrs., 3 min., 45 sec. at an average speed of 82.47 mph.

June 20 The 46th annual **Belmont Stakes** was won by Luke McLuke, with a time of 2:20. The jockey was M. Buxton.

July 4 At the **Henley Royal Regatta** in England, an American crew for the first time won the top event when the Harvard eight won the Grand Challenge Cup. Another American crew, the Union Boat Club of Boston, took second.

Aug. 15 In the **Davis Cup** international tennis challenge round, the U.S. was defeated by Australia three matches to two. The U.S. champion, Maurice E. McLoughlin, won both his singles matches, beating Norman E. Brookes and Anthony F. Wilding.

Aug. 21 Walter Hagen captured the **U.S. Open golf title** at Midlothian Country Club, Blue Island, Ill., edging amateur Charles "Chick" Evans, Jr., with a 290 total for his first important victory.

Sept. 1 The **U.S. Lawn Tennis Association singles championships** were won by Mary K. Browne in the women's division and R. Norris Williams II in the men's division.

Oct. 9-13 The **Boston Braves** capped their miraculous rise in the National League standing from eighth place on July 18 to a pennant with a clean sweep of one of Connie Mack's greatest Philadelphia teams in the 11th annual World Series.

1915

Clarence C. Pell won the first of 12 national racquets singles titles he was to win in a period of 19 years.

JESSE OWENS

Jesse Cleveland Owens
b. Danville, Ala., Sept. 12, 1913
d. Tucson, Ariz., Mar. 31, 1980

Jesse Owens is popularly recalled for making a hash of Adolf Hitler's racial theories in Berlin at the 1936 Olympic Games. All he did in those games was win four Olympic gold medals against the world's best. In terms of sports achievements, however, his greatest day came a year earlier. At the National Collegiate Track and Field Meet on May 25, 1935, Owens, an Ohio State University student, put on an astounding display. He equaled the 100-yard dash mark, set new records in the 220-yard dash and the 220-yard low hurdles, and ended with what was then a new world record for the long jump, 26 feet, 8 1/4 inches.

Even before then, Jesse Owens had amazed the sports world with his 10-second 100-yard dash while he was in junior high school. Then, in 1933, at the National Interscholastic Championships, he ran the 100-yard dash in 9.4 seconds and also won the 200-yard dash and the long jump.

At the Berlin Olympics in August 1936, the great black athlete put on his best-known display, receiving great applause from the spectators but being pointedly ignored by Hitler. Owens won his four gold medals in the 100-meter and 200-meter dashes, in the long jump, and as a member of the 400-meter relay team. In the process, he tied one record and broke two others.

In an Associated Press poll in 1950, Jesse Owens was voted the greatest track athlete of the first half of the century. After retiring, he appeared in professional exhibitions and was active with the Illinois athletic and youth commissions.

The **first major ice show** in the U.S. opened at the Hippodrome in New York City. Called *Flirting in St. Moritz,* it featured the German ice ballerina Charlotte (Oelschagel), supported by a Berlin ice ballet group. The show was an instant success and ran for 300 days.

This year's **national college football championship** was won by Cornell, with a record of nine wins, no losses, no ties.

Ty Cobb set a **major league record for bases stolen** in one season, 96. The record stood until 1962, when Maury Wills stole 104 bases. In 1974 Lou Brock shattered the record again with 118 steals.

During Cobb's career, he set more records than any other player in the history of baseball.

A new **record for the mile run** was set in Cambridge, Mass., by Norman Taber, who completed the distance in 4:12.6, nearly 2 sec. under the old record.

The **NHL Stanley Cup** was won by the Vancouver Millionaires, who swept the Ottawa Senators in three straight games.

Feb. 24 At the **Westminster Kennel Club** dog show, Ch. Matford Vic, a wire fox terrier owned by George W. Quintard of Bay Shore, Long Island, N.Y., took best-in-show.

ALICE MARBLE

b. Beckworth, Calif., Sept. 28, 1913

Alice Marble was not the winningest tennis player ever, but the style of play she developed brought about a dramatic and fundamental change in the women's game. She favored the serve and volley game in place of the usual baseline style, and it was not long before her way of playing was widely copied.

Marble's first love was baseball, but at about age 15 she began playing tennis on public courts in San Francisco. She was doing well in tournament play until 1934, when she was stricken with an illness variously diagnosed by doctors. Marble collapsed while playing in the French championships. She battled hard to recover and in 1936 won her first U.S. championship. She was also U.S. champion from 1938 to 1940 and won the Wimbledon crown in England in 1939.

That year, Marble and her partners also won the women's and the mixed doubles for an unusual triple crown.

With Sarah Palfrey Cooke, Marble won the U.S. women's doubles title for four consecutive years, 1937, 1938, 1939, and 1940. She also played on winning Wightman Cup teams in 1933, 1937, 1938, 1939, and 1940.

The Associated Press named Alice Marble the outstanding woman athlete of the year in 1939, and she was elected to the International Tennis Hall of Fame in 1964.

> *Losers walking around with money in their pockets are always dangerous, not to be trusted. Some horse always reaches out and grabs them.*
>
> Bill Barich

Apr. 5 The **world heavyweight boxing championship** was won by Jess Willard, who defeated Jack Johnson in a 23-round bout in Havana, Cuba. It was not clear whether a blow by Willard or the blazing sun caused Johnson's descent to the canvas, which was described as a slow sinking.

Apr. 19 The 19th **Boston Marathon** was won by Edouard Fabre of Montreal, Canada, with a time of 2 hrs., 31 min., 41.2 sec.

May 6 **Babe Ruth,** pitching for the Boston Red Sox, hit his first home run off Yankee pitcher Jack Warhop at the Polo Grounds, New York City.

May 8 The 41st annual **Kentucky Derby** was won by Regret, the first filly to win the race, with a time of 2:05⅖. The jockey was Joe Notter.

May 17 The 49th annual **Preakness Stakes** was won by Rhine Maiden, with a time of 1:58. The jockey was D. Hoffman.

May 31 The fifth annual **Indianapolis 500** auto race was won by Ralph De Palma, completing the 500-mi. course in 5 hrs., 33 min., 55.51 sec., at an average speed of 89.84 mph.

June 5 The 47th annual **Belmont Stakes** was won by The Finn, with a time of 2:18⅖. The jockey was G. Byrne.

June 12 The **U.S. Lawn Tennis Association singles championships** were won by Molla Bjurstedt of Norway in the women's division, the first foreigner to do so, and William M. Johnston in the men's division (Sept. 8). This year the men's championships were moved from Newport, R.I., to the West Side Tennis Club in Forest Hills, N.Y. The women's championships would be moved there from Philadelphia in 1921.

June 18 The **U.S. Open golf tournament** was won by an amateur from Long Island, N.Y., Jerome D. Travers. Travers was the second amateur to stand off the pros.

July 27 The **American Lawn Bowls Association** was formed in Buffalo, N.Y., by bowlers representing clubs in Boston, Brooklyn, and Buffalo. It became the controlling body in the U.S. for bowls.

Oct. 8-13 The 12th annual **World Series** was won

JOE LOUIS

Joseph Louis Barrow
b. Lafayette, Ala., Mar. 13, 1914
d. Las Vegas, Nev., Apr. 12, 1981

Joe Louis, the son of a sharecropper, grew up in Detroit in the home of his stepfather. He began his boxing career as an amateur when he was 18 and in 1934 won the AAU light heavyweight title. Louis turned pro and won his first pro fight on July 4, 1934. He went on to win 23 bouts, including knockouts of Primo Carnera and Max Baer, both former heavyweight champions. On June 19, 1936, however, the Brown Bomber was knocked out in the 12th round of a fight with Max Schmeling of Germany.

Louis attained his goal of heavyweight champion on June 22, 1937, in Chicago, when he knocked out titleholder Jim Braddock in the eighth round. Louis then had his revenge against Schmeling on June 22, 1938, when he knocked Schmeling out in the first round. Louis went on to defend his title 25 times, although he quickly ran out of well-qualified contenders and his opponents soon were known collectively as the Bum of the Month Club. Louis fought and won his last fight before retiring, on June 25, 1948, when he knocked out a future champion, Jersey Joe Walcott, in the 11th round.

Louis, undefeated since becoming champion, announced his retirement on March 1, 1949. Despite having earned about $5,000,000, Louis was deep in debt—especially to the Internal Revenue Service—and attempted a comeback in 1950. He lost a decision to Ezzard Charles, the new champion, in a 15-round fight. Once more, on October 27, 1951, Louis tried but was knocked out in the eighth round by Rocky Marciano. This was only the second time he had been knocked out in 71 fights, and he had lost only one other bout.

The Brown Bomber is regarded by many as the best heavyweight boxer ever. Although his footwork was slow, his reflexes were exceedingly fast and his punches paralyzing. Louis served in the Army in World War II, giving boxing exhibitions for troops in many parts of the world.

SAMMY "SLINGING SAMMY" BAUGH

Samuel Adrian Baugh
b. Temple, Tex., Mar. 17, 1914

Sammy Baugh was the football player who made passing, in both quality and quantity, the primary requirement for a quarterback, especially in the professional game. After starring in high school athletics in Sweetwater, Texas, Baugh and his passing game made Texas Christian University a football power from 1934 to 1936.

Joining the Washington Redskins of the NFL, Slinging Sammy led his team to a league championship in 1937, his first season. It was his passing that did the trick, and the entire nation stood in awe at his prowess. Baugh's career lasted for 16 seasons, during which he paced the Redskins to five division titles, and one more championship, in 1942. In six of these seasons, Slinging Sammy was the leading passer in the league.
At retirement in 1952, Baugh held

many records, since surpassed. He had passed 3016 times, gained 22,085 yards with these passes, and had a completion average of 56.5%. Other records included most passing attempts in a season, 210, and most touchdown passes, 187.
Baugh was head football coach at Hardin-Simmons University, Abilene, Texas, from 1955 to 1959. He is in the Pro Football Hall of Fame.

by the Boston Red Sox (AL), who beat the Philadelphia Phillies (NL) four games to one. It was a low-scoring series, with the winning Red Sox making a total of only 12 runs. Harry Hooper and Duffy Lewis, both outfielders, drove in 8 of the 12, Hooper hitting two home runs and Lewis hitting one.

Dec. 21 The Federal League, entangled in a **baseball antitrust suit** being heard in a U.S. District Court under Judge Kenesaw Mountain Landis, finally signed an amicable settlement with the older leagues. Star Federal players now acquired by various National and American League teams included Eddie Roush, Benny Kauff, Howard Ehmke, Max Flack, Jack Tobin, and Bill McKechnie.

1916

This year's **national college football championship** was won by Pittsburgh, with a record of eight wins, no losses, no ties.

The **NHL Stanley Cup** was won by the Montreal Canadiens over Portland. The Canadiens outscored Portland by 15 goals to 13.

Jan. 1 In the second **Tournament of Roses Association football game** (the first had been played in 1902), and the first annual game, Washington State defeated Brown 14-0. This

game marked the beginning of the annual football contest that in 1923 came to be called the Rose Bowl game.

Jan. 17 The **Professional Golfers Association** (PGA) had its beginning at a luncheon in New York City given by Rodman Wanamaker, of the Wanamaker department store family, and attended by many top golfers. On Feb. 7 an organizing committee established the new association, drew up tentative bylaws, and chose a permanent committee. The first professional tournament under PGA auspices, played under match play rules and held at the Siwanoy Golf Course in Bronxville, N.Y., on Apr. 10, was won by Jim Barnes, of Great Britain, with a 1-up victory over Jock Hutchison.

Feb. 25 At the **Westminster Kennel Club** dog show, Ch. Matford Vic, a wire fox terrier owned by George W. Quintard of Bay Shore, Long Island, N.Y., took best-in-show for the second year in a row.

Apr. 1 National **championships in women's swimming**, both indoors and outdoors, were held for the first time by the AAU. The five events offered were races at 440 and 880 yards, 1 mi., and long distance, plus one diving contest.

Apr. 19 The 20th **Boston Marathon** was won by Arthur V. Roth of Roxbury, Mass., with a time of 2 hrs., 27 min., 16.4 sec.

May 13 The 42nd annual **Kentucky Derby** was won by George Smith, with a new record time of 2:04. The jockey was Johnny Loftus.

May 16 The 40th annual **Preakness Stakes** was

BABE DIDRIKSON

Mildred Ella Didrikson Zaharias
b.   Port Arthur, Tex., June 26, 1914
d.   Galveston, Tex., Sept. 27, 1956

In 1950, toward the end of Babe Didrikson's life, an Associated Press poll voted her the greatest woman athlete of the preceding half century. From youth she had shown remarkable athletic abilities and by age 16 was known throughout Texas as the star forward of the undefeated, state-champion Beaumont High School girls' basketball team.

In 1931, Babe Didrikson entered nine of ten events at the annual AAU women's track and field meet and finished first in seven of them. In the 1932 AAU meet, she entered eight events, taking first place in five and winning an honored place with the U.S. Olympic team. And at the 1932 Summer Olympics in Los Angeles, Didrikson entered three events, the maximum allowed, winning two gold medals and one silver medal.

In 1935, she took up golf and within months had won the Texas State Women's Golf Championship. Declared a professional by the USGA because she had received income from appearances in basketball and baseball exhibitions, Didrikson later reapplied for amateur status, which she secured in 1943.

Babe Didrikson married George Zaharias, a wrestler, in 1938. In 1946 and 1947, she stunned the sports world by winning 17 golf touraments in a row, including the 1946 U.S. Women's Amateur Championship. Also in 1947, she became the first American to win the British Women's Amateur Championship. Turning pro, she won the 1948 U.S. Women's Open.

Between 1948 and 1952, she won 24 tournaments, finishing second in 15 others. She won her second U.S. Women's Open in 1950 and her third in 1954, a year after surgery for cancer. She won two more tournaments in 1955, but illness forced her off the links.

In 1949, Babe and George Zaharias, Fred Corcoran, and Patty Berg founded the Ladies Professional Golf Association.

---

won by Damrosch, with a time of 1:54⅘. The jockey was Linus McAtee.

May 30   The sixth **Indianapolis 500** auto race was won by Dario Resta. This year the course distance was 300 mi. Resta completed the race in 3 hrs., 34 min., 17 sec., at an average speed of 84 mph. The race was not run in 1917 or 1918.

June 10   The 48th annual **Belmont Stakes** was won by Friar Rock, with a time of 2:22. The jockey was E. Haynes.

June 12   The **U.S. Lawn Tennis Association singles championships** were won by Molla Bjurstedt in the women's division and R. Norris Williams II in the men's division (Sept. 6).

June 15   **Boy Scouts of America** was incorporated by a bill signed by Pres. Woodrow Wilson.

June 30   The **U.S. Open golf tournament** was won by another amateur, Charles "Chick" Evans, Jr. His 286 total at the Minikahda Club, Minneapolis, stood as the record low until 1936. The competition was suspended until 1919 because of U.S. entry into World War I in 1917.

July 22   A **double soccer championship** was achieved by a team representing Bethlehem Steel Company, which added the National Cup to its earlier victory in the American Challenge Cup. Eighty-eight teams entered the competition for the National Cup, a trophy donated by

---

MARION LADEWIG

b.   Grand Rapids, Mich., Oct. 30, 1914

Marion Ladewig is generally conceded to be the best woman bowler of all time. Perhaps some of her success can be attributed to the fact that, as she has reported, she bowled every day of the year from 1940 through 1962. Ladewig won her first championship, the Western Michigan Golden Pin Classic, in 1940.

Her accomplishments from then through the end of her competitive career are unmatched. She won seven women's national all-star titles, the last coming in 1959. Ladewig was named woman bowler of the year nine times, in 1950 through 1954, 1957 through 1959, and 1963. She holds the record eight-game average, 247.6. Ladewig was elected to the Women's International Bowling Congress Hall of Fame in 1964.

JOE DIMAGGIO

Joseph Paul DiMaggio
b. Martinez, Calif., Nov. 25, 1914

Joe DiMaggio's skill in center field and at the plate was equaled only by the grace with which he played baseball and has lived his life. He is, of course, remembered first for his great feat of hitting safely in 56 consecutive major league games. The streak began on May 15, 1941, and ended on July 17. During that time, he had 91 hits, including 15 home runs. This streak was at the heart of his achievement of getting on base in 84 consecutive games. A fact less

well known is his 1933 accomplishment of hitting safely in 61 consecutive games while with San Francisco of the Pacific Coast League.

Known both as Joltin' Joe and as the Yankee Clipper, DiMaggio played for 13 years with the New York Yankees, from 1936 to 1951, with three years out for military service in World War II. He was the American League batting champion in 1939, winning with a .381 average, and in 1940, winning with a .352 average. He was the league's most valuable player in 1939, 1941, and 1947. He

hit 351 home runs, 33rd on the all-time list, and he ended his career with a batting average of .325.

DiMaggio played in ten World Series, hit eight home runs, and batted .271. In a 1936 regular season game, he hit two home runs in one inning, and three times in his career he hit three home runs in a single game. Quiet and unassuming, DiMaggio let his deeds on the playing field speak for themselves. He was elected to the Baseball Hall of Fame in 1955, as soon as he became eligible.

Sir Thomas Dewar to encourage soccer in the U.S.

July 30 The *New York Times* reported that **women golf players** were much restricted as to when they were allowed to play most courses. The Garden City, N.Y., Golf Club allowed women to play only on Monday and Friday mornings, and they had to tee off by 11 A.M. The Upper Montclair, N.J., Country Club had about 20 women members, who were not allowed to play on holidays. They were allowed on the course on Saturday mornings and on Sundays after 3 P.M.

Aug. 21-26 Prizes for **women trapshooters** were

awarded for the first time at the Grand American Handicap events in St. Louis, Mo. The three leading markswomen were Mrs. F. A. Johnson, Mrs. L. G. Vogel, and Mrs. D. J. Dalton.

Sept. 30 The **longest baseball winning streak** on record was stopped at 26 games when the New York Giants (NL) were beaten 8-3 by the Boston Braves in the second game of a double header.

Oct. 7 In the **most lopsided game in football history,** Georgia Tech defeated Cumberland College, of Lebanon, Tenn., by a score of 222-0.

Oct. 7-12 The 13th annual **World Series** was won by the Boston Red Sox (AL), defeating the

DON BUDGE

John Donald Budge
b. Oakland, Calif., June 13, 1915

Don Budge, a somewhat reluctant tennis player who showed little interest in the game until he was 15, went on to become the first player to complete the grand slam of tennis by winning the U.S., British, French, and Australian men's singles in the same year. This goal was reached on September 24, 1938, when he defeated Gene Mako in four sets at

Forest Hills, New York, for the U.S. championship.

Budge's first successful year was 1937, when he won the U.S. and British championships. At Wimbledon he defeated Baron Gottfried von Cramm of Germany in a hard-fought five-set match. In both 1936 and 1938, he won the U.S. men's doubles with Mako as partner. Budge played a leading role in 1937 in winning the Davis Cup over England and had a similar role in retaining it

against Australia the next year.

Budge had no weak spots in his game, always pressing his opponents, especially with his backhand. He had the distinction in 1937 of being the first tennis player to win the James E. Sullivan Memorial Award for best American amateur athlete of the year. Budge turned professional in 1939, then retired from tennis in 1941 to enter business. He is a member of the International Tennis Hall of Fame.

George Edward Arcaro
b. Cincinnati, Ohio, Feb. 16, 1916

Only two other jockeys, Willie Shoemaker and Johnny Longden, have won more races in their careers than Eddie Arcaro, whose total at retirement in 1962 was 4779. In his 31 years in horse racing, Arcaro rode 24,092 mounts and won purses totaling $30,039,543.

Arcaro rode his first race when he was 15 but had to go out 46 times before riding a winner. He went on to win the Kentucky Derby five times, in 1938, 1941, 1945, 1948, and 1952; the Preakness Stakes six times, 1941, 1948, 1950, 1951, 1955, and 1957; and the Belmont Stakes also six times, 1941, 1942, 1945, 1948, 1952, and 1955. In addition, Arcaro became the first jockey to win the Triple Crown twice, in 1941 and 1948.

Arcaro was suspended for a year, beginning in September 1942, because he almost rode into the fence a jockey who had cut in on him at the start of a race. He admitted he was after the offender. Standing 5 feet 2 inches tall and weighing 114 pounds during his long career, Arcaro is now enjoying his earnings. His agent once said of Arcaro: "He's the only jockey who subscribes to [both] the *Racing Form* and the *Wall Street Journal.*"

Brooklyn Dodgers (NL) four games to one. In the second game, a 14-inning thriller, Babe Ruth gave up only six hits while going the route on the mound. The Red Sox won 2-1.

Nov. 29 The **Women's National Bowling Association,** now the Women's International Bowling Congress, was organized in St. Louis, Mo. In its first tournament, the team championship was won by the Progress team of St. Louis and the all-event title by Mrs. A. J. Koester, also of St. Louis.

Dec. 21 The growing popularity of **trapshooting** was reported on by the *New York Times.* In ten years the sport had grown so rapidly that it now attracted 675,000 shooters, who belonged to 5000 clubs and spent $12 million a year on ammunition.

1917

The **Women's Swimming Association of New York was formed** as a swimming club for amateurs. For a decade WSA swimmers, particularly Gertrude Ederle, dominated amateur competitive swimming.

The **American crawl** was born when Charlotte Boyle and Claire Galligan of the Women's Swimming Association of New York modified the Australian crawl with a new six-beat kick and achieved record-breaking success. The stroke, improved in details by Johnny Weissmuller in 1920, went to become used almost universally by freestyle swimmers.

This year's **national college football championship** was won by Georgia Tech, with a record of nine wins, no losses, no ties.

The **NHL Stanley Cup** championship was won by the Seattle Metropolitans, who defeated the Montreal Canadiens three games to one.

Jan. 1 The third **Tournament of Roses Association football game** (Rose Bowl) was won by Oregon over Pennsylvania, 14-0.

Feb. 23 At the **Westminster Kennel Club** dog show, Ch. Conejo Wycollar Boy, a wire fox terrier owned by Mrs. Roy A. Rainey of Huntington, Long Island, N.Y., took best-in-show.

Apr. 19 The 21st **Boston Marathon** was won by William K. Kennedy of Port Chester, N.Y., with a time of 2 hrs., 28 min., 37 sec.

May 2 The **first double no-hit nine-inning baseball game** in the major leagues was played in Chicago. Jim Vaughn of the Chicago Cubs and Fred Toney of Cincinnati both pitched full games without allowing a hit. The Reds scored in the tenth inning to win 1-0.

May 12 The 42nd annual **Preakness Stakes** was won by Kalitan, with a time of 1:54⅗. The jockey was E. Haynes.

May 12 The 43rd annual **Kentucky Derby** was won by Omar Khayyam, with a time of 2:04⅗. The jockey was Charles Borel.

May 28 Benny Leonard won the **lightweight boxing championship** when he knocked out the British titleholder, Freddie Welsh, in the ninth

SID LUCKMAN

Sidney Luckman
b.   Brooklyn, N.Y., Nov. 21, 1916

If any one player proved the value of football's T formation, it was Sid Luckman. The most striking demonstration of the efficacy of this formation came on December 8, 1940, when the Chicago Bears met the Washington Redskins for the National Football League championship. It was Luckman's second year with the Bears and his first as regular starting quarterback. When coach George Halas and quarterback Luckman led the Bears to a 73–0 rout of the Redskins, the T formation was acclaimed.

Luckman owed the start of his career as a great quarterback to natural talent and the coaching he received under Lou Little at Columbia. He then played 12 seasons for the Bears, from 1939 to 1950. In addition to winning the NFL title in 1940, the Chicago eleven also won in 1941, 1943, and 1946. In the 1940 game, Luckman's last game before joining the armed forces, he threw five touchdown passes. Earlier that season, on November 14, he set a league record that has been tied but never surpassed, completing seven touchdown passes in a game.

Luckman is in both the College Hall of Fame and the Pro Football Hall of Fame.

round of a bout in New York City. Leonard went on to hold the title until he retired in 1924. In all, Leonard fought 209 times and lost only five bouts.

June 16   The 49th annual **Belmont Stakes** was won by Hourless, in a new track record time of 2:17⅘. The jockey was Jimmy Butwell.

June 23   Ernie Shore of the Boston Red Sox pitched an unusual **perfect game** against Washington. Babe Ruth started for Boston, walked the first batter, protested the call, and was ejected from the game. Shore came in, and the base runner tried to steal second and was thrown out. The next 26 batters went down in order in the 4-0 Boston victory.

June 23   The **U.S. Lawn Tennis Association singles championships** were won by Molla Bjurstedt in the women's division and R. Lindley Murray in the men's division (Aug. 25).

Aug. 19   The first baseball game played in New York City's **Polo Grounds** resulted in the arrest of managers John McGraw of the New York Giants and Christy Mathewson of the Cincinnati Reds for violating a law prohibiting Sunday ball playing.

Oct. 6-15   The 14th annual **World Series** was won

ARCHIE MOORE

Archibald Lee Moore
b.   Benoit, Miss., Dec. 13, 1916?

There is some question about the year of Archie Moore's birth, but none about his fighting ability, which made him one of the two or three best boxers, pound for pound, the U.S. has ever produced. Son of a farm laborer, Moore grew up in St. Louis, Missouri, living with his aunt and uncle, and spent 22 months in reform school for stealing before joining the Civilian Conservation Corps (CCC) in 1934.

Moore had his first professional fight in 1936 as a middleweight and won his first 13 bouts by knockouts before losing three. After touring Australia in 1940 and winning all seven of his fights there, he was out of action because of illness until 1942. In St. Louis, on December 17, 1952, Moore became light heavyweight champion by defeating Joey Maxim in a 15-round unanimous decision.

Moore attempted to step up to the heavyweight title on July 21, 1955, when he took on the champion, Rocky Marciano, in Yankee Stadium, in New York City. Although Moore accomplished a rare feat by knocking Marciano down in the second round, he was knocked out by Marciano in the ninth. With the title vacant because of Marciano's retirement, Moore again attempted to take the crown on November 30, 1956, but Floyd Patterson became champion when he knocked Moore out in the fifth round at Chicago. Moore, of course, was not a young man at the time; indeed, he was at least 39 years old.

In his career, Moore had 220 professional fights and won 136 of them by knockouts. A heavyset man, Moore was a hard puncher as well as a skilled boxer.

RED AUERBACH

Arnold Jacob Auerbach
b. Brooklyn, N.Y., Sept. 20, 1917

Red Auerbach is the winningest coach in pro basketball history and is likely to hold that title for some years at least. A player of modest distinction in high school and at George Washington University, he did some high school and college coaching, then served in the Navy in World War II.

Auerbach became a pro basketball coach in 1946, when he took over the Washington Capitols for three winning seasons. For the 1949–1950 season, he headed the Tri-Cities team without great success. Auerbach then took the reins of the Boston Celtics and coached them for 16 seasons, 1950–1951 through 1965–1966, when he retired.

During his regime Boston was the most successful team in the National Basketball Association. His Celtics did not have a single losing season, although in 1954–1955 they just broke even. They won their first NBA championship under Auerbach in 1957 and won eight more by 1966, the last in his farewell year. In regular season play, Auerbach's teams won 938 games and lost 379 for a percentage of .662. In postseason play, they won 99 games and lost 69, a percentage of .589.

Coaching on the sideline, Auerbach had a low boiling point and often screamed at the officials. He was named NBA coach of the year in 1965, and in 1980 the Professional Basketball Writers' Association voted him the greatest coach in the history of the NBA. After retiring as coach, Auerbach became president and general manager of the Celtics. He was named to the Basketball Hall of Fame in 1968.

---

by the Chicago White Sox (AL), who defeated the New York Giants (NL) four games to two. Urban "Red" Faber won three for the White Sox, and Eddie Collins had an outstanding series, batting .409.

1918

This year's **national college football championship** was won by Pittsburgh, with a record of four wins, one loss, no ties.

The fourth **Tournament of Roses Association football game** (Rose Bowl) was won by the Mare Island Marines, who defeated the Camp Lewis Army team 19-7.

The **NHL Stanley Cup** championship was won by the Toronto Arenas, who defeated the Vancouver Millionaires three games to two.

For this year's **Boston Marathon,** individual competition was suspended because of the war. A service team race was won by Camp Devens.

Feb. 23 At the **Westminster Kennel Club** dog show, Ch. Haymarket Faultless, a bull terrier owned by R. H. Elliot, took best-in-show.

Mar. 7 U.S. **figure skating championships** were won by Mrs. Seton R. Beresford of Great Britain, women's singles; Nathaniel W. Niles of Boston, men's singles; and Theresa Weld of Boston and Nathaniel W. Niles, pairs.

May 11 The 44th annual **Kentucky Derby** was won by Exterminator, one of the great American racehorses, with a time of 2:10⅘. The jockey was Willie Knapp.

May 15 The 43rd annual **Preakness Stakes** was run in two sections this year. The first was won by War Cloud, with a time of 1:53⅗. The jockey was Johnny Loftus. The second was won by Jack Hare, Jr., with a time of 1:53⅖. The jockey was C. Peak.

June 15 The 50th annual **Belmont Stakes** was won by Johren, with a time of 2:20⅖. The jockey was Frankie Robinson.

June 22 The **U.S. Lawn Tennis Association singles championships** were won by Molla Bjurstedt, for the fourth time in a row, in the women's division and R. Lindley Murray over William T. "Bill" Tilden in the men's division (Sept. 3).

Aug. 2 Because of the **manpower shortage** during World War I, Secretary of War Newton D. Baker ordered major league baseball to terminate its season on September 1 but permitted the World Series to be played.

Sept. 5-11 The 15th annual **World Series** was won by the Boston Red Sox (AL), who beat the Chicago Cubs (NL) four games to two. Carl Mays and Babe Ruth both won two games for

PATTY BERG

Patricia Jane Berg
b. Minneapolis, Minn., Feb. 13, 1918

Patty Berg took up golf at the age of 12 and just three years later won the Minneapolis city championship. In 1935, when only 17, she lost the final match of the women's national amateur championship to the veteran Glenna Collett Vare. Three years later, she won this event. Berg turned professional in 1940 and won the first U.S. Women's Open, played in 1946.

By 1962, when she retired, Berg had won 55 tournaments, 42 of them on the LPGA tour. During the U.S. Women's Open in 1959, she sank a hole-in-one, making her the first woman ever to record an ace in USGA competition.

Berg's activities off the course on behalf of golf have contributed at least as much as her playing did to making women's golf both popular and profitable for the players. She was a founder and first president of the LPGA and in 1951 was one of the first four players elected to the LPGA Hall of Fame. Berg has received numerous honors, including Associated Press Athlete of the Year three times, in 1938, 1943, and 1955. In 1978, the LPGA established the Patty Berg Award, to be given for outstanding contributions to women's golf.

---

the Red Sox. It was in this series that Ruth ran his record for scoreless innings pitched in a series to 29⅔ innings. Each player on the winning team received $1102.51, the all-time low payment to World Series winners.

Dec. 16 **William Harrison "Jack" Dempsey,** less than a year away from winning the world heavyweight boxing title, knocked out Carl Morris in 14 sec. at New Orleans. On July 27, at Harrison, N.J., he had stopped Fred Fulton in 18 sec.

1919

The governing body of **motorcycling,** the Motorcycle and Allied Trades Association, created two basic classes of competition, one for stock machines and the other for track speed events.

Suzanne Lenglen revolutionized women's tennis dress and startled spectators by appearing for matches in a short-sleeved, one-piece pleated dress worn over shorts, without a petticoat. Not until 1929 did women cast aside stockings for tennis. In 1937

MARGARET OSBORNE DU PONT

b. Joseph, Oreg., Mar. 4, 1918

The achievements of Margaret du Pont as a singles tennis player, substantial as they were, are somewhat overshadowed by her unmatched success in women's doubles, usually teaming up with her friend Louise Brough, who was also one of her main opponents in singles. Overall, du Pont was ranked among the top ten women players of the year 14 times and in 1948 was ranked number one.

In singles she won the French title in 1946, her first major victory, and again in 1949. She won the U.S. championship in 1948, 1949, and 1950. In du Pont's first victory in that tournament, she upset the favored Brough, with the final set going to 15–13. She also won the crown at Wimbledon in 1947 but lost it to Brough in both 1949 and 1950.

Together with Brough, du Pont won the U.S. women's doubles 12 times, from 1942 to 1950 and from 1955 to 1957; the Wimbledon doubles in 1946, 1948, 1950, and 1954; and the French in 1946, 1947, and 1949. With other partners, du Pont added the U.S. doubles title in 1941 and 1958. In U.S. championships she won a record number of titles, 25 in all. In 1962, 16 years after she won her first championship at Wimbledon, du Pont teamed with Neale Fraser to capture the Wimbledon mixed doubles. She was a member of the Wightman Cup team ten times between 1946 and 1962.

Du Pont's game was powerful, featuring a terrific volley and backhand smash. She and Brough were elected to the International Tennis Hall of Fame in the same year, 1967.

TED WILLIAMS

Theodore Samuel Williams
b. San Diego, Calif., Aug. 30, 1918

A rangy left-handed-hitting outfielder, Ted Williams displayed unusual talent at the plate. He was both consistent and powerful. Consider his 1942 record, when he led the American League in batting with a .356 average, in home runs with 36, and in runs batted in with 137.

After playing in the minor leagues, Williams joined the Boston Red Sox in 1949 and played for them through 1960, except for his service in World War II, from 1943 to 1945, and again in the Korean War, in 1952 and 1953. Had it not been for the seasons Williams missed, his record

would have been even more impressive. Williams led the league in batting in 1941, 1942, 1946, 1947, 1948, 1957, and 1958. He also led in home runs in 1941, 1942, 1947, and 1949.

His career total of 521 homers ties him for ninth place. With 2654 hits, he had a career batting average of .344. That pitchers feared him is shown by his 2019 bases on balls, second only to the record held by Babe Ruth, and he struck out only 709 times. In 1957, he got on base 16 consecutive times with four home runs, two singles, nine walks, and one hit-by-pitch.

Williams appeared in only one World Series, in 1946, when the Red

Sox lost to the St. Louis Cardinals. After his playing days, he managed Washington from 1969 to 1971 and stayed on for one more year when the franchise moved and became the Texas Rangers. His record as a manager was 273 won and 364 lost.

Williams would never play up to the crowds; in fact, he seemed to resent the fans and positively disliked reporters. In 1956, he was fined $5000 by the Red Sox for spitting at fans and newspapermen. He had been fined lesser amounts for similar offenses twice before. Williams was elected to the Baseball Hall of Fame in 1966.

Alice Marble introduced shorts to the hallowed venues of tennis.

This year's **national college football championship** was won by Harvard, with a record of nine wins, no losses, one tie.

The **NHL Stanley Cup** championship was halted because of an outbreak of influenza, which incapacitated several players and killed one. The Seattle Metropolitans and Montreal Canadiens were tied at two games each, with one tie game.

Jan. 1 The fifth **Tournament of Roses Association football game** (Rose Bowl) was won by the Great Lakes Naval Training Station team, which beat the Mare Island Marines 17-0.

Feb. 22 At the **Westminster Kennel Club** dog show, Ch. Briergate Bright Beauty, an Airedale owned by G. L. L. Davis of St. Louis, Mo., took best-in-show.

Feb. 22-26 The horseshoe pitchers of the U.S. held their **annual world championship** for the first time in the winter and also for the first time in the South. It was held at St. Petersburg, Fla. Another first was the pitching distance, 40 ft., now standardized. The winner was Fred Burst of Columbus, Ohio. At the tourney's end, the players organized the National League of Horseshoe and Quoit Pitchers.

Apr. 19 The 23rd **Boston Marathon** was won by

Carl W. A. Linder of Quincy, Mass., in 2 hrs., 29 min., 13 sec.

Apr. 28 The first recorded **delayed parachute jump** was performed by Leslie Irvin, whose plane took off from McCook Field near Dayton, Ohio. Jumping from 1500 ft. with a manually released parachute, Irvin delayed several seconds in free fall before pulling the cord. Prior to this feat it had been believed that such a jumper would lose consciousness so rapidly that he would not have time to pull the cord.

May 10 The 45th annual **Kentucky Derby** was won by Sir Barton, ridden by Johnny Loftus, with a time of 2:09⅘. Sir Barton, ridden by Loftus, went on to win the Preakness and Belmont Stakes, thereby becoming the first horse to win racing's Triple Crown.

May 14 The 44th annual **Preakness Stakes** was won by Sir Barton, with a time of 1:53. The jockey was Johnny Loftus.

May 31 The seventh annual **Indianapolis 500** auto race marked the resumption of the racing classic after a two-year hiatus. Howard Wilcox won, completing the course in 5 hrs., 40 min., 42.87 sec., at an average speed of 88.05 mph.

June 11 The first postwar **U.S. Open golf tournament** was won by Walter Hagen at Brae Burn Country Club, West Newton, Mass., with a 301

BOB FELLER

Robert William Andrew Feller
b. Van Meter, Iowa, Nov. 3, 1918

Right-hander Bob Feller's fastball made him one of major league baseball's leading pitchers for 18 seasons between 1936 and 1956. He played for the Cleveland Indians and was in the U.S. armed forces from 1942 to 1944. His records and achievements might have been even more impressive had he not lost those three seasons.

In Rapid Robert's career, he won

266 games and lost 162 for a percentage of .621. He struck out 2581 batters, placing him 14th on the all-time list. His earned run average was 3.25. Six times Feller won 20 or more games in a season. In his first start for Cleveland, on August 23, 1936, when he was only 17, he fanned 15 batters, one short of the American League record. He bettered this mark on October 2, 1938, when he struck out 18 Detroit batters for a new major league record, but Cleveland lost the game.

Feller pitched a total of three no-hit games and 12 one-hitters. His first no-hit game came on opening day, April 16, 1940, against the Chicago White Sox. His second came on April 3, 1946, and he pitched his third—a modern record for pitchers at that time—on July 5, 1951.

Feller appeared in only one World Series, that of 1948 against the Boston Braves, and he lost both games he pitched. He was elected to the Baseball Hall of Fame in 1962.

total and a playoff victory over Michael Brady.

June 11   The 51st annual **Belmont Stakes** was won by Sir Barton, with a time of 2:17⅖. The jockey was Johnny Loftus. This victory completed Sir Barton's Triple Crown.

June 21   The **U.S. Lawn Tennis Association singles championships** were won by Hazel Hotchkiss in the women's division and William M. Johnston over Bill Tilden in the men's division (Sept. 4).

July 4   The **world heavyweight boxing championship** was won by Jack Dempsey, who knocked out Jess Willard in the third round of their bout in Toledo, Ohio.

Sept. 20   The **PGA golf tournament** was won by Jim Barnes, who defeated Fred McLeod in the final round, 6 and 5, at Engineers Country Club, Roslyn, N.Y.

Oct. 1-9   The 16th annual **World Series** was won by the Cincinnati Reds (NL), who defeated the Chicago White Sox (AL) five games to three in a best-of-nine series, which the major leagues adopted from 1919 through 1921. This was the infamous series in which seven White Sox players agreed to throw the series to Cincinnati. The only principal players who were untainted by the scandal were Eddie Collins, second base; Ray Schalk, catcher; Nemo Leibold, right

JACKIE ROBINSON

Jack Roosevelt Robinson
b. Cairo, Ga., Jan. 31, 1919
d. Stamford, Conn., Oct. 24, 1972

Jackie Robinson is remembered, even by those who know little about sports, as the baseball player who broke the color bar in the major leagues. He was a fine fielder at second base, a consistent hitter, and a constant threat on the base paths. He had starred at baseball, football, basketball, and track at UCLA and served in the U.S. Army from 1942 to 1945, emerging as a lieutenant, before Branch Rickey signed him for

the Brooklyn Dodgers. He was sent first to the Montreal Royals of the International League, where on April 18, 1946, he became the first black to play in that organization.

On April 11, 1947, Robinson played his first major league game. It was an exhibition game between the Dodgers and the New York Yankees. He met considerable prejudice at first, being subjected to racial insults and segregation in eating and housing. Encouraged by Branch Rickey, president of the Dodgers, Robinson stuck it out and so paved the way for the many others of his

race who followed him into professional baseball.

He played for ten years with Brooklyn, being voted rookie of the year in 1947 and most valuable player in 1949, when he also led the National League in batting with a .342 average. Over his career, he batted .311, with 1518 hits, 137 home runs, 197 stolen bases, and 740 bases on balls. Robinson appeared in six World Series between 1947 and 1956. In 1962, he became the first black elected to the Baseball Hall of Fame.

fielder; and pitchers Red Faber and Dickie Kerr. Kerr won two games despite the machinations of his subverted teammates.

Oct. 30 The **spitball and shineball** were outlawed by the rules committees of baseball's two major leagues. Application of any foreign substance to the baseball by a pitcher was made unacceptable.

1920

A **new type of sailboat,** sold under the trademark name of Sailfish, was produced at Waterbury, Conn., by Alexander Bryan and Cortland Heyniger. Later they added two Super Sailfish models and a Sunfish. This began the era of boardboats, or sailing surfboards, which accelerate rapidly, plane, and require agility to manage.

The **Harmsworth Cup** was won for the first time by a U.S. entry, Gar Wood's *Miss America.* Later versions of *Miss America* also won the cup, donated by Lord Northcliffe, an English newspaper publisher.

The **first national tournament for women horseshoe pitchers** was won by Marjorie Voorhies.

The **Negro National League** was formed to play professional baseball. It was followed by the Negro Eastern League in 1921. Both failed in the Great Depression and were succeeded in 1936 by a two-division Negro American League.

William H. Foster, a founding father of skeet shooting, became associate editor of *National Sportsman* and *Hunting and Fishing.* Skeet shooting rules were now specific, and Foster's articles on the sport gave it the boost it needed to attract new adherents across the nation.

This year's **national college football championship** was won by California, with a record of nine wins, no losses, no ties.

Jan. 1 The sixth **Tournament of Roses Association football game** (Rose Bowl) was won by Harvard, which edged out Oregon 7-6.

Jan. 5 The New York Yankees purchased **Babe Ruth** from the Boston Red Sox for $125,000. In 1919, transformed from a top-notch pitcher to an outfielder, Ruth had hit a record 29 home runs. In 1920 he hit 54 for New York. No other player has had so profound an effect on the style of the game.

Feb. 14 At the **Westminster Kennel Club** dog show, Ch. Conejo Wycollar Boy, a wire fox terrier owned by Mrs. Roy A. Rainey of Huntington, Long Island, N.Y., took best-in-show.

Mar. 20 **U.S. figure skating championships** were won by Sherwin C. Badger, men's singles; Theresa Weld, women's singles; and Theresa Weld and Nathaniel W. Niles, pairs (Mar. 21).

Apr. 1 The **NHL Stanley Cup** championship was won by the Ottawa Senators, who took the fifth game of the series to beat the Seattle Metropolitans three games to two.

Apr. 19 The 24th **Boston Marathon** was won by Peter Trivoulidas of Greece with a time of 2 hrs., 29 min., 31 sec.

Apr. 20-Sept. 12 At the **Olympic Games** in Antwerp, Belgium, the U.S. won the unofficial team championship, winning nine gold medals. Finland was the second-place team. The team of 15 U.S. women swimmers was the first to gain full

TOM HARMON

Thomas Dudley Harmon
b. Rensselaer, Ind., Sept. 28, 1919

Tom Harmon remains the University of Michigan's greatest football hero and one of the best college players ever. Unlike many college stars, however, he did not have a career of consequence in pro football.

A star in high school, he entered Michigan in 1937 and in his three varsity years as a running back scored 33 touchdowns and 237 points. He was chosen for the all-American team in 1939 and 1940 and in the latter year also won the Heisman Trophy.

An airplane pilot in World War II,

Harmon was twice reported missing but both times turned up safely. After the war, he played for one season with the Los Angeles Rams of the NFL, 1946–1947, and then retired to become a sportscaster. Harmon is a member of the College Football Hall of Fame.

SUGAR RAY ROBINSON

Walker Smith
b. Detroit, Mich., May 3, 1920

Not only has Sugar Ray Robinson won and lost more boxing titles than any other fighter, but he is also generally acknowledged to be the best fighter of his day, pound for pound. About 1938 he adopted the name Ray Robinson from another fighter. The "Sugar" was added later after a sportswriter declared him "the sweetest fighter . . . sweet as sugar."

As an amateur, Robinson won all of his 89 bouts, including, in 1939, the Golden Gloves featherweight title. Turning pro in 1940, he won 122 of his first 123 fights. After military service, from 1943 to 1945, he won the welterweight championship from Tommy Bell in 1946. He then stepped up to the middleweight title in February 1951, when he knocked out Jake La Motta. That same year, he lost this title to Randy Turpin and then won it back.

On June 25, 1952, Robinson tried for the light heavyweight championship but, falling victim to heat prostration, lost to Joey Maxim in the 13th round. In December 1955, he won the middleweight championship for the third time when he defeated Bobo Olson.

Thereafter, Robinson lost, regained, and again lost the middleweight title in 1957. Finally, on March 25, 1958, he regained this title for the fifth time, defeating Carmen Basilio, thereby setting his unequaled record for winning and losing a championship. In 1960, he lost this title for the last time, to Tom Pender.

Robinson retired in 1965, having won 175 of 202 bouts, more than half by knockouts. Both defensively and offensively, he was a superior boxer, lightning fast and a devastating combination puncher.

---

status as part of the U.S. Olympic team. Ethelda Bleibtrey won the 100-m. freestyle, Aileen Riggin won the springboard dive competition, and the U.S. won the 400-m. freestyle relay. Charlie Paddock won the 100-m. dash with a time of 10.8 sec., and Duke Kahanamoku won the 100-m. freestyle swimming event in 1 min., 1.4 sec. He had also won this event in the 1912 Olympics.

May 1 The **longest game (in innings) ever played** in the major leagues was pitched by Joe Oeschger of the Boston Braves and Leon Cadore of the Brooklyn Robins. They dueled in Braves Field to a 26-inning 1-1 tie called by darkness.

May 8 The 46th annual **Kentucky Derby** was won by Paul Jones, with a time of 2:09. The jockey was T. Rice.

May 18 The 45th annual **Preakness Stakes** was won by Man o' War, with a time of 1:51 3/5. The jockey was Clarence Kummer.

May 31 The eighth **Indianapolis 500** auto race was won by Gaston Chevrolet, completing the 500-mi. course in 5 hrs., 38 min., 32 sec., at an average speed of 88.62 mph.

June 4 The American single sculls champion, **John B. Kelly, Sr., was barred** from the Royal Henley Regatta in England. He was the leading oarsman of the Vesper Boat Club of Philadelphia, which had been banned from Henley previously because of alleged infringements of the amateur code. Kelly won the Olympic single sculls title later this year.

June 12 The 52nd annual **Belmont Stakes** was won by Man o' War, with a time of 2:14 1/5. The jockey was Clarence Kummer.

June 26 In the **3000-m. walk** at Philadelphia, William Plant set a new American record of 12 min., 51 2/5 sec. during the Olympic tryouts.

July 3 At the **Wimbledon** tennis championships in England, Bill Tilden won the men's singles title, defeating Australian Gerald Patterson in four sets.

July 9-16 The **Davis Cup** international tennis challenge round, for the first time since 1913, was won by the U.S., which swept Australia in five straight matches. The U.S. team comprised "Big Bill" Tilden and William M. "Little Bill" Johnston.

July 15-27 The **America's Cup** was successfully defended by the U.S. yacht *Resolute*, defeating

---

Say it ain't so, Joe!

Attributed to a young fan confronting Joe Jackson of the Chicago White Sox, after hearing that Jackson had conspired with gamblers to fix the 1919 World Series

the British challenger *Shamrock IV* three races to two.

Aug. 13 The U.S. **Open golf tournament** was won by veteran Ted Ray of England, with a 295 total at the Inverness Club, Toledo, Ohio.

Aug. 16 Ray Chapman, shortstop for the Cleveland Indians, was **struck in the head** by a fastball thrown by pitcher Carl Mays of the New York Yankees, at the Polo Grounds in New York City. Chapman never regained consciousness. His death on the next day was major league baseball's first and only game-related fatality.

Aug. 21 The **PGA golf tournament** was won by Jock Hutchison in a 1-up victory over J. Douglas Edgar at Flossmoor Country Club, Flossmoor, Ill.

Sept. The **Walker Law,** legalizing boxing in New York State and regulating the conduct of boxing matches, was passed. The subsequent success of boxing in New York led to similar legislation in other states.

Sept. 6 The **U.S. Lawn Tennis Association singles championships** were won by Bill Tilden in the men's division and Molla Bjurstedt Mallory in the women's division (Sept. 25). It took Tilden five sets to turn back William M. Johnston.

Sept. 17 The **forerunner of the National Football League,** the American Professional Football Association, was founded in an automobile showroom in Canton, Ohio. Twelve teams paid a fee of $100 each to obtain franchises. The

MAN O' WAR'S LAST VICTORY

On October 12, 1920, the racehorse that 30 years later would be voted the greatest thoroughbred of the first half of the twentieth century closed out a spectacular career with a convincing seven-length victory in a match race at the Kenilworth track in Windsor, Ontario, Canada. With Jockey Kummer up, 3-year-old champion Man o' War, owned by Samuel D. Riddle of Glen Riddle, Pennsylvania, was opposed by Sir Barton, a 3-year-old owned by Commander J. K. L. Ross of Canada. Sir Barton was considered by some to have a real chance of besting the great Man o' War, known affectionately as Big Red, which had been bought as a yearling by Riddle for $5000 and would later bring an offer of $1 million from another owner, an offer that was refused.

The two-horse race was to be run at a distance of a mile and a quarter, with a $75,000 purse to the winner. Perfect autumn weather prevailed, ideal for racing, and the track was fast, so there would be no excuse for the loser. In attendance were 21,000 fans, the largest crowd assembled at a Canadian track up to that time. They were eager to have the chance of seeing the great Man o' War

perform. Many of those present had come from the United States and from remote parts of Canada to see the race, and they filled all available Ontario hotel rooms.

What they would witness was far from a thrilling match race. Indeed, Jockey Keogh aboard Sir Barton would say after the race that he knew his horse was through by the time it had run the first sixteenth of a mile. Newsmen in attendance called the race a ridiculously easy win for Man o' War, since the horse was never fully extended. Yet the race was not without interest for those who saw it.

The horses were required to break from a standing start, and Man o' War was caught flatfooted by the fast-breaking Sir Barton. Within the first 60 yards, however, Man o' War had drawn even with Sir Barton and never was headed again. Power and speed paid off for Big Red, and though the time of 2:03 for the mile and a quarter was not especially fast, it was almost 7 seconds below the previous Kenilworth track record. And this was accomplished by a horse that was not challenged seriously. In fact, Jockey Kummer on Big Red held his mount back in the

last quarter mile, and track fans who saw the race claimed later that Man o' War, eager to run, was straining at the bit.

For once, the betting fans had been right in their assessment of the outcome of the match race. By the time the betting windows closed, $132,000 had been bet on the winning horse and only $14,000 on the loser. Thus a bet of $2 brought the winning ticketholder only $2.10, which translates into odds of 1–20 on the winner.

For Man o' War, the $75,000 purse brought lifetime earnings to $249,465, more than any other U.S.-trained horse until that date and fourth among the thoroughbreds of the entire world. Raced in 1919 and 1920, Big Red won 20 of a total of 21 races. The one loss came at Saratoga, New York, in August 1919, when an aptly named horse defeated the great thoroughbred by half a length. The horse was named Upset, and it must be said out of respect for Man o' War that Upset carried 15 pounds less weight in the race.

The otherwise undefeated Man o' War was retired to stud after the victory over Sir Barton, and it was in retirement that Big Red died in 1947.

STAN MUSIAL

Stanley Frank Musial
b. Donora, Pa., Nov. 21, 1920

Stan Musial began his baseball career as a pitcher in the minor leagues and became a highly competent outfielder and first baseman in the majors, but he is remembered and respected most for his consistency as a hitter. With the St.Louis Cardinals from 1941 to 1963, he ended his career with a total of 3630 hits, a National League record at the time.

Voted his league's most valuable player in 1943, 1946, and 1948, Stan the Man also led the league in batting in those years, and from 1950 through 1952 and again in 1957, he won a total of seven batting titles. His best average was .376 in 1948, and his career batting average was .331. Musial ranks sixth in the big leagues in runs scored, 1949, and he batted in a total of 1951 runs.

Musial hit 475 home runs, 16th highest of all time, and in six seasons had 30 or more, his high being 39 in 1948. On May 2, 1954, Musial hit five home runs in a doubleheader, a record not equaled until 1972. In the all-star game of July 12, 1955, he hit a home run in the bottom of the 12th inning that won the game for the National League. Musial appeared in four World Series, 1942, 1943, 1944, and 1946, of which the Cardinals won three.

In 1956, the *Sporting News* named Musial the best baseball player of the decade, with Joe DiMaggio second. Musial was elected to the Baseball Hall of Fame in 1969.

---

association went out of business after one season but started up again in 1921 with 13 teams. The Chicago Staleys, who in 1922 became the Chicago Bears, won the championship.

Sept. 28 In what came to be known as the **Black Sox scandal,** eight players of the Chicago White Sox team of 1919 were indicted on charges of fixing the outcome of the World Series of that year, in which the favored Sox were defeated by the Cincinnati Reds.

Oct. 5-12 The 17th annual **World Series** was won by the Cleveland Indians (AL), who beat the Brooklyn Dodgers (NL) five games to two. Stan Covaleski, allowing two runs and 15 hits in 27 innings, won three games for the Indians.

Oct. 10 **Two firsts in World Series play** highlighted Cleveland's 8-1 victory over Brooklyn. Outfielder Elmer Smith of Cleveland hit a grand slam home run in the first inning. In the fifth inning, Cleveland second baseman Bill Wambsganss pulled off an unassisted triple play when he snared a liner near second base while Brooklyn runners were moving on a hit-and-run play.

Nov. 12 Seeking to **reestablish public confidence** in major league baseball, the club owners turned to Judge Kenesaw Mountain Landis and chose him commissioner of baseball, with absolute powers, for a term of seven years. The previous three-man National Commission was discarded.

Nov. 25 The **first radio broadcast of a college football game** was made over station WTAW of College Station, Tex., which carried an ac-count of the Texas-Texas A&M contest. The first coast-to-coast college football broadcast was made on Oct. 28, 1922. It was the Chicago-Princeton game, played in Chicago.

Dec. 13 The **heavyweight wrestling championship,** catch-as-catch-can style, was won by Ed "Strangler" Lewis, who pinned the defending champion, Joe Stecher, after nearly 2 hrs. of wrestling. Noting that women were "conspicuous in the gathering," the *New York Times* reported that they "shouted with a fervor which rivaled that of the male spectators."

Dec. 23 Jigoro Kano, the originator of **judo,** demonstrated the martial art that was said to be replacing jujitsu in Japan before an audience of several hundred men at the New York Athletic Club. Kano, over 60, presented judo as a plan for physical, mental, and moral culture as well as a martial art.

1921

Paddle tennis had its start this year, when Rev. Frank Peer Beal, associate minister of the Judson Memorial Church at Washington Square, New York City, laid out a court of half the dimensions of a tennis court and raised an impromptu net on the floor of the church gymnasium.

The **U.S. polo team** recaptured the Westchester

Cup by defeating Great Britain at Hurlingham, 11-4 and 10-6. The U.S. team members were Louis E. Stoddard, Thomas Hitchcock, Jr., J. Watson Webb, and Devereux Milburn. The trophy was successfully defended by U.S. teams about every three years until the outbreak of World War II.

This year's **national college football championship** was won by Cornell, with a record of eight wins, no losses, no ties.

The **NHL Stanley Cup** was won by the Ottawa Senators, who defeated the Vancouver Millionaires three games to two.

Jan. 1 The seventh **Tournament of Roses Association football game** (Rose Bowl) was won by California, who beat Ohio State 28-0.

Feb. 12 At the **Westminster Kennel Club** dog show, Ch. Midkiff Seductive, a cocker spaniel owned by W. T. Payne of Kingston, Pa., took best-in-show.

Feb. 26-27 **U.S. figure skating championships** were won in Philadelphia by Theresa Weld Blanchard, women's singles; Sherwin C. Badger, men's singles; and Theresa Weld Blanchard and Nathaniel W. Niles, pairs.

Apr. 19 The 25th **Boston Marathon** was won by Frank Zuna of New York City, with a time of 2 hrs., 18 min., 57.6 sec.

May 6 The **American Soccer League** was formed by eight leading northeastern professional clubs at a meeting held at the Hotel Astor in New York City. Most of the clubs were sponsored by industrial concerns.

May 6 The catch-as-catch-can **world heavyweight championship** was won by Stanislaus

Zbyszko in New York City, who defeated Strangler Lewis in 23 min., 17 sec.

May 7 The 47th annual **Kentucky Derby** was won by Behave Yourself, with a time of 2:04$\frac{1}{5}$. The jockey was Charles Thompson.

May 10 The **National Horseshoe Pitching Association** of the U.S. was incorporated in the state of Ohio by members of the National League of Horseshoe and Quoit Pitchers, who wanted an organization devoted solely to horseshoes.

May 16 The 46th annual **Preakness Stakes** was won by Broomspun, with a time of 1:54$\frac{1}{5}$. The jockey was F. Coltiletti.

May 30 The ninth annual **Indianapolis 500** auto race was won by Tommy Milton, completing the course in 5 hrs., 34 min., 44.65 sec., at an average speed of 89.62 mph.

June 11 The 53rd annual **Belmont Stakes** was won by Grey Lag, with a time of 2:16$\frac{4}{5}$. The jockey was Earl Sande.

June 17-18 The **first NCAA track and field championships** were held at the U. of Chicago. There were entries from 62 colleges and universities. The U. of Illinois won this first championship with 20$\frac{1}{4}$ points. Notre Dame was second with 16$\frac{3}{4}$, and Iowa third with 12$\frac{1}{4}$.

June 25 Jock Hutchison, of Chicago, became the **first American to win the British Open.**

June 29 At the **Wimbledon** tennis championships, Elizabeth Ryan won the women's singles title. Bill Tilden won the men's title on July 2, defeating B. I. C. Norton of South Africa.

July 2 The **world heavyweight boxing championship** was defended by Jack Dempsey, who

WARREN SPAHN

Warren Edward Spahn
b. Buffalo, N.Y., Apr. 23, 1921

Warren Spahn won a career total of 363 games, more than any other left-handed pitcher in major league baseball, and ranks fifth among all winning pitchers. He suffered 243 career losses, for a winning percentage of .597. Spahn set his record over 24 years, beginning with the Boston Braves—later the Milwaukee Braves—between 1942 and 1964. There was time out for World War II service, in which he won a battlefield commission in the European theater. Spahn ended his career with the New York Mets and the San Francisco Giants in 1965.

Spahn pitched 63 shutouts, placing him sixth in this category, and had an earned run average of 3.09. On September 7, 1963, he became a 20-game winner for the 13th season, tying the record set by Christy Mathewson. His superior control is reflected in his totals of 2583 strikeouts and only 1434 bases on balls.

He appeared in the World Series of 1948, 1957, and 1958, winning four games and losing three. Spahn did not retire until he was 43 years old and was elected to the Baseball Hall of Fame in 1973.

OTTO GRAHAM

Otto Everett Graham
b. Waukegan, Ill., Dec. 6, 1921

As quarterback of the Cleveland Browns from 1946 to 1955, before the merger of the American Football League with the National, Otto Graham was the league's dominant player at his position. In his first year as a professional, he led the Browns to a 14–9 victory for the league championship over the New York Yankees. In that game, his best of the year, Graham completed 16 of 27 passes.

On December 24, 1950, Graham did even better, leading the Browns to a 30–28 victory for another league championship over the Los Angeles Rams. He completed 22 of 32 passes for four touchdowns and 298 yards.

Graham played college football at Northwestern University, where he made all-American in 1943, and he served in the Navy during 1944 and 1945 before becoming a pro. After his playing days ended, from 1959 to 1966, Graham was football coach and athletic director at the U.S. Coast Guard Academy. After a stint, from 1966 to 1968, as general manager and head coach of the Washington Redskins, he returned to the Academy as athletic director, serving from 1970 to 1985.

Graham was elected to the College Football Hall of Fame in 1955 and the Pro Football Hall of Fame in 1965.

---

knocked out Georges Carpentier in the fourth round. This was the first fight with a $1,000,000 gate and the first championship fight to be broadcast over the radio.

July 22 The **U.S. Open golf tournament** was won by Jim Barnes at Columbia Country Club, Chevy Chase, Md. His 289 total edged out Walter Hagen, Leo Diegel, Jock Hutchison, and Fred McLeod.

Aug. 1 A new **roller skating speed record** was set in competition at Reading, Pa., by Frank Klopp, international amateur champion, of Philadelphia. He skated 1 mi. in 2 min., 40⅗ sec.

Aug. 3 The Chicago White Sox baseball players charged with **fixing the 1919 World Series** were acquitted and freed on a technicality. Despite their acquittal, Commissioner Kenesaw Mountain Landis immediately announced that the men would never again be allowed to play professional baseball.

Aug. 20 The **U.S. Lawn Tennis Association singles championships** were won by Molla Bjurstedt Mallory in the women's division and Bill Tilden over Wallace F. Johnson in the men's division (Sept. 19). The women's tournament had been moved to Forest Hills, N.Y. and the men's to Philadelphia, where it would remain for two more years.

Sept. 3 The **Davis Cup** international tennis challenge round was won by the U.S., defeating the Japanese team in five straight matches.

Sept. 28 The **PGA golf tournament** was won by Walter Hagen with a 3 and 2 win over Jim Barnes at Inwood Country Club, Far Rockaway, N.Y.

Oct. 5 The **first radio coverage of the World Series** was carried by a wireless station set up at the Electrical Show at the 71st Regiment Armory in New York City and by station WJZ in Newark, N.J. Both stations carried play-by-play bulletins. The first actual play-by-play coverage began in 1922.

Oct. 5-13 The 18th annual **World Series** was won by the New York Giants (NL), who beat the New York Yankees (AL) five games to three. A bad arm kept Babe Ruth out of the last three games, and Giant pitching silenced Yankee bats. The Yankee team batting average was a puny .207.

1922

Water skiing was invented by Minnesotan Ralph W. Samuelson.

The **first men's national volleyball championship** was played at Pittsburgh, Pa., with the Brooklyn, N.Y., YMCA the winner.

Paddle tennis spread rapidly in New York City after the director of recreation of the Department of Parks had allowed suitable park space to be used for the game. Play on certain city streets followed. A tournament, the first, was won by Dalio Santini.

Princeton won the **first intercollegiate polo**

championship, played by three-man teams indoors.

The **NHL Stanley Cup** was won by the Toronto St. Pats, who defeated the Vancouver Millionaires three games to two.

This year's **national college football championship** was won by Cornell, with a record of eight wins, no losses, no ties.

Jan. 1   The eighth **Tournament of Roses Association football game** (Rose Bowl) was played to a scoreless tie by Washington and Jefferson College and California.

Jan. 22   The **International Star Class Yacht Racing Association** was launched at the Hotel Astor, New York City. Actually founded in 1921, the vigorous association pushed sales of the 22-ft., 9-in. one-design boat into more than 30 countries, including Russia. The Star was the first class chosen for Olympic competition.

Feb. 15   At the **Westminster Kennel Club** dog show, Ch. Boxwood Barkentine, an American airedale owned by Frederic C. Hodd of Brookline, Mass., took best-in-show.

Mar. 3   Strangler Lewis regained the **world heavyweight wrestling title** by beating Stanislaus Zbyszko two falls to one at Wichita, Kans.

Mar. 7   **U.S. figure skating championships** were won by Theresa Weld Blanchard, women's singles; Sherwin C. Badger, men's singles; and Theresa Weld Blanchard and Nathaniel W. Niles, pairs.

Mar. 11   The **first IC4A indoor track meet** was held at the 2nd Regiment Armory in New York City. Cornell's team finished first, with Dartmouth second and Pennsylvania third. Leroy Brown of Dartmouth set a new world indoor record for the high jump when he cleared 6 ft., 4⅞ in.

Mar. 25   **Johnny Weissmuller,** age 17, set the first two of his many world swimming records, for 300 yards and for 300 m.

Apr.   The board of governors of the **Amateur Athletic Union** was requested to provide competitions for women. Swimming and track and field were the first AAU women's sports. In January 1923 the AAU approved registration for women in all the sports under its jurisdiction.

Apr. 16   The famous sharpshooter **Annie Oakley,** who had been a star of Buffalo Bill's Wild West Show from 1885 to 1902, demonstrated that she still retained her skill when she broke 100 clay targets in a row in a trapshooting event at Pinehurst, N.C. This was believed to be a record for women shooters.

Apr. 19   The 26th **Boston Marathon** was won by Clarence H. DeMar of Melrose, Mass., in a record time of 2 hrs., 18 min., 10 sec., breaking the old record by 47.53 sec.

May 13   The 48th annual **Kentucky Derby** was won by Morvich, with a time of 2:04⅗. The jockey was Albert Johnson.

May 13   The 47th annual **Preakness Stakes** was won by Pillory, with a time of 1:51⅗. The jockey was L. Morris.

May 20   The **suspension of Babe Ruth and Bob Meusel,** imposed in the fall of 1921 by Commissioner Kenesaw Mountain Landis, ended. Ruth and his fellow Yankee outfielder had gone on a barnstorming tour after the 1921 World Series in the face of explicit disapproval by the Commissioner. Landis thus established the finality of his decisions.

May 30   The tenth annual **Indianapolis 500** auto race was won by Jimmy Murphy, completing the 500-mi. course in 5 hrs., 17 min., 30.79 sec., for a record average speed of 94.48 mph.

June 10   The 54th annual **Belmont Stakes** was won by Pillory, with a time of 2:18⅘. The jockey was C. H. Miller.

June 14   The **PGA golf tournament** was won by Gene Sarazen, who defeated Emmet French in the final round, 4 and 3, at Oakmont Country Club, Oakmont, Pa.

July 15   Gene Sarazen won the **U.S. Open golf tournament** at Skokie Country Club, Glencoe, Ill., his last-round 68 edging out Bobby Jones and John Black.

Aug. 19   The **U.S. Lawn Tennis Association singles championships** were won by Molla Bjurstedt Mallory in the women's division and Bill Tilden in the men's division (Sept. 6). Both won for the third consecutive time, Mrs. Mallory for the sixth time overall. Tilden was hard put to defeat William M. Johnston in five sets.

Aug. 28   The **oldest American international team golf match,** the Walker Cup, between the U.S. and Great Britain, was established with the opening of play at the National Golf Links of America, Southampton, N.Y. The U.S. team won the match 8-4.

Aug. 31-Sept. 5   The **Davis Cup** international tennis challenge round was won for the third straight year by the U.S., defeating Australia four matches to one.

Oct. 4-8 The 19th annual **World Series** was won by the New York Giants (NL), who took four of five games from the New York Yankees (AL). The second game of the series (Oct. 5) had ended in a 3-3 tie after ten innings when the game was called on account of darkness. Babe Ruth was held to two hits in 17 appearances, and his team's batting average for the series was only .203.

Oct. 20 Lt. Harold Harris became the first member of the **Caterpillar Club** by parachuting from a defective airplane during a test flight at McCook Field in Dayton, Ohio. Members of the Caterpillar Club are those who have escaped death by using a parachute.

Nov. **Howie Morenz,** age 20, played his first professional ice hockey game for the Montreal Canadiens. For 15 years he was to be the outstanding forward in professional hockey.

1923

Stanley W. Pearson, of Philadelphia, won the national squash racquets championship for the sixth time in the last seven competitions for it. The string was interrupted only in 1920 by Charles C. Peabody of Boston.

The **U.S. Paddle Tennis Association** was formed, known at first and until 1926 as the American Paddle Tennis Association, a name later adopted as well by the Platform Paddle Tennis Organization.

The **North American figure skating championships** for men, women, pairs, and fours were initiated as a competition for teams representing the U.S. and Canada, to be held every two years, with the countries alternating as hosts.

A concrete stadium for tennis matches replaced the former wooden stands at the **West Side Tennis Club** in Forest Hills, N.Y. The first Wightman Cup match was the inaugural event. In 1924 the national championships returned to the West Side Tennis Club after three years at Germantown, Philadelphia.

Mrs. George W. Wightman, the former U.S. women's champion, who played under her maiden name, Hazel Hotchkiss, donated the **Wightman Cup** for tennis team competition between the U.S.

and England. It was first contested this year, with the U.S. winning 7-0 at Forest Hills, N.Y.

This year's **national college football championship** was won by Illinois, with a record of eight wins, no losses, no ties.

The **NHL Stanley Cup** was won by the Ottawa Senators, who beat the Vancouver Millionaires three games to one. They also defeated the Edmonton Eskimos in two straight games.

Jan. The **Amateur Athletic Union** (AAU) authorized registration for women in all sports under its governance.

Jan. 1 The ninth **Tournament of Roses Association football game,** which was officially renamed the Rose Bowl game this year, was won by Southern California, beating Penn State 14-3.

Jan. 9 The **Amateur Trapshooting Association of America** was founded. At the same time it took over control of the sport from the Interstate Manufacturers Trapshooting Association. The permanent home of the association, in Vandalia, Ohio, was dedicated in 1924, and the Grand American tournaments are held there annually. The Trapshooting Hall of Fame and Museum was dedicated in Vandalia in 1969.

Feb. 15-16 U.S. figure skating championships were won by Theresa Weld Blanchard, women's singles; Sherwin C. Badger, men's singles; and Theresa Weld Blanchard and Nathaniel W. Niles, pairs.

Apr. 12-13 The **first three-weapon championships** of the Intercollegiate Fencing Association were held at the Hotel Astor, New York City. Army won the overall three-weapon trophy as well as the saber and épée titles. Harvard won in foils.

Apr. 18 The New York **Yankees opened Yankee Stadium,** "the house that Ruth built," before 74,200 fans, with 25,000 turned away. Fittingly, Babe Ruth hit a three-run home run off Howard Ehmke as the Yanks beat the Boston Red Sox 4-1.

Apr. 18 Charley Robertson, a pitcher for the Chicago White Sox, pitched a **perfect game** against the Detroit Tigers, with no runner reaching first base. This was the third such game since the adoption of modern pitching rules, and the first since 1908.

Apr. 19 The 27th **Boston Marathon** was won by Clarence H. DeMar of Melrose, Mass., in 2 hrs., 23 min., 47.35 sec.

May 2-3 The **first nonstop transcontinental**

LOUISE BROUGH

Althea Louise Brough
b. Oklahoma City, Okla., Mar. 11, 1923

Although Louise Brough won the women's tennis singles title in the United States, England, and Australia, she is remembered equally for the many doubles titles she captured. She was given tennis lessons as a birthday present when she was 14. Ten years later, in 1947, she became the American women's singles champion. She never won it again but was runner-up five times.

Brough was more successful in England, where she won the singles crown at Wimbleton for three straight years, 1948, 1949, and 1950, and again in 1955. She was also runner-up three times. At the 1948 and 1950 Wimbledon events, Brough became only the third person to win the triple crown, taking not only the singles but also the women's doubles and the mixed doubles. The Australian title was hers in 1950.

With her favorite partner, Margaret Osborne du Pont, Brough won the U.S. doubles 12 times, from 1942 to 1950, and in 1955, 1956, and 1957; the Wimbledon doubles five times,

1946, 1948, 1949, 1950, and 1954; the French doubles three times, 1946, 1947, and 1949; and the Australian doubles in 1950 with Doris Hart. She also scored victories in both the U.S. and Wimbledon mixed doubles four times each. As a member of the Wightman Cup team, 1946–1957, she won all 22 of her matches.

Brough's game exploited the strength of her backhand and her steady serve. She was elected to the International Tennis Hall of Fame in 1967.

---

flight was made by two U.S. Army lieutenants, John A. MacReady and Oakley G. Kelly. Taking off from Roosevelt Field, on Long Island, N.Y., they flew their single-engine Fokker T-2 monoplane 2700 miles to San Diego, Calif., in 26 hrs., 50 min.

May 12 The 48th annual **Preakness Stakes** was won by Vigil, with a time of 1:53⅗. The jockey was Benny Marinelli.

May 19 The 49th annual **Kentucky Derby** was won by Zev, with a time of 2:05⅖. The jockey was Earl Sande, scoring his first Kentucky Derby victory.

May 30 The 11th annual **Indianapolis 500** auto race was won by Tommy Milton, completing the 500-mi. course in 5 hrs., 29 min., 50.17 sec., at an average speed of 90.95 mph.

June 9 The 55th annual **Belmont Stakes** was won by Zev, with a time of 2:19. The jockey was Earl Sande.

July 15 The U.S. **Open golf tournament** was won by amateur golfer Bobby Jones. Tied at the end of four rounds with Bobby Cruikshank at 296, Jones scored a 76 in the playoff, while Cruikshank carded a 78.

Aug. 18 The **U.S. Lawn Tennis Association women's singles championship** was won by 17-year-old Helen Wills over Molla Bjurstedt Mallory, ending Mallory's eight-year domination of the event.

Aug. 30-Sept. 1 The **Davis Cup** international tennis challenge round was won for the fourth year in a row by the U.S., defeating Australia four matches to one. On Sept. 1, Bill Tilden and R. Norris Williams won a memorable doubles victory over James O. Anderson and John B. Hawkes to clinch the U.S. win.

Sept. 14 **Jack Dempsey retained his title** by knocking out Argentina's Luis Firpo, the "Wild Bull of the Pampas," in 57 sec. of the second round. In the first round, after Firpo had been knocked down seven times, he hit Dempsey so hard that Dempsey went through the ropes and into the laps of sportswriters. They pushed him back into the ring and saved Dempsey's title. In the brief fight, Firpo was downed ten times and Dempsey twice.

Sept. 15 The **U.S. Lawn Tennis Association men's singles championship** was won by Bill Tilden over William M. Johnston, this time in straight sets. The women's singles championship had been won on Aug. 18 by Helen Wills.

Sept. 29 The first AAU-sponsored **track and field meet for women** was held in Newark, N.J. After eight events, the Prudential Insurance Athletic Association of Newark was the team winner with 22 points. Runner-up was the Meadowbrook Club of Philadelphia with 19. A new world mark for the baseball throw was set by Elinor Churchill of the Robinson Female Seminary, Exeter, N.H., who threw the ball 284 ft., 5¾ in.

Sept. 29 The **PGA golf tournament** was won by Gene Sarazen, who beat Walter Hagen 1 up in

38 holes at Pelham Country Club, Pelham, N.Y.

Oct. 10-15 The 20th annual **World Series** was won by the New York Yankees (AL), defeating the New York Giants (NL) four games to two. Yankee bats came to life against Giant pitching. Babe Ruth hit .368, including three home runs. The team batting average was a respectable .293.

Oct. 20 In the **first international horse race in the U.S.,** an American horse, Zev, winner of the Kentucky Derby and the Belmont Stakes, defeated Papyrus, winner of the English Derby, by five lengths at Belmont Park, N.Y.

1924

The **first U.S. woman swimmer** to break records wholesale was Sybil Bauer. This year she broke 21 U.S. records.

Gerald Robarts, of England, became the first foreign player to win the U.S. squash racquets championship.

The **first national women's sailing championship** was won by the Cohasset Yacht Club, with Ruth Sears as skipper.

In soccer, the **National Amateur Cup,** emblematic of U.S. amateur soccer championship, was donated by the United States Soccer Football Association. Bad weather prevented completion of the tournament this year.

This year Rogers Hornsby of the St. Louis Cardinals set a **new major league batting record.** He batted .424, the highest ever for a season in modern

THE FIERCEST HEAVYWEIGHT FIGHT EVER

A champion knocked entirely out of the ring, his challenger downed ten times in less than two full rounds—these bare facts characterize the hard-to-believe 3 minutes and 57 seconds of a bout for the heavyweight championship of the world, a bout that has never been surpassed for excitement and ferocity in the history of professional heavyweight boxing. The bout took place on September 14, 1923, at the Polo Grounds in New York City. It pitted defending champion Jack Dempsey, the Manassa Mauler, against challenger Luis Angel Firpo, the Wild Bull of the Pampas. Firpo was taller than Dempsey and outweighed him by 24 pounds.

Ringside seats were priced at $27.50, the cheapest reserved seats went for $11, and general admission was $3.30. Scalpers were demanding and getting as much as $150 for a choice seat, and by the time the fighters entered the ring, 85,800 fans were on hand. Outside the Polo Grounds, another 25,000 fans who

had been denied admission rioted almost out of control of the small army of New York's Finest that had been mobilized for the event.

From the opening bell the fight was an all-out slugging match in which neither contestant seemed likely to survive the first round. Dempsey knocked Firpo down seven times and closed in for the kill. Much to Dempsey's surprise, Firpo unloaded a long and powerful right-hand punch to Dempsey's jaw, and the champion sailed through the ropes and out of the ring. His head and torso disappeared from view, and all that fans could see was a pair of white-clad legs writhing in the air above the laps of sportswriters at ringside. With their help, the dazed Dempsey got back into the ring, where he staggered somehow into a clinch and managed to keep Firpo from finishing him off.

At the end of the round, Dempsey tried his best to recover his senses so that he could once more come out swinging. Sure enough, Dempsey

caught Firpo with a right and decked him. Firpo got up after a count of 2. Dempsey downed him again, this time for a count of 5 before Firpo got up from the canvas. But the Wild Bull was groggy, and Dempsey promptly nailed him with a left to the jaw and, as Firpo began to sink once again, with a murderous right. Bleeding at the mouth, Firpo tried to roll over and rise to his feet, but just as the referee was reaching the count of 10, Firpo stiffened and went out.

Dempsey was criticized later for standing over Firpo while the Argentinian was down, but it was Dempsey's speed, agility, and rapid hitting plus his indomitable spirit while on the defensive that made the difference. Never before or after would a champion more fully earn the winner's purse in a heavyweight bout—$468,750—nor would a loser more fully earn his purse of $156,250. Indeed, as one wag figures it, Luis Firpo earned $15,625 each time he was sent to the canvas.

ROCKY MARCIANO

Rocco Francis Marchegiano
b. Brockton, Mass., Sept. 1, 1923
d. Des Moines, Iowa, Aug. 31, 1969

Rocky Marciano first tried baseball as a professional sports career but, after taking up boxing, won 27 of 30 amateur fights and turned pro in 1947. In the course of his campaign for the heavyweight title, Marciano on October 26, 1951, became the second person ever to knock out Joe Louis, the former titleholder, who was attempting a comeback.

On September 23, 1952, Marciano won the championship when he knocked out Jersey Joe Walcott in the 13th round. Before retiring on Apr. 27, 1956, Marciano successfully defended his title six times, including victories over Ezzard Charles, a former champion, and Archie Moore, the light heavyweight champion, who was attempting to move up to the top weight class. Marciano retired undefeated with a professional record of 49 wins, all but six of them by knockouts.

At 5 feet, 11 inches, Marciano was not a big heavyweight, but he more than made up for lack of size by being ever on the attack and packing a big punch. Marciano was killed in an airplane crash the day before his 46th birthday.

baseball. His mark erased that of Napoleon "Nap" Lajoie, who had hit .422 for the American League's Philadelphia Athletics in 1901.

The **American Trapshooting Association** divorced itself from subsidies by gun and ammunition manufacturers and changed its name to the Amateur Trapshooting Association. Today it represents 50 state trapshooting organizations.

The **first shuffleboard club** in the U.S. was organized at St. Petersburg, Fla., which soon became the nation's shuffleboard capital.

This year's **national college football championship** was won by Notre Dame, with a record of ten wins, no losses, no ties.

Jan. 1 The tenth **Rose Bowl** football game was fought to a 14-14 tie by Washington and Navy.

Jan. 25-Feb. 4 The **first Winter Olympics** were held at Chamonix, France. The U.S. finished fourth in the unofficial team standings, behind Norway, Finland, and Great Britain, and won one gold medal.

Feb. 13 At the **Westminster Kennel Club** dog show, Ch. Barberryhill Bootlegger, a Sealyham terrier owned by Bayard Warren, took best-in-show.

Feb. 18 **U.S. figure skating championships** were won in Philadelphia by Theresa Weld Blanchard, women's singles; Sherwin C. Badger, men's singles; and Theresa Weld Blanchard and Nathaniel W. Niles, pairs.

Mar. 5 Frank Carauna of Buffalo, N.Y., became the **first bowler to roll two perfect games in succession.**

Mar. 25 The **NHL Stanley Cup** was won by the Montreal Canadiens, who defeated the Vancouver Millionaires in two straight games and the Calgary Tigers in two straight games.

Apr. 11-12 The **first national collegiate men's swimming championships** were held, under

LOUISE SUGGS

Mae Louise Suggs
b. Atlanta, Ga., Sept. 7, 1923

A founder and charter member of the Ladies Professional Golf Association and its president three times, Louise Suggs has contributed to the welfare of women's golf by her activities both on and off the golf course. When only 17, she won the Georgia State Amateur title; in 1947, the U.S. Amateur; and the following year, the British Amateur. She had begun to play golf at the age of 10 under her father's guidance.

Suggs turned professional in July 1948 and in the next year won the Women's Open, the first time she played it. She repeated this victory in 1952 and took the LPGA championship in 1957. In all, Suggs had 50 career victories, the last coming in 1961. Only three other women pros have won more tournaments.

In 1951, Suggs was the first woman elected to the LPGA Hall of Fame, and in 1966 she became the first woman ever elected to the Georgia Athletic Hall of Fame.

BILLY HAUGHTON

William Haughton
b. Gloversville, N.Y., Nov. 2, 1923
d. Valhalla, N.Y., July 15, 1986

Billy Haughton was known as the most complete horseman in the sport of harness racing. He was a leading driver for many years, served as director of the U.S. Trotting Association, and had three sons who became drivers.

Haughton won all the important

races at one time or another, including four triumphs in the Hambletonian, in 1974, 1976, 1977, and 1980. One of his sons, Tommy, took this event in 1982. Haughton won the triple crown of harness racing—the Hambletonian, the Yonkers Futurity, and the Kentucky Futurity—in 1968 and was inducted into the Harness Racing Hall of Fame that same year.

Haughton ranked fourth in both

number of races won (4910) and purses earned ($40,200,000). He was also a leading trainer of trotters and pacers. He died on July 15, 1986, ten days after suffering severe head injuries in an accident at Yonkers Raceway.

NCAA auspices, at the U.S. Naval Academy, Annapolis, Md. Team points were not awarded until 1937.

Apr. 19 The 28th **Boston Marathon** was won by Clarence H. DeMar of Melrose, Mass., who broke both the Boston Marathon and Olympic Marathon records with a time of 2 hrs., 29 min., 40.15 sec.

May 4-July 27 At the **Summer Olympics** in Paris, France, the U.S. took first place in unofficial team standings for the eighth consecutive time and won 45 gold medals. American wrestlers won four of the seven gold medals in their events: Robin Reed, featherweight; Russel Vis, lightweight; John T. Spellman, light heavyweight; and Harry Steele, heavyweight. In swimming events, Johnny Weissmuller won three gold medals—in the 100-m. and 400-m. races and as a member of the 800-m. freestyle relay team. In the running high jump, Harold Osborn set a new Olympic record of 6 ft., 5^{15}/$_{16}$ in.

May 12 The **PGA golf tournament** was won by Walter Hagen with a 2-up victory over Jim Barnes at French Lick (Indiana) Country Club.

May 12 The 49th annual **Preakness Stakes** was won by Nellie Morse, with a time of 1:57^1/$_5$. The jockey was Johnny Merimee.

May 17 The 50th annual **Kentucky Derby** was won by Black Gold, with a time of 2:05^1/$_5$. The jockey was John D. Mooney.

May 30 The 12th annual **Indianapolis 500** auto race was won by Lora L. Corum, completing the 500-mi. course in a record 5 hrs., 5 min., 23.51 sec., at an average speed of 98.23 mph.

June 6 The **U.S. Open golf tournament** was won

by Cyril Walker, who beat Bobby Jones by three strokes. Play was at Oakland Hills Country Club, Birmingham, Mich.

June 7 The 56th annual **Belmont Stakes** was won by Mad Play, with a time of 2:18^4/$_5$. The jockey was Earl Sande.

July 19-21 At the **Olympic Games** held in Paris, the U.S. swept all five tennis titles, notably Vincent Richards over Henri Cochet of France in men's singles, and Helen Wills over Emilienne Vlasto of France in women's singles.

July 24-26 The newly organized **American Motorcyclist Association,** successor to two previous organizations, staged its first event, a three-day rally and race meet at Toledo, Ohio. By 1925 the AMA was conducting 14 national title races in events ranging from 3 to 100 mi.

Aug. 16 The **U.S. Lawn Tennis Association singles championships** were won by Helen Wills in the women's division and Bill Tilden in the men's division, again over William M. Johnston in straight sets (Sept. 2).

Sept. 11-13 The **Davis Cup** international tennis challenge round was won for the fourth year running by the U.S., defeating Australia in five straight matches. Bill Tilden and William M. Johnston starred.

Oct. 4-10 The 21st annual **World Series** was won by the Washington Senators (AL), defeating the New York Giants (NL) four games to three. The great Walter Johnson finally made it to the World Series. He lost games one and five but won a thriller in relief in game seven, 4-3 in 12 innings.

Oct. 18 In what many consider **college football's**

Louis Ray Groza
b. Martins Ferry, Ohio, Jan. 25, 1924

Lou Groza earned his nickname by the consistency and quality of his place kicking as well as the total number of points he scored. After his college career, he joined the Cleveland Browns, then part of the American Football League.

Groza spent his entire pro career from 1946 to 1967 with the Browns and was an outstanding offensive tackle and place kicker. In all his games in the AFL and NFL, which Cleveland joined in 1950, he scored 1349 points. Of this total, 641 came on point-after-touchdown kicks, 702 on field goals, and 6 on a lone touchdown. His total places him sixth among all-time leading scorers.

Groza led the league five times in number of field goals. His best remembered field goal came on December 24, 1950, when the Browns were playing the Los Angeles Rams for the NFL championship. With 20 seconds left, Groza booted a 16-yard field goal that gave Cleveland the victory 30–28.

Groza was elected to the Pro Football Hall of Fame in 1974.

---

greatest individual performance, Harold "Red" Grange, the "Galloping Ghost of the Gridiron," led Illinois to victory over Michigan 39-14 when he ran for touchdowns the first five times he carried the ball and passed for another touchdown. Grange's longest run was 90 yards, and he rushed for a total of 402 yards. After college, Grange played in professional football and was largely responsible for starting the sport on the road to great popularity.

Dec. 31 **Exterminator,** one of the great American racehorses, was retired after eight years of racing. The horse had won 50 of 100 races, including the 1918 Kentucky Derby.

1925

The **National Skeet Shooting Association** was founded. It held its first national skeet shooting championships in 1927.

The term *banjo hit* was coined by Snooks Dowd of the Jersey City Giants to describe a fly ball hit weakly into the outfield for a base hit. The term was created from the sound of the ball against the bat, calling to mind the plucking of a banjo string.

The **national college football championship** was won by Alabama, with a record of ten wins, no losses, no ties.

The **NHL Stanley Cup** was won by the Victoria Cougars, who defeated the Montreal Canadiens three games to one.

Jan. 1 The 11th **Rose Bowl** football game was won by Notre Dame, defeating Stanford 27-10.

Jan. 3 The St. Petersburg, Fla., Kennel Club opened the **oldest greyhound track in the world.** Known as Derby Lane, it still operates at the same site. Three of its running events are the oldest continuing greyhound races in the U.S.

Jan. 8 The **heavyweight wrestling title** was won at Kansas City, Mo., by Wayne "Big" Munn over the defending champion, Strangler Lewis. Munn won two falls out of three.

Feb. 12 At the **Westminster Kennel Club** dog show, Ch. Governor Moscow, a pointer owned by Robert F. Maloney, took best-in-show.

Feb. 15 **U.S. figure skating championships** were won in Boston by Beatrix Loughran, women's singles; Nathaniel W. Niles, men's singles; and Theresa Weld Blanchard and Nathaniel W. Niles, pairs.

Feb. 26 A **merger of horseshoe and quoit pitching organizations,** begun in 1921, was finalized at Lake Worth, Fla., at the world tournament being conducted there.

Mar. 8 **Lady Byng** of Vimy, France, donated a cup to be awarded annually to the professional hockey player judged by newspaper sports edi-

> *I don't want anybody going out there to die for dear old Notre Dame. Hell, I want you fighting to stay alive!*
>
> Knute Rockne

1 GEORGE MIKAN

George Lawrence Mikan, Jr.
b. Joliet, Ill., June 18, 1924

George Mikan was the first superstar of professional basketball in the 1940s and 1950s, when it was struggling to become a popular spectator sport. He first played for Chicago of the National Basketball League in the 1946–1947 season, played the next season with Minneapolis of the NBL, and after that, through 1955–1956, also played

with the Lakers, by then part of the National Basketball Association.

Mikan scored 11,764 points in his career and had a game average of 22.6 points. He was in nine playoff series and four all-star games. Mikan's highest total in a game was 61, and he led the NBA in scoring in 1949, 1950, and 1952. NBL teams he played with won titles in 1947 and 1948.

Mikan was voted the most valuable player in the NBL in 1948. He

played college basketball at De Paul University, where he became an all-American in 1944 and 1945 and led the team to victory in the National Invitation Tournament in 1945. Mikan coached at Minneapolis in 1957–1958, winning 9 and losing 30. After retiring, he was named commissioner of the new America Basketball Association for the 1968–1969 season. He was elected to the Basketball Hall of Fame in 1959.

---

tors to be the most sportsmanlike player. For the 1924-1925 season, the winner was Frank Nighbor, center for the Ottawa Senators.

Apr. 11 The **AAU all-around gymnastics title** was won by Alfred Jochim of Brooklyn, N.Y. He continued to hold the title through 1930 and then triumphed again in 1933 for a total of seven championships.

Apr. 20 The 29th **Boston Marathon** was won by Charles L. Mellor of Chicago, with a time of 2 hrs., 33 min., 0.35 sec.

May 8 The 50th annual **Preakness Stakes** was won by Coventry, with a time of 1:59. The jockey was Clarence Kummer.

May 16 The 51st annual **Kentucky Derby** was won by Flying Ebony, with a time of 2:07⅗. The jockey was Earl Sande, who was still recovering from a spill he had taken at Saratoga Springs, N.Y., in 1924. It was his first mount in months and his second Kentucky Derby victory.

May 30 The **heavyweight wrestling title** was regained by Strangler Lewis at Michigan City, Ind., when he defeated Wayne "Big" Munn two falls out of three.

May 30 The 13th annual **Indianapolis 500** auto race was won by Peter DePaolo, completing the 500-mi. course in 4 hrs., 56 min., 39.47 sec. for a record average speed of 101.13 mph.

June 5 The **U.S. Open golf tournament** was won by Willie Macfarlane, who beat Bobby Jones by one stroke in the second round of a playoff. Both scored 75 in the first playoff round. In the second, Macfarlane posted a 72 to beat Jones by one stroke.

June 13 The 57th annual **Belmont Stakes** was won by American Flag, with a time of 2:16⅘. The jockey was Albert Johnson.

Aug. 24 The **U.S. Lawn Tennis Association singles championships** were won by Helen Wills over Kathleen McKane of England, for the third time running, in the women's division and by Bill Tilden, for the sixth time in a row, in the men's division (Sept. 19). William M. Johnston lost to the champion only after a thrilling five-set battle.

Sept. 12 The **Davis Cup** international tennis challenge round was won for the sixth straight time by the U.S., defeating France in five straight matches. Bill Tilden and William M. Johnston in singles and Vincent Richards and R. Norris Williams in doubles formed unbeatable combinations.

Sept. 26 The **PGA golf tournament** was won for the second time in a row and third time overall by Walter Hagen at Olympia Fields (Illinois) Country Club, with a 6 and 5 win over Bill Mehlhorn.

Sept. 26 The newly renamed **National Hockey League** (NHL) became truly international in scope when applications for membership by teams representing New York City and Pittsburgh were accepted. Boston had been admitted in 1924.

Oct. 7-15 The 22nd annual **World Series** was won by the Pittsburgh Pirates (NL), who beat the Washington Senators (AL) four games to three. In this series, Walter Johnson won games one and four but was pounded in game seven, losing 9-7. The Senators' veteran shortstop, Roger Peckinpaugh, set the unenviable record of eight errors in a World Series.

Oct. 11 The **last Pulitzer Trophy airplane race** was won by Lt. Cy Bettis, who flew an Army Curtiss Racer at a speed of 248.99 mph at Mitchell Field, Long Island, N.Y. The first Pulitzer Trophy race was held at the same location in 1920. It was won by Lt. C. C. Moseley, who flew a Verville-Packard at 156.537 mph. The Army Curtiss Racer, which also won the Schneider Trophy, is on exhibit at the National Air and Space Museum in Washington.

Dec. 15 A new **Madison Square Garden** in New York City was formally opened with a hockey game that was watched by 17,000 persons. The Montreal Canadiens defeated the New Yorks, later called Americans, 3-1. This was the third Garden. The first had been built in 1879. It was replaced in 1890 by an elegant structure designed by the firm of McKim, Mead, and White. The third Garden was in turn replaced by the fourth and present Madison Square Garden, 31st to 33rd streets between Seventh and Eighth avenues.

1926

The name *softball* was proposed by Walter Hakanson at a meeting of the National Recreation Congress, and by 1930 it was accepted throughout the U.S. When invented in 1887, softball had been called indoor baseball but had moved outdoors. In the meantime it flourished under a variety of names: mush ball, playground ball, kitten ball, and ladies' baseball.

Curley Fredericks, on an Indian motorcycle, **broke the 2-mi./min. barrier** on a closed track by averaging 120.3 mph on a 1¼-mile track at Salem, N.H.

Jay Gould, amateur court tennis champion since 1906, retired from singles play. He continued to play

RED GRANGE ON A RAMPAGE

Harold "Red" Grange, also known as the Galloping Ghost of the Gridiron, on October 14, 1924, put on the greatest display of ball-carrying ever seen in college football, justifying—as if justification were needed—his place on the 1923 all-American team. Playing at home in Urbana, Illinois, before 67,000 spectators, the University of Illinois halfback scored five touchdowns even though he played about three quarters of the game.

To start the action off, Grange took the opening kickoff and ran it back 90 yards for a touchdown. In the course of that run, he twice crisscrossed the field, and by the time he went over the goal line with the ball, the official clock showed that only 10 seconds of the game had elapsed. The crowd was delirious, and the Michigan team knew why Grange was said to run with the speed of a deer.

The next time Illinois took possession of the ball, Grange on the first play ran 65 yards around right end for another touchdown. By this time the spectators were screaming with delight. A few minutes later, on another run around right end, he ran 55 yards for his third touchdown and, before the end of the first quarter, took off on a 45-yard touchdown jaunt. Grange had excellent interference from his teammates, and his ability to dodge, swivel, and generally befuddle his would-be tacklers completed the job each time. In the first quarter, Red Grange had run a total of 255 yards in four touchdown plays.

The Associated Press, in reporting the game, said Grange "has a way of dodging, almost coming to a complete stop before whirling in another direction, that leaves his tacklers flatfooted and amazed."

With Illinois ahead by 27 points after only one quarter, 24 of them scored by Grange, he was taken out and did not return until the third period. He climaxed a series of plays, including his 23-yard pass to a teammate, with a final 10-yard rush for his fifth score of the day. As a finale to this unique exhibition of talent, in the fourth quarter Grange passed again for 23 yards for the final Illinois score.

In all, Red Grange handled the ball 21 times and gained 402 yards, including five touchdowns that he scored and a sixth that came on a pass he had thrown. Of the 39 points Illinois scored, 30 belonged to Red.

Will there ever be another Galloping Ghost of the Gridiron? Ask the crowd of 70,000 spectators who showed up for Grange's first game as a pro in 1925, with the Chicago Bears.

GLENN DAVIS

b. Claremont, Calif., Dec. 26, 1924

Along with a West Point teammate, fullback Felix "Doc" Blanchard, halfback Glenn Davis was a sensational college football running back of the mid-1940s. The pair were known as Mr. Inside (Blanchard) and Mr. Outside (Davis) for the paths they took in carrying the ball, and they brought a steady string of victories to Army and excitement to spectators.

In high school in California, Davis earned 16 letters in football, baseball, basketball, and track. At West Point, in three seasons of varsity football, he played in all the games of Army's 29-game winning streak. By the end of his college career in 1946, Davis had scored 51 touchdowns in 35 games, while Blanchard registered 38. Davis's best season was 1944, when he scored 20 touchdowns. Together, Davis and Blanchard accounted for 537 of the 1179 points scored by Army in its three unbeaten seasons. In 1946, Davis was awarded the Heisman Trophy. Davis played pro football for the Los Angeles Rams but did not repeat his collegiate success.

doubles, winning five more titles with W. C. Wright, Jr.

The **Intercollegiate Soccer Football Association of America** was formed to succeed the Intercollegiate Association Football League. Six more eastern institutions joined immediately. By 1952 there would be over 70 member colleges, by 1972 over 200, with another 300 or more colleges playing regularly scheduled games.

The **NHL Stanley Cup** championship was won by the Montreal Maroons, who defeated the Victoria Cougars three games to one.

This year's **national college football championship** was won by Stanford, with a record of ten wins, no losses, one tie.

Jan. 1 The 12th annual **Rose Bowl** football game was won by Alabama, defeating Washington 20-19.

Jan. 16 Two **rifle shooting records** were set by L. Samuel Moore, a Newton, Mass., high school senior. In 8 hrs. of continuous firing with a .22-caliber rifle, he hit 244 course "A" bull's-eyes. On Feb. 24 Moore, firing prone on a 50-ft. range in the cellar of his home, scored 3000 consecutive bull's-eyes between 8 A.M. and 5 P.M.

Feb. The adoption of *skeet* as the official name for what had been known as shooting around the clock resulted from articles about the sport appearing this month in *National Sportsman* and *Hunting and Fishing* magazines. At the same time that rules were announced, a prize of $100 was offered for the most appropriate name. About 10,000 entries were received, and the winning name was submitted by Mrs. Gertrude Hurlbutt of Dayton, Mont., who suggested that *skeet* was an old Scandinavian form of *shoot*.

MICKEY WRIGHT

Mary Kathryn Wright
b. San Diego, Calif., Feb. 14, 1925

Perhaps the best golfer the Ladies Professional Golf Association has ever produced, Mickey Wright was certainly the outstanding woman golfer of the 1960s. With 82 career victories, 79 of them in a nine-year span, she is second only to Kathy Whitworth in this respect. She won the U.S. Golf Association Junior Girls' Championship in 1952 and turned pro in 1955.

Wright's major tournament victories were the LPGA in 1958 and 1960 and the women's U.S. Open in 1958, 1959, 1961, and 1964. In 1962 and again in 1963, she won four consecutive LPGA events. In the latter year, she captured 13 of the 32 events on the tour. In addition, she was the leading money winner four years in a row, from 1961 to 1964, and leader in the number of tournaments won in six years, 1958, 1960, 1961, 1962, 1963, and 1964.

Wright ended regular tournament play in 1970 but in 1985 teamed with Kathy Whitworth to play in the Legends of Golf tourney. The Vare Trophy, for low average score, went to her five times. Wright's tall and powerful build, combined with a classic swing, made her a long-ball hitter who could drive 270 yards off the tee. Mickey Wright was inducted into the LPGA Hall of Fame in 1964.

> *Honey, I just forgot to duck.*
>
> Jack Dempsey, on the telephone with his wife, explaining why he lost the heavyweight title to Gene Tunney

Feb. **U.S. figure skating championships** were won in Boston by Beatrix Loughran, women's singles; Chris R. Christienson, men's singles; and Theresa Weld Blanchard and Nathaniel W. Niles, pairs.

Feb. 13 At the **Westminster Kennel Club** dog show, Ch. Signal Circuit, a wire fox terrier owned by Halleston Kennels, took best-in-show.

Apr. 19 The 30th **Boston Marathon** was won by John C. Miles of Nova Scotia in a record time of 2 hrs., 25 min., 40.25 sec.

May 10 The 51st annual **Preakness Stakes** was won by Display, with a time of 1:59⅘. The jockey was Johnny Maiben.

May 15 The 52nd annual **Kentucky Derby** was won by Bubbling Over, with a time of 2:03⅘. The jockey was Albert Johnson.

May 31 The 14th annual **Indianapolis 500** auto race was won by Frank Lockhart, with a time of 4 hrs., 10 min., 14.95 sec., for an average speed of 95.904 mph. This year the race distance was 400 miles.

June 12 The 58th annual **Belmont Stakes** was won by Crusader, with a time of 2:32⅕. The jockey was Albert Johnson. Beginning with this year, the distance for the Belmont became a mile and a half.

July 10 The **U.S. Open golf tournament** was won for the second time by Bobby Jones at the Scioto Country Club, Columbus, Ohio, with a 293 total.

Aug. 6 The **first woman to swim the English Channel** was Gertrude Ederle of New York City, 19, who accomplished the feat in 14 hrs., 31 min.

Aug. 23 The **U.S. Lawn Tennis Association women's singles championship** was won by Molla Bjurstedt Mallory, who achieved a seventh title in a close match with Elizabeth Ryan. Illness prevented Helen Wills from playing.

Aug. 24 A **plane and its pilot were lowered by parachute** for the first time from a height of 2400 ft. near El Segundo, Calif. The pilot was R. Carl Oelze of the Naval Reserve. Plane and pilot weighed about 1800 lbs., and the craft, with power off, suffered only slight damage.

Aug. 30 The **first Hambletonian Stakes,** the premier event in harness racing, was won at Syracuse, N.Y., by Guy McKinney in two straight heats. The driver was Nat Ray.

Sept. 11 The **Davis Cup** international tennis challenge round was won for the seventh time in a row by the U.S., defeating France four matches to one at Philadelphia. This proved to be the last triumph for the marvelous team of Bill Tilden, William H. Johnston, Vinnie Richards, and R. Norris Williams.

Sept. 16 **Bill Tilden's six-year reign** as the U.S. Lawn Tennis Association men's singles champion was ended by Henri Cochet of France in the quarterfinals. On this day also, Jean Borotra of France defeated William M. Johnston, and René Lacoste of France eliminated R. Norris Williams. The era of French supremacy in tennis was at hand. On Sept. 18 Lacoste won the title.

Sept. 23 The **world heavyweight boxing championship** was won by Gene Tunney in a ten-round decision over Jack Dempsey in Philadelphia..

Sept. 25 The **PGA golf tournament** was again won by Walter Hagen, this time at the Salisbury Golf Club, Westbury, N.Y. His victim was Leo Diegel, 5 and 3.

Sept. 25 The **National Hockey League** admitted into membership the New York Rangers and teams in Chicago and Detroit, as yet unnamed. The ten-team league was divided into two divisions: the Canadian, with four Canadian teams and the New York Americans, and the American, with the other five American teams.

Fall Charles C. "Cash and Carry" Pyle, a U.S. promoter, organized the **first tour of professional tennis players,** featuring the internationally famous French star Suzanne Lenglen. Other members of the troupe were Mary K. Browne, Vincent Richards, Howard Kinsey, Harvey Snodgrass, and Paul Feret.

Oct. 2-10 The 23rd annual **World Series** was won by the St. Louis Cardinals (NL), who defeated the New York Yankees (AL) four games to three. In the seventh inning of the final game, with the Cardinals leading 3-2, the Yankees filled the bases with two out and Tony Lazzeri

BOB RICHARDS

Robert Eugene Richards
b. Champaign, Ill., Feb. 20, 1926

Bob Richards, an ordained clergyman, was the first pole vaulter, and so far the only one, to win his event at two consecutive Olympics. At the 1952 Games, he vaulted 14 feet, 11⅛ inches and, in 1956, 14 feet, 11½ inches, an Olympic record at the time. While at the 1956 Games in Melbourne, Australia, he delivered several church sermons as well as demonstrations in the art of pole vaulting.

Richards turned to athletics and religion early in life. At the age of 8 he could chin himself 30 times. In 1946, at the age of 20, he was ordained a minister of the Church of the Brethren. He first participated in the Olympics in 1948, coming in third in the pole vault. By 1951, he had increased his best heights to a little over 15 feet, a formidable mark at the time. His best vault was made in February 1957, when he reached 15 feet, 6 inches.

Richards also competed in the decathlon and won the U.S. title three times, in 1951, 1954, and 1955. In 1951, he received the Sullivan Trophy, given to the year's outstanding athlete not only for skill but also for sportsmanship. After he retired from competition, Richards became pastor of the Church of the Brethren in Long Beach, California.

---

at bat. Lazzeri was in his first year in the majors and had hit 18 home runs in the regular season. Cardinal manager Rogers Hornsby called on Grover Cleveland Alexander as relief pitcher. The 39-year-old veteran struck Lazzeri out and held off Yankee hitters to the end.

1927

Twenty-six nations were now competing for the **Davis Cup.**

Walter Johnson, pitcher for the Washington Senators (AL), ended the last season of his 20-year career by setting two major league career records. Johnson had pitched a total of 113 shutouts and struck out 3503 batters.

The **first Golden Gloves** amateur boxing matches were held this year, sponsored by the New York *Daily News.*

This year's **national college football championship** was won by Illinois, with a record of seven wins, no losses, one tie.

Jan. The **all-black basketball team** soon to be known as the Harlem Globetrotters initiated gypsy tours that ultimately made them basketball's outstanding attraction in cities large and small around the world. Their manager-promoter was Abe Saperstein.

Jan. 1 The 13th **Rose Bowl** football game was played to a 7-7 tie by Alabama and Stanford.

Feb. 10-11 **U.S. figure skating championships** were won by Beatrix Loughran, women's singles; Nathaniel W. Niles, men's singles; and Theresa Weld Blanchard and Nathaniel W. Niles, pairs.

Feb. 12 At the **Westminster Kennel Club** dog show, Ch. Pinegrade Perfection, a Sealyham terrier owned by Frederic C. Brown, took best-in-show.

Apr. 5 **Johnny Weissmuller** swam the 200-m. freestyle in a record 2:08, beating his old record by more than 7 sec. On the same day, he lowered his 100-yard record to 51.0 sec., a mark that was to stand for 17 years.

Apr. 7-13 The **NHL Stanley Cup** was won by the Ottawa Senators, who beat the Boston Bruins in two games and tied them in two games. The shares of the winners came to about $1000, with $600 shares going to losing players.

Apr. 19 The 31st **Boston Marathon** was won for the fifth time by Clarence H. DeMar of Melrose, Mass., with a time of 2 hrs., 40 min., 22.2 sec.

May 7 The **first Blackwell Cup crew race** was won by Yale at Derby, Conn., with Columbia second and Pennsylvania third. The cup was donated by the family of George E. Blackwell of the Columbia class of 1880 for an annual race among the three schools.

May 9 The 52nd annual **Preakness Stakes** was won by Bostonian, with a time of 2:01⅗. The jockey was Whitey Abel.

May 14 The 53rd annual **Kentucky Derby** was won by Whiskery, with a time of 2:06. The jockey was Linus McAtee.

May 30 The 15th annual **Indianapolis 500** auto race was won by George Soulders, completing the 500-mi. course in 5 hrs., 7 min., 33.08 sec., at an average speed of 97.545 mph.

June 4 In the **first Ryder Cup competition,** a team of American professional golfers defeated a British team 9½ to 2½ at Worcester, Mass. The trophy was donated by a British merchant for match play biennially on sites alternating between Great Britain and the U.S.

June 11 The 59th annual **Belmont Stakes** was won by Chance Shot, with a time of 2:32⅖. The jockey was Earl Sande.

June 16 The **U.S. Open golf tournament** was won by Tommy Armour at Oakmont Country Club, Oakmont, Pa. His 301 score was matched by Harry Cooper, but Armour won the playoff by three strokes.

July 2 At the **Wimbledon** tennis championships, Helen Wills won the women's singles title. Her victory was the first by an American woman since May Sutton's in 1907. Other titles won by U.S. players were men's doubles, Francis T. Hunter and Bill Tilden (July 4); women's doubles, Helen Wills and Elizabeth Ryan (July 5); and mixed doubles, Francis T. Hunter and Elizabeth Ryan (July 5).

Aug. 30 The **U.S. Lawn Tennis Association singles championship** was won by Helen Wills, who defeated Betty Nuthall of England in the finals.

Sept. 10 The **Davis Cup** international tennis challenge round was won by France. The French challengers defeated the defending U.S. team three matches to two. On the final day, Bill Tilden lost to René Lacoste, and William M. Johnston to Henri Cochet.

Sept. 14 **Bill Tilden** was vanquished in the quarterfinals of the U.S. Lawn Tennis Association singles championship, falling victim to Henri Cochet of France in a dramatic five-set battle at Forest Hills, N.Y. Though Big Bill would win additional major events in the five years before he turned professional, he would never again experience the invincibility of his play from 1920 to 1926. On this day also, Little Bill Johnston and R. Norris Williams lost to Jean Borotra and René Lacoste, respectively. U.S. supremacy had passed to the French.

Sept. 16 The **U.S. Lawn Tennis Association men's singles championship** was won by René Lacoste of France.

Sept. 22 In what became known as the **long-count fight,** Gene Tunney retained the heavyweight boxing title in a return bout with Jack Dempsey, the man he had dethroned. In the seventh round of the fight in Chicago, Dempsey floored Tunney but failed to go to a neutral

JACK KELLY

John B. Kelly, Jr.
b. Philadelphia, Pa., May 24, 1927
d. Philadelphia, Pa., Mar. 2, 1985

Jack Kelly not only was one of the finest oarsmen the U.S. has produced, but was also able with his skill to avenge a slight to his father, John Kelly, Sr., also a superb sculler. At single sculls in the mid-1940s, the younger Kelly was beaten only twice in more than 30 races.

His most satisfying victory came on July 5, 1947, when he took the Diamond Sculls at the Henley Royal Regatta in England. In 1920, his father had been refused entry in this race because he belonged to the Vesper Boat Club of Philadelphia, which had been barred from competition at Henley on the grounds of alleged infringement of amateur rules. At the time, though, it was said the elder Kelly was turned down because he was "not a gentleman," that is, he had been a bricklayer. Eventually, he became a wealthy contractor.

The younger Kelly won the Diamond Sculls again in 1949 and also won the U.S. single sculls title eight times, including five years in succession, from 1952 to 1956. He was not successful at the Olympics, however, where four times he failed to win in either single or double sculls, beginning in 1948. Kelly retired from rowing in 1960.

He served as president of the Amateur Athletic Union from 1970 to 1972 and took an active part in modernizing international regulations concerning amateur athletes. Among his siblings was Grace Kelly, who became a movie star and princess of Monaco.

John Kelly, Sr. (born in Philadelphia on Oct. 4, 1890; died in Philadelphia on June 20, 1960), was the first American to win an Olympic sculling title. He was victor in the single and double sculls in 1920 and the doubles in 1924, rowing with a cousin, Paul Costello. Kelly Senior won a total of 88 races.

STANLEY DANCER

1 9 2 7

b. New Egypt, N.J., July 25, 1927

A farm boy who left school after the eighth grade, Stanley Dancer began his association with harness racing as a $50-a-week stable boy at Roosevelt Raceway, Long Island, New York. It was there also, in May 1947, that Dancer for the first time became a winning driver. By 1950, he was training a dozen trotters and pacers as well as driving in many races each year.

At the end of 1986, Dancer ranked 17th among winning drivers with 3707 victories. Among these were four triumphs in harness racing's premier event, the Hambletonian, in 1968, 1972, 1975, and 1983. In 1972, he won harness racing's triple crown with wins in the Hambletonian, the Yonkers Futurity, and the Kentucky Futurity.

Dancer won 132 races in 1962 and led in money winnings with $760,343. Two years later, he became the first driver to top the $1,000,000 mark. He has since passed $14,000,000 in total winnings. A member of the Harness Racing Hall of Fame, Dancer says: "A horse is like a child. You like to watch them grow up. You never know what they are going to do next."

---

corner. As a result, the referee did not start counting Tunney out for 4 or 5 sec., thus giving the champion time to regain his feet. Tunney won on a decision after ten rounds. The gate receipts of $2,658,660 set a record, and Tunney received $990,445 as his share.

Sept. 27 The second annual **Hambletonian Stakes,** moved to Lexington, Ky., because the event was rained out at Saratoga in August and September, was won by Isola's Worthy in straight heats. The driver was Marvin Childs.

Sept. 30 **Babe Ruth** hit his 60th home run of the season, setting a major league record that would stand for many seasons. The Yankee slugger would finally be surpassed by Roger Maris, also of the Yankees, in the 1961 season.

Oct. 5-8 The 24th annual **World Series** was won by the New York Yankees (AL), who swept the Pittsburgh Pirates (NL) in four straight games. The Yankees this year fielded one of the most powerful teams of all time, with four outstanding pitchers—Waite Hoyt, George Pipgras, Herb Pennock, and Wilcy Moore—and were never in danger. Ruth hit .400, and shortstop Mark Koenig hit .500.

Nov. 5 The **PGA golf tournament** was won by Walter Hagen, for an unmatched fourth time in a row and a fifth overall. He slipped by Joe Turnesa, 1 up.

ALTHEA GIBSON

Althea Bison Gibson Darben
b. Silver, S.C., Aug. 25, 1927

Althea Gibson's path to becoming the first world-class black woman tennis player began in the Harlem section of New York City, where she played paddle tennis under Police Athletic League auspices. By 1945, she was the National Negro Girls' champion and then, from 1947 to 1957, the titleholder of the black American Tennis Association.

By 1952, Gibson was ranked in the top ten, regardless of race, and held first place in 1957–1958. In 1956, she won the French women's championship. On September 8, 1957, Gibson became the first black to win the U.S. women's championship when she defeated the favored Louise Brough. Also in 1957, she became the first black to win the title at Wimbledon. Gibson repeated both victories in 1958. Gibson also won all but one of the matches she played as a member of the Wightman Cup team.

After Gibson's first Wimbledon victory, she was given a ticker tape parade up Broadway in New York City on July 11, 1957. Gibson had first broken the color barrier in 1950, when she played in the U.S. championships at Forest Hills, New York, and again at Wimbledon in 1951. "Nothing was easy for Althea," said Mary Hare, an English player, who once practiced with Gibson when no U.S. player would do so. As a star, Gibson hit the ball hard and took the offensive. She retired from competition in 1958 and was named to the International Tennis Hall of Fame in 1971.

GEORGE BLANDA

George Frederick Blanda
b. Youngwood, Pa., Sept. 17, 1927

To pro football players who watched George Blanda pass and kick field goals and points after touchdown, he must have seemed ageless. Beginning in 1949, Blanda played for 27 seasons in all with the Chicago Bears, Baltimore Colts, Houston Oilers, and

Oakland Raiders, in that order.

Son of a coal miner father and one of 11 children, Blanda in high school played football and basketball and was a one-man track team. At the University of Kentucky, he was a varsity quarterback and was graduated in 1949.

Although it has been more than a decade since Blanda retired, he still

holds the record for most points scored in a career, 2002. He achieved this total with nine touchdowns, 943 points after touchdown, and 335 field goals. A sportswriter summed Blanda up this way: "A marvelous arm, a keen mind, a competitive fire that may be matchless in our time."

1928

The **United States Volleyball Association** (USVBA) was founded at a meeting at the Yale Club in New York City for the purpose of representing the sport nationally and internationally and for conducting an annual open championship. It is now the national governing body of the sport.

The **ocean-sailing yacht *Ninca,*** owned by Paul Hammond, won the fourth sailing of the Fastnet Race, from Cowes, Isle of Wight, around Fastnet Rock off southern Ireland, and back to Plymouth, England. It was the first U.S. victory. The time was 101 hrs., 48 min., 20 sec.

Platform paddle tennis, a modified form of paddle tennis played on a permanent or heavy portable platform, was introduced at Scarsdale, N.Y., by its inventors, Fessenden Blanchard and James K. Cogs-

well. The first platform was erected on Cogswell's property.

Joe Petrali won the **motorcycle hill-climb championship** for the first time. He would repeat in 1929, 1932, and 1933, while also winning five national dirt-track championships.

In the **first recorded game of men's field hockey** in the U.S., the Westchester Biltmore Men's Field Hockey Club defeated the Germantown Cricket Club 2-1.

The **first polo competition** for the Cup of the Americas between the U.S. and Argentina was won by the U.S. team, two matches to one, at Meadow Brook Club, Westbury, N.Y.

The **first match for the Intercollegiate Rifle Team Trophy** was won by George Washington U. Teams consist of five members. The trophy was presented to the National Rifle Association by the Sons of the American Revolution.

An important improvement in **surfboards** was

GORDIE HOWE

Gordon Howe
b. Floral, Sask., Canada, Mar. 21, 1928

The most durable player in National Hockey League history is Gordie Howe, who played for the Detroit Red Wings for 26 years, from 1946 to 1971. On top of that, he then, with two sons, joined the Houston Aeros of the American Hockey League in 1973 and in 1979 went

back to the NHL with the Hartford Whalers. He was director of player development there from 1980 to 1982.

Howe ended his career with a record 1767 games played in the NHL. This durability helped give him the career leadership of 801 goals and 1049 assists for a total of 1850 points. Howe also holds the record for the most 30-goal seasons. He was named most valuable player six

times, in 1952, 1953, 1957, 1958, 1960, and 1963, and was on the league's all-star team 21 times.

Howe's career was not all fun. He suffered a severe concussion in 1950, had several broken bones, and is said to have taken about 500 stitches in his face. In any event, Howe is not only the greatest forward in the history of ice hockey, but quite likely the best all-around player ever.

BETSY RAWLS

Elizabeth Earle Rawls
b. Spartanburg, S.C., May 4, 1928

One of the founders of the Ladies Professional Golf Association in 1951, Betsy Rawls is also one of the players of the 1950s and 1960s who had much to do with increasing the popularity and status of women's golf. Rawls was a successful amateur, although she did not play the game until she was 17. Her first important victory as a pro came in 1951, when she won the first of her four U.S. Women's Open tournaments. Her other victories came in 1952, 1957, and 1960.

On her way to 55 career victories as a pro, third best in LPGA play, Rawls twice won the LPGA championship, in 1959 and 1969. In 1959 she won ten tournaments and in 1952 and 1957 also had the most wins. Rawls retired in 1975 and then, for six years, was tournament director of the LPGA in a period of extensive growth. She became a member of the LPGA Hall of Fame in 1960.

---

made by Tom Blake, who produced a hollow board that brought the weight of surfboards down to 70-100 lbs., well below the 125- to 150-lb. weight of redwood boards. In 1935, Blake introduced fins for surfboards, making them more controllable. In the late 1940s, Bob Simmons invented very light surfboards made of styrofoam and plywood. In 1957 came the first boards of polyurethane foam.

The **original Celtics,** playing their home games in New York, disbanded after dominating the American Basketball League, formed in 1925. They had finished the 1927-1928 season with a record of 109 wins in 120 games. The Celtics had started in 1915 as a semiprofessional team.

This year's **national college football championship** was won by Georgia Tech, with a record of ten wins, no losses, no ties.

Jan. 1 The 14th **Rose Bowl** football game was won by Stanford, edging out Pittsburgh 7-6.

Feb. 11-19 At the second **Winter Olympics** in St. Moritz, Switzerland, the U.S. finished second in team standings and won two gold medals.

Feb. 15 At the **Westminster Kennel Club** dog show, Ch. Talavera Margaret, a wire-haired fox terrier owned by Reginald M. Lewis of Ridgefield, Conn., took best-in-show.

Feb. 21 The **world heavyweight wrestling championship** was won by Strangler Lewis, who took two out of three falls from Joe Stecher at St. Louis, Mo.

Mar. 4 A transcontinental footrace that was dubbed the **Bunion Derby** began in Los Angeles, when 199 men started a 3422 mi. race to New York City. Prize money of $48,500 was offered by the promoter, Cash and Carry Pyle, who failed to profit from his venture because of bad weather, small crowds in towns through which the weary runners passed, and the reluctance of sponsors along the way to put up much money. Eventually, Andy Payne, 19, of Claremore, Okla., won with a time of 573 hrs., 4 min., 34 sec.

Mar. 27 **U.S. figure skating championships** were won by Maribel Y. Vinson, women's singles; Roger Turner, men's singles; and Maribel Y. Vinson and Thornton Coolidge, pairs.

Apr. 5-14 The **NHL Stanley Cup** was won by the New York Rangers, defeating the Montreal Canadiens three games to two.

Apr. 19 The 32nd **Boston Marathon** was won by Clarence H. DeMar of Melrose, Mass., who gained his sixth marathon win with a time of 2 hrs., 37 min., 7.8 sec.

May 11 The 53rd annual **Preakness Stakes** was won by Victorian, with a time of 2:00⅕. The jockey was Raymond "Sonny" Workman.

May 19 The 54th annual **Kentucky Derby** was won by Reigh Count, with a time of 2:10⅖. The jockey was Charles Lang.

May 30 The 16th annual **Indianapolis 500** auto race was won by Louis Meyer, completing the 500-mi. course in 5 hrs., 1 min., 33.75 sec., at an average speed of 99.482 mph.

June 9 The 60th annual **Belmont Stakes** was won by Vito, with a time of 2:33⅕. The jockey was Clarence Kummer.

June 24 The **U.S. Open golf tournament** was won by Johnny Farrell, who beat Bobby Jones by one stroke in a 36-hole playoff, necessitated by a tie at the end of 18. Play was at Olympia Fields (Illinois) Country Club.

July 7 At the **Wimbledon** tennis championships, Helen Wills won the women's singles title for the second year in a row. The mixed doubles

DOLPH SCHAYES

Adolph Schayes
b. New York City, May 19, 1928

As a pro basketball player, Dolph Schayes set records, since surpassed in most cases but notable in their time. On December 12, 1960, he became the first pro player to score more than 15,000 career points. He ended his career with 19,249 and a game average of 18.2. Between February 17, 1952, and December 27, 1961, he played in 764 consecutive games, finally being forced to end his streak because he suffered a broken cheekbone in a collision with another player.

Schayes played college basketball for New York University, then was drafted in 1948 by Syracuse of the National Basketball League, which became the National Basketball Association the next year. Schayes played for Syracuse for 15 seasons and moved on to Philadelphia for his last season, 1963–1964, when the Syracuse franchise was transferred. In his career he had 11,256 rebounds and 3072 assists.

Schayes is tied with others at 15 for most playoff series, and he was on the all-star team six times, in 1952, 1953, 1954, 1955, 1957, and 1958. He led the league in rebounding in 1951 and in free throw percentage in 1958, 1960, and 1962. After his playing career ended, Schayes coached Philadelphia from 1963 to 1966 and Buffalo from 1970 to 1972. His record as a coach was 151 wins and 172 losses. Later he was the NBA supervisor of referees. Schayes was voted coach of the year for 1964 and was elected to the Basketball Hall of Fame in 1972.

title was won by Elizabeth Ryan teamed with P. D. B. Spence of South Africa.

July 26 The **world heavyweight boxing championship** was successfully defended by Gene Tunney, who scored a 12th-round knockout over Tom Heeney in a bout in New Zealand. Shortly after, Tunney announced his retirement.

July 29-Aug. 12 At the **Summer Olympics** in Amsterdam, Netherlands, the U.S. took first place in team standings and won 24 gold medals. U.S. athletes set 17 new Olympic records and seven world records. Paul Desjardins, U.S. diving champion, earned two perfect scores of 10 in the springboard diving event, the first perfect scores awarded in modern Olympic competition. Martha Norelius picked up her second consecutive gold medal in the 400-m. freestyle, the first woman swimmer to win consecutive gold medals in an event. In the shot put, John Kuck set a new Olympic record of 52 ft., 11^{11}/$_{16}$ in. Women's track events were included for the first time, and Elizabeth Robinson won the 100-m. dash in 12.2 sec.

Aug. 20-22 David White was the winner of the singles competition at the **first National Tournament of the American Lawn Bowls Association,** held at Hartford, Conn.

Aug. 27 The third annual **Hambletonian Stakes** was won at Saratoga, N.Y., by Spencer in two straight heats. The driver was William H. Leese.

Aug. 27 The **U.S. Lawn Tennis Association singles championships** were won by Helen Wills over Helen Hull Jacobs in the women's division and Henri Cochet of France over Francis T. Hunter in the men's division (Sept. 17).

Oct. 4-9 The 25th annual **World Series** was won by the New York Yankees (AL), who swept the St. Louis Cardinals (NL) in four straight games. Babe Ruth smashed ten hits in 16 times at bat for a .625 series average, including three home runs.

Oct. 6 The **PGA golf tournament** was won by Leo Diegel, who won the final round 6 and 5 over Al Espinosa.

Dec. 26 **Johnny Weissmuller** announced his retirement from amateur swimming competition. In eight years of top-level competition, he had never lost a freestyle race. At one time he held all the world records in freestyle swimming at distances from 50 to 880 yards.

1929

Golf clubs with steel shafts came into use.

The **Intercollegiate Women's Fencing Association** was founded by Bryn Mawr, Cornell, New York U., and Pennsylvania. The first championship was held this year at Cornell, with NYU the winner. There now are 44 members of the association, which changed its name in 1971 to the National Intercollegiate Women's Fencing Association.

1 BOB COUSY

Robert Joseph Cousy
b. New York City, Aug. 9, 1928

Bob Cousy was rather short for a modern pro basketball player, standing 6 feet, 1 inch tall, but his speed and fast break more than made up for his lack of height. He demonstrated this at Holy Cross, where he made the all-American team in his sophomore year.

Except for one year, Cousy spent his 14-year pro career with the Boston Celtics. He played for them from 1950–1951 through 1962–1963 and retired until the 1969–1970 season, when he played for Cincinnati. In all he scored 16,960 points in regular season play, with an average of 18.4 points a game and with 4786 rebounds.

The Celtics made the league playoffs every year that Cousy played for them, and in those games he scored another 2018 points. He was a major factor in Boston's six National Basketball Association championships, in 1957, 1959, 1960, 1961, 1962, and 1963. Cousy was the NBA's most valuable player in 1957. He ranks third in career assists with 6955 and led the league in this category eight times. Cousy played in 13 all-star games.

After retiring, Cousy coached Boston College for six seasons, from 1963 to 1969, during which time the Crusaders won 117 games, lost 38, and were in the National Invitation Tournament three times and the NCAA Tournament twice. Cousy went on to coach for five seasons with Cincinnati and Kansas City-Omaha, where he was not as successful, ending with 141 victories and 209 defeats. His last position in sports was as commissioner of the American Soccer League from 1975 to mid-season of 1980. Cousy was elected to the Basketball Hall of Fame in 1970.

The **world heavyweight boxing championship** was up for grabs this year. Max Schmeling of Germany became a contender after successful fights against Johnny Risko (Feb. 1) and Paulino Uzcudun (June 27). Jack Sharkey defeated William L. "Young" Stribling in a ten-round bout (Feb. 27). Schmeling and Sharkey met each other in a championship fight in 1930.

This year's **national college football championship** was won by Notre Dame, with a record of nine wins, no losses, no ties.

Jan. 1 The 15th **Rose Bowl** football game was won by Georgia Tech, which edged out California 8-7. During the game, a confused California player ran 60 yards with the ball in the wrong direction before being tackled near the Georgia Tech goal line by one of his fellow players.

Jan. 4 The **world heavyweight wrestling title** was won by Gus Sonnenberg, who beat Strangler Lewis at Boston. Sonnenberg got one fall, then butted Lewis out of the ring five times. After the first butt, Lewis refused to return to the ring, and the referee disqualified him.

Feb. 13 At the **Westminster Kennel Club** dog show, Ch. Laund Loyalty of Bellhaven, a collie owned by Mrs. Florence B. Ilch of Red Bank, N.J., took best-in-show. It was the first time in the show's history that a puppy won the top honor.

Feb. 19 **U.S. figure skating championships** were won by Maribel Y. Vinson, women's singles; Roger Turner, men's singles; and Maribel Y. Vinson and Thornton Coolidge, pairs.

Mar. 28-29 The **NHL Stanley Cup** was won by the Boston Bruins, who took two straight games from the New York Rangers.

Apr. 4 The **first AAU national wrestling championships,** Greco-Roman style, were concluded at Teutonia Hall in New York City. There was competition in seven weight classes.

Apr. 19 The 33rd **Boston Marathon** was won by Johnny Miles of Hamilton, Ontario, with a time of 2 hrs., 33 min., 8.8 sec.

May 10 The 54th annual **Preakness Stakes** was won by Dr. Freeland, with a time of 2:01⅗. The jockey was Louis Schaefer.

May 18 The 55th annual **Kentucky Derby** was won by Clyde Van Dusen, with a time of 2:10⅘. The jockey was Linus McAtee.

May 30 The 17th annual **Indianapolis 500** auto race was won by Ray Keech of Philadelphia, completing the 500-mi. course in 5 hrs., 7 min., 25.42 sec., at an average speed of 97.585 mph.

Everybody likes to be a Monday morning quarterback. It's so easy to call the plays a day or two later.

Knute Rockne

DICK BUTTON

Richard Totten Button
b. Englewood, N.J., July 18, 1929

During 1948 and 1949, while Dick Button was a student at Harvard, he became the first person to hold at one time the five major titles in figure skating: U.S., North American, European, world, and Olympic. He had not begun receiving instruction in the sport until 1942, and he entered his first competitive event in 1943, when he finished second in the Eastern States Novice Class.

From 1946 to 1952, Button was easily the dominant male figure skater of the world. In 1946, he won the U.S. title and held it every year through 1952. In 1947 he became the first American since 1923 to win the North American championship. He also won it in 1949 and 1951.

Button took the European championship in 1948, the last time Americans were allowed to compete in this event. In that year and again in 1952, he won the gold medal at the Olympics. On top of all that,

Button won the world title five consecutive times, from 1948 to 1952.

He was not only a winner but a skater who changed the sport. Button opened a new era of athleticism and at the 1952 Olympics was the first to achieve a real triple loop jump. Turning professional, Button signed to appear with the Ice Capades in 1953. He became a lawyer in 1953 and also worked as a television sports commentator.

June 8 The 61st annual **Belmont Stakes** was won by Blue Larkspur, with a time of 2:32⅘. The jockey was Mack Garner.

June 30 At Winged Foot, Mamaroneck, N.Y., the **U.S. Open golf tournament** was won by Bobby Jones, who beat a hapless Al Espinosa by 23 strokes in a playoff, 141-164.

July 5 At the **Wimbledon** tennis championships in England, the women's singles title was won for the third straight year by Helen Wills. On July 6 the men's doubles was won by Wilmer Allison and John Van Ryn, and the mixed doubles was won by Helen Wills and Francis T. Hunter.

Aug. 24 The **U.S. Lawn Tennis Association sin-** gles championships were won for the sixth time by Helen Wills over Helen Hull Jacobs in the women's division and by Bill Tilden, for the seventh time, in the men's division, over Francis T. Hunter (Sept. 14).

Sept. 26 **Forward passing** within any of the three zones was made permissible in professional hockey.

Oct. 8 The fourth annual **Hambletonian Stakes** was won by Walter Dear in straight heats at Lexington, Ky. The driver was Walter Cox. In 1930 the race was moved to Goshen, N.Y., where it was held until 1956.

Oct. 8-14 The 26th annual **World Series** was won by the Philadelphia Athletics (AL), who beat the

ARNOLD PALMER

Arnold Daniel Palmer
b. Youngstown, Ohio, Sept. 10, 1929

To Arnold Palmer, along with Jack Nicklaus, belongs a large share of the credit for making golf a popular spectator sport, a television attraction, and a very profitable game for the professionals. Both golfers play an aggressive game, are capable of brilliant shots, and have personalities that attract attention bordering on adulation. In the case of Palmer, his following during his

heyday was so fervent that it was known as Arnie's Army.

Palmer got his hands on his first golf club at age 3 and was taught by his father, who was a country club pro. He played golf at Wake Forest, which he entered in 1947, and then spent three years in the Coast Guard. Returning to golf, Palmer won the U.S. Amateur championship in 1954 and in November of that year turned professional.

His first important victory came in August 1955, when he won the Canadian Open. Since then he has

won the Masters in 1958, 1960, 1962, and 1964, becoming the first player to win this tournament four times. Palmer triumphed in the U.S. Open in 1960 and the British Open two years in succession, 1961 and 1962, but has never won a PGA championship.

In 1967, Palmer became the first golfer to pass the $1,000,000 mark in earnings. In recent years, Palmer has played more or less regularly on the Seniors tour and, win or lose, continues to be a leading attraction.

JIM JACOBS

b. St. Louis, Mo., Feb. 18, 1930

The most successful handball player ever, Jim Jacobs dominated the game in the late 1950s and the 1960s. He learned to play the game in Hollywood and won his first national four-wall championship in 1955 while attending UCLA. He held this U.S. Handball Association title for the next two years, then won again in 1960, 1964, and 1965 for a total of six championships.

In 1956, he became the first person to win all three major four-wall singles titles in the same year when he also triumphed in the national AAU and YMCA championships. He won six doubles titles, in 1960, 1962, 1963, 1965, 1967, and 1968, all but the first of these with Marty Decatur as his partner.

Jacobs had everything a handball player needed: speed, power, control, and stamina. He wore down his opponents. In 1979, a poll taken by *Handball* magazine found general agreement that he was the best.

Chicago Cubs (NL) four games to one. Connie Mack, manager of the Athletics, surprised fans by starting pitcher Howard Ehmke in the first game. Ehmke, who had pitched in only 11 games all season, responded by striking out 13 Cubs and winning the game by 3 to 1. Ehmke's strikeouts set a new record for a series game.

Dec. 7 The **PGA golf tournament** was won for the second year in a row by Leo Diegel. This time, at Hillcrest Country Club, Los Angeles, he defeated Johnny Farrell, 6 and 4.

1930

The first **women's squash racquets** singles champion was the Boston sportswoman Eleanora Sears.

Paddle tennis was being played in the parks and playgrounds of 165 cities, the National Recreation Association reported. The number grew to 470 cities by 1940.

Once again, the official **baseball was made livelier,** with the manufacturers once again disclaiming any change in specifications. Batting averages soared in the decade following, abetted by the increased willingness of umpires to discard balls discolored or scuffed in the course of play.

Competition between **professional tennis players and amateurs** was proposed by the delegates from England and the U.S. to the International Federation of Tennis Associations. Twenty member nations voted in the negative to defeat the initiative.

Jan. 1 The 16th **Rose Bowl** football game was won by Southern California, defeating Pittsburgh 47-14.

Feb. 12 At the **Westminster Kennel Club,** Ch. Pendley Calling of Blarney, a wire-haired fox

EARL ANTHONY

Earl Roderick Anthony
b. Kent, Wash., Apr. 27, 1930

Considering the number of bowling tournaments Earl Anthony has entered and the number he has won, it is not surprising that Anthony is pro bowling's first millionaire in terms of prize money won. He turned pro in 1970 and 11 years later was elected to the pro bowlers' hall of fame.

One of Anthony's attributes is his constant activity. He bowls often and in all parts of the country. As a result, he has a record, as of the end of 1986, of 41 Professional Bowlers Association titles and of having finished among the top five contestants in 145 tournaments. In 1975 he was the first bowler to earn more than $100,000 in a year.

Anthony's other honors have also been substantial. He won the PBA national championship tournament six times, in 1973, 1974, 1975, 1981, 1982, and 1983, and was the American Bowling Congress Master Champion in 1977 and 1984. In 1977 Anthony set the PBA 18-game scoring record of 4515 and in 1970 the 24-game record of 5825.

terrier owned by John G. Bates of Morristown, N.J., took best-in-show.

Mar. 22-23 U.S. **figure skating championships** were won by Maribel Y. Vinson, women's singles; Roger Turner, men's singles; and Beatrix Loughran and Sherwin C. Badger, pairs.

Apr. 1-3 The **NHL Stanley Cup** was won by the Montreal Canadiens, who swept the Boston Bruins in two straight games.

Apr. 6 The **first transcontinental glider tow** ended in New York City's Van Cortland Park eight days and 2816 mi. after leaving San Diego, Calif. The pilot of the glider *Eaglet* was Frank Hawks, who was towed by J. D. Jernigen in a two-place biplane. The pair made 19 hops totaling 35 hrs. of actual flying time.

Apr. 19 The **Boston Marathon** was won for the seventh time by Clarence H. DeMar of Melrose, Mass., with a time of 2 hrs., 34 min., 48.2 sec.

May 9 The 55th annual **Preakness Stakes** was won by Gallant Fox, with a time of 2:00⅗. The jockey was Earl Sande.

May 17 The 56th annual **Kentucky Derby** was won by Gallant Fox, with a time of 2:07⅗. The jockey was Earl Sande, who scored his third Derby victory.

May 30 The 18th annual **Indianapolis 500** auto race was won by Billy Arnold, who completed the 500-mi. course in 4 hrs., 58 min., 39.72 sec., at an average speed of 100.44 mph.

June 7 The 62nd annual **Belmont Stakes** was won by Gallant Fox with a winning time of 2:31⅗. The jockey was Earl Sande. This was the second time that a horse had won the Triple Crown.

June 12 The **world heavyweight boxing championship** was won by Max Schmeling of Germany. Schmeling was awarded the victory after Jack Sharkey fouled him in the fourth round of the bout in New York City.

July 4 At the **Wimbledon** tennis championships, the women's singles title was won by Helen Wills Moody over Elizabeth Ryan. Other titles taken by Americans were men's singles, Bill Tilden, at age 37, over Wilmer Allison (July 5); women's doubles, Helen Wills Moody and Elizabeth Ryan (July 5); men's doubles, Wilmer Allison and John Van Ryn (July 7).

July 12 The **U.S. Open golf tournament** was won by Bobby Jones. This year Jones also won the British Open, the American Amateur, and the British Amateur, a feat that has never yet been matched by another player. On Nov. 17, Jones announced his retirement from competitive golf, having won 13 of the 27 major tournaments he entered.

Aug. 23 The **U.S. Lawn Tennis Association singles championships** were won by Betty Nuthall of England in the women's division and John H. Doeg over Francis X. Shields in the men's division (Sept. 13).

Aug. 26 A **rattlesnake bit an airplane pilot** 4500 ft. in the air over Kansas. P. "Happy" Wiggins, a salesman whose hobby was flying, was bitten twice but managed to throw the snake out of the cockpit. Wiggins landed near a farmhouse, where he was treated, and he eventually recovered. It was believed that the rattler found its way into the plane while the plane was in its hangar.

BOB MATHIAS

Robert Bruce Mathias
b. Tulare, Calif., Nov. 7, 1930

Bob Mathias was not only the first man ever to win the Olympic decathlon twice but also the youngest male athlete ever to win an Olympic gold medal. Just out of high school, he triumphed in the decathlon in 1948 in a floodlighted, near-midnight finish of the grueling event in London. In his 1952 repeat victory, he set a new Olympic record of 7887 points, since surpassed. Two other Americans, Milton Campbell and Floyd Simmons, finished second and third that year.

In high school, Mathias starred at basketball, football, and track. At Stanford University, he was the star fullback of the football team and once ran 96 yards for a touchdown against the University of Southern California. Between his two Olympic triumphs, he won four successive U.S. decathlon titles.

Standing 6 feet, 3 inches tall and weighing just over 200 pounds, Mathias was a superb athlete in both appearance and condition. After he retired from athletics in 1966, he was elected to the U.S. House of Representatives from a California district.

THE ONLY GOLF GRAND SLAM EVER

On September 27, 1930, on the 29th hole of the National Amateur, played at the Merion Cricket Club in Ardmore, Pennsylvania, Bobby Jones made his place secure among golf immortals by achieving a goal no one else has since managed or probably ever will. Until that great day, it had been thought no one ever would win the golfing grand slam, but Bobby Jones was equal to the task in taking the necessary fourth and climactic single-season victory in golfing's severest test. No wonder he was called the best golfer of his day and still is said by most to be the best of all time.

Jones, who never turned professional, began his quest for the four major titles that constitute the golf grand slam by winning the British Amateur tournament at the St. Andrews Golf Club in Scotland on May 31, 1930. He defeated Roger Wethered in match play, 7 and 6. Next, at Hoylake, England, on June 20, Jones added the British Open championship to his skein with a four-round total of 291, two strokes better than the runners-up, American professionals Leo Diegel and Macdonald Smith. This win made Jones the first golfer since 1890 to win the British Amateur and the British Open in the same year. Forty years between double victories gives some idea of the calibre of Bobby Jones on the links.

But there was more to come. Back in the United States, on July 12, at the Interlachen Country Club in Minneapolis, Minnesota, Jones added

his third major title, the United States Open. He finished with a total of 287 strokes, two better than Macdonald Smith, again runner-up to Jones.

To cap his triumphant year, in the final of the United States amateur championship at Merion, Jones defeated Gene Homans in match play, 8 and 7. It was fitting that Jones would make his run at the final leg of a grand slam at Merion, for it was there that Jones, at age 14, had made his debut in championship golf.

The decisive match with Gene Homans was played on a day of strong winds, but Jones was equal to the task and with this victory became the first man to win the United States Amateur title five times in all. Golf writer William D. Richardson, writing in the *New York Times,* said Jones demonstrated once again that he had "come closer to mastering the intricacies of the game than anyone else."

Accurately sensing that golf history would be made that day, 18,000 spectators jammed the course. The end for Homans came on a 415-yard, par 4 hole. Both sides of the fairways were 12 deep in spectators, respectfully silent as the players teed off. The hole had two level fairways and a green that resembled an island surrounded on three sides by deep woods.

Homans, first off the tee, drove strongly but a bit to the left on the fairway. Then Bobby Jones hit his tee shot and sent it flying almost 300 yards. Homans, on his second shot,

hit the green but somewhat long. Bobby's approach also landed on the green, closer to the pin than the approach shot by Homans, but short of the pin. The caddy handed Jones his faithful putter, Calamity Jane, which Jones had used to advantage thousands of times before. Jones put the ball just to the side of the hole. He was a sure par 4, and if Homans two-putted, they would halve the hole, and the match would belong to Bobby. Homans putted, and the moment the ball left his putter, Homans knew he had missed. Immediately, he rushed to Jones's side to congratulate him on the victory, and the crowd went wild. It was only the contingent of Marines and other guards stationed around the green that kept the crowd from swamping Jones.

A great landmark had been reached in the long history of golf. While commentators have said that Jones, in winning 8 and 7, had not had one of his best days on a course, they also recognized that his ability to stroke consistently, especially when the chips were down, enabled him to capitalize on the wildness that Homans showed that day. By the 22nd hole, Jones was nine up, and on the last nine holes played, only once was Jones a stroke over par.

Characteristically, after the great year for Bobby Jones that was 1930, and having no further golf worlds to conquer, he retired from competitive golf. To this day, his name is recognized as synonymous with golfing excellence.

Aug. 27 The fifth annual **Hambletonian Stakes** was won at Goshen, N.Y., by Hanover's Bertha in the second and third heats. The driver was Thomas Berry.

Sept. A **craze for miniature golf** was sweeping the country. By this time there were about 30,000 miniature golf courses, in which nearly $125,000,000 was invested. For a dime or so,

one played with a putter on a course covered with artificial grass and trapped with tin pipes and other obstacles.

Sept. 13 The **PGA golf tournament** was won by Tommy Armour by defeating Gene Sarazen in the final round, 1 up, at Flushing Meadows Country Club, Flushing, N.Y.

Sept. 13-17 The **America's Cup** was successfully

defended by the yacht *Enterprise,* which defeated the British challenger, *Shamrock V,* in four straight races.

Oct. 1-8 The 27th annual **World Series** was won by the Philadelphia Athletics (AL), who defeated the St. Louis Cardinals (NL) four games to two. The combined pitching of Lefty Grove and George Earnshaw was just too much for the Cardinals. They won two games each.

Dec. 16 It was announced that the first AAU **James E. Sullivan Memorial Trophy** for outstanding amateur athlete of the year would be awarded to Bobby Jones, who had just retired from golf. The annual award was established to honor an athlete who did the most to advance the cause of good sportsmanship.

1931

The **first platform tennis court** to be built by an established tennis club was opened for play at Fox Meadow Tennis Club in Scarsdale, N.Y.

Bill Tilden, arguably the greatest amateur player in tennis history, turned pro and went on tour. In the years to follow, the top amateurs regularly followed suit, including Ellsworth Vines, Fred J. Perry, Don Budge, and Alice Marble.

The **National Shuffleboard Association** was formed and the rules of the game rewritten. Two annual tournaments were to be held, one in winter and played in Florida and the other in summer played in a northern state. The winners in 1931 were Carl Bailey and Carl Breece, respectively. Women's championships were begun in 1932, summer, and in 1933, winter.

This year's **national college football championship** was won by Southern California, with a record of ten wins, one loss, no ties.

Jan. 1 The 17th **Rose Bowl** football game was won by Alabama, defeating Washington State 24-0.

Feb. 12 At the **Westminster Kennel Club** dog show, Ch. Pendley Calling of Blarney, a wire-haired fox terrier owned by John G. Bates, took best-in-show for the second consecutive year.

Mar. 21 U.S. figure skating championships were won in Boston by Maribel Y. Vinson, women's singles; Roger F. Turner, men's singles; and Beatrix Loughran and Sherwin C. Badger, pairs.

Mar. 28 The first **table tennis national championship** for men was won by Marcus Schussheim, of New York, who took the title in three straight games over his opponent in the final match. The matches were held at the Hotel Pennsylvania and were sponsored by the American Ping-Pong Association. The game was still known in some quarters as Ping-Pong.

WILLIE MAYS

Willie Howard Mays, Jr.
b. Fairfield, Ala., May 6, 1931

A superb outfielder, batter, and base runner, Willie Mays was the most talented all-around baseball player of his era. Known as the Say Hey Kid because of the locution he employed in greeting friends, Mays ranked near the top in many categories and at one time or other won almost every award available.

Mays spent most of his big league career with the Giants, first in New York and then in San Francisco, from 1951 to 1972, and finished his career in 1973 with the New York

Mets. His best-known record puts him in third place in career home runs with 660. He had 3283 hits, ninth highest; 2062 runs, fifth highest; 1903 runs batted in; and a career batting average of .302. Mays struck out 1526 times, the 14th highest number, but he also had 1464 bases on balls, 11th highest. He was also the first player to reach the 300 mark both in home runs and stolen bases.

As rookie of the year in the National League in 1951, Mays began collecting awards in his initial season. He was the most valuable player in 1954 and again 11 years

later. With a .345 average in 1954, he was also the league batting champion. On defense he set a record by making 7095 putouts.

As a slugger, Mays was always at or near the top, leading the National League in home runs in 1955, 1962, 1964, and 1965. His best year was 1965, when he hit 52 home runs. On April 30, 1961, he became the ninth player in major league history to hit four home runs in one game. Mays appeared in four World Series and was elected to the Baseball Hall of Fame in 1979.

WILLIE SHOEMAKER

William Lee Shoemaker
b.   Fabens, Tex., Aug. 19, 1931

Willie Shoemaker, the most successful American jockey ever, set records almost from the start of his career. Winning his first race in 1949, when he was 18, Shoemaker needed only two years to become the leading money winner of the year in 1951, a feat he achieved ten times in all. In 1956 he became the first American jockey to win purses totaling more than $2,000,000 in a single year.

By July 1987, Shoemaker had an unmatched record of 8681 wins. Despite all these victories, Shoemaker never rode a Triple Crown winner, but he did win the Kentucky Derby four times, in 1955, 1959, 1965, and 1986; the Belmont Stakes five times, in 1957, 1959, 1962, 1967, and 1975; and the Preakness Stakes twice, in 1963 and 1967.

An unusual and embarrassing moment in Shoemaker's career occurred in the 1957 Kentucky Derby. While riding Gallant Man, Shoemaker misjudged the finish line

and allowed Iron Liege to win. For his error, the stewards suspended him for 15 days for "gross carelessness."

Generally known as the Shoe, Shoemaker was earlier called the Silent Shoe because of his natural reserve. His racing weight is 98 pounds on a 4-foot, 11-inch frame. Willie Shoemaker was elected to the Racing Hall of Fame in 1958.

Apr. 3-14   The **NHL Stanley Cup** was won by the Montreal Canadiens, who defeated the Chicago Black Hawks three games to two.

Apr. 20   The 35th **Boston Marathon** was won by James Henigan of Medford, Mass., with a time of 2 hrs., 46 min., 45.8 sec.

May 9   The 56th annual **Preakness Stakes** was won by Mate, with a time of 1:59. The jockey was George Ellis.

May 13   In the celebrated **false start race** at Jamaica, N.Y., the entire field of horses went completely around the track before they were recalled. Rideaway and Clock Tower came in first and second, respectively, in the false start. In the official race, Clock Tower came in first and Rideaway finished second.

May 16   The 57th annual **Kentucky Derby** was won by Twenty Grand, in a new Derby record time of 2:01⅘, which held until 1941. The jockey was Charles Kurtsinger.

May 23   The **first national women's gymnastic championship** was won by Roberta C. Ranck of Philadelphia as all-around champion. In the contest, held in Springfield, Mass., Dorothy M. Rossenbach of Buffalo, N.Y., took second place.

May 30   The 19th annual **Indianapolis 500** auto race was won by Louis Schneider, completing the 500-mi. course in 5 hrs., 10 min., 27.94 sec., at an average speed of 96.629 mph.

June 13   The 63rd annual **Belmont Stakes** was won by Twenty Grand, with a time of 2:29⅗. The jockey was Charles Kurtsinger.

July   Plans and specifications for a **one-design**

racing sailboat, the 15½-ft. *Snipe,* appeared in the July issue of *Rudder.* Conceived by Florida's West Coast Racing Association as a small racer portable on a trailer, the *Snipe* became the largest class of racing sailboats in the world. The Snipe Class Sailing Association was founded in 1931, and its first world championships were held in 1932.

July 3-4   At the **Wimbledon** tennis championships, the men's singles title was won by Sidney B. Wood, Jr., 20, the youngest winner yet in the history of the event. The men's doubles title was won by George Lott, Jr., and John Van Ryn, and the mixed doubles was won by George Lott, Jr., and Mrs. L. A. Harper.

July 6   The **U.S. Open golf tournament** was won by Billy Burke, who beat amateur George Von Elm by one stroke after two 36-hole playoffs, necessitated by repeated tie scores. Play was at the Inverness Club, Toledo, Ohio.

July 13   **Bill Tilden,** having left the amateur ranks, captured the national professional tennis championship from Vinnie Richards, who had held the title since he turned pro in 1927.

Aug. 14   The sixth annual **Hambletonian Stakes** was won at Goshen, N.Y., by Calumet Butler in the second and third heats. The driver was Richard McMahon.

Aug. 20   The **U.S. Lawn Tennis Association singles championships** were won by Helen Wills Moody in the women's division and by 19-year-old Ellsworth Vines over George Lott in the men's division (Sept. 12).

Sept. 19 The **PGA golf tournament** was won by Tom Creavy in a 2-1 victory over Denny Shute.

Oct. 1-10 The 28th annual **World Series** was won by the St. Louis Cardinals (NL), who beat the Philadelphia Athletics (AL) four games to three. Centerfielder Pepper Martin made all the difference for the Cardinals. He batted .500, with 12 hits in 24 times at bat; ran wild on the bases, stealing five; and made a glittering catch in the ninth inning of the final game with two Athletics on base, two out, and the score 4-2.

Dec. 28 The **U.S. figure skating championships** were won by Maribel Y. Vinson, women's singles; Roger F. Turner, men's singles; and Beatrix Loughran and Sherwin C. Badger, pairs.

1932

The **Field Hockey Association of America** was founded by Henry K. Greer.

Jan. 1 The 18th **Rose Bowl** football game was won by Southern California, defeating Tulane 21-12. Southern California, with a record of ten wins, one loss, no ties, won the national college football championship.

Jan. 1 Effective this date, the **official golf ball** of the USGA weighed 1.62 oz. and measured 1.68 in. in diameter.

Feb. 4-13 At the 1932 **Winter Olympics** in Lake Placid, N.Y., the third such games in history and the first held in the U.S., the U.S. team won ten gold medals and the unofficial team championship. Both the two-man and the four-man bobsled teams took gold medals, the four-man team being captained for the second time by Billy Fiske.

Feb. 9 The **only bobsled run in the U.S.** was opened for the Winter Olympics on Mount Van Hoevenberg, at Lake Placid. The run, designed by Stanislaus Zentzytski, is over 5000 ft. long, and its average drop of 10% is punctuated by 26 major curves, some with nearly perpendicular walls 30 ft. high.

Feb. 13 At the **Westminster Kennel Club** dog show, Ch. Nancolleth Markable, a pointer owned by Giralda Farms, took best-in-show.

Apr. 5-9 The **NHL Stanley Cup** was won by the Toronto Maple Leafs, who defeated the N.Y. Rangers in three straight games.

Apr. 19 The 36th **Boston Marathon** was won by Paul DeBruyn of New York with a time of 2 hrs., 33 min., 36.4 sec.

May 7 The 58th annual **Kentucky Derby** was won by Burgoo King, with a time of 2:05⅕. The jockey was Eugene James.

MICKEY MANTLE

Mickey Charles Mantle
b. Spavinaw, Okla., Oct. 20, 1931

Mickey Mantle, one of the best players in the history of baseball and a member of the best team of the 1950s and 1960s, had a memorable career. In 1951, he replaced another star, Joe DiMaggio, in center field for the New York Yankees and, except when out with more than his share of injuries, played steadily as the regular center fielder through 1968. In Mantle's Yankee career, he played in 2401 games; hit 536 home runs, seventh best of all time; and had a career batting average of .298. He struck out 1710 times but, as a switch hitter feared regardless of which side of the plate he batted from, was walked 1734 times. He had 2415 hits in 8102 times at bat and scored 1677 runs, the all-time 21st highest. Mantle was voted most valuable player in the American League in 1956, 1957, and 1962 and won the league batting championship in 1956 with an average of .353.

It is as a slugger that Mantle is best remembered. He hit 30 or more home runs in nine seasons and led the league in homers in 1955, 1956, 1958, and 1960. His best years were 1956 and 1961, when he hit 52 and 56 homers respectively. In Washington, on April 17, 1953, he hit what was judged to be the longest home run since the days of Babe Ruth, a shot that traveled 565 feet.

Mantle had a major role in the Yankee record of 12 league championships during the years in which he starred, and this team success in turn enabled him to set a number of World Series records. He played in 65 series games, second only to the record set by Yogi Berra; hit 18 home runs, a record; scored the most runs, 43; had the most runs batted in, 40; had the most bases on balls, 43; and had the most strikeouts, 54. Mantle entered the Baseball Hall of Fame in 1974.

Andrea Mead Lawrence
b. Rutland, Vt., Apr. 19, 1932

Andrea Mead, who grew up at a ski center operated by her parents, learned to ski not long after she learned to walk. She entered competition when she was 11 and at 14 won the slalom trial for the 1948 Olympics. At the Games, however, Lawrence did not distinguish herself, placing 25th in the downhill after suffering a bad fall.

Beginning in 1949, Mead's career took off, when she won the U.S. downhill, slalom, and combined. In 1951, she raced only on the international circuit, winning 10 of 16 events and finishing second in four others. In the next year she won the U.S. downhill and slalom titles and repeated in 1955. She also took the giant slalom in 1953.

Andrea Mead married another skier, David Lawrence, and the third of their five children was born only

four months before the 1956 Olympic games. She made the U.S. team but did not win any medals, finishing tied for fourth in the giant slalom. Andrea Mead Lawrence remains the only American skier to have won two gold medals in a single Olympics.

May 9   The 57th annual **Preakness Stakes** was won by Burgoo King, with a time of 1:59⅘. The jockey was Eugene James.

May 30   The 20th **Indianapolis 500** auto race was won by Fred Frame of Los Angeles, completing the 500-mi. course in 4 hrs., 48 min., 3.79 sec., at an average speed of 104.144 mph.

June 4   The 64th annual **Belmont Stakes** was won by Faireno, with a time of 2:32⅘. The jockey was Tommy Malley.

June 21   The world **heavyweight boxing championship** was won by Jack Sharkey, who took a 15-round decision over Max Schmeling of Germany in New York City, thus returning the title to the U.S.

June 25   The **U.S. Open golf tournament** was won by Gene Sarazen, a decade after his earlier win. His 286 total at Fresh Meadow (New York) Country Club, was the lowest in 20 years.

July 1   At the **Wimbledon** tennis championships, Helen Wills Moody won the women's singles title, in the final match beating Helen Hull Jacobs. H. Ellsworth Vines, Jr., won the men's singles on July 2, defeating England's H. W. "Bunny" Austin.

July 30-Aug. 14   At the 1932 **Summer Olympics** in Los Angeles, the U.S. won 16 gold medals and the unofficial team championship. Eleanor Holm, 18, won the 100-m. backstroke. She went on to win 29 U.S. championships and break seven backstroke records. Eddie Tolan won both the 100- and 200-m. dashes and set new Olympic records in both with times of 10.3 sec. and 21.2 sec., respectively. In women's track

and field events, Mildred "Babe" Didrikson won the 80-m. hurdles in 11.7 sec. and the javelin throw with a toss of 143 ft., 4 in.

July 31   The **U.S. Davis Cup team** lost a close 3-2 decision to the French in Paris when Jean Borotra defeated Wilmer Allison in five sets after Ellsworth Vines had evened the competition at 2-2 by defeating Henri Cochet in the fourth match.

Aug. 17   The seventh running of the **Hambletonian Stakes** was won in the fourth heat by The Marchioness. The driver was William Caton.

Aug. 21   The **U.S. Lawn Tennis Association women's singles championship** was won by Helen Hull Jacobs. She had finally succeeded in winning the title after trying for seven years. Her opponent in the final match was Carolyn Babcock.

Sept. 3   The **U.S. Lawn Tennis Association men's singles championship** was won by Ellsworth Vines in a straight-set victory over Henri Cochet of France. Vines earlier had won at Wimbledon. Not since Bill Tilden won in 1921 had an American won at Wimbledon and Forest Hills in the same year.

Sept. 4   The **PGA golf tournament** was won by Olin Dutra at Keller Golf Club, St. Paul, Minn. In the final round he defeated Frank Walsh, 4 and 3.

Sept. 28-Oct. 2   The 29th annual **World Series** was won by the New York Yankees (AL), who swept the Chicago Cubs (NL) in four games. In game three, Babe Ruth taunted Cub pitcher

Charley Root by either—this question is moot—holding up his arm to indicate the two-strike count on him or pointing to the center-field bleachers. Whatever the fact, Ruth then drove a homer into those bleachers. It was Ruth's last World Series home run, and the game extended the Yankees' winning streak in World Series play to 12 straight.

1933

Breaststroke swimmer Henry Myers caused consternation among U.S. swimming meet judges in breaststroke competition by employing the **butterfly,** a stroke in which the arms emerge from the water and fling forward. He had copied the style from a German swimmer, Erich Rademacher. Myers correctly insisted that nothing in the rules for the breaststroke prohibited his method.

Katherine Rawls, all-around aquatic performer, won four events at the national championships: springboard diving, at which she was an Olympic medalist in 1932 and 1936; the 880-yard freestyle; the 200-m. breaststroke; and the difficult 300-m. individual medley.

Synchronized swimming was given its first public demonstration by the Modern Mermaids at the Century of Progress Exposition (World's Fair) in Chicago.

The **first totalizator** (tote board) used at an American racetrack was installed at Arlington Park, Chicago. This completely electrical device, invented and built in the U.S. in 1927, printed and issued betting tickets at the rate of 50 a minute. It then sorted, added, and transmitted totals to indicator boards, flashing new information to racing fans at the track every 90 sec. These machines came into use at all major tracks run under the parimutuel system. Depending on the size of the track, from 100

to 350 vending machines operated by 400 to 900 men and women were used at each park.

Jan. 1 In **college football bowl games,** the results were Miami (Fla.) 7, Manhattan 0 in the first annual Orange Bowl; and Southern California 35, Pittsburgh 0 in the Rose Bowl. The 1932 national collegiate football championship was won by Southern California, with a record of ten wins, no losses, no ties.

Feb. 15 At the **Westminster Kennel Club** dog show, Ch. Warland Protector of Shelterock, an Airedale terrier owned by S. M. Stewart, took best-in-show.

Feb. 26 In ice hockey, the **Boston Olympics,** representing the U.S., won the world's amateur championship by defeating Canada in the final round.

Mar. 18 U.S. **figure skating championships** were won in New Haven, Conn., by Maribel Y. Vinson, women's singles; Roger Turner, men's singles; Maribel Y. Vinson and George E. B. Hill, pairs.

Apr. 3 A record was set for the **longest game in the history of North American hockey.** It lasted 1 hr., 44 min., and 46 sec. of overtime beyond the 1 hr. of regulation play. A goal by Ken Doraty gave the Toronto Maple Leafs a 1-0 victory over the Boston Bruins.

Apr. 4-13 The **NHL Stanley Cup** was won by the New York Rangers, who defeated the Toronto Maple Leafs three games to one.

Apr. 19 The 37th **Boston Marathon** was won by Leslie Pawson of Pawtucket, R.I., with a time of 2 hrs., 31 min., 1.6 sec.

May 6 The 59th annual **Kentucky Derby** was won by Broker's Tip, with a time of 2:06⅘. The jockey was Don Meade. This was the second straight year in which the Derby was won by a horse owned and bred by Col. E. R. Bradley.

May 13 The 57th annual **Preakness Stakes** was won by Head Play, with a time of 2:02. The jockey was Charles Kurtsinger.

May 30 The 21st **Indianapolis 500** auto race was won by Louis Meyer of Huntington Park, Calif., completing the 500-mi. course in 4 hrs., 48 min., 0.75 sec., at an average speed of 104.162 mph.

June 10 The U.S. **Open golf tournament** was won by Johnny Goodman, the last amateur to win this event. His 287 total at North Shore Country Club, Glen View, Ill., was sufficient to edge Ralph Guldahl.

June 10 The 65th annual **Belmont Stakes** was

1 THE BAMBINO POINTS THE WAY

In the fifth inning of the third game of the 1932 World Series, on October 1, the mighty Babe Ruth of the New York Yankees came to bat for the third time. The scene was Wrigley Field, Chicago, and the principal actors in the drama were not the Babe and Charlie Root, the Chicago starting pitcher. They were the 49,986 loyal Cubs fans who had come to cheer on their heroes, who were locked in bitter struggle with the Yankees. The Cubs were down 2–0 in the series and tied 4–4 in the game when the Babe came to bat.

Ruth had failed to hit one of his specials in the first two games, and the fans had been on him during batting practice before the third game. In response, when he came to bat in the first inning, he drove in three runs with a homer. But now it was the fifth inning. The Cubs had come back, and with the score tied, the fans really went at Ruth. And what did the Babe do? Of course he hit a home run. This was not in itself an unusual occurrence. In fact, this was the Babe's 15th World Series homer, a new record for home run production. So why the fuss?

What made this home run extraordinary is that everyone present on that day believed that Ruth actually called the shot, not only proclaiming that he would hit a big one but that it would go precisely where he wanted it to go.

The story began to build in the fourth inning, with the Cubs at bat. Playing right field, the Bambino made a heroic but futile stab at a low line drive hit by Cub shortstop Billy Jurges. The partisan crowd loudly made known its pleasure at the missed catch, and good-natured as usual, Ruth doffed his cap to the crowd in a grand gesture. The fans went wild.

Now, a few minutes later, the Yankee slugger came to bat with a man on base, and the drama was ready to reach its climax. According to a *New York Times* report the following day, "In no mistaken motions the Babe notified the crowd that the nature of his retaliation would be a wallop right out of the confines of the park." Charlie Root threw two balls and two strikes, and Ruth after each pitch held his fingers high in the air to show what the count was or, perhaps, when the count reached 2 and 2, to show where he would hit the next pitch. Ruth's nonchalance served to raise the crowd's taunting to new heights. And then, on the next pitch, Ruth connected. Not for a moment was there any doubt that it would be a home run. The ball went high, straight out to center, and disappeared behind the angle formed by the scoreboard and the right-field

bleachers, just where the Babe had seemed to be pointing.

It was one of the longest homers ever hit, and the good baseball fans of Chicago applauded wildly to show their appreciation of the mighty blow, even though it was to prove decisive in putting the Cubs three down in the series.

There always has been some question as to whether Ruth actually intended to point to where he was going to hit a home run or whether he was simply gesturing to show the count. Over the years that followed, Ruth seemed at times to confirm the story and at other times to deny it. Whatever the truth, the Yankees went on to whitewash the Cubs, taking them four straight.

Overlooked by most baseball fans is the fact that Lou Gehrig also had two home runs for the Yankees on that memorable day. As happened so often in Gehrig's career, people were so taken by a Babe Ruth special that they overlooked Gehrig's achievement. For the record, therefore, in the 1932 Series Gehrig had three home runs to Ruth's two, nine hits to Ruth's five, eight runs batted in to Ruth's six, and nine runs scored to Ruth's six. Gehrig batted .529 in the series, and Ruth batted only .333.

won by Hurryoff, with a time of 2:32⅗. The jockey was Mack Garner.

June 29 The **world heavyweight boxing championship** was won by the Italian giant, Primo Carnera, who knocked out Jack Sharkey at Long Island City Bowl, N.Y., in the sixth round.

July 6 In the **first all-star baseball game,** the American League defeated the National League by a score of 4-2. The game was held at Comiskey Park in Chicago before 49,200 fans. Babe Ruth's home run off Bill Hallahan of the Cardinals and his single provided the margin of victory.

July 8 The **Wimbledon** women's singles championship was won by Helen Wills Moody.

July 15-22 The **first solo flight around the world** was made by Wiley Post. Taking off from Floyd Bennett Field on Long Island, N.Y., he flew his Lockheed Vega, *Winnie Mae,* around the globe in 7 days, 18 hrs., 49.5 min., returning to his starting point.

July 28-31 The **national horseshoe pitching championship** was held in Chicago in conjunction with the World's Fair. The contests were held at Soldier's Field, home of the Chicago Bears football team. Ted Allen won the

BILL HARTACK

William Hartack, Jr.
b. Colver, Pa., Dec. 9, 1932

Although Bill Hartack holds none of the major records for jockeys, he has been a consistent winner during years of steady riding, one of two dozen or so jockeys who have won more than 4000 races. From 1955 to 1957, he set a record for the number of races won annually over consecutive years, and it took more than 25 years for anyone to match his mark.

Hartack rode five Kentucky Derby winners, in 1957, 1960, 1962, 1964, and 1969; three Preakness winners, in 1956, 1964, and 1969; and one Belmont Stakes winner in 1960. He has been a member of the National Museum of Racing Hall of Fame since 1959.

---

first of his 13 singles titles, covering 1933-1959. The first black to enter this world championship tournament was Guy H. Marshbanks.

Aug. The **first national softball tournament** was held in Chicago. Forty men's teams and 15 women's teams competed. Chicago teams won both the men's fast pitch and the women's championship, the former title going to the J. L. Friedman Boosters and the latter to the Great Northern Laundry team. The Amateur Softball Association of America was organized this summer and began to stabilize rules and increase the popularity of the game.

Aug. 13 The **PGA golf tournament** was won by Gene Sarazen after a ten-year lapse. In the final round he defeated Willie Goggin, 5 and 4.

Aug. 16 The eighth annual **Hambletonian Stakes** was won in the fourth heat by Mary Reynolds. The driver was Ben White.

Aug. 26 The **U.S. Lawn Tennis Association** women's singles championship was won by Helen Hull Jacobs, to whom Helen Wills Moody defaulted in the third set because of back and hip pain. In the finals of the men's division, on Sept. 10, Frederick J. "Fred" Perry of England became the first English player to win the title since Hugh Doherty won in 1903. Perry defeated Jack Crawford of Australia in the final round.

Oct. 3-7 The 30th annual **World Series** was won by the New York Giants (NL), defeating the Washington Senators (AL) four games to one. Carl Hubbell won two games and allowed no earned runs in 20 innings for the Giants. Mel Ott led the team's attack with two home runs and a .389 average.

Dec. 12 **Eddie Shore,** rugged defenseman of the Boston Bruins, seriously injured Ace Bailey of the Toronto Maple Leafs by an illegal trip, which triggered an attack on Shore by Toronto's Red Horner and a general melee in the Boston Garden.

Dec. 17 In the **first National Football League (NFL) championship playoff,** the Chicago

---

BOB PETTIT

Robert Lee Pettit, Jr.
b. Baton Rouge, La., Dec. 12, 1932

Bob Pettit stayed home in Baton Rouge to play college basketball for Louisiana State, where he made all-American in 1954. Scoring 1893 points, he had a more than respectable game average of 27.4. He was drafted into the National Basketball Association in the first round in 1954 by Milwaukee, whose franchise transferred to St. Louis after the 1954–1955 season, and Pettit remained with the Hawks for the rest of his career, which ended with the 1964–1965 season.

He was a high scorer in the NBA, becoming the first player, on November 13, 1964, to reach a career total of more than 20,000 points. By the end of his career, he had 20,880, now 14th on the all-time list. His game average of 26.4 places him in a tie for fourth place, and his 12,849 rebounds are ninth best. He was in playoff series nine times and had a game average of 25.5 points.

Pettit led the NBA in scoring in 1956 and 1959 and in rebounding in 1956 and helped the Hawks win the NBA championship in 1958. Pettit was the league's rookie of the year in 1955 and most valuable player in 1956 and 1959. He was named to the all-star team in every year of his career except the last. Pettit was elected to the Basketball Hall of Fame in 1970.

JOHNNY UNITAS

John Constantine Unitas
b. Pittsburgh, Pa., May 7, 1933

Several college football coaches turned down Johnny Unitas as a college prospect. He weighed only 145 pounds when he left high school, so he was considered too small for the game. Only the University of Louisville offered him a scholarship. During those years, Louisville's football team did not have an impressive record, but Unitas completed 245 of 502 passes and registered 27 touchdowns in his college career.

Unitas's start in pro football was equally discouraging. Pittsburgh drafted him in 1955 but released him almost at once. He took a construction job and played semipro football until February 1956, when the Baltimore Colts decided to take a chance on him. By 1957, he was voted the most valuable player in the National Football League, and on December 12, 1958, he maneuvered the Colts to the league championship, 23–17, in an overtime game with the New York Giants that is generally regarded as the most exciting football game ever played.

Unitas remained with the Colts through 1972, then played with the San Diego Chargers until he retired in July 1974. Most of the records he set have been broken, but he still holds one: most consecutive games, 47, in which a quarterback threw one or more touchdown passes. Unitas is a member of the Pro Football Hall of Fame.

Bears defeated the New York Giants 23-21 to become NFL champions of 1933. This year the NFL was divided into eastern and western divisions, the leaders of the divisions meeting in a playoff game to determine the league winner. Previously, the league championship went to the team with the highest winning percentage.

1934

The **first rope tow for skiers** in the U.S. was installed at Woodstock, Vt. A Model T Ford provided the power for a rope that took skiers 500 ft. upward. The charge for skiing was $1 a day.

The **lawn bowling** national singles championship was won by Fred Chaplin, Jr., of Brooklyn, N.Y. Chaplin was 16 years old.

College basketball proved its appeal for metropolitan sports fans this year when Ned Irish, a New York sportswriter turned promoter, booked several college teams to play doubleheaders in New York City's Madison Square Garden. Intersectional collegiate competition had begun.

The **penalty shot** made its appearance in ice hockey.

Jan. 1 In **college football bowl games,** the results were Duquesne 33, Miami (Fla.) 7 in the Orange Bowl, and Columbia 7, Stanford 0 in the Rose Bowl. Al Barabas won the game for Columbia by carrying the ball for a touchdown on a hidden-ball play. The 1933 national collegiate football championship was won by Michigan, with a record of seven wins, no losses, one tie.

Jan. 14 For a **ski jump contest,** railroad boxcars brought 43,000 cubic ft. of snow from the Sierra Nevada to Berkeley, Calif. Fifty thousand people watched as Roy Mikkelson, national champion, from a platform 60 ft. high, jumped 125 ft., not up to his usual jumps under normal conditions.

Feb. 14 At the **Westminster Kennel Club** dog show, Ch. Flornell Spicy Bit of Halleston, a wire fox terrier owned by Halleston Kennels, took best-in-show.

Mar. 10 **U.S. figure skating championships** were won in Philadelphia by Suzanne Davis, women's singles; Roger Turner, men's singles; and Grace E. Madden and James L. Madden, pairs.

Mar. 25 The **first annual Masters golf tournament,** held in Augusta, Ga., was won by Horton Smith, who defeated Craig Wood by one stroke, 284-285.

Apr. 3-10 The **NHL Stanley Cup** was won by the Chicago Black Hawks, who defeated the Detroit Red Wings three games to one.

Apr. 19 The 38th **Boston Marathon** was won by Dave Komonen of Ontario, Canada, with a time of 2 hrs., 32 min., 53.8 sec.

May 5 The 60th annual **Kentucky Derby** was won by Cavalcade, with a time of 2:04. The jockey was Mack Garner.

May 12 The 59th annual **Preakness Stakes** was won by High Quest, with a time of 1:58⅕. The jockey was Robert Jones.

HANK AARON

Henry Louis Aaron
b. Mobile, Ala., Feb. 5, 1934

Both Hank Aaron's great skills and his long career in major league baseball, 23 years, account for the records Aaron has compiled. Beginning in the Negro American League and moving on to the minor leagues, Aaron began his major league career in 1954 as a right-handed hitting outfielder with the Milwaukee Braves of the National League. Aaron played for the Braves for all but the last two years of his career, 1975 and 1976. In those seasons he played for the Milwaukee Brewers of the American League, the Braves having become the Atlanta Braves in 1966.

Aaron's most noteworthy feat was to better Babe Ruth's career record of 714 home runs. On April 8, 1974, in Atlanta and on national television, 39 years after Ruth hit number 714, Aaron belted number 715. By the time Aaron retired, his total was 755, and his best year for home runs was 1971, when he hit 47.

Along the way Aaron accumulated other records. His 2297 total runs batted in ranks first; he is second, tied with Ruth, in runs scored, 2174; second in number of times at bat, 12,364; third in number of hits, 3771; and third in games played, 3298. From 1955 to 1975, a total of 21 consecutive years, Aaron was named to the National League all-star team.

A quiet and unassuming man, Aaron since retirement as a player has been vice president and director of player development for the Atlanta Braves. He is in the Baseball Hall of Fame.

May 30 The 22nd **Indianapolis 500** auto race was won by Bill Cummings of Indianapolis, completing the 500-mi. course in 4 hrs., 46 min., 5.2 sec., at an average speed of 104.863 mph.

June 9 The 66th annual **Belmont Stakes** was won by Peace Chance, with a time of 2:29⅕. The jockey was Wayne D. Wright.

June 9 The **U.S. Open golf tournament** was won at Merion Cricket Club, Ardmore, Pa., by Olin Dutra. His 293 total bested Gene Sarazen by one stroke.

June 14 The **world heavyweight boxing championship** was won by Max Baer, who scored a technical knockout over Primo Carnera in the 11th round of a fight held before a crowd of 48,495 in New York City.

June 25 The **heavyweight wrestling championship** was won by Jim Londos, who defeated Jim Browning in a match at Madison Square Garden, New York City.

July 10 The second annual **baseball all-star game** was won by the American League, 9-7. It will live forever in the memories of fans as the game in which Carl Hubbell fanned five immortals in a row: Babe Ruth, Lou Gehrig, Jimmy Foxx, Al Simmons, and Joe Cronin.

BILL RUSSELL

William Fenton Russell
b. Monroe, La., Feb. 12, 1934

In 1980, the Professional Basketball Writers' Association voted Bill Russell the greatest player in the history of the National Basketball Association. Before that he was generally considered the best college basketball player of his time. He played for the University of San Francisco and made it an outstanding defensive team. Russell led the team to successive NCAA championships in 1955 and 1956.

Drafted by the Boston Celtics, Russell played for them throughout his pro career, from 1956 to 1969, during which time the Celtics won the NBA championship 11 times. Playing center, Russell changed the game by his skill at blocking shots and grabbing rebounds. In the latter category, his 21,620 career total is second highest. He scored 14,522 points, a game average of 15.1, and had 4100 assists. In 1960, he set a one-game record of 51 rebounds, which was later broken by Wilt Chamberlain's 55.

In 1966, Russell became the first black coach in NBA history, and he played on and coached the Celtics for three seasons, during which they won two league championships. He also coached Seattle from 1973 to 1977. His complete record as a coach was 324 victories and 249 losses.

Russell collected many honors in the course of his pro career, such as most valuable player five times, in 1958, 1961, 1962, 1963, and 1965; member of the all-star team in 12 of his 13 years; and leader in rebounding in 1957, 1958, 1964, and 1965. He was elected to the Basketball Hall of Fame in 1974.

ROBERTO CLEMENTE

Roberto Walker Clemente
b.   Carolina, P.R., Aug. 18, 1934
d.   Near San Juan, P.R., Dec. 14,
      1972

A tragic accident ended Roberto Clemente's brilliant baseball career, but Clemente had long since proved he would be one of the all-time stars of baseball. He played the outfield for 18 years, from 1955 to 1972, for the Pittsburgh Pirates and was their major resource. He took part in two World Series, 1960 and 1971, both of which the Pirates won, four games to three.

In individual achievements, Clemente was four times the National League batting champion, in 1961, 1964, 1965, and 1967. He was voted the league's most valuable player in 1966 and was 12 times chosen for its all-star teams. He is one of only 16 players to have accumulated 3000 or more hits in a career, and he ended with exactly that number. Clemente had 240 home runs and a lifetime batting average of .317. As a batter, no type of pitch baffled him, and as a fielder, he had a remarkable throwing arm that made base

runners extra cautious.

Clemente died in an airplane crash in the sea off San Juan, Puerto Rico. He had been escorting relief supplies for the victims of an earthquake in Nicaragua. The Baseball Hall of Fame waived its five-year waiting period after a player's retirement and immediately elected him to membership. Clemente remains a national hero in Puerto Rico.

July 29   The **PGA golf tournament** was won by Paul Runyan at Park Country Club, Williamsville, N.Y. He defeated Craig Wood in the final round, 1 up in 38 holes.

Aug. 15   The ninth annual **Hambletonian Stakes** was won in the fourth heat by Lord Jim. The driver was Hugh P. Parshall.

Aug. 19   The **U.S. Lawn Tennis Association singles championships** were won by Helen Hull Jacobs in the women's division and Fred Perry of Great Britain in the men's division (Sept. 12).

Sept. 17-25   The **America's Cup** was successfully defended by the U.S. yacht *Rainbow,* which defeated the British challenger *Endeavour* four races to two.

Oct. 3-9   The 31st annual **World Series** was won by the St. Louis Cardinals (NL), defeating the Detroit Tigers (AL) four games to three. Dizzy and Daffy Dean were the winning pitchers in the four Cardinal wins, taking two each. In the sixth inning of the final game, Ducky Medwick slid hard into Detroit third baseman Marv Owen, and a brief fight ensued. When Medwick went out to left field to take his position, he was showered with fruit and debris by fans in the bleachers. To enable play to resume, Judge Kenesaw Mountain Landis, the baseball commissioner, ordered Medwick to leave the game and police to protect the field. The Cards went on to win by the score of 11-0. Medwick batted .379 for the series and drove in five runs.

Nov.   The **American Paddle Tennis Association**

was formed by the Fox Meadow Tennis Club of Scarsdale, N.Y., the Manursing Island Club of Rye, N.Y., and the Field Club of Greenwich, Conn., pioneers in platform paddle tennis.

Dec.   The **leading money winner in professional golf** for this year was Paul Runyan, who won $6767. After expenses he netted $2.

Dec. 9   The **NFL championship** was won by the New York Giants, defeating the Chicago Bears 30-13.

1935

The **butterfly stroke** over a 200-yard distance became a recognized event in the NCAA men's swimming championships. The new event was won by Jack Kasley of the U. of Michigan. The fish-tail kick for the butterfly was first permitted in the 1957 championships.

A new **basketball rule** prohibited an offensive player, with or without the ball, from remaining within the free-throw lane for more than 3 sec. This eliminated so-called basket hanging and increased the speed of the game.

The first annual **Heisman Trophy,** for outstanding college football player of 1935, was voted to Chicago halfback Jay Berwanger. The trophy,

ROGER MARIS

Roger Eugene Maris
b. Hibbing, Minn., Sept. 10, 1934
d. Houston, Tex., Dec. 15, 1985

When Roger Maris hit 61 home runs in 1961, one more than the great Babe Ruth hit in 1927, he broke a record many old-time baseball fans hoped would never be bettered. His 61st came on October 1 at Yankee Stadium, in the last game of the season. Controversy still surrounds the feat, because teams played 162 games in 1961 but only 154 in 1927. The baseball commissioner ruled that the record book must show this difference in the number of games played.

Maris entered the major leagues in 1957 with the Cleveland Indians and the next year played part of the season for the Indians and then went to Kansas City. He joined the Yankees as an outfielder in 1960 and ended his career as a member of the St. Louis Cardinals in 1967 and 1968. In his 12 years in the majors, Maris hit 275 home runs and had a batting average of .260. He hit 39 home runs in 1960 and 33 in 1962, his best years except for 1961. Maris was voted the most valuable player in the American League in 1960 and 1961.

He appeared in seven World Series, five with the Yankees, from 1960 through 1964, and twice with the Cardinals, in 1967 and 1968. In the 44 Series games Maris played, he hit six home runs.

The controversy over his accomplishment in 1961 appeared to affect Maris and cause him to retire from baseball early. He died of lymphatic cancer when he was only 51.

---

named for John W. Heisman, who was an excellent college football player and then a coach over a period of several decades beginning in 1892, was established to honor "the outstanding college football player in the United States."

Jan. 1 In **college football bowl games,** the results were Bucknell 26, Miami (Fla.) 0 in the Orange Bowl; Alabama 29, Stanford 13 in the Rose Bowl; and Tulane 20, Temple 14 in the first annual Sugar Bowl. Two teams were named 1934 national college football champions in votes by two sports organizations: Minnesota, with a record of eight wins, no losses, no ties, and Alabama, with ten wins, no losses, no ties.

Feb. 9 **U.S. figure skating championships** were won in New Haven, Conn., by Maribel Y. Vinson, women's singles; Robin H. Lee, men's singles; Maribel Y. Vinson and George E. B. Hill, pairs.

Feb. 13 At the **Westminster Kennel Club** dog show, Ch. Nunsoe Duc de la Terrace, a standard poodle owned by Blakeen Kennels, took best-in-show.

Apr. 2 The **first woman trainer of thorough-bred race horses** was licensed by the Jockey Club of the U.S. She was Mary Hirsch, 22-year-old daughter of the well-known race horse trainer Max Hirsch.

ELGIN BAYLOR

Elgin Gay Baylor
b. Washington, D.C., Sept. 16, 1934

Elgin Baylor played basketball at both the College of Idaho and Seattle University and was drafted in 1958 as a first round selection by the Minneapolis Lakers. He spent his 14-year career with the Lakers, who moved to Los Angeles after the 1959–1960 season. Baylor was an all-around player whose impressive career was cut short in 1972 by recurring knee trouble.

During his career, he scored 23,149 points, 11th on the career list, with a game average of 27.4, second best. Baylor also appeared in 12 postseason playoff series, scoring 3623 points, and in 11 all-star games, in which he registered 218 points. On November 11, 1960, in a game against the New York Knicks, Baylor scored 71 points, an NBA record at the time. He still shares the record for the most field goals in a championship game, 22, against Boston, April 14, 1962.

After retiring, Baylor coached New Orleans from 1976 through 1979, without great success, the team winning 86 games while losing 135. Baylor was rookie of the year in 1959 and was selected for the all-star team ten times. He was elected to the Basketball Hall of Fame in 1976.

MAUREEN "LITTLE MO" CONNOLLY

Maureen Catherine Connolly Brinker
b. San Diego, Calif., Sept. 17, 1934
d. Dallas, Tex., June 21, 1969

Maureen Connolly was the first woman to complete the grand slam of tennis, winning the U.S., British, French, and Australian championships in 1953. Her most spectacular victory in the sweep came at Wimbledon on July 4, 1953, when she defeated Doris Hart in the tennis equivalent of a slugging match, 8–6, 7–5. Earlier, when she was 13, she had won the national junior championship.

Little Mo's first major victory came in 1951, when she became the second youngest woman and the youngest in 47 years to win the U.S. title, defeating Shirley Fry in three sets. The victory came two weeks before her 17th birthday. After this 1951 victory, she lost only four matches during the rest of her career.

Connolly retained the U.S. title in 1952 and also won at Wimbledon that year as well as in 1954 and in France in 1954. Connolly was still only 17 when she won that first Wimbledon title, defeating Louise Brough in straight sets to become the

youngest American to win this championship since 1905. She played on the Wightman Cup teams from 1951 to 1954 and won all her matches.

Connolly had always loved horses, and her husband was an expert horseman. In July 1954, she suffered a serious leg injury in a riding accident and was forced to retire from tennis. She helped other players as a coach but died of cancer before her 35th birthday. Connolly became a member of the International Tennis Hall of Fame in 1968.

Apr. 4-9 The **NHL Stanley Cup** was won by the Montreal Maroons, who defeated the Toronto Maple Leafs in three straight games.

Apr. 8 The second annual **Masters golf tournament** was won by Gene Sarazen, who won in a playoff round against Craig Wood. Sarazen's second shot on the 15th hole ended in the cup for a double eagle 2, which erased Wood's three-stroke lead.

Apr. 19 The 39th **Boston Marathon** was won by John Kelley of Arlington, Mass., with a time of 2 hrs., 32 min., 7.4 sec.

Apr. 26 **Frank Boucher** of the New York Rangers was given permanent possession of the Lady Byng Trophy for the most sportsmanlike player in the NHL. Boucher had won it for 7 of the 11

years of the trophy's history. It was announced that a new trophy would be awarded in the next year.

May 4 The 61st annual **Kentucky Derby** was won by Omaha, with a time of 2:05. The jockey was Willis Saunders.

May 11 The 60th annual **Preakness Stakes** was won by Omaha, with a time of 1:58²⁄₅. The jockey was Willis Saunders.

May 24 The **first night baseball game** to be played in the major leagues drew 25,000 fans to a game in Cincinnati in which the Reds defeated the Philadelphia Phillies 2-1. Pres. Franklin D. Roosevelt switched on the floodlights from Washington, D.C.

May 30 The 23rd **Indianapolis 500** auto race

A. J. FOYT

Anthony Joseph Foyt, Jr.
b. Houston, Tex., Jan. 16, 1935

On several counts, A. J. Foyt is the most successful American auto racing driver in the history of the sport. By the age of 18, he was already well known among stock car racers and fans. In 1958, he finished 16th in his first Indianapolis 500. Three years and three attempts later, in 1961,

Foyt won this demanding event. Since then, Foyt has won the Indy three more times, in 1964, 1967, and 1977. He has also finished second twice.

Badly injured in races in both 1965 and 1966, Foyt nevertheless came back in 1967, teaming with Dan Gurney to become the first Americans to win the 24 Hours of Le Mans, in France.

Foyt has won the U.S. Auto Club Championship seven times, in 1960, 1961, 1963, 1964, 1967, 1975, and 1979. This record is unmatched by any other driver. He has also taken the USAC stock car championship three times. In the course of his many victories, Foyt has also won more prize money than any other USAC driver.

TENLEY ALBRIGHT

Tenley Emma Albright
b. Newton Centre, Mass., July 18, 1935

In spite of a mild case of polio when Tenley Albright was 11 years old, she went on to become the first American woman figure skater to win the world championship, in 1953, and an Olympic gold medal, in 1956. She had learned to skate at age 9, and this sport helped her recover from the effects of her illness.

Albright was only 16 when she won her first U.S. championship, and she repeated this triumph in the next four years. When only 17, on February 15, 1953, she won the world championship at Davos, Switzerland. She earned this title again in 1955 but lost it the next year to her younger rival, Carol Heiss.

In the 1956 Olympics, Albright became the first American woman to win the gold medal in figure skating, but two weeks later, skating on an injured ankle, she lost her world title to Heiss.

Albright became a surgeon and is an authority on sports medicine. In 1979 she was the first woman to become an officer of the U.S. Olympic Committee.

---

was won by Kelly Petillo of Los Angeles, Calif., completing the 500-mi. course in 4 hrs., 42 min., 22.71 sec., at an average speed of 106.240 mph.

June 8 The 67th annual **Belmont Stakes** was won by Omaha, with a time of 2:30⅗. The jockey was Willis Saunders. Omaha became the third horse to win horse racing's Triple Crown.

June 8 The **U.S. Open golf tournament** was won by Sam Parks, Jr., at Oakmont (Pennsylvania) Country Club. His winning total of 299 was the result of lightning-fast greens that enraged the competitors.

June 13 The **world heavyweight boxing championship** was won by James J. Braddock over Max Baer on points in 15 rounds.

July 6 At the **Wimbledon** tennis championships, the women's singles title was won by Helen Wills Moody over Helen Hull Jacobs in a close three-set match. This was Moody's seventh Wimbledon victory, achieved after a two-year absence from tournament play.

July 8 The third annual **baseball all-star game** was won by the American League 4 to 1. The press chided the National League clubs for not taking the game seriously.

Aug. 13 The **first roller derby** began in Chicago under the auspices of promoter Leo Seltzer. At first the derby was an endurance contest, but by 1937 it had become a team sport with both men's and women's teams and bodily contact allowed. Still later it became a popular TV attraction, first shown on CBS on Nov. 29, 1948.

Aug. 14 The tenth running of the **Hambletonian Stakes** was won in two straight heats by Greyhound. The driver was Sep Palin.

Aug. 15-31 The **first national skeet shooting championships** were held at Cleveland, Ohio. The overall title was won by Henry Joy with a score of 517. The 12-gauge award went to Lovel

---

RAFER JOHNSON

Rafer Lewis Johnson
b. Hillsboro, Tex., Aug. 18, 1935

Rafer Johnson was a star athlete in four sports in high school and went on to success in track at UCLA, all this despite a serious injury. At age 14, he caught his leg in a conveyor belt. In 1955, he won the decathlon at the Pan-American Games in Mexico City and established himself forever as a great American athlete.

Johnson was the favorite to win the decathlon at the 1956 Olympics in Melbourne, Australia, but a knee injury forced him out of the long jump entirely, and he finished second in the decathlon to Milton Campbell, another American. He then set his aim at the 1960 Games. On July 9, 1960, Johnson turned in what was at the time a world record score of 8683 in the combined AAU national championships and the Olympic tryouts. Then, on September 6 at Rome, he won the decathlon with a score of 8392, an Olympic mark since exceeded.

1
9
3
5

PAUL HORNUNG

Paul Vernon Hornung
b. Louisville, Ky., Dec. 23, 1935

The career of magnificent running back Paul Hornung, called the Golden Boy of Football, was marred by his suspension from National Football League play for 11 months beginning in April 1963. He was accused of gambling. Alex Karras of the Detroit Lions was suspended at the same time. Neither was accused of betting against his own team, but NFL rules forbid a player to bet on any football game.

Hornung first made his mark in football at Notre Dame, where he was an all-American in 1955 and winner of the Heisman Trophy in 1956. Out of college, he joined the Green Bay Packers and played for them for nine seasons. Under Coach Vince Lombardi, Hornung became the sparkplug of an offense that won the NFL championship for three years running, 1960 to 1962.

In 1960, Hornung set a record for scoring in a season with 176 points—15 touchdowns, 41 points after touchdowns, and 15 field goals. The next year, he was voted most valuable player in the league. His most spectacular performance came on December 12, 1965, when this talented halfback ran for five touchdowns.

Hornung is a member of the College Football Hall of Fame and the Pro Football Hall of Fame.

S. Pratt, a clerk in a sporting goods store, with a score of 244 out of 250 targets.

Sept. 11 The **U.S. Lawn Tennis Association singles championship** was won by Helen Hull Jacobs, for the fourth consecutive time, in the women's division and Wilmer L. Allison over Sidney B. Wood, Jr., in the men's division (Sept. 12).

Oct. 2-7 The 32nd annual **World Series** was won by the Detroit Tigers (AL), defeating the Chicago Cubs (NL) four games to two. It was the first win ever for Detroit. Tommy Bridges won two games, and Pete Fox, an outfielder, and Charley Gehringer, the great second basemen, were the Tigers' heavy hitters. Fox hit for a .385 average, and Gehringer .375.

Oct. 20 An **outlaw bronco,** Black Bottom, which no man had ever been able to ride successfully, broke its neck and died while throwing a rider at a rodeo in Oklahoma City, Okla.

Oct. 23 The **PGA golf tournament** was won by Johnny Revolta, with a 5 and 4 win over Tommy Armour in the final round.

Dec. 15 The **NFL championship** was won by the Detroit Lions, defeating the New York Giants 26-7.

SANDY KOUFAX

Sanford Koufax
b. Brooklyn, N.Y., Dec. 30, 1935

Expert opinion has it that if Sandy Koufax had not retired prematurely after the 1966 season because of an arm ailment, he might have become the greatest pitcher in baseball history. A left-hander with great speed and a fine curve, Koufax had been blazing his way through the National League for a dozen years and had compiled an overall record of 165 wins and 87 losses, for a percentage of .655 and an earned run average of 2.76.

Koufax was a local boy who made good. Born in Brooklyn, he joined the Dodgers there in 1955 and went with them in 1958 to California when they became the Los Angeles Dodgers. He played in four World Series, 1959, 1963, 1965, and 1966, winning four games and losing three. In the 1963 series, Koufax struck out 23 Yankees in four games, a record. In the first game, he struck out 15 batters. On September 9, 1965, he pitched a perfect game against the Chicago Cubs, the eighth perfect game in National League history. With this performance, Koufax also became the first pitcher ever to hurl four no-hit games.

In his career, Koufax struck out 2396 batters and walked only 817. He won the Cy Young Award three times, in 1963, 1965, and 1966, and was named to the Baseball Hall of Fame in 1972.

1936

Platform paddle tennis this year became a popular off-season sport for tennis players, following the development by Donald K. Evans of 12-ft.-high wire walls kept under uniform tension around the platform.

The opening of the *Ice Follies,* produced by Oscar Johnson, Edward Shipstad, and Roy Shipstad, marked the beginning of a modern era of ice shows featuring the world's leading figure and acrobatic skaters. It was followed by *Ice Capades, Sonja Henie Ice Revue, Hollywood Ice Review,* and *Holiday on Ice.*

In **polo,** the Cup of the Americas, contested by Argentina and the U.S., was won by Argentina, two matches to none, at Meadow Brook Club, Westbury, N.Y. The U.S. recaptured the trophy in 1939, but since World War II Argentinian supremacy in polo has been almost unchallenged.

William H. Foster and the publishers of *National Sportsman* and *Hunting and Fishing* introduced refinements in the rules of skeet shooting and began featuring the sport. By 1940 the National Skeet Shooting Association had grown to 50,000 members, about 1000 of them women.

Basketball was named an Olympic sport, and James Naismith was honored internationally as its creator. At the Summer Olympics in Berlin, Germany, in August, the U.S. won the first of its seven consecutive gold medals in basketball.

The **American Badminton Association** was formed. Badminton's popularity expanded rapidly in the 1930s.

The **Baseball Hall of Fame** was established in Cooperstown, N.Y., by a group of baseball leaders. A shrine and museum were planned to honor the players considered immortals of the game.

Jan. 1 In **college football bowl games,** the results were Catholic U. 20, Mississippi 19 in the Orange Bowl; Stanford 7, Southern Methodist 0 in the Rose Bowl; and Texas Christian 3, Louisiana State 2 in the Sugar Bowl. The national college football championship for 1935 was awarded to Minnesota, with a record of eight wins, no losses, no ties, and SMU, with 12 wins, one loss, no ties.

Feb. 5-16 At the **Winter Olympics** in Garmisch-Partenkirchen, Germany, the U.S. won two gold medals and placed fifth in the unofficial team scoring after Norway, Germany, Sweden, and Finland. One of the U.S. gold medals was won by the two-man bobsled team.

Feb. 12 At the **Westminster Kennel Club** dog show, Ch. Saint Margaret Magnificent of Clairedale, a Sealyham terrier owned by the Clairedale Kennels, took best-in-show.

Feb. 13 **U.S. figure skating championships** were won in Chicago by Maribel Y. Vinson, women's singles; Robin H. Lee, men's singles; Maribel Y. Vinson and George E. B. Hill, pairs; and Marjorie Parker and Joseph K. Savage, dance.

Mar. 18 The **women's world table tennis championship** was won by an American for the first time. Ruth Hughes Aaron took the title at the

JIM BROWN

James Nathaniel Brown
b. Simon Island, Ga., Feb. 17, 1936

From 1957 to 1965, the most awe-inspiring ball-carrier in professional football was Jim Brown of the Cleveland Browns. As another player said, "The best way to tackle Brown is to hold on and wait for help."

A star athlete in high school, Brown attended Syracuse University, where he won letters in football, lacrosse, basketball, and track. In his final college football game in 1956, Brown scored 43 points in a 61–7 rout of Colgate.

In 1957, Brown's first year as a pro, he gained 942 yards rushing and was named rookie of the year. His career was a continuing saga of league or personal records broken, and he was named the best back of the decade 1950–1960. His prowess in rushing made him a drawing card with fans, and in 1963 he was paid $45,000, then the highest salary of any pro football player.

On November 1, 1964, Brown became the first back to pass the 10,000-yard mark in rushing. In his nine-year career, he gained a total of 12,312 yards, an average of 5.2 yards a carry in 2359 attempts. This record has since been surpassed by Walter Payton, but Brown still holds the lifetime record for touchdowns, 126.

Brown retired in 1965 and became a movie actor. He was elected to the Pro Football Hall of Fame in 1971.

A WEEK OF TRIUMPH FOR JESSE OWENS

If anyone needed proof that Adolf Hitler's racial theory of Aryan supremacy was wrong, Jesse Owens, the great black American track star, provided the data and did so dramatically. At the 1936 Olympic Games in Berlin, with Hitler in attendance on some days, Owens won four gold medals and set or tied a record in each of his events. A stone-faced Hitler looked aside every time Owens or one of the other black athletes at the games was awarded a gold medal.

On August 3, before a capacity crowd of 110,000, Owens won the 100-meter dash in 10.3 seconds, equaling the world and Olympic records. To make matters worse for Hitler, Ralph Metcalfe, another black member of the United States team, placed second in the event.

(Metcalfe, holder of many track titles in his day, won the United States National Championship in the 100-meter dash from 1932 through 1934 and the 200-meter dash from 1932 through 1936.) Hitler was present for this one-two finish in the dash and also for the hammer throw, in which German athletes finished one-two. In public, the dictator did not congratulate any of the four medal winners, but later he met privately with the two German athletes to offer his congratulations.

On August 4, before another capacity crowd, Jesse Owens won the long jump, then known as the broad jump, by leaping 26 feet, 5 inches to set a new Olympic record. On August 5, Owens won his third gold medal when he took the 200-meter dash in 20.7 seconds,

setting a world and Olympic record. Finally, on August 9, Owens ran the first leg of the 400-meter relay, passing the baton on with a lead of 4 yards. The United States team added another 11 yards to its lead by the time the race was over. The time of 39.8 seconds was to stand as an Olympic record for 20 years.

So impressive was the Olympic performance by Owens that an Associated Press poll taken in 1950 voted him the greatest track athlete of the first half of the century. While only the most dedicated of sports fans know of this honor, almost everyone interested in sports knows the 1936 Olympics as the games in which an individual athlete, by his performance, made an eloquent statement about brotherhood and democracy.

---

international tournament in Prague, Czecho-slovakia.

Mar. 24 The **longest hockey game** to date in National Hockey League history—2 hrs., 56 min., 30 sec.—saw the Detroit Red Wings defeat the Montreal Maroons 1-0. The time exceeded the old mark, set April 3, 1933, by nearly 12 min.

Apr. 3 In the **shortest boxing bout fought with gloves,** Al Carr defeated Lew Massey in New Haven, Conn., in a bout recorded as lasting 10 sec. of the first round. The fight was actually stopped after 7 sec., with Massey out cold. The shortest fight seen on national television was held 50 years later, on July 26, 1986, when Mike Tyson knocked out Marvin Frazier in 30 sec. of the first round.

Apr. 5-11 The **NHL Stanley Cup** was won by the Detroit Red Wings, who defeated the Toronto Maple Leafs three games to one.

Apr. 6 The **Masters golf tournament** was again won by Horton Smith, with a 285 total, one better than Harry Cooper.

Apr. 20 The 40th **Boston Marathon** was won by Ellison Brown of Alton, R.I., with a time of 2 hrs., 33 min., 40.8 sec.

May 2 The 62nd annual **Kentucky Derby** was

won by Bold Venture, with a time of 2:03⅗. The jockey was Ira Hanford.

May 16 The 61st annual **Preakness Stakes** was won by Bold Venture, with a time of 1:59. The jockey was George Woolf.

May 27 The **first woman coxswain** of a men's college varsity crew was Sally Stearns, who coxed Rollins College in a race against Marietta College.

May 30 The 24th **Indianapolis 500** auto race was won by Louis Meyer of Huntington Park, Calif., completing the 500-mi. course in 4 hrs., 35 min., 3.39 sec., at an average speed of 109.069 mph.

June 6 The 68th annual **Belmont Stakes** was won by Granville, with a time of 2:30. The jockey was Jimmy Stout.

June 6 The **U.S. Open golf tournament** was won by Tony Manero, whose 282 was a record for a 72-hole title event. Play was at the Baltusrol Golf Club, Springfield, N.J.

July 4 At the **Wimbledon** tennis championships in England, the women's singles title was won by Helen Hull Jacobs, who after four previous losses in the final round crowned her career with the elusive victory.

July 7 The fourth annual **baseball all-star game**

WILT CHAMBERLAIN

Wilton Norman Chamberlain
b. Philadelphia, Pa., Aug. 21, 1936

Wilt the Stilt Chamberlain stands out among basketball players not just because of his 7-foot, 1-inch height but also because of the numerous records he set. In his first varsity game at the University of Kansas, he scored 52 points, and in the two years he played there, Kansas won 42 of 50 games. After college, Chamberlain played in 1958–1959 with the clever and entertaining Harlem Globetrotters.

After being drafted by the Philadelphia Warriors, Chamberlain began a 14-year pro career, between 1959 and 1973, that took him from Philadelphia to San Francisco to Philadelphia to Los Angeles to Philadelphia to San Francisco to Philadelphia, and back to Los Angeles. In the course of this seemingly vagabond career, he scored 31,419 points in regular season play, second highest, and averaged 30.1 points per game, putting him in first place. In addition, he ranks first in rebounds with 23,924.

Chamberlain appeared in 13 playoff series and on 13 all-star teams. He had the honor in 1960 of being selected not only as rookie of the year but also as most valuable player. The latter award went to him three more times, in 1966, 1967, and 1968. His records are more than remarkable: the only National Basketball Association player to score 3000 and 4000 points in a season; single-game record for most points, 100; most field goals attempted in a game, 63, and most field goals made, 36, on March 2, 1962; most single-game rebounds, 55; and most consecutive field goals, 35. Chamberlain led the NBA in field goal percentage nine times between 1961 and 1973.

After retiring as a player, he coached San Diego of the American Basketball Association in 1973–1974, the team finishing with a 37–47 record. Chamberlain was selected for the Basketball Hall of Fame in 1978.

---

was won by the National League, which beat the American League 4-1. It was the first time the National League had won the event. Lon Warneke, of the Cubs, stopped an American League rally in the seventh inning to preserve the win, following six strong innings pitched by Dizzy Dean and Carl Hubbell.

Aug. 5-16 At the **Summer Olympics** in Berlin, Germany, the U.S. won 20 gold medals and placed second in the unofficial team scoring, behind Germany. The star of the games was the U.S. athlete Jesse Owens, who won four gold medals in the 100- and 200-meter dashes, the long jump, and as a member of the 400-m. relay team.

Aug. 12 The 11th running of the **Hambletonian Stakes** was won in two straight heats by Rosalind. The driver was Ben White.

Sept. 12 In the **U.S. Lawn Tennis Association singles championships,** Alice Marble unseated Helen Jacobs in three sets in the women's division. Fred Perry of England became the first foreigner to win the men's singles title three times running, in a close five-set victory over Don Budge.

Sept. 30-Oct. 6 The 33rd annual **World Series** was won by the New York Yankees (AL), defeating the New York Giants (NL) four games to two. Except for Carl Hubbell and Hal Schu-

macher's winning games, the Yankee hitters were uncontrollable, especially outfielder Jake Powell, with a .425 average; third baseman Red Rolfe, with .400; and Joe DiMaggio, with .346. The team batted .302 and outscored the Giants 43-23. In the second game, the Yankees set a new series record by winning 18-4. Every player had at least one hit and scored at least one run.

Nov. 22 The **PGA golf tournament** was won by Denny Shute at Pinehurst, N.C. He defeated Jimmy Thomson in the final round, 3 and 2.

Dec. 1 The **Heisman Trophy** for outstanding college football player of 1936 was voted to Yale end Larry Kelley.

Dec. 4 A **coast-to-coast trip on roller skates** was achieved by Norman Skelly, 28, a roller rink operator, and John Shefuga, 27, both of Boston. They arrived in Los Angeles after having left Boston on Oct. 2. They skated during 55 days of their trip. Skelly returned east by hitchhiking to New York City.

Dec. 13 The **NFL championship** was won by the Green Bay Packers, defeating the Boston Redskins 21-6.

Dec. 27 A **ski rack for automobiles** was reported by the *New York Times* as one of the developments of the year in the motor world. Made by the Auto-Ski-Rack Co., of New York

City, the device would hold as many as five pairs of skis on the top of a car "without scratching."

Dec. 30 **Basketball's potential for excellence** in individual performance and its popularity as a spectator sport were brought to new heights by the one-handed shot maker from Stanford U., Hank Luisetti, at Madison Square Garden, New York City. By a score of 45-31, before 17,623 fans, Stanford defeated Long Island U., previously undefeated in 43 games. Luisetti scored 15 points.

Dec. 31 Effective Jan. 1, 1938, **no more than 14 golf clubs** would be allowed in tournament play, the USGA announced. The move was expected to make caddies' lives easier and speed up the game.

1937

Michigan U. swimmers won the first **NCAA men's swimming championships** at which team points were awarded. Michigan repeated in 1938-1941, edging Ohio State and Yale. One of these three won the title in every year through 1962, except for 1960, when Southern California topped Michigan.

The **world horseshoe pitching championship,** men's singles, was won by Fernando Isais. In the period 1937-1958, Isais would capture nine titles. He or Ted Allen won every men's individual championship held between 1933 and 1959 except one. Guy Zimmerman won in 1954.

The **first amateur roller skating championships** were held at the Arena Gardens in Detroit. The speed skating title was won by Lloyd Christopher of St. Louis. Seventeen skating clubs met here to organize and develop amateur competition. This year the Roller Skating Rink Operators of America was formed, to be followed later by the U.S. Amateur Federation of Roller Skating.

Baseball is 90 percent mental. The other half is physical.

Yogi Berra

Congress passed the **Pittman-Robertson Federal Aid in Wildlife Restoration Act,** placing a 10% excise tax on sporting arms and ammunition, to be used for the benefit of wildlife and nature conservation.

Duck hunters organized Ducks Unlimited, a private organization for the betterment of waterfowl and waterfowling by attention to wetlands and fowl nesting habitats.

The popular DN class of **ice yachts** resulted from a contest sponsored by the *Detroit News.* In 1953 the DN class organization was formed, and the first North American Championship Regatta was held. In 1972 the DN Association changed its name to the International Ice Yacht Racing Association and planned a DN World Gold Cup Regatta for 1973.

A new **basketball rule** eliminated the center jump after a basket. This speeded up the game and increased spectator interest.

The **first national badminton championships** to be held were won by Walter R. Kramer in men's singles and Mrs. Del Barkhuff in women's singles.

Jan. 1 In **college football bowl games,** the results were Texas Christian 16, Marquette 6 in the first annual Cotton Bowl; Duquesne 13, Mississippi State 12 in the Orange Bowl; Pittsburgh 21, Washington 0 in the Rose Bowl; and Santa Clara 21, Louisiana State 14 in the Sugar Bowl. This season the Associated Press, in its first poll of football sportswriters, ranked Minnesota the leading national college football team of 1936.

Jan. 20 Announcement was made of the election to the **Baseball Hall of Fame** of Nap Lajoie, second baseman; Tris Speaker, outfielder; and Cy Young, pitcher.

Feb. 3-6 **World table tennis titles** were won by U.S. men's and women's teams at Baden, Austria. The U.S. men defeated Hungary in the final, 5½ matches to 3½, to win the Swathling Cup. The U.S. women defeated Czechoslovakia three matches to one to win the Corbillon Cup.

Feb. 11 At the **Westminster Kennel Club** dog show, Ch. Flornell Spicy Piece of Halleston, a wire fox terrier owned by Halleston Kennels, took best-in-show.

Feb. 13 U.S. **figure skating championships** were won in Chicago by Maribel Y. Vinson, women's singles; Robin H. Lee, men's singles; Maribel Y. Vinson and George E. B. Hill, pairs; and Nettie C. Prantel and Harold Hartshorne, dance.

Mar. 6 A **revolver marksman outshot an**

archer in a contest at Utica, N.Y. Firing a .38-caliber revolver at 15 yards, Lt. Dennis J. Janiekwicz of the Utica police department scored 267 out of 300 bull's-eyes to 242 for the archer, Grant Merriman.

Apr. 4   The **Masters golf tournament** was won by Byron Nelson. His 283 was two strokes better than the 285 carded by Ralph Guldahl.

Apr. 6-15   The **NHL Stanley Cup** was won by the Detroit Red Wings, who defeated the New York Rangers three games to two.

Apr. 19   The 41st **Boston Marathon** was won by Walter Young of Verdun, Quebec, Canada, with a time of 2 hrs., 33 min., 20 sec.

May 8   The 63rd annual **Kentucky Derby** was won by War Admiral, with a time of 2:03⅕. The jockey was Charles Kurtsinger.

May 15   The 62nd annual **Preakness Stakes** was won by War Admiral, with a time of 1:58⅖. The jockey was Charles Kurtsinger.

May 30   The **PGA golf tournament** was again won by Denny Shute, with a 1-up, 37-hole victory over Harold "Jug" McSpaden in the final round.

May 31   The 27th **Indianapolis 500** auto race was won by Wilbur Shaw of Indianapolis, completing the 500-mi. course in 4 hrs., 24 min., 7.8 sec., at an average speed of 113.580 mph.

June 5   The 69th annual **Belmont Stakes** was won by War Admiral, with a time of 2:28⅗. The jockey was Charles Kurtsinger. War Admiral thus became the fourth horse to win the Triple Crown.

June 12   The **U.S. Open golf tournament** was won by Ralph Guldahl at Oakland Hills Country Club, Birmingham, Mich. Sam Snead finished second.

June 22   The **world heavyweight boxing championship** was won by Joe Louis, who knocked out James J. Braddock in the eighth round at Chicago.

July 2   At the **Wimbledon** tennis championship in England, the men's singles championship was won by Don Budge, who defeated Baron Gottfried von Cramm of Germany in straight sets. Budge and Gene Mako won the doubles title over von Cramm and Heiner Henkel.

July 7   The fifth annual **baseball all-star game** was won by the American League, which defeated the National League 8-3 and picked up its fourth victory in the event. Lou Gehrig's big homer off Dizzy Dean and his double off Van Lingle Mungo together were enough for the American League victory.

July 27   The **Davis Cup** international tennis challenge round was won by the U.S. team, which defeated Great Britain four matches to one.

July 31-Aug. 5   The **America's Cup** was successfully defended by the yacht *Ranger,* which won four straight races from the British challenger, *Endeavour II.*

Aug.   Jack Milne of Pasadena, Calif., became the first U.S. **motorcyclist** to win the world championship in speedway—short-track, dirt-oval—racing at Wembley, near London, England, before 85,000 fans.

Aug. 12   The 12th running of the **Hambletonian Stakes** was won in straight heats by Shirley Hanover. The driver was Henry Thomas.

Sept. 4   The first **women's bicycle riding championships** were held in Buffalo, N.Y. Doris Kopsky, of Belleville, N.J., won the 1-mi. race in 4 min., 22.4 sec.

Sept. 11   The **U.S. Lawn Tennis Association sin-**

RICHARD PETTY

Richard Lee Petty
b.   Randleman, N.C., July 2, 1937

Richard Petty, on the basis of races run and racing victories, is the king of the road among racing car drivers. Considering winnings, miles driven, and records set, only A. J. Foyt is in the same class.

Petty's outstanding achievement thus far is his string of seven victories in the Daytona 500—no one else has won it more than twice—coming in 1964, 1966, 1971, 1973, 1974, 1979, and 1981. Petty has also been the National Association for Stock Car Auto Racing (NASCAR) Grand National Champion seven times, in 1964, 1967, 1971, 1972, 1974, 1975, and 1979. Petty holds the NASCAR record for most races, 1000 as of mid-June 1986, and the most won, 200.

He belongs to a car-racing family. Petty's father, Lee, was NASCAR Grand National Champion in 1954, 1958, and 1959 and won the first Daytona 500 in 1961. Richard's son, Kyle, is also a racing driver.

A TENNIS MATCH TO REMEMBER

When the two star tennis players took the court at Wimbledon on July 20, 1937, they were matched in the decisive encounter of the Davis Cup interzone finals between Germany and the United States. It was expected by all who followed tennis that Baron Gottfried von Cramm, representing Germany, would lose to Don Budge, the best player on the United States squad. Budge, with a big serve and marvelous forehand, had taken von Cramm in straight sets just weeks before in British title play at Wimbledon. With the team score 2–2 in matches, things looked good for a U.S. Davis Cup victory.

To the surprise of the spectators, however, as soon as play began it became apparent that Budge was not in top form and that von Cramm was playing superb tennis. Von Cramm started things off by holding service in the first game without allowing Budge a single point. It was not going to be an easy day for Budge. Yet despite Budge's poor stroking and lethargic play, so close was the first set that it went to 14 games, with von Cramm winning 8–6. The second set was more of the same—hard-fought points, with Budge hanging in at 5–5 until von Cramm broke his service in the 11th game and went on to win the set 7–5. Budge seemed at times to be on the verge of rousing himself, but he did not play his best. Now he was down 2–0 in sets.

The third set was a different story. Budge moved into a 4–2 lead after six games and held on to win the set 6–4. And the fourth set was a rout. It took Budge only 5 minutes to win the first four games, losing only five points in the four games, and von Cramm appeared to be through. The set ended with Budge winning handily, 6–2.

Now the players took their positions to play the fifth and deciding set. Budge, who had shown what he really could do in the previous set, confounded the spectators. Von Cramm broke Budge's service in the fourth game to take a 3–1 lead and held service to extend his lead to 4–1. Budge, realizing it was now or never, began rushing the net and managed to tie the set at 4–4. Von Cramm fought back, and the tide turned again. But von Cramm was clearly tiring, and while the score went to 5–5 and then to 6–6, the dam finally burst in the 13th game.

With the final set at 6–6, von Cramm was playing the game of his life against a Budge who knew the pangs of self-doubt. Budge showed his stamina and the quality of tennis of which he was capable by breaking von Cramm's service once more, with von Cramm again failing to score a point. Was von Cramm through? In the 14th game, with Budge serving, von Cramm extended Budge fully and managed to reach game point twice. The game went to 16 points before von Cramm finally caved in. It came on a brilliant forehand placement beyond the reach of von Cramm's backhand, to win the final point for Budge and, with that point, to take the set 8–6 and the match three sets to two. The display of savvy tennis in that final game brought the reserved Wimbledon crowd to its feet in a well-deserved tribute to both players.

The victory by Budge over a valiant opponent gave the United States the right to play against England, defending holder of the Davis Cup. The U.S. triumphed 4–1, Budge taking two singles matches and, with Gene Mako, winning the doubles. The United States had not won the Davis Cup in ten years, but, again with Budge on the squad, the United States won the cup in 1938 as well. On that occasion the opponent was Australia, and again Budge was largely responsible for the successful Cup defense.

But it is the last match of the 1937 interzone final that remains in people's memories and is still recalled as a brilliant display of tennis at its best.

---

gles championships** were won by Don Budge in the men's division and Anita Lizana of Chile in the women's division.

Sept. 25 The New York City **paddle tennis championships,** male and female at several age levels, concluded. Sixty-eight thousand players entered. The men's singles championship was won by Pat Lillis, age 17.

Oct. 6-10 The 34th annual **World Series** was won by the New York Yankees (AL), defeating the New York Giants (NL) four games to one. It was almost a repetition of the 1936 series. Hubbell was the only Giant winning pitcher, and Lefty Gomez won two for the Yankees. The final game was noteworthy for Gomez, who went all the way and drove in the winning run with a single in the fifth inning. His lifetime batting average, over 14 seasons, was .147. The Yankees' Tony Lazzeri hit .400 for the series.

Nov. 30 The **Heisman Trophy** for outstanding college football player of 1937 was voted to Yale quarterback Clint Frank.

Dec. 11 Former heavyweight wrestling champion **Strangler Lewis,** in announcing his retire-

John Sherman Rutherford III
b. Coffeyville, Kans., Mar. 12, 1938

Johnny Rutherford became a racing driver in 1959 and since then has won 26 championship races. His most important victories have been his three first-place finishes in the Indianapolis 500, in 1974, 1976, and 1980. With the 1980 win, Rutherford became the first driver ever to win the Indy twice from the pole position.

At Daytona Beach, Florida, in 1963, he set a new record for stock cars. He was the U.S. Auto Club national sprint champion in 1965 and the USAC national driving champion in 1980.

Rutherford, not eloquently, has said: "I am a firm believer in the fact that a person can do anything in this world he or she wants to as long as you have desire."

---

ment, criticized the changed state of professional wrestling. He said the new type of "slam-bang" grappling was "terrible and awful." Pro wrestling was becoming entertainment, complete with fixed matches, heroes and villains, and camp followers. After World War II, with the advent of television, the trend was accentuated, and this type of wrestling attracted large numbers of viewers. Wrestlers took such names as Gorgeous George, Lord Carlton, Haystack Calhoun, and The Gorilla, who was, of course, wheeled to the ring in a cage. Amateur wrestling, as sponsored by the AAU and the NCAA and as part of the Olympics and the Pan-American Games, remains an authentic sport requiring skill and stamina.

Dec. 12 The **NFL championship** was won by the Washington Redskins, defeating the Chicago Bears 28-21.

1938

The **Amateur Hockey Association** of the U.S. (AHAUS) initiated championships to compete with those sponsored by the Amateur Athletic Union (AAU).

Jan. 1 In **college football bowl games,** the results were Rice 28, Colorado 14 in the Cotton Bowl; Auburn 6, Michigan State 0 in the Orange Bowl; California 13, Alabama 0 in the Rose Bowl; and Santa Clara 6, Louisiana State 0 in the Sugar Bowl. This season the AP poll selected Texas Christian as the national collegiate champions of 1937.

Jan. 18 Election to the **Baseball Hall of Fame** of Grover Cleveland Alexander, the pitcher, was announced.

Feb. 12 At the **Westminster Kennel Club** dog show, Ch. Daro of Maridor, an English setter owned by Maridor Kennels, took best-in-show.

Feb. 26 **U.S. figure skating championships** were won in Ardmore, Pa., by Joan Tozzer, women's singles; Robin H. Lee, men's singles; Joan Tozzer and M. Bernard Fox, pairs; and Nettie C. Prantel and Harold Hartshorne, dance.

Mar. 16 The **National Invitational Tournament** (NIT), sponsored by the Metropolitan Basketball Writers Association of New York, was won by Temple, which crushed Colorado, 60-36. This first major season-ending tournament, held in Madison Square Garden, New York City, was a huge promotional success.

Apr. 4 The **Masters golf tournament** was won by Henry Picard, who defeated Ralph Guldahl and Harry Cooper by two strokes.

Apr. 5-12 The **NHL Stanley Cup** was won by the Chicago Black Hawks, who defeated the Toronto Maple Leafs three games to one.

Apr. 19 The 42nd **Boston Marathon** was won by Leslie Pawson of Pawtucket, R.I., with a time of 2 hrs., 35 min., 34.8 sec.

May 7 The 64th annual **Kentucky Derby** was won by Lawrin, with a time of 2:04⅕. The jockey was Eddie Arcaro.

May 14 The 63rd annual **Preakness Stakes** was won by Dauber, with a time of 1:59⅘. The jockey was Maurice Peters.

May 30 The 25th **Indianapolis 500** auto race was won by Floyd Roberts of Van Nuys, Calif., completing the 500-mi. course in 4 hrs., 15 min., 58.40 sec., at an average speed of 117.200 mph.

May 31 Barney Ross lost the **welterweight boxing championship** to Henry Armstrong in a bruising 15 rounds at Long Island City, N.Y. It was to be the last important match in Ross's career. Earlier, Ross had held two titles at the same time. He won the lightweight championship on June 23, 1933, in ten rounds in Chicago with Tony Canzoneri. Less than a year later, on May 28, 1934, at Long Island City, he took the welterweight title from Jimmy McLarnin in 15 rounds. The New York State Athletic Commission ruled that thereafter Ross must announce before any fight which title he was defending. Ross went on to lose the welterweight title on Sept. 17, 1934, and win it back once more on May 28, 1935, before losing the title yet again in the 1938 match with Armstrong.

June 4 The 70th annual **Belmont Stakes** was won by Pasteurized, with a time of 2:29⅖. The jockey was Jimmy Stout.

June 11 The **U.S. Open golf tournament** was won for the second year in a row by Ralph Guldahl, with a 284 score. Play was at the Cherry Hills Club, Denver, Colo.

June 15 Johnny Vander Meer pitched his **second no-hit, no-run game** in a row. The Cincinnati left-hander pitched his team to a 6-0 win over the Brooklyn Dodgers at Ebbets Field before 38,748 fans, who had come out to see the first night game played in the New York area. Vander Meer's previous no-hitter was pitched in daylight a few days before, in Cincinnati, with the Reds winning 3-0 against Boston.

July 1 At the **Wimbledon** tennis championships in England, the men's singles title was won by Don Budge in a quick triumph over Bunny Austin of England. The next day Helen Wills Moody won the women's singles.

July 6 The sixth annual **baseball all-star game** was won by the National League, which defeated the American League 4 to 1.

July 16 The **PGA golf tournament** was won by Paul Runyan. In the final round he routed Sam Snead, 8 and 7.

Aug. 10 The 13th running of the **Hambletonian Stakes** was won in two straight heats by McLin Hanover. The driver was Henry Thomas.

Sept. 5 In the **Davis Cup** international tennis matches, the U.S. defeated Australia three matches to two in the challenge round, with Don Budge starring.

Sept. 17 The **U.S. Lawn Tennis Association singles championships** were won by Don Budge in the men's division and Alice Marble over Nancy Wynne of Australia in the women's division. By his victory, Budge completed the grand slam of tennis, the national championships of Australia, France, England, and the U.S.

Oct. 5-9 The 35th annual **World Series** was won by the New York Yankees (AL), defeating the Chicago Cubs (NL) in four straight games. The Yankees were at it again in this sweep of the Cubs. Pitchers Red Ruffing, Lefty Gomez, and Monte Pearson were in charge. Bill Dickey, the Yankee catcher, and Joe Gordon, the second baseman, both hit .400 with six hits apiece.

Nov. 28 The **Heisman Trophy** for outstanding college football player of 1938 was voted to Texas Christian quarterback Davey O'Brien.

Dec. 11 The **NFL championship** was won by the

JERRY WEST

Jerome Alan West
b. Cheylan, W.Va., May 28, 1938

Jerry West's varsity basketball record at West Virginia University was so good that he was chosen as the second selection in the first round of the National Basketball Association's 1960 draft by the Minneapolis Lakers. In college he had made all-American twice and in 1959 was voted the outstanding player of the NCAA tournament.

The Minneapolis franchise was transferred to Los Angeles before West started pro play, so he spent his 14-year career from 1961 through 1974 with the Los Angeles Lakers. His play as a guard was memorable, and he excelled at setting up plays. This is shown by his 2435 assists, sixth highest ever. He also scored 25,192 points, tenth best, with a third best average of 27 points per game. West had 5376 rebounds.

He led the NBA in assists in 1972 with 747 and in scoring in 1970 with 2309 points and a 31.2 average. He still holds the record for most free throws in a season, 840 in 1966. He was on the league all-star team ten times.

West coached Los Angeles from 1976 to 1979, with a record of 145 victories and 101 defeats. He was elected to the Basketball Hall of Fame in 1979.

OSCAR "BIG O" ROBERTSON

Oscar Palmer Robertson
b. Charlotte, Tenn., Nov. 24, 1938

Oscar Robertson was the great-grandson of a slave and attended all-black Crispus Attucks High School in Indianapolis, Indiana. Playing basketball there, he was a major factor in a 45-game winning streak and two state championships. His college career at the University of Cincinnati was equally impressive. In 1958, he was the first sophomore to be named college player of the year, and he also received this honor

from the *Sporting News* in each of the next two years. In this same period, the *Sporting News* chose him for its all-American team.

Robertson was drafted by the Cincinnati Royals into the National Basketball Association in the first round, but before starting to play for them, he served as cocaptain of the U.S. basketball team that won the gold medal at the 1960 Olympics. He played for Cincinnati for ten years and then for four more years for the Milwaukee Bucks before retiring in 1973.

His career total of 26,710 points is sixth highest, his game average of 25.7 seventh best. As a guard, he had 9887 rebounds and 2931 assists, indicating his value as a playmaker. Robertson led the league in assists in 1961, 1962, 1964, 1965, 1966, 1968, and 1969. He was on the all-star team from 1961 to 1969, rookie of the year in 1961, and most valuable player in 1964. Robertson was elected to the Basketball Hall of Fame in 1979.

New York Giants, defeating the Green Bay Packers 23-17.

1939

The **American Water Ski Association** was organized, and the first national championships were held. Over 400 local water ski clubs are now affiliated with the AWSA.

Little League Baseball was founded in Williamsport, Pa., by Carl Stotz, George Bebble, and Bert Bebble. They were the managers of the first three teams, named Lundy Lumber, Lycoming Dairy, and Jumbo Pretzel.

James Bean, a student at Mount View High School in Thorndike, Maine, played field hockey with the school's girls team. Bean wore a kilt.

Archers in California organized the **National Field Archery Association** to promote interest in the freehand shooting used in field archery.

Another great **U.S. polo team** defeated Great Britain, challenging for the Westchester Cup, 11-7 and 9-4, at Westbury, N.Y. Michael Phipps, Thomas Hitchcock Jr., Stewart Iglehart, and Winston F. C. Guest made up the U.S. team. For Hitchcock, rated the greatest polo player of all time, this was his last appearance in an international match. He was killed during World War II.

David G. Freeman won the **national badminton men's singles championship** for the first of four successive times. When play resumed after World War II, Freeman won the championship in 1947 and 1948 and then retired. He returned to win it once again in 1953.

Winter The **Penguin-class dinghy** began its career as a popular, small, safe, inexpensive one-design racing sailboat when the first models were built in Virginia by Chesapeake Bay sailors to a design by P. L. Rhodes. It rapidly became one of the largest classes in the world, especially in the Northeast, Southern California, and the Chicago region. Winter (frostbite) racing often employs Penguins.

Jan. The **Lightning class** 19-ft. racing sailboat was introduced at the New York Motor Boat Show. Twenty boats were already being built to plans of boatbuilders Sparkman and Stephens. An International Lightning Class Association was quickly formed. Sales here and internationally increased rapidly after World War II.

Jan. 1 In **college football bowl games,** the results were St. Mary's 20, Texas Tech 13 in the Cotton Bowl; Tennessee 17, Oklahoma 0 in the Orange Bowl; Southern California 7, Duke 3 in the Rose Bowl; and Texas Christian 15, Carnegie Tech 7 in the Sugar Bowl. This season the AP poll chose Texas A&M as national collegiate champion of 1938.

Jan. 7 The **United States Trotting Association** was incorporated and became the governing body of American harness racing.

BOBBY HULL

Robert Marvin Hull, Jr.

b. Point Anne, Ont., Canada, Jan. 3, 1939

Probably the hardest shot in ice hockey—one of his shots was timed at 116.3 mph—and one of the fastest skaters ever—he was timed at 29.4 miles per hour—Bobby Hull had a remarkably productive career in the National Hockey League. He began skating at age 3 and in 1957 joined the Chicago Black Hawks, with whom he remained for 16 seasons. He led the team to the Stanley Cup championship in the 1960–1961 season, the first title for Chicago since 1938.

Hull was the NHL's leading scorer in 1960, 1962, and 1966, setting a new record in the 1966 season with 54 goals and 97 points. In his career in the league, he ranks 14th in points scored, with 1170—610 goals and 560 assists (fourth highest)—in 1063 games. Hull's honors include being voted most valuable player in 1965 and 1966 and winner of the Lady Byng Trophy for sportsmanship in 1965.

Hull was the first player in the NHL to score 50 goals in a season more than once: 50 in 1961–1962, 54 in 1965–1966, and 52 in 1966–1967.

On June 27, 1972, Hull jumped to the new World Hockey Association in a deal reported to be worth $2,500,000. He played for the Winnipeg Jets and was voted most valuable player for the 1972–1973 season. Hull returned to the NHL with the Hartford Whalers in 1979–1980. He is generally regarded as the best left wing in ice hockey history.

Jan. 21 U.S. **figure skating championships** were won in St. Paul, Minn., by Robin E. Lee, men's singles; Joan Tozzer, women's singles; Joan Tozzer and M. Bernard Fox, pairs; and Sandy Macdonald and Harold Hartshorne, dance.

Jan. 24 Election to the **Baseball Hall of Fame** was announced for Eddie Collins, Wee Willie Keeler, and George Sisler. On May 2, during the centennial celebration of baseball, six more baseball immortals were added to the Hall of Fame: Adrian C. "Cap" Anson, Charles A. Comiskey, William A. Cummings, William Ewing, Charles "Old Hoss" Radbourn, and Albert G. Spaulding.

Feb. 15 At the **Westminster Kennel Club** dog show, Ch. Ferry von Rauhfelsen of Giralda, a Doberman pinscher owned by Giralda Farms, took best-in-show.

Mar. 23 The second **NIT basketball championship** was won by Long Island U., beating Loyola of Chicago 44-32. LIU finished its season undefeated.

Mar. 27 The **National Collegiate Athletic Association** (NCAA) for the first time conducted its own national intercollegiate basketball championship. The final game, played at Northwestern U., Evanston, Ill., before 5000 fans, was won by Oregon over Ohio State 46-33. After World War II, the NCAA tournament pulled away from its NIT rival in popularity.

Apr. 2 The **Masters golf tournament** was won by Ralph Guldahl. With 279, he led Sam Snead by a stroke.

Apr. 6-16 The **NHL Stanley Cup** was won by the Boston Bruins, who defeated the Toronto Maple Leafs four games to one.

Apr. 19 The 43rd **Boston Marathon** was won by Ellison Brown of Alton, R.I., with a time of 2 hrs., 28 min., 51.8 sec.

May 2 "Ironman" **Lou Gehrig,** legendary first baseman, took himself out of the lineup after 2130 consecutive games played for the New York Yankees, beginning on June 1, 1925. Although Gehrig did not know it, he was suffering from a rare form of muscular degeneration, which caused his death on June 2, 1941. The Baseball Writers Association moved on Dec. 7, 1939, to place Gehrig in the Baseball Hall of Fame without going through a formal election process.

May 6 The 65th annual **Kentucky Derby** was won by Johnstown, with a time of 2:03⅖. The jockey was Jimmy Stout. Johnstown had been trained by Sunny Jim Fitzsimmons, who had trained two previous Derby winners, Gallant Fox and Omaha.

May 13 The 64th annual **Preakness Stakes** was won by Challedon, with a time of 1:59⅘. The jockey was George Seabo.

May 30 The 27th annual **Indianapolis 500** auto race was won by Wilbur Shaw of Indianapolis, who completed the 500-mi. course in 4 hrs., 20 min., 47.41 sec., at an average speed of 115.035

William Caleb Yarborough
b. Timmonsville, S.C., Mar. 27, 1939

Cale Yarborough is one of the most successful of the auto racing drivers who participate primarily in events of the National Association for Stock

Car Auto Racing (NASCAR). He was grand national champion for three consecutive years, from 1976 to 1978. As of the end of 1986, he was the tenth all-time busiest NASCAR driver, having participated in 525 races.

Among his victories have been four

in the Daytona 500, in 1968, 1977, 1983, and 1984 and four in the Southern 500, in 1968, 1973, 1974, and 1978.

---

mph. Floyd Roberts, the 1938 winner, died in a crash during the race.

June 3 The 71st annual **Belmont Stakes** was won by Johnstown, with a time of 2:29³⁄₅. The jockey was Jimmy Stout.

June 12 The National **Baseball Hall of Fame** and Museum at Cooperstown, N.Y., was dedicated.

June 12 The **U.S. Open golf tournament** was won by Byron Nelson, after a three-way playoff with Craig Wood and Denny Shute. This was the tournament in which Sam Snead led all the way to the final hole, where he carded an 8 and lost out.

July 7-8 At the **Wimbledon** tennis championships in England, Robert L. "Bobby" Riggs won the men's singles title and Alice Marble won the women's singles. Riggs and Elwood T. Cooke took the men's doubles, Marble and Sarah Palfrey Fabyan the women's doubles, and Riggs and Marble won the mixed doubles. Only Suzanne Lenglen of France, in 1920, had previously swept the three women's titles.

July 11 The seventh annual **baseball all-star game** was won by the American League, which

beat the National League 3-1 at Yankee Stadium in New York City.

July 17 The **PGA golf tournament** was won by Henry Picard. In the final round, he beat Byron Nelson 1 up for 37 holes.

Aug. 9 The 14th annual **Hambletonian Stakes** was won in straight heats by Peter Astra. The driver was H. M. Parshall.

Sept. 5 In **Davis Cup** play, the U.S. lost the trophy to Australia. Adrian Quist and John Bromwich defeated Bobby Riggs and Frank Parker in the last singles matches.

Sept. 17 The **U.S. Lawn Tennis Association singles championships** were won by Bobby Riggs over S. Welby Van Horn in the men's division and by Alice Marble in the women's division. As she had done at Wimbledon earlier, Miss Marble swept the women's singles and doubles and won in the mixed doubles.

Oct. 4-8 The 36th annual **World Series** was won by the New York Yankees (AL), sweeping the Cincinnati Reds (NL) in four games. In this fourth consecutive world championship, the Yankees took the final game by tying it in the

---

JOANNE CARNER

JoAnne Gunderson Carner
b. Kirkland, Wash., Apr. 4, 1939

In view of JoAnne Carner's overall record, it is not surprising that she is the last amateur to have won an LPGA event, the 1969 Burdine's Invitational at Miami. She began playing golf when she was 10 and won five national amateur titles, in

1957, 1960, 1962, 1966, and 1968, before turning professional in 1970. It goes without saying that she won her first pro tournament.

Carner has 42 career victories and, prior to a winless 1986, had won at least one tournament for 12 consecutive years. She is the only woman to have won the USGA Junior, the U.S. amateur, and the

U.S. Women's Open titles. In money won, Carner ranks second among women golfers, with $2,013,991 in earnings as of December 1986.

She became, in 1982, the tenth member of the LPGA Hall of Fame and, in 1985, the tenth woman to be inducted into the World Golf Hall of Fame.

AL UNSER

b. Albuquerque, N.Mex., May 29, 1939

Al Unser is the most successful member of a very successful auto racing family. He has won the Indianapolis 500 three times, in 1970, 1971, and 1978. In 1971, he completed the race with an average speed of 157.735 miles per hour,

then an Indy record. In 1978, he became the fifth driver in history to win the Indy three times and in this race his older brother Bobby (born in Albuquerque, N.Mex., on Feb. 20, 1934) finished sixth.

Al Unser has also won the Pocono 500 three times, in 1976, 1978, and 1980, and the Pikes Peak Hill Climb, in 1964 and 1965. In 1970, he was

the U.S. Auto Club national champion driver.

Bobby Unser has also won the Indy 500 three times, in 1968, 1975, and 1981, and was the USAC national champion in 1968 and 1974.

In 1983, Al's son, Al, Jr., also raced in the Indy 500, placing third, right behind his father.

---

ninth with two runs and scoring three runs on Reds errors in the tenth to win 7-4. It was not a great series. Neither team batted well, the Yankees going .206 and the Reds .203.

Oct. 25 A new **bowling record** for three games was set by Albert Brandt, of Lockport, N.Y., who scored 886.

Dec. 6 The **Heisman Trophy** for outstanding college football player of 1939 was awarded to Iowa halfback Nile Kinnick, Jr.

Dec. 10 The **NFL championship** was won by the Green Bay Packers, defeating the New York Giants 27-0.

1940

Lt. Harry Reeves of the Detroit police department won the first of his six national **pistol target shooting** championships over a 15-year period. No competition was held in five of the years.

Racetrack attendance was 8,500,000 for the year. Some $408,500,000 was bet in parimutuel pools, and $16,145,182 was gathered by states in revenue. By 1952 these figures would rise to 26,434,-903 attendance, $1,915,220,517 bet, and $119,266,959 in revenue earned by states.

Jan. 1 In **college football bowl games** the results were Clemson 6, Boston College 3 in the Cotton Bowl; Georgia Tech 21, Missouri 7 in the Orange Bowl; Southern California 14, Tennessee 0 in the Rose Bowl; and Texas A&M 14,

KATHY WHITWORTH

Kathrynne Anne Whitworth
b. Monahans, Tex., Sept. 27, 1939

A leading figure in women's golf both on and off the course, Kathy Whitworth has won more women's tournaments, a total of 88, than any other player, even though she never took the women's U.S. Open. She played golf as a teenager, turned professional in December 1958, and won her most recent tournament in 1985.

Whitworth has on her record a great variety of accomplishments: three times Ladies Professional Golf Association champion, in 1967, 1971, and 1975; seven times player of the year; seven times winner of the Vare Trophy, given for low average score; eight times the leading LPGA money winner; and the first woman to reach $1 million in career earnings. She now stands fifth in that category with $1,666,762 as of the end of 1986. She is also

credited with 11 holes-in-one.

Whitworth is known as a long-ball hitter, but it is her putting that is most outstanding. She was inducted into the LPGA Hall of Fame in 1975. Active in LPGA affairs, Whitworth was president in 1970 and has worked to increase the number of tournaments and the prize money offered.

LEE TREVINO

Lee Buck Trevino
b. Dallas, Tex., Dec. 1, 1939

Lee Trevino's volubility and happy-go-lucky ways have made him a popular member of the professional golfers' tour. He also happens to be one of the best and most astute players of the game. After quitting grade school, he did some greenskeeping and caddying before spending four years in the U.S.

Marines, where, he admits, he spent a lot of time playing golf on Okinawa.

Turning pro in 1966, Trevino was voted rookie of the year in 1967. His initial major victory came in 1968 at the U.S. Open, where he became the first player ever to shoot all four rounds of the event under par. In 1970, he was the leading money winner on the PGA tour. The following year, Trevino won the

Open for the second time and won five tournaments between April and July. In 1971, he also triumphed in the British Open and repeated in 1972. Trevino's most recent major win was the 1974 PGA.

He is not noted for the gracefulness of his swing, but he wins tournaments, money, and the loyalty of his many fans.

Tulane 13 in the Sugar Bowl. This season the AP poll selected Minnesota as national collegiate champion of 1939.

Feb. 10 **U.S. figure skating championships** were won in Cleveland, Ohio, by Eugene Turner, men's singles; Joan Tozzer, women's singles; Joan Tozzer and M. Bernard Fox, pairs; and Sandy Macdonald and Harold Hartshorne, dance.

Feb. 14 At the **Westminster Kennel Club** dog show, Ch. My Own True Brucie, a cocker spaniel owned by H. E. Mellenthin, took best-in-show.

Mar. 15 In the third **NIT basketball championship,** Colorado defeated Duquesne in the final round, 51-40, before 15,201 fans. Sophomore Bob Doll of Colorado scored 15 points and was voted most valuable player.

Mar. 30 The **NCAA basketball championship** was won by Indiana U., defeating the U. of Kansas 60-42.

Apr. 2-13 The **NHL Stanley Cup** was won by the New York Rangers, who defeated the Toronto Maple Leafs four games to two.

Apr. 7 The **Masters golf tournament** was won by Jimmy Demaret, who beat Lloyd Mangrum by four strokes.

Apr. 13 The **first 15-ft. pole vault in history** was accomplished by Cornelius Warmerdam, competing for the San Francisco Olympic Club at Berkeley, Calif. On June 29 at Fresno, Calif., he bettered this mark by $1\frac{7}{8}$ in. He retired from competition in 1943 after having vaulted 15 ft. or more 43 times.

Apr. 19 The 44th **Boston Marathon** was won by

CAROL HEISS

Carol Elizabeth Heiss Jenkins
b. New York City, Jan. 20, 1940

Early in Carol Heiss's career, she was regularly beaten by Tenley Albright in figure skating competition, but in 1956 she turned the tables and became the dominant woman performer in her sport. Heiss began skating on roller skates given her on her fourth birthday, but later that year she shifted to ice skates and by the time she was 11 had taken the national novice title.

By 1953, she was runner up to Albright in the U.S. championships and, in 1956, second to her in the Olympics. Heiss's winning streak began with the U.S. title in 1957, which she held through 1960, and at the 1960 Olympics she won the gold medal. Meanwhile, in 1956, she defeated Albright for the world championship and held that title through 1960. Heiss was North American titleholder in 1957 and 1959.

Heiss was a strong, athletic skater

whose freestyle skating was fast and dashing. She married a fellow figure skating champion, Hayes Alan Jenkins, on April 30, 1960. Jenkins won the men's figure skating championship at the 1956 Olympics and held the U.S. championship from 1953 to 1956. Carol's younger siblings, Nancy and Bruce, also took up figure skating. Nancy finished second to her sister in the 1959 U.S. championships.

JACK NICKLAUS

Jack William Nicklaus
b.   Columbus, Ohio, Jan. 21, 1940

Jack Nicklaus began to play golf under his father's tutelage at the age of 10, and this extraordinary athlete won the Ohio Open while he was in high school. At Ohio State University from 1957 to 1962, he won the U.S. amateur championship twice. His first victory came in 1959, the second in 1961. At age 21, in December 1961, Nicklaus turned professional.

Already considered the best golfer since Bobby Jones, Nicklaus won the U.S. Open in 1962 by beating Arnold Palmer in a playoff. He was the youngest winner of this tournament in nearly 40 years. Since then, Nicklaus has won three more Opens, in 1967, 1972, and 1980.

Overall, Nicklaus has triumphed in more major tournaments than any other golfer to date. He won both the PGA and the Masters in 1963 and since then has won the PGA in 1971, 1973, 1975, and 1980. Even more remarkable is his record in the Masters, which he has won five more times since 1963, in 1965, 1966, 1972, 1975, and 1986. The 1986 victory at age 46 made him the oldest player ever to win this event. In addition, Nicklaus won the British Open in 1966, 1970, and 1978.

Known as the Golden Bear, both because of his blond hair and a tendency toward plumpness in his early playing days, Nicklaus is one of the most popular players on the PGA tour. He has also won more prize money than any other golfer, having passed the $4,000,000 mark. He plays in fewer tournaments than formerly and devotes much of his time to various interests, among which is designing golf courses.

Gérard Côte of St. Hyacinthe, Quebec, Canada, with a record time of 2 hrs., 28 min., 28.6 sec.

May 4   The 66th annual **Kentucky Derby** was won by Gallahadion, with a time of 2:05. The jockey was Carroll Bierman.

May 11   The **first intercollegiate gymnastics team championship** was won by the U. of Illinois in Chicago. Three clubs with more points than Illinois had only one participant each and so were ineligible for the team championship.

May 11   The 65th annual **Preakness Stakes** was won by Bimelech, with a time of 1:58⅗. The jockey was Fred A. Smith.

May 30   The 28th **Indianapolis 500** auto race was won by Wilbur Shaw of Indianapolis, completing the 500-mi. course in 4 hrs., 22 min., 31.17 sec., at an average speed of 114.277 mph. It was his third win, his second in a row.

June 8   The 72nd annual **Belmont Stakes** was won by Bimelech, with a time of 2:29⅗. The jockey was Fred A. Smith.

June 9   The **U.S. Open golf tournament** was won by W. Lawson Little. Tied with Gene Sarazen at 287 after four rounds, Little won the playoff, 70-73.

July 9   The eighth annual **baseball all-star game** was won by the American League, which defeated the National League 1-0.

Aug. 14   The 15th annual **Hambletonian Stakes** was won in straight heats by Spencer Scott. The driver was Fred Egan.

Sept. 2   The **PGA golf tournament** was won by

HERVÉ FILION

b.   Angers, Que., Canada, Feb. 1, 1940

Considering the driving records Hervé Filion had set by the time he was 47, in 1987, Filion's place in harness racing seems unlikely ever to be surpassed. On May 24, 1987, he won his 10,000th race, at Yonkers Raceway, New York. No other driver has come near this mark. He has raced more than 60,000 times, and the purses he has won total more than $52,000,000.

Filion grew up on a farm in a remote part of Quebec, where he became well acquainted with horses at an early age. He first raced when he was 12, and the next year, he won his first race. After arriving in the United States in 1961, he soon established himself as a winner. Filion began racing at one track in the daytime and another at night on the same day, a practice he has continued.

In 1957, Filion became the youngest driver ever elected to the Harness Racing Hall of Fame, and he has received the Lou Marsh Trophy as Canada's leading professional athlete.

FRAN TARKENTON

Francis Asbury Tarkenton
b. Richmond, Va., Feb. 3, 1940

The holder of more professional football passing records than any other quarterback thus far, Fran Tarkenton got an early start by playing football at the age of 10. At Athens, Georgia, he was a high school all-state quarterback and at the University of Georgia an all-American. In his senior year, Georgia had a 9–1 record and defeated Missouri in the Orange Bowl 14–0.

Drafted by Minnesota of the National Football League, Tarkenton soon became the Vikings' starting quarterback, making a spectacular debut in which he completed 17 of 23 passes and steered the Vikings to a 37–17 upset of the favored Chicago Bears. By 1966, however, Tarkenton and the Minnesota coach, Norm Van Brocklin, were not getting along well, and Tarkenton was benched. He resigned and was traded to the New York Giants on March 7, 1967, with whom he starred until his return to the Vikings

in 1972. He remained with the Vikings until he retired in 1978. By that time, he had set several records for passing that still stand: most yards gained, lifetime, 47,003; most passes completed, lifetime, 3686; most passes attempted, lifetime, 6467.

A quiet and friendly person, Tarkenton has been active in the Fellowship of Christian Athletes. He says, "I feel I was put here for more reasons than to throw a football."

Byron Nelson. He defeated Sam Snead in the final round, 1 up at Hershey (Pennsylvania) Country Club.

Sept. 9 The **U.S. Lawn Tennis Association singles championships** were won by W. Donald McNeill over Bobby Riggs in the men's division and Alice Marble in the women's division.

Oct. 2-8 The 37th annual **World Series** was won by the Cincinnati Reds (NL), defeating the Detroit Tigers (AL) four games to three. The Reds came back from a 2-3 deficit on a 4-0 win by Bucky Walters in game six and a 2-1 win by Paul Derringer in game seven. This was Cincinnati's first World Series victory in 21 years.

Oct. 4 Henry Armstrong lost the **welterweight boxing title** after having defended it successfully 20 times. He was beaten by Fritzie Zivic in a 15-round decision in New York City. Armstrong had been the only boxer ever to hold

three titles at the same time. He won the featherweight crown in 1937 and both the welterweight and lightweight titles the next year. Armstrong retired in 1945 after 175 bouts, of which he won 144.

Nov. 27 The **Heisman Trophy** for outstanding college football player of 1940 was voted to Michigan back Tom Harmon.

Dec. 8 The **NFL championship** was won by the Chicago Bears, who defeated the Washington Redskins by the incredible score of 73-0.

MARIO ANDRETTI

Mario Gabriel Andretti
b. Montona, Italy, Feb. 28, 1940

Arriving in the United States in 1955 and becoming a citizen in 1959, Mario Andretti two years later launched a full-time career as a racing car driver. In another four years, he became the U.S. Auto Club

National Champion, a title he also won in 1966 and 1969.

In 1965, Andretti finished third in his first Indy 500 and won it in 1969, in his fifth try. In 1978 he won the World Grand Prix Driver Championship, the first and so far the only U.S. citizen to achieve this honor. He took the International

Race of Champions that same year.

Andretti's record includes a variety of other victories, including the 1969 Pikes Peak Hill Climb; the 1970 and 1972 Sebring Twelve-Hours, with codrivers; the 1971 South Africa Grand Prix; and the 1973 Twenty-Four Hours of Daytona.

JOHN HAVLICEK

John J. Havlicek
b. Martins Ferry, Ohio, Apr. 8, 1940

After playing basketball and football for Ohio State for three years, John Havlicek in 1962 had to choose between pro football and pro basketball. He was drafted by the Cleveland Browns as a wide receiver but accepted a first-round draft by the Boston Celtics to play in the National Basketball Association.

Hondo, as he was known to his many fans, became a mainstay of the Celtics and played for them for 16 years, when the team won eight NBA championships, in 1963, 1964, 1965, 1966, 1968, 1969, 1974, and 1976.

In a game on January 11, 1974, Havlicek became the eighth player to score over 20,000 points in a career. He ended with 26,395 points, now eighth highest for regular season play. His average per game was 20.8 points. He had 8007 rebounds and

6114 assists, seventh highest. In 1976, he scored 1000 points or more for the 14th season in a row, a record.

The Celtics made the league playoffs in 13 of Havlicek's 16 years with the team, and he scored 3776 points. He also played on 13 all-star teams. Havlicek was an outstanding forward who was strong defensively. He was elected to the Basketball Hall of Fame in 1983.

1941

The **first amateur synchronized swimming** group was formed by Katherine Curtis, a physical education instructor at the U. of Wisconsin.

Jan. 1 In **college football bowl games,** the results were Texas A&M 13, Fordham 12 in the Cotton Bowl; Mississippi State 14, Georgetown 7 in the Orange Bowl; Stanford 21, Nebraska 13 in the Rose Bowl; and Boston College 19, Tennessee 13 in the Sugar Bowl. This season the AP poll chose Minnesota as national collegiate champion of 1940.

Feb. 1 **U.S. figure skating championships** were won in Boston by Jane Vaughn, women's sin-

gles; Eugene Turner, men's singles; Donna Atwood and Eugene Turner, pairs; and Sandy Macdonald and Harold Hartshorne, dance.

Feb. 13 At the **Westminster Kennel Club** dog show, Ch. My Own True Brucie, a cocker spaniel owned by H. E. Mellenthin, took best-in-show for the second year.

Mar. 24 In the fourth **NIT championship,** Long Island U. defeated Ohio U. 56-42 before 18,377 fans. Frank Baumholtz, with 19 points, starred for LIU.

Mar. 29 The **NCAA basketball championship** was won by Wisconsin, who defeated Washington State 39-34.

Apr. 6 The **Masters golf tournament** was won by Craig Wood. His score of 280 beat Byron Nelson by three strokes.

WILMA RUDOLPH

Wilma Glodean Rudolph
b. St. Bethlehem, Tenn., June 23, 1940

Wilma Rudolph in childhood suffered various illnesses, including polio, which made it impossible for her to walk without braces until she was 8 years old. By the time she was 16, however, she had exercised and developed her muscles to such an extent that she was winning

statewide dash events in high school track meets.

Rudolph qualified for the 1956 Olympics and won a bronze medal as part of a relay team, but her time of glory came in the 1960 Olympics in Rome. There she was the only competitor in the games to win three gold medals, taking the 100- and 200-meter dashes and running on the winning 400-meter relay team. The team, comprising Rudolph and three

of her classmates at Tennessee State University, set a record of 44.4 seconds.

On July 9, 1960, Rudolph set a world record of 22.9 seconds for the 200-meter dash. In February 1961, in New York, Rudolph tied the 60-yard dash mark of 6.9 seconds and later the same year set a new 100-meter world record of 11.2 seconds.

PELÉ

Edson Arantes do Nascimento
b. Três Corações, Brazil, Oct. 23, 1940

Conceded to be the best soccer player in the world, Pelé completed a record-shattering career in Brazil that made him a national hero before coming to the United States in 1975 to play for the New York Cosmos of the North American Soccer League. His arrival was a much needed shot in the arm for a sport and a league that were not thriving.

Pelé became a professional at 16, when he joined the Santos team and played for them through 1974. In this period, he was largely responsible for Brazil's three world championships in 1958, 1962, and 1970. He made his first appearance in the United States in 1966, when the Santos club defeated Milan International 4–1.

During Pelé's time with the Cosmos, they won the NASL championship in 1977 by defeating the Seattle Sounders on August 28, 2–1. It was Pelé's last game for the Cosmos. It was reported that he had received $7,000,000 for his three-year contract, and this apparently made him the highest paid athlete in the world.

Pelé played inside left forward and was noted for his cool manner and the way he planned offensive moves. He scored 1281 career goals, 65 of them for the Cosmos. His outstanding skill and his outgoing personality made him popular with fans everywhere.

Apr. 6-12 The **NHL Stanley Cup** was won by the Boston Bruins, who swept the Detroit Red Wings in four straight games.

Apr. 19 The 45th **Boston Marathon** was won by Leslie Pawson of Pawtucket, R.I., with a time of 2 hrs., 30 min., 38 sec.

May 3 The 67th annual **Kentucky Derby** was won by Whirlaway, with a time of 2:01⅖, a new Derby record. The jockey was Eddie Arcaro, who had won the event in 1938.

May 10 The 66th annual **Preakness Stakes** was won by Whirlaway, with a time of 1:58⅘. The jockey was Eddie Arcaro.

May 30 The 29th **Indianapolis 500** auto race was won by Mauri Rose and Floyd Davis, completing the 500-mi. course in 4 hrs., 20 min., 36.24 sec., at an average speed of 115.117 mph. The next Indy 500 race was not held until 1946.

June 7 The **U.S. Open golf tournament** was won by Craig Wood at Colonial Country Club, Fort Worth, Tex., with a 284 total. This was the last time the U.S. Open would be played until 1946.

June 7 The 73rd annual **Belmont Stakes** was won by Whirlaway, with a time of 2:31. The jockey was Eddie Arcaro. Whirlaway thus became the fifth horse to win racing's Triple Crown.

July 8 The ninth annual **baseball all-star game** was won by the American League, which defeated the National League 7-5. A homer by Ted Williams with two on base, two out in the bottom of the ninth did the trick.

July 13 The **PGA golf tournament** was won by Vic Ghezzi, with a 1-up 38-hole victory over Byron Nelson.

July 17 Yankee center fielder **Joe DiMaggio's hitting streak** was ended by Cleveland Indian pitchers Al Smith and Jim Bagby, Jr., and by third baseman Ken Keltner, who made two great stops of hard DiMaggio smashes down the baseline. DiMaggio had hit safely in 56 consecutive games, a major league record that still stands. The day before, Dimaggio hit two singles and a double, giving him a total of 91 hits in 223 times at bat during his streak.

Aug. 6 The 16th annual **Hambletonian Stakes** was won in the third heat by Bill Gallon. The driver was Lee Smith. It was the first time since 1934 that an extra heat was needed to decide the event.

Sept. 7 The **U.S. Lawn Tennis Association singles championships** were won by Bobby Riggs over Frank Kovacs in the men's division and by Sarah Palfrey Cooke in the women's division.

Sept. 28 **Ted Williams** of the Boston Red Sox finished the season with a batting average of .4057. Entering a last-day doubleheader at .3995, Williams hammered out six hits in eight times at bat, including a home run. He became the sixth American League player since 1900 to

---

I zigged when I should have zagged.

Jack Roper, explaining the knockout he suffered at the hands of Joe Louis

MUHAMMAD ALI

Cassius Marcellus Clay, Jr.
b. Louisville, Ky., Jan. 17, 1942

The man who later called himself The Greatest began to learn to box at the age of 12, first fought as an amateur for six years, and won 100 of his 108 fights. In 1960 Cassius Clay captured the light heavyweight gold medal at the Olympics and on October 29, 1960, triumphed in his first professional bout.

Clay's path to the heavyweight championship was steady, and he achieved this goal on February 25, 1964, when he knocked out the titleholder, Sonny Liston, in the seventh round of a 15-round bout. The next day, Clay announced that he had become a Black Muslim and had taken the name Muhammad Ali.

A year later, in the shortest heavyweight title fight in history, Ali knocked out Liston in 1 minute of the first round of a rematch on May 25, 1965.

In June 1967, Ali refused induction into the U.S. armed forces on the grounds of his religious belief and was convicted of draft evasion. The WBA and the New York State Athletic Commission stripped him of his title, but Ali was able to return to boxing after the Supreme Court on June 20, 1970, overturned his conviction on technical grounds.

Clay did not regain his title until October 30, 1974, when he knocked out George Foreman in the eighth round of a fight in Kinshasa, Zaire. Ali called the fight "the rumble in the jungle." In a 15-round split decision,

Ali lost his championship to Leon Spinks on February 15, 1978, but regained it on September 15, 1978, with a unanimous decision over Spinks. Ali retired but in 1980 attempted a comeback. The effort ended in disappointment when the new champion, Larry Holmes, beat him.

Many experts agree that Ali was the greatest, although he is much criticized for his boastfulness. He liked to predict in verse the outcome of his fights, saying, "They'll all fall in the round I call." He described his fighting style as "Float like a butterfly, sting like a bee." Ali, now in physical decline, is 6 feet 3 inches tall and was at his fighting best at about 220 pounds.

---

reach the .400 level, the first in either league since Bill Terry's .401 in 1930.

Oct. 1-6 The 38th annual **World Series** was won by the New York Yankees (AL), defeating the Brooklyn Dodgers (NL) four games to one. The series is remembered best for its fourth game. The Dodgers, behind two games to one, were ahead by 4-3 when the Yankees came up for their final at-bats. With two out and nobody on, catcher Mickey Owen failed to catch the ball after the batter, Tommy Henrich, swung and missed the pitch that would have meant the third out. Henrich made it to first, and the floodgates were open. The Yankees won 7-4 on hits by Joe DiMaggio and Charley Keller, a walk to Bill Dickey, and another hit by Joe Gordon.

Nov. 27 **Professional tennis ranks** swelled with the signing of Bobby Riggs and Frank Kovacs, following the earlier signings of Don Budge and Fred Perry by sportsman-promoter Alexis Thompson.

Dec. 9 The **Heisman Trophy** for outstanding college football player was voted to Minnesota back Bruce Smith.

Dec. 21 The **NFL championship** was won by the Chicago Bears, who defeated the New York Giants 37-9.

1942

The Brooklyn Americans **ice hockey team folded.** Until 1941 it had been known as the New York Americans. The NHL was down to six teams, where it would stay until 1967. The schedule for each team was increased from 48 games to 50.

Jan. 1 In **college football bowl games,** the results were Alabama 29, Texas A&M 21 in the Cotton Bowl; Georgia 40, Texas Christian 26 in the Orange Bowl; Oregon State 20, Duke 16 in the Rose Bowl; and Fordham 2, Missouri 0 in the Sugar Bowl. This season the AP poll chose Ohio State as national collegiate champion of 1941.

Jan. 9 The world **heavyweight boxing championship** was successfully defended, for the 20th time, by Joe Louis, who knocked out Buddy Baer in the first round.

Jan. 20 Elected to the **Baseball Hall of Fame** was Rogers Hornsby, the second baseman and seven-time National League batting champion.

Feb. 12 At the **Westminster Kennel Club** dog show, Ch. Wolvey Pattern of Edgerstowne, a West Highland white terrier owned by Mrs. John G. Winant, took best-in-show.

PHIL ESPOSITO

Philip Anthony Esposito
b.   Sault Ste. Marie, Ont., Canada,
     Feb. 20, 1942

After signing a contract with hockey's Chicago Black Hawks in 1962, Phil Esposito was promoted to the Black Hawks after one season in a minor league. In 1967, he was traded to the Boston Bruins, then in last place. By the end of his third season with the Bruins, they had jumped to third, due in large measure to the play of this outstanding skater.

Esposito's rise to stardom was rapid. In 1969 and again in 1974, he was named most valuable player in the NHL. Also in 1969 and again for four consecutive years, from 1971 to 1974, he was the league's leading scorer. In the 1970–1971 season, Esposito set a new scoring record of 76 goals and 52 points. By the end of the 1985–1986 season, Esposito ranked third in career scoring, with 717 goals, 873 assists, and 1590 points in his career.

Playing for Team Canada against

the USSR in September 1972, Esposito led his team to victory in an eight-game series, with four wins, three losses, and one tie. He played for the New York Rangers from 1975 on and retired as a player in 1981. He is now general manager of the Rangers. In the course of his career, Esposito set a number of season records, such as most seasons with 20 or more goals.

Feb. 21 **U.S. figure skating championships** were won in Chicago by Jane Vaughn Sullivan, women's singles; Bobby Specht, men's singles; Doris Schubach and Walter Noffke, pairs; and Edith B. Whetstone and Alfred N. Richards, Jr., dance.

Mar. 28 The **NCAA basketball championship** was won by Stanford, who defeated Dartmouth 53-38.

Apr. 4-18 The **NHL Stanley Cup** was won by the Toronto Maple Leafs, who defeated the Detroit Red Wings four games to three. Toronto became the first team to win the Stanley Cup after losing the first three games.

Apr. 12 The **Masters golf tournament** was won for the second time by Byron Nelson. His play-

off 69 edged Ben Hogan's 70 for the green jacket.

Apr. 19 The 46th **Boston Marathon** was won by Joe Smith of Medford, Mass., with a time of 2 hrs., 26 min., 51.2 sec.

May 2 The 68th annual **Kentucky Derby** was won by Shut Out, with a time of 2:04⅖. The jockey was Wayne D. Wright.

May 9 The 67th annual **Preakness Stakes** was won by Alsab, with a time of 1:57. The jockey was Basil James.

May 31 The **PGA golf tournament** was won by Sam Snead, with a final round 2 and 1 win over Jim Turnesa at Seaview Country Club, Atlantic City, N.J.

June 6 The 74th annual **Belmont Stakes** was won

ROGER STAUBACH

Roger Thomas Staubach
b.   Cincinnati, Ohio, Feb. 5, 1942

Roger Staubach began playing football at age 7 and starred on his high school team. Twenty-five colleges offered him scholarships, but Staubach chose the Naval Academy, where he played varsity football and baseball. Staubach won the Heisman Trophy in 1963 and during his collegiate career set an NCAA record for quarterbacks by completing

66.4% of his passes while achieving a total of 4235 yards rushing and passing.

Having completed his commitment to the Navy, he joined the Dallas Cowboys of the National Football League in 1969, became the first-string quarterback midway through the 1971 season, and held that job through the 1977 season. The Cowboys won Super Bowl VI on January 16, 1972, by a score of 24–3 against Miami, and Staubach was

voted the most valuable player in the game. He also led Dallas to victory in Super Bowl XII on January 15, 1978, by a score of 27–10 over Denver.

Staubach ranks second on the all-time passing list of the NFL with 22,700 yards and 1685 completions. He is in the College Football Hall of Fame and the Pro Football Hall of Fame.

ANGEL CORDERO

Angel Tomas Cordero
b.   San Juan, P.R., Nov. 8, 1942

Although Angel Cordero's mounts have never won the Triple Crown of thoroughbred racing, Cordero ranks near the very top of the all-time list

of successful jockeys. As of December 1986, he was third in career purses with $109,958,510. Fourth in total number of races won, he brought home his 6000th mount on July 28, 1987.

Cordero rode to victory in the

Kentucky Derby in 1974, 1976, and 1985; in the Preakness Stakes in 1980 and 1984; and in the Belmont Stakes in 1976. For 11 years in succession, he was the leading rider at Saratoga and was named jockey of the year in 1982.

---

by Shut Out, with a time of 2:29⅕. The jockey was Eddie Arcaro.

July 6   The tenth annual **baseball all-star game** was won by the American League, which scored three runs in the first inning in beating the National League 3-1.

Aug. 12   The 17th annual **Hambletonian Stakes** was won in three heats by The Ambassador. The driver was Ben White.

Sept. 6-7   The **U.S. Lawn Tennis Association singles championships** were won by Frederick R. "Ted" Schroeder, Jr., over Frank Parker in the men's division and by Pauline M. Betz over Louise Brough in the women's division.

Sept. 30-Oct. 5   The 39th annual **World Series** was won by the St. Louis Cardinals (NL), defeating the New York Yankees (AL) four games to one. Johnny Beazley won two games, including the final game, which was tied by the Cardinals on a two-run homer by Whitey Kurowski, the Cards' third baseman. Enos Slaughter, Stan Musial, Walker Cooper, and Kurowski simply outplayed the favored Yankee team, which led in almost all the statistics by series end but never made it beyond the fifth game.

Oct. 16   The **freezing of titles** for boxing champions serving in the armed forces was announced as the policy of the National Boxing Association for the duration of the war. Heavyweight champ Joe Louis, serving in the U.S. Army, was one of those affected.

Dec. 8   The **Heisman Trophy** for outstanding college football player was voted to Georgia halfback Frank Sinkwich.

Dec. 13   The **NFL championship** was won by the Washington Redskins, who defeated the Chicago Bears 14-6.

1943

Jan. 1   In **college football bowl games,** the results were Texas 14, Georgia Tech 7 in the Cotton Bowl; Alabama 37, Boston College 21 in the Orange Bowl; Georgia 9, UCLA 0 in the Rose Bowl; and Tennessee 14, Tulsa 7 in the Sugar Bowl. This season the AP poll chose Ohio State as national collegiate champion of 1942.

Feb. 12   At the **Westminster Kennel Club** dog show, Ch. Pitter Patter of Piperscroft, a miniature poodle owned by Mrs. P. H. B. Frelinghuysen, took best-in-show.

Mar. 8   **U.S. figure skating championships** were won in New York City by Gretchen Merrill, women's singles; Arthur R. Vaughn, Jr., men's singles; Doris V. Schubach and Walter Noffke, pairs; and Marcella May and James Lochead, Jr., dance.

Mar. 30   The **NCAA basketball championship** was won by the U. of Wyoming, which defeated Georgetown 56-43 despite the absence of ailing star forward Jim Pollard, who later became a high-scoring forward for the Minneapolis Lakers. Ken Sailors scored 16 for the Cowboys.

Apr. 1-8   The **NHL Stanley Cup** was won by the Detroit Red Wings, who swept the Boston Bruins in four games.

Apr. 18   The 47th **Boston Marathon** was won by Canadian Gérard Côte with a time of 2 hrs., 28 min., 25.8 sec.

May 1   The 69th annual **Kentucky Derby** was won by Count Fleet, with a time of 2:04. The jockey was Johnny Longden.

May 8   The 68th annual **Preakness Stakes** was won by Count Fleet, with a time of 1:57⅖. The jockey was Johnny Longden.

June 5   The 75th annual **Belmont Stakes** was won

JOE NAMATH

Joseph William Namath
b. Beaver Falls, Pa., May 31, 1943

Joe Namath is generally regarded as the best quarterback of his day, but in his heyday, Broadway Joe was as well known for his swinging life style as he was for his skill as a pro football quarterback.

At the University of Alabama, from 1961 to 1965, Namath led the Crimson Tide to an undefeated season in 1964, and Coach Bear Bryant said of Namath that he was "the greatest athlete I have coached."

When Namath signed a contract with the New York Jets for $387,000 in January 1965, he unwittingly gave birth to two movements. One was to bring about a merger of the American and the National football leagues by helping the former achieve equality of play while attracting more fans. The other was to launch a remarkable inflation in salaries paid to pro football stars.

Although troubled by injuries that resulted in operations on his knees, Namath showed remarkable willingness and ingenuity that would lead the Jets to heights the team had

never before approached. In 1967, he passed for 4007 yards, at that time a season record. His finest moment came in 1969, when the Jets won the American League title but were decided underdogs against the Baltimore Colts, at the time champions of the National League. In Super Bowl III, however, Joe Namath outwitted the Colts, completed 17 of 28 passes, and led the Jets to a 16–7 victory.

---

by Count Fleet, with a time of 2:28⅕. The jockey was Johnny Longden. Count Fleet thus became the sixth horse to win racing's Triple Crown.

July 13 The 11th annual **baseball all-star game** was won by the American League, which beat the National League 5 to 3.

Aug. 11 The 18th annual **Hambeltonian Stakes** was won in the third heat by Volo Song. The driver was Ben White, scoring his fourth Hambletonian win.

Sept. 5 The **U.S. Lawn Tennis Association singles championships** were won by Lt. Joseph R. Hunt over John A. "Jack" Kramer in the men's division and Pauline M. Betz in the women's division.

Fall A new **pitching record** for the twentieth century was set by New York Giants relief pitcher Ace Adams, who pitched in 70 games this past season, only one of them a complete game for him. Adams closed the season with a record of 11 wins and 7 losses. His ERA was 2.82.

Oct. 5-11 The 40th annual **World Series** was won by the New York Yankees (AL), defeating the St. Louis Cardinals (NL) four games to one. Spud Chandler won two games for the Yankees, and ten Cardinal errors took St. Louis out of the series.

Dec. 3 The **Heisman Trophy** for outstanding college football player of 1943 was awarded to Notre Dame quarterback Angelo Bertelli. Because of military obligations, he could not attend the award ceremony.

Dec. 26 The **NFL championship** was won by the Chicago Bears, who defeated the Washington Redskins 41-21.

1944

The **first woman to receive the prestigious Sullivan Award,** honoring the outstanding amateur athlete of the year, was swimmer Ann Curtis.

Jan. 1 In **college football bowl games,** the results were Randolph Field 7, Texas 7 in the Cotton Bowl; Louisiana State 19, Texas A&M 14 in the Orange Bowl; Southern California 29, Washington 0 in the Rose Bowl; and Georgia Tech 20, Tulsa 18 in the Sugar Bowl. This season the AP poll chose Notre Dame as national collegiate champion of 1943.

Feb. 12 At the **Westminster Kennel Club** dog show, Ch. Flornell Rare-Bit of Twin Ponds, a Welsh terrier owned by Mrs. Edward P. Alker, took best-in-show.

Feb. 27 **U.S. figure skating championships** were won by Gretchen Merrill, women's singles; Doris Schubach and Walter Noffke, pairs; and Marcella May and James Lochead, Jr., dance. There was no men's singles competition this year.

ARTHUR ASHE

Arthur Robert Ashe
b. Richmond, Va., July 10, 1943

Arthur Ashe began playing tennis at age 7 on a segregated playground. He went on to become the first world-class black male player. Ashe had a tennis scholarship at UCLA, from which he was graduated in 1966, and went on to win his first major tennis victory in 1968, when he was an Army lieutenant. That year, he won both the amateur national title and the first U.S. Open championship.

Ashe in 1970 won the Australian Open, and in 1975 the British title at Wimbledon. In his climb to that title, he defeated his fellow American Jimmy Connors on July 5 in four sets and became the first black man to win a championship at Wimbledon.

Meanwhile, Ashe became involved in racial controversy when South Africa denied him permission to play there in 1970. Ashe carried his fight to the United Nations and the World Tennis Union, asking that South Africa be barred from international competition. In 1973 Ashe was allowed to compete there.

Ashe was a member of the U.S.

Davis Cup team from 1963 on and played a large part in recapturing the trophy from Australia in 1968. Later he became the nonplaying captain of the team, spending much time and energy getting representative American teams together.

Turning professional in 1970, Ashe in 1972 became the first American tennis player to earn more than $100,000 in a year. He was still a top player when, in 1978, he suffered the first of his heart attacks and had surgery, ending his playing days.

Mar. 28 The **NCAA basketball championship** was won by Utah, which defeated Dartmouth 42-40. Arnold Ferrin led the Utes with 22 points.

Mar. 28 Two new **basketball rules** were adopted by the NCAA/AAU Joint Basketball Rules Committee. The first forbade goal-tending, touching the ball on its downward flight on a field goal shot, unless the ball is obviously short of the basket. The second rule change increased from four to five the number of personal fouls a player may make before being ejected from a game.

Apr. 4-13 The **NHL Stanley Cup** was won by the Montreal Canadiens, who defeated the Chicago Black Hawks in four straight games.

Apr. 19 The 48th **Boston Marathon** was won by Gérard Côte, with a time of 2 hrs., 31 min., 50.4 sec. It was his second consecutive and third career win in the event.

May 6 The 70th annual **Kentucky Derby** was won by Pensive, with a time of 2:04⅕. The jockey was Conn McCreary.

May 13 The 69th annual **Preakness Stakes** was won by Pensive, with a time of 1:59⅕. The jockey was Conn McCreary.

June 3 The 76th annual **Belmont Stakes** was won by Bounding Home, with a time of 2:32⅕. The jockey was G. L. Smith.

June 10 The **youngest baseball player** in major league history, 15-year-old Joe Nuxhall, pitched

BILL BRADLEY

William Warren Bradley
b. Crystal City, Mo., July 28, 1943

Bill Bradley is the only former pro basketball star to sit in the U.S. Senate. Before being elected to that post as a Democrat from New Jersey in 1978 and again in 1984, he was better known for his athletic ability. He had begun playing basketball when he was 9, and in high school he was considered the best player in Missouri. At Princeton he proved himself one of the best college

players in the country. The *Sporting News* named him college player of the year in 1964 and 1965, and picked him for its all-American team three times, in 1963, 1964, and 1965.

On graduating in 1965, Bradley was drafted by the New York Knicks but preferred to go to Oxford University for two years as a Rhodes scholar. On his return to the U.S., Bradley joined the Knicks for the 1967–1968 season and remained with them for his entire pro

basketball career, retiring after the 1976–1977 season.

Bradley was not a high scorer, registering 9217 points for an average of 12.4 per game, but he was a cool playmaker who kept the Knicks moving. The Knicks won the NBA championship in 1970 and 1973. Both modest and frugal, Bradley was known to his teammates as Dollar Bill. His book *Life on the Run* (1976) is a classic of the sports book genre. Bradley was elected to the Basketball Hall of Fame in 1982.

Larry Edward Mahan
b.   Brooks, Oreg., Nov. 21, 1943

Larry Mahan and Tom Ferguson are the outstanding performers in modern American rodeo. Mahan began competing in high school and won the Arizona All-Around Cowboy title in 1962. He turned professional the next year.

Mahan won his first World Champion All-Around Cowboy title in 1966, repeated this feat in each of the next four years, and then won again in 1973. He and Ferguson are the only ones to have achieved six such titles. Mahan also earned two bull riding world championships. In 1977, he cut down his rodeo appearances and last appeared in a

saddle bronc event in 1981.

When Mahan appeared on the rodeo scene, he sported long curly hair and somewhat flashy clothes that set him apart from the usual cowboy stereotype. In retirement, Mahan was the star of the movie *The Great American Cowboy,* which won an Academy Award as the best documentary feature of 1972.

---

two-thirds of an inning for the Cincinnati Reds in a lopsided 18-0 loss to the St. Louis Cardinals. Nuxhall gave up five runs in the ninth on two hits, five walks, and one wild pitch. He went on to an excellent career, winning 135 games and losing 117, with an ERA of 3.90.

June 10   A rare **triple dead heat** ended a horse race run at the Aqueduct track on Long Island, N.Y. In the Carter Handicap, Bossuet, Brownie, and Wait a Bit crossed the finish line together.

July 11   The 12th annual **baseball all-star game** was won by the National League, which defeated the American League 7-1. The victory margin was the largest ever in an all-star game.

Aug. 9   The 19th annual **Hambletonian Stakes** was won by Yankee Maid in straight heats. The driver was Henry Thomas.

Aug. 20   The **PGA golf tournament** was won by Robert Hamilton, a relatively unknown pro from Indiana who upset Byron Nelson in the final round, 1 up.

Sept. 3   The **U.S. Lawn Tennis Association singles championships** were won by U.S. Army Sgt. Frank A. Parker in the men's division and Pauline M. Betz in the women's division.

Oct. 2   Charges that **professional gamblers** were inducing college basketball players to throw games were aired by Forrest C. "Phog" Allen, coach at Kansas U. He urged college presidents to take action to prevent a "scandal that will stink to high heaven." His warning was not acted on.

Oct. 4-9   The 41st **World Series** was won by the St. Louis Cardinals (NL), defeating the St. Louis Browns (AL) four games to two. World War II had a positive effect on baseball when the Browns played its first World Series ever but lost to its powerful rival. Against the likes of

Mort Cooper, Max Lanier, and Ted Wilks, the Browns batted .183.

Dec. 2   The **Heisman Trophy** for outstanding college football player of 1944 was voted to Ohio State quarterback Leslie Horvath.

Dec. 17   The **NFL championship** was won by the Green Bay Packers, who defeated the New York Giants 14 to 7.

Winter   **Maurice "Rocket" Richard,** high-scoring professional hockey forward, began his 14-year career with the Montreal Canadiens.

1945

Jan. 1   In **college football bowl games,** the results were Oklahoma A&M 34, Texas Christian 0 in the Cotton Bowl; Tulsa 26, Georgia Tech 12 in the Orange Bowl; Southern California 25, Tennessee 0 in the Rose Bowl; and Duke 29, Alabama 26 in the Sugar Bowl. This season the AP poll chose Army as national collegiate champion of 1944.

Jan. 20   Ten new members, all old-timers, were elected to the **Baseball Hall of Fame:** Roger Bresnahan, Dennis Brouthers, Frederick C. Clarke, James J. Collins, Edward J. Delahanty, Hugh Duffy, Hughey A. Jennings, Michael J. Kelly, James H. O'Rourke, and "Uncle" Wilbert Robinson.

Jan. 26   The **New York Yankees** baseball club was sold by Edward G. Barrow and the heirs of the late Jacob Ruppert to a syndicate headed by Lawrence MacPhail and including Daniel

Topping and Del Webb for an estimated price of $2,800,000.

Feb. 13 At the **Westminster Kennel Club** dog show, Ch. Shieling's Signature, a Scottish terrier owned by Mr. and Mrs. T. H. Snethen, took best-in-show.

Mar. 2-5 **U.S. figure skating championships** were won in New York City by Gretchen Merrill, women's singles; Donna Jeanne Pospisil and Jean Pierre Brunet, pairs; and Kathe Mehl Williams and Robert J. Swenning, dance. There was no men's singles competition this year.

Mar. 19 **Torger Tokle,** Norwegian-born American champion ski jumper, was killed in action while fighting with the U.S. Army in Italy. In 1942, he set a new American ski jump record of 289 ft. In his career, Tokle broke 24 records and won 42 of 48 tournaments he entered.

Mar. 27 **Basketball players' heights** reached new heights this season. George Mikan, 6-ft., 9-in. center for DePaul U., starred as his team defeated Bowling Green in the final round of the National Invitation Tournament. Even taller than Mikan were Bowling Green's Don Otten (6 ft., 11½ in.) and Bob Kurland of Oklahoma A&M (7 ft.).

Mar. 27 The **NCAA basketball championship** was won by Oklahoma A&M, which defeated New York U., 49-45. On March 29 the Aggies defeated DePaul, winner of the National Invita-

tion Tournament, 52-44, in a Red Cross benefit game.

Apr. 6-22 The **NHL Stanley Cup** was won by the Toronto Maple Leafs, who defeated the Detroit Red Wings four games to three.

Apr. 19 The 49th **Boston Marathon** was won by John Kelley of West Acton, Mass., with a time of 2 hrs., 30 min., 40.2 sec.

Apr. 24 Albert B. "Happy" Chandler, junior Senator from Kentucky, was elected **commissioner of baseball** by the unanimous vote of major league club owners. Chandler was named to a seven-year term, succeeding Kenesaw Mountain Landis, who had died on November 25, 1944.

June 9 The 71st annual **Kentucky Derby** was won by Hoop Jr., with a time of 2:07. The jockey was Eddie Arcaro, who scored his third Kentucky Derby victory.

June 16 The 70th annual **Preakness Stakes** was won by Polynesian, with a time of 1:58⅘. The jockey was Wayne D. Wright.

June 23 The 77th annual **Belmont Stakes** was won by Pavot, with a time of 2:30⅕. The jockey was Eddie Arcaro.

July This year's **all-star game** was canceled at government request.

July 15 The **PGA golf tournament** was won by Byron Nelson, who defeated Sam Byrd in the final round. This year Nelson won 19

BILLIE JEAN KING

Billie Jean Moffitt King
b. Long Beach, Calif., Nov. 22, 1943

Billie Jean King has been prominent and successful as a tennis player and as a crusader for women's equality in sports, especially in the matter of amounts of prize money awarded. On October 3, 1971, she became the first woman athlete in any sport to earn more than $100,000 in a year and at Wimbledon in 1979 won her 20th, and record-breaking, title.

King began to play tennis when she was 11. Within a dozen years she was capturing championships in the United States and abroad. King's

first major victory was the singles title at Wimbledon in 1966, which she also won in 1967, 1968, 1972, 1973, and 1975. Her first U.S. championship came in 1967 and was repeated in 1971, 1972, and 1974. She was the French champion in 1972 and the Australian winner in 1968.

With various partners, King has captured many doubles titles: four in the United States championship tournament, in 1967, 1974, 1978, and 1980; and an astounding ten at Wimbledon, in 1961, 1962, 1965, 1967, 1968, 1970, 1971, 1972, 1973, and 1979. She also has various mixed doubles titles to her credit.

King's most publicized victory came on September 20, 1973, against Bobby Riggs, a male professional tennis player who had made disparaging remarks about women's tennis and women in general. He had previously challenged Margaret Smith Court and defeated her, winning as much by his antics as his tennis. King proved to be a different proposition. She overwhelmed Riggs in three straight sets, nearly driving him to exhaustion.

King retired from competitive tennis in 1984 but continued to work to improve the position of women in sports.

of 31 tournaments, eleven of them in succession.

Aug. 8 The 20th annual **Hambletonian Stakes** was won by Titan Hanover in straight heats. The driver was Harry Pownall, Sr.

Aug. 10 The **Brooklyn Dodgers** baseball club gained new owners as the controlling interest was acquired by Branch Rickey, Walter O'Malley, and John L. Smith.

Sept. 2 The **U.S. Lawn Tennis Association singles championships** were won by Sgt. Frank A. Parker over William F. Talbert in the men's division and by Sarah Palfrey Cooke over Pauline M. Betz in the women's division.

Oct. 3-10 The 42nd annual **World Series** was won by the Detroit Tigers (AL), defeating the Chicago Cubs (NL) four games to three. The Cubs sent in Hank Borowy to pitch the final game on one day's rest. He failed to finish the first inning, in which Detroit scored five runs and then proceeded to coast to a 9-3 win.

Oct. 14 The **NFL's longest losing streak** ended when the Chicago Cardinals, after losing 29 consecutive games, defeated the Chicago Bears 16-7. The Cardinals had lost all 20 of their 1943 and 1944 games. After their victory over the Bears, the Cardinals lost their last six games of the season.

Dec. 4 The **Heisman Trophy** for outstanding college football player of 1945 was voted to Army back Felix "Doc" Blanchard.

Dec. 16 The **NFL championship** was won by the Cleveland Rams, who defeated the Washington Redskins 15-14.

1946

The **Basketball Association of America** (BAA) was organized. It was to become the first strong professional basketball league.

It gets late early out there.

Yogi Berra, on having trouble with the sun at Yankee Stadium in autumn

The **National Hockey League schedule** was increased from 50 games in a season to 60. In 1949 it would be increased to 70 and in 1967 to 74.

Jan. 1 In **college football bowl games,** the results were Texas 40, Missouri 27 in the Cotton Bowl; Miami (Fla.) 13, Holy Cross 6 in the Orange Bowl; Alabama 34, Southern California 14 in the Rose Bowl; and Oklahoma A&M 33, St. Mary's 13 in the Sugar Bowl. This season the AP poll chose Army as national collegiate champion of 1945.

Feb. 13 At the **Westminster Kennel Club** dog show, Ch. Hetherington Model Rhythm, a wire-haired fox terrier owned by Mr. and Mrs. T. H. Carruthers III, took best-in-show.

Mar. 2-3 **U.S. figure skating championships** were won in Chicago by Gretchen Merrill, women's singles; Richard Button, men's singles; and Donna Jeanne Pospisil and Jean Pierre Brunet, pairs; Anne Davies and Carleton C. Hoffner, Jr., dance.

Mar. 23 The **NCAA basketball championship** was won by Oklahoma A&M, which defeated California 52-35. Bob Kurland was outstanding for the Aggies.

Mar. 30-Apr. 9 The **NHL Stanley Cup** was won by the Montreal Canadiens, who defeated the Boston Bruins four games to one.

Apr. 7 The **Masters golf tournament** was won by Herman Keiser, who finished one stroke ahead of Ben Hogan, 282-283.

Apr. 20 The 50th annual **Boston Marathon** was won by Stylianos Kyriakides of Greece, with a time of 2 hrs., 29 min., 27 sec.

Apr. 23 Eleven new members, all old-timers, were elected to the **Baseball Hall of Fame:** Jesse Burkett, Frank Chance, John Chesbro, John J. Evers, Clark Griffith, Ed Walsh, Tom McCarthy, Joe "Iron Man" McGinnity, Eddie Plank, Joe Tinker, and Rube Waddell.

May 4 The 72nd annual **Kentucky Derby** was won by Assault, with a time of 2:06⅗. The jockey was Warren Mehrtens.

May 11 The 71st annual **Preakness Stakes** was won by Assault, with a time of 2:01⅖. The jockey was Warren Mehrtens.

May 30 After a five-year hiatus, the 30th **Indianapolis 500** auto race was won by George Robson of Los Angeles, completing the course in 4 hrs., 21 min., 16.70 sec., at an average speed of 114.820 mph.

June 1 The 78th annual **Belmont Stakes** was won

1 9 4 6 DON SCHOLLANDER

Donald Arthur Schollander
b. Charlotte, N.C., Apr. 30, 1946

Don Schollander was the first swimmer ever to win four gold medals at one Olympics. He did this in 1964 at Tokyo, winning the 100- and 400-meter freestyle races and as a member of the 400- and 800-meter relays. In the 400-meter freestyle, he set a world record of 4 minutes, 12.2 seconds.

Schollander began swimming when he was 9 years old and at 15 went to the Santa Clara (California) Swim Club for expert coaching. A year later, in April 1962, he set his first U.S. record, 4 minutes, 18.3 seconds in the 440-yard freestyle. In July 1963, he became the first to swim the 200-meter in under 2 minutes, with a mark of 1:58. He later reduced his time for this event to 1:54.3. In all, between July 1967 and August 1968, Schollander set nine new records.

During most of Schollander's victorious career, he was a student at Yale and was the 100-yard intercollegiate champion in 1968. At the Pan American Games of 1967, he won the 200-meter event but was less successful at the 1968 Olympics, where he qualified only for the 200-meter freestyle and did not win the gold.

Schollander trained for perfection, and his effortless crawl style belied his speed.

---

by Assault, with a time of 2:30⅘. The jockey was Warren Mehrtens. Assault became the seventh horse to win racing's Triple Crown.

June 16 The **U.S. Open golf tournament** was won by Lloyd Mangrum, who defeated Byron Nelson and Vic Ghezzi by one stroke after the threesome had tied at the end of the first play-off round.

July 6 At the **Wimbledon** tennis championships in England, Yvon Petra of France won the men's single title and Pauline M. Betz won the women's singles title. Louise Brough and Margaret Osborne won the women's doubles, and Tom Brown and Jack Kramer won the men's doubles.

July 9 The 13th annual **baseball all-star game** was won by the American League, which shut out the National League 12-0. Ted Williams went four for four, including two home runs, before his Boston fans in Fenway Park.

Aug. 8 The 21st annual **Hambletonian Stakes** was won in the third heat by Chestertown. The driver was Tom Berry.

Aug. 25 The **PGA golf tournament** was won by Ben Hogan, with a 6 and 4 win over Ed "Porky" Oliver in the final round at the Portland, Oreg., Golf Club.

Sept. 1 The **first perfect national tournament score** in the five-eighths ounce plug accuracy event of the National Association of Angling and Casting Clubs was scored by Joe Halbleib, of Louisville, Ky., at the casting championships held in Indianapolis.

Sept. 1 The **first U.S. Women's Open golf tour-**

nament was won in Spokane, Wash., by Patty Berg. At match play, Berg defeated Betty Jameson in the final round.

Sept. 8 The **U.S. Lawn Tennis Association singles championships** were won by Jack Kramer over Tom Brown in the men's division and Pauline M. Betz over Doris Hart in the women's division.

Oct. 6-15 The 43rd annual **World Series** was won by the St. Louis Cardinals (NL), defeating the Boston Red Sox (AL) four games to three. In the eighth inning of the final game, Enos Slaughter scored the winning run by racing home from first base on a line drive single to left center by Harry Walker that the center fielder, Leon Culberson, threw to shortstop Johnny Pesky. Pesky hesitated in relaying to the catcher, a fatal hesitation when one is trying to cut down a Slaughter at the plate. On Oct. 3 the Cardinals had won the first National League playoff, beating the Brooklyn Dodgers two games straight.

Oct. 16 **Gordie Howe** scored the first goal in his record-setting career, which ended in 1980.

Dec. 3 The **Heisman Trophy** for outstanding college football player of 1946 was voted to Army halfback Glenn Davis.

Dec. 15 The **NFL championship** was won by the Chicago Bears, who defeated the New York Giants 24-14.

Dec. 26 In the **Davis Cup** international tennis matches, the U.S. defeated Australia 5-0, regaining the trophy lost to Australia in 1939. The U.S. team was the first to fly to Australia. Team members were Jack Kramer, Ted Schroeder, Frank

Parker, Tom Brown, Billy Talbert, and Gardnar Mulloy. Schroeder took Jack Bromwich in five sets in the opening match, and the U.S. went on to sweep the Aussies 5-0, the worst defeat ever inflicted on a defending team.

1947

Charles M. P. Brinton, of Philadelphia, won the **national squash racquets championship** for the fourth consecutive time, bridging the World War II years, when the event was canceled.

Little League baseball's first world series was held at Williamsport, Pa., where all later series have also been held. The winner was a hometown team, Maynard Little League.

Master Sergeant **Huelet Benner** of the U.S. Army won the pistol target shooting championship, interrupting the string of victories by Harry Reeves. Benner would also win the title six times, over an 11-year span that included one year in which no competition was held.

Jan. 1 In **college football bowl games,** the results were Arkansas 0, Louisiana State 0 in the Cotton Bowl; Rice 8, Tennessee 0 in the Orange Bowl; Illinois 45, UCLA 14 in the Rose Bowl; and Georgia 20, North Carolina 10 in the Sugar Bowl. This season the AP poll chose Notre Dame as national collegiate champion of 1946.

Feb. 13 At the **Westminster Kennel Club** dog show, Ch. Warlord of Mazelaine, a boxer owned by Mr. and Mrs. R. C. Kettles, Jr., took best-in-show.

Mar. 9 **U.S. figure skating championships** were won in Berkeley, Calif., by Gretchen Merrill, women's singles; Richard T. "Dick" Button, men's singles; Yvonne Sherman and Robert Swenning, pairs; Lois Waring and Walter H. Bainbridge, Jr., dance.

Mar. 15 **Vincent "Vinnie" Richards** was named commissioner of the World Professional Tennis League. League president Tony Owen announced that players in the first tournament for $10,000 in prize money would include Don Budge, Bobby Riggs, Fred Perry, Frank Kovacs, and George Lott.

Mar. 25 The **NCAA basketball championship** was won by Holy Cross, which defeated the U. of Oklahoma 58-47. George Kaftan of Holy Cross was voted most valuable player.

Apr. 6 The **Masters golf tournament** was won for the second time by Jimmy Demaret. His 281 bested Byron Nelson by two strokes.

Apr. 8-19 The **NHL Stanley Cup** was won by the Toronto Maple Leafs, who defeated the Montreal Canadiens four games to two.

Apr. 10 **Jackie Robinson** became the first black player to achieve major league baseball status when the Brooklyn Dodgers bought his contract from the Montreal Royals, of the International League. He appeared in a Dodgers uniform at Ebbets Field the next day, in time for the first game of an exhibition series with the Yankees.

Apr. 19 The 51st **Boston Marathon** was won by Yun Bok Sun of Seoul, Korea, with a time of 2 hrs., 25 min., 39 sec.

Apr. 22 The first **championship of the Basketball Association of America** (BAA) was won by the Philadelphia Warriors over the Chicago

LAFFIT PINCAY

Laffit Pincay, Jr.
b. Panama City, Panama, Dec. 19, 1946

In terms of purses won, Pincay is the most successful jockey ever. He leads in career purse earnings with $116,146,205; in single season earnings with $13,353,299, in 1985; and as winner of the richest one-race

purse, $2,000,000 in the 1985 Jersey Derby. He was the leading money winner for five consecutive years, from 1970 to 1974.

Money earnings are not Pincay's only claim to fame in the world of thoroughbred racing. He ranks second in career victories, with 6721 as of July 1987, and he won three consecutive Belmont Stakes, 1982,

1983, and 1984. He also rode Swale to a Kentucky Derby win in 1984. Pincay has been given the award as outstanding jockey five times, in 1971, 1973, 1974, 1979, and 1985. He was elected to the National Museum of Racing Hall of Fame in 1975.

JIM RYUN

James Ronald Ryun
b. Wichita, Kans., Apr. 29, 1947

Although the many track records Jim Ryun set have since been broken, according to many authorities there never was a better middle-distance runner. Despite his nearsightedness, impaired hearing, and various allergies, Ryun in 1963 was able to run the mile in 4 minutes, 1.7 seconds, faster than any other high school runner had ever done. Later that same year he became the first high school runner to run the mile in under 4 minutes. His time was 3 minutes, 59 seconds.

From 1965 through 1967, Ryun set and broke records with admirable regularity: 1965, a new U.S. mile record of 3:55.3; 1966, a new U.S. 2-mile record, 8:25.2; 1966, another mile record, 3:53.7, which he broke later that year with a 3:51.3; June 1967, still another world record for the mile, 3:51.1, in the AAU championship, which Ryun won by 40 yards, and in the next month, a world record for the 1500 meters, 3:33.1.

Ryun's great disappointment came in the 1964 Olympics. Suffering from a head cold, he lost in the semifinals of the 1500-meter run. In the 1968 Olympics he placed second to Kipchogue Keino of Kenya.

Stags, four games to one. Starring for the winners was Joe Fulks, with 34 points in the final game.

May 3 The 73rd annual **Kentucky Derby** was won by Jet Pilot, with a time of 2:06⅘. The jockey was Eric Guerin.

May 10 The 72nd annual **Preakness Stakes** was won by Faultless, with a time of 1:59. The jockey was Douglas Dodson.

May 30 The 31st **Indianapolis 500** auto race was won by Mauri Rose of Chicago, completing the 500-mi. course in 4 hrs., 17 min., 52.17 sec., at an average speed of 116.338 mph.

May 31 The 79th annual **Belmont Stakes** was won by Phalanx, with a time of 2:29⅖. The jockey was Ruperto Donoso.

June 15 The **U.S. Open golf tournament** was won by Lew Worsham, who beat Sam Snead by one stroke on the last green in an 18-hole play-off. At the end of the regular rounds at the St. Louis, Mo., Country Club, they had been tied at 282.

June 24 The **PGA golf tournament** was won by Jim Ferrier. He defeated Chick Harbert in the final round, 2 and 1, at the Plum Hollow Country Club, Detroit.

June 29 The **U.S. Women's Open golf tournament,** now a medal-play event, was won by Betty Jameson at the Forest Country Club, Greensboro, N.C. Jameson's 72-hole total was 295.

July 4-5 At the **Wimbledon** tennis championships in England, Jack Kramer won the men's singles title and Margaret Osborne won the women's singles. Kramer teamed with Robert Falkenburg to win the men's doubles, Doris Hart and Patricia Canning Todd won the women's doubles, and Louise Brough teamed with John E. Bromwich of Australia to win the mixed doubles.

July 5 Oarsman **John B. Kelly, Jr.,** won the Diamond Challenge Sculls at the Henley Royal Regatta in England. On July 2, 1949, he repeated his victory. Kelly's father, John B. Kelly, Sr., had been barred from participating in this same event in 1920.

July 8 The 14th annual **baseball all-star game** was won by the American League, defeating the National League 2-1. Hal Newhouser, Spec Shea, Walt Masterson, and Joe Page allowed but five hits, one a homer by Johnny Mize.

July 21 The **Baseball Hall of Fame** inducted Carl Hubbell, Lefty Grove, Mickey Cochrane, and Frank Frisch, as well as 11 old-timers elected to the Hall of Fame in 1946.

Aug. 6 The 22nd annual **Hambletonian Stakes** was won in the third heat by Hoot Mon. The driver was S. F. Palin.

Sept. 4 The **National Hockey League** adopted a players' pension plan. Funding was to be obtained from annual contributions by the players; two-thirds of the proceeds of a new, annual all-star game; and 25 cents from each paid admission to postseason playoff games.

Sept. 14 The **U.S. Lawn Tennis Association singles championships** were won by Jack Kramer over Frank Parker in the men's division and Louise Brough in the women's division. Kramer lost only one set during the entire tournament.

PETE MARAVICH

Peter Press Maravich
b.   Aliquippa, Pa., June 22, 1947
d.   Pasadena, Calif., Jan. 5, 1988

Pete Maravich more than made good in pro basketball, but the records he set in his college career are even more impressive. At Louisiana State, where his father was coach, he scored 3667 points, a college career record that still stands, as does his game average of 44.5 points scored. Against Alabama on February 7, 1970, Maravich registered 69 points, and he led the NCAA in scoring in 1968, 1969, and 1970. He was named college player of the year in 1970 by the *Sporting News* and made its all-American team three times, in 1968, 1969, and 1970. His record totals for field goals and free throws attempted brought him the nickname Pistol Pete.

Drafted into the National Basketball Association by Atlanta in 1970, Maravich played four seasons there, was traded to the New Orleans Jazz in 1974, moved with the Jazz to Utah in 1979, but finished the season with Boston. In his career, he scored 15,948 points in regular-season play with a game average of 24.2, the 12th highest. He led the NBA in the 1976–1977 season with 2273 points and a point average of 31.1.

Maravich appeared in four playoff series and averaged 18.7 points per game. He also played in four all-star games. Maravich was elected to the Basketball Hall of Fame in 1987. His sudden death at age 40 came just after playing in a schoolyard game of basketball.

Sept. 30-Oct. 6 The 44th annual **World Series** was won by the New York Yankees (AL), defeating the Brooklyn Dodgers (NL) four games to three. The sixth game of this subway series lives in memory, because Dodgers outfielder Al Gionfriddo robbed Joe DiMaggio of a score-tying home run on a 415-ft. drive with two aboard. Joe Page saved games one and seven for the Yankees. In game four, Floyd Bevens had a no-hitter going until there were two outs in the ninth. With two men aboard, Harry "Cookie" Lavagetto, the Dodgers third baseman, doubled off the right-field wall to give his team a 3-2 victory.

Fall Jack Kramer turned pro and **organized an extensive national circuit** for matches between his tennis players. Kramer later took his players to Europe. His player associates included Bobby Riggs, Pancho Segura, and Don Budge. Virtually every year, additional players joined the traveling company, most notably Pancho Gonzales and Tony Trabert.

Oct. 13 The **National Hockey League** held its first all-star game at Toronto, the All-Stars defeating the Toronto Maple Leafs 4-3.

Oct. 23 The **United States Women's Curling Association** was founded in Milwaukee, Wis., by representatives of five Midwest clubs. By 1987

O. J. SIMPSON

Orenthal James Simpson
b.   San Francisco, Calif., July 9, 1947

No one was surprised when, in 1970, a National Collegiate Sports Services poll rated O. J. Simpson, a running back, the best college football player of the 1970s. He had set records at the University of Southern California and led its team to prominence. The Trojans were the number one college team in 1966, and Simpson played a large part in the team's victory in the Rose Bowl in 1968, when they defeated Indiana 14–3. He won the Heisman Trophy that year and set a rushing record of 1309 yards. On top of all this, Simpson was a sprinter who in 1967 was a member of a 440-yard relay team that established a world record.

Joining the Buffalo Bills of the American Football League in 1969, Simpson became one of the stars, along with Joe Namath, who made that league competitive with the National Football League and led to a merger of the two leagues. With his speed and his timing, Simpson began to set records. His record season total of 2003 yards gained in 1973 stood for ten years. His total of 23 touchdowns in 1975 is still a record for a season, and he ranks fifth among rushers with a lifetime record of 11,236 yards in 1404 carries in 11 seasons, for an average gain of 4.7 yards.

After his retirement from football, he became an actor and a sports commentator on television. He is in both the College Football Hall of Fame and the Pro Football Hall of Fame.

BILL RODGERS

William Henry Rodgers
b. Hartford, Conn., Dec. 23, 1947

When Bill Rodgers was in his prime, he was generally judged to be the best marathon runner in the world. Yet he did not get off to an auspicious start in his event, having had to drop out of the 1973 Boston Marathon at 20 miles because he suffered cramps and dehydration. Two years later, however, he began his winning streak by taking the Boston race in 2 hours, 9 minutes, 55 seconds, at that point the fastest time ever turned in by an American.

The next year, 1976, Rodgers began a record-setting streak of four consecutive victories in the New York City Marathon, ending in 1979. He did almost as well in the Boston Marathon, winning three more times, in 1978, 1979, and 1980. In the 1979 race, Rodgers ran his own best time, 2 hours, 9 minutes, 27 seconds. In December 1977, Rodgers won the Japanese Invitational Marathon. In his career, Rodgers set records for the 10-mile and 25-kilometer distances.

Rodgers was an outspoken critic of the U.S. boycott of the 1980 Olympics and in 1981 helped organize the Association of Road Running Athletes to promote distance running as a professional sport.

---

the association had grown to 88 clubs and 4600 individual members.

Oct. 29 A new **professional basketball rule** raised from five to six the number of personal fouls calling for ejection from the game.

Dec. 2 The **Heisman Trophy** for outstanding college football player of 1947 was voted to Notre Dame quarterback Johnny Lujack.

Dec. 28 The **NFL championship** was won by the Chicago Cardinals, who defeated the Philadelphia Eagles 28-21.

Dec. 30 In the **Davis Cup** international tennis challenge round, the U.S. defeated Australia four matches to one. Ted Schroeder and Jack Kramer once again were too much for the Australians, beating them 4-1. The only U.S. loss came in the doubles, when Schroeder and Kramer lost to Jack Bromwich and Dinny Pails.

1948

Richard D. "Dick" Pope Sr., founder of Cypress Gardens near Winter Haven, Fla., signed **Willa Worthington,** reigning queen of women water skiers, as prima ballerina of his water ski show and instructor of his Aquamaids. She was the show's star attraction for a decade.

The **Amateur Athletic Union** approved synchronized swimming as a competitive sport. In 1963 it initiated annual age-group synchronized swimming competitions.

Jan. 1 In **college football bowl games,** the results were Southern Methodist 13, Penn State 13 in the Cotton Bowl; Georgia Tech 20, Kansas 14 in the Orange Bowl; Michigan 49, Southern California 0 in the Rose Bowl; and Texas 27, Alabama 7 in the Sugar Bowl. This season the AP poll chose Notre Dame as national collegiate champion of 1947.

Jan. 30-Feb. 8 At the **Winter Olympics** in St. Moritz, Switzerland, the U.S. won three gold medals and finished third in unofficial team standings, behind Sweden and Switzerland. Gretchen Fraser won the first gold medal ever by an American in a skiing event when she took the title in the women's special slalom.

Feb. 12 At the **Westminster Kennel Club** dog show, Ch. Rock Ridge Night Rocket, a Bedlington terrier owned by Mr. and Mrs. William A. Rockefeller, took best-in-show.

Feb. 13 At the **world figure skating championships** in Davos, Switzerland, the men's singles title was won by Richard T. "Dick" Button, the first U.S. skater to win the men's title. Button, who entered Harvard College later this year, would win four more titles in succession before turning professional and studying law.

Mar. 20 The NCAA initiated **collegiate ice hockey playoffs,** Michigan beating Dartmouth in the final round at Colorado Springs. The growth of college hockey and the increasing popularity of the professional game hastened the end of club amateur hockey, played primarily by former college players. Two of the clubs that played for a time were the St. Nicks, at the St. Nicholas Arena in New York City, and the Boston Hockey Club.

Mar. 20 A new **safety program for professional boxers** was announced by the National Boxing Association. The program called for more thorough physical examinations, long layoffs after knockout defeats, a mandatory count of 8 after knockdowns, and the use of heavily padded 8-oz. gloves.

Mar. 23 The **NCAA basketball tournament** was won by Kentucky, which defeated Baylor 58-42. Alex Groza and Ralph Beard were outstanding for the winners.

Apr. 3 **U.S. figure skating championships** were won in Colorado Springs, Colo., by Gretchen Merrill, women's singles, her sixth consecutive win; Dick Button, men's singles; Karol and Peter Kennedy, pairs; and Lois Waring and Walter H. Bainbridge, Jr., dance.

Apr. 7-14 The **NHL Stanley Cup** was won for the second year in a row by the Toronto Maple Leafs, who defeated the Detroit Red Wings in four straight games.

Apr. 11 The **Masters golf tournament** was won by Claude Harmon by a five-stroke margin over Cary Middlecoff.

Apr. 19 The 52nd **Boston Marathon** was won by Canadian Gérard Côte with a time of 2 hrs., 31 min., 2 sec. It was his fourth win.

May 1 The 74th annual **Kentucky Derby** was won by Citation, with a time of 2:05⅖. The jockey was Eddie Arcaro.

May 15 The 73rd annual **Preakness Stakes** was won by Citation, with a time of 2:02⅗. The jockey was Eddie Arcaro.

May 25 The **PGA golf tournament** was won by Ben Hogan, who defeated Mike Turnesa in the final round, 7 and 6.

May 31 The 32nd **Indianapolis 500** auto race was won by Mauri Rose, completing the 500-mi. course in 4 hrs., 10 min., 23.33 sec., at an average speed of 119.814 mph. It was his second consecutive win.

June 12 The 80th annual **Belmont Stakes** was won by Citation, with a time of 2:28⅕. Citation thus became the seventh horse in history to win the Triple Crown of racing. The jockey was Eddie Arcaro, who chalked up his second Triple Crown victory.

June 12 Ben Hogan won the **U.S. Open golf tournament** at Riviera Country Club, Los Angeles, with a tournament record-breaking score of 276, five strokes lower than Ralph Guldahl's previous tournament record. Hogan's rounds were 67, 72, 68, and 69.

June 25 The **world heavyweight boxing championship** was successfully defended by Joe Louis, who defeated "Jersey Joe" Walcott in an 11-round bout. After the fight, Louis announced that he was retiring from the ring.

July 2 At the **Wimbledon** tennis championships in England, Robert Falkenburg won the men's singles title. The next day Louise Brough won the women's singles, then teamed with Margaret Osborne du Pont to win the women's doubles and with John E. "Jack" Bromwich of Australia to win the mixed doubles. Only Suzanne

BOBBY ORR

Robert Gordon Orr
b. Parry Sound, Ontario, Canada,
    Mar. 20, 1948

Bobby Orr began ice skating at 4, was taken in hand by the Boston Bruins when he was 12, and began playing for them when he was 18, the earliest age at which a skater is eligible for the National Hockey League. Almost immediately, Orr became the best defenseman in the league and certainly the highest

scorer for a player on the back line.

Orr was soon picking up honors and awards, becoming rookie of the year in 1967. That same year, he underwent surgery for torn cartilage in a knee. In later years, he had his left shoulder broken, his nose broken six times, and innumerable stitches taken, but he never slowed down. He was always a vigorous and fearless player, a tough man on the ice.

Orr's dominance as a defenseman

is shown by the fact that he won the James Norris Trophy eight years in succession, from 1968 to 1975. At the same time, he was twice the winner of the Art Ross Trophy for leading scorers, in 1970 and 1975. Such feats have resulted in his being named the league's most valuable player in 1970, 1971, and 1972.

Orr played his final season, 1976–1977, with the Chicago Black Hawks.

1 PEGGY FLEMING

9
4
9

Peggy Gale Fleming Jenkins
b.   San Jose, Calif., July 27, 1948

In 1964, when Peggy Fleming was only 15 years old, she became the youngest person ever to win the U.S. women's figure skating championship. By so doing, she also captured the hearts of Americans. Fleming had begun skating when she was nine. Two years later she won her first title in the Pacific Coast Juvenile competition.

Fleming first competed in the Olympics in 1964, finishing sixth. Four years later she won the gold medal at Grenoble, France, the only gold medal in skating taken by the United States at the 1968 Games. Meanwhile, Fleming held the U.S. title through 1968 and was twice North American champion. To crown her achievements, she won the world title for three consecutive years, from 1966 to 1968.

Fleming then retired from amateur

skating and appeared in *Ice Follies* and *Holiday on Ice* as well as in television specials. She has been active in promoting women's sports and as a goodwill ambassador for UNICEF. Fleming's style was one of grace and romance. As the *New York Times* once put it, her skating was a "victory of the ballet over the Ice Follies approach to figure skating."

Lenglen and Alice Marble had previously won the women's triple crown.

July 13   The 15th annual **baseball all-star game** was won by the American League, which beat the National League 5 to 2.

July 29-Aug. 14   At the **Summer Olympics** in London, England, the U.S. won 33 gold medals and the unofficial team championship. Wilbur Thompson set a new Olympic record in the shot put with a toss of 56 ft., 2 in. Robert Mathias won the decathlon and repeated his victory in the 1952 Olympics, becoming the first athlete ever to win consecutive Olympics decathlons.

Aug. 11   The 23rd annual **Hambletonian Stakes** was won in straight heats by Demon Hanover. The driver was Harrison Hoyt.

Aug. 15   The **U.S. Women's Open golf tournament** was won by Mildred "Babe" Didrikson Zaharias at the Atlantic City (New Jersey) Country Club. Betty Hicks placed second.

Sept. 6   In the **Davis Cup** international tennis challenge round, the U.S. won its fifth straight match from Australia, sweeping the round 5-0 and retaining the trophy. Ted Schroeder and Frank Parker and the doubles team of Billy Talbert and Gardnar Mulloy blanked Adrian Quist and Billy Sidwell.

Sept. 19   The **U.S. Lawn Tennis Association singles championships** were won by 20-year-old Pancho Gonzales in the men's division in a three-set victory in the finals over Eric Sturgess of South Africa. In the women's division, Margaret Osborne du Pont outlasted Louise Brough to win the women's title.

Oct. 6-11   The 45th annual **World Series** was won by the Cleveland Indians (AL), defeating the Boston Braves (NL) four games to two in an undistinguished championship series. The Indians had won the American League pennant on Oct. 4 by beating the Boston Red Sox 8-3 in a single-game playoff, the first time a playoff was needed in the league.

Oct. 26   **American rodeo performers** were expelled from Switzerland after they became embroiled in a free-for-all with spectators and police in Geneva. The 40 cowboys and cowgirls were escorted to the French border.

Dec. 8   The **Heisman Trophy** for outstanding college football player of 1948 was voted to Southern Methodist back Doak Walker.

Dec. 19   The **NFL championship** was won by the Philadelphia Eagles, who defeated the Chicago Cardinals 7-0.

1949

G. Diehl Mateer, Jr., of Philadelphia, won the first of 11 **national squash racquets doubles championships.** This year, and in victories in 1950 and 1953, his partner was Hunter H. Lott, Jr., also of Philadelphia.

Jan. 1   In **college football bowl games,** the results were Southern Methodist 21, Oregon 13 in

178

b. Waterloo, Iowa, Oct. 25, 1948

In the world of amateur wrestling, Dan Gable is both the best wrestler and the most successful coach ever. In high school in Waterloo, Ohio, he won 64 matches and lost one in three years. At Iowa State University, from 1967 to 1970, he won 118 matches and lost one. The loss came in the NCAA finals, when he was a senior. Prior to that he had been undefeated in 182 consecutive bouts.

Gable became the University of Iowa's head wrestling coach in August 1976 after having been assistant coach for four years. Since then his matmen have won 11 consecutive Big Ten titles, from 1977 to 1987, taking 72 matches without a loss. In addition, Hawkeye wrestlers have won nine consecutive NCAA championships, from 1978 to 1986, finishing third in 1977 and second in 1987. Gable's overall coaching record is 167 wins, 7 losses, and 2 ties.

At the 1972 Olympics, Gable won the gold medal in the 149.5-pound class, never giving up a point to an opponent. He also won titles at the Pan American Games. At the 1984 Olympic Games, he was head coach of the U.S. freestyle team, which won seven gold and two silver medals. Gable was named to the Wrestling Hall of Fame in 1980.

---

the Cotton Bowl; Texas 41, Georgia 28 in the Orange Bowl; Northwestern 20, California 14 in the Rose Bowl; and Oklahoma 14, North Carolina 6 in the Sugar Bowl. This season the AP poll chose Michigan as national collegiate champion of 1948.

Feb. 8 A **U.S. four-man bobsled team** led by Stan Benham won the world championship at Lake Placid, N.Y.

Feb. 15 At the **Westminster Kennel Club** dog show, Ch. Mazelaine's Zazarac Brandy, a boxer owned by Mr. and Mrs. John P. Wagner, took best-in-show.

Feb. 17 At the **world figure skating championships,** held in Paris, France, Dick Button won the men's singles title.

Feb. 22 A new **pro basketball scoring record** was set by George Mikan of the Minneapolis Lakers, who scored 48 points as the Lakers defeated the New York Knicks, 101-74. On Jan. 31, 1950, a sportswriters' poll named Mikan the greatest basketball player of the half-century, with Hank Luisetti of Stanford the runner-up.

Mar. 13 **U.S. figure skating championships** were won in Ardmore, Pa., by Yvonne Sherman, women's singles; Dick Button, men's singles; Karol and Peter Kennedy, pairs; and Lois Waring and Walter H. Bainbridge, Jr., dance.

Mar. 26 The **NCAA basketball championship** was won by Kentucky, which defeated Oklahoma State 46-36. Alex Groza, Kentucky center, was voted most valuable player.

Apr. 8-16 The **NHL Stanley Cup** was won for the third consecutive year by the Toronto Maple Leafs, defeating the Detroit Red Wings in a four-game sweep.

Apr. 10 The **Masters golf tournament** was won by Sam Snead, whose 282 total beat out Lloyd Mangrum and Johnny Bulla by three strokes.

Apr. 19 The 53rd **Boston Marathon** was won by Karl Gosta Leandersson of Sweden, with a time of 2 hrs., 31 min., 50.8 sec.

May 7 The 75th annual **Kentucky Derby** was won by Ponder, with a time of 2:04⅕. The jockey was Steve Brooks.

May 14 The 74th annual **Preakness Stakes** was won by Capot, with a time of 1:56. The jockey was Ted Atkinson.

May 30 The 33rd **Indianapolis 500** auto race was won by Bill Holland of Reading, Pa., completing the 500-mi. course in a record time of 4 hrs., 7 min., 15.97 sec., at an average speed of 121.327 mph.

May 31 The **PGA golf tournament** at the Hermitage Country Club, Richmond, Va., was won by Sam Snead. In the final round, he defeated Johnny Palmer, 3 and 2.

June 11 At Medinah (Illinois) Country Club, the **U.S. Open golf tournament** was won by Cary Middlecoff with a 286. Sam Snead and Clayton Heafner tied for second. Ben Hogan, recuperating from injuries suffered in a serious automobile accident, did not play.

June 11 The 81st **Belmont Stakes** was won by Capot, with a time of 2:30⅕. The jockey was Ted Atkinson.

June 13 The **Baseball Hall of Fame** inducted five new members: Three Finger Brown,

He can run, but he can't hide.

Joe Louis, explaining why he would win his
bout with Billy Conn

pitcher; Charley Gehringer, second baseman;
Kid Nichols, pitcher; Herb Pennock, pitcher;
and Harold "Pie" Traynor, third baseman.

June 22 The **world heavyweight boxing championship** was won by Ezzard Charles, who defeated Joe Walcott on points in a 15-round bout in Chicago. Joe Louis had announced his retirement as champion on Mar. 1, and the National Boxing Association recognized the winner of this bout as the new champion.

July 1-2 At the **Wimbledon** tennis championships in England, Ted Schroeder won the men's singles title after clawing his way through five-set victories over Frank Sedgman of Australia, Eric Sturgess of South Africa, and Jaroslav Drobny of Czechoslovakia. Louise Brough had an easier time of it in winning the women's singles. Brough and Margaret Osborne du Pont won the women's doubles, and Frank Parker and Pancho Gonzales won the men's doubles.

July 12 The 16th annual **baseball all-star game** was won by the American League, which beat the National League 11-7. It was a long day for pitchers. There were 25 hits and 18 runs, and the National League infield and catchers committed five errors.

Aug. 3 The **National Basketball Association** (NBA) was formed by the merger of the Basketball Association of America and an older midwestern circuit called the National Basketball League.

Aug. 10 The 24th annual **Hambletonian Stakes** was won in straight heats by Miss Tilly. The driver was Fred Egan.

Aug. 28 In the **Davis Cup** international tennis challenge round, the U.S. won the final two matches from Australia to take the round 4-1 and retain the trophy. Both Pancho Gonzales and Ted Schroeder twice beat Frank Sedgman and Billy Sidwell in singles matches, but Billy Talbert and Gardnar Mulloy lost in doubles to Sidwell and Jack Bromwich.

Sept. 5 The **U.S. Lawn Tennis Association men's singles championship** was again won

by Pancho Gonzales in the men's division over Ted Schroeder in a marathon five-set match. Margaret Osborne du Pont defeated Doris Hart for the women's title. Gonzales shortly after the competition turned pro.

Sept. 20 **Pancho Gonzales** turned pro, signing a one-year contract with promoter Bobby Riggs that guaranteed him $60,000 in the first year. A Gonzales-Jack Kramer tour was announced, starting at New York City's Madison Square Garden on Oct. 25.

Sept. 25 At Landover, Md., the **U.S. Women's Open golf tournament** was won by Louise Suggs, who beat Babe Didrikson Zaharias by 14 strokes.

Oct. 5-9 The 46th annual **World Series** was won by the New York Yankees (AL), defeating the Brooklyn Dodgers (NL) four games to one. Although two of the games were close, the series had no special interest, but it was noteworthy because it was the first World Series victory for Casey Stengel in what would turn out to be an enviable record with the Yankees.

Dec. 7 The **Heisman Trophy** for outstanding college football player of 1949 was awarded to Notre Dame end Leon Hart.

Dec. 8 The **color bar in fencing** was broken when the Amateur Fencers League of America voted to admit members "regardless of color or race." The action came as the result of application for membership by two blacks who were members of the Columbia U. fencing team.

Dec. 18 The **NFL championship** was won by the Philadelphia Eagles, who defeated the Los Angeles Rams 14-0.

1950

Racquetball, first called paddle rackets, a cross between squash racquets and handball, was invented by Joe Sobek, a former squash racquets and tennis professional, at Greenwich, Conn.

Jan. 1 In **college football bowl games,** the results were Rice 27, North Carolina 13 in the Cotton Bowl; Santa Clara 21, Kentucky 12 in the Orange Bowl; Ohio State 17, California 14 in the Rose Bowl; and Oklahoma 35, Louisiana State 0

TOM WATSON

Thomas Sturges Watson
b. Kansas City, Mo., Sept. 4, 1949

When first playing on the pro golf tour, Tom Watson exhibited a perky manner and friendly grin that qualified him for the role of Tom Sawyer. His golfing skills, however, made it seem as though he had been around for years. Already successful as an amateur, Watson turned pro in 1971, after graduation from Stanford University.

Watson won his first major victory in 1975, in the most difficult of all tournaments, the British Open. In fact Watson is by far the most successful American player ever to compete in this event. After his initial victory, he won it four more times, in 1977, 1980, 1982, and 1983. One other player has won the Open more times, but Watson holds such British Open records as lowest 72-hole score at both Muirfield (271 in 1980) and Turnberry (268 in 1977) and best finish by a winner, 65, at Turnberry in 1977.

He has also won the Masters twice, in 1977 and 1981, and the U.S. Open in 1982 but has never triumphed in the PGA. In 1977, Watson won five tournaments and the next year won six. For three successive years, from 1977 to 1979, he was the leading money winner, and in 1979 he became the first golfer to pass the $400,000 mark. Also in 1979, he became the first to win the Byron Nelson Classic three times. Watson has won the Vardon Trophy for the year's best average score seven times.

---

in the Sugar Bowl. This season the AP poll chose Notre Dame as national collegiate champion of 1949.

Jan. 29 Jack Dempsey was named the **greatest fighter of the past 50 years** in an Associated Press poll of sportswriters and broadcasters. He received 251 votes to 104 for Joe Louis.

Feb. 5 A **U.S. four-man bobsled team** led by Stan Benham won the world championship at Cortina d'Ampezzo, Italy, repeating the 1949 victory of a team led by Benham.

Feb. 8 **Man o' War** was named the greatest horse of the first half of the century by an Associated Press poll. Known as a horse that excelled as sprinter and distance runner, Man o' War ran as a 2-year-old and a 3-year-old, winning 20 out of 21 starts and breaking five track records.

Feb. 14 At the **Westminster Kennel Club** dog show, Ch. Walsing Winning Trick of Edgerstoune, a Scottish terrier owned by Mrs. John G. Winant, took best-in-show.

Mar. 7 At the **world figure skating championships** in London, England, Dick Button won the men's singles title for the third consecutive year. Americans Michael McGean and Lois Waring won the ice dancing championship, a new event this year. Americans Peter and Karol Kennedy won the pairs' figure skating championship. The Kennedy team was the first U.S. team to win this event.

Mar. 19 The **U.S. Women's Open golf tournament,** held at Wichita, Kans., was won by Babe Didrikson Zaharias, with Betsy Rawls second.

Mar. 24 **U.S. figure skating championships**

BRUCE JENNER

b. Mt. Kisco, N.Y., Oct. 28, 1949

Bruce Jenner almost in a single day became the world's idea of the complete, all-around athlete when he won the decathlon at the 1976 Olympic Games in Montreal, Canada. It was the first U.S. victory in this event since 1968. In winning, Jenner established a new Olympic record of 8618 points. This mark stood until the 1984 Games, when Daley Thompson of Great Britain scored 8797 points.

A descendant of Edward Jenner, the English physician who discovered the method for vaccinating against smallpox, Bruce Jenner first tried the decathlon while in college. He also played football and excelled at water skiing. He competed in the decathlon at the 1972 Olympics, finishing tenth.

After graduating from college in 1973, Jenner took a part-time job so that he could spend 8 hours a day training for the next Olympics. During this period, he won 12 of 13 decathlons in which he competed.

Jenner says the physical work of an athlete is done before the competiton. Nervous pressure then takes over.

LARRY HOLMES

b. Cuthbert, Ga., Nov. 3, 1949

Larry Holmes was a fighting heavyweight champion whose only loss came when he attempted to better Rocky Marciano's record of retiring undefeated after 49 fights. A school dropout at 13, Holmes began his march to the title by becoming an amateur boxer in 1970. In three years as an amateur, he won 19 of 22 fights. He won his first professional bout in March 1973 and within a month was ranked eighth among heavyweights.

Holmes's first important bout came in March 1978, when he won a decision over Ernie Shavers. An even bigger fight took place three months later, on June 9, when he won the World Boxing Council championship at Las Vegas in a split decision over the titleholder, Ken Norton. Holmes remained WBC champion until 1983 and then was the International Boxing Federation champ until 1985.

Holmes was an active defender of his title, beating Norton in a return bout in 1978, ending Muhammad Ali's attempt to regain the title by beating Ali in a TKO in October 1980, and winning decisions over Trevor Berbick and Leon Spinks in 1981. The end of his reign for Holmes came on September 21, 1985, when Michael Spinks beat him in a unanimous 15-round decision. Spinks repeated his victory on April 19, 1986, in a split decision. On January 22, 1988, at Atlantic City, N.J., Holmes was knocked out in the fourth round of a championship fight with Mike Tyson. Holmes was 38 years old, whereas the victor was only 21.

Holmes held the heavyweight title longer than anyone since Joe Louis, defended it 21 times, and ended his career with a record of 48 wins and only 3 defeats. Thirty-four of his wins were knockouts. Gentle and soft-spoken, Holmes, whose first job was in a car wash, once said of his retirement: "I'll be washing cars, but this time they'll be mine."

---

were won in Sherburne Pass, Vt., by Yvonne Sherman, women's singles; Dick Button, men's singles; Karol and Peter Kennedy, pairs; and Lois Waring and Michael McGean, dance.

Mar. 28 The **NCAA basketball championship** was won by CCNY, defeating Bradley U. 71-68. This was a rematch of the NIT championship game on Mar. 18, which CCNY won 69-61. CCNY thus became the only team to win both major postseason basketball events in the same season. After this dual victory, the rules were changed to prevent participation by any team in both tournaments.

Spring The **first black basketball player** drafted by an NBA club, Charles "Chuck" Cooper of Duquesne U., was acquired by the Boston Celtics and became the first black to play in the NBA. This season Washington signed two black players, Earl Lloyd of West Virginia State and Harold Hunter of North Carolina College, and on May 24 the New York Knicks acquired Nat "Sweetwater" Clifton, ace center for the Harlem Globetrotters.

Apr. 8-23 The **first NBA (National Basketball Association) basketball championship** was won by the Minneapolis Lakers, who beat the Syracuse Nationals four games to two. George Mikan scored 40 points for the Lakers in their sixth-game 110-95 victory.

Apr. 9 The **Masters golf tournament** was won for the third time by Jimmy Demaret. Jim Ferrier trailed by two strokes.

Apr. 11-23 The **NHL Stanley Cup** was won by the Detroit Red Wings, defeating the New York Rangers four games to three.

Apr. 19 The 54th **Boston Marathon** was won by Ham Kee Yong, 19, of Seoul, Korea, with a time of 2 hrs., 32 min., 39 sec. He was the youngest runner ever to win the event.

May 6 The 76th annual **Kentucky Derby** was won by Middleground, with a time of 2:01⅗, just ⅕ sec. shy of the Derby record. The jockey was Bill Boland.

May 20 The 75th annual **Preakness Stakes** was won by Hill Prince, with a time of 1:59⅕. The jockey was Eddie Arcaro.

May 31 The 34th **Indianapolis 500** auto race was won by Johnny Parsons of Van Nuys, Calif., completing the course (shortened to 345 mi. because of rain) in 2 hrs., 46 min., 55.97 sec., at an average speed of 124.002 mph.

June 10 The 82nd annual **Belmont Stakes** was won by Middleground, with a time of 2:28⅗. The jockey was Bill Boland.

June 10 At the Merion Cricket Club, Ardmore, Pa., at the end of regulation play, the **U.S. Open golf tournament** was deadlocked. Ben Hogan, Lloyd Mangrum, and George Fazio were in a three-way tie. On the next day Hogan, in a remarkable comeback after his 1949 auto accident, won an 18-hole playoff round, beating Mangrum by four strokes and Fazio by six strokes.

June 27 The **PGA golf tournament** was won by Chandler Harper at the Scioto Country Club, Columbus, Ohio.

June 29 In soccer's **World Cup** play, the poorly regarded U.S. team shocked England by defeating its team 1-0 in Rio de Janeiro. The U.S. was eliminated by Chile on July 2 by a score of 5-2.

July 7 At the **Wimbledon** tennis championships in England, the men's singles title was won by Budge Patty. The next day Louise Brough won the women's singles over Margaret Osborne du Pont. Louise Brough and du Pont won the women's doubles, and Brough teamed with Eric Sturgess of South Africa to win the mixed doubles.

July 11 The 17th annual **baseball all-star game** was won by the National League, defeating the American League 4-3 on homers by Ralph Kiner and Red Schoendienst in the 14th inning. Earlier, Ted Williams slammed into the left field wall when making a fine catch of a Ralph Kiner drive. Williams broke his elbow and was out of play for the rest of the season, taking the Boston Red Sox out of the pennant race.

Aug. 9 The 25th annual **Hambletonian Stakes** was won in straight heats by Lusty Song. The driver was Delvin Miller.

Aug. 22 The **first black tennis player** to be accepted in competition for the national championship was announced. She was Althea Gibson.

Aug. 26 In the **Davis Cup** international tennis challenge round, the Australian team led by Frank Sedgman and Ken McGregor, losing only one singles match, won its third straight victory over the U.S. The Australian doubles team of Frank Sedgman and Jack Bromwich defeated Ted Schroeder and Gardnar Mulloy in five sets.

Sept. 5 The **U.S. Lawn Tennis Association singles championships** were won by Arthur Larsen in the men's division and Margaret Osborne du Pont in the women's division.

Sept. 27 The **world heavyweight boxing championship** was retained by Ezzard Charles in a 15-round bout in New York, when he won a unanimous decision over the former champion, Joe Louis, who was attempting a comeback.

Oct. 4-7 The 47th annual **World Series** was won by the New York Yankees (AL), defeating the Philadelphia Phillies (NL) in four straight games. Dubbed the Whiz Kids, the Phillies lost the first three by one run in each game. Yankee pitchers Vic Raschi, Allie Reynolds, Ed "Steady Eddie" Lopat, and Whitey Ford were superb. Combined, they had an earned run average of 0.73.

Dec. 12 The **Heisman Trophy** for outstanding college football player of 1950 was voted to Ohio State back Vic Janowicz.

Dec. 24 The **NFL championship** was won by the Cleveland Browns, who defeated the Los Angeles Rams 30–28.

MARK SPITZ

Mark Andrew Spitz
b. Modesto, Calif., Feb. 10, 1950

Mark Spitz was the first, and remains the only, person to have won seven gold medals in one Olympics. This he did in 1972 at the Games held in Munich, when he was victorious in the 100- and 200-meter freestyle and butterfly events and was a member of three winning relay teams. This climax to his career indicated why he was considered the best swimmer of his time and one of the greatest ever.

Spitz had his first swimming lesson when he was 8 and was already being encouraged by his father to think only of winning. At Indiana University he led the swim team to four national championships, winning eight events himself. At the Pan American games in 1967, he won five races. At the Olympic Games in Mexico City in 1968, he was a disappointment to himself and others when he won only a single bronze medal.

Spitz retired after the 1972 Olympics, by which time he had set a total of 23 world and 35 U.S. records.

TOM FERGUSON

Thomas Ferguson
b.   Tahlequah, Okla., Dec. 20, 1950

Tom Ferguson and Larry Mahan have won far more honors and set more records than any other professional cowboys. Ferguson first attracted attention while attending California Polytechnic State University, when he led his school's 1973 rodeo team to the national collegiate championship. He was already also a professional.

Ferguson and Mahan are the only performers to have won the world championship All-Around Cowboy title six times, and Ferguson is the only one who did it in consecutive years, 1974 to 1979. He was the first to win $100,000 in a single season, 1978, and his career earnings of $1,049,744 as of the end of 1986 are the highest.

Ferguson's specialties are calf roping and steer wrestling, and he holds world championships in these events.

1951

Fred Bear of Grayling, Mich., secured a **patent for the use of fiberglass** on the compression side of hunting bows. It transformed bowmaking from an individual art to a logical production process. The heat-controlled process enabled the bonding of the bow units in a single operation. Mass production of bows of consistent weight and quality accelerated the growing popularity of archery.

Jan. 1   In **college football bowl games,** the results were Tennessee 20, Texas 14 in the Cotton Bowl; Clemson 15, Miami (Fla.) 14 in the Orange Bowl; Michigan 14, California 6 in the Rose Bowl; and Kentucky 13, Oklahoma 7 in the Sugar Bowl. This season a UPI poll of football coaches selected Oklahoma as national collegiate champion of 1950, as did the annual AP poll.

Feb. 2-4   **U.S. figure skating championships** were won in Seattle, Wash., by Dick Button, men's singles, his sixth consecutive win; Sonya Klopfer, women's singles; Karol and Peter Kennedy, pairs; and Carmel and Edward L. Bodel, dance.

Feb. 3   The **largest purse** to date in horse racing, $144,323, was won by Great Circle in the Santa Anita Maturity at Santa Anita Park, Arcadia, Calif. The jockey was Willie Shoemaker.

Feb. 13   At the **Westminster Kennel Club** dog show, Ch. Bang Away of Sirrah Crest, a boxer owned by Dr. and Mrs. R. C. Harris, took best-in-show.

Feb. 18   **Collegiate basketball's greatest scandal,** whispered about for weeks, broke open when Manhattan District Attorney Frank S. Hogan ordered the arrest of three CCNY players on bribery charges. Also arrested were two professional gamblers and two intermediaries. The arrests marked the beginning of a game-fixing scandal that would eventually involve college teams across the country. Most of the

PAT BRADLEY

Patricia Ellen Bradley
b.   Westford, Mass., Mar. 24, 1951

From 1980 through 1986, Pat Bradley was the dominant woman golfer. As an indication of her success, consider that in 1986 she became the first LPGA player to record $2,000,000 in earnings. She attained this goal ten weeks before JoAnne Carner matched her.

Bradley's total at the end of the 1986 season was $2,286,218.

Bradley had a successful amateur career in New England before entering Florida International University, where she was named an all-American college golfer in 1970. Between 1980 and 1986, Bradley won six major tournaments, including the Open in 1981. Her best year was 1986, when she won three of the four major women's tournaments: the Nabisco Dinah Shore, the LPGA, and the Du Maurier.

Bradley's record of winning $100,000 or more for nine consecutive years is unmatched by any other woman golfer. In 365 LPGA events, she has been in the top ten 206 times.

participants in the CCNY scandal confessed or ultimately pleaded guilty and received suspended sentences.

Feb. 25-Mar. 9 The **first Pan-American Games** were held in Buenos Aires, Argentina. The U.S. finished second in unofficial team score, behind Argentina.

Feb. 26 At the **world figure skating championships** in Milan, Italy, Dick Button won the men's singles title for the fourth consecutive year.

Mar. 27 The **NCAA basketball championship** was won by Kentucky, which defeated Kansas State 68-58. Bill Spivey led Kentucky's scorers with 22 points.

Apr. 7 The **Masters golf tournament** was won by Ben Hogan with a 280 total, beating Robert Riegel by two strokes.

Apr. 7-21 The **NBA basketball championship** was won by the Rochester Royals, who beat the New York Knicks 79-75 in the final game of a seven-game series. With the score 75-75, Bob Davis hit two foul shots, and Jack Coleman scored a lay-up in the final seconds.

Apr. 7-June 3 The **American Bowling Congress** held its first masters tournament. The singles title was won by Lee Jouglard of Detroit, and the five-man team title by the C. B. O'Malley group of Chicago.

Apr. 11-21 The **NHL Stanley Cup** was won by the Toronto Maple Leafs, who defeated the Montreal Canadiens four games to one.

Apr. 19 The 55th **Boston Marathon** was won by Shigeki Tanaka, 19, of Japan, with a time of 2 hrs., 27 min., 45 sec.

May 5 The 77th annual **Kentucky Derby** was won by Count Turf, with a time of 2:02⅗. The jockey was Conn McCreary, gaining his second Derby win.

May 19 The 76th annual **Preakness Stakes** was won by Bold, with a time of 1:56⅖. The jockey was Eddie Arcaro, scoring his fourth Preakness win.

I had many years that I was not so successful as a ball player, as it is a game of skill.

Casey Stengel

May 30 The 45th **Indianapolis 500** auto race was won by Lee Wallard of Altamont, N.Y., completing the 500-mi. course in a record 3 hrs., 57 min., 38.05 sec., at an average speed of 126.244 mph.

June 13 The **first boxing match on closed-circuit television** pitted Joe Louis against Lee Savold, of New York City. Louis knocked out Savold in the sixth round in his attempt to launch a comeback for the heavyweight title.

June 16 The **U.S. Open golf tournament** was won for the second year in a row by Ben Hogan, with a score of 287 at the Oakland Hills Country Club, Birmingham, Mich.

June 16 The 83rd annual **Belmont Stakes** was won by Counterpoint, with a time of 2:29. The jockey was David Gorman.

Summer The **Harlem Globetrotters** played in a game before 75,000 basketball fans in the Olympic Stadium at Berlin, Germany. It was the largest crowd to date to attend a basketball game.

July 3 The **PGA golf tournament** at Oakmont, Pa., was won by Sam Snead. His 7 and 6 triumph over Walter Burkemo gave him his third PGA victory.

July 6-7 At the **Wimbledon** tennis championships in England, Dick Savitt won the men's singles title over Ken McGregor of Australia, and Doris Hart won the women's singles over Shirley Fry. Hart and Fry won the women's doubles.

July 10 What the *New York Times* called "**the most amazing upset in 25 years of boxing history**" occurred in London when British boxer Randy Turpin defeated Sugar Ray Robinson in 15 rounds. Robinson was making his first defense of the middleweight title he had won on Feb. 14, when he beat Jake LaMotta. It was only his second loss in an 11-year career, during which he had won 133 bouts. Turpin had never fought a bout of more than eight rounds before. On Sept. 12, Robinson regained his championship when he knocked Turpin out in the tenth round of a bout in New York City.

July 10 The 18th annual **baseball all-star game** was won by the National League, which defeated the American League 8-3. Home runs by Stan Musial, Bob Elliott, Gil Hodges, and Ralph Kiner provided six runs for the winning team.

July 14 The **first horse to win $1,000,000** was Citation. The great thoroughbred's total earnings reached $1,085,760 upon winning the Hol-

THE HOMER BROOKLYN NEVER FORGOT

As late as August 11, 1951, the New York Giants were 13½ games behind the Brooklyn Dodgers in the race for the National League pennant. The experts regarded the Dodgers as the wonder team. After all, the Brooklyn stars were Jackie Robinson, Roy Campanella, Gil Hodges, Duke Snider, Pee Wee Reese, and Carl Furillo. How could they fail to win the pennant?

But in the heat of summer, something went awry. The Dodgers began to falter, and the New York Giants picked up steam. In their final 47 games of the season, the Giants went on to win 39 and lose only 8, for a percentage of .829. Lightning had indeed struck, and the two teams ended the season in a flatfooted tie for first place. League rules called for them to play a best-two-out-of-three playoff series to decide the pennant winner.

In the first game of the playoff, on October 1, Giant momentum appeared unstoppable, and the Giants won 3 to 1. The following day, however, Dodger bats crushed the Giants, and the final score was Brooklyn 10, New York 0.

Now it was October 3, and the playoffs came back to the Polo Grounds for the final game, winner take all. It was the first time a playoff series had ever gone the full distance.

Because the game was played on the Jewish New Year, only 34,320 paying fans were in attendance in a ballpark that could hold almost 30,000 more. But all over New York City millions of fans listened by radio to see how the rivalry of the two boroughs would be settled, at least for that year.

At the end of seven innings, with both teams' aces on the mound, the score was tied 1–1. It was Don Newcombe for the Dodgers and Sal "the Barber" Maglie for the Giants. In the eighth inning, the Barber began to falter. The Dodgers scored three times, and it looked as though it was all over for the Giants. But in the last of the ninth it was Newcombe's turn to falter. He gave up three hits and one run before being yanked. With two men on base, up to the mound came Ralph Branca, a strong young pitcher with a 13–12 record behind him for the season. The batter was Bobby Thomson, the Giant third baseman, and he had already hit safely twice in the game.

Branca did not wind up with men on base, but he still threw hard for strike one. He pitched again, and this time Thomson connected. The ball carried into the lower left-field stands, barely clearing the wall at the 315-foot mark, and three runs scored. The game was over and the

Giants, by a score of 5–4, had gained the right to represent the National League in yet another Subway Series.

Over the borough of Brooklyn settled a cloud of gloom that even a winter and the following spring, with its promise of renewed hope, failed to dissipate. Indeed, it is believed that Brooklyn has never recovered from that fateful blow off the bat of Bobby Thomson.

What happened next was a letdown. The Yanks beat the Giants 4–2 in the World Series. The teams were tied after four games, but the Yankees showed their batting strength by swamping the Giants 13–1 in the fifth game behind the five-hit pitching of "Steady Eddie" Lopat. The sixth game was much closer. The Giants outhit the Yankees and almost evened the score in the ninth inning, when they scored twice, but the final score was 4–3, Yankees.

The big baseball story of 1951, however, was not the World Series. It was one hit, Bobby Thomson's ninth-inning homer off Ralph Branca, a blow that still has Brooklyn fans muttering to themselves nearly four decades later. And what of the unfortunate Branca? He went into decline, pitching for four more seasons but winning only 12 more games before he retired at age 30.

---

lywood Gold Cup at Inglewood, Calif. The bay horse had run out of the money only once in 45 starts during a four-year career.

July 18 The **world heavyweight boxing championship** was won by Jersey Joe Walcott, who knocked out Ezzard Charles in the seventh round at Pittsburgh, Pa. At 37 Walcott was the oldest fighter to gain the title.

July 23 The **Baseball Hall of Fame** inducted Jimmy Foxx, first baseman, who had a career slugging average of .609, and Mel Ott, longtime star outfielder and star slugger for the New York Giants.

Aug. 9 The 26th annual **Hambletonian Stakes** was won in straight heats by Mainliner. The driver was Guy Crippen.

Aug. 26 **Bernarr MacFadden,** 83-year-old physical culturist and publisher, parachuted 1500 ft. from an airplane into the Hudson R. off Alpine, N.J. He was picked out of the water by a launch he had hired for the purpose, apparently none the worse for his adventure.

Sept. 4 The **U.S. Lawn Tennis Association singles championships** were won by Frank Sedgman of Australia over Victor Seixas in the men's division and 16-year-old Maureen Connolly in the women's division. Sedgman was the first Australian to win the U.S. men's title.

Sept. 16 The **U.S. Women's Open golf tournament** was won by Betsy Rawls, who edged Louise Suggs at Atlanta, Ga.

Sept. 19 A new **commissioner of baseball,** Ford C. Frick, president of the National League, was elected after at least 50 ballots by the team owners. Frick began his career as a sportswriter.

Oct. 4-10 The 48th annual **World Series** was won by the New York Yankees (AL), who defeated the New York Giants (NL) four games to two. Casey Stengel won his third series in three tries. Joe DiMaggio, who had one home run and drove in five, played his last series. The Giants had won the National League pennant in a playoff series by beating the Brooklyn Dodgers two games to one in a spectacular ninth-inning comeback in the third game of the league playoff played on Oct. 3. The playoff was clinched when Bobby Thomson, of the Giants, hit a home run off Dodger relief pitcher Ralph Branca to win the game by a score of 5-4.

Oct. 5 Two leading **featherweight boxers were punished for rough tactics** in a bout held on Sept. 26 in New York City. Sandy Saddler, the champion, was suspended indefinitely, and Willie Pep, the former champion, had his boxing license revoked. The action was taken by the New York State Athletic Commission, stating: "You violated every rule in the book." In the fight Pep was unable to continue after the ninth round because of a badly cut eye. Saddler and Pep had fought five times since 1948. In his career Pep fought 241 professional bouts, winning 65 by knockouts and 164 by decisions. Between 1940 and 1943 he had a string of 62 consecutive victories.

Dec. 4 The **Heisman Trophy** for outstanding college football player of 1951 was voted to Princeton tailback Richard William Kazmaier.

Dec. 23 The **NFL championship** was won by the Los Angeles Rams, who defeated the Cleveland Browns 24-17.

Dec. 27 The **Davis Cup was lost** by the U.S. team to Australia by three matches to two. Both U.S. singles players, Vic Seixas and Ted Schroeder, beat Marvin Rose but lost to Frank Sedgman. In the key doubles match, Sedgman and Ken McGregor defeated Schroeder and Tony Trabert.

1952

In swimming, the **butterfly** was authorized and regulated by the *Fédération internationale de natation amateur* (International Amateur Swimming Federation). The characteristic flying arms—over-the-water recovery of the arms—had been employed, as unforbidden, by enterprising U.S. breaststrokers. In recognizing the butterfly arm motion, the new regulation stipulated simultaneous up-and-down movements of the legs and feet in a vertical plane. The rules for the breaststroke event were tightened at the same time.

Final rounds for the **Mallory Cup,** emblematic of the North American sailing championship, were conducted at Mystic, Conn. The winning skipper was Cornelius Shields, representing the Yacht Racing Association of Long Island.

Alastair B. Martin, reigning U.S. **amateur court tennis champion,** unsuccessfully challenged Pierre Etchebaster, the French world's open champion, who resided in New York City. Etchebaster, the greatest court tennis player of modern times, was 58 years old and had reigned since 1928. He retired in 1954.

The first match was held for the **Randle Women's International Team Trophy.** The Randle Trophy goes to the winning ten-woman team in a small-bore rifle match, sponsored by the National Rifle Association. The American women's teams won for the first 13 years before the British triumphed in 1965.

National championship whitewater slalom racing made its first official appearance in the U.S. on the Brandywine R. in Delaware.

Jan. 1 In **collegiate football bowl games,** the results were Kentucky 20, Texas Christian 7 in the Cotton Bowl; Georgia Tech 17, Baylor 14 in the Orange Bowl; Illinois 40, Stanford 7 in the Rose Bowl; and Maryland 28, Tennessee 13 in the Sugar Bowl. This season the AP poll chose Tennessee as national collegiate champion of 1951, as did the UPI poll.

Jan. 15 The **first bonspiel for women curlers** in the New York area was held at St. Andrews Golf Club in Westchester County. The Utica, N.Y., Curling Club took first place with the Nashua, N.H., Country Club second. The *New York Times* described the players as "gaily attired, comely participants" who wore "gay, colorful tartans."

Jan. 19 Participation of **blacks in golf tournaments** was approved by the PGA.

Feb. 12 At the **Westminster Kennel Club** dog show, Ch. Rancho Dobe's Storm, a Doberman pinscher owned by Mr. and Mrs. Len Carey, took best-in-show.

Feb. 15-25 At the **Winter Olympics** in Oslo, Norway, the U.S. won four gold medals and finished second in the unofficial team standings.

Feb. 29 At the **world figure skating championships** in Paris, France, Dick Button won the men's singles title for the fifth consecutive year.

Mar. 15 The **first Sebring 12-hr. auto race** was won by the driving team of H. Gray and L. Kulok in a Frazer Nash. In 1953 this race became a round in the Sports Car World Championship.

Mar. 26 The **NCAA basketball championship** was won by Kansas, which defeated St. John's 80-63. Clyde Lovelette scored 33 points for Kansas.

Mar. 28 U.S. **figure skating championships** were won in Colorado Springs, Colo., by Dick Button, men's singles, his seventh consecutive win; Tenley Albright, women's singles; Karol and Peter Kennedy, pairs, their fifth consecutive win; and Lois Waring and Michael McGean, dance.

Apr. 5 In the AAU **national wrestling championships** at Ithaca, N.Y., Henry Wittenberg won the 191-lb. title for the eighth time. A CCNY graduate and member of the New York City Police Department, Wittenberg defeated Enzo Marinelli, of Syracuse U. Wittenberg won a gold medal at the 1948 Olympics and over a period of 13 years won more than 350 bouts.

Apr. 6 The **Masters golf tournament** was won for the second time by Sam Snead, whose 386 total led Jack Burke, Jr., by four strokes.

Apr. 10-15 The **NHL Stanley Cup** was won by the Detroit Red Wings, defeating the Montreal Canadiens in four straight games. The Red Wings had also swept the Toronto Maple Leafs in the semifinals in four straight games.

Apr. 12-15 The **NBA basketball championship** was won by the Minneapolis Lakers, who beat the New York Knicks four games to three. George Mikan, Jim Pollard, and Vern Mikkelsen overpowered the Knicks for Minneapolis.

Apr. 19 The 56th **Boston Marathon** was won by

Doroteo Flores of Guatemala, with a time of 2 hrs., 31 min., 53 sec.

Apr. 25 An **automatic pinsetter** was approved by the American Bowling Congress. The invention was mostly the work of Fred Schmidt, in cooperation with the American Machine and Foundry Co. Inventors had been trying since the 1890s to perfect such a device.

May 3 The 78th annual **Kentucky Derby** was won by Hill Gail, with a time of 2:01⅗, a fifth of a second off the Derby record set in 1941 by Whirlaway. The jockey was Eddie Arcaro, winning his fifth Derby victory.

May 7 The 84th annual **Belmont Stakes** was won by One Count, with a time of 2:30⅕. The jockey was Eddie Arcaro.

May 17 The 77th annual **Preakness Stakes** was won by Blue Man, with a time of 1:57⅖. The jockey was Conn McCreary.

May 30 The 46th **Indianapolis 500** auto race was won by Troy Ruttman, 22, from California, the youngest driver to win the 500-mi. race. He completed the course in a record 3 hrs., 52 min., 41.88 sec., at an average speed of 128.922 mph.

June 14 The **U.S. Open golf tournament,** at Dallas, Tex., was won by Julius Boros, who beat Ed "Porky" Oliver by four strokes and Ben Hogan, the defending champion, by five.

June 25 The **PGA golf tournament,** held at Louisville, Ky., was won by Jim Turnesa with a 1-up victory over Chick Harbert in the final round.

June 29 The **U.S. Women's Open golf tournament** was won by Louise Suggs. Her 284 lead beat Betty Jameson and Marlene Bauer by seven strokes.

July 5 At the **Wimbledon** tennis championships in England, Maureen Connolly won the women's singles title over Louise Brough. Doris Hart and Shirley Fry won the women's doubles.

July 8 The 19th annual **baseball all-star game** was won by the National League, which beat the American League 3-2. Jackie Robinson and Hank Sauer hit home runs for the winners.

July 19-Aug. 3 At the **Summer Olympics** in Helsinki, Finland, the U.S. won 40 gold medals and finished first in the unofficial team standings. Dr. Sammy Lee became the first person to win consecutive gold medals in platform diving. In 1953 he won the Sullivan Award, honoring the nation's outstanding amateur athlete of the

1887	Ellen F. Hansell	1938	Alice Marble
1888	Bertha L. Townsend	1939	Alice Marble
1889	Bertha L. Townsend	1940	Alice Marble
1890	Ellen C. Roosevelt	1941	Sarah Palfrey Cooke
1891	Mabel E. Cahill	1942	Pauline Betz
1892	Mabel E. Cahill	1943	Pauline Betz
1893	Aline M. Terry	1944	Pauline Betz
1894	Helen M. Helwig	1945	Sarah Palfrey Cooke
1895	Juliette P. Atkinson	1946	Pauline Betz
1896	Elisabeth H. Moore	1947	Louise Brough
1897	Juliette P. Atkinson	1948	Margaret Osborne du Pont
1898	Juliette P. Atkinson	1949	Margaret Osborne du Pont
1899	Marion Jones	1950	Margaret Osborne du Pont
1900	Myrtle McAteer	1951	Maureen Connolly
1901	Elisabeth H. Moore	1952	Maureen Connolly
1902	Marion Jones	1953	Maureen Connolly
1903	Elisabeth H. Moore	1954	Doris Hart
1904	May C. Sutton	1955	Doris Hart
1905	Elisabeth H. Moore	1956	Shirley Fry
1906	Helen Homans	1957	Althea Gibson
1907	Evelyn Sears	1958	Althea Gibson
1908	Maud Bargar-Wallach	1959	Maria Bueno
1909	Hazel V. Hotchkiss	1960	Darlene Hard
1910	Hazel V. Hotchkiss	1961	Darlene Hard
1911	Hazel V. Hotchkiss	1962	Margaret Smith
1912	Mary K. Browne	1963	Maria Bueno
1913	Mary K. Browne	1964	Maria Bueno
1914	Mary K. Browne	1965	Margaret Smith
1915	Molla Bjurstedt	1966	Maria Bueno
1916	Molla Bjurstedt	1967	Billie Jean King
1917	Molla Bjurstedt	1968	Margaret Smith Court
1918	Molla Bjurstedt	1968	Virginia Wade (Open)
1919	Hazel Hotchkiss Wightman	1969	Margaret Smith Court
1920	Molla Bjurstedt Mallory	1970	Margaret Smith Court
1921	Molla Bjurstedt Mallory	1971	Billie Jean King
1922	Molla Bjurstedt Mallory	1972	Billie Jean King
1923	Helen Wills	1973	Margaret Smith Court
1924	Helen Wills	1974	Billie Jean King
1925	Helen Wills	1975	Chris Evert
1926	Molla Bjurstedt Mallory	1976	Chris Evert
1927	Helen Wills	1977	Chris Evert
1928	Helen Wills	1978	Chris Evert
1929	Helen Wills	1979	Tracy Austin
1930	Betty Nuthall	1980	Chris Evert Lloyd
1931	Helen Wills Moody	1981	Tracy Austin
1932	Helen Hull Jacobs	1982	Chris Evert Lloyd
1933	Helen Hull Jacobs	1983	Martina Navratilova
1934	Helen Hull Jacobs	1984	Martina Navratilova
1935	Helen Hull Jacobs	1985	Hana Mandlikova
1936	Alice Marble	1986	Martina Navratilova
1937	Anita Lizana	1987	Martina Navratilova

year. William Parry O'Brien won the shot put with a throw of 57 ft., 1½ in. At the 1956 Olympic Games he repeated his triumph and set a new Olympic and world record of 60 ft., 11 in.

July 21 The **Baseball Hall of Fame** inducted two outstanding hitters, Harry Heilmann and Paul "Big Poison" Waner.

Aug. 2 **American boxers took five championships** in the Olympics in Helsinki, Finland, and won the unofficial team title for the first time. Norvel Lee, who won the light heavyweight title, was voted outstanding boxer of the games.

Aug. 7 The 27th annual **Hambletonian Stakes** was won in the third heat by Sharp Note. The driver was 74-year-old Bion Shively.

Sept. 7 The **U.S. Lawn Tennis Association singles championships** were won for the second year in a row by Frank Sedgman of Australia in the men's division, this time over Gardnar Mulloy, and by Maureen Connolly in the women's division.

Sept. 23 The **world heavyweight boxing championship** was won by Rocky Marciano, who knocked out Jersey Joe Walcott in the 13th round of a bout in Philadelphia. It was Marciano's 43rd straight win as a professional boxer, with no losses.

Oct. 1-7 The 49th annual **World Series** was won by the New York Yankees (AL), defeating the Brooklyn Dodgers (NL) four games to three. Veteran pitchers Vic Raschi and Allie Reynolds pulled the Yankees through to victory in games six and seven. The margin of victory in the final game was provided by Mickey Mantle's sixth-inning home run.

Dec. 2 The **Heisman Trophy** for outstanding college football player of 1952 was voted to Oklahoma halfback Billy Vessels.

Dec. 17 Archie Moore won the **light heavyweight boxing championship** when he defeated Joey Maxim in 15 rounds at St. Louis, Mo. Born in 1915 or 1916, he was the oldest boxer ever to hold the title in this class, and he retained it for ten years. In all, Moore fought 229 times and won 111 of his bouts by knockouts. He tried twice for the heavyweight crown but lost both times.

Dec. 28 The **NFL championship** was won by the Detroit Lions, who defeated the Cleveland Browns 17-7.

1953

Jan. 1 In **college football bowl games,** the results were Texas 16, Tennessee 0 in the Cotton Bowl; Alabama 61, Syracuse 6 in the Orange Bowl; Southern California 7, Wisconsin 0 in the Rose Bowl; and Georgia Tech 24, Mississippi 7 in the Sugar Bowl. This season the AP poll chose Michigan State as national collegiate champion of 1952, as did the UPI poll.

Feb. 1 A U.S. **four-man bobsled team** led by Lloyd Johnson won the world championship at Garmisch-Partenkirchen, West Germany.

Feb. 10 At the **Westminster Kennel Club** dog show, Ch. Rancho Dobe's Storm, a Doberman pinscher owned by Mr. and Mrs. Len Carey, took best-in-show.

Feb. 10 At the **world figure skating championships** in Switzerland, Hayes Alan Jenkins won the men's singles title and Tenley Albright won the women's singles. For Jenkins, this was the first of four consecutive world singles championships. Albright, the first U.S. woman figure skater to win in this competition, would win again in 1955.

Mar. 16 **Bill Veeck,** president of the St. Louis Browns, failed to obtain approval of American League club owners for his bid to move his franchise to Baltimore. At the end of the 1953 season, Veeck sold his controlling interest to a Baltimore syndicate, and league approval of the transfer followed.

Mar. 18 The **NCAA basketball championship** was won by Indiana, defeating Kansas 69-68. Don Schlundt scored 30 points for Indiana.

Mar. 18 Transfer of the **Boston Braves** baseball franchise to Milwaukee was unanimously approved by the National League owners. This year Milwaukee led both leagues in attendance with a total of 1,826,397 paid admissions. This was the first shift of a major league franchise in 50 years.

Mar. 21 A new **NBA playoff record** was set by Bob Cousy of the Boston Celtics, who scored 50 points as the Celtics defeated the Syracuse Nationals 111-105 in four overtime periods. At season's end, the sensational first-year playmaker from Holy Cross was named to the all-pro team for the first of what were to be ten consecutive years.

UNITED STATES TENNIS ASSOCIATION
Men's Championship

Year	Champion	Year	Champion
1881	Richard D. Sears	1935	Wilmer Allison
1882	Richard D. Sears	1936	Fred Perry
1883	Richard D. Sears	1937	Don Budge
1884	Richard D. Sears	1938	Don Budge
1885	Richard D. Sears	1939	Bobby Riggs
1886	Richard D. Sears	1940	Donald McNeill
1887	Richard D. Sears	1941	Bobby Riggs
1888	Henry Slocum, Jr.	1942	Fred Schroeder
1889	Henry Slocum, Jr.	1943	Joseph Hunt
1890	Oliver S. Campbell	1944	Frank Parker
1891	Oliver S. Campbell	1945	Frank Parker
1892	Oliver S. Campbell	1946	Jack Kramer
1893	Robert D. Wrenn	1947	Jack Kramer
1894	Robert D. Wrenn	1948	Pancho Gonzales
1895	Fred H. Hovey	1949	Pancho Gonzales
1896	Robert D. Wrenn	1950	Arthur Larsen
1897	Robert D. Wrenn	1951	Frank Sedgman
1898	Malcolm Whitman	1952	Frank Sedgman
1899	Malcolm Whitman	1953	Tony Trabert
1900	Malcolm Whitman	1954	Vic Seixas
1901	William A. Larned	1955	Tony Trabert
1902	William A. Larned	1956	Ken Rosewall
1903	Hugh L. Doherty	1957	Mal Anderson
1904	Holcombe Ward	1958	Ashley Cooper
1905	Beals C. Wright	1959	Neale Fraser
1906	William J. Clothier	1960	Neale Fraser
1907	William A. Larned	1961	Roy Emerson
1908	William A. Larned	1962	Rod Laver
1909	William A. Larned	1963	Rafael Osuna
1910	William A. Larned	1964	Roy Emerson
1911	William A. Larned	1965	Manuel Santana
1912	Maurice McLoughlin	1966	Fred Stolle
1913	Maurice McLoughlin	1967	John Newcombe
1914	R. Norris Williams II	1968	Arthur Ashe
1915	William Johnston	1969	Rod Laver
1916	R. Norris Williams II	1970	Ken Rosewall
1917	R. Lindley Murray	1971	Stan Smith
1918	R. Lindley Murray	1972	Ilie Nastase
1919	William Johnston	1973	John Newcombe
1920	Bill Tilden	1974	Jimmy Connors
1921	Bill Tilden	1975	Manuel Orantes
1922	Bill Tilden	1976	Jimmy Connors
1923	Bill Tilden	1977	Guillermo Vilas
1924	Bill Tilden	1978	Jimmy Connors
1925	Bill Tilden	1979	John McEnroe
1926	René Lacoste	1980	John McEnroe
1927	René Lacoste	1981	John McEnroe
1928	Henri Cochet	1982	Jimmy Connors
1929	Bill Tilden	1983	Jimmy Connors
1930	John H. Doeg	1984	John McEnroe
1931	Ellsworth Vines	1985	Ivan Lendl
1932	Ellsworth Vines	1986	Ivan Lendl
1933	Fred Perry	1987	Ivan Lendl
1934	Fred Perry		

Mar. 28 U.S. **figure skating championships** were won in Hershey, Pa., by Tenley Albright, women's singles; Hayes Alan Jenkins, men's singles; Carole Ann Ormaca and Robin Greiner, pairs; and Carol Ann Peters and Daniel C. Ryan, dance.

Apr. 4-10 The **NBA basketball championship** was won by the Minneapolis Lakers, who defeated the New York Knickerbockers four games to one. Play was rough, and four Knicks fouled out in the final game.

Apr. 9-16 The **NHL Stanley Cup** was won by the Montreal Canadiens, who defeated the Boston Bruins four games to one.

Apr. 12 At the **first AAU amateur Greco-Roman wrestling tournament,** held in Toledo, Ohio, the heavyweight title was won by Bill Kerslake of Cleveland, Ohio. He held the title through 1959.

Apr. 12 The **Masters golf tournament** was won a second time by Ben Hogan. His 274 beat Porky Oliver by five strokes.

Apr. 20 The 57th **Boston Marathon** was won by Keizo Yamada of Japan, with a time of 2 hrs., 18 min., 51 sec., the fastest time recorded for a marathon.

May 2 The 79th annual **Kentucky Derby** was won by Dark Star, with a time of 2:02. The jockey was Henry Moreno.

May 23 The 78th annual **Preakness Stakes** was won by Native Dancer, with a time of 1:57⅘. The jockey was Eric Guerin.

May 30 The 37th **Indianapolis 500** was won by Bill Vukovich of Fresno, Calif., in 3 hrs., 53 min., 0.69 sec., at an average speed of 128.740 mph.

June 13 The 85th annual **Belmont Stakes** was won by Native Dancer, with a time of 2:28⅗. The jockey was Eric Guerin.

June 13 The **U.S. Open golf tournament** was won by Ben Hogan, who beat Sam Snead by six strokes to become the third person in history to win the tournament four times. The tournament was played at Oakmont, Pa.

June 28 The **U.S. Women's Open golf tournament** at Rochester, N.Y., was won by Betsy Rawls, who beat Jacqueline Pung of Hawaii by six strokes in an 18-hole playoff.

July 3 At the **Wimbledon** tennis championships in England, Victor Seixas won the men's singles title over Kurt Nielsen of Denmark. The next day Maureen Connolly won the women's singles over Doris Hart. Hart and Shirley Fry won the women's doubles, and Hart and Vic Seixas won the mixed doubles.

July 7 The **PGA golf tournament** was won by Walter Burkemo at Birmingham, Mich. In the final round, he defeated Felice Terza, 2 and 1.

July 14 The 20th annual **baseball all-star game** was won by the National League 5-1.

July 27 The **Baseball Hall of Fame** inducted Dizzy Dean and Al Simmons.

Aug. 12 The 28th annual **Hambletonian Stakes** was won in the third heat by Helicopter. The driver was Harry Harvey.

Sept. 7 The **U.S. Lawn Tennis Association men's singles championship** was won by Tony Trabert over Victor Seixas in straight sets. In the women's division, Maureen Connolly won for the third successive year, repeating her 1952 victory over Doris Hart.

Sept. 16 Transfer of the **St. Louis Browns** baseball franchise to Baltimore, Md., was approved by the American League, the Browns to begin the 1954 season as the Baltimore Orioles.

Sept. 30-Oct. 5 The 50th annual **World Series** was won by the New York Yankees (AL), defeating the Brooklyn Dodgers (NL) four games to two. This was the first time a team had won five consecutive World Series. In the final game, Carl Furillo hit a two-run homer that tied the score at 3-3 in the top of the ninth, but Billy Martin singled home the series-winning run in the Yankees' half of the ninth. For Martin, a .257 hitter during the regular season, it was his 12th hit in the series, which set a record for hits in a six-game series.

Nov. 9 The U.S. **Supreme Court** ruled 7-2 that baseball was not subject to antitrust laws, holding that baseball is a sport, not a business.

Dec. 8 The **Heisman Trophy** for outstanding college football player of 1953 was voted to Notre Dame back Johnny Lattner.

Dec. 27 The **NFL championship** was won by the Detroit Lions, who defeated the Cleveland Browns 17-16.

1954

The **American Motorcyclist Association** initiated the Grand National Series, raced on four different types of dirt tracks, plus pavement racing. Winners three or more times in the early years of the series were Joe Leonard, Carroll Resweber, and Bart Markel.

The **Lawn Tennis Hall of Fame** and Tennis Museum was opened at Newport, R.I.

Judy Devlin, later Mrs. G. C. K. Hashman, won the first of her many women's badminton championships. From 1954 to her retirement in 1967, she won 12 national singles championships, 11 in women's doubles (nine with her sister Susan), and eight mixed doubles titles. She also captured ten all-England women's singles championships, badminton's unofficial world championship.

Jan. 1 In **college football bowl games,** the results were Rice 28, Alabama 6 in the Cotton Bowl; Oklahoma 7, Maryland 0 in the Orange Bowl; Michigan State 28, UCLA 20 in the Rose Bowl; and Georgia Tech 42, West Virginia 19 in the Sugar Bowl. This season the AP poll and the UPI poll chose Maryland as national collegiate champion of 1953.

Feb. 2 A new **individual basketball scoring record** for a player from a small college was set by Bevo Francis of Rio Grande College, who scored 113 points in a 134-91 victory over Hillsdale.

Feb. 9 At the **Westminster Kennel Club** dog show, Ch. Carmor's Rise and Shine, a cocker spaniel owned by Mrs. Carl E. Morgan, took best-in-show.

Feb. 14 A new **individual basketball scoring record** for a player from a major college was set by Frank Selvy of Furman College, who made 100 points in a 149-95 victory over Newberry College.

Feb. 17 At the **world figure skating championships** in Oslo, Norway, Hayes Alan Jenkins won the men's singles title.

Feb. 21 The **National Ski Hall of Fame** was founded in Ishpeming, Mich. Its first four members were inducted in Feb. 1956. They were Arthur J. "Red" Barth, Askel Holter, Edward F. Taylor, and Carl Tellefsen.

Mar. 19 U.S. **figure skating championships** were won in Los Angeles by Tenley Albright, women's singles; Hayes Alan Jenkins, men's singles; Carole Ann Ormaca and Robin Greiner, pairs; and Carmel and Edward L. Bodel, dance.

Mar. 20 The **NCAA basketball championship** was won by La Salle, defeating Bradley 92-76. Tom Gola starred for La Salle.

Mar. 31-Apr. 12   The **NBA basketball champion-ship** was won by the Minneapolis Lakers, who defeated the Syracuse Nationals four games to one.

Apr. 4-16   The **NHL Stanley Cup** was won by the Detroit Red Wings, defeating the Montreal Canadiens four games to three.

Apr. 12   The **Masters golf tournament** was won by Sam Snead, who beat Ben Hogan by one stroke in a playoff round. This was the third green jacket win for Snead, and his last.

Apr. 19   The 58th **Boston Marathon** was won by Viekko Karanen of Finland, with a time of 2 hrs., 20 min., 39 sec.

Apr. 23   Two **new basketball rules** were adopted by the NBA. A 24-sec. time limit was set for a team to shoot at the basket from the time it gained possession of the ball. The NBA also limited each team to six personal fouls in a quarter, after which two free throws would be awarded to the other team.

May 1   The 80th **Kentucky Derby** was won by De-termine, with a time of 2:03. The jockey was Ray York.

May 8   The first **shot put of more than 60 ft.** was achieved by William Parry O'Brien at Los An-geles. His throw was officially measured at 60 ft., 5¼ in.

May 22   The 79th annual **Preakness Stakes** was won by Hasty Road, with a time of 1:57⅖. The jockey was Johnny Adams.

May 31   The 38th **Indianapolis 500** auto race was won by Bill Vukovich, completing the course in a record 3 hrs., 49 min., 17.27 sec., at an average speed of 130.840 mph. It was his second consec-utive win.

June 12   The 86th annual **Belmont Stakes** was won by High Gun, with a time of 2:30⅘. The jockey was Eric Guerin.

June 19   The **U.S. Open golf tournament** at Balti-more County Club, Springfield, N.J., was won by Ed Furgol, by a single shot over Gene Littler, amateur champion recently turned pro. This was the first golf tournament to be televised nationally.

July 3   The **U.S Women's Open golf tourna-ment** was won by Babe Didrikson Zaharias at Salem, Mass.

July 3   At the **Wimbledon** tennis championships in England, Maureen Connolly won the women's singles title over Louise Brough. Brough and Margaret Osborne du Pont won the women's doubles, and Vic Seixas and Doris Hart won the mixed doubles.

July 13   The 21st annual **baseball all-star game** was won by the American League, defeating the National League 11-9. The game, a slugfest, was enlivened by six home runs, four by the win-ners. Al Rosen, Cleveland Indians third base-man, hit a pair of homers to produce five runs for the winners.

July 20   The meteoric career of **Maureen Con-nolly,** one of the great women tennis players, was ended tragically at age 19 by a fatal horseback riding accident. Hard-hitting "Little Mo" won the U.S. women's singles title in 1951-1953, the Wimbledon crown in 1952-1954. In 1953 she achieved the women's tennis grand slam by winning the Australian, French, En-glish, and U.S. women's titles. In four years of Wightman Cup play, "Little Mo" never lost a match.

July 27   The **PGA golf tournament** at St. Paul, Minn., was won by Chick Harbert, with a final-round, 4 and 3 win over Walter Burkemo.

Aug. 4   The 29th annual **Hambletonian Stakes** was won in straight heats by Newport Dream. The driver was Adelbert Cameron.

Aug. 5   The first **elections to the Boxing Hall of Fame** enshrined 24 fighters of the past and pre-sent. The leading modern pugilists elected were Jack Dempsey, Joe Louis, and Henry Arm-strong. Fifteen boxers of the pioneer era were also chosen, among them John L. Sullivan, James J. "Gentleman Jim" Corbett, and Jack Johnson.

Aug. 9   The **Baseball Hall of Fame** inducted nine new members: Edward G. Barrow, baseball ex-ecutive; Thomas H. Connolly, umpire; Chief Bender, pitcher; Bill Dickey, catcher; Bill Klem, umpire; Rabbit Maranville, infielder; Bill Terry, first baseman and manager; Bobby Wallace, pitcher; and Harry Wright, center fielder and manager.

Sept. 6   The **U.S. Lawn Tennis Association sin-gles championships** were won by Vic Seixas over Rex Hartwig of Australia in the men's divi-sion and Doris Hart in the women's division.

Sept. 29-Oct. 2   The 51st annual **World Series** was won by the New York Giants (NL), defeating the Cleveland Indians (AL) in four straight games. Cleveland, with its glittering pitching staff of Bob Lemon, Early Wynn, Bob Feller, and Mike Garcia, was humbled by a pinch hitter

WALTER PAYTON

Walter Jerry Payton
b. Columbia, Miss., July 25, 1954

According to all the statistics, Walter Payton is the best running back ever to play in the National Football League. In 11 seasons through 1986, he has amassed 14,860 yards in 3371 carries, for an average of 4.4 yards. When the yards he has gained after catching passes are included, Payton's total offensive yardage comes to 17,304.

Payton did not play football until his junior year in high school because he was more interested in being a drummer in the band. At Jackson State University, he set an NCAA record for most points, 464, and was graduated in 3½ years with a degree in education for the deaf.

Drafted by the Chicago Bears in 1975, Payton helped them to their first winning season in ten years and their first playoff berth in 14. Against Minnesota on November 20, 1977, he set the record for most yards gained rushing in one game, 275. In 1977, he was the youngest person to be named most valuable player by the NFL. Payton now ranks fourth in lifetime touchdowns scored, with 109. Of this total, 98 were scored by rushing and 11 as a pass receiver.

Payton's success as a running back seems to depend more on his acceleration than on his speed. After the 1983 season, he signed a Bears contract guaranteeing him $240,000 a year for life.

---

named Dusty Rhodes, who hit two home runs, drove in seven runs, and batted .667, with four hits in six at-bats. With game one tied 2-2 and two men on, slugger Vic Wertz hit a fly ball to deep center in the Polo Grounds. Willie Mays turned his back to the plate and caught the ball over his shoulder at a point estimated to be 460 ft. from home plate. He then whirled and threw the ball to the infield to prevent the base runners from advancing. From that point on, the Giants were destined to win the series.

Nov. 8   The transfer of the **Philadelphia Athletics** baseball franchise to Kansas City, Mo., was approved by the American League.

Nov. 30   The **Heisman Trophy** for outstanding college football player of 1954 was voted to Wisconsin back Alan Ameche.

Dec. 26   The **NFL championship** was won by the Cleveland Browns, who defeated the Detroit Lions 56-10.

Dec. 28   The **Davis Cup** international tennis challenge round was won by the U.S., which defeated Australia three matches to two. Tony Trabert and Vic Seixas represented the U.S.

1955

Synchronized swimming was added to the competition at the Pan-American Games.

Jan. 1   In **college football bowl games,** the results were Georgia Tech 14, Arkansas 6 in the Cotton Bowl; Duke 34, Nebraska 7 in the Orange Bowl; Ohio State 20, Southern California 7 in the Rose Bowl; and Navy 21, Mississippi 0 in the Sugar Bowl. This season the AP poll chose Ohio State as national collegiate champion of 1954. The UPI poll selected UCLA.

Feb. 15   At the **Westminster Kennel Club** dog show, Ch. Kippax Fearnought, a bulldog owned by Dr. John A. Saylor, took best-in-show.

Feb. 16-17   At the **world figure skating championships** in Vienna, Austria, Hayes Alan Jenkins won the men's singles title and Tenley Albright won the women's singles title.

Mar. 12-26   At the second **Pan-American Games** in Mexico City, Mexico, the U.S. took first place in the unofficial team championships, followed by Argentina and Mexico.

Mar. 19   The **NCAA basketball championship** was won by San Francisco, defeating La Salle 77-63. Bill Russell starred for San Francisco.

Mar. 21-Apr. 10   The **NBA basketball championship** was won by the Syracuse Nationals, who beat the Fort Wayne Pistons four games to three.

Apr. 1-2   **U.S. figure skating championships** were won in Colorado Springs, Colo., by Hayes Alan Jenkins, men's singles; Tenley Albright, women's singles; Robin Greiner and Carole Ann Ormaca, pairs; and Carmel and Edward L. Bodel, dance.

Apr. 3-14   The **NHL Stanley Cup** was won by the Detroit Red Wings, who defeated the Montreal Canadiens four games to three.

Apr. 10 The **Masters golf tournament** was won by Cary Middlecoff, whose 279 beat Ben Hogan by seven strokes.

Apr. 19 The 59th **Boston Marathon** was won by Hideo Hamamura of Japan, with a record time of 2 hrs., 18 min., 22 sec.

May 7 The 81st annual **Kentucky Derby** was won by Swaps, with a time of 2:01⁴/₅. The jockey was Willie Shoemaker.

May 28 The 80th annual **Preakness Stakes** was won by Nashua, with a time of 1:54³/₅. The jockey was Eddie Arcaro.

May 30 The 39th **Indianapolis 500** auto race was won by Bob Sweikert of Indianapolis, completing the course in 3 hrs., 53 min., 59.53 sec., at an average speed of 128.209 mph. Bill Vukovich, seeking his third consecutive win, was killed in a four-car crash.

June 11 The 87th annual **Belmont Stakes** was won by Nashua, with a time of 2:29. The jockey was Eddie Arcaro, who won this race for the sixth time, tying James McLaughlin's record..

June 19 The **U.S. Open golf tournament** was won by Jack Fleck, who beat favored Ben Hogan by three strokes in a playoff round. Play was at the Olympic Country Club, San Francisco.

July 1-2 At the **Wimbledon** tennis championships in England, Tony Trabert won the men's singles title over Kurt Nielsen of Denmark.

Louise Brough won the women's singles over Beverly Baker Fleitz, and Vic Seixas and Doris Hart won the mixed doubles.

July 2 The **U.S. Women's Open golf tournament,** held at Wichita, Kans., was won by Fay Crocker of Uruguay, the first foreign winner. Her 299 led Mary Lena Faulk and Louise Suggs by four strokes.

July 12 The 22nd annual **baseball all-star game** was won by the National League, which beat the American League 6-5 in 12 innings. The winning run was scored on the first pitch in the bottom of the 12th on a home run into the right-field bleachers by Stan Musial.

July 17 The **first LPGA golf tournament** was won by Beverly Hanson. At the end of the 54-hole event, Hanson and Louise Suggs were tied. Hanson won the playoff by three strokes.

July 25 The **Baseball Hall of Fame** inducted six new members: Home Run Baker, Joe DiMaggio, Gabby Hartnett, Ted Lyons, Ray Schalk, and Dazzy Vance.

July 26 In a **record for horseshoe pitching,** Ted Allen had 72 successive ringers at Murray, Utah. Horseshoe pitchers regard this as the equivalent of 72 consecutive strikes in bowling.

July 26 The **PGA golf tournament** was won by Doug Ford at Detroit. In the final round, he defeated Cary Middlecoff, 4 and 3.

Aug. 3 The 30th annual **Hambletonian Stakes**

CHRIS "CHRISSIE" EVERT LLOYD

Christine Marie Evert Lloyd
b. Ft. Lauderdale, Fla., Dec. 21, 1954

Not only is Chris Evert one of the best women tennis players in history, but she was also perceived from the start of her career as the all-American girl athlete. On her first appearance at the U.S. Open in 1971, unseeded Chrissie became the focus of attention, and after four victories her matches were moved to center court.

Chrissie first played tennis when she was 6 and was coached by her father, a professional tennis teacher. In 1974, having turned pro on her 18th birthday, she won her first major titles, the French and British. She repeated her French victory in 1975, the year in which she also won the U.S. Open for the first time. Evert held the U.S. title through 1978 and won it again in 1980 and 1982, for a total of six victories. Meanwhile, she also triumphed at Wimbledon twice more, in 1976 and 1981; added four more French titles, in 1979, 1980, 1985, and 1986; and won in Australia in 1982 and 1984.

In one period, from August 1973 to May 1979, Evert won 125 consecutive matches on clay courts. Overall she has won more than 100 titles and has played on the Wightman Cup team ten times. In the later years of her career, Evert's chief rival has been a younger tennis great, Martina Navratilova. The two have played more than 60 matches, and the Czech-born player has gradually gained the ascendancy.

Nevertheless, Evert has remained the queen of the courts in popularity. Her cool looks and style of play endear her to spectators. Her coolness, though, hides a strong determination to win, supported by her steady baseline play and her powerful two-handed backhand. Evert is the first woman to have earned more than $1,000,000 in tennis.

EDWIN MOSES

b.   Dayton, Ohio, Aug. 31, 1955

Track history's longest winning streak came to an end on June 4, 1987, when Edwin Moses lost a 400-meter hurdles race in Madrid to Danny Harris, another American. Moses had won 122 consecutive races, his last previous loss coming ten years before, on August 26, 1977.

Moses, however, has enough outstanding triumphs to his credit that no one can doubt his world stature as a hurdler. In 1976 and again in 1984—the U.S. did not participate in the 1980 Olympics—Moses won the gold medal in the 400-meter hurdles, an event that includes ten high hurdles and so requires strength and precision as well as speed. His 1976 time of 47.64 seconds set a world record. Moses went a step further on Aug. 31, 1983, when at Koblenz, West Germany, he set a new world record of 47.02 seconds in this event. In Rome, on September 3, 1987, when Moses was 32 years old, he beat 29-year-old Harald Schmid and 21-year-old Danny Harris in the 400-meter intermediate hurdles in the world championships of track and field. His time was 47.46 seconds, beating both men by .02 in near-90 degree heat.

A graduate of Morehouse College, Moses is still active and was the first U.S. athlete to be chosen as a delegate to the International Amateur Athletic Union. Small wonder. Of the 15 sub-47.50 times recorded for the 400-meter hurdles in track competition, Moses has 12.

---

was won in straight heats by Scott Frost. The driver was Joe O'Brien.

Aug. 26-28   The **Davis Cup** international tennis challenge round was swept by the Australian team of Ken Rosewall, Lewis Hoad, and Rex Hartwig, who beat the American team five matches to none. The Australians clinched the cup on Aug. 27, when Hoad and Hartwig defeated Tony Trabert and Vic Seixas in a rousing five-set doubles match.

Sept. 11   The **U.S. Lawn Tennis Association singles championships** were won by Tony Trabert over Ken Rosewall of Australia in the men's division and Doris Hart in the women's division. Both winners shortly turned pro.

Sept. 16   Formation of the **United States Auto Club** (USAC) was completed. The USAC sanctions four major categories of auto races. On Mar. 17, 1956, it opened its office and museum in a new building on the grounds of the Indianapolis Speedway, Indianapolis, Ind.

Sept. 28-Oct. 4   The 52nd annual **World Series** was won by the Brooklyn Dodgers (NL), who defeated the New York Yankees (AL) four games to three. Johnny Podres pitched a brilliant shutout in the final game. The score was 2-0, and it was the first time a team had won a seven-game series after losing the first two games. Gil Hodges drove in both runs for the Dodgers. It was Sandy Amoros, the Dodger left fielder, who made history in the seventh game of the series with a desperate lunging catch of a Yogi Berra line drive with two men on base in the sixth to save the shutout.

Fall   **Tennis balls with nylon and Dacron** in their covers were successfully introduced by manufacturers.

Dec. 8   The **Heisman Trophy** for outstanding college football player of 1955 was voted to Ohio running back Howard Cassady.

Dec. 26   The **NFL championship** was won by the Cleveland Browns, who defeated the Los Angeles Rams 38-14.

1956

Hashim Khan, Pakistani professional squash racquets player, succeeded G. Diehl Mateer, Jr., of the U.S. as men's open champion. Hashim was the first of several members of the Khan family who for 30 years dominated the event, winning 25 open championships among them.

In **horseshoe pitching**, Vicki Chapelle won the first of her nine women's singles championships, spanning 20 years.

The introduction of **neoprene wetsuits** for surf-

Winning isn't everything. It's the only thing.
Vince Lombardi

b. Kansas City, Mo., Feb. 22, 1956

Ranking third on the LPGA all-time money list as of 1986, with $1,806,648 in earnings, Amy Alcott has been a consistent tournament winner with 26 titles to her credit. After a short but successful amateur career, she joined the LPGA tour in 1975 and became Rookie of the Year.

Alcott's best year was 1980, when she won the U.S. Women's Open and three other tournaments, with an average round of 71.51, for which she won the Vare Trophy. She has won other important tournaments, such as the Nabisco-Dinah Shore Invitational in 1983 and the Mazda Hall of Fame Championship in 1986. The 1986 season marked the 12th consecutive season in which Alcott won at least one tourney, tying her with JoAnne Carner in that respect.

Alcott was awarded the 1986 Founders Cup, which recognizes contributions to the betterment of society by LPGA members. In the off-season she likes to spend part of her time as a short order cook at the Butterfly Bakery in Los Angeles. "The pressure of getting an order right," Alcott says, "is greater than sinking a putt."

---

ing, by Jack O'Neill, of Santa Cruz, Calif., made surfing a year-round sport in colder climates and extended surfing farther north than before.

Televised National Hockey League games played on Saturday afternoons were broadcast for the first time.

Jan. 1 In **college football bowl games,** the results were Mississippi 14, Texas Christian 13 in the Cotton Bowl; Oklahoma 20, Maryland 6 in the Orange Bowl; Michigan State 17, UCLA 14 in the Rose Bowl; and Georgia Tech 7, Pittsburgh 0 in the Sugar Bowl. This season both the AP poll and the UPI poll chose Oklahoma as national collegiate champion of 1955.

Jan. 26-Feb. 5 At the **Winter Olympics** in Cortina d'Ampezzo, Italy, the U.S. won two gold medals. Hayes Alan Jenkins and Tenley Albright took top honors in singles figure skating competitions.

Feb. 14 At the **Westminster Kennel Club** dog show, Ch. Wilber White Swan, a toy poodle owned by Bertha Smith, took best-in-show.

Feb. 17 At the **world figure skating championships** in Garmisch-Partenkirchen, West Germany, Hayes Alan Jenkins won the men's singles title for the fourth year in a row. The next day Carol Heiss won the women's singles. She would go on to win four more consecutive world figure skating championships.

Mar. 16 **U.S. figure skating championships** were won in Philadelphia by Hayes Alan Jenkins, men's singles; Tenley Albright, women's singles; Carole Ann Ormaca and Robin Greiner, pairs; and Joan Zamboni and Roland Junso, dance.

Mar. 23 The **NCAA basketball championship** was won by San Francisco, defeating Iowa 83-71. San Francisco's Bill Russell starred offensively and defensively.

Mar. 24 The **first Sebring Grand Prix** road race was run at Sebring, Fla. This most important road race in the U.S. was won by Juan Manuel of Argentina and Eugenio Castellotti of Italy in a Ferrari. A Ferrari also finished second, with Luigi Musso of Italy and Harry Schell of the U.S. at the wheel.

Mar. 31-Apr. 7 The **NBA basketball championship** was won by the Philadelphia Warriors, who defeated the Fort Wayne Pistons four games to one.

Mar. 31-Apr. 10 The **NHL Stanley Cup** was won by the Montreal Canadiens, who defeated the Detroit Red Wings four games to one.

Apr. 8 The **Masters golf tournament** was won by Jack Burke, Jr., who came from eight strokes behind to beat Ken Venturi by one stroke.

Apr. 19 The 60th **Boston Marathon** was won by Antti Viskari of Finland, with a record time of 2 hrs., 14 min., 14 sec.

Apr. 27 Rocky Marciano, **undefeated heavyweight boxing champion,** retired. He had won all 49 of his bouts, including six in defense of the championship and 43 by knockouts. His record has never been matched.

May 5 The 82nd annual **Kentucky Derby** was won by Needles, with a time of 2:03⅖. The jockey was Dave Erb.

May 19 The 81st annual **Preakness Stakes** was won by Fabius, with a time of 1:58⅖. The jockey was Bill Hartack.

May 30 The 40th **Indianapolis 500** auto race was won by Patrick Francis Flaherty of Chicago,

KURT THOMAS

b.   Terre Haute, Ind., Mar. 29, 1956

Kurt Thomas is the best male gymnast America has produced so far and the first to give the country a standing of some consequence in international competition in this sport. He might well have been the first American gold medalist in gymnastics at the Olympics had the United States participated in the 1980 Games.

Thomas began learning gymnastics when he was 14, and at Indiana University he was an all-American. At the Pan American Games in 1976, he finished third in the all-around competition, best of any American.

Thomas won the U.S. championship three years in a row, from 1978 to 1980, and gained medals in both 1978 and 1979 at the World Championships: a gold in 1978, the first such for an American in nearly half a century, and two gold and three silver in 1979, one of the silver being in the all-around category.

completing the 500-mi. course in 3 hrs., 53 min., 59.13 sec., at an average speed of 128.490 mph.

June 16   The 88th annual **Belmont Stakes** was won by Needles, with a time of 2:29⅘. The jockey was Dave Erb.

June 16   The **U.S. Open golf tournament** was won for the second time by Cary Middlecoff, who beat Ben Hogan and Julius Boros by one stroke at Rochester, N.Y.

June 24   The **LPGA golf tournament** was won by Marlene Bauer Hagge in a sudden-death playoff with Patty Berg.

July 7   At the **Wimbledon** tennis championships in England, Shirley Fry won the women's singles title. Althea Gibson teamed with Angela Buxton of Great Britain to win the women's doubles, and Shirley Fry and Vic Seixas won the mixed doubles.

July 10   The 23rd annual **baseball all-star game** was won by the National League, which beat the American League 7-3.

July 16   The **Ringling Brothers and Barnum & Bailey Circus** performed its last show under canvas. Rising costs for a tented show had forced the move to performances in permanent structures.

July 23   The **Baseball Hall of Fame** inducted two active major league managers: Joe Cronin, former shortstop of the Boston Red Sox, and Hank Greenberg, former first baseman and outfielder of the Cleveland Indians.

July 25   The **PGA golf tournament** was won by Jack Burke, Jr., at the Blue Hill Country Club, Milton, Mass. He defeated Ted Kroll in the final round, 3 and 2.

July 29   The **U.S. Women's Open golf tournament** was won by Kathy Cornelius in a playoff with runner-up Barbara McIntyre.

Aug. 11   A **record perfect 100** in the skish accuracy fly event was scored by Steve Aleshi of Kansas City, Mo., at the national fly and plug casting tournament held in San Francisco. (*Skish* refers to casting at a target on dry land.)

Aug. 18   The 31st annual **Hambletonian Stakes** was won in straight heats by The Intruder. The driver was Ned Bower.

Sept. 9   The **U.S. Lawn Tennis Association singles championships** were won by Ken Rosewall of Australia over his teammate Lewis Hoad in the men's division and Shirley Fry over Althea Gibson in the women's division.

Oct. 3-10   The 53rd annual **World Series** was won by the New York Yankees (AL), defeating the Brooklyn Dodgers (NL) four games to three. In Game five, on Oct. 8, Yankee right-hander Don Larsen pitched the first perfect game in World Series history, beating Brooklyn 2-0. No Dodger batter reached first base.

Nov. 22-Dec. 8   At the **Summer Olympics** in Melbourne, Australia, the U.S. won 32 gold medals and finished second in the unofficial team standings, behind the USSR. Pat McCormick won gold medals in both springboard and platform diving, repeating her double gold triumph in the 1952 games. Bobby Morrow won both the 100- and 200-m. dashes with times of 10.5 sec. and 20.6 sec., respectively. Bob Richards won the pole vault, repeating his victory at the 1952 games.

Nov. 30   The **world heavyweight boxing championship** was won by Floyd Patterson, who knocked out Archie Moore in the fifth round in Chicago to win the title vacated by Rocky Marciano on Apr. 27. Patterson, 21, was the youngest fighter to win the championship.

Dec. 4   The **Heisman Trophy** for outstanding col-

lege football player of 1956 was voted to Notre Dame quarterback Paul Hornung.

Dec. 17 **America's Cup** competition was opened to 12-m. class racing yachts when the New York State Supreme Court approved revisions in the deed of gift under which the races were held. The revisions dropped the requirement that challenge yachts had to sail to the site of the match on their own bottoms and reduced the minimum length at waterline from 65 ft. to 44 ft. This ended the era of the large, heavy-sailed, long-masted J-class sloops that had dominated the America's Cup races. The next match, in 1958, and all subsequent matches were contested by 12-m. yachts.

Dec. 30 The **NFL championship** was won by the New York Giants, who defeated the Chicago Bears 47-7.

1957

A **deep-V hull for powerboats** was invented by designer C. Raymond Hunt. The hull cushioned shock in rough water and increased seaworthiness.

The first Huntington Beach, Calif., **surfing contest** was held. By 1964 this developed into the U.S. Surfing Championships, now called the U.S. Amateur Surfing Championships. The contests rotate among California, the East Coast, Hawaii, and Texas.

A new **baseball attendance record** for the National League was set by the Milwaukee Braves, who drew 2,215,404 fans to home games this year.

Jan. 1 In **college football bowl games,** the results were Texas Christian 28, Syracuse 27 in the Cotton Bowl; Colorado 27, Clemson 21 in the Orange Bowl; Iowa 35, Oregon State 19 in the Rose Bowl; and Baylor 13, Tennessee 7 in the Sugar Bowl. This season both the UPI poll and the AP poll chose Oklahoma as national collegiate champion of 1956.

Jan. 12 The **best competitive average in skeet shooting** for 1956 was achieved for the first time by a woman, it was announced by the National Skeet Shooting Association. Mrs. Carol Mandel of Chicago led all skeet shooters, men and women, and set three world's records. She had a run of 610 consecutive targets.

Jan. 13 **Wilt Chamberlain,** a sophomore standing a shade over 7 ft., 1 in. playing center for the U. of Kansas basketball team, led the nation's collegiate scorers. By the end of his collegiate career, Wilt the Stilt would become the highest-scoring player in college basketball history.

MARTINA NAVRATILOVA

b. Prague, Czechoslovakia, Oct. 10, 1956

Winner of her first tennis tournament when she was 8, Martina Navratilova became women's champion of Czechoslovakia in 1972 and held that title continuously until she defected to the U.S. on Sept. 7, 1975, during the U.S. Open tournament. Within three years, Navratilova was well on her way to becoming the dominant woman player in international competition, overtaking Chris Evert Lloyd, who had reigned for several years.

Navratilova's first major victory was at Wimbledon in 1978. She won the English title again the next year

and then for six consecutive years, from 1982 to 1987. This record of eight victories at Wimbledon tied the record set earlier by Helen Wills Moody. Meanwhile, Navratilova won the U.S. Open in 1983, 1984, 1986, and 1987; the French title in 1982 and 1984; and the Australian in 1981, 1983, and 1985.

In 1984, she became only the third woman player ever to achieve the grand slam by winning all four of the major tournaments in a year. In doubles, Navratilova has won seven times at Wimbledon, with different partners, including in 1976 archrival Chris Evert Lloyd. She has such records as 90 victories and only 3 losses in 1982 and an 86–1 record in

1983. In 1987, she was a triple winner in the U.S. Open, becoming the first triple winner in a grand slam tournament in 14 years.

Navratilova is a left-handed player with a serve that has been timed at 93 miles per hour. Her serve-and-volley game has kept her high in the women's list even in 1987, when younger players, especially Steffi Graf of West Germany, have threatened her. In 1987, for example, she defeated Graf in the final match of the U.S. Open singles competition. Behind Navratilova's power and skill is her basic reliance on superb physical conditioning.

NANCY LOPEZ

Nancy Marie Lopez Knight
b.   Torrance, Calif., Jan. 6, 1957

Nancy Lopez was introduced to the game of golf by her father and by age 11 was beating him. She triumphed in the New Mexico Women's Open when she was 12. In high school, Lopez was the only female member of the golf team, and as an 18-year-old senior, she placed second in the U.S. Women's Open.

Nancy Lopez made a most spectacular appearance in women's big-time golf. The year was 1978, and it was the first full season for the golfer. She won nine tournaments, one of them the LPGA, and a record-breaking five in a row. She was named rookie of the year, player of the year, and winner of the Vare Trophy. Finally, she set a new record for earnings by a rookie, a total of $189,813.

With this beginning it is not surprising that, by winning her 35th tournament on Feb. 8, 1986, Lopez qualified to become the 11th member of the LPGA Hall of Fame. However, she had to wait until July for induction because she had not completed ten years as an LPGA member. Lopez's best season since 1978 was 1985, when she won five tournaments, including the LPGA again, and 21 times finished in the top ten in the 25 tournaments she entered. By the end of the 1986 season, her total earnings were $1,711,079.

Feb. 11   The **National Hockey League Players Association** was formed, and the members elected Ted Lindsay of the Detroit Red Wings as president.

Feb. 12   At the **Westminster Kennel Club** dog show, Ch. Shirkhan of Grandeur, an Afghan hound owned by Sunny Shay and Dorothy Chenade, took best-in-show.

Feb. 28-Mar. 3   At the **world figure skating championships** in Colorado Springs, Colo., Carol Heiss won the women's singles title and David Jenkins, the brother of Hayes Alan Jenkins, won the men's singles. David Jenkins would go on to win two more consecutive world figure skating titles.

Mar. 15-16   **U.S. figure skating championships** were won in Berkeley, Calif., by Carol Heiss, women's singles; David Jenkins, men's singles; Ronald and Nancy Ludington, pairs; and Sharon McKenzie and Bert Wright, dance.

Mar. 23   The **NCAA basketball championship** was won by North Carolina, which beat Kansas 54-53 in three overtime periods.

Mar. 27-30   The **first men's national curling championship** was held in Chicago, with the Hibbing, Minn., Curling Club winning the title over the Minot, N.Dak., Curling Club by a score of 12-6.

Mar. 30-Apr. 3   The **NBA basketball championship** was won by the Boston Celtics, defeating the St. Louis Hawks four games to three. Forward Tommy Heinsohn scored 37 points for Boston in the final game, which went to double overtime and ended with Boston winning 125-123.

Apr. 6-16   The **NHL Stanley Cup** was won by the Montreal Canadiens, who defeated the Boston Bruins four games to one.

Apr. 7   The **Masters golf tournament** was won by Doug Ford, whose 283 led Sam Snead by three strokes.

Apr. 12   A **new nine-game bowling record** of a total of 2088 pins was set by Jim Spalding of Louisville, Ky., at the American Bowling Congress national championship tournament at Fort Worth, Tex. The previous record of 2070 was set in 1937 by Max Stein of Belleville, Ill.

Apr. 12-14   Leah Thall "Ping" Neuberger won her eighth **women's national singles table tennis championship** and third in a row. Four years later she added a ninth title, her first having come in 1947. Neuberger also won the Canadian singles title 11 times and the U.S. doubles championship 12 times.

Apr. 20   The 61st **Boston Marathon** was won by John J. Kelley of West Acton, Mass., with a time of 2 hrs., 20 min., 5 sec. He was the first U.S. runner to win the event since 1945.

May 4   The 83rd annual **Kentucky Derby** was won by Iron Liege, with a time of 2:02⅕. The jockey was Bill Hartack.

May 18   The 82nd annual **Preakness Stakes** was won by Bold Ruler, with a time of 1:56⅕ . The jockey was Eddie Arcaro.

May 30   The 41st **Indianapolis 500** auto race was won by Sam Hanks of Pacific Palisades, Calif., completing the 500-mi. course in 3 hrs., 41 min., 14.25 sec., at an average speed of 135.601 mph.

June 10   The **LPGA golf tournament** was won by Louise Suggs at Pittsburgh, Pa., with a 285 total.

PHIL MAHRE

Philip Mahre
b. White Pass, Wash., May 10, 1957

When Phil Mahre took first place overall in World Cup skiing competition in 1981, something no other American skier had ever done, he proved what was already pretty much conceded. He was the best American skier ever.

In 1980, Mahre had won second place in the slalom at the Olympics held at Lake Placid, New York. He was the only American skier to win a medal there. Four years later, in Yugoslavia, he did better, coming away with the gold medal. He has also won seven World Cup medals for individual events.

Mahre's accomplishments have come despite three serious injuries,

any one of which might have put a lesser athlete out of competition for good. In 1974, he suffered a broken leg in an avalanche, broke a leg again in 1975 while going down an amusement park slide, and suffered a severe ankle break in the World Cup races in 1979.

Mahre's identical twin Steve is also a world-class competitor in alpine skiing events.

June 15 The 89th annual **Belmont Stakes** was won by Gallant Man, with a time of 2:26⅗. The jockey was Willie Shoemaker.

June 15 The **U.S. Open golf tournament** was won by Dick Mayer. In 98-degree heat, Mayer beat defending champion Cary Middlecoff by seven strokes in a playoff round at the Inverness Club, Toledo, Ohio.

June 29 The **U.S. Women's Open golf tournament** was won by Betsy Rawls after the apparent winner, Jacqueline Pung, was disqualified for turning in an incorrect card.

July 6 At the **Wimbledon** tennis championships in England, Althea Gibson defeated Darlene Hard to win the women's singles title. She then teamed with Hard to win the women's doubles. Gardnar Mulloy and Budge Patty won the men's doubles. Hard teamed with Mervyn Rose of Australia to win the mixed doubles. Mulloy, at

age 42, was the oldest man ever to win a Wimbledon championship.

July 9 The 24th annual **baseball all-star game** was won by the American League, defeating the National League 6-5.

July 19 The **first U.S. runner to break the 4-min. mile** was Don Bowden, who ran the mile in 3:58.7 at Stockton, Calif. (Englishman Roger Bannister had turned in a 3:59.4 in 1954.)

July 21 The **PGA golf tournament** was won by Lionel Hebert, with a 2 and 1 final-round victory over Dow Finsterwald at Dayton, Ohio.

July 22 The **Baseball Hall of Fame** inducted Sam Crawford, who held the major league record for career triples (312), and Joe McCarthy, former manager of the Chicago Cubs, New York Yankees, and Boston Red Sox. McCarthy led the Yankees to eight American League pennants and seven World Series victories.

JOAN BENOIT

Joan Benoit-Samuelson
b. Cape Elizabeth, Maine, May 16, 1957

Joan Benoit's first interest in sports was skiing, but after she broke a leg in that sport she took up running to get back in shape. She subsequently became America's foremost female distance runner. In her senior year in high school, Benoit qualified for the Junior Olympics.

The second time Benoit ran in the

Boston Marathon, in 1979, she won with a time of 2 hours, 35 minutes, 15 seconds, a record that stood for only two years. She came back in 1983 to win the same event and set another record, 2 hours, 22 minutes, 42 seconds. At this time Benoit was running over 100 miles a week, but she eased off when signs of overtraining began to appear.

Benoit's finest triumph came in the 1984 Olympics, when she won the first women's marathon ever included

in the games. Her time was 2 hours, 24 minutes, 52 seconds. Moreover, she defeated Grete Waitz, who previously had beaten Benoit in 10 of the 11 races in which they had competed together.

At various times, Benoit has set U.S. records for distances of 10 to 25 kilometers. In 1984, she and Olympic gymnastic champion Mary Lou Retton shared honors as the Women's Sports Foundation Sportswoman of the Year.

Aug. 20 **Transfer of the New York Giants** baseball team to San Francisco next spring was announced by Horace Stoneham, president of the National Exhibition Company, which owned the team franchise. On October 8 the Brooklyn Baseball Club, owner of the Dodgers, announced it would begin play in Los Angeles in 1958.

Aug. 23 **Little League baseball's** championship was won for the first time by a team from a foreign country, Monterrey Industrial Little League, Monterrey, Mexico. Pitcher A. Macias pitched a perfect game for Monterrey.

Aug. 27 The 32nd annual **Hambletonian Stakes** was won by Hickory Smoke in the fifth and deciding heat of a split-field contest. The driver was John Simpson, Sr. This was the first Hambletonian to be run at Du Quoin, Ill. The classic was held there until 1981, when it was moved to East Rutherford, N.J.

Sept. 8 The **U.S. Lawn Tennis Association singles championships** were won by Malcolm Anderson of Australia over Ashley Cooper, another Australian, in the men's division. Althea Gibson defeated Louise Brough in the women's division. Gibson was the first black to win the title.

Sept. 9-11 The singles title at the **first U.S. championships of the American Lawn Bowls Association,** held at Whitefield, N.H., was won by Leonard Schofield.

Oct. 2-10 The 54th annual **World Series** was won by the Milwaukee Braves (NL), defeating the New York Yankees (AL) four games to three. Lew Burdette was the star of the series as he became the seventh pitcher in history to win three games in a World Series. He beat the Yankees 4-2 in the second game, shut them out 1-0 in the fifth game, and shut them out again 5-0 in the seventh game. Henry "Hank" Aaron hit three home runs in the series and batted .393 for Milwaukee.

Nov. 16 Notre Dame ended Oklahoma's **longest winning streak in college football** with a 7-0 victory to stop a string of 47 wins by the Sooners. On Oct. 31, 1959, Nebraska ended Oklahoma's 74-game winning streak in the Big Eight Conference with a 25-21 victory.

Nov. 16 A new **NBA rebound record** was set by Bill Russell of the Boston Celtics, who brought down 49 rebounds in a 111-89 Boston triumph over the Philadelphia Warriors. Russell, in his second season as a professional, had made basketball fans conscious once again of the art of defense.

Dec. 3 The **Heisman Trophy** for outstanding college football player of 1957 was voted to Texas A&M halfback John Crow.

Dec. 29 The **NFL championship** was won by the Detroit Lions, who defeated the Cleveland Browns 59-14.

1958

Jan. 1 In **college football bowl games,** the results were Navy 20, Rice 7 in the Cotton Bowl; Oklahoma 48, Duke 21 in the Orange Bowl; Ohio State 10, Oregon 7 in the Rose Bowl; and Mississippi 39, Texas 7 in the Sugar Bowl. This season the AP poll chose Auburn as national collegiate champion of 1957. The UPI poll selected Ohio State.

Jan. 12 A new **lifetime pro basketball scoring record** was set by Adolph "Dolph" Schayes of the Syracuse Nationals, in a 135-109 win over the Detroit Pistons. Schayes had logged 11,770 career points, erasing the previous record of 11,764 set by George Mikan. Schayes reached 15,000 points on Jan. 12, 1960, and 19,209 points by the time he retired.

Feb. 11 At the **Westminster Kennel Club** dog show, Ch. Puttencove Promise, a standard poodle owned by Puttencove Kennels, took best-in-show.

Feb. 14-15 At the **world figure skating championships** in Paris, France, David Jenkins won the men's singles title. Carol Heiss won the women's singles title for the third consecutive year.

Mar. 18 **Oscar Robertson,** 19-year-old basketball player at the U. of Cincinnati, was named colle-

Football isn't a contact sport, it's a collision sport. Dancing is a contact sport.

Vince Lombardi

giate player of the year in a United Press International poll of sportswriters and broadcasters. His competition included such other future pro stars as Elgin Baylor, Wilt Chamberlain, and Dave Gambee.

Mar. 22 The **NCAA basketball championship** was won by Kentucky, which defeated Seattle 84-72. Vern Hatton and Johnny Cox scored a total of 35 points in Kentucky's second-half comeback.

Mar. 25 The **world middleweight boxing championship** was regained for an unprecedented fifth time by Sugar Ray Robinson, who outpointed Carmen Basilio in 15 rounds at Chicago.

Mar. 28-29 **U.S. figure skating championships** were won in Minneapolis, Minn., by Carol Heiss, women's singles; David Jenkins, men's singles; Ronald and Nancy Ludington, pairs; and Andree Anderson and Donald Jacoby, dance.

Mar. 29-Apr. 12 The **NBA basketball championship** was won by the St. Louis Hawks, who defeated the Boston Celtics four games to two. In the final game, Bob Pettit of the Hawks scored 50 points, a new NBA record for a regulation-time playoff game.

Apr. 8 The **U.S. Men's Curling Association** was founded. In 1976 the word *Men's* was dropped. The association is the national body of the sport.

Apr. 8-20 The **NHL Stanley Cup** was won by the Montreal Canadiens, who defeated the Boston Bruins four games to two.

Apr. 16 The **Masters golf tournament** was won by Arnold Palmer, who beat Doug Ford by one stroke.

Apr. 19 The 62nd **Boston Marathon** was won by Franjo Mihalic of Yugoslavia, with a time of 2 hrs., 25 min., 54 sec.

May 3 The 84th annual **Kentucky Derby** was won by Tim Tam, with a time of 2:05. The jockey was Ismael Valenzuela.

May 17 The 83rd annual **Preakness Stakes** was won by Tim Tam, with a time of 1:57⅕. The jockey was Ismael Valenzuela.

May 30 The 42nd annual **Indianapolis 500** auto race was won by Jimmy Bryan of Phoenix, Ariz., completing the 500-mi. course in 3 hrs., 44 min., 13 sec., at an average speed of 133.791 mph.

June 7 The 90th annual **Belmont Stakes** was won by Cavan, with a time of 2:30⅕. The jockey was Pete Anderson.

June 8 The **LPGA golf tournament** was won by Mary K. "Mickey" Wright, whose 288 at Pittsburgh led Fay Crocker by six strokes.

June 14 In **Wightman Cup** play, Great Britain defeated the U.S. 4 to 3 at Wimbledon. It was the first British win since 1930.

June 14 The **U.S. Open golf tournament** at the Southern Hills Country Club, Tulsa, Okla., was won by Tommy Bolt, best known for his temper tantrums and club throwing. His 283 total led newcomer Gary Player by four strokes.

July 5 At the **Wimbledon** tennis championships in England, Althea Gibson won the women's singles title by defeating Angela Mortimer of

ERIC HEIDEN

Eric Arthur Heiden
b. Madison, Wis., June 14, 1958

Although Eric Heiden's records have been broken since the end of his competitive skating career, Heiden is still generally rated the best speed skater ever. His greatest feat came in the Olympics held at Lake Placid, New York, in 1980. Not only did he win the 500-, 1000-, 1500-, 5000-, and 10,000-meter races, but he set a new record in each event. He also

became the only person ever to win five gold medals in individual events at Olympic Games.

Heiden always trained hard. He competed in the 1976 Olympics, when he was 18, but did no better than seventh place in the 1500-meter event. His record improved rapidly, and in 1977 Heiden became the first American to win the men's all-around world speed skating championship. He lost the title in 1980, when he finished second in

the cumulative standings to Hilbert van der Duim of the Netherlands.

After Eric Heiden's 1980 victories at the Olympics, he retired from competition. As a racer, Heiden had a very powerful body and was able to get off to a fast start. His sister Beth is also a speed skater. She competed in the 1980 winter games and won the bronze medal in the 3000-meter event and finished seventh in the 1500-meter race.

MARY DECKER SLANEY

Mary Teresa Decker Slaney
b. Flemington, N.J., Aug. 4, 1958

Despite injuries and enforced layoffs in almost every year of her track career, Mary Slaney has regularly set U.S. and world records at distances from 800 to 10,000 meters. She registered her first world mark when only 15. Perhaps she was doing too much too soon, for she developed shin splints so severe as to require

surgery in 1977 and 1978.

As of September 1987, Slaney held the world record among women for the mile, 4 minutes, 16.71 seconds, which she set on August 21, 1985. Her U.S. records, set between July 16, 1982, and August 25, 1985, are for the 800-, 1500-, 3000-, 5000-, and 10,000-meter distances. At the world championships in Helsinki in 1983, Slaney won gold medals in the 1500- and 3000-meter races. Her

great disappointment came at the 1984 Olympics, when she was favored to win the 3000-meter run but tripped and fell after an entanglement with Zola Budd of Great Britain and was unable to finish.

In 1982, Slaney became the first woman to be given the Jesse Owens Award, presented annually to the best U.S. track and field athlete.

England. Gibson then teamed with Maria Bueno of Brazil to win the women's doubles.

July 8 The 25th annual **baseball all-star game** was won by the American League, beating the National League 4-3.

July 13 The **U.S. Women's Open golf tournament** was won by Mickey Wright by five strokes over Louise Suggs at Bloomfield Hills, Mich.

July 20 The **PGA golf tournament,** held at Havertown, Pa., was won by Dow Finsterwald. For the first time, the tournament called for medal play. Billy Casper was runner-up.

Aug. 6 A new **world 400-m. hurdles record,** 49.2 sec., was set by Glenn Davis of Columbus, Ohio, during a meet in Budapest, Hungary.

Aug. 27 The 33rd annual **Hambletonian Stakes** was won in the third heat by Emily's Pride. The driver was Flave Nipe.

Sept. 7 The **U.S. Lawn Tennis Association singles championships** were won by Ashley Cooper of Australia over fellow Australian Malcolm Anderson in the men's division and by Althea Gibson over Darlene Hard in the women's division.

Sept. 20-27 The **America's Cup** was defended by the U.S. 12-m. sloop *Columbia,* which defeated the British challenger, *Sceptre,* in four straight races.

Oct. 1-9 The 55th annual **World Series** was won by the New York Yankees (AL), defeating the Milwaukee Braves (NL) four games to three by winning the last three games, the first time a team had done this since the 1925 Pittsburgh victory over Washington. Yogi Berra, the Yan-

kee catcher, marked his tenth World Series, tying records set by Babe Ruth and Joe DiMaggio.

Nov. 5 The **first ascent of El Capitan** in Yosemite National Park was accomplished by a three-man team consisting of Warren Harding and two college students, George Whitmore and Wayne Merry. El Capitan is a perpendicular granite cliff, the top of which is 3604 ft. above the valley floor.

Dec. 2 The **Heisman Trophy** for outstanding college football player of 1958 was voted to Army back Pete Dawkins.

Dec. 28 The **NFL championship** was won by the Baltimore Colts, who defeated the New York Giants 23-17.

Dec. 31 The U.S. regained the **Davis Cup** when Alejandro "Alex" Olmedo defeated Australian Ashley Cooper in a decisive singles match that gave the U.S. a 3-2 victory.

1959

Bob Kiphuth, physical educator and head coach of swimming at Yale, retired. In his 42 years at Yale, the teams he coached lost only ten times in intercollegiate contests and won 38 Eastern Intercollegiate titles and 4 NCAA championships, finishing second ten times.

The **first national amateur racquetball cham-**

SUDDEN DEATH FOR THE FOOTBALL GIANTS

Bert Bell, commissioner of the National Football League, called the game the greatest he had ever seen, and the *New York Times* reported that the 68¼ minutes of play "left most of the 64,185 spectators limp." The game under discussion—fans still talk about it—was played on December 28, 1958, at Yankee Stadium in New York City. In overtime, the Baltimore Colts won the National Football League Championship by beating the New York Giants 23 to 17.

A field goal put the Giants on the scoreboard first, and they held the lead until the second quarter, when the Colts scored two touchdowns plus two conversions to put Baltimore ahead 14-3 at the half. In the third quarter and for most of the final quarter, it was the Giants who dominated. Frank Gifford, the Giant halfback whose fumbles had set up the two Colt second-quarter touchdowns, caught a 15-yard touchdown pass from 37-year-old quarterback Charlie Conerly. After a successful try for the point after touchdown, the Giants were down 14-10.

Later in the third quarter, with the Colts in possession at the Giant 1-yard line, everything seemed about to collapse for the Giants. But their defense held off a Colt attack, and the Giant offense immediately caught fire. The big offensive play came on a Conerly pass to left end Kyle Rote, who caught the ball and headed down the field, with fans screaming. Everything seemed to turn to ashes for New York when Rote fumbled on the 25-yard line, but Giant back Alex Webster recovered and took the ball to the 1-yard line. With a touchdown and conversion, the Giants led at the end of the third period and well into the final period by 17–14. New York fans were in seventh heaven.

Hometown euphoria quickly disappeared as Colt quarterback Johnny Unitas passed and masterminded his team down the field. When the Colts reached the Giant 13-yard line, only 8 seconds remained on the clock. Unitas knew prime field goal territory when he saw it. In came reliable Steve Myrha, the Colt kicking specialist, who was not about to fail his team. A boot of 20 yards tied the score at 17–17, and Giants fans fell silent.

Under rules that had been adopted not long before the game, the teams went into sudden-death overtime, for the first time in regular league competition. The Giants won the toss and elected to receive. Their offense was equal to the task. The Giants went deep into Colt territory before relinquishing the ball on a try for a first down that missed by inches. The Colts took over, and again Unitas was brilliant, driving Baltimore 80 yards in 13 plays and completing four of six passes. The Colts made it to the Giant 1-yard line, and Unitas handed off the ball to fullback Alan "Horse" Ameche. The rest, as they say, was history. The Horse plunged across the goal line to make the final score 23–17, and the game was over. The league championship had been decided in 8 minutes, 15 seconds of overtime.

Such games are the stuff fans' dreams are made of, but for every winner in football, there is a loser. And this time the loss was bitter for the home team. Unitas that day, according to sports pundit Arthur Daley, was the "best pitcher Baltimore has had since Iron Man Joe McGinnity before the turn of the century." Yet no passer can excel without a gifted receiver, and on that day in 1958 it was Ray Berry, a Colt end, who caught 12 Unitas passes for a total of 178 yards.

---

pionships were held in New Britain, Conn. Victor Lugli won the singles title, and Joe Granski and Norman Steinberg won the doubles championship.

The **Lacrosse Foundation** was organized and housed at Johns Hopkins U., Baltimore. Known until 1975 as the Lacrosse Hall of Fame Federation, it also maintains a lacrosse museum and library, and sponsors an annual superstar game.

The success of the movie *Gidget* popularized Malibu Beach and made **surfing** a fad. The Beach Blanket movies that followed also increased interest and participation in the sport.

Jacques Plante, goalie for the Montreal Canadiens, this season wore a padded plastic mask. He was the first goalie to do so.

Jan. 1 In **college football bowl games,** the results were Texas Christian 0, Air Force 0 in the Cotton Bowl; Oklahoma 21, Syracuse 6 in the Orange Bowl; Iowa 38, California 12 in the Rose Bowl; and Louisiana State 7, Clemson 0 in the Sugar Bowl. This season both the UPI and AP polls chose Louisiana State as national collegiate champion of 1958.

Jan. 31-Feb. 1 U.S. **figure skating championships** were won in Rochester, N.Y., by Carol Heiss, women's singles; David Jenkins, men's singles; Nancy and Ronald Ludington, pairs; and Andree Anderson Jacoby and Donald Jacoby, dance.

Feb. 7 A **flight duration record** was set by Robert Timm and John Cook when they landed their Cessna plane at McCarran Airfield, Las Vegas, Nev. Taking off on Dec. 4, 1958, they had remained in the air for 64 days, 22 hrs., 19 min., 5 sec. The plane had flown the equivalent of six times around the world and been refueled in the air many times.

Feb. 9-10 At the **Westminster Kennel Club** dog show, Ch. Fontclair Festoon, a miniature poodle owned by Dunwalke Kennels, took best-in-show.

Feb. 15 A **U.S. four-man bobsled team** led by Art Tyler won the world championship at St. Moritz, Switzerland.

Feb. 21 In the *Yachting* magazine **One-of-a-Kind Regatta** beginning this day at Miami, Fla., the best-designed catamarans outstripped 40 representative boats of the fastest single-hull racing classes. Three types of catamarans finished first, second, and fourth on corrected time. Sales of racing and day-sailing catamarans zoomed.

Feb. 22 The **first Daytona 500 auto race,** on the new International Speedway at Daytona Beach, Fla., was won by Lee Petty, driving a 1959 Oldsmobile 88 at an average speed of 135.521 mph. John Beauchamp, driving a Ford Thunderbird, had originally been declared the winner in a photo finish. On Feb. 25, after an examination of moving and still pictures, the decision was changed.

Feb. 26-28 At the **world figure skating championships** in Colorado Springs, Colo., Carol Heiss won the women's singles title for the fourth year in a row. David Jenkins won the men's singles.

Feb. 27 In the **highest-scoring basketball game** to date, the Boston Celtics beat the Minneapolis Lakers 173-139 in the Boston Garden.

Mar. 21 The **NCAA basketball championship** was won by California, defeating West Virginia 71-70, despite Jerry West's 28 points for West Virginia.

Apr. 4-9 The **NBA basketball championship** was won by the Boston Celtics, who defeated the Minneapolis Lakers in a four-game sweep. It was the first sweep ever in NBA title play.

Apr. 5 The **Masters golf tournament** was won by Art Wall by one stroke over Fred Hawkins.

Apr. 9-18 The **NHL Stanley Cup** was won for the fourth year in a row by the Montreal Canadiens, who defeated the Toronto Maple Leafs four games to one.

Apr. 20 The 63rd **Boston Marathon** was won by Eino Oksanen of Finland, with a time of 2 hrs., 22 min., 42 sec.

May 2 The 85th annual **Kentucky Derby** was won by Tomy Lee, with a time of 2:02⅕. The jockey was Willie Shoemaker.

May 16 The 84th annual **Preakness Stakes** was

JOHN MCENROE

John Patrick McEnroe, Jr.
b. Wiesbaden, West Germany, Feb. 16, 1959

John McEnroe at age 8 reached the semifinals of a tennis tournament at his prep school. How he behaved during play there does not seem to have been recorded, but as soon as he entered adult matches he was perceived as an *enfant terrible* (in plain words, a brat) by many observers. He complained about linesmen's calls, he berated officials in impolite language, and as a result he was vastly unpopular.

Even those who disliked his manners had to admit, however, that McEnroe was rapidly becoming one of the best male tennis players in the world. He demonstrated this by winning the U.S. championship three years in succession, 1979, 1980, and 1981, and again in 1984. McEnroe also won the British championship at Wimbledon in 1981, 1983, and 1984.

One of the greatest matches he has ever played was one he lost to Bjorn Borg at Wimbledon on July 5, 1980. Playing for the title, the two struggled for 4 hours, 53 minutes before Borg won. The score was 1–6, 7–5, 6–3, 6–7, 7–6. In the fourth set, in which they played a 34-point tiebreaker, McEnroe was on the wrong end of match point seven times before taking the set. In 1979, one year after turning professional, McEnroe earned $800,000, and he became a millionaire by the time he was 20. Like other top male players of today, McEnroe features a very aggressive, hard-hitting game in every respect. He has said of himself, "My biggest strength is that I don't have any weaknesses." He remains controversial and belligerent, having been fined $7500 and suspended from tournament play for two months on September 5, 1987, for his tantrums and for obscene language addressed to officials in a match during the U.S. Open.

won by Royal Orbit, with a time of 1:57. The jockey was Willie Harmatz.

May 25 A Louisiana ban on **boxing matches between blacks and whites** was declared unconstitutional by the U.S. Supreme Court.

May 30 The 43rd **Indianapolis 500** auto race was won by Roger Ward of Indianapolis, Ind., completing the 500-mi. course in 3 hrs., 40 min., 49.20 sec., at an average speed of 135.857 mph.

June 4 A **distance record for a single-engine airplane** was set by Max Conrad when he landed at Los Angeles International Airport. In his Piper Comanche he had flown an official distance of 7668.5 mi. nonstop from Casablanca, Morocco, in 58 hrs., 36 min.

June 13 The 91st annual **Belmont Stakes** was won by Sword Dancer, with a time of 2:28⅖. The jockey was Willie Shoemaker.

June 13 The **U.S. Open golf tournament** was won by Billy Casper.

June 26 The **world heavyweight boxing championship** was won by Ingemar Johansson of Sweden, who knocked out Floyd Patterson in the third round of a bout in New York City.

June 27 The **U.S. Women's Open golf tournament** was won by Mickey Wright over runner-up Louise Suggs with a winning total of 287.

July 3 **Alex Olmedo,** the U.S. tennis star born in Peru, won the men's singles title at Wimbledon, beating Australia's Rod Laver in straight sets.

July 6 The **LPGA golf tournament** was won by Betsy Rawls by one stroke over Patty Berg at French Lick, Ind.

July 7 Two **baseball all-star games** were played this year. The first was won on this date by the National League, beating the American League 5-4. On Aug. 3 the American League won the second game 5-3.

July 20 The **Baseball Hall of Fame** inducted Zach Wheat, former outfielder for the Brooklyn Dodgers.

Aug. 2 The **PGA golf tournament** was won by Bob Rosburg, at the Minneapolis Golf Club.

Aug. 14 Formation of the **American Football League** was announced in Chicago. The league began play in 1960 with eight teams. The leading sponsor of the organization was the Texas millionaire Lamar Hunt, who had been refused an NFL franchise.

Aug. 27-Sept. 7 At the third **Pan-American Games,** held at Soldier Field, Portage Park, and several other sites in Chicago, the U.S. won the unofficial team championship. Argentina was second.

Aug. 28-31 In the **Davis Cup** international tennis challenge round, Australia beat the defending U.S. team three matches to two.

Sept. 2 The 34th annual **Hambletonian Stakes** was won in straight heats by Diller Hanover. The driver was Frank Ervin.

Sept. 13 The **U.S. Lawn Tennis singles championships** were won by Neale Frazer of Australia over Alex Olmedo in the men's division and by Maria Bueno of Brazil over Darlene Hard in the women's division.

Oct. 8 The 56th annual **World Series** was won by the Los Angeles Dodgers (NL), defeating the Chicago White Sox (Al) four games to two. Star of the series was Larry Sherry, Los Angeles relief pitcher, with two wins and two saves. Ted Kluszewski's three homers and ten runs batted in for the White Sox were to no avail. The Dodgers had won the National League pennant by sweeping two games from the Milwaukee Braves in a league playoff.

Nov. 8 A new **pro basketball scoring record** was set by Elgin Baylor, forward for the Minneapolis Lakers. He scored 64 points in a Laker victory over the Boston Celtics at Minneapolis. Baylor erased the old mark of 63 set by Joe Fulks in 1949.

Nov. 28 In the **NCAA's first soccer playoffs** for the men's collegiate title, St. Louis U. defeated Bridgeport U. 5-2 at Bridgeport, Conn.

Dec. 1 The **Heisman Trophy** for outstanding college football player of 1959 was awarded to Billy Cannon, halfback for Louisiana State U.

Dec. 27 The **NFL championship** was won by the Baltimore Colts, defeating the New York Giants 31-16.

1960

Racquetball became the new name of paddle rackets. The International Racquetball Association was formed, supplanting the original Paddle Racquets Association.

The **amateur world championship of ice hockey,** sponsored by the International Ice Hockey

Federation, was won by the U.S. team. Ever since, the USSR has dominated the event.

Jan. 1 In **college football bowl games,** the results were Syracuse 23, Texas 14 in the Cotton Bowl; Georgia 14, Missouri 0 in the Orange Bowl; Washington 44, Wisconsin 8 in the Rose Bowl; and Mississippi 21, Louisiana State 0 in the Sugar Bowl. This season both the AP and UPI polls chose Syracuse as national collegiate champion of 1959.

Jan. 2 The **U.S. chess championship** was successfully defended by Brooklyn's 16-year-old chess wonder, Bobby Fischer, in a tournament in New York City.

Jan. 12 **Dolph Schayes** of the Syracuse Nationals became the first NBA player to score more than 15,000 career points.

Jan. 22 The world **middleweight boxing championship** was won by Paul Pender, who defeated Sugar Ray Robinson in a 15-round split decision.

Jan. 30 **U.S. figure skating championships** were won in Seattle by Carol Heiss, women's singles; David Jenkins, men's singles; Ronald and Nancy Ludington, pairs; and Margie Ackles and Charles Phillips, Jr., dance.

Feb. 6 **Bill Russell,** basketball center for the Boston Celtics, pulled down 51 rebounds, breaking his old record of 49, as the Celtics defeated the Syracuse Nationals 124-100 at Boston.

Feb. 8-9 At the **Westminster Kennel Club** dog show, Ch. Chik T'Sun, a Pekingese owned by Mr. and Mrs. C. C. Venable, took best-in-show.

Feb. 18-28 At the **Winter Olympics** in Squaw Valley, Calif., the unofficial team championship was won by the USSR. Sweden was second and the U.S. was third. David Jenkins of the U.S. won the gold medal in men's figure skating. His brother Hayes had won the same event four years earlier. The U.S. ice hockey team beat the USSR team 3-2, and went on to become the first U.S. ice hockey champions by trouncing Czechoslovakia 9-4.

Feb. 21 **Wilt Chamberlain,** center for the Philadelphia Warriors, set a new basketball scoring record for Madison Square Garden, with 58 points against the New York Knicks. In this, his first year in the NBA, Chamberlain scored 50 or more points four times in the season, an NBA record.

Feb. 23 Demolition of **Ebbets Field,** home park of the Brooklyn Dodgers (now the Los Angeles Dodgers), was begun. An apartment project was to replace the aging structure.

Mar. 2-5 At the **world figure skating championships** in Vancouver, British Columbia, Canada,, Carol Heiss won the women's singles title.

Mar. 19 The **NCAA basketball championship** was won by Ohio State, which defeated California 75-55. The Buckeyes' team included Jerry Lucas, John Havlicek, and Larry Siegfried.

Mar. 25 **Wilt Chamberlain** announced his retirement from professional basketball. He decried the rough tactics by opponents on the court and admitted that racial difficulties he encountered as a black had influenced his decision. Chamberlain relented later in the year and signed another pro basketball contract.

Mar. 27-Apr. 9 The **NBA basketball championship** was won by the Boston Celtics, who beat the St. Louis Hawks four games to three. The final victory, 122-103, set off a tumultuous demonstration by the hometown crowd at the Boston Garden, especially for Bob Cousy and Bill Russell.

Apr. 7-14 The **NHL Stanley Cup** was won by the Montreal Canadiens, who defeated the Toronto Maple Leafs in four straight games to become the first team to win the cup five times in a row.

Apr. 10 The **Masters golf tournament** was won for the second time by Arnold Palmer, whose 282 beat Ken Venturi by one stroke. Palmer birdied the final two holes.

Apr. 19 The 64th **Boston Marathon** was won by Paavo Kotila of Finland, with a time of 2 hrs., 20 min., 54 sec.

May 7 The 86th annual **Kentucky Derby** was won by Venetian Way, with a time of 2:02$\frac{2}{5}$. Bill Hartack was the jockey.

May 21 The 85th annual **Preakness Stakes** was won by Bally Ache, with a time of 1:57$\frac{3}{5}$. The jockey was Bob Ussery.

May 30 The 44th **Indianapolis 500** auto race was won by Jim Rathmann of Miami, Fla., completing the 500-mi. course in 3 hrs., 36 min., 11.36 sec., at an average speed of 138.767 mph.

June Carleton Mitchell's yawl *Finisterre* won the biennial 635-mi. **Newport-Bermuda ocean yacht race,** on the basis of corrected time, for the third time in a row. This record has never been equaled.

June 11 The 92nd annual **Belmont Stakes** was won by Celtic Ash, with a time of 2:29$\frac{3}{5}$. The jockey was Bill Hartack.

	WINNER	SPORT		WINNER	SPORT
1930	Bobby Jones	Golf	1959	Parry O'Brien	Shotput
1931	Barney Berlinger	Track and field			
1932	Jim Bausch	Track and field	1960	Rafer Johnson	Decathlon
1933	Glenn Cunningham	Track	1961	Wilma Rudolph	Track and field
1934	Bill Bontron	Track	1962	Jim Beatty	Track and field
1935	Lawson Little	Golf	1963	John Pennel	Track and field
1936	Glenn Morris	Track	1964	Don Schollander	Swimming
1937	Don Budge	Tennis	1965	Bill Bradley	Basketball
1938	Don Lash	Track	1966	Jim Ryun	Track and field
1939	Joe Burk	Rowing	1967	Randy Matson	Track and field
			1968	Debbie Meyer	Swimming
1940	Greg Rice	Track and field	1969	Bill Toomey	Decathlon
1941	Leslie MacMitchell	Track and field			
1942	Cornelius Warmerdam	Pole vault	1970	John Kinsella	Swimming
1943	Gil Dodds	Track and field	1971	Mark Spitz	Swimming
1944	Ann Curtis	Swimming	1972	Frank Shorter	Marathon
1945	Felix "Doc" Blanchard	Football	1973	Bill Walton	Basketball
1946	Y. Arnold Tucker	Football	1974	Rick Wohlhuter	Track
1947	John B. Kelly, Jr.	Rowing	1975	Tim Shaw	Swimming
1948	Bob Mathias	Decathlon	1976	Bruce Jenner	Decathlon
1949	Dick Button	Figure skating	1977	John Naber	Swimming
			1978	Tracy Caulkins	Swimming
1950	Fred Wilt	Track and field	1979	Kurt Thomas	Gymnastics
1951	Bob Richards	Pole vault			
1952	Horace Ashenfelter	Track and field	1980	Eric Heiden	Speed Skating
1953	Sammy Lee	Diving	1981	Carl Lewis	Track and field
1954	Mal Whitfield	Track and field	1982	Mary Decker Tabb	Track and field
1955	Harrison Dillard	Track and field	1983	Edwin Moses	Track and field
1956	Patricia McCormick	Diving	1984	Greg Louganis	Diving
1957	Bobby Jo Morrow	Track and field	1985	Joan Benoit	Marathon
1958	Glenn Davis	Track and field	1986	Jackie Joyner	Track and field

June 14 Jake LaMotta, former middleweight boxing champion, **confessed he had thrown a fight** in 1947. Testifying before a Senate committee, LaMotta said he was told he would have to take a dive if he wanted a shot at the title.

June 18 The **U.S. Open golf tournament** at Cherry Hills, Denver, Colo., was won by Arnold Palmer, who beat amateur Jack Nicklaus by two strokes. After an erratic start, Palmer recovered. On the first nine of the final round, he shot a record-tying 30 to bolt into the lead, which he held with a strong 35 for the closing nine holes.

June 20 The **world heavyweight boxing championship** was won by Floyd Patterson, who defeated Ingemar Johansson in a fifth-round knockout in New York City. Patterson thus be-

came the first fighter in boxing history to regain the heavyweight championship.

July 2 The **longest delayed drop by a parachutist** was achieved by Capt. Joseph W. Kittinger, Jr., who fell 41,000 ft. at a speed of up to more than 600 mph before opening his chute over New Mexico. Kittinger was about 19.5 mi. up when he jumped and was in free-fall for 16 min., 30 sec.

July 2 At the **Wimbledon** tennis championships in England, Dennis Ralston teamed with Rafael Osuna of Mexico to win the men's doubles title. Darlene Hard teamed with Rod Laver of Australia to win the mixed doubles and with Maria Bueno of Brazil to win the women's doubles.

July 4 The **LPGA golf tournament** was won by

Mickey Wright, who became the first person to win the championship twice.

July 13 The second **baseball all-star game** of this year was won 6-0 by the National League, thus sweeping the 1960 games. On July 11, the National League had won the first game 5-3.

July 23 The **U.S. Women's Open golf tournament,** held at Worcester, Mass., was won by Betsy Rawls, who became the first person to win the title four times.

July 24 At Akron, Ohio, the **PGA golf tournament** was won by Jay Hebert, beating Jim Ferrier by one stroke.

Aug. 25-Sept. 11 At the **Summer Olympics** in Rome, Italy, the U.S. won 34 gold medals and took second place in the team standings, behind the USSR. Glenn Davis won the 400-m. hurdles in a new Olympic time of 49.3 sec. He had also won this event at the 1956 Olympics, with a slightly slower time, and thus was the first ever to triumph in this event twice. In 1960 he also won a gold medal in the 1600-m. relay. In winning the pole vault at 15 ft., 5 1/8 in., Don Bragg became the first vaulter to clear more than 15 ft. at the Olympics. In the women's events, Wilma Rudolph took the gold medal in both the 100- and 200-m. dashes in times of 11 sec. and 24 sec., respectively. Bob Webster won the platform dive and repeated this triumph at the 1964 games.

Aug. 31 The 35th annual **Hambletonian Stakes** was won in the fourth heat by Blaze Hanover. The driver was Joe O'Brien.

Sept. 17 The **U.S. Lawn Tennis Association singles championships** were won by Neale Fraser of Australia over Rod Laver in the men's division and by Darlene Hard of California in the women's division. Hard defeated Maria Bueno of Brazil.

Oct. 5-13 The 57th **World Series** was won by the Pittsburgh Pirates (NL), defeating the New York Yankees (AL) four games to three. In a wild seventh game, the Pirates scored five runs in the eighth inning to move ahead 9-7, but the Yankees came back with two in the ninth to tie the score. In the bottom of the ninth, Bill Mazeroski, the Pirate second baseman, undid the Yankees' heroics with a 400-ft. drive over the left-field wall.

Oct. 18 **Casey Stengel,** successful manager of the New York Yankees baseball team since 1949, was fired. Although the official announcement stated that Stengel had reached retirement age, he attributed the dismissal to a controversy with the club owners.

Nov. 16 Elgin Baylor set a new **pro basketball scoring record.** The Los Angeles Lakers forward increased his NBA single-game scoring record to 71 points at New York City's Madison Square Garden against the New York Knicks.

Nov. 25 A new **pro basketball rebound record** was set by Wilt Chamberlain, who erased Bill Russell's record of 51 by grabbing 55 rebounds in a losing Philadelphia game against the Boston Celtics.

Nov. 29 The **Heisman Trophy** for outstanding college football player of 1960 was voted to Navy halfback Joe Bellino.

Dec. 26 The **NFL championship** was won by the Philadelphia Eagles, who defeated the Green Bay Packers 17-13.

1961

Little League baseball extended its program by launching a Senior League for boys 13 to 15.

The **American League,** now ten teams strong, increased its 154-game schedule to 162 games.

The **Washington Senators** baseball franchise was moved to Minneapolis-St. Paul, where the team would be called the Minnesota Twins. A new franchise was granted to Washington, where the team would remain until 1971. The franchise was then moved to Dallas-Fort Worth, where the team would be called the Texas Rangers. A tenth team, called the California Angels, was added to the American League with a franchise for Los Angeles. The team later moved to Anaheim, in Orange County, Calif.

The **National Skeet Shooting Association** initiated an event named Champion of Champions. This called for each contestant to use four different guns, with 25 targets each. The first winner was Miner Cliett of Childersburg, Ala.

The **U.S. Surfing Association** was founded at Huntington Beach, Calif., in an attempt to combat the increasingly negative image surfing and surfers had acquired. The name was changed to the U.S. Surfing Federation in 1979. The federation is the official governing body of amateur surfing.

Jan. 1 In **college football bowl games,** the results were Duke 7, Arkansas 6 in the Cotton Bowl; Missouri 21, Navy 14 in the Orange Bowl; Washington 17, Minnesota 7 in the Rose Bowl; and Mississippi 14, Rice 6 in the Sugar Bowl. This season both the AP and UPI polls chose Minnesota as national collegiate champion of 1960.

Jan. 2 The **AFL championship** for 1960 was won by the Houston Oilers, who defeated the Los Angeles Chargers 24-16.

Jan. 27-29 **U.S. figure skating championships** were won in Colorado Springs, Colo., by Laurence Owen, women's singles; Bradley Lord, men's singles; Maribel Owen and Dudley Richards, pairs; and Diane Sherbloom and Larry Pierce, dance.

Feb. 14 At the **Westminster Kennel Club** dog show, Ch. Cappoquin Little Sister, a toy poodle owned by Florence Michelson, took best-in-show.

Feb. 25 A **world record for glider altitude** was set by Paul F. Bikle, Jr., who soared 46,266 ft. over the Mojave Desert in California.

Mar. 12 The **LPGA golf tournament** was won by Mickey Wright, her third win in four years. Her margin over Louise Suggs was a whopping nine strokes.

Mar. 13 The **world heavyweight boxing championship** was successfully defended by Floyd Patterson, who knocked out Ingemar Johansson in the sixth round in Miami Beach, Fla.

Mar. 17 Another **basketball point-shaving scandal** was revealed when Manhattan District Attorney Frank S. Hogan arrested two professional gamblers and implicated players from two colleges. In April, ten more colleges and 14 more players were named. In September, Seton Hall U. announced it would withdraw from further tournament competition and play its home games in its own gymnasium.

Mar. 25 The **NCAA basketball championship** was won by Cincinnati, defeating the defending champions, Ohio State, 70-65 and ending the Buckeyes' 32-game winning streak.

Apr. 2-11 The **NBA basketball championship** was won by the Boston Celtics, who defeated the St. Louis Hawks four games to one. This was Boston's third consecutive title.

Apr. 6-16 The **NHL Stanley Cup** was won by the Chicago Black Hawks, who defeated the Detroit Red Wings four games to two.

Apr. 10 The **Masters golf tournament** was won by Gary Player of South Africa. The first foreign golfer to win the event, he edged Arnold Palmer and amateur Charley Coe by one stroke.

Apr. 19 The 65th **Boston Marathon** was won by Eino Oksanen of Finland, with a time of 2 hrs., 23 min., 29 sec.

May 4 An **altitude record for balloons** was set by two U.S. Navy officers, Malcolm D. Ross and Victor G. Prather, when they reached 113,740 ft. in their research vehicle. They took off from the USS *Antietam* in the Gulf of Mexico. Prather was killed during recovery of the balloon.

May 6 The 87th annual **Kentucky Derby** was won by Carry Back, with a time of 2:04. The jockey was John Sellers.

May 20 The 86th annual **Preakness Stakes** was

WAYNE GRETZKY

b. Brantford, Ont., Canada, Jan. 26, 1961

No other player in National Hockey League history has become a star and a leading scorer as quickly as Wayne Gretzky. He learned to skate when he was 6, and his career with the Edmonton Oilers began in 1979, when he was only 18.

Gretzky immediately began to set records. In the 1979–1980 season, he became the youngest player ever to score 50 or more goals and 100 or more points in a season. In 1980 he became the youngest hockey player ever to be named most valuable player. Gretzky won this honor every year through 1986. In 1980, he also won the Lady Byng Trophy, given for sportsmanship. Gretzky has been the league's leading scorer in every year he has played since 1981.

By the end of the 1986–1987 season, his eighth, Gretzky was already fourth on the career scoring list, with 543 goals, 971 assists, and 1520 points. He also set a record for most Stanley Cup playoff points, 183.

Experts say Gretzky looks awkward, but he has great balance and is able to anticipate the flow of the action. His hockey prowess has made Gretzky Canada's best-known living athlete.

won by Carry Back, with a time of 1:57⅗. The jockey was John Sellers.

May 30 Frankie Carbo was convicted in Los Angeles of **trying to cut in on a boxing champion's earnings.** Carbo, reputed to be the underworld boss of professional boxing, and four others were accused of trying to muscle in on the contract of Don Jordan, a former welterweight champion, and threatening him with bodily harm.

May 30 The 45th **Indianapolis 500** auto race was won by A. J. Foyt, completing the 500-mi. course in 3 hrs., 35 min., 37.49 sec., at an average speed of 139.130 mph, a new race record.

June 3 The 93rd annual **Belmont Stakes** was won by Sherluck, with a time of 2:29⅗. The jockey was Braulio Baeza.

June 5 The **three-point basketball field goal** was adopted by the newly formed American Basketball League (ABL), for a field goal made from behind a line on the court 22 ft. from the basket. The ABL, an eight-team circuit organized by Abe Saperstein, opened its season on Oct. 27. Its first and only league championship was won on Apr. 9, 1962, by the Cleveland Pipers, who defeated the Kansas City Steers 106-102 at Kansas City, Mo. The league lost $1,500,000 in its first season, and midway through the 1962-1963 season suspended operation. It shared its name with an earlier pro league that had been organized in the mid-1920s and had fielded teams, with interruptions, into the 1940s but also failed to establish itself as a national league.

June 9 In a **college basketball bribery** scandal, four former players were indicted in New York City in connection with a point-shaving plot, in which players would deliberately control the score of a game as instructed by gamblers. Two gamblers, Aaron Wagman and Joseph Hacken, were named as coconspirators. Both had been indicted earlier on related charges in the grand jury probe that began on Apr. 4. As the summer progressed, further revelations and indictments showed the practice of point-shaving to be widespread.

June 17 The **U.S. Open golf tournament** was won by Gene Littler at Birmingham, Mich. His sparkling 68 in the final round enabled him to edge out Doug Sanders and Bob Goalby.

July 1 The **U.S. Women's Open golf tournament** was won by Mickey Wright, who beat defending champion Betsy Rawls by six strokes.

July 8 At the **Wimbledon** tennis championships in England, the women's doubles title was won by Karen Hantze and Billie Jean Moffitt. Chuck McKinley lost to Rod Laver of Australia in the men's singles finals.

July 24 The **Baseball Hall of Fame** inducted former outfielders Max Carey and William R. "Billy" Hamilton.

July 25 The south face of **Mt. McKinley was climbed for the first time** by a team of Italian mountain climbers led by R. Cassin. Three climbers were hospitalized with frostbite after scaling the Alaskan peak.

July 30 The **PGA golf tournament** was won by Jerry Barber, who beat Don January by one stroke in a playoff round at Olympia Falls, Ill.

July 31 The second **baseball all-star game** of the year ended in a 1-1 tie at the end of the ninth inning due to rain. It was the first tie in the history of the event. The first game (July 11) had been won in ten innings by the National League, 5-4.

Aug. 26 The **International Hockey Hall of Fame** was officially opened at Toronto.

Aug. 30 The 36th annual **Hambletonian Stakes** was won in two straight heats by Harlan Dean, setting a new record with a combined time of 3:57⅖. The driver was Jimmy Arthur.

Sept. 10 The **World Driving Championship** was won for the first time by an American, Phil Hill.

Sept. 10 The **U.S. Lawn Tennis Association singles championships** were won by Roy Emerson of Australia over his teammate Rod Laver in the men's division and by Darlene Hard for the second year running in the women's division.

Oct. 1 **Roger Maris** of the New York Yankees, in the last (162nd) game of the season, hit his 61st home run of the season off Tracy Stallard, of the Boston Red Sox. He thus surpassed Babe Ruth's record of 60, set in 1927 in a 154-game season. In the first 154 games, Maris had hit 59. Record books still cite both Ruth's and Maris's achievements.

Oct. 4-9 The 58th annual **World Series** was won by the New York Yankees (AL), beating the Cincinnati Reds (NL) four games to one. In the fourth game, won by the Yankees 7-0, Whitey Ford set a new record for scoreless innings in World Series play. He left the game after the

CARL LEWIS

Frederick Carlton Lewis
b. Birmingham, Ala., July 1, 1961

Carl Lewis would seem to have the correct genes for superior performance in track and field events. His father had been a track star at Tuskegee Institute, and his mother competed in the hurdles at the 1951 Pan American Games. His sister Carol, two years younger, is a star in her own right in sprints, hurdles, and the high jump.

By the time Lewis was in high school, he was already rated the top athlete of his age. Because the United States withdrew from the 1980 Olympics, Lewis had no chance to compete that year. In 1981, at the NCAA indoor championships, he won the 100-meter dash and the long jump, the first time anyone had triumphed in both an NCAA track event and field event. He repeated this feat in the outdoor championships of that year.

In August 1983, Lewis won three gold medals at the World Championships in Helsinki, Finland—in the 100-meter dash, in the long jump, and as a member of the 400-meter relay team. His chance to star in the Olympics finally came in 1984, and he responded by becoming the only athlete since Jesse Owens, in 1936, to win four gold medals in track and field events. His victories came in the 100-meter dash, the 200-meter dash, the 400-meter relay, and the long jump.

---

fifth inning because of injuries, but he had run his string of scoreless innings to 32, surpassing Babe Ruth's record of $29\frac{2}{3}$ scoreless innings, set in 1918.

Nov. The so-called **TV instant replay** was introduced in this season's football coverage by ABC Television Sports. The process, which enables immediate playback of live coverage, in slow motion when desired, was soon copied by the other networks and used in other sports also.

Dec. 4 The **world heavyweight boxing championship** was successfully defended by Floyd Patterson, who knocked out Tom McNeeley in the fourth round of a bout in Toronto, Canada.

Dec. 6 The **Heisman Trophy** for outstanding college football player of 1961 was voted to Syracuse halfback Ernie Davis.

Dec. 24 The **AFL championship** was won by the Houston Oilers, who defeated the San Diego Chargers 10-3.

Dec. 31 The **NFL championship** was won by the Green Bay Packers, who defeated the New York Giants 37-0.

1962

The **International Catamaran Challenge Trophy** was initiated following a challenge from England. England won 4-1 and beat back challenges from the U.S. and Australia for a decade.

The **first inboard powerboat** to exceed 200 mph, *Miss U.S.I,* reached 200.49 mph in a run at Guntersville, Ala.

New **National League baseball franchises** were awarded to the New York Mets and the Houston Astros. This brought the National League to a total of ten teams.

A **UPI survey of horse racing** showed that the sport was enjoying great popularity. In the 24 states with legalized betting at racetracks, 33,881,860 fans bet a total of $2,679,461,505. Attendance was up 1.28% over 1961, and betting was up 5.57%. Mrs. Richard C. du Pont's Kelso was named horse of the year for the third straight year. Kelso earned $254,585 to boost lifetime earnings to $1,011,940, becoming the fifth horse in racing history to top the $1,000,000 mark.

Jan. 1 In **college football bowl games,** the results were Texas 12, Mississippi 7 in the Cotton Bowl; Louisiana State 25, Colorado 7 in the Orange Bowl; Minnesota 21, UCLA 3 in the Rose Bowl; and Alabama 10, Arkansas 3 in the Sugar Bowl. This season both the AP and UPI polls chose Alabama as national collegiate champion of 1961.

Feb. 2 The **first person to vault 16 ft.** was a Marine Corps corporal, John Uelses, at the Millrose Games in Madison Square Garden in New York City. Using a springy fiberglass pole, he cleared 16 ft., ¼ in. On the following night, in Boston, he raised the mark to 16 ft., ¾ in.

Feb. 3-4 **U.S. figure skating championships** were won in Boston by Barbara Roles Pursley, women's singles; Monty Hoyt, men's singles;

1962

Dorothyann Nelson and Pieter Kollen, pairs; and Yvonne Littlefield and Peter Betts, dance.

Feb. 10 Jim Beatty, the **first American to break the 4-min. mile indoors,** was clocked at 3:58.9 in Los Angeles, a new indoor record. On June 8, also in Los Angeles, he set a new world record of 8:29.8 for 2 mi. Beatty went on to win the James E. Sullivan Memorial Trophy as the outstanding amateur athlete of 1962.

Feb. 13 At the **Westminster Kennel Club** dog show, Ch. Elfinbrook Simon, a West Highland white terrier, took best-in-show.

Mar. 2 The **first basketball player to score 100 points** in a game was Wilt Chamberlain, star of the Philadelphia Warriors, who made 36 goals and 28 foul shots in a game against the New York Knicks, for a 169-147 victory at Hershey, Pa. The teams' combined total of 316 points surpassed the Boston-Minneapolis record of 312 points set on Feb. 27, 1959.

Mar. 5 The **last Bendix Trophy airplane race** was won by a B-58 bomber, which flew a round trip from Los Angeles to New York and back in 4 hrs., 42 min., 32 sec., at an average speed of 1214.71 mph. The first Bendix Trophy race, on Sept. 3, 1931, was won by Major (later Lt. Gen.) James H. Doolittle, who flew a Laird Racer from Burbank, Calif., to Cleveland, Ohio, in 9 hrs., 10 min., 21 sec., at an average speed of 223.058 mph.

Mar. 24 The **NCAA basketball championship** was won by Cincinnati, which defeated Ohio State 71-59. Center Paul Hogue was the dominating Cincinnati player.

Apr. 3 **Boxing-related deaths** since the turn of the century numbered about 450, according to Nat Fleischer, editor of *Ring* magazine, it was reported in the *New York Times.* There had already been four boxing deaths this year.

Apr. 3 **Eddie Arcaro,** considered by many to be the greatest American jockey in modern turf history, retired from racing. During his 31-year

career he rode 4779 winners and won purses totaling $30,039,543.

Apr. 7-18 The **NBA basketball championship** was won for the fourth consecutive time by the Boston Celtics, defeating the Los Angeles Lakers four games to three. Bob Cousy, Bill Sharman, Tommy Heinsohn, and Bill Russell were too much for Wilt Chamberlain and the other Lakers. Russell scored 30 points in the final game and made 44 rebounds as the Celtics won 110-107 in overtime.

Apr. 9 The **Masters golf tournament** was won by Arnold Palmer, who beat Gary Player and Dow Finsterwald in a three-way playoff after all three had posted four-round totals of 280.

Apr. 10-22 The **NHL Stanley Cup** was won for the first time since 1951 by the Toronto Maple Leafs, who beat the Chicago Black Hawks four games to two.

Apr. 19 The 66th **Boston Marathon** was won for the third time, second time in a row, by Eino Oksanen of Finland, with a time of 2 hrs., 23 min., 48 sec.

May 5 The 88th annual **Kentucky Derby** was won by Decidedly, with a time of 2:00⅖. The jockey was Bill Hartack.

May 19 The 87th annual **Preakness Stakes** was won by Green Money, with a time of 1:56⅕. The jockey was Johnny Rotz.

May 30 The 46th **Indianapolis 500** auto race was won by Roger Ward, who completed the 500-mi. course in 3 hrs., 33 min., 50 sec. for a new race record of 140.293 mph.

June 9 The 94th annual **Belmont Stakes** was won by Jaipur, with a time of 2:28⅘. The jockey was Willie Shoemaker.

June 17 The **U.S. Open golf tournament,** at Oakmont, Pa., was won by Jack Nicklaus, who beat Arnold Palmer by three strokes in a playoff. Nicklaus had turned pro in January.

June 30 The **U.S. Women's Open golf tournament** was won by Murle Lindstrom at Myrtle Beach, S.C.

July 7 At the **Wimbledon** tennis championships in England, Karen Hantze Susman won the women's singles title by defeating Mrs. V. Sukova of Czechoslovakia in the finals. Susman teamed with Billie Jean Moffitt to win the women's doubles, and Margaret Osborne du Pont paired with Neale Fraser of Australia to win the mixed doubles.

July 10 The first **baseball all-star game** of 1962

It just shows you how easy this business is.

Casey Stengel, speaking to the press after his fledgling New York Mets beat his old team, the Yankees, 4–3 on March 23, 1962

was won by the National League, which beat the American League 3-1. The second game, on July 30, was won by the American League, 9-4. In late November the leagues decided to return to playing a single all-star game each year.

July 22   The **PGA golf tournament** was won by Gary Player of South Africa, who became the first nonresident of the U.S. to win the championship. Play was at the Aronimink Golf Club, Newtown Square, Pa.

July 23   The **Baseball Hall of Fame** inducted Bob Feller, Bill McKechnie, Jackie Robinson, and old-timer Edd Roush.

Aug. 29   The 37th annual **Hambletonian Stakes** was won in straight heats by A.C.'s Viking. The driver was Sanders Russell.

Sept. 8   The **richest purse in thoroughbred racing history,** $357,250, was offered in the Arlington-Washington Futurity, a race for 2-year-olds. The winner's share, $142,250, went to Candy Spots.

Sept. 10   The **U.S. Lawn Tennis Association singles championships** were won by Rod Laver of Australia in the men's division and Margaret Smith of Australia in the women's division. With his win, Laver completed a grand slam of the four top world amateur championships, the Australian, French, British, and U.S. tournaments. It was only the second such sweep, preceded by that of Don Budge in 1938.

Sept. 15-25   The **America's Cup** was successfully defended by the U.S. 12-m. yacht *Weatherly,* which defeated the Australian challenger *Gretel* four races to one. It was the closest competition in years and the first time since 1934 that the U.S. entry failed to sweep the first four races.

Sept. 25   The **world heavyweight boxing championship** was won by Sonny Liston, who knocked out defending champion Floyd Patterson in 2 min. and 6 sec. of the first round.

Sept. 27   The **New York Mets,** a new National League baseball team, finished their first season under former Yankees manager Casey Stengel. The Mets lost 120 of the 160 games they played, but the fans loved them. Nearly 1,000,000 came to the Polo Grounds and paid to witness the heroic ineptitude of the players and the antics of their manager.

Oct.   **Maury Wills,** shortstop for the Los Angeles Dodgers, stole 104 bases this season, breaking Ty Cobb's record of 96, established in 1915.

Oct. 4-16   The 59th annual **World Series** was won

LADIES' PROFESSIONAL GOLF ASSOCIATION CHAMPIONS

1955	Beverly Hanson
1956	Marlene Hagge
1957	Louise Suggs
1958	Mickey Wright
1959	Betsy Rawls
1960	Mickey Wright
1961	Mickey Wright
1962	Judy Kimball
1963	Mickey Wright
1964	Mary Mills
1965	Sandra Haynie
1966	Gloria Ehret
1967	Kathy Whitworth
1968	Sandra Post
1969	Betsy Rawls
1970	Shirley Englehorn
1971	Kathy Whitworth
1972	Kathy Ahern
1973	Mary Mills
1974	Sandra Haynie
1975	Kathy Whitworth
1976	Betty Burfeindt
1977	Chako Higuchi
1978	Nancy Lopez
1979	Donna Caponi Young
1980	Sally Little
1981	Donna Caponi Young
1982	Jan Stephenson
1983	Patty Sheehan
1984	Patty Sheehan
1985	Nancy Lopez
1986	Pat Bradley
1987	Jan Geddes

by the New York Yankees (AL), defeating the San Francisco Giants (NL) four games to three. The Yankees' Ralph Terry escaped with a 1-0 win in the final game when Bobby Richardson snared Willie McCovey's line drive with two base runners on the move. This was the last out of the game. The Giants had won the National League pennant by beating the Los Angeles Dodgers two games to one in a league playoff. The Giants won the playoff by scoring four runs in the ninth inning of the third game. The final score was 6-4.

Oct. 7   The **LPGA golf tournament** was won by Judy Kimball at the Stardust Country Club, Las Vegas, Nev.

Nov. 24   The **first North American karate tour-**

PROFESSIONAL GOLFERS' ASSOCIATION CHAMPIONS

1916	Jim Barnes	1952	Jim Turnesa
1917–18	(tournament not held)	1953	Walter Burkemo
		1954	Chick Harbert
1919	Jim Barnes	1955	Doug Ford
1920	Jock Hutchinson	1956	Jack Burke, Jr.
1921	Walter Hagen	1957	Lionel Hebert
1922	Gene Sarazen	1958	Dow Finsterwald
1923	Gene Sarazen	1959	Bob Rosburg
1924	Walter Hagen	1960	Jay Hebert
1925	Walter Hagen	1961	Jerry Barber
1926	Walter Hagen	1962	Gary Player
1927	Walter Hagen	1963	Jack Nicklaus
1928	Leo Diegel	1964	Bobby Nichols
1929	Leo Diegel	1965	Dave Marr
1930	Tommy Armour	1966	Al Geiberger
1931	Tom Creavy	1967	Don January
1932	Olin Dutra	1968	Julius Boros
1933	Gene Sarazen	1969	Ray Floyd
1934	Paul Runyan	1970	Dave Stockton
1935	Johnny Revolta	1971	Jack Nicklaus
1936	Denny Shute	1972	Gary Player
1937	Denny Shute	1973	Jack Nicklaus
1938	Paul Runyan	1974	Lee Trevino
1939	Henry Picard	1975	Jack Nicklaus
1940	Byron Nelson	1976	Dave Stockton
1941	Vic Ghezzi	1977	Lanny Wadkins
1942	Sam Snead	1978	John Mahaffey
1943	(tournament not held)	1979	Dave Graham
		1980	Jack Nicklaus
1944	Bob Hamilton	1981	Larry Nelson
1945	Byron Nelson	1982	Ray Floyd
1946	Ben Hogan	1983	Hal Sutton
1947	Jim Ferrier	1984	Lee Trevino
1948	Ben Hogan	1985	Hubert Green
1949	Sam Snead	1986	Bob Tway
1950	Chandler Harper	1987	Larry Nelson
1951	Sam Snead		

nament was held in Madison Square Garden, New York City. Sixty-four contestants took part, and the black belt title was won by Gary Alexander of Jersey City, N.J.

Nov. 27 The **Heisman Trophy** for outstanding college football player of 1962 was voted to Oregon State quarterback Terry Baker.

Dec. 23 The **AFL championship** was won by the Dallas Texans, who defeated the Houston Oilers 20-17. The game went to two extra quarters and was decided on a field goal by Tommy Brooker.

Dec. 30 The **NFL championship** was won for the second year running by the Green Bay Packers, who defeated the New York Giants 16-7.

1963

Jan. 1 In **college football bowl games,** the results were Louisiana State 13, Texas 0 in the Cotton Bowl; Alabama 17, Oklahoma 0 in the Orange Bowl; Southern California 42, Wisconsin 37 in the Rose Bowl; and Mississippi 17, Arkansas 13 in the Sugar Bowl. This season the AP and UPI polls chose Southern California as national collegiate champion of 1962.

Feb. 9-10 **U.S. figure skating championships** were won in Long Beach, Calif., by Lorraine Hanlon, women's singles; Thomas Litz, men's singles; Judianne and Jerry Fotheringill, pairs; and Sally Schantz and Stanley Urban, dance.

Feb. 12 At the **Westminster Kennel Club** dog show, Ch. Wakefield's Black Knight, an English springer spaniel owned by Mrs. W. J. S. Borie, took best-in-show.

Mar. 23 The **NCAA basketball championship** was won by Loyola, of Chicago, which defeated the U. of Cincinnati 60-58. The underdog Loyola team pulled out an overtime victory after trailing by 15 points.

Apr. 7 The **Masters golf tournament** was won by Jack Nicklaus, who beat Tony Lema by one stroke.

Apr. 9-18 The **NHL Stanley Cup** was won by the Toronto Maple Leafs, who defeated the Detroit Red Wings four games to one.

Apr. 19 The 67th **Boston Marathon** was won by Aurele Vandendriessche of Belgium with a record time of 2 hrs., 18 min., 58 sec., beating the course record set in 1957 by 1 min., 7 sec.

Apr. 20-May 5 At the fourth **Pan-American Games** in São Paulo, Brazil, the U.S. won the unofficial team championship with 108 gold medals. Brazil was second with 14 gold medals.

Apr. 24 The Boston Celtics' brilliant guard **Bob Cousy,** 34, retired from competition after leading the team to its fifth straight NBA championship. The Celtics had downed the Los Angeles Lakers four games to two (Apr. 14-24).

May 1   The **first American to climb Mt. Everest** was James W. Whittaker, who was accompanied only by a Sherpa guide.

May 4   The 89th annual **Kentucky Derby** was won by Chateaugay, with a time of 2:01⅘. The jockey was Braulio Baeza.

May 18   The 88th annual **Preakness Stakes** was won by Candy Spots, with a time of 1:56⅕. The jockey was Willie Shoemaker.

May 22   **Four Americans scaled Mt. Everest** from the opposite side from which James. W. Whittaker had conquered it three weeks earlier. They were Barry C. Bishop, Luther G. Jerstad, William F. Unsold, and Thomas Hornbein.

May 30   The 47th annual **Indianapolis 500** auto race was won by Parnelli Jones, completing the course in 3 hrs., 29 min., 35.40 sec., at an average speed of 143.137 mph.

June 8   The 95th annual **Belmont Stakes** was won by Chateaugay, with a time of 2:30⅕. The jockey was Braulio Baeza.

June 23   The **U.S. Open golf tournament** was won by Julius Boros, who beat Arnold Palmer and Jacky Cupit in a playoff. To mark the 50th anniversary of Francis Ouimet's victory over Vardon and Ray, the event was returned to the scene of that pivotal event in U.S. golf history, the Country Club of Brookline, Mass.

Summer   The **Greyhound Hall of Fame** was dedicated in Abilene, Kans., and three racing dogs were the first to be named to it: Rural Rube, Flashy Sir, and Real Huntsman. Rural Rube set a world record of 31 sec. for the 5/16th-mi. course on June 30, 1940. Flashy Sir was the sensation of the racetracks between 1944 and 1947. Real Huntsman set a record, never equaled, of 27 consecutive victories.

July 6   At the **Wimbledon** tennis championships in England, Chuck McKinley won the men's singles championship, defeating Fred Stolle of Australia in straight sets. Billie Jean Moffitt lost the women's finals to Margaret Smith of Australia.

July 9   The **baseball all-star game** was won by the National League, which beat the American League 5-3.

July 20   The **U.S. Women's Open golf tournament** was won by Mary Mills at the Kenwood Country Club, Cincinnati, Ohio.

July 21   The **PGA golf tournament** was won by Jack Nicklaus, with a 279 score at Dallas, Tex.

July 22   The **world heavyweight boxing championship** was successfully defended by Sonny Liston, who knocked out Floyd Patterson in 2 min., 10 sec. of the first round.

Aug. 5   The **Baseball Hall of Fame** inducted John G. Clarkson, Elmer H. Flick, Sam Rice, and Eppa Rixey.

Aug. 5   Craig Breedlove set an unofficial **world land speed record** of 407.6 mph on the Bonneville Salt Flats in Utah, driving a sleek 3-ton, three-wheeled, jet-powered auto. The U.S. Auto Club established a new class for its records, jet-powered vehicles.

Aug. 18   **Jon Tarantino,** the outstanding figure in American Casting Association's national championships in the late 1950s and early 1960s, won its two major trophies, scoring 393 out of a possible 400 in the four accuracy events.

Aug. 24   **Little League baseball's** championship game in Williamsport, Pa., was covered for the first time by a national television network on ABC's *Wide World of Sports,* a relationship that continues.

Aug. 24   **Don Schollander** of Santa Clara, Calif., became the first person to break the 2-min. mark for the 200-m. freestyle swim. At Osaka, Japan, he won the event with the time of 1:58.4.

Aug. 24   John Pennel became the **first person to pole-vault 17 ft.,** reaching 17 ft., ¾ in. at a meet in Miami, Fla.

Aug. 28   The 38th annual **Hambletonian Stakes** was won in the third heat by Speedy Scot. The driver was Ralph Baldwin.

Sept. 8   The **U.S. Lawn Tennis Association singles championships** were won by Rafael Osuna of Mexico over Frank Froehling in the men's division and Maria Bueno of Brazil in the women's division.

Sept. 29   **Stan "The Man" Musial** played his last game for the St. Louis Cardinals, retiring at 42 to take an executive position with the club. In his 22 years in baseball, all with the Cards, the great hitter set or tied 17 major league and 30 National League records.

Oct. 2-6   The 60th annual **World Series** was won by the Los Angeles Dodgers (NL), who swept the New York Yankees (AL) in four games. Dodger pitcher Sandy Koufax set a new series record by striking out 15 players in the opening game. Koufax, Don Drysdale, and Johnny Podres throttled the Yankees, who ended with a team batting average of .171 for the series.

Oct. 13   The **LPGA golf tournament** was won by

Mickey Wright. It was her fourth win in six years, again at Las Vegas, Nev.

Nov. 8 A **riot at Roosevelt Raceway** in Westbury, Long Island, N.Y., was sparked when six of eight trotters in the sixth race were involved in a pileup. Fans who had bet on the daily double were outraged when the race was declared official. They rioted and started a $20,000 fire. In the melee, 20 people were injured.

Nov. 26 The **Heisman Trophy** for outstanding college football player of 1963 was voted to Navy quarterback Roger Staubach.

Dec. 17 A **new free-fall record** was set by a 13-man U.S. Air Force team when they fell 41,000 ft. before opening their parachutes. This surpassed the former record by 4350 ft., set by a Soviet team.

Dec. 26-29 The U.S. regained the **Davis Cup,** which it had lost in 1959, by beating the Australian team three matches to two. Chuck McKinley and Dennis Ralston represented the U.S.

Dec. 31 The **NFL championship** was won by the Chicago Bears, who defeated the New York Giants 14-0.

1964

Jan. 1 In **college football bowl games,** the results were Texas 28, Navy 6 in the Cotton Bowl; Nebraska 13, Auburn 7 in the Orange Bowl; Illinois 17, Washington 7 in the Rose Bowl; and Alabama 12, Mississippi 7 in the Sugar Bowl. This season both the AP and UPI polls chose Texas as national collegiate champion of 1963.

Jan. 5 The 1963 **AFL championship** was won by the San Diego Chargers, who defeated the Boston Patriots 51-10.

Jan. 11-12 U.S. figure skating championships

There are three important things in life: family, religion, and the Green Bay Packers.

Vince Lombardi

were won in Cleveland, Ohio, by Peggy Fleming, women's singles; Scott Allen, men's singles; Judianne and Jerry Fotheringill, pairs; and Darlene Streich and Charles D. Fetter, Jr., dance.

Jan. 29-Feb. 9 At the **Winter Olympics** in Innsbruck, Austria, the U.S. finished eighth in the unofficial team standings, taking one gold, two silver, and three bronze medals.

Feb. 11 At the **Westminster Kennel Club** dog show, Ch. Courtenay Fleetfoot of Pennyworth, a whippet owned by Pennyworth Kennels, took best-in-show.

Feb. 25 The **world heavyweight boxing championship** was won by Cassius Clay, who later changed his name to Muhammad Ali, in a bout in Miami Beach, Fla., when Sonny Liston could not answer the bell for the seventh round because of an injury to his left arm. Ali announced he would give Liston a rematch, but the World Boxing Association (WBA), claiming it had a rule forbidding return bouts, declared the heavyweight title vacant and made plans for an elimination tournament. When their contender, Cleveland Williams, was shot by Texas highway police, the WBA postponed its plans until 1965. The Ali-Liston bout, scheduled for Nov. 16 in Boston, was called off 70 hrs. before the bell, after Ali entered a hospital for an operation.

Mar. 21 The **NCAA basketball championship** was won by UCLA, which defeated Duke U. 98-83. The victory climaxed a perfect season for UCLA, which won all 30 of its games, the first major team to have an undefeated season since 1957. Walt Hazzard and Gail Goodrich shone for the Bruins.

Apr. 11-25 The **NHL Stanley Cup** was won for the third year in a row by the Toronto Maple Leafs, who beat the Detroit Red Wings four games to three.

Apr. 12 The **Masters golf tournament** was won by Arnold Palmer for the fourth time, with a score of 276, second lowest in the history of the event.

Apr. 17 The **first woman to fly around the world solo** was Jerrie Mock, who completed her flight when she landed at Columbus, Ohio. She began the trip on Mar. 19, made 21 stops, and flew a total of 22,858.8 mi. in her single-engine plane.

Apr. 18-26 The **NBA basketball championship** was won for the sixth time in a row by the Boston Celtics, who defeated the San Francisco

	DRIVER	AVERAGE SPEED (m.p.h.)		DRIVER	AVERAGE SPEED (m.p.h.)
1911	Ray Harroun	74.59	1951	Lee Wallard	126.244
1912	Joe Dawson	78.72	1952	Troy Ruttman	128.922
1913	Jules Goux	75.93	1953	Bill Vukovich	128.740
1914	René Thomas	82.47	1954	Bill Vukovich	130.840
1915	Ralph DePalma	89.84	1955	Bob Sweikert	128.209
1916	Dario Resta	84.00	1956	Pat Flaherty	128.490
1917–18	(not held)		1957	Sam Hanks	135.601
1919	Howard Wilcox	88.05	1958	Jimmy Bryan	133.791
			1959	Rodger Ward	135.857
1920	Gaston Chevrolet	88.62			
1921	Tommy Milton	89.62	1960	Jim Rathmann	138.767
1922	Jimmy Murphy	94.48	1961	A. J. Foyt	139.130
1923	Tommy Milton	90.95	1962	Rodger Ward	140.293
1924	L.L. Corum/	98.23	1963	Parnelli Jones	143.137
	Joe Boyer		1964	A. J. Foyt	147.350
1925	Peter DePaolo	101.13	1965	Jim Clark	150.686
1926	Frank Lockhart	95.904	1966	Graham Hill	144.317
1927	George Souders	97.545	1967	A. J. Foyt	151.207
1928	Louis Meyer	99.482	1968	Bobby Unser	152.882
1929	Ray Keech	97.585	1969	Mario Andretti	156.867
1930	Billy Arnold	100.448	1970	Al Unser	155.749
1931	Louis Schneider	96.629	1971	Al Unser	157.735
1932	Fred Frame	104.144	1972	Mark Donohue	162.962
1933	Louis Meyer	104.162	1973	Gordon Johncock	159.036
1934	Bill Cummings	104.863	1974	Johnny Rutherford	158.589
1935	Kelly Petillo	106.240	1975	Bobby Unser	149.213
1936	Louis Meyer	109.069	1976	Johnny Rutherford	148.725
1937	Wilbur Shaw	113.580	1977	A. J. Foyt	161.331
1938	Floyd Roberts	117.200	1978	Al Unser	161.363
1939	Wilbur Shaw	115.035	1979	Rick Mears	158.889
1940	Wilbur Shaw	114.277	1980	Johnny Rutherford	142.862
1941	Floyd Davis/	115.117	1981	Bobby Unser	139.029
	Mauri Rose		1982	Gordon Johncock	162.029
1942–45	(not held)		1983	Tom Sneva	162.117
1946	George Robson	114.820	1984	Rick Mears	162.962
1947	Mauri Rose	116.338	1985	Danny Sullivan	152.982
1948	Mauri Rose	119.814	1986	Bobby Rahal	170.722
1949	Bill Holland	121.327	1987	Al Unser	162.175
1950	Johnnie Parsons	124.002			

Warriors four games to one. The Celtics had an easy time of it.

Apr. 20 The **Boston Marathon** was won for the second time in a row by Aurele Vandendries-sche of Belgium, with a time of 2 hrs., 19 min., 59 sec.

May 2 The 90th annual **Kentucky Derby** was won by Northern Dancer, with a time of 2:00. The jockey was Bill Hartack.

May 16 The 89th annual **Preakness Stakes** was won by Northern Dancer, with a time of 1:56⅘. The jockey was Bill Hartack.

May 30   The 48th annual **Indianapolis 500** auto race was won by A. J. Foyt, completing the course in 3 hrs., 23 min., 35.83 sec., at an average speed of 147.350 mph.

May 31   In the **longest baseball game** ever played, the San Francisco Giants beat the New York Mets 8-6 after 7 hrs., 23 min. of the second game of a double header. The end came in the 23rd inning, matching the fourth-longest game in innings played.

June 6   The 96th annual **Belmont Stakes** was won by Quadrangle, with a time of 2:28⅖. The jockey was Manuel Ycaza. A new world record for bets placed in a single day was set, as fans poured $5,834,896 into the mutuel machines on nine races at Aqueduct Race Track.

June 20   The **U.S. Open golf tournament** was won by Ken Venturi, who beat Tommy Jacobs by two strokes. Venturi's final two rounds of 66 and 70 on the final day in suffocating heat at the Congressional Club, Washington, D.C., were among the most dramatic ever.

June 21   A **perfect baseball game,** the first in a regular season since 1922, was pitched by Jim Bunning of the Philadelphia Phillies in a 6-0 victory over the New York Mets at Shea Stadium, Queens, New York.

July 7   The **baseball all-star game** was won by the National League, which defeated the American League 7-4.

July 12   The **U.S. Women's Open golf tournament** was won for the fourth and final time by Mickey Wright, who beat Ruth Jessen by two strokes in a playoff. Wright had dominated women's golf for seven years.

July 16   **Little League baseball,** by an act of Congress signed by Pres. Lyndon B. Johnson on this day, was granted a Congressional Charter of Federal Incorporation, the only U.S. sport to be so recognized.

July 19   The **PGA golf tournament** was won by Bobby Nichols, who beat both Arnold Palmer and Jack Nicklaus by three strokes at the Columbus (Ohio) Country Club.

July 27   The **Baseball Hall of Fame** inducted seven new members: Luke Appling, Red Faber, Burleigh Grimes, Miller Huggins, Tim Keefe, Heinie Manush, and John Montgomery Ward.

July 31   The **first glider flight of more than 600 mi.** in the U.S. was achieved by Alvin Parker, who soared 647.17 mi. in a Sisu sailplane.

Aug. 13   The **New York Yankees were bought** by

That feller runs splendid but he needs help at the plate, which coming from the country chasing rabbits all winter give him strong legs, although he broke one falling out of a tree, which shows you can't tell, and when a curve ball comes he waves at it and if pitchers don't throw curves you have no pitching staff, so how is a manager going to know whether to tell boys to fall out of trees and break legs so he can run fast even if he can't hit a curve ball?

Casey Stengel

the Columbia Broadcasting System. CBS obtained an 80% interest in the club with an option to acquire the remaining 20% within five years.

Sept. 2   The 39th annual **Hambletonian Stakes** was won by Ayres in two heats, setting a new race record of 1:56⅘ in the first heat.

Sept. 12   In the **New Hampshire Sweepstakes,** the first legal sweepstakes in U.S. horse racing history, six persons won the first prize of $100,000 at Rockingham Park in Salem, N.H.

Sept. 13   The **U.S. Lawn Tennis Association singles championships** were won by Roy Emerson of Australia over teammate Fred Stolle in the men's division and by Maria Bueno of Brazil in the women's division.

Sept. 15-21   The **America's Cup,** yachting's oldest trophy, was successfully defended by the U.S racer *Constellation,* which easily beat the British challenger *Sovereign* in four races off Newport, R.I.

Sept. 25-28   For the first time in the history of **Davis Cup** tennis competition, the international challenge round was played on clay courts. The play took place in Cleveland, Ohio, and Roy Emerson and Fred Stolle of Australia beat the U.S. defenders, Chuck McKinley and Dennis Ralston, three matches to two.

Oct. 4   The **LPGA golf tournament** was won by Mary Mills, who beat Mickey Wright by two strokes at Las Vegas, Nev.

Oct. 7-15   The 61st annual **World Series** was won by the St. Louis Cardinals (NL), defeating the New York Yankees (AL) four games to three. Catcher Tim McCarver hit .478 for the Cardinals, while Bob Gibson, the Cardinal pitcher, struck out 31 batters in three games, a Series record. He had just enough left to stave off a Yankee rally late in game seven. Mickey Mantle of the Yankees hit his 16th Series homer, breaking the record held by Babe Ruth.

Oct. 10-24 At the **Summer Olympics** in Tokyo, Japan, the U.S. won the unofficial team championship with 36 gold medals. Don Schollander became the first swimmer to win four gold medals, taking first place in the 100- and 400-m. freestyle and helping win the 400- and 800-m. freestyle relays. Warren Jay Cowley won the 400-m. hurdles in 49.6 sec. In winning the pole vault at 16 ft., 8¾ in., Fred Hansen became the first to exceed 16 ft. at the Olympics. In the women's events, Wyomia Tyus won the 100-m. dash with a time of 11.4 sec. and won the event again in 1968 in 11 sec. flat.

Nov. 1 Setting a new **lifetime pro football rushing record,** Jim Brown became the first player to rush for more than 10,000 yards. Playing for the Cleveland Browns, the running back ended the season with a total of 10,135 yards. In 1965, the last season of Brown's nine-year professional football career, he rushed for a total of 12,312 yards.

Nov. 13 **Bob Pettit,** forward for the St. Louis Hawks, became the first basketball player in the NBA to score 20,000 points in a career. By the time Pettit retired, he had scored 20,880 points in 11 seasons.

Nov. 24 The **Heisman Trophy** for outstanding college football player of 1964 was voted to Notre Dame quarterback John Huarte.

Dec. 26 The **AFL championship** was won by the Buffalo Bills, who defeated the San Diego Chargers 20-7.

Dec. 27 The **NFL championship** was won by the Cleveland Browns, who swept the Baltimore Colts 27-0.

1965

Swimming's International Hall of Fame was founded at Fort Lauderdale, Fla., with funds raised by private citizens. On Dec. 27 the city formally dedicated a ten-lane public pool. The building that would house the hall of fame, to be completed in 1966, was to stand adjacent to the city pool.

Professional surfing began with the holding of the Tom Morey Noseriding Contest in Ventura, Calif. This was the first surfing contest to offer cash prizes.

Jan. 1 In **college football bowl games,** the results were Arkansas 10, Nebraska 7 in the Cotton Bowl; Texas 21, Alabama 17 in the Orange Bowl; Michigan 34, Oregon State 7 in the Rose Bowl; and Louisiana State 13, Syracuse 10 in the Sugar Bowl. This season the AP and UPI polls chose Alabama as national college football champion of 1964.

Feb. 13 **U.S. figure skating championships** were won at Lake Placid, N.Y., by Peggy Fleming, 16, in the women's singles; Gary Visconti, men's singles; Vivian and Ronald Joseph, pairs; and Kristin Fortune and Dennis Sveum, dance.

Feb. 15-16 At the **Westminster Kennel Club** dog show, Ch. Carmichael's Fanfare, a Scottish terrier owned by Mr. and Mrs. Charles C. Stalter, took best-in-show.

Mar. 15-18 The **Scotch Cup,** emblematic of the world curling championship, was won by the U.S. for the first time. At Perth, Scotland, the Bud Somerville rink of Superior, Wis., defeated the Canadians, who had won for six consecutive years previously. The U.S. repeated its victory in 1974 and 1978.

Mar. 19 **Bill Bradley,** Princeton basketball star, captivated sports fans by leading his otherwise undistinguished team to within two victories of the NCAA championship. Princeton was defeated in the semifinals by UCLA, 108-89. Bradley accepted and fulfilled a Rhodes Scholarship before signing a lucrative contract with the New York Knicks.

Mar. 20 The **NCAA basketball championship** was won by UCLA, which defeated Michigan 91-80. Gail Goodrich scored 42 points for UCLA.

People have started asking me if we've got any talent on this team. Well, I tell them, if we start winning games we'll have talent. But since we're getting beat to death, no, we don't.

Joe Namath

Apr. 9 The **Houston Astrodome,** largest indoor arena in the world, opened in Houston, Tex., with an exhibition game between the Houston Astros and the New York Yankees. Pres. Lyndon B. Johnson was among the honored guests. Costing $20,500,000, the stadium covers 9.5 acres, with an inside diameter of 642 ft. and a height of 208 ft. For baseball, the Astrodome seats 45,000; for boxing, 66,000.

Apr. 11 The **Masters golf tournament** was won by Jack Nicklaus by nine strokes, a tournament record. His score of 271 bested Ben Hogan's 1953 record by three strokes.

Apr. 17-May 1 The **NHL Stanley Cup** was won by the Montreal Canadiens, who defeated the Chicago Black Hawks four games to three.

Apr. 18-25 The **NBA basketball championship** was won for the seventh straight year by the Boston Celtics, who defeated the Los Angeles Lakers four games to one. It was another easy one for Boston, despite high scoring by Lakers star Jerry West.

Apr. 19 The 69th **Boston Marathon** was won by Morio Shigematsu of Japan with a time of 2 hrs., 16 min., 33 sec.

May 1 The 91st annual **Kentucky Derby** was won by Lucky Debonair, with a time of 2:01⅕. The jockey was Willie Shoemaker.

May 15 The 90th annual **Preakness Stakes** was won by Tom Rolfe, with a time of 1:56⅕. The jockey was Ron Turcotte.

May 25 The **world heavyweight boxing championship** was successfully defended by Muhammad Ali, who knocked out Sonny Liston about a minute into the first round of a rematch. Few fans saw the punch that floored Liston. Despite Ali's win, the World Boxing Association maintained that its heavyweight title belonged to Ernie Terrell, who had outpointed Eddie Machen on Mar. 5. Ali retained the National Boxing Association title.

May 31 The 49th annual **Indianapolis 500** auto race was won by Jim Clark of Scotland, completing the course in 3 hrs., 19 min., 5.34 sec., at a record average speed of 150.686 mph.

June 5 The 97th annual **Belmont Stakes** was won by Hail to All, with a time of 2:28⅖. The jockey was Johnny Sellers.

June 21 At St. Louis, Mo., the **U.S. Open golf tournament** was won by Gary Player of South Africa, when he defeated Kel Nagle by three strokes in a playoff. Player became the third man to win golf's four top pro titles. Only Gene Sarazen and Ben Hogan had previously taken the U.S. and British Opens, the Masters, and the PGA.

July 4 The **U.S. Women's Open golf tournament** was won by Carol Mann by two strokes over Kathy Cornelius at Northfield, N.J.

July 13 The **baseball all-star game** was won by the National League, which beat the American League 6-5.

July 26 The **Baseball Hall of Fame** inducted James F. "Pud" Galvin. During Galvin's 16-year career as a pitcher, from 1875 to 1892, he won 365 games.

Aug. 15 The **PGA golf tournament** was won by Dave Marr over Jack Nicklaus and Billy Casper at Ligonier, Pa.

Aug. 30 Mets manager **Casey Stengel announced his retirement** after 55 years in baseball. On July 25, just a few days before his 75th birthday, he had broken his hip in a fall. Mets coach Wes Westrum became interim manager and at season's end was given the job of manager.

Sept. 1 The 40th running of the **Hambletonian Stakes** was won in the fourth heat by Egyptian Candor, with a time of 2:10⅕. The driver was Del Cameron.

Sept. 9 A **perfect baseball game** was pitched by Sandy Koufax of the Los Angeles Dodgers (NL) against the Chicago Cubs. Koufax fanned 14 batters in the 1-0 victory. It was the fourth no-hit game of his career, a major league record, and only the eighth perfect game in baseball history.

Sept. 12 The **U.S. Lawn Tennis Association singles championships** were won by Manuel Santana of Spain over Cliff Drysdale of South Africa in the men's division and by Margaret Smith of Australia in the women's division.

Sept. 26 The **LPGA golf tournament** was won by Sandra Haynie, who beat C. A. Creed by one stroke at Las Vegas, Nev.

Oct. 6-14 The 62nd annual **World Series** was won by the Los Angeles Dodgers (NL), defeating the Minnesota Twins (AL) four games to three. In the seventh game, on Oct. 14, Sandy Koufax pitched his second Series shutout, blanking the Twins 2-0. He pitched his first shutout in game five.

Nov. 1 The **first women's softball world championship,** held in Melbourne, Australia, was

NATIONAL INVITATION TOURNAMENT WINNERS

1938	Temple	1963	Providence
1939	Long Island University	1964	Bradley
1940	Colorado	1965	St. John's (New York City)
1941	Long Island University	1966	Brigham Young
1942	West Virginia	1967	Southern Illinois
1943	St. John's (New York City)	1968	Dayton
1944	St. John's (New York City)	1969	Temple
1945	DePaul	1970	Marquette
1946	Kentucky	1971	North Carolina
1947	Utah	1972	Maryland
1948	St. Louis	1973	Virginia Tech
1949	San Francisco	1974	Purdue
1950	CCNY	1975	Princeton
1951	Brigham Young	1976	Kentucky
1952	La Salle	1977	St. Bonaventure
1953	Seton Hall	1978	Texas
1954	Holy Cross	1979	Indiana
1955	Duquesne	1980	Virginia
1956	Louisville	1981	Tulsa
1957	Bradley	1982	Bradley
1958	Xavier (Cincinnati)	1983	Fresno State
1959	St. John's (New York City)	1984	Michigan
1960	Bradley	1985	UCLA
1961	Providence	1986	Ohio State
1962	Dayton	1987	Southern Mississippi

won by the Australian team, which defeated the favored American Raybestos Brakettes 1-0 in the final.

Nov. 5 A **women's auto speed record** was set by Margaret Laneive Breedlove, who drove the car of her speed-king husband, Craig Breedlove, 308.56 mph on the Bonneville Salt Flats, Utah.

Nov. 17 William D. Eckert, 56, a retired Air Force general, was named **commissioner of baseball** by the major league club owners. Eckert, a surprise choice, succeeded retiring commissioner Ford C. Frick.

Nov. 22 **Muhammad Ali** stopped ex-champ Floyd Patterson in the 12th round of what had been billed as a fight for the heavyweight championship. Although the bout had been set up by Jim Deskin, new head of the World Boxing Association, that organization afterward classified Ali as merely the top contender for the crown the WBA had given to Ernie Terrell on Mar. 5.

Nov. 23 The **Heisman Trophy** for outstanding college football player of 1965 was voted to USC halfback Mike Garrett.

Dec. 26 The **AFL football championship** was won by the Buffalo Bills, who defeated the San Diego Chargers 23-0.

Dec. 26 In an **NFL Western Conference playoff,** the Green Bay Packers defeated the Baltimore Colts 13-10 in sudden death overtime. The Packers went on to play the Cleveland Browns for the league title on Jan. 2, 1966.

1966

An **electronic timing device** was used for the first time at an NCAA swimming championship, held this year at the Air Force Academy at Colorado Springs, Colo.

The National League franchise of the **Milwaukee**

Braves baseball team was transferred to Atlanta, Ga.

Jan. 1 In **college football bowl games,** the results were Louisiana State 14, Arkansas 7 in the Cotton Bowl; Alabama 39, Nebraska 28 in the Orange Bowl; UCLA 14, Michigan State 12 in the Rose Bowl; and Missouri 20, Florida 18 in the Sugar Bowl. This season the AP poll chose Alabama as national collegiate champion of 1965; the UPI poll selected Michigan State.

Jan. 2 The 1965 **NFL championship** was won by the Green Bay Packers, who defeated the Cleveland Browns 23-12.

Jan. 29 **U.S. figure skating championships** were won by Peggy Fleming, women's singles; Scott Allen, men's singles; Cynthia and Ronald Kauffman, pairs; and Kristin Fortune and Dennis Sveum, dance.

Feb. 15 At the **Westminster Kennel Club** dog show, Ch. Zeloy Mooremaides, a wire fox terrier owned by Marion G. Bunker, took best-in-show.

Feb. 27 At the **world figure skating championships** in Davos, Switzerland, Peggy Fleming won the women's singles title. She would go on to win a total of three consecutive world figure skating titles.

Mar. 5 A new indoor **record pole vault** of 17 ft., ¼ in. was set by Bob Seagren in Albuquerque, N.Mex.

Mar. 12 **Bobby Hull** of the Chicago Black Hawks scored his 51st hockey goal of the season against the New York Rangers in Chicago. Hull thus became the first player to score more than 50 in a season; he ultimately ran the total to 54.

Mar. 12 Jockey **Johnny Longden,** 59, retired after 40 years of racing and after riding his 6032nd winner—the most ever for a jockey—in the San Juan Capistrano Handicap at Santa Anita, Calif.

Mar. 19 The **NCAA basketball championship** was won by Texas Western College, now the U.

Open the window, Aunt Minnie—here it comes.

Pittsburgh Pirates sportscaster Rosey Rosewell, whenever a Pirate hit a home run in Forbes Field

of Texas, El Paso, which defeated Kentucky 72-65.

Apr. 11 The **Masters golf tournament** was won for the third time by Jack Nicklaus, who became the first golfer to win two years in a row. To do it, he shot a 70 in a playoff with Tommy Jacobs and Gay Brewer. Jacobs had a 72, Brewer a 78.

Apr. 17-28 The **NBA basketball championship** was won by the Boston Celtics, who beat the Los Angeles Lakers four games to three, thus enabling coach Red Auerbach to retire with his eighth successive championship. On Apr. 18, Bill Russell, Celtic center, was named to succeed Auerbach as the Celtics' coach. Auerbach became the team's general manager, and Russell became the first black to coach a major U.S. sports team.

Apr. 19 The 70th **Boston Marathon** was won by Kenji Kimihara of Japan with a time of 2 hrs., 17 min., 11 sec. Among the competitors was Roberta Gibb Bingay, the first woman ever to run in this event. She finished well ahead of about half the men.

Apr. 24-May 5 The **NHL Stanley Cup** was won by the Montreal Canadiens, who defeated the Detroit Red Wings four games to two for their second consecutive NHL championship.

May 7 The 92nd annual **Kentucky Derby** was won by Kauai King, with a time of 2:02. The jockey was Donald Brumfield.

May 21 The 91st annual **Preakness Stakes** was won by Kauai King, with a time of 1:55⅖. The jockey was Donald Brumfield.

May 30 At the 50th annual **Indianapolis 500** auto race, nearly half of the 33 starters were involved in a first-lap crash, but only one driver was hurt. Graham Hill led the six finishers, completing the course in 3 hrs., 27 min., 52.53 sec., for an average speed of 144.317 mph.

June 4 The 98th annual **Belmont Stakes** was won by Amberoid, with a time of 2:29⅗. The jockey was Bill Boland.

June 8 A **merger** of the National and American football leagues, effective in 1970, was announced. The move provided for a common draft of college players in 1967, putting an end to costly competition between the leagues. It also set up a Super Bowl game between the league champions in the 1966-1967 season.

June 20 The **U.S. Open golf tournament,** at the Olympic Club, San Francisco, was won by Billy

Casper, who beat Arnold Palmer in a playoff, 69-73.

June 25 **Buckpasser** set a new world record of 1:32⅗ for the mile in winning the Arlington Classic. The horse also became the first 3-year-old to win more than $1,000,000. Kauai King, the Derby and Preakness winner this year, went lame in the race and was retired from racing three days later.

July 2 At the **Wimbledon** tennis championships in England, Billie Jean King beat Maria Bueno of Brazil to win the women's singles championship.

July 2-3 The **world decathlon record** of 8089 points, held by C. K. Yang, was bested twice at Salina, Kans., by Russ Hodge (8130) and Bill Toomey (8234).

July 3 The **U.S. Women's Open golf tournament** was won by Sandra Spuzich, who edged Carol Mann by one stroke at Minneapolis.

July 9 **Jack Nicklaus** won the British Open with a 282 at Muirfield. He thereby joined Gene Sara-

zen, Ben Hogan, and Gary Player as the only men to have won the four major golf championships of the world. The other events are the PGA, the Masters, and the U.S. Open.

July 12 The **baseball all-star game** was won by the National League, which defeated the American League 2-1 in the tenth inning.

July 16-17 At a long-awaited **five-nation swimming meet** in Moscow, the U.S. won 11 of the 17 events. The USSR won the other six.

July 17 A new **record for the mile run,** 3:51.3, was set by Jim Ryun, a 19-year-old college freshman, trimming 2.3 sec. from the world record.

July 23 A new outdoor **pole vault record** of 17 ft., 6¼ in. was set by John Pennel of Los Angeles.

July 24 The **PGA golf tournament** was won by Al Geiberger with a 280 at the Firestone Country Club, Akron, Ohio.

July 25 The **Baseball Hall of Fame** inducted two new members: Casey Stengel, who managed the New York Yankees to ten American League

Basketball
NATIONAL COLLEGIATE ATHLETIC ASSOCIATION TOURNAMENT WINNERS

Year	Winner	Year	Winner
1939	Oregon	1964	UCLA
1940	Indiana	1965	UCLA
1941	Wisconsin	1966	Texas Western
1942	Stanford	1967	UCLA
1943	Wyoming	1968	UCLA
1944	Utah	1969	UCLA
1945	Oklahoma A&M	1970	UCLA
1946	Oklahoma A&M	1971	UCLA
1947	Holy Cross	1972	UCLA
1948	Kentucky	1973	UCLA
1949	Kentucky	1974	North Carolina State
1950	CCNY	1975	UCLA
1951	Kentucky	1976	Indiana
1952	Kansas	1977	Marquette
1953	Indiana	1978	Kentucky
1954	La Salle	1979	Michigan State
1955	San Francisco	1980	Louisville
1956	San Francisco	1981	Indiana
1957	North Carolina	1982	North Carolina
1958	Kentucky	1983	North Carolina State
1959	California	1984	Georgetown
1960	Ohio State	1985	Villanova
1961	Cincinnati	1986	Louisville
1962	Cincinnati	1987	Indiana
1963	Loyola (Illinois)		

pennants and seven World Series wins from 1949 to 1960, and Ted Williams, former outfielder for the Boston Red Sox and six-time American League batting champion.

Aug. 23 The newly formed **North American Soccer League** (NASL) elected James P. McGuire as its president. The league increased the number of its franchises to 11 teams and planned its first games for 1968.

Aug. 31 The 41st annual **Hambletonian Stakes** was won in two heats by Kerry Way. The driver was Frank Ervin.

Sept. 11 The **U.S. Lawn Tennis Association singles championships** were won by Fred Stolle of Australia over teammate John Newcombe in the men's division. Maria Bueno of Brazil defeated Nancy Richey in the women's division to win her fourth U.S. title.

Sept. 25 The **LPGA golf tournament** was won by Gloria Ehret, who beat Mickey Wright by three strokes at Las Vegas, Nev.

Oct. 5-9 The 63rd annual **World Series** was won by the Baltimore Orioles (AL), who swept the Los Angeles Dodgers (NL) in four straight games, the last three being shutouts. Dave McNally, Jim Palmer, Wally Bunker, and Moe Drabowsky held Dodger hitters to a series batting average of .142. The Orioles' average was only .200.

Nov. 1 The **first men's softball world championship** was held in Mexico City. Twelve countries entered teams, and the American team won with ten straight victories.

Nov. 19 In the **collegiate football game of the year,** the undefeated teams of Michigan State and Notre Dame battled to a 10-10 tie at East Lansing, Mich.

Nov. 22 The **Heisman Trophy** for outstanding college football player of 1966 was voted to quarterback Steve Spurrier of the U. of Florida.

Nov. 27 A new **NFL scoring record** was set when the Washington Redskins defeated the New York Giants 72-41. Washington's score was the second highest ever for one team, and the combined total of 113 was the highest ever scored in a game.

Dec. 20 In an **expansion of basketball franchises,** the National Basketball Association granted a franchise to Seattle. On Jan. 11, 1967, it awarded the league's 12th franchise to San Diego.

1967

Professional soccer had two leagues in operation. The North American Soccer League, which in March was renamed the United Soccer Association (USA, 12 franchises), imported entire European teams. The National Professional Soccer League (NPSL) signed individual players in ten franchises, domestic and foreign. The Los Angeles Wolves (England's Wolverhampton Wanderers) captured the USA title on July 15, and the Oakland Clippers won the NPSL crown on Sept. 9.

Jan. 2 In **college football bowl games,** the results were Georgia 24, Southern Methodist 9 in the Cotton Bowl (Dec. 31, 1966); Florida 27, Georgia Tech 12 in the Orange Bowl; Purdue 14, Southern California 13 in the Rose Bowl; and Alabama 34, Nebraska 7 in the Sugar Bowl. This year the AP and UPI polls selected Notre Dame as national collegiate champion of 1966.

Jan. 15 The first annual **Super Bowl** was won by the Green Bay Packers (NFL), who defeated the Kansas City Chiefs (AFL) 35-10. The Packers had won the NFL championship Jan. 1 by beating the Dallas Cowboys 34-27. The same day the Chiefs won the AFL championship over the Buffalo Bills, 31-7.

Jan. 18-21 **U.S. figure skating championships** were won in Omaha, Nebr., by Peggy Fleming, women's singles; Gary Visconti, men's singles; Cynthia and Ronald Kauffman, pairs; and Lorna Dyer and John Carrell, dance.

Feb. 2 The **American Basketball Association** (ABA) began operations, with George Mikan as commissioner. The league had two divisions: East, comprising New York, Pittsburgh, Indianapolis, Minneapolis, and New Orleans, and West, including Dallas, Houston, Kansas City, Oakland, and Anaheim. On Mar. 6 Louisville was awarded the 11th ABA franchise. The new league failed to lure stars from the NBA.

Feb. 14 At the **Westminster Kennel Club** dog show, Ch. Bardene Bingo, a Scottish terrier owned by E. H. Stuart, took best-in-show.

Feb. 28-Mar. 4 At the **world figure skating championships** in Vienna, Austria, Peggy Fleming fell during her freestyle event but went on to win the women's singles title for the second year in a row.

Mar. 25 The **NCAA basketball championship**

was won for the third time in four years by undefeated UCLA, which beat Dayton 79-64. UCLA's center, sophomore Lew Alcindor, who later changed his name to Kareem Abdul-Jabbar, had an all-time high season field goal percentage of .667 in this, his first varsity year.

Apr. 9   The **Masters golf tournament** was won by Gay Brewer by one stroke over Bobby Nichols.

Apr. 14-24   The **NBA basketball championship** was won by the Philadelphia 76ers, who defeated the San Francisco Warriors four games to two.

Apr. 19   The 71st annual **Boston Marathon** was won by Dave McKenzie of New Zealand in a record 2 hrs., 15 min., 45 sec.

Apr. 20-May 2   The **NHL Stanley Cup** was won by the Toronto Maple Leafs, who beat the Montreal Canadiens four games to two.

May 6   The 93rd annual **Kentucky Derby** was won by Proud Clarion, with a time of 2:00³⁄₅. The jockey was Bob Ussery.

May 14   New York Yankees outfielder **Mickey Mantle,** at Yankee Stadium, hit his 500th career home run, becoming the sixth player to reach that mark.

May 20   The 92nd annual **Preakness Stakes** was won by Damascus, with a time of 1:55¹⁄₅. The jockey was Willie Shoemaker.

May 31   The 51st annual **Indianapolis 500** auto race, started on May 30 and postponed by rain after 18 laps, was won by A. J. Foyt, completing the course in 3 hrs., 18 min., 24.22 sec. at an average speed of 151.207 mph. Andy Granatelli's turbine-engine car, driven by Parnelli Jones, allowed in the race over protests by owners of piston cars, led until the final three laps, when its transmission failed.

June 3   The 99th annual **Belmont Stakes** was won by Damascus, with a time of 2:28⁴⁄₅. The jockey was Willie Shoemaker.

June 18   The **U.S. Open golf tournament** was won by Jack Nicklaus at Baltusrol Golf Club, Springfield, N.J., with a score of 275, one stroke better than the record set by Ben Hogan in 1948. Arnold Palmer finished second.

June 20   **Muhammad Ali** was given a five-year sentence and fined $10,000 for refusing to be drafted for military service. Boxing authorities had earlier stripped him of his world title, rejecting his claim to exemption as a minister of the Nation of Islam.

June 23   A new **world record for the mile** was

set by Jim Ryun, who shaved 0.2 sec. from his old record with a time of 3:51.1 in the AAU championships at Bakersfield, Calif. At the same meet, Paul Wilson cleared 17 ft. 7³⁄₄ in., a new world record for the outdoor pole vault.

July 2   The **U.S. Women's Open golf tournament** was won by Catherine Lacoste, an amateur from France, daughter of former tennis star René Lacoste, and at 22 the youngest to win the crown.

July 8   At the **Wimbledon** tennis championships in England, Billie Jean King swept the women's singles; the women's doubles, with Rosemary Casals; and the mixed doubles, with Owen Davidson of Australia. In her final singles match, King defeated Ann Haydon Jones of England.

July 9   The **LPGA golf tournament** was won by Kathy Whitworth. Her 284 was one stroke better than Shirley Englehorn's 285. The event this year was moved from Las Vegas, where it had been held for six years, to the Pleasant Valley Country Club in Sutton, Mass.

July 11   The **baseball all-star game** was won by the National League, which defeated the American League 2-1 in 15 innings, the longest all-star game yet played.

July 14   **Eddie Mathews** of the Houston Astros became the seventh player to hit 500 home runs. He had scored most of his home runs while playing for the Milwaukee Braves.

July 23-Aug. 6   At the fifth **Pan-American Games** in Winnipeg, Canada, the U.S. won the unofficial team championship, taking 120 gold medals. Ronald Owen Laird won the 20-km. walk championship. Laird did much to raise race walking standards in the U.S., winning more than 50 national titles and setting several records. In both 1967 and 1973, he took third place in the Lugano Cup 20-km. walk in Switzerland, an unusual accomplishment for a non-European race walker.

July 24   The **PGA golf tournament** was won by Don January in a playoff with Don Massengale, 69-71, at Denver, Colo.

July 24   The **Baseball Hall of Fame** inducted Branch Rickey, Red Ruffing, and Lloyd "Little Poison" Waner.

Aug. 27   In a mass parachute descent, **16 sky divers were killed** when their pilot mistook his plane's location and they fell into Lake Erie near Huron, Ohio. Two others were rescued

NATIONAL BASKETBALL ASSOCIATION
Championship Finals

	WINNER	LOSER	GAMES
1950	Minneapolis Lakers	Syracuse Nationals	4–2
1951	Rochester Royals	New York Knicks	4–3
1952	Minneapolis Lakers	New York Knicks	4–3
1953	Minneapolis Lakers	New York Knicks	4–1
1954	Minneapolis Lakers	Syracuse Nationals	4–3
1955	Syracuse Nationals	Fort Wayne Pistons	4–3
1956	Philadelphia Warriors	Fort Wayne Pistons	4–3
1957	Boston Celtics	St. Louis Hawks	4–3
1958	St. Louis Hawks	Boston Celtics	4–2
1959	Boston Celtics	Minneapolis Lakers	4–0
1960	Boston Celtics	St. Louis Hawks	4–3
1961	Boston Celtics	St. Louis Hawks	4–1
1962	Boston Celtics	Los Angeles Lakers	4–3
1963	Boston Celtics	Los Angeles Lakers	4–2
1964	Boston Celtics	San Francisco Warriors	4–1
1965	Boston Celtics	Los Angeles Lakers	4–1
1966	Boston Celtics	Los Angeles Lakers	4–3
1967	Philadelphia 76ers	San Francisco Warriors	4–2
1968	Boston Celtics	Los Angeles Lakers	4–2
1969	Boston Celtics	Los Angeles Lakers	4–3
1970	New York Knicks	Los Angeles Lakers	4–3
1971	Milwaukee Bucks	Baltimore Bullets	4–0
1972	Los Angeles Lakers	New York Knicks	4–1
1973	New York Knicks	Los Angeles Lakers	4–3
1974	Boston Celtics	Milwaukee Bucks	4–3
1975	Golden State Warriors	Washington Bullets	4–0
1976	Boston Celtics	Phoenix Suns	4–2
1977	Portland Trail Blazers	Philadelphia 76ers	4–2
1978	Washington Bullets	Seattle Supersonics	4–3
1979	Seattle Supersonics	Washington Bullets	4–1
1980	Los Angeles Lakers	Philadelphia 76ers	4–2
1981	Boston Celtics	Houston Rockets	4–2
1982	Los Angeles Lakers	Philadelphia 76ers	4–2
1983	Philadelphia 76ers	Los Angeles Lakers	4–0
1984	Boston Celtics	Los Angeles Lakers	4–3
1985	Los Angeles Lakers	Boston Celtics	4–2
1986	Boston Celtics	Houston Rockets	4–2
1987	Los Angeles Lakers	Boston Celtics	4–2

from the lake. The 18 had jumped from 20,000 ft. under conditions of poor visibility.

Aug. 30 The 42nd annual **Hambletonian Stakes** was won in straight heats by Speedy Streak. The driver was Adelbert "Del" Cameron.

Sept. 10 The **U.S. Lawn Tennis Association singles championships** were won by John Newcombe of Australia over Clark Graebner in the men's division and by Billie Jean King over Ann Haydon Jones of England in the women's division. King became the first woman to sweep the U.S. and British singles, doubles, and mixed doubles championships since Alice Marble's sweep in 1939.

Sept. 12-18 The **America's Cup** was successfully defended by the U.S. yacht *Intrepid,* which

Washington, first in war, first in peace, last in the American League.

Popular saying, referring to the hapless Washington Senators

swept the Australian challenger *Dame Pattie* in four straight races.

Sept. 24 Pro **football kicking records** were smashed when Jim Bakken of the St. Louis Cardinals scored seven field goals in one game.

Oct. Addition of six **new professional ice hockey teams** doubled the size of the National Hockey League. They were Los Angeles, Oakland, Minnesota, Philadelphia, Pittsburgh, and St. Louis.

Oct. 4-12 The 64th annual **World Series** was won by the St. Louis Cardinals (NL), who defeated the Boston Red Sox (AL) four games to three. The Cardinals ended Boston's impossible dream, as Red Sox fans termed it, led by Lou Brock's .414 batting average and his seven stolen bases in the series. Bob Gibson pitched three of the Cardinals' four victories.

Oct. 18 Another **baseball franchise change** was announced. Transfer of the Kansas City Athletics to Oakland, Calif., was approved by the American League. The owners also voted to expand the league to 12 teams, the two new teams to be in Kansas City, Mo., and Seattle, Wash.

Nov. 28 The **Heisman Trophy** for outstanding college football player of 1967 was voted to UCLA quarterback Gary Beban.

Dec. 14 **Wimbledon** officials defied tradition and the world's major tennis associations by accepting the principle of open tennis, allowing pros as well as amateurs to compete and offering substantial money prizes.

Dec. 31 The **NFL championship** was won by the Green Bay Packers, who defeated the Dallas Cowboys 21-17 with a touchdown scored from the 1-yard line by quarterback Bart Starr with 13 sec. remaining in the game.

Dec. 31 The **AFL championship** was won by the Oakland Raiders, who routed the Houston Oilers 40-7.

Indiana U. swimmers won the **NCAA Division I men's team championship,** the first of their six consecutive national collegiate titles.

Swimmer **Debby Meyer received the Sullivan Award** for the outstanding amateur athlete of the year.

Little League baseball extended its program by launching a Big League for boys 16 to 18.

The **Baseball Players Association,** guided by attorney Marvin Miller, opened negotiations with team owners. Over a five-year period, these discussions greatly improved players' salaries and pensions and limited the application of the reserve clause in their contracts.

New baseball franchises were awarded to the San Diego Padres and to the Montreal Expos, which became the first major league franchise outside the U.S.

Jan. 1 In **college football bowl games,** the results were Texas A&M 20, Alabama 16 in the Cotton Bowl; Oklahoma 26, Tennessee 24 in the Orange Bowl; USC 14, Indiana 3 in the Rose Bowl; and Louisiana State 20, Wyoming 13 in the Sugar Bowl. This season the AP and UPI polls chose USC as national collegiate champion of 1967.

Jan. 4-5 The two **professional soccer leagues** merged to form a 17-team North American Soccer League (NASL).

Jan. 14 **Super Bowl II** was won by the Green Bay Packers (NFL), who defeated the Oakland Raiders (AFL) 33-14 for their second Super Bowl victory. Shortly thereafter, the Packers' coach, Vince Lombardi, retired to an executive post with the team. The Packers had won the NFL title on Dec. 31, 1967, by beating the Dallas Cowboys 21-17. On the same day, the Raiders had clinched the AFL title by beating the Houston Oilers 40-7.

Jan. 19-20 **U.S. figure skating championships** were won by Peggy Fleming, women's singles; Tim Wood, men's singles; Cynthia and Ronald Kauffman, pairs; and Judy Schwomeyer and James Sladky, dance.

Jan. 22 In a **National Basketball Association expansion,** new franchises were awarded to Milwaukee in the league's eastern division, and Phoenix in the western division.

1
9
6
8

MARY LOU RETTON

b. Fairmont, W.Va., Jan. 24, 1968

Mary Lou Retton's achievements marked the appearance on the international gymnastic competition scene of a new style of athlete. Instead of the thin ballet dancer type, Retton is compact and muscular. At 3 inches under 5 feet tall and weighing 95 pounds, she has been described as a cast-iron toy truck, but she ruled women's gymnastics in the first half of the 1980s.

Retton began taking gym lessons at age 5 and at age 8 won the beginners' class state title in West Virginia. By late 1982, when Retton was 14, she was winning in international competition, for example, in the all-around in the Sanlam Cup in South Africa. In 1983, she won the American Cup and Japan's Chunichi Cup. Retton went on to win the American Cup again in 1984, when she scored 39.50 points out of a possible 40, and again in 1985.

The climax of her career was her gold medal in all-around gymnastics at the 1984 Olympics in Los Angeles. There she had a perfect vault for 10 points and then repeated the feat. She took the silver medal in one individual event and bronze medals in two others.

An outgoing bundle of energy, characterized as "not a little flower, but a little flyer," Retton was the first gymnast to be elected to the U.S. Olympic Hall of Fame.

Feb. 6-18 At the 1968 **Winter Olympics** in Grenoble, France, the unofficial team championship was won by Norway. The U.S. won only one gold medal, that taken by figure skater Peggy Fleming.

Feb. 13 At the **Westminster Kennel Club** dog show, Ch. Stingray of Derrybah, a Lakeland terrier owned by Mr. and Mrs. James A. Farrell, Jr., took best-in-show.

Mar. 2 At the **world figure skating championships** in Geneva, Switzerland, the women's singles title was won for the third straight year by Peggy Fleming. The 19-year-old from Colorado Springs, Colo., then announced her retirement from competitive skating.

Mar. 4 Joe Frazier was awarded the **world heavyweight boxing championship** by Illinois, Maine, Massachusetts, New York, Pennsylvania, and Texas after he knocked out Buster Mathis in the tenth round of a fight in New York City. Muhammad Ali had previously been stripped of the title.

Mar. 23 The **NCAA basketball championship** was won by UCLA, which defeated North Carolina 78-55. Lew Alcindor (Kareem Abdul-Jabbar) starred for UCLA, scoring 34 points.

Mar. 30 The **distinction between amateurs and professionals** in national tennis competition was abolished by the International Lawn Tennis Association and the U.S. Lawn Tennis Association, which bowed to the pressure of players and the public.

Apr. The first sanctioned **tennis tournament open to amateurs and professionals** was held at Bournemouth, England.

Apr. 14 The **Masters golf tournament** was won by Bob Goalby after the tournament leader, Roberto de Vicenzo of Argentina, was penalized for having signed an incorrect scorecard.

Apr. 18-May 4 The **first ABA basketball championship** was won by the Pittsburgh Pipers, who beat the New Orleans Buccaneers four games to three.

Apr. 19 The 72nd annual **Boston Marathon** was won by Ambrose Burfoot, with a time of 2 hrs., 22 min., 17 sec. Burfoot was the first U.S. runner to win the race since 1957.

Apr. 21-May 2 The **NBA basketball championship** was won by the Boston Celtics, who defeated the Los Angeles Lakers four games to two.

Apr. 27 The **world heavyweight boxing championship** was won by Jimmy Ellis in a 15-round decision over Jerry Quarry in Oakland, Calif. The bout was the final match in an eight-man elimination tournament to fill Muhammad Ali's place and was recognized by the World Boxing Association.

May 4 The 94th annual **Kentucky Derby** was won by Dancer's Image, with a time of 2:02⅕. The jockey was Bob Ussery. Three days later Dancer's Image was disqualified when traces of a pain-killing drug were found in tests, and Forward Pass, ridden by Ismael Valenzuela, was declared the winner. This was the first recalled race in Derby history. Peter Fuller, owner of Dancer's Image, challenged the recall. Finally, on Dec. 23, the Kentucky Racing Commission ruled that Dancer's Image had won the race but not the purse.

230

May 5-11 The **NHL Stanley Cup** was won by the Montreal Canadiens, who swept the St. Louis Blues in four straight games.

May 8 A **perfect baseball game** was pitched by Jim "Catfish" Hunter of the Oakland Athletics, in leading his team to a 4-0 victory over the Minnesota Twins. This was the first American League perfect game since 1922. The Oakland team had transferred from Kansas City at the end of the 1967 season.

May 18 The 93rd annual **Preakness Stakes** was won by Forward Pass, with a time of 1:56⅘. The jockey was Ismael Valenzuela.

May 27 **George Halas,** a leading figure in the National Football League since the 1920s and owner of the Chicago Bears, retired as coach of the Bears.

May 30 The 52nd annual **Indianapolis 500** auto race was won by Bobby Unser, who completed the course in 3 hrs., 16 min., 13.76 sec. at a new record average speed of 152.882 mph.

June 1 The 100th annual **Belmont Stakes** was won by Stage Door Johnny, setting a new track record of 2:27⅕. The jockey was Heliodoro Gustines.

June 8 **Don Drysdale** of the Los Angeles Dodgers set a new record for consecutive scoreless innings pitched. His 58⅔ innings surpassed the 56-inning record set in 1913 by Walter Johnson. Drysdale's new record went into the books as 58 innings when the Baseball Writers Association decided to determine records on the basis of full innings.

June 16 The **U.S. Open golf tournament,** held at Rochester, N.Y., was won by Lee Trevino, who beat Jack Nicklaus by four strokes and became the first person in the tournament's history to play all four rounds under par.

Hockey
STANLEY CUP WINNERS 1926–1987

1926	Montreal Maroons	1957	Montreal Canadiens
1927	Ottawa Senators	1958	Montreal Canadiens
1928	New York Rangers	1959	Montreal Canadiens
1929	Boston Bruins	1960	Montreal Canadiens
1930	Montreal Canadiens	1961	Chicago Black Hawks
1931	Montreal Canadiens	1962	Toronto Maple Leafs
1932	Toronto Maple Leafs	1963	Toronto Maple Leafs
1933	New York Rangers	1964	Toronto Maple Leafs
1934	Chicago Black Hawks	1965	Montreal Canadiens
1935	Montreal Maroons	1966	Montreal Canadiens
1936	Detroit Red Wings	1967	Toronto Maple Leafs
1937	Detroit Red Wings	1968	Montreal Canadiens
1938	Chicago Black Hawks	1969	Montreal Canadiens
1939	Boston Bruins	1970	Boston Bruins
1940	New York Rangers	1971	Montreal Canadiens
1941	Boston Bruins	1972	Boston Bruins
1942	Toronto Maple Leafs	1973	Montreal Canadiens
1943	Detroit Red Wings	1974	Philadelphia Flyers
1944	Montreal Canadiens	1975	Philadelphia Flyers
1945	Toronto Maple Leafs	1976	Montreal Canadiens
1946	Montreal Canadiens	1977	Montreal Canadiens
1947	Toronto Maple Leafs	1978	Montreal Canadiens
1948	Toronto Maple Leafs	1979	Montreal Canadiens
1949	Toronto Maple Leafs	1980	New York Islanders
1950	Detroit Red Wings	1981	New York Islanders
1951	Toronto Maple Leafs	1982	New York Islanders
1952	Detroit Red Wings	1983	New York Islanders
1953	Montreal Canadiens	1984	Edmonton Oilers
1954	Detroit Red Wings	1985	Edmonton Oilers
1955	Detroit Red Wings	1986	Montreal Canadiens
1956	Montreal Canadiens	1987	Edmonton Oilers

June 24 The **LPGA golf tournament** was won by Sandra Post of Canada, who beat Kathy Whitworth in a playoff to become the first non-U.S. player and the first rookie on the LPGA tour to win the event, held at the Pleasant Valley Country Club, Sutton, Mass.

July 5 After a contract impasse over salary, **Wilt Chamberlain was traded** by the Philadelphia 76ers to the Los Angeles Lakers for three players and cash.

July 6 At the **Wimbledon** tennis championships in England, Billie Jean King won the women's singles title for the third straight year, defeating Judy Tegart of Australia. King and Rosemary Casals won the women's doubles title for the second year running.

July 7 The **U.S. Women's Open golf tournament** was won by Susie Maxwell Berning. Mickey Wright was runner-up at Moslem Springs, Pa.

July 9 The **baseball all-star game** was won by the National League, which beat the American League 1-0.

July 21 The **PGA golf tournament** was won by Julius Boros, whose 281 beat Arnold Palmer and Bob Charles by one stroke at San Antonio, Tex.

July 22 The **Baseball Hall of Fame** inducted three new members, all former outfielders: Kiki Cuyler, Goose Goslin, and Joe Medwick.

July 27-Aug. 6 Horseshoe pitcher **Elmer Hohl** set two world records and tied another at the horseshoe world championship at Keene, N.H. He scored 572 points in 200 shoes, just 28 shy of perfection; 88.2% for a complete tournament; and a perfect game, 30 ringers in 30 shoes. The only previous perfect game, 44 ringers in 44 shoes, in world championship play was pitched by Guy Zimmerman in 1948.

Aug. 24 A new **horse racing record** for the mile was set by Dr. Fager, who ran the distance in 1:32⅕ at Arlington Park in Arlington, Ill. This year Dr. Fager was voted horse of the year and then was retired to stud.

Aug. 25 The 43rd annual **Hambletonian Stakes** was won in two heats by Nevele Pride, driven by Stanley Dancer.

Sept. 9 The **first U.S. Open tennis championships** were won by Arthur Ashe over Tom Okker of the Netherlands in the men's singles division and by Virginia Wade of England (Sept.

8) in an upset over Billie Jean King in the women's singles division.

Sept. 28 The **first North American Soccer League (NASL) championship** was won by the Atlanta Chiefs, who beat the San Diego Toros 3-0. The first game of the two-game total-goal playoff championship, played on Sept. 21, had ended in a scoreless tie.

Oct. 2-10 The 65th annual **World Series** was won for the first time since 1945 by the Detroit Tigers (AL), who beat the St. Louis Cardinals (NL) four games to three. In the first game, Bob Gibson struck out seventeen Tigers to break the record of fifteen, held by Sandy Koufax. It was the sixth straight series victory for Gibson, tying the record held by Lefty Gomez and Red Ruffing. Tiger pitcher Mickey Lolich pitched and won three complete games, beating Bob Gibson in game seven, 4-1.

Oct. 12-27 At the **Summer Olympics** in Mexico City, the U.S. won 45 gold medals and took first place in the unofficial team standings. Despite the altitude, many records were broken, and spectacular performances were turned in by Bob Beamon, who broke the world broad jump record by 21 in. with a jump of 29 ft., 2½ in., and Dick Fosbury, who won the high jump at 7 ft., 4½ in., going over the bar backward. Al Oerter of the U.S. won the discus throw for the fourth time, having also won in the three previous Olympics. He was the only athlete ever to win the gold medal four times in a row in the same event. On Oct. 18 two U.S. track stars, Tommy Smith and John Carlos, were suspended from competition after giving the black power salute, a clenched fist raised high over the head, at an awards ceremony. Smith and Carlos had won the gold and bronze medals for the 200-m. dash.

Nov. 17 In what became known as the *Heidi game,* a critical football game between the New York Jets and the Oakland Raiders televised on NBC, the network cut off the last minute of the game to broadcast a production of a children's program, *Heidi.* Oakland, behind at the time, scored twice in 9 sec. to win 43-32.

Nov. 26 The **Heisman Trophy** for outstanding college football player of 1968 was voted to USC running back O. J. Simpson.

Dec. 3 The **Baseball Rules Committee** adopted changes designed to produce more scoring. The legal height of the pitcher's mound was

HAMBLETONIAN WINNERS

	HORSE	DRIVER		HORSE	DRIVER
1926	Guy McKinney	N. Ray	1957	Hickory Smoke	J. Simpson, Sr.
1927	Iosola's Worthy	M. Childs	1958	Emily's Pride	F. Nipe
1928	Spencer	W. Lessee	1959	Diller Hanover	F. Ervin
1929	Walter Dear	W. Cox	1960	Blaze Hanover	J. O'Brien
1930	Hanover's Bertha	T. Berry	1961	Harlan Dean	J. Arthur
1931	Calumet Butler	R. McMahon	1962	A.C.'s Viking	S. Russell
1932	The Marchioness	W. Caton	1963	Speedy Scot	R. Baldwin
1933	Mary Reynolds	B. White	1964	Ayres	J. Simpson, Sr.
1934	Lord Jim	H. Parshall	1965	Egyptian Candor	A. Cameron
1935	Greyhound	S. Palin	1966	Kerry Way	F. Ervin
1936	Rosalind	B. White	1967	Speedy Streak	A. Cameron
1937	Shirley Hanover	H. Thomas	1968	Nevele Pride	S. Dancer
1938	McLin Hanover	H. Thomas	1969	Lindy's Pride	H. Beissinger
1939	Peter Astra	H. Parshall	1970	Timothy T.	J. Simpson, Jr.
1940	Spencer Scott	F. Egan	1971	Speedy Crown	H. Beissinger
1941	Bill Gallon	L. Smith	1972	Super Bowl	S. Dancer
1942	The Ambassador	B. White	1973	Flirth	R. Baldwin
1943	Volo Song	B. White	1974	Christopher T.	W. Haughton
1944	Yankee Maid	H. Thomas	1975	Bonefish	S. Dancer
1945	Titan Hanover	H. Pownall	1976	Steve Lobell	W. Haughton
1946	Chestertown	T. Berry	1977	Green Speed	W. Haughton
1947	Hoot Mon	S. Palin	1978	Speedy Somolli	H. Beissinger
1948	Demon Hanover	H. Hoyt	1979	Legend Hanover	G. Sholty
1949	Miss Tilly	F. Egan	1980	Burgomeister	W. Haughton
1950	Lusty Song	D. Miller	1981	Shiaway St. Pat	R. Remmen
1951	Mainliner	G. Crippen	1982	Speed Bowl	T. Haughton
1952	Sharp Note	B. Shively	1983	Duenna	S. Dancer
1953	Helicopter	H. Harvey	1984	Historic Free	B. Webster
1954	Newport Dream	A. Cameron	1985	Prakas	W. O'Donnell
1955	Scott Frost	J. O'Brien	1986	Nuclear Kosmos	U. Thoresen
1956	The Intruder	N. Bower	1987	Mack Lobell	J. Campbell

reduced from 15 to 10 in., and the strike zone was reduced from between the shoulders and the knees to between the tops of the knees and the armpits of the batter when taking his normal stance.

Dec. 6 Baseball commissioner **William D. Eckert was relieved** of his post at a meeting of team owners.

Dec. 26-28 In Australia, the **Davis Cup** international tennis round was won, for the first time since 1963, by the U.S., which beat Australia four matches to one. Arthur Ashe starred.

1969

Becoming the **youngest male swimmer to conquer the English Channel,** Jon Erickson of the U.S. crossed from France to England in 11 hrs., 23 min. He was 14 years old. In 1964 Leonore Modell, also 14, had become the youngest female to swim the Channel. Her time was 15 hrs., 27 min.

Elizabeth "Liz" Allan won all three events (jumping, slalom, tricks) in the three major championships of water skiing—the Nationals, the World, and the Masters. In the decade ending with her retirement in 1975, Allan dominated her sport as few other female competitors have.

The **international racquetball championship,** held in St. Louis, Mo., was won by Bud Muehleisen.

Twelve of the 17 franchises of the **North American Soccer League** were dropped for financial reasons. The NASL was kept alive by the five remaining teams.

New baseball franchises were awarded this year to the Kansas City Royals and the Seattle Pilots. The Pilots subsequently moved to Milwaukee, becoming the Milwaukee Brewers. In this same year, the 12-team major leagues formed two divisions in each league, with playoff games between division winners for the pennants and the right to play in the World Series.

Jan. 1   In **college football bowl games,** the results were Texas 36, Tennessee 13 in the Cotton Bowl; Penn State 15, Kansas 14 in the Orange Bowl; Ohio State 27, Southern California 16 in the Rose Bowl; and Arkansas 16, Georgia 2 in the Sugar Bowl. This season the AP and UPI polls chose Ohio State as national collegiate champion of 1968.

Jan. 12   **Super Bowl III** was won by the New York Jets (AFL), who defeated the Baltimore Colts (NFL) 16-7 to gain the first AFL victory. On Dec. 31, 1968, the Jets had won the AFL championship by beating the Oakland Raiders 27-23. The same day, the Colts had won the NFL title from the Cleveland Browns, 34-0.

Feb. 1-2   **U.S. figure skating championships** were won in Seattle, Wash., by Tim Wood, men's singles; Janet Lynn, women's singles; Cynthia and Ronald Kauffman, pairs (their fourth consecutive win); and Judy Schwomeyer and James Sladky, dance.

Feb. 2   At the **Westminster Kennel Club** dog show, Ch. Glamoor Good News, a Skye terrier owned by Walter F. Goodman, took best-in-show.

Feb. 4   **Bowie Kuhn** was named commissioner of Baseball pro tem by the 24 major league club owners. Kuhn, a Wall Street lawyer, was a compromise choice after a deadlock among supporters of Michael Burke and Charles S. Feeney.

Feb. 7   Diana Crump became the **first woman jockey** to race at a U.S. parimutuel track. At Hialeah, Fla., she rode her first mount to a tenth-place finish in a field of 12.

Feb. 22   The **first winning woman jockey** at a U.S. thoroughbred track was Barbara Jo Rubin, with a victory at Charles Town, W.Va.

Feb. 25   A **boycott of spring training** by baseball players was ended with the signing of a three-year pact. Club owners agreed to increase their pension contributions and to reduce eligibility for a pension to four years.

Feb. 28   At the **world figure skating championships** in Colorado Springs, Colo., Tim Wood won the men's singles title. He would win the title once more, in the 1970 championships.

Mar. 22   The **NCAA basketball championship** was won by UCLA, sparked by center Kareem Abdul-Jabbar, defeating Purdue 97-72. Still known as Lew Alcindor, Abdul-Jabbar became the first player to win the tourney's most valuable player award three years in a row.

Apr. 13   The **Masters golf tournament** was won by George Archer, one stroke ahead of Tom Weiskopf, George Knudson, and Billy Casper.

Apr. 21   The 73rd **Boston Marathon** was won by Yoshiaki Unetani of Japan with a record time of 2 hrs., 13 min., 49 sec.

Apr. 23-May 5   The **NBA basketball championship** was won by the Boston Celtics, who beat the Los Angeles Lakers four games to three. In the decisive game, the Celtics barely held off a Laker rally that brought L.A. from 103-94 to 103-102. Boston finally pulled away, to win 107-102. Following this, the Celtics' tenth victory in 11 years, player-coach Bill Russell announced his retirement as a player.

Apr. 27-May 4   The **NHL Stanley Cup** was won by the Montreal Canadiens, who swept the St. Louis Blues in four straight games.

Apr. 30-May 7   The **ABA basketball championship** was won by the Oakland Oaks, who beat the Indiana Pacers four games to one.

May 3   The 95th **Kentucky Derby** was won by Majestic Prince, with a time of 2:01⅘. The jockey was Bill Hartack.

May 10   Plans for the 1970 **pro football merger** of the AFL and NFL were completed. The new Na-

---

Prizefighting offers a profession to men who might otherwise commit murder in the street.

Norman Mailer

---

tional Football League was to have two conferences of 13 teams each. The old NFL was renamed the National Football Conference (NFC), and three of its teams (Baltimore, Cleveland, and Pittsburgh) were shifted to the new American Football Conference.

May 17 The 94th **Preakness Stakes** was won by Majestic Prince, with a time of 1:55⅗. The jockey was Bill Hartack.

May 30 The 53rd **Indianapolis 500** auto race was won by Mario Andretti, completing the 500-mile course in 3 hrs., 11 min., 14.71 sec. for a new record average speed of 156.867 mph. It was Andretti's first win in the classic race.

June 6 **Joe Namath,** quarterback of the New York Jets, announced he would retire from football rather than give up his interest in a restaurant that Commissioner Pete Rozelle said was a hangout for gamblers. On July 18 Namath reversed his decision.

June 7 The 101st **Belmont Stakes** was won by Arts and Letters, with a time of 2:28⅘. The jockey was Braulio Baeza. Majestic Prince lost its chance at the triple crown, finishing five lengths back.

June 8 In ceremonies at Yankee Stadium, star outfielder **Mickey Mantle formally retired** after 18 years with the Yankees.

June 15 The **U.S. Open golf tournament** was won by Orville Moody by a single stroke ahead of Deane Beman, Al Geiberger, and Bob Rosburg, at Houston, Tex.

June 21 A new **world pole vault record** was set by John Pennel, who cleared the bar at 17 ft., 10½ in. in a meet at Sacramento, Calif.

June 24-25 In the **longest tennis match in Wimbledon history,** Pancho Gonzales, 41, eight-time world's professional champion, defeated the much younger Charles Pasarell in a 112-game match taking 5 hr., 12 min. over two days. Gonzales had lost the first two sets on June 24 before play was postponed due to darkness. On the next day Gonzales returned to take the next three sets and score the most memorable upset of the 1969 Wimbledon games.

June 29 The **U.S. Women's Open Golf tournament** was won by Donna Caponi, whose 291 score led Peggy Wilson by a stroke at Pensacola, Fla.

July 23 The **baseball all-star game** was won for the seventh year in a row by the National League, beating the American League 9-3.

1935	Tulane 20, Temple 14
1936	Texas Christian 3, Louisiana State 2
1937	Santa Clara 21, Louisiana State 14
1938	Santa Clara 6, Louisiana State 0
1939	Texas Christian 15, Carnegie Tech 7
1940	Texas A&M 14, Tulane 13
1941	Boston College 19, Tennessee 13
1942	Fordham 2, Missouri 0
1943	Tennessee 14, Tulsa 7
1944	Georgia Tech 20, Tulsa 18
1945	Duke 29, Alabama 26
1946	Oklahoma A&M 33, St. Mary's (California) 13
1947	Georgia 20, North Carolina 10
1948	Texas 27, Alabama 7
1949	Oklahoma 14, North Carolina 6
1950	Oklahoma 35, Louisiana State 0
1951	Kentucky 13, Oklahoma 7
1952	Maryland 28, Tennessee 13
1953	Georgia Tech 24, Mississippi 7
1954	Georgia Tech 42, West Virginia 19
1955	Navy 21, Mississippi 0
1956	Georgia Tech 7, Pittsburgh 0
1957	Baylor 13, Tennessee 7
1958	Mississippi 39, Texas 7
1959	Louisiana State 7, Clemson 0
1960	Mississippi 21, Louisiana State 0
1961	Mississippi 14, Rice 6
1962	Alabama 10, Arkansas 3
1963	Mississippi 17, Arkansas 13
1964	Alabama 12, Mississippi 7
1965	Louisiana State 13, Syracuse 10
1966	Missouri 20, Florida 18
1967	Alabama 34, Nebraska 7
1968	Louisiana State 20, Wyoming 13
1969	Arkansas 16, Georgia 2
1970	Mississippi 27, Arkansas 22
1971	Tennessee 34, Air Force Academy 13
1972	Oklahoma 40, Auburn 22
1973	Oklahoma 14, Penn State 0
1974	Notre Dame 24, Alabama 23
1975	Nebraska 13, Florida 10
1976	Alabama 13, Penn State 6
1977	Pittsburgh 27, Georgia 3
1978	Alabama 35, Ohio State 6
1979	Alabama 14, Penn State 7
1980	Alabama 24, Arkansas 9
1981	Georgia 17, Notre Dame 0
1982	Pittsburgh 24, Georgia 20
1983	Penn State 27, Georgia 23
1984	Auburn 9, Michigan 7
1985	Nebraska 28, Louisiana State 10
1986	Tennessee 35, Miami 7
1987	Nebraska 30, Louisiana State 15
1988	Syracuse 16, Auburn 16

July 27 The **LPGA golf tournament** was won by Betsy Rawls by four strokes over Susie Berning and Carol Mann at Kiamesha Lake, N.Y.

July 28 The **Baseball Hall of Fame** inducted Stan Musial, Roy Campanella, Waite Hoyt, and Stan Coveleski.

Aug. 13 **Bowie Kuhn,** temporary commissioner of baseball since February, was formally appointed to that post with a seven-year contract.

Aug. 13-20 The **first world championships in field archery** were held at Valley Forge, Pa. Richard Braustetter of Creve Coeur, Ill., won the men's title, and Irma Danielson of Sweden won the women's title.

Aug. 17 The **PGA golf tournament,** at Dayton, Ohio, was won by Ray Floyd by one stroke over Gary Player. The tournament was marred by the actions of civil rights demonstrators, who harassed Gary Player on Aug. 16. The demonstrators objected to the inclusion in the tournament of a golfer from the Republic of South Africa, which refused to allow black athletes to play in tournaments in that country.

Aug. 19 **Swimmer Debby Meyer** completed her two-year assault on world records in women's freestyle events, during which she set 15 new marks from 200 to 1500 m. In the 1500 m., perhaps her strongest event, Meyer drove the record down from 18:11 to 17:19.9. At the 1968 Olympic Games she had won gold medals in races at 200, 400, and 800 m. She was the first woman swimmer to win three individual titles in one Olympic competition.

Aug. 23 A **Little League** team from Taiwan won the Little League world championship. Over the next 12 years, teams from Taiwan would win nine more Little League titles.

Aug. 27 The 44th running of the **Hambletonian Stakes** was won in two straight heats by Lindy's Pride. The driver was Howard Beissinger.

Aug. 31 A new **standardbred racing record** for the mile was set by Nevele Pride, which ran 1:54⅘ in a time trial, breaking the mile record of 1:55⅕ set by Greyhound in 1938.

Sept. The **North American Soccer League** title was won by the Kansas City Spurs, who edged the second-place Atlanta Chiefs at season's end. There were no playoffs this year.

Sept. 7-8 The **U.S. Open tennis singles championships** were won by Margaret Smith Court of Australia (Sept. 7) in the women's division and Rod Laver of Australia (Sept. 8) in the

men's division. With his victory, Laver completed the grand slam of tennis by winning the top four international championships—the Australian, French, Wimbledon, and U.S. singles titles. Laver had won the grand slam once before, in 1962.

Sept. 19-21 The **Davis Cup** was successfully defended by the U.S., defeating Rumania in five straight matches.

Sept. 22 San Francisco Giants outfielder **Willie Mays hit his 600th home run,** becoming the only player other than Babe Ruth to reach that mark.

Oct. 7 **Fourteeen blacks were dropped from the U. of Wyoming football team** after they defied the coach's ban against protests and wore black armbands in support of a stand by the Black Students' Alliance. The BSA wanted the university to sever sports ties with Brigham Young U., a school run by a Mormon church group, which had barred blacks from the church ministry.

Oct. 11-16 The **World Series** was won by the New York Mets (NL), who won four straight games from the Baltimore Orioles (AL) after losing the opener. After being down 3-0 in the final game, they came on to tie the score with two runs in the sixth inning and one in the seventh. A hit by Ron Swoboda put the Mets ahead in the bottom of the eighth, and the New York team held its lead to win 5-3. The amazing Mets, organized only 7 years earlier, had been in ninth place at one point in the season and had climaxed their climb to the top of the league by beating the Atlanta Braves in three straight games to take the National League pennant. The Orioles had swept three games from the Minnesota Twins for the American League pennant.

Oct. 18 A new **football field goal record** was set by Chester Marcol of Hillsdale College in Michigan, who kicked a 62-yard field goal, the longest on record for either amateur or pro football.

Nov. 26 The **Heisman Trophy** for outstanding college football player of 1969 was awarded to Oklahoma halfback Steve Owens.

Dec. 6 A **football controversy** over honors for the top college football team was fueled when Pres. Richard Nixon presented the U. of Texas team with a plaque honoring it as the best in the nation following its 15-14 defeat of Arkansas. The presentation had been protested to no effect by Gov. Raymond P. Shafer of Pennsyl-

1937	Texas Christian 16, Marquette 6
1938	Rice 28, Colorado 14
1939	St. Mary's (California) 20, Texas Tech 13
1940	Clemson 6, Boston College 3
1941	Texas A&M 13, Fordham 12
1942	Alabama 29, Texas A&M 21
1943	Texas 14, Georgia Tech 7
1944	Randolph Field 7, Texas 7
1945	Oklahoma A&M 34, Texas Christian 0
1946	Texas 40, Missouri 27
1947	Louisiana State 0, Arkansas 0
1948	Southern Methodist 13, Penn State 13
1949	Southern Methodist 21, Oregon 13
1950	Rice 27, North Carolina 13
1951	Tennessee 20, Texas 14
1952	Kentucky 20, Texas Christian 7
1953	Texas 16, Tennessee 0
1954	Rice 28, Alabama 6
1955	Georgia Tech 14, Arkansas 6
1956	Mississippi 14, Texas Christian 13
1957	Texas Christian 28, Syracuse 27
1958	Navy 20, Rice 7
1959	Air Force 0, Texas Christian 0
1960	Syracuse 23, Texas 14
1961	Duke 7, Arkansas 6
1962	Texas 12, Mississippi 7
1963	Louisiana State 13, Texas 0
1964	Texas 28, Navy 6
1965	Arkansas 10, Nebraska 7
1966	Louisiana State 14, Arkansas 7
1967	Georgia 24, Southern Methodist 9
1968	Texas A&M 20, Alabama 16
1969	Texas 36, Tennessee 13
1970	Texas 21, Notre Dame 17
1971	Notre Dame 24, Texas 11
1972	Penn State 30, Texas 6
1973	Texas 17, Alabama 13
1974	Nebraska 19, Texas 3
1975	Penn State 41, Baylor 20
1976	Arkansas 31, Georgia 10
1977	Houston 30, Maryland 21
1978	Notre Dame 38, Texas 10
1979	Notre Dame 35, Houston 34
1980	Houston 17, Nebraska 14
1981	Alabama 30, Baylor 2
1982	Texas 14, Alabama 12
1983	Southern Methodist 7, Pittsburgh 3
1984	Georgia 10, Texas 9
1985	Boston College 45, Houston 28
1986	Texas A&M 36, Auburn 16
1987	Ohio State 28, Texas A&M 12
1988	Texas A&M 35, Notre Dame 10

vania, who noted that Penn State had been undefeated through 30 games in three years.

Dec. 11-12 A new **world record decathlon score** of 8417 was set by Bill Toomey at the Southern Pacific AAU meet held at UCLA.

1970

A **frank book about professional baseball** was published. It was *Ball Four*, written by retired pitcher Jim Bouton, who had played for most of his career with the New York Yankees. The public discussion that ensued made it a best seller.

The **Dingell-Hart Bill** was adopted by Congress, making a 10% excise tax on handguns available for wildlife conservation. A similar tax was levied on archery equipment in 1972.

Jan. 1 In **college football bowl games,** the results were Texas 21, Notre Dame 17 in the Cotton Bowl; Penn State 10, Missouri 3 in the Orange Bowl; USC 10, Michigan 3 in the Rose Bowl; and Mississippi 27, Arkansas 22 in the Sugar Bowl. This season the AP and UPI polls chose Texas as national college champion of 1969.

Jan. 11 **Super Bowl IV** was won by the Kansas City Chiefs (AFL), who defeated the Minnesota Vikings (NFL) 23-7. On Jan. 4 the Chiefs had won the AFL championship by beating the Oakland Raiders 17-7. On the same day, the Vikings took the NFL title by beating the Cleveland Browns 27-7.

Jan. 28 U.S. **black tennis player** Arthur Ashe was denied a visa by the South African government to compete in the South African open championship. Ashe was finally allowed to enter and play there in November 1973.

Feb. 6 The **NBA expanded** to 18 teams for the 1970-1971 basketball season. New franchises were granted to Buffalo and Cleveland in the eastern division and to Houston and Portland in the western division.

Feb. 6-7 **U.S. figure skating championships** were won at Tulsa, Okla., by Tim Wood, men's singles; Janet Lynn, women's singles; Jo Jo Starbuck and Kenneth Shelley, pairs; and Judy Schwomeyer and James Sladky, dance.

Feb. 10 At the **Westminster Kennel Club** dog

show, Ch. Arriba's Prima Donna, a boxer owned by Dr. and Mrs. P. J. Pagano of Pelham Manor, N.Y., took best-in-show.

Feb. 16 The **world heavyweight boxing championship** was awarded to Joe Frazier, who knocked out Jimmy Ellis in the fifth round in New York City. The bout settled a three-year-old controversy over the title.

Feb. 21 The **American Women's Lawn Bowls Association** was founded at Santa Anita, Calif., by 81 women bowlers. The organization sponsors annual national open and U.S. singles and pairs championships.

Mar. 7 At the **world figure skating championships** at Ljubljana, Yugoslavia, Tim Wood won the men's singles title for the second year in a row.

Mar. 21 The **NCAA basketball championship** was won for the fourth straight time by UCLA, which defeated Jacksonville U. 80-69. Curtis Rowe and Sidney Wicks were UCLA's high scorers.

Mar. 31 The **Seattle Pilots' (AL) baseball franchise** was sold by its owners to Milwaukee interests. After only one year in Seattle, the Pilots became the Milwaukee Brewers. The transfer was made a few days before the opening of the season, thus bringing a major league team back to Milwaukee after a four-year absence.

Spring Outfielder **Curt Flood,** traded by the St. Louis Cardinals to Philadelphia over the winter, refused to report to training camp and instituted proceedings against the reserve clause in baseball's player contracts. He wanted freedom to choose the team he played for. A New York court turned him down, and he resolved to sit out the season.

Apr. 13 The **Masters golf tournament** was won by Billy Casper, who beat Gene Littler by five strokes in a playoff round after they had tied at 279.

Apr. 20 The 74th annual **Boston Marathon** was won by Ron Hill of Great Britain, with a time of 2 hrs., 10 min., 30 sec., a new U.S. marathon record.

Apr. 22 **Tom Seaver** of the New York Mets tied the major league strikeout record of 19 in one game, with ten of them in a row. The record had been set by Steve Carlton, of the Philadelphia Phillies, in 1969. In 1974, it was matched by Nolan Ryan, pitching for the California Angels.

Apr. 24-May 8 The **NBA basketball championship** was won for the first time in 24 years by the New York Knicks, who beat the Los Angeles Lakers four games to three. Guard Walt Frazier starred for the Knicks, scoring 36 points in the seventh game for a 113-99 win.

May 2 The 96th annual **Kentucky Derby** was won by Dust Commander, with a time of 2:03²/₅. The jockey was Mike Manganello.

May 3-10 The **NHL Stanley Cup** was won for the first time in 29 years by the Boston Bruins, who swept the St. Louis Blues in four straight games.

May 15-25 The **ABA basketball championship** was won by the Indiana Pacers, who beat the Los Angeles Stars four games to two.

May 16 The 95th annual **Preakness Stakes** was won by Personality, with a time of 1:56¹/₅. The jockey was Eddie Belmonte.

May 30 The 54th **Indianapolis 500** auto race was won by Al Unser, completing the course in 3 hrs., 12 min., 37.04 sec., at an average speed of 155.749 mph.

June 6 The 102nd annual **Belmont Stakes** was won by High Echelon, with a time of 2:34. The jockey was John Rotz.

June 15 The **LPGA golf tournament** was won by Shirley Englehorn, who beat Kathy Whitworth by four strokes in an 18-hole playoff.

June 18-20 A new **world 440-yard hurdles record** of 48.8 sec. was set at the NCAA outdoor championships by Ralph Mann of Brigham Young U.

June 21 The **U.S. Open golf tournament** was won by Tony Jacklin of Great Britain, who led runner-up Dave Hill by five strokes to become the first Englishman to win the tournament in 50 years.

July 4 At the **Wimbledon** tennis championships, the women's doubles title was won by Billie Jean King and Rosemary Casals for the third time in four years. Casals teamed with Ilie Nastase of Rumania to win the mixed doubles title. Margaret Smith Court of Australia defeated Billie Jean King in the women's finals in a 2½-hr. match.

July 5 The **U.S. Women's Open golf tournament** was won for the second year running by Donna Caponi, who beat Sandra Spuzich and Sandra Haynie by one stroke.

July 14 The **baseball all-star game** was won by the National League for the eighth consecutive year, defeating the American League team 5-4 in the 12th inning.

1933	Miami 7, Manhattan 0		1961	Missouri 21, Navy 14
1934	Duquesne 33, Miami 7		1962	Louisiana State 25, Colorado 7
1935	Bucknell 26, Miami 0		1963	Alabama 17, Oklahoma 0
1936	Catholic 20, Mississippi 19		1964	Nebraska 13, Auburn 7
1937	Duquesne 13, Mississippi State 12		1965	Texas 21, Alabama 17
1938	Auburn 6, Michigan State 0		1966	Alabama 39, Nebraska 28
1939	Tennessee 17, Oklahoma 0		1967	Florida 27, Georgia Tech 12
1940	Georgia Tech 21, Missouri 7		1968	Oklahoma 26, Tennessee 24
1941	Mississippi State 14, Georgetown 7		1969	Penn State 15, Kansas 14
1942	Georgia 40, Texas Christian 26		1970	Penn State 10, Missouri 3
1943	Alabama 37, Boston College 21		1971	Nebraska 17, Louisiana State 12
1944	Louisiana State 19, Texas A&M 14		1972	Nebraska 38, Alabama 6
1945	Tulsa 26, Georgia Tech 12		1973	Nebraska 40, Notre Dame 6
1946	Miami 13, Holy Cross 6		1974	Penn State 16, Louisiana State 9
1947	Rice 8, Tennessee 0		1975	Notre Dame 13, Alabama 11
1948	Georgia Tech 20, Kansas 14		1976	Oklahoma 14, Michigan 6
1949	Texas 41, Georgia 28		1977	Ohio State 27, Colorado 10
1950	Santa Clara 21, Kentucky 13		1978	Arkansas 31, Oklahoma 6
1951	Clemson 15, Miami 14		1979	Oklahoma 31, Nebraska 24
1952	Georgia Tech 17, Baylor 14		1980	Oklahoma 24, Florida State 7
1953	Alabama 61, Syracuse 6		1981	Oklahoma 18, Florida State 17
1954	Oklahoma 7, Maryland 0		1982	Clemson 22, Nebraska 15
1955	Duke 34, Nebraska 7		1983	Nebraska 21, Louisiana State 20
1956	Oklahoma 20, Maryland 6		1984	Miami 31, Nebraska 30
1957	Colorado 27, Clemson 21		1985	Washington 28, Oklahoma 17
1958	Oklahoma 48, Duke 21		1986	Oklahoma 25, Penn State 10
1959	Oklahoma 21, Syracuse 6		1987	Oklahoma 42, Arkansas 8
1960	Georgia 14, Missouri 0		1988	Miami 20, Oklahoma 14

July 24 A **nine-point tie-breaking** scoring innovation for tennis, instituted on an experimental basis by the International Lawn Tennis Association, was approved for use in the U.S. National Open. Wimbledon followed suit.

July 27 The **Baseball Hall of Fame** inducted Lou Boudreau, Earl Combs, Ford C. Frick, and Jesse Haines.

Aug. 16 The **PGA golf tournament** was won by Dave Stockton, who topped Arnold Palmer and Bob Murphy by two strokes.

Aug. 29-31 The **Davis Cup** international tennis challenge round was won by the U.S., which swept West Germany in five straight matches.

Sept. 2 The 45th annual **Hambletonian Stakes** was won by Timothy T. in three heats. The driver was John Simpson, Jr., who at 27 was the youngest person ever to win the trotting classic.

Sept. 2-13 The **U.S. Open tennis singles cham-** pionships were won by 35-year-old Ken Rosewall of Australia over teammate Tony Roche in the men's division and by Margaret Smith Court of Australia over Rosemary Casals in the women's division.

Sept. 6-13 The **North American Soccer League championship** was won by the Rochester Lancers, who bested the Washington Darts four goals to three in a two-game, total-goal playoff.

Sept. 7 A new **world record for winning mounts** was set by Willie Shoemaker, who broke Johnny Longden's record by winning his 6033rd race, at Del Mar, Calif.

Sept. 13 The **first New York City Marathon** was won by Gary Muhrcke of the Millrose Athletic Association, with a time of 2 hrs., 31 min., 38.2 sec. Of the 126 starters, 55 finished the 26-mi., 385-yard course.

Sept. 15-28 The **America's Cup** was successfully defended by the U.S. yacht *Intrepid*, which beat the British challenger *Gretel II* four races to one. In the second race *Gretel II* was disqualified because it collided with *Intrepid* at the beginning of the race, the first such forfeit in the history of the yachting classic.

Sept. 24 **Women professional tennis players rebelled** against the differences between prize money offered to men and women by promoter Jack Kramer. Nine players, led by Billie Jean King, signed up instead for a tournament sponsored by the Philip Morris Company's Virginia Slims, which upped the winner's prize from $1500 to $5000.

Oct. Capt. **Margaret Murdock** (U.S. Army), the only woman competitor in the three-position free-rifle matches at the 40th World Shooting Championships held at Phoenix, Ariz., captured the gold medal in the standing position. She was the first woman to do so. She also won the Ladies Standard Rifle Championship. Fifty nations were represented at the 13-day meet. Most of the awards were won by representatives of the USSR and the U.S.

Oct. At the world gymnastic championships, **Kathy Rigby** became the first American gymnast, male or female, to win a medal. She earned a silver medal in the balance beam.

Oct. The **National Hockey League** added the Vancouver Canucks and the Buffalo Sabres to its roster of teams.

Oct. 2 Fourteen members of the **Wichita State University football team** were killed when their chartered plane crashed in the Rocky Mts.

Oct. 3 The first **strike by umpires** in baseball history began. Umpires walked out in a dispute over the pay scale for their work in the league playoffs and World Series. A crew of Triple A League umpires worked the opening National League playoff game between Cincinnati and Pittsburgh without incident.

Oct. 15 The 67th **World Series** was won by the Baltimore Orioles (AL), defeating the Cincinnati Reds four games to one. Oriole bats and Brooks Robinson's brilliant play at third base proved decisive. Robinson batted .428 and Paul Blair .474 for the winning team. On Oct. 5 the Orioles had clinched the American League pennant by sweeping the Minnesota Twins in three games; the Reds had taken the National League pennant by beating the Pittsburgh Pirates three straight.

Oct. 23 A new **land speed record** of 622.407 mph

was set by Gary Gabelich of Long Beach, Calif. He drove a rocket-powered car at the Bonneville Salt Flats in Utah.

Nov. 8 A new **football field goal record** of 63 yards was set by Tom Dempsey of the New Orleans Saints in a two-point win over the Detroit Lions. The kick came in the final play of the game and gave the Saints a 19-17 upset victory. Dempsey, 23, was born with only half a right foot (his kicking foot) and a stub of a right hand.

Nov. 14 Forty-three players and coaches of the **Marshall University football team** died when their chartered plane crashed in Kenova, W. Va.

Nov. 24 The **Heisman Trophy** for outstanding college football player of 1970 was voted to Stanford quarterback Jim Plunkett.

1971

The **American Motorcyclist Association** affiliated with the *Fédération internationale motocycliste,* after a decade of negotiation. International competition in motocross events thrived.

In **professional soccer,** a franchise was awarded to the New York Cosmos, which brought the North American Soccer League up to eight teams.

The **Coronation Cup** replaced the Westchester Cup as the polo trophy for matches between the U.S. and Great Britain. The trophy was given for a one-game match played annually at Hurlingham, England. The U.S. this year won the first contest 9-6.

The **rules for women's basketball** were changed to conform with those of the men's game.

Jan. 1 In **college football bowl games,** the results were Notre Dame 24, Texas 11 in the Cotton Bowl; Nebraska 17, Louisiana State 12 in the Orange Bowl; Stanford 27, Ohio State 17 in the Rose Bowl; and Tennessee 34, Air Force 13 in the Sugar Bowl. This season the AP poll selected Nebraska as national collegiate champion of 1970. The UPI poll chose Texas.

Jan. 17 **Super Bowl V** was won in the final 5 sec. by the Baltimore Colts (AFC), who beat the Dallas Cowboys (NFC) 16-13 on a field goal by Jim

1902	Michigan 49, Stanford 0		1952	Illinois 40, Stanford 7
1903–15	(not played)		1953	Southern California 7, Wisconsin 0
1916	Washington 14, Brown 0		1954	Michigan State 28, UCLA 14
1917	Oregon 14, Pennsylvania 0		1955	Ohio State 20, Southern California 7
1918	Mare Island Marines 19, Camp Lewis 7		1956	Michigan State 17, UCLA 14
1919	Great Lakes 17, Mare Island Marines 0		1957	Iowa 35, Oregon State 19
1920	Harvard 7, Oregon 6		1958	Ohio State 10, Oregon 7
1921	California 28, Ohio State 0		1959	Iowa 38, California 12
1922	Washington and Jefferson 0, California 0		1960	Washington 44, Wisconsin 8
1923	Southern California 14, Penn State 3		1961	Washington 17, Minnesota 7
1924	Navy 14, Washington 14		1962	Minnesota 21, UCLA 3
1925	Notre Dame 27, Stanford 10		1963	Southern California 42, Wisconsin 37
1926	Alabama 20, Washington 19		1964	Illinois 17, Washington 7
1927	Alabama 7, Stanford 7		1965	Michigan 34, Oregon State 7
1928	Stanford 7, Pittsburgh 6		1966	UCLA 14, Michigan State 12
1929	Georgia Tech 8, California 7		1967	Purdue 14, Southern California 13
1930	Southern California 47, Pittsburgh 14		1968	Southern California 14, Indiana 3
1931	Alabama 24, Washington State 0		1969	Ohio State 27, Southern California 16
1932	Southern California 21, Tulane 12		1970	Southern California 10, Michigan 3
1933	Southern California 35, Pittsburgh 0		1971	Stanford 27, Ohio State 17
1934	Columbia 7, Stanford 0		1972	Stanford 13, Michigan 12
1935	Alabama 29, Stanford 13		1973	Southern California 42, Ohio State 17
1936	Stanford 7, Southern Methodist 0		1974	Ohio State 42, Southern California 21
1937	Pittsburgh 21, Washington 0		1975	Southern California 18, Ohio State 17
1938	California 13, Alabama 0		1976	UCLA 23, Ohio State 10
1939	Southern California 7, Duke 3		1977	Southern California 14, Michigan 6
1940	Southern California 14, Tennessee 0		1978	Washington 27, Michigan 20
1941	Stanford 21, Nebraska 13		1979	Southern California 17, Michigan 10
1942	Oregon State 20, Duke 16		1980	Southern California 17, Ohio State 16
1943	Georgia 9, UCLA 0		1981	Michigan 23, Washington 6
1944	Southern California 29, Washington 0		1982	Washington 28, Iowa 0
1945	Southern California 25, Tennessee 0		1983	UCLA 24, Michigan 14
1946	Alabama 34, Southern California 14		1984	UCLA 45, Illinois 9
1947	Illinois 45, UCLA 14		1985	Southern California 20, Ohio State 17
1948	Michigan 49, Southern California 0		1986	UCLA 45, Iowa 28
1949	Northwestern 20, California 14		1987	Arizona State 22, Michigan 15
1950	Ohio State 17, California 14		1988	Michigan State 20, Southern California 17
1951	Michigan 14, California 6			

O'Brien. On Jan. 3 the Colts had beaten the Oakland Raiders 27-17 to win the AFC championship and the Cowboys had topped the San Francisco 49ers 17-10 for the NFC championship.

Jan. 28-31 *U.S. figure skating championships* were won by John Misha Petkevich, men's singles; Janet Lynn, women's singles; Jo Jo Starbuck and Kenneth Shelley, pairs; and Judy Schwomeyer and James Sladky, dance.

Feb. 16 At the **Westminster Kennel Club** dog show, Ch. Chinoe's Adamant James, an English springer spaniel owned by Milton E. Prickett of Lexington, Ky., took best-in-show.

Feb. 28 The **PGA golf tournament** was won by Jack Nicklaus, who topped Billy Casper by three strokes.

Mar. 8 The **world heavyweight boxing championship** was defended by Joe Frazier in a unanimous 15-round decision over Muhammad Ali. The fight, one of the richest sports events in history, grossed nearly $20,000,000, largely through receipts from closed-circuit television.

Mar. 27 The **NCAA basketball championship** was won for the fifth straight year by UCLA, which beat Villanova 68-62. Villanova's Howard Porter was voted the tournament's most valuable player.

Apr. 8 The first legal **off-track betting** (OTB) system in the U.S. went into operation in New York City.

Apr. 10-14 A U.S. **table tennis team** visited the People's Republic of China and played several exhibition matches in Peking. The unprecedented invitation by the Chinese also included visas for seven Western newsmen, reversing a policy that had been maintained since the new government took power in 1949. The event turned out to be a signal from the Chinese that they were ready to consider diplomatic relations with the U.S. after the long lapse since 1949.

Apr. 11 The **Masters golf tournament** was won by Charles Coody, who beat Jack Nicklaus and Johnny Miller by two strokes.

Apr. 19 The **Boston Marathon** was won by Alvaro Mejía of Colombia, with a time of 2 hrs., 18 min., 45 sec.

Apr. 30 The **NBA basketball championship** was won by the Milwaukee Bucks in a four-game rout of the Baltimore Bullets. It was only the second time a team had swept the NBA finals. Oscar Robertson starred for the Bucks.

May 1 The 97th annual **Kentucky Derby** was won by Canonero II, with a time of 2:03⅕. The jockey was Gustavo Avila.

May 4-18 The **NHL Stanley Cup** was won by the Montreal Canadiens, who defeated the Chicago Black Hawks four games to three.

May 15 The 96th annual **Preakness Stakes** was won by Canonero II, with a new track record time of 1:54. The jockey was Gustavo Avila.

May 18 The **ABA basketball championship** was won by the Utah Stars, who beat the Kentucky Colonels four games to three.

May 29 The 55th annual **Indianapolis 500** auto race was won for the second year in a row by Al Unser, who completed the 500-mi. course in 3 hrs., 10 min., 11.56 sec., at a new record average speed of 157.735 mph.

June 5 The **first NCAA national championships** were held at Hofstra U., Hempstead, N.Y. Cornell defeated Maryland 12-6 in the title game.

June 5 The 103rd annual **Belmont Stakes** was won by Pass Catcher, with a time of 2:30⅖. The jockey was Walter Blum.

June 13 The **LPGA golf tournament** was won by Kathy Whitworth.

June 21 The **U.S. Open golf tournament** was won by Lee Trevino, who beat Jack Nicklaus by two strokes in a playoff. On July 10 Trevino won the British Open, becoming the fourth U.S. player to win both championships in the same year.

June 27 The **U.S. Women's Open golf tournament** was won by JoAnne Gunderson Carner.

June 28 **Muhammad Ali** won a four-year legal battle when the Supreme Court overturned his 1967 conviction for draft evasion. In an 8-0 decision the court found that he qualified as a conscientious objector.

July 3 The **outstanding standardbred horses of the century** were selected by the Hall of Fame of the Trotter. Greyhound was named the best trotter, and Bret Hanover the top pacer. Greyhound raced from 1934 to 1940, set 25 world records, and won 71 of 82 starts. Bret Hanover won 62 of 68 races between 1964 and 1966.

July 3 At the **Wimbledon** tennis championships, the women's doubles title was won for the fourth time in five years by Billie Jean King and Rosemary Casals. King teamed with Owen Davidson of Australia to win the mixed doubles title. Stan Smith of the U.S. lost to John Newcombe of Australia in a five-set match marked by battering serves and booming overhead smashes.

July 13 The **baseball all-star game** was won by the American League, beating the National League 6-4 for its first all-star victory since 1962.

July 30-Aug. 12 At the **Pan-American Games** in Cali, Colombia, the U.S. won 105 gold medals and ranked first in team standings, followed by Cuba and Canada.

Aug. 9 The **Baseball Hall of Fame** inducted eight new members: Dave Bancroft, Jake Beckley, Chick Hafey, Harry Hooper, Joe Kelley, Rube Marquard, Satchel Paige, and George Weiss.

Aug. 26 It was announced that the **New York Giants** football team would move to New Jersey after completion of a 75,000-seat stadium to be opened there in 1975.

Sept. 1 The 46th annual **Hambletonian Stakes** was won in straight heats by Speedy Crown. The driver was Howard Beissinger.

Sept. 5-15 The **U.S. Open tennis singles championships** were won by Stan Smith over Jan Kodes of Czechoslovakia in the men's division and Billie Jean King over Rosemary Casals in the women's division. It was the first time in 16 years that both titles were won by U.S. players.

Sept. 9 **Gordie Howe,** one of the all-time greats of the NHL, announced his retirement at age 43 to take a job in the front office of the Detroit Red Wings, his team for 25 seasons.

Sept. 19 The **North American Soccer League championship** was won by the Dallas Tornado, defeating the Atlanta Chiefs 2-0 in the final game of a three-game playoff.

Sept. 19 The second annual **New York City Marathon** was won by Norman Higgins of New London, Conn., with a time of 2 hrs., 22 min., 54.2 sec.

Sept. 21 The **Washington Senators,** often fondly described by baseball fans as "first in war, first in peace, and last in the American League," would move to Texas for the 1972 season, it was announced. The team was soon renamed the Texas Rangers.

Sept. 24 A new professional ice hockey league, the **World Hockey Association (WHA),** with 12 franchises—11 determined and one still to be chosen—announced its intention to begin play in Oct. 1972.

Oct. 3 **Billie Jean King** became the first woman professional tennis player to win over $100,000 in one year when she won $4000 in a Virginia Slims-Thunderbird tournament held in Phoenix.

Oct. 8-11 The **Davis Cup** international tennis challenge round was won by the U.S., defeating Rumania three matches to two. This year it was decided to abolish the challenge round. Beginning in 1972, the defending team would be required to play through the entire competition.

Oct. 9-17 The 68th annual **World Series,** the first to be played at night, was won by the underdog Pittsburgh Pirates (NL), who beat the Baltimore Orioles (AL) four games to three. Roberto Clemente, the Pirates' right fielder, and Manny Sanguillen, their catcher, had hot bats. Clemente hit .414 and two home runs, while Sanguillen hit .379. Steve Blass won games three and seven. On Oct. 5, Baltimore had completed a three-game sweep over the Oakland Athletics to take the American League championship. On Oct. 6, the Pirates had clinched the National

League pennant, beating the San Francisco Giants three games to one.

Oct. 30 A new **college football rushing record** was set by Ed Marinaro of Cornell, who scored a three-year career total of 4132 yards.

Nov. 18 A bill outlawing **hunting from airplanes** was signed by Pres. Richard Nixon.

Nov. 25 The **Heisman Trophy** for outstanding college football player of the year was awarded to Auburn quarterback Pat Sullivan.

1972

The **American Motorcyclist Association** initiated its 250-cc and 500-cc professional motocross events—races conducted on a closed but irregular course between 0.5 and 2.0 mi. long, including sharp right and left turns and terrain that requires gear changing. At Daytona Beach, Fla., in the first such race in the U.S., Jim Weinert was the winner.

Jan. 1 In **college football bowl games,** the results were Penn State 30, Texas 6 in the Cotton Bowl; Nebraska 38, Alabama 6 in the Orange Bowl; Stanford 13, Michigan 12 in the Rose Bowl; and Oklahoma 40, Auburn 22 in the Sugar Bowl. This season the AP and UPI polls picked Nebraska as national collegiate champion of 1971.

Jan. 8 In a major ruling on **college sports eligibility,** the NCAA announced that beginning in the fall, freshmen would be permitted to play on varsity football and basketball teams.

Jan. 14-16 **U.S. figure skating championships** were won by Ken Shelley, men's singles; Janet Lynn, women's singles, for the fourth year in a row; Jo Jo Starbuck and Kenneth Shelley, pairs; and Judy Schwomeyer and James Sladky, dance, for the fifth consecutive year.

Jan. 16 **Super Bowl VI** was won by the Dallas Cowboys (NFC), who defeated the Miami Dolphins (AFC) 24-3. On Jan. 2 the Cowboys had stopped the San Francisco 49ers 14-3 for the NFC championship, and the Dolphins had defeated the Baltimore Colts 21-0 for the AFC title.

Feb. 3-13 At the **Winter Olympics** at Sapporo, Japan, U.S. athletes won three gold medals. The USSR was first, with eight gold medals, followed

Football
HEISMAN MEMORIAL
TROPHY WINNERS

1935	Jay Berwanger, Chicago
1936	Larry Kelley, Yale
1937	Clinton Frank, Yale
1938	Davey O'Brien, Texas Christian
1939	Nile Kinnick, Iowa
1940	Tom Harmon, Michigan
1941	Bruce Smith, Minnesota
1942	Frank Sinkwich, Georgia
1943	Angelo Bertelli, Notre Dame
1944	Leslie Horvath, Ohio State
1945	Felix "Doc" Blanchard, Army
1946	Glenn Davis, Army
1947	John Lujack, Notre Dame
1948	Doak Walker, Southern Methodist
1949	Leon Hart, Notre Dame
1950	Vic Janowicz, Ohio State
1951	Dick Kazmaier, Princeton
1952	Billy Vessels, Oklahoma
1953	John Lattner, Notre Dame
1954	Alan Ameche, Wisconsin
1955	Howard Cassady, Ohio State
1956	Paul Hornung, Notre Dame
1957	John Crow, Texas A&M
1958	Pete Dawkins, Army
1959	Billy Cannon, Louisiana State
1960	Joe Bellino, Navy
1961	Ernie Davis, Syracuse
1962	Terry Baker, Oregon State
1963	Roger Staubach, Navy
1964	John Huarte, Notre Dame
1965	Mike Garrett, Southern California
1966	Steve Spurrier, Florida
1967	Gary Beban, UCLA
1968	O. J. Simpson, Southern California
1969	Steve Owens, Oklahoma
1970	Jim Plunkett, Stanford
1971	Pat Sullivan, Auburn
1972	John Rodgers, Nebraska
1973	John Cappelletti, Penn State
1974	Archie Griffin, Ohio State
1975	Archie Griffin, Ohio State
1976	Tony Dorsett, Pittsburgh
1977	Earl Campbell, Texas
1978	Billy Sims, Oklahoma
1979	Charles White, Southern California
1980	George Rogers, South Carolina
1981	Marcus Allen, Southern California
1982	Herschel Walker, Georgia
1983	Mike Rozier, Nebraska
1984	Doug Flutie, Boston College
1985	Bo Jackson, Auburn
1986	Vinnie Testaverde, Miami
1987	Tim Brown, Notre Dame

by East Germany, Switzerland, and the Netherlands, all with four.

Feb. 15 At the **Westminster Kennel Club** dog show, Ch. Chinoe's Adamant James, an English springer spaniel owned by Dr. Milton E. Prickett of Lexington, Ky., took best-in-show for the second consecutive year.

Mar. 2 The New York State Athletic Commission decided to **let women journalists into dressing rooms** at boxing and wrestling matches. The women had to be properly accredited and allowed in when "the male contestants are properly attired."

Mar. 12 **World Championship Tennis, Inc.,** refused to permit the tennis players it had under contract to enter the Wimbledon tournament. No settlement could be worked out between WCT and the International Lawn Tennis Association and various national associations until just after this year's Wimbledon.

Mar. 15 The owners of the **Cincinnati Royals** basketball team moved their NBA franchise to Kansas City. Mo., for the 1972-1973 season.

Mar. 19 The **Association for Intercollegiate Athletics for Women** (AIAW) held its first women's collegiate basketball championship. Immaculata College defeated West Chester State 52-48.

Mar. 25 The **NCAA basketball championship** was won by UCLA, defeating Florida State 81-76 and maintaining its 45-game winning streak. Bill Walton and Henry Bibby starred for UCLA.

Apr. The **first Albuquerque (N.Mex.) International Balloon Festival** was held with 14 balloons and crews participating. The main attraction was a mass ascent of the 14 craft. This annual affair now attracts about 500 balloons and features a variety of events.

Apr. 1 The **first major league baseball strike** in history began as players walked out over a pension dispute. The strike was settled on Apr. 13.

Managing a ball club is the most vulnerable job in the world. . . . If you don't win, you're going to be fired. If you do win, you've only put off the day you're going to be fired.

Leo Durocher

The season began on Apr. 15, ten days late. Games not played were canceled.

Apr. 9 The **Masters golf tournament** was won by Jack Nicklaus.

Apr. 17 The 76th annual **Boston Marathon** was won by Olavi Suomalainen of Finland, with a time of 2 hrs., 15 min., 39 sec. The first women's competition was won by Nina Kuscsik of Huntington, Long Island, N.Y., with a time of 3 hrs., 8 min., 58 sec.

Apr. 28 In a settlement of the **1968 Kentucky Derby controversy,** a Kentucky appeals court awarded the prize money to the second-place winner, Forward Pass. The winner, Dancer's Image, was disqualified from the money, but not the win, because the horse had been given a pain-killing drug before the race.

Apr. 30-May 11 The **NHL Stanley Cup** was won for the second time in three years by the Boston Bruins, who defeated the New York Rangers four games to two.

May 6 The 98th annual **Kentucky Derby** was won by Riva Ridge, with a time of 2:01⅘. The jockey was Ron Turcotte.

May 7 The **NBA basketball championship** was won by the Los Angeles Lakers, who defeated the New York Knicks four games to one. It was the Lakers' first NBA championship.

May 20 The **ABA basketball championship** was won by the Indiana Pacers, who beat the New York Nets four games to two.

May 20 The 97th annual **Preakness Stakes** was won by Bee Bee Bee, with a time of 1:55⅗. The jockey was Eldon Nelson.

May 27 The 56th **Indianapolis 500** auto race was won by Mark Donohue, with a time of 3 hrs., 4 min., 5.54 sec., for a new record average speed of 162.962 mph.

June A U.S. **lawn bowling** team composed of William Miller, Clive Forrester, and Richard Folkins won the world championship for triples at Worthing, England. The initial world championships (singles, doubles, triples, and fours) had been held at Sydney, Australia, in 1966. They were planned to be held every four years.

June 10 The 104th annual **Belmont Stakes** was won by Riva Ridge, with a time of 2:28. The jockey was Ron Turcotte.

June 11 The **LPGA golf tournament** was won by Kathy Ahern.

June 18 The **U.S. Open golf tournament** was won for the third time by Jack Nicklaus, tying the record of 13 major golf titles set by Bobby Jones. As in this year's Masters, Bruce Crampton finished second, three strokes behind.

June 19 In a decision bearing on **baseball's reserve clause,** the Supreme Court ruled major league baseball exempt from antitrust statutes, thus ending Curt Flood's 1970 suit against organized baseball. The Court called the exemption from these statutes an "anomaly" and called on Congress to correct the situation through legislation.

June 23 **Collegiate athletics** for women was advanced immeasurably by the signing today by Pres. Richard Nixon of the Higher Education Act of 1972. Title IX of this congressional act in effect barred sex bias in athletics and other activities at colleges receiving federal assistance. Equality of women's programs, facilities, and coaching soon followed.

June 27 **Bobby Hull** announced that he was jumping from the Chicago Black Hawks to the Winnipeg Jets of the World Hockey Association. The chief inducement was a ten-year contractual package of $2,500,000 plus $1,000,000 as a bonus for signing as a player-coach.

July 2 A new **world pole vault record** of 18 ft., 5¾ inches was set by Bob Seagren, using a fiberglass pole in a meet at Eugene, Oreg.

July 2 The **U.S. Women's Open golf tournament** was won by Susie Maxwell Berning over Kathy Ahern.

July 7 At the **Wimbledon** tennis championships in England, Billie Jean King won the women's singles title by defeating Evonne Goolagong of Australia. On July 9, Stan Smith won the men's singles title by defeating Ilie Nastase of Rumania in five sets, completing the first U.S. singles sweep since 1955. King teamed with Betty Stove of the Netherlands to win the women's doubles, and Rosemary Casals teamed with Nastase to take the mixed doubles title.

July 13 In an unprecedented **football team swap,** Robert Isray made a no-cash trade of his Los Angeles Rams for Carroll Rosenbloom's Baltimore Colts.

July 25 The **baseball all-star game** was won by the National League, beating the American League 4-3 in the tenth inning.

Aug. 6 The **PGA golf tournament** was won by Gary Player of South Africa.

Aug. 7 The **Baseball Hall of Fame** inducted eight new members: Yogi Berra, Josh Gibson, Lefty Gomez, Will Harridge, Sandy Koufax, Buck Leonard, Early Wynn, and Ross Youngs.

Golf
UNITED STATES OPEN WINNERS
Women

1946	Patty Berg	1967	Catherine LaCoste
1947	Betty Jameson	1968	Susie Berning
1948	Babe Didrikson Zaharias	1969	Donna Caponi
1949	Louise Suggs	1970	Donna Caponi
1950	Babe Didrikson Zaharias	1971	JoAnne Carner
1951	Betsy Rawls	1972	Susie Berning
1952	Louise Suggs	1973	Susie Berning
1953	Betsy Rawls	1974	Sandra Haynie
1954	Babe Didrikson Zaharias	1975	Sandra Palmer
1955	Fay Crocker	1976	JoAnne Carner
1956	Katherine Cornelius	1977	Hollis Stacy
1957	Betsy Rawls	1978	Hollis Stacy
1958	Mickey Wright	1979	Jerilyn Britz
1959	Mickey Wright	1980	Amy Alcott
1960	Betsy Rawls	1981	Pat Bradley
1961	Mickey Wright	1982	Janet Alex
1962	Murle Lindstrom	1983	Jan Stephenson
1963	Mary Mills	1984	Hollis Stacy
1964	Mickey Wright	1985	Kathy Baker
1965	Carol Mann	1986	Jane Geddes
1966	Sandra Spuzich	1987	Laura Davies

Aug. 26 The **North American Soccer League championship** was won by the New York Cosmos, who defeated the St. Louis Stars 2-1.

Aug. 26-Sept. 11 At the **Summer Olympics** in Munich, West Germany, the U.S. won 33 gold medals to the Soviet Union's 50. Swimmer Mark Spitz set an Olympic record by winning seven gold medals. Frank Shorter was the first U.S. athlete in 64 years to win the gold medal for the marathon, and the U.S. basketball team lost for the first time since the game was introduced in 1936. In wrestling, the U.S. won three gold, two silver, and one bronze medal, the best showing ever in this sport when both the U.S. and the USSR competed. On Sept. 5, Arab terrorists entered the Olympic village, killed two Israeli coaches, and took nine Israeli athletes hostage. All nine were killed, along with a number of terrorists, in a shootout at the Munich airport. The Olympic Games were suspended for the first time in modern history. They were resumed on Sept. 6 after a memorial service for the dead athletes.

Aug. 30 The 47th annual **Hambletonian Stakes** was won in straight heats by Super Bowl, driven by Stanley Dancer.

Sept. 9-10 The **U.S. Open tennis singles championships** were won by Billie Jean King for the third time in the women's division and by Ilie Nastase of Rumania over Arthur Ashe in the men's division.

Sept. 10 The **U.S. Olympic basketball team was defeated** by the USSR team 51-50 in a game marked by a hectic and disputed final 3 sec. A U.S. protest that the clock was incorrect was denied. The defeat ended the 63-game winning streak of the U.S. in Olympic basketball competition.

Oct. The **World Hockey Association (WHA)** began play with a 12-franchise circuit, split into two divisions. The NHL countered by adding the New York Islanders and the Atlanta Flames.

Oct. 1 The third annual **New York City Marathon** was won by Sheldon Karlin, with a time of 2 hrs., 27 min., 52.8 sec. A separate women's competition was boycotted by its ten entrants, who were permitted to run in the main race after a 10-min. sit-in. The first woman to finish was Nina Kuscsik, with an official time of 3 hrs., 18 min., 41 sec.

Oct. 13-15 The **Davis Cup** tennis championship was successfully defended by the U.S., defeat-

ing Rumania three matches to two in Buchar-
est.

Oct. 14-22 The **World Series** was won by the
Oakland Athletics (AL), defeating the Cincinnati Reds (NL) four games to three. A second-
string Oakland catcher, Gene Tenace, was his
team's hero. He drove in nine runs and tied a
World Series record with four home runs. On
Oct. 11 the Reds had won the National League
pennant by beating the Pittsburgh Pirates three
games to two. The next day the Athletics won
the American League title over the Detroit
Tigers, three games to two.

Oct. 29 Two possible origins of the **Frisbee,**
which became popular on college campuses,
were reported by the *New York Times.* One
version says that a Yale student began it by
throwing a church collection plate 200 ft. on the
campus. Another version reported that it got its
name at Yale after World War II, when students
took to throwing empty pie plates that came
from the Frisbie Bakery.

Nov. In soccer the NCAA initiated a **playoff series**
for its college division (Division II) teams similar to the series for its Division I teams. The first
championship was won by Southern Illinois U.,
Edwardsville, Ill., where the series was held.

Nov. 6 What was billed as the first intercollegiate
game of **Ultimate Frisbee** was played at New
Brunswick, N.J., between Rutgers and Princeton. The schools 103 years earlier had played
the first game of football in the U.S., with Rutgers beating Princeton by 6-4. Rutgers also won
at Ultimate Frisbee. The score this time was
29-27. The new game was copyrighted by Columbia High School of Maplewood, N.J., which
had developed it as a team sport. Ultimate Frisbee combines basketball and football, but a
player may not run with the Frisbee, and points
are scored by completing a pass of a Frisbee
over the goal line. Seven-person teams play 24-
min. halves.

Dec. 5 The **Heisman Trophy** for outstanding college football player was awarded to Nebraska
running back Johnny Rodgers.

Nice guys finish last.

Leo Durocher

Dec. 31 **Roberto Clemente,** star outfielder for
the Pittsburgh Pirates, died in an airplane accident en route to San Juan, P.R. He had a lifetime
major league batting average of .317 and hit 240
home runs in his 18 years in the majors, all of
them with the Pirates.

1973

A **baseball players' strike** was averted when an
agreement was reached between owners and players that allowed a player with ten years of service,
the last five with the same club, to refuse a trade
made without his consent. Coupled with this was an
arbitrator's decision that any player without a contract was a free agent and could make any deal on
his own. Thus, the reserve rule was undermined.

Winter First place in the first **Gold Cup World DN
Championships** for iceboats, held at Gull
Lake, Mich., was won by Ain Vilde of Estonia,
USSR. Tim Woodhouse of Michigan, previously
a three-time North American champion, in 1974
became the first American to win the cup, at a
site near Warsaw, Poland. The site of this annual meet alternates between North America
and Europe.

Jan. 1 In **college football bowl games,** the results were Texas 17, Alabama 13 in the Cotton
Bowl; Nebraska 40, Notre Dame 6 in the Orange
Bowl; Southern California 42, Ohio State 17 in
the Rose Bowl; and Oklahoma 14, Penn State 0
in the Sugar Bowl (Dec. 31, 1972). This season
the AP and UPI polls chose Southern California
as national college football champion of 1972.

Jan. 11 The **designated hitter rule** was adopted
by the American League on a three-year trial
basis by the owners of the 24 major league
clubs. It permitted American League teams to
use a pinch hitter for the pitcher whenever it
was the pitcher's turn to bat, without requiring
the pitcher to leave the game. The change was
designed to stimulate fan interest in a period
when American League attendance was slump-
ing.

Jan. 14 **Super Bowl VII** was won by the Miami
Dolphins (AFC), defeating the Washington Redskins (NFC) 14-7. On Dec. 31, 1972, the Dolphins

Golf
UNITED STATES OPEN WINNERS
Men

1901	Willie Anderson	1946	Lloyd Mangrum
1902	L. Auchterlonie	1947	Lew Worsham
1903	Willie Anderson	1948	Ben Hogan
1904	Willie Anderson	1949	Cary Middlecoff
1905	Willie Anderson	1950	Ben Hogan
1906	Alex Smith	1951	Ben Hogan
1907	Alex Ross	1952	Julius Boros
1908	Fred McLeod	1953	Ben Hogan
1909	George Sargent	1954	Ed Furgol
1910	Alex Smith	1955	Jack Fleck
1911	John McDermott	1956	Cary Middlecoff
1912	John McDermott	1957	Dick Mayer
1913	Francis Ouimet	1958	Tommy Bolt
1914	Walter Hagen	1959	Billy Casper
1915	Jerome Travers	1960	Arnold Palmer
1916	Chick Evans	1961	Gene Littler
1917–18	(tournament	1962	Jack Nicklaus
	not held	1963	Julius Boros
1919	Walter Hagen	1964	Ken Venturi
1920	Edward Ray	1965	Gary Player
1921	Jim Barnes	1966	Billy Casper
1922	Gene Sarazen	1967	Jack Nicklaus
1923	Bobby Jones	1968	Lee Trevino
1924	Cyril Walker	1969	Orville Moody
1925	Willie MacFarlane	1970	Tony Jacklin
1926	Bobby Jones	1971	Lee Trevino
1927	Tommy Armour	1972	Jack Nicklaus
1928	John Farrell	1973	Johnny Miller
1929	Bobby Jones	1974	Hale Irwin
1930	Bobby Jones	1975	Lou Graham
1931	William Burke	1976	Jerry Pate
1932	Gene Sarazen	1977	Hubert Green
1933	John Goodman	1978	Andy North
1934	Olin Dutra	1979	Hale Irwin
1935	Sam Parks	1980	Jack Nicklaus
1936	Tony Manero	1981	David Graham
1937	Ralph Guldahl	1982	Tom Watson
1938	Ralph Guldahl	1983	Larry Nelson
1939	Byron Nelson	1984	Fuzzy Zoeller
1940	Lawson Little	1985	Andy North
1941	Craig Wood	1986	Ray Floyd
1942–45	(tournament	1987	Scott Simpson
	not held)		

had defeated the Pittsburgh Steelers 21-17 for the AFC championship and the Redskins had beaten the Dallas Cowboys 26-3 for the NFC title.

Jan. 22 The **world heavyweight boxing championship** was won by George Foreman, who defeated Joe Frazier in a second-round knockout in Kingston, Jamaica. On Sept. 1 he defended the title with a one-round knockout of Joe Roman in Tokyo, Japan.

Jan. 24-27 **U.S. figure skating championships** were won in Bloomington, Minn., by Gordon

McKellen, Jr., men's singles; Janet Lynn, women's singles; Melissa and Mark Militano, pairs; and Mary Karen Campbell and Johnny Johns, dance.

Jan. 27 A new **college basketball winning streak** was set by UCLA, which won its 61st consecutive game, over Notre Dame at South Bend, Ind., 82-63. This broke the old record set by San Francisco U. in 1956. On Jan. 19, 1974, Notre Dame would beat UCLA 71-70, again at South Bend, to halt UCLA's winning streak at 88 games.

Feb. 18 At the **Westminster Kennel Club** dog show, Ch. Acadia Command Performance, a standard poodle owned by Edward B. Jenner and Jo Ann Sering, took best-in-show.

Mar. The **first Iditarod Trail Sled Dog Race** was run, from Anchorage to Nome, Alaska. The winner was Dick Wilmarth, of Red Devil, Alaska, in a time of 20 days, 49 min., and 41 sec.

Mar. 1 **Robyn Smith** became the first woman jockey to win a stakes race when she rode North Sea to victory in the Paumonok Handicap at Aqueduct Raceway, Queens, N.Y.

Mar. 3 The **U.S. Lawn Tennis Association** informed the West Side Tennis Club, Forest Hills, N.Y., that it must convert its grass courts to a synthetic surface or face loss of the tournament.

Mar. 4-June 6 The **International Track Association** launched its first season of professional meets.

Mar. 5 Terms of the **first comprehensive basketball contract** between the NBA and the Players Association were announced. They included the highest minimum salary in professional sports, $20,000, and pension benefits of $720 for each season played.

Mar. 24 The second **AIAW basketball championship** was won by Immaculata College, beating Queens College 59-52 for its second women's college championship.

Mar. 26 The **NCAA basketball championship** was won for the seventh consecutive year by UCLA, defeating Memphis State 87-66. Bill Walton scored 44 points for UCLA.

Apr. 9 **Otto Kerner,** former governor of Illinois, was sentenced to three years in prison and fined $50,000 for his role in an illegal racetrack scheme.

Apr. 9 The **Masters golf tournament** was won by Tommy Aaron.

Apr. 9 Warring ended between **professional women's tennis** groups and the U.S. Lawn Tennis Association over the sanctioning of tournaments and scheduling. An agreement was reached on Apr. 27 and was approved by the players on Apr. 30.

Apr. 17 The **Boston Marathon** was won by Jon Anderson of Oregon, with a time of 2 hrs., 16 min., 3 sec. He was the first U.S. winner in four years. The first woman to cross the finish line was Jacqueline Hansen of California, with a time of 3 hrs., 5 min., 59 sec.

Apr. 28-May 12 The **ABA basketball championship** was won by the Indiana Pacers, who defeated the Kentucky Colonels four games to three.

Apr. 29-May 10 The **NHL Stanley Cup** was won by the Montreal Canadiens, who defeated the Chicago Black Hawks four games to two.

May 5 The 99th annual **Kentucky Derby** was won by Secretariat, with a record time of 1:59⅖. The jockey was Ron Turcotte.

May 6 The **first World Hockey Association championship** was won by the New England Whalers, defeating the Winnipeg Jets four games to one.

May 10 The **NBA basketball championship** was won by the New York Knicks, who beat the Los Angeles Lakers four games to one. Willis Reed played Wilt Chamberlain to a standstill, while teammates Earl Monroe, Walt Frazier, and Bill Bradley piled up big scores for the Knicks.

May 13 **Bobby Riggs,** 55-year-old former tennis champion, easily defeated Margaret Smith Court, leading women's professional player, at Ramona, Calif., in a match instigated by Riggs's put-downs of women's tennis. The winner-take-all prize was $10,000. Income from national television was substantial.

May 19 The 98th annual **Preakness Stakes** was won by Secretariat, with a time of 1:55. The jockey was Ron Turcotte.

May 21 The **first athletic scholarship awarded to a woman** was given to Lynn Genesko, a swimmer from Woodbridge, N.J., by the U. of Miami (Fla.).

May 27 A new **track record** for the 880-yard run was set by Rick Wohlhuter, who ran the distance in 1:44.6 at the AAU meet in Los Angeles.

May 30 The 57th **Indianapolis 500** auto race was won by Gordon Johncock, who completed the abbreviated race (332.5 mi.) in 2 hrs., 5 min.,

26.59 sec. at an average speed of 159.014 mph.

June 9 The 105th annual **Belmont Stakes** was won by Secretariat, with a time of 2:24, thus becoming the ninth horse to win racing's Triple Crown. The jockey was Ron Turcotte. Secretariat set a world record for the 1.5 mi. distance on a dirt track and also set a record for the largest margin of victory in the Belmont, 31 lengths.

June 10 The **LPGA golf tournament** was won by Mary Mills, with a score of 288.

June 17 The **U.S. Open golf tournament** was won by Johnny Miller, who carded a 63 in his final round.

June 19 **Janet Lynn,** five-time U.S. figure skating champion, signed a three-year, $1,455,000 contract with the Ice Follies.

July 7-8 At the **Wimbledon** tennis championships in England, Billie Jean King won the women's singles title for the second straight year. King teamed with Rosemary Casals to win the women's doubles and with Owen Davidson of Australia to win the mixed doubles. Jimmy Connors teamed with Ilie Nastase of Rumania to take the men's doubles. Many tennis professionals boycotted the championship because the International Lawn Tennis Federation had suspended Yugoslavian player Nikki Pilic for refusing to play on the Yugoslavian Davis Cup team.

July 20 **Bruce Lee,** a popularizer of martial arts, died at age 32. His appearance in the TV series *The Green Hornet* in 1966 and the movie *Enter the Dragon* in 1973, in which he used his judo-karate talents, started a boom in interest in the martial arts in the U.S.

July 22 The **U.S. Women's Open golf tournament** was won by Sue Berning with a score of 290.

July 24 The **baseball all-star game** was won by the National League, beating the American League 7 to 1. A record number of players, 28 National League and 26 American League, played in the game.

Aug. 3 **World Team Tennis,** a newly organized 16-team professional tennis league, announced plans for the 1974 season and began to put together teams of men and women players under contract with the league.

Aug. 6 The **Baseball Hall of Fame** inducted five new members: Roberto Clemente, Billy Evans, Monte Irvin, George Kelly, and Warren Spahn.

Aug. 12 The **PGA golf tournament** was won at Lost Tree Village, Fla., by Jack Nicklaus, with a score of 277.

Aug. 25 The **North American Soccer League championship** was won by the Philadelphia Atoms, who defeated the Dallas Tornado 2-0.

Aug. 29 The 48th annual **Hambletonian Stakes** was won by Flirth in straight heats. The driver was Ralph Baldwin.

Aug. 29-Sept. 9 The **U.S. Open tennis singles championships** were won by John Newcombe of Australia over teammate Ken Rosewall in the men's division and by Margaret Smith Court of Australia, for the fifth time, in the women's division, over Evonne Goolagong.

Sept. 20 In a nationally televised tennis match billed as the **Battle of the Sexes,** Billie Jean King beat Bobby Riggs in three straight sets and won the $100,000 winner-take-all purse.

Sept. 25 **Willie Mays,** completing his career with the New York Mets, retired at season's end after 22 years in the majors. He was honored in a ceremony today at Shea Stadium in New York City. Mays, who had played for most of his career with the Giants, had a career total of 660 home runs.

Sept. 30 The fourth annual **New York City Marathon** was won by Tom Fleming of Bloomfield, N.J., with a course record time of 2 hrs., 21 min., 54.2 sec. Of the 12 women entrants, the first to finish was Nina Kuscsik of Long Island, N.Y., with a time of 2 hrs., 57 min., 7 sec.

Oct. 3 Formation of the **World Football League,** a new pro football league, was announced. Some NFL players were lured to the new group by high salary offers, and the sponsors spoke of expanding to foreign countries. However, with no TV revenue and small crowds, the league on Oct. 22, 1975, announced it was going out of business. Its ten teams were then playing the league's second season.

Oct. 13-21 The **World Series** was won for the second year in a row by the Oakland Athletics (AL), defeating the New York Mets (NL) four games to three. Ken Holtzman pitched two winning games for Oakland, and the Mets outhit the Athletics .253 to .212. Although a series "ain't over until it's over," the Mets never had a chance in the final game, losing 5-2. Oakland shortstop Bert Campaneris and Reggie Jackson hit two-run homers in the third inning. The Mets had won the National League pennant on Oct. 10 by beating the Cincinnati Reds three

MASTERS TOURNAMENT WINNERS

1934	Horton Smith	1962	Arnold Palmer
1935	Gene Sarazen	1963	Jack Nicklaus
1936	Horton Smith	1964	Arnold Palmer
1937	Byron Nelson	1965	Jack Nicklaus
1938	Henry Picard	1966	Jack Nicklaus
1939	Ralph Guldahl	1967	Gay Brewer
1940	Jimmy Demaret	1968	Bob Goalby
1941	Craig Wood	1969	George Archer
1942	Byron Nelson	1970	Billy Casper
1943–45	(tournament not held)	1971	Charles Coody
		1972	Jack Nicklaus
1946	Herman Keiser	1973	Tommy Aaron
1947	Jimmy Demaret	1974	Gary Player
1948	Claude Harmon	1975	Jack Nicklaus
1949	Sam Snead	1976	Ray Floyd
1950	Jimmy Demaret	1977	Tom Watson
1951	Ben Hogan	1978	Gary Player
1952	Sam Snead	1979	Fuzzy Zoeller
1953	Ben Hogan	1980	Severiano Ballesteros
1954	Sam Snead	1981	Tom Watson
1955	Cary Middlecoff	1982	Craig Stadler
1956	Jack Burke	1983	Severiano Ballesteros
1957	Doug Ford	1984	Ben Crenshaw
1958	Arnold Palmer	1985	Bernhard Langer
1959	Art Wall, Jr.	1986	Jack Nicklaus
1960	Arnold Palmer	1987	Larry Mize
1961	Gary Player		

games to two. This made manager Yogi Berra the only manager besides Joe McCarthy to win pennants in both major leagues. The Athletics had won the American League title on Oct. 11, beating the Baltimore Orioles three games to two.

Nov. 30-Dec. 2 The **Davis Cup** tennis championship was won by Australia, in Cleveland, Ohio. The Australians beat the U.S. in five straight matches.

Dec. 1 **Jack Nicklaus** won the Disney World Open, becoming the first professional golfer to hit a career total of $2,000,000 in winnings.

Dec. 8 The **Heisman Trophy** for outstanding college football player of 1973 was voted to Penn State back John Cappelletti.

Dec. 16 A new **NFL rushing record** was set by O. J. Simpson, running back for the Buffalo Bills, who broke Jim Brown's 1963 total of 1863 yards. Simpson later set a new pro record of 2003 yards.

1974

Swimmers of the **U. of Southern California** edged Indiana U. 339-338 for the NCAA men's national championship, ending Indiana's string of six consecutive titles.

There were now 33,900,000 **tennis players** in the U.S., according to a Nielsen report.

Jan. 1 In **college football bowl games,** the results were Nebraska 19, Texas 3 in the Cotton Bowl; Penn State 16, Louisiana State 9 in the Orange Bowl; Ohio State 42, USC 21 in the Rose Bowl; and Nebraska 13, Florida 10 in the Sugar Bowl (Dec. 31, 1973). This season the AP poll chose Notre Dame as national college football champion of 1973. The UPI poll selected Alabama.

Jan. 4 In the **NCAA men's soccer match** for the 1973 title, St. Louis U. defeated UCLA by a score of 2-1 in overtime in the Orange Bowl. This was the winner's ninth title in the 14 years since playoffs began. In addition, St. Louis shared the title with Michigan State in 1967 when, in inclement weather, their game was declared a tie.

Jan. 13 **Super Bowl VIII** was won by the Miami Dolphins, defeating the Minnesota Vikings 24-7 for their second consecutive Super Bowl win. On Dec. 30, 1973, the Dolphins had defeated the Oakland Raiders 27-10 for the NFC championship, becoming the first team in NFL history to go through an entire season undefeated. Also on that day, the Vikings defeated the Dallas Cowboys 27-10 for the AFC championship.

Jan. 24 **World Championship Tennis** (WCT), the organization of professional tennis players, severed its ties with the U.S. Lawn Tennis Association, WCT head Lamar Hunt announced.

Feb. 6-9 **U.S. figure skating championships** were won in Providence, R.I., by Gordon McKellen, Jr., men's singles; Dorothy Hamill, women's singles; Melissa Militano and Johnny Johns, pairs; and Colleen O'Connor and Jim Millns, dance.

Feb. 12 At the **Westminster Kennel Club** dog show, Ch. Gretchenhof Columbia River, a German short-haired pointer owned by Dr. Richard P. Smith of Hayward, Calif., took best-in-show.

Feb. 20 **Gordie Howe,** high-scoring Detroit forward, retired since Sept. 9, 1971, returned to professional hockey with the Houston Aeros of the WHA. His four-year pact guaranteed him $1,000,000 and the chance to play on the same team with his sons Marty and Mark.

Mar. 23 The third annual **AIAW basketball championship** was won by Immaculata College, defeating Mississippi State 68-53. It was Immaculata's third consecutive women's college title.

Mar. 24 The **NCAA basketball championship** was won by North Carolina State U., defeating Marquette 76-64. David Thompson was North Carolina's outstanding player. UCLA, defeated in the semifinals, had won seven consecutive titles.

Apr. 8 **Hank Aaron** of the Atlanta Braves (NL) hit his 715th career home run in Atlanta against the Los Angeles Dodgers, breaking the record set decades earlier by the great Babe Ruth. Aaron finished the year with a career total of 733 homers.

Figure Skating
**UNITED STATES
MEN'S SINGLES CHAMPIONS**

1946	Dick Button
1947	Dick Button
1948	Dick Button
1949	Dick Button
1950	Dick Button
1951	Dick Button
1952	Dick Button
1953	Hayes Jenkins
1954	Hayes Jenkins
1955	Hayes Jenkins
1957	David Jenkins
1958	David Jenkins
1959	David Jenkins
1960	David Jenkins
1961	Bradley Lord
1962	Monty Hoyt
1963	Tommy Litz
1964	Scott Allen
1965	Gary Visconti
1966	Scott Allen
1967	Gary Visconti
1968	Tim Wood
1969	Tim Wood
1970	Tim Wood
1971	John Petkevich
1972	Ken Shelley
1973	Gordon McKellen
1974	Gordon McKellen
1975	Gordon McKellen
1976	Terry Kubicka
1977	Charles Tickner
1978	Charles Tickner
1979	Charles Tickner
1980	Charles Tickner
1981	Scott Hamilton
1982	Scott Hamilton
1983	Scott Hamilton
1984	Scott Hamilton
1985	Brian Boitano
1986	Brian Boitano
1987	Brian Boitano

Apr. 14 The **Masters golf tournament** was won by Gary Player, who earned his second green jacket with a score of 278.

Apr. 15 The 78th annual **Boston Marathon** was won by Neil Cusack of Ireland, with a time of 2 hrs., 13 min., 39 sec. The first woman to finish was Michiko "Miki" Gorman of Los Angeles, with a time of 2 hrs., 47 min., 11 sec.

Apr. 25 **Football rule changes** were announced by the NFL, including a 15-min. sudden death period to avoid tie games and the moving of goalposts 10 yards back from the goal lines to make it more difficult to score a field goal.

Apr. 28-May 12 The **NBA basketball championship** was won by the Boston Celtics, who took their 12th title in 18 years by beating the Milwaukee Bucks four games to three. It was defense that did it for the Celtics, especially in the final game, won by the score of 102-87.

Apr. 30-May 10 The **ABA basketball championship** was won by the New York Nets, who beat the Utah Stars four games to one.

May 4 The 100th annual **Kentucky Derby** was won by Cannonade, with a time of 2:04. The jockey was Angel Cordero.

May 7-19 The **NHL Stanley Cup** was won by the Philadelphia Flyers, who beat the Boston Bruins four games to two.

May 18 The 99th annual **Preakness Stakes** was won by Little Current, with a time of 1:54⅗. The jockey was Miguel Rivera.

May 25 The NCAA conducted its **first national collegiate Division II lacrosse championships** at SUNY, Cortland, N.Y. It initiated Division III playoffs in 1980.

May 26 The 58th **Indianapolis 500** auto race was won by Johnny Rutherford, who completed the 500-mi. course in 3 hrs., 9 min., 10.06 sec., at an average speed of 158.589 mph.

June 8 The 106th annual **Belmont Stakes** was won by Little Current, with a time of 2:29⅕. The jockey was Miguel Rivera.

June 12 **Little League baseball** announced that its teams would be open to girls. In so doing, and in the face of numerous legal challenges to the exclusion of girls, Little League officials "deferred to the changing social climate."

June 16 The **U.S. Open golf tournament** was won by Hale Irwin, beating Forrest Fezler by two strokes at Winged Foot, Mamaroneck, N.Y. Irwin scored a seven-over-par 287.

June 23 The **LPGA golf tournament** was won by Sandra Haynie, followed by JoAnne Carner, who won six events this year.

July 5 At the **Wimbledon** tennis championships in England, Chris Evert won the women's singles title over Olga Morozova of the USSR. On July 6, Jimmy Connors won the men's singles title over Ken Rosewall of Australia. Peggy Michel teamed with Evonne Goolagong of Aus-

tralia to win the women's doubles, and Billie Jean King teamed with Owen Davidson of Australia to win the mixed doubles for the fourth time.

July 21 The **U.S. Women's Open golf tournament** was won by Sandra Haynie, who birdied the final two holes to edge past Carol Mann and Beth Stone by one stroke, at LaGrange, Ill.

July 23 The **baseball all-star game** was won by the National League, beating the American League 7-2 for its 11th win in 12 years. First baseman Steve Garvey starred at bat and in the field for the winners.

Aug. 11 The **PGA golf tournament** was won by Lee Trevino, beating Jack Nicklaus by one stroke at El Paso, Tex.

Aug. 12 The **Baseball Hall of Fame** inducted six new members: James "Cool Papa" Bell, a star in Negro league play; Sunny Jim Bottomley, Jocko Conlan, Whitey Ford, Mickey Mantle, and Samuel Thompson.

Aug. 20 A **pitching speed record** was set by Nolan Ryan, pitcher for the California Angels. In a game against Detroit, he threw a pitch that was clocked by infrared radar at 100.9 mph. The previous record belonged to Bob Feller of Cleveland, who was clocked in 1946 at 98.6 mph. In 1973, Ryan had 383 strikeouts for the season.

Aug. 25 The **North American Soccer League championship** was won by the Los Angeles Aztecs, who defeated the Miami Toros 4-3.

Aug. 29 **Moses Malone**, 6 ft., 11 in., 210-lb., 19-year-old high school basketball star from Petersburg, Va., signed a contract with the Utah Stars (ABA) that guaranteed him a salary of between $150,000 and $200,000 a year, with bonuses and incentives attached. He became the first player to go directly from high school into major league professional basketball.

Aug. 30 The 49th **Hambletonian Stakes** was won by Christopher T in the third heat of a split-field competition. The driver was Bill Haughton, who picked up his first Hambletonian win in a career total of more than 3800 victories.

Sept. 2 Two teams of women played the **longest softball game ever**, at Parsippany, N.J. The game went 620 innings and was staged as a benefit for the Muscular Dystrophy Foundation.

Sept. 9 The **U.S. Open tennis singles championships** were won by Jimmy Connors over

Ken Rosewall of Australia in the men's division and by Billie Jean King over Evonne Goolagong of Australia in the women's division.

Sept. 10 **Lou Brock** of the St. Louis Cardinals (NL) broke the major league record set by Maury Wills, 104 stolen bases in a season. Brock completed steal 105 in a home game against the Philadelphia Phillies. He finished the year with 118 and his National League career in 1979 with a record of 938 stolen bases.

Sept. 10-17 The **America's Cup** was successfully defended by the U.S. yacht *Courageous,* which won four straight races from the Australian challenger Southern *Cross.*

Sept. 29 The fifth annual **New York City Marathon** was won by Dr. Norbert Sander, Jr., of New York City, with a time of 2 hrs., 26 min., 30 sec. The first woman to complete the race was Kathy Switzer of New York City, with a time of 3 hrs., 7 min., 29 sec.

Oct. 3 **Frank Robinson** became the first black manager in major league baseball when he signed a $175,000-a-year contract as player-manager with the Cleveland Indians.

Oct. 5 David Kunst completed a **walk around the world.** He had begun it on June 10, 1970. It had been reported that George Schilling had accomplished this feat between June 1897 and June 1904, but this claim was not confirmed.

Oct. 12-17 The **World Series** was won for the third straight year by the Oakland Athletics (AL), who beat the Los Angeles Dodgers four games to one. After making four successful appearances in relief, pitcher Rollie Fingers was voted most valuable player. Fingers won one game and saved two for Oakland. Oakland broke a 2-2 tie with a run in the seventh inning of the fifth game when Joe Rudi pulled a pitch high into the second deck of the left field grandstand in Oakland. On Oct. 9, the Athletics had won the American League pennant, beating the Baltimore Orioles three games to one. On the same day, the Dodgers took the National League pennant from the Pittsburgh Pirates, winning three games to one.

Oct. 17 The **world championship in women's softball** was won for the first time by an American team. At Stratford, Conn., the Raybestos Brakettes defeated Japan in the final game 3-0.

Oct. 30 The **world heavyweight boxing championship** was regained by Muhammad Ali,

Figure Skating
UNITED STATES WOMEN'S SINGLES CHAMPIONS

1943	Gretchen Merrill
1944	Gretchen Merrill
1945	Gretchen Merrill
1946	Gretchen Merrill
1947	Gretchen Merrill
1948	Gretchen Merrill
1949	Yvonne Sherman
1950	Yvonne Sherman
1951	Sonya Klopfer
1952	Tenley Albright
1953	Tenley Albright
1954	Tenley Albright
1955	Tenley Albright
1956	Tenley Albright
1957	Carol Heiss
1958	Carol Heiss
1959	Carol Heiss
1960	Carol Heiss
1961	Laurence Owen
1962	Barbara Pursley
1963	Lorraine Hanlon
1964	Peggy Fleming
1965	Peggy Fleming
1966	Peggy Fleming
1967	Peggy Fleming
1968	Peggy Fleming
1969	Janet Lynn
1970	Janet Lynn
1971	Janet Lynn
1972	Janet Lynn
1973	Janet Lynn
1974	Dorothy Hamill
1975	Dorothy Hamill
1976	Dorothy Hamill
1977	Linda Fratianne
1978	Linda Fratianne
1979	Linda Fratianne
1980	Linda Fratianne
1981	Elaine Zayak
1982	Rosalynn Sumners
1983	Rosalynn Sumners
1984	Rosalynn Sumners
1985	Tiffany Chin
1986	Debi Thomas
1987	Jill Trenary

who triumphed over George Foreman with an eighth-round knockout in Kinshasa, Zaire.

Nov. 11 Competition in the **Little League world series** was seriously impaired when foreign teams were barred from participating. Japan and Taiwan had won seven of the last eight baseball championships.

Dec. 15 Jim "Catfish" Hunter, Oakland pitcher, was ruled a **free agent** by arbitrator Peter Seitz because the team owner, Charles O. Finley, had failed to live up to the terms of Hunter's contract. Twenty clubs began bidding for the star pitcher.

Dec. 20 The **NFL player reserve system** was ruled illegal by Federal Judge William Sweigert. Under the so-called Rozelle rule, named for NFL commissioner Pete Rozelle, the league could decide which team a player would play for even after his contract with a team was completed. The ruling, handed down in an antitrust suit filed by quarterback Joe Kapp, meant that such players in future could negotiate with any team they chose.

Dec. 27 The **Heisman Trophy** for outstanding college football player of 1974 was awarded to Ohio State running back Archie Griffin.

1975

Jan. 1 In **college football bowl games,** the results were Penn State 41, Baylor 20 in the Cotton Bowl; Notre Dame 13, Alabama 11 in the Orange Bowl; USC 18, Ohio State 17 in the Rose Bowl; and Nebraska 13, Florida 10 in the Sugar Bowl (Dec. 31, 1974). This season the AP poll chose Oklahoma as national college football champion, and the UPI poll chose USC.

Jan. 12 **Super Bowl IX** was won by the Pittsburgh Steelers (AFC), who defeated the Minnesota Vikings (NFC) 16-6 for their first Super Bowl win. On Dec. 29, 1974, the Steelers had beaten the Oakland Raiders 24-13 for the AFC championship and the Vikings had defeated the Los Angeles Rams 14-10 for the NFC title.

Jan. 31-Feb. 2 **U.S. figure skating championships** were won in Oakland, Calif., by Gordon McKellen, Jr., men's singles; Dorothy Hamill, women's singles; Melissa Militano and Johnny Johns, pairs; and Colleen O'Connor and Jim Millns, dance.

Feb. 11 At the **Westminster Kennel Club** dog show, Ch. Sir Lancelot of Barvan, an old English sheepdog owned by Mr. and Mrs. Ronald Vanward of Newmarket, Ontario, Canada, took best-in-show.

Feb. 16 **Jimmy Connors** won the National Indoor Tennis tournament, becoming the first player to win the event three consecutive times.

Feb. 22 A **women's basketball doubleheader** at Madison Square Garden in New York City drew 11,969 spectators. In the feature attraction, Immaculata College defeated Queens College 65-61.

Mar. 22 The fourth annual **AIAW basketball championship** was won by Delta State, which defeated the three-time women's national champion, Immaculata College, 90-81.

Mar. 31 The **NCAA basketball championship** was won for the tenth time in 12 years by UCLA, defeating the U. of Kentucky 92-85. On Mar. 29, UCLA coach John Wooden had announced he was retiring, after compiling a 620-147 career record.

Apr. 13 The **Masters golf tournament** was won for the fifth time by Jack Nicklaus. His long putt for a birdie on the 70th hole provided him with a one-stroke margin over Johnny Miller and Tom Weiskopf.

Apr. 21 The 79th annual **Boston Marathon** was won by Bill Rodgers of Boston, with a time of 2 hrs., 9 min., 55 sec., the fastest time to date by a U.S. runner. The first woman to finish was Liane Winter of West Germany, with a time of 2 hrs., 42 min., 24 sec.

May A **cricket team from India,** the Hyderabad Blues, at Randalls Island, N.Y., played a team of New York players fielded by the U.S. Cricket Association. The visitors' tour reflected the return of cricket to favor in the U.S. Some 200 cricket clubs now participate in league or tournament play.

May 3 The 101st annual **Kentucky Derby** was won by Foolish Pleasure, with a time of 2:02. The jockey was Jacinto Vasquez.

May 13-22 The **ABA basketball championship** was won by the Kentucky Colonels, who defeated the Indiana Pacers four games to one.

May 15-27 The **NHL Stanley Cup** was won for the second straight year by the Philadelphia Flyers, defeating the Buffalo Sabres four games to two.

May 17 The 100th annual **Preakness Stakes** was won by Master Derby, a longshot, with

Baseball
AMERICAN LEAGUE BATTING CHAMPIONS

	PLAYER	TEAM	AVERAGE
1901	Nap Lajoie	Philadelphia	.422
1902	Nap Lajoie	Philadelphia/ Cleveland	.378
1903	Nap Lajoie	Cleveland	.355
1904	Nap Lajoie	Cleveland	.377
1905	Elmer Flick	Cleveland	.306
1906	George Stone	St. Louis	.358
1907	Ty Cobb	Detroit	.350
1908	Ty Cobb	Detroit	.324
1909	Ty Cobb	Detroit	.377
1910	Ty Cobb	Detroit	.385
1911	Ty Cobb	Detroit	.420
1912	Ty Cobb	Detroit	.410
1913	Ty Cobb	Detroit	.390
1914	Ty Cobb	Detroit	.368
1915	Ty Cobb	Detroit	.369
1916	Tris Speaker	Cleveland	.386
1917	Ty Cobb	Detroit	.383
1918	Ty Cobb	Detroit	.382
1919	Ty Cobb	Detroit	.384
1920	George Sisler	St. Louis	.407
1921	Harry Heilmann	Detroit	.394
1922	George Sisler	St. Louis	.420
1923	Harry Heilmann	Detroit	.403
1924	Babe Ruth	New York	.378
1925	Harry Heilmann	Detroit	.393
1926	Heinie Manush	Detroit	.378
1927	Harry Heilmann	Detroit	.398
1928	Goose Goslin	Washington	.379
1929	Lew Fonseca	Cleveland	.369
1930	Al Simmons	Philadelphia	.381
1931	Al Simmons	Philadelphia	.390
1932	Dale Alexander	Detroit/Boston	.367
1933	Jimmy Foxx	Philadelphia	.356
1934	Lou Gehrig	New York	.363
1935	Buddy Myer	Washington	.349
1936	Luke Appling	Chicago	.388
1937	Charlie Gehringer	Detroit	.371
1938	Jimmy Foxx	Boston	.349
1939	Joe DiMaggio	New York	.381
1940	Joe DiMaggio	New York	.352
1941	Ted Williams	Boston	.406
1942	Ted Williams	Boston	.356
1943	Luke Appling	Chicago	.328
1944	Lou Boudreau	Cleveland	.327
1945	George Stirnweiss	New York	.309
1946	Mickey Vernon	Washington	.353
1947	Ted Williams	Boston	.343
1948	Ted Williams	Boston	.369

(continued)

AMERICAN LEAGUE BATTING CHAMPIONS *(Continued)*

	PLAYER	TEAM	AVERAGE
1949	George Kell	Detroit	.343
1950	Billy Goodman	Boston	.354
1951	Ferris Fain	Philadelphia	.344
1952	Ferris Fain	Philadelphia	.327
1953	Mickey Vernon	Washington	.337
1954	Bobby Avila	Cleveland	.341
1955	Al Kaline	Detroit	.340
1956	Mickey Mantle	New York	.353
1957	Ted Williams	Boston	.388
1958	Ted Williams	Boston	.328
1959	Harvey Kuenn	Detroit	.353
1960	Pete Runnels	Boston	.320
1961	Norm Cash	Detroit	.361
1962	Pete Runnels	Boston	.326
1963	Carl Yastrzemski	Boston	.321
1964	Tony Oliva	Minnesota	.323
1965	Tony Oliva	Minnesota	.321
1966	Frank Robinson	Baltimore	.316
1967	Carl Yastrzemski	Boston	.326
1968	Carl Yastrzemski	Boston	.301
1969	Rod Carew	Minnesota	.332
1970	Alex Johnson	California	.329
1971	Tony Oliva	Minnesota	.337
1972	Rod Carew	Minnesota	.318
1973	Rod Carew	Minnesota	.350
1974	Rod Carew	Minnesota	.364
1975	Rod Carew	Minnesota	.359
1976	George Brett	Kansas City	.333
1977	Rod Carew	Minnesota	.388
1978	Rod Carew	Minnesota	.333
1979	Fred Lynn	Boston	.333
1980	George Brett	Kansas City	.390
1981	Carney Lansford	Boston	.336
1982	Willie Wilson	Kansas City	.332
1983	Wade Boggs	Boston	.361
1984	Don Mattingly	New York	.343
1985	Wade Boggs	Boston	.368
1986	Wade Boggs	Boston	.357
1987	Wade Boggs	Boston	.363

a time of 1:56²⁄₅. The jockey was Darrel McHargue.

May 18-25 The **NBA basketball championship** was won by the Golden State Warriors, who swept the Washington Bullets in four games. Sound defense plus Rick Barry's high scoring produced the third four-game final round sweep in NBA history.

May 18-28 U.S. athletes, in their **first track and field meet in China,** won 91 of 99 events.

May 30 The 59th **Indianapolis 500** auto race, cut short by rain, was won by Bobby Unser, who completed 435 mi. in 2 hrs., 54 min., 55.08 sec., at an average speed of 149.213 mph.

June 1 The **LPGA golf tournament** was won by Kathy Whitworth.

June 3 It was reported that **Pelé,** the 34-year-old Brazilian soccer star (born Edson Arantes do Nascimento), would come out of retirement to play for the New York Cosmos. His three-year, $7,000,000 contract made him the highest-paid team athlete in the world. For most of Pelé's career, he played for Santos of Brazil. He played his first game for the Cosmos on June 15.

June 3 Guidelines concerning **women in school sports,** affirming the right of women to equal participation in athletics, were sent by the Department of Health, Education and Welfare to public schools and colleges receiving federal aid.

June 7 The 107th annual **Belmont Stakes** was won by Avatar, with a time of 2:28⅕. The jockey was Willie Shoemaker.

June 23 The **U.S. Open golf tournament** was won by Lou Graham, who beat John Mahaffey in a playoff after they tied at 287 at the end of 72 holes.

July 4-5 At the **Wimbledon** tennis championships in England, Billie Jean King defeated Evonne Goolagong Cawley of Australia to win her sixth women's singles title. Arthur Ashe, by defeating Jimmy Connors, became the first black to win the men's singles title. The men's doubles was won by Vitas Gerulaitis and Sandy Mayer. Ann Kiyomura teamed with Kazuko Sawamatsu of Japan to win the women's doubles, and Marty Riessen teamed with Margaret Smith Court of Australia to win the mixed doubles.

July 15 The **baseball all-star game** was won by the National League, defeating the American League 6-3. A three-run ninth inning National League attack on Catfish Hunter and Rich Gossage wiped out a Carl Yastrzemski three-run pinch-hit home run.

July 18 The first pro athlete indicted for a **crime committed during play,** Dave Forbes of the Boston Bruins hockey team saw his trial for criminal assault end in a hung jury. The prosecution decided not to seek a retrial in the case, alleging excessive force used on an opponent.

July 20 The **U.S. Women's Open golf tournament** was won by Sandra Palmer. She carded a 295 at Dallas, Tex.

Aug. 3 The Superdome in New Orleans, La., the **largest indoor sports arena in the world,** was dedicated. The building covers 13 acres, holds 71,647 spectators for a football game, and cost $173,000,000 to construct.

Aug. 10 The **PGA golf tournament** was won by Jack Nicklaus, who beat Bruce Crampton and Tom Weiskopf by two strokes with a score of 276. This made 16 major titles won by Nicklaus, three more than Bobby Jones's career total.

Aug. 18 The **Baseball Hall of Fame** inducted five new members: Earl Averill; Bucky Harris; Billy Herman; Rudy Johnson, a Negro league star; and Ralph Kiner.

Aug. 24 The **North American Soccer League championship** was won by the Tampa Bay Rowdies, who beat the Portland Timbers 2-0.

Aug. 30 The 50th annual **Hambletonian Stakes** was won in the third and fourth heats by Bonefish. The driver was Stanley Dancer.

Sept. 1 **Tom Seaver,** pitcher for the New York Mets, set a new major league record of eight consecutive years with 200 strikeouts or more in a season.

Sept. 6-7 The **U.S. Open tennis singles championships** were won by Chris Evert over Evonne Goolagong Cawley in the women's division and by Manuel Orantes of Spain over Jimmy Connors in the men's division.

Sept. 28 The sixth annual **New York City Marathon** was won by Tom Fleming of New York City, with a course record time of 2 hrs., 19 min., 27 sec. The first woman to finish was Kim Merritt of Wisconsin, with a time of 2 hrs., 46 min., 14 sec.

Oct. 1 In what he called the **Thriller in Manila,** fought in the Philippines, heavyweight champion Muhammad Ali defeated Joe Frazier in 14 rounds in Ali's fourth title defense of the year.

Oct. 11-22 The **World Series** was won by the Cincinnati Reds (NL), who beat the Boston Red Sox (AL) four games to three. The Reds won the series in the last inning of the seventh game when, with two out, a hit by Joe Morgan scored Ken Griffey and gave the Reds the game 4-3. This was Cincinnati's first World Series victory in 35 years. On Oct. 7 the Reds had beaten the Pittsburgh Pirates in three straight games for the National League pennant and the Red Sox had swept the Oakland Athletics in three straight.

Oct. 16-26 At the seventh **Pan-American Games** in Mexico City, Mexico, the U.S. won 116 gold medals and first place in the unofficial team standings, followed by Cuba, Canada, and Mexico.

Oct. 22 The **World Football League was disbanded** 12 weeks into its second season because of declining attendance and lack of a national television contract.

Dec. 6 The **Heisman Trophy** for outstanding college football player of 1975 was voted to Ohio State running back Archie Griffin, the first player to win the trophy twice.

1976

U.S. **archer Darrel Pace set a world's record** for the individual men's event with a score of 2571. This achievement continued the 20-year tradition of dominance by U.S. athletes in target archery.

A **new baseball franchise** was awarded to Seattle, the team becoming known as the Seattle Mariners. The Toronto Blue Jays also won a franchise. They were the second team outside the U.S. to be franchised by professional baseball.

Jan. 1 In **college football bowl games,** the results were Arkansas 31, Georgia 10 in the Cotton Bowl; Oklahoma 14, Michigan 6 in the Orange Bowl; UCLA 23, Ohio State 10 in the Rose Bowl; and Alabama 13, Penn State 6 in the Sugar Bowl (Dec. 31, 1975). This season the AP and UPI polls chose Oklahoma as national college champion of 1975.

Jan. 9 A new **pole vault record** of 18 ft., 1¼ in. was set by Dan Ripley at a National Invitational Indoor Track meet in College Park, Md.

Jan. 10-11 U.S. **figure skating championships** were won in Colorado Springs, Colo., by Dorothy Hamill, women's singles; Terry Kubicka, men's singles; Tai Babilonia and Randy Gardner, pairs; and Colleen O'Connor and Jim Millns, dance.

Jan. 18 **Super Bowl X** was won by the Pittsburgh Steelers (AFC), who defeated the Dallas Cowboys (NFC) 21-17 to pick up their second straight victory. On Jan. 4 the Steelers had beaten the Oakland Raiders 16-10 for the AFC championship and the Cowboys had beaten the Los Angeles Rams 37-7 for the NFC title.

Feb. 4 Two new baseball **free agents** were an-

nounced, pitchers Andy Messersmith of the Los Angeles Dodgers and Dave McNally of the Montreal Expos. The decision was made by U.S. District Court Judge John W. Oliver, who upheld a ruling by arbitrator Peter Seitz. Later in the month, all club owners except Bill Veeck of the Chicago White Sox responded by locking their players out of spring training camp.

Feb. 4-15 At the **Winter Olympics** in Innsbruck, Austria, the U.S. won three gold medals and tied with West Germany for third place, behind the USSR and East Germany. Dorothy Hamill, who won a gold medal on Feb. 13, emerged from the games as an Olympic star. Bill Koch of the U.S. became the first American to win a medal in the Nordic events when he took second place in the 30 kilometer cross country race.

Feb. 10 At the **Westminster Kennel Club** dog show, Ch. Jo-Ni's Red Baron of Crofton, a Lakeland terrier owned by Virginia Dickson of La Habra, Calif., took best-in-show.

Mar. 6 At the **world figure skating championships** in Göteborg, Sweden, Dorothy Hamill won the women's singles title.

Mar. 13 Sheila Young, U.S. speed skater, set a **women's world record** of 40.68 sec. in the 500-m. event at an international speed skating meet held at Davos, Switzerland.

Mar. 27 The fifth **AIAW basketball championship** was won by Delta State College, defeating Immaculata College 69-64 to win its second consecutive title.

Mar. 29 The **NCAA basketball championship** was won by Indiana, defeating Michigan 86-68. Indiana ended the season with a perfect record, the seventh team in NCAA history to do so.

Apr. 11 The **Masters golf tournament** was won by Ray Floyd, who beat Ben Crenshaw by eight strokes and tied the tournament record of 271 set by Jack Nicklaus in 1965.

Apr. 17 **Mike Schmidt,** of the Philadelphia Phillies, set a modern National League record by hitting four consecutive home runs in a single game. Schmidt drove in nine runs, and his final homer for the day broke a 15-15 tie in the game

Float like a butterfly, sting like a bee.

Muhammad Ali, describing his style of boxing

259

against the Chicago Cubs. The Phillies won 18-16.

Apr. 19 The 80th annual **Boston Marathon** was won by Jack Fultz of Arlington, Va., with a time of 2 hrs., 20 min., 19 sec. The first woman to finish was Kim Merritt of Kenosha, Wis., with a time of 2 hrs., 47 min., 19 sec.

May 1 The 102nd **Kentucky Derby** was won in an upset by Bold Forbes, with a time of 2:01⅗. The jockey was Angel Cordero, Jr.

May 1-13 The **ABA basketball championship** was won by the New York Nets, who defeated the Denver Nuggets four games to two to take their second championship in three years.

May 9-16 The **NHL Stanley Cup** was won for the 19th time by the Montreal Canadiens, who swept the Philadelphia Flyers in four straight games.

May 15 The 101st **Preakness Stakes** was won by Elocutionist, with a time of 1:55. The jockey was John Lively.

May 23-June 6 The **NBA basketball championship** was won for the 13th time in 20 seasons by the Boston Celtics, defeating the Phoenix Suns four games to two. Jo Jo White starred for Boston throughout the series.

May 30 The 60th **Indianapolis 500** auto race, shortened to 255 mi. because of rain, was won by Johnny Rutherford, with a time of 1 hr., 42 min., 52.46 sec., at an average speed of 148.725 mph.

May 30 The **LPGA golf tournament** was won by Betty Burfeindt, beating Judy Rankin by one stroke.

June 5 The 108th **Belmont Stakes** was won by Bold Forbes, with a time of 2:29. The jockey was Angel Cordero, Jr.

June 15 **Charles O. Finley,** owner of the Oakland Athletics, sold three of his ace players, Vida Blue, Rollie Fingers, and Joe Rudi, to other clubs for $3,500,000. On June 18, baseball commissioner Bowie Kuhn voided the sale as not being good for baseball.

June 17 In a **basketball merger,** the 18 teams of the NBA merged with four of the six remaining teams of the ABA: the New York (later New Jersey) Nets, Indiana Pacers, Denver Nuggets, and San Antonio Spurs.

June 20 The **U.S. Open golf tournament** was won by 22-year-old Jerry Pate, who beat Tom Weiskopf and Al Geiberger by two strokes. John Mahaffey took an early lead but faded in the final holes.

July 2-3 At the **Wimbledon** tennis championships in England, Chris Evert won the women's singles title over Evonne Goolagong Cawley. Brian Gottfried teamed with Paul Ramirez of Mexico to win the men's doubles, and Evert teamed with Martina Navratilova of Czechoslovakia to win the women's doubles.

July 11 The **U.S. Women's Open golf tournament** was won by JoAnne Carner for the second time, with a two-stroke victory over defending champion Sandra Palmer in an 18-hole playoff.

July 12 A change in the **baseball reserve clause** was agreed to by major league owners and players. The new rule allowed players to become free agents after five years.

July 13 The **baseball all-star game** was won for the fifth straight year by the National League, beating the American League 7-1. Home runs by George Foster and Cesar Cedeno were more than enough for the winning team.

July 17-Aug. 1 At the **Summer Olympics** in Montreal, Canada, the U.S. won 34 gold medals and finished second in the unofficial team standings behind the USSR. Among the stars of the games was decathlon champion Bruce Jenner. On July 31, U.S. boxers won five of the 11 titles. The U.S. winners were Leon Spinks (light heavyweight), Michael Spinks (middleweight), Ray Leonard (light welterweight), Howard Davis (lightweight), and Leo Randolph (flyweight).

Aug. 9 The **Baseball Hall of Fame** inducted six new members: Oscar Charleston, a star of the old Negro leagues; Roger Connor; Cal Hubbard, umpire; Bob Lemon; Freddy Lindstrom; and Robin Roberts.

Aug. 16 The **PGA golf tournament** was won by Dave Stockton, repeating his victory of 1970.

Aug. 27 A new type of **sexual discrimination** in sports was highlighted when transsexual Renee Richards, formerly Richard Raskind, an eye surgeon, was barred from competing at the U.S. Open tennis championships at Forest Hills, N.Y., after refusing to submit to a chromosome qualification test. A year later a court reversed the ruling.

Aug. 28 The **North American Soccer League championship** was won by the Toronto Metros, who beat the Minnesota Kicks 3-0.

Sept. 4 The 51st **Hambletonian Stakes** was won by Steve Lobell in four heats. The driver was Billy Haughton. Three hours after the final heat,

Baseball
NATIONAL LEAGUE BATTING CHAMPIONS

	PLAYER	TEAM	AVERAGE
1901	Jesse Burkett	St. Louis	.376
1902	Ginger Beaumont	Pittsburgh	.357
1903	Honus Wagner	Pittsburgh	.355
1904	Honus Wagner	Pittsburgh	.349
1905	Cy Seymour	Cincinnati	.377
1906	Honus Wagner	Pittsburgh	.339
1907	Honus Wagner	Pittsburgh	.350
1908	Honus Wagner	Pittsburgh	.354
1909	Honus Wagner	Pittsburgh	.339
1910	Sherry Magee	Philadelphia	.331
1911	Honus Wagner	Pittsburgh	.334
1912	Heinie Zimmerman	Chicago	.372
1913	Jake Daubert	Brooklyn	.350
1914	Jake Daubert	Brooklyn	.329
1915	Larry Doyle	New York	.320
1916	Hal Chase	Cincinnati	.339
1917	Edd Roush	Cincinnati	.341
1918	Zack Wheat	Brooklyn	.335
1919	Edd Roush	Cincinnati	.321
1920	Rogers Hornsby	St. Louis	.370
1921	Rogers Hornsby	St. Louis	.397
1922	Rogers Hornsby	St. Louis	.401
1923	Rogers Hornsby	St. Louis	.384
1924	Rogers Hornsby	St. Louis	.424
1925	Rogers Hornsby	St. Louis	.403
1926	Bubbles Hargrave	Cincinnati	.353
1927	Paul Waner	Pittsburgh	.380
1928	Rogers Hornsby	Boston	.387
1929	Lefty O'Doul	Philadelphia	.398
1930	Bill Terry	New York	.401
1931	Chick Hafey	St. Louis	.349
1932	Lefty O'Doul	Brooklyn	.368
1933	Chuck Klein	Philadelphia	.368
1934	Paul Waner	Pittsburgh	.362
1935	Arky Vaughan	Pittsburgh	.385
1936	Paul Waner	Pittsburgh	.373
1937	Joe Medwick	St. Louis	.374
1938	Ernie Lombardi	Cincinnati	.342
1939	Johnnie Mize	St. Louis	.349
1940	Debs Garms	Pittsburgh	.355
1941	Pete Reiser	Brooklyn	.343
1942	Ernie Lombardi	Boston	.330
1943	Stan Musial	St. Louis	.357
1944	Dixie Walker	Brooklyn	.357
1945	Phil Cavaretta	Chicago	.355
1946	Stan Musial	St. Louis	.365
1947	Harry Walker	St. Louis/ Philadelphia	.363
1948	Stan Musial	St. Louis	.376

(continued)

NATIONAL LEAGUE BATTING CHAMPIONS *(Continued)*

	PLAYER	TEAM	AVERAGE
1949	Jackie Robinson	Brooklyn	.342
1950	Stan Musial	St. Louis	.346
1951	Stan Musial	St. Louis	.355
1952	Stan Musial	St. Louis	.336
1953	Carl Furillo	Brooklyn	.344
1954	Willie Mays	New York	.345
1955	Richie Ashburn	Philadelphia	.338
1956	Hank Aaron	Milwaukee	.328
1957	Stan Musial	St. Louis	.351
1958	Richie Ashburn	Philadelphia	.350
1959	Hank Aaron	Milwaukee	.355
1960	Dick Groat	Pittsburgh	.325
1961	Roberto Clemente	Pittsburgh	.351
1962	Tommy Davis	Los Angeles	.346
1963	Tommy Davis	Los Angeles	.326
1964	Roberto Clemente	Pittsburgh	.339
1965	Roberto Clemente	Pittsburgh	.329
1966	Matty Alou	Pittsburgh	.342
1967	Roberto Clemente	Pittsburgh	.357
1968	Pete Rose	Cincinnati	.335
1969	Pete Rose	Cincinnati	.348
1970	Rico Carty	Atlanta	.366
1971	Joe Torre	St. Louis	.363
1972	Billy Williams	Chicago	.333
1973	Pete Rose	Cincinnati	.338
1974	Ralph Garr	Atlanta	.353
1975	Bill Madlock	Chicago	.354
1976	Bill Madlock	Chicago	.339
1977	Dave Parker	Pittsburgh	.338
1978	Dave Parker	Pittsburgh	.334
1979	Keith Hernandez	St. Louis	.344
1980	Bill Buckner	Chicago	.324
1981	Bill Madlock	Pittsburgh	.341
1982	Al Oliver	Montreal	.331
1983	Bill Madlock	Pittsburgh	.323
1984	Tony Gwynn	San Diego	.351
1985	Willie McGee	St. Louis	.353
1986	Tim Raines	Montreal	.334
1987	Tony Gwynn	San Diego	.370

Steve Lobell went into shock and nearly died of exhaustion. The near-disaster prompted officials and owners to demand modification of the rules so that horses would not have to run four races in one day.

Sept. 11-12 The **U.S. Open tennis singles championships** were won by Chris Evert in the women's division and by Jimmy Connors over Bjorn Borg of Sweden in the men's division. Marty Riessen shared the men's doubles title with Tom Okker of the Netherlands.

Sept. 28 The **United States Croquet Association** (USCA) was founded by four clubs: the Westhampton Mallet Club, the Green Gables Croquet Club (Spring Lake, N.J.), the Palm Beach Croquet Club, and the Croquet Club of

Bermuda. The association drew up new rules for the six-wicket standard game. It sponsors annual national championships.

Oct. 8 Chris Chandler and Bob Cormack **reached the top of Mt. Everest.** They became the 54th and 55th mountaineers to accomplish the feat. Chandler and Cormack were members of the American Bicentennial Everest Expedition. Two women who were members of the 12-person team, Barbara Roach and Arlene Blum, reached the 21,000 ft. level, about 8000 ft. below the summit.

Oct. 16-21 The **World Series** was won in a four-game sweep by the Cincinnati Reds (NL) over the New York Yankees (AL). Games two and three were played in temperatures more suitable for football, drawing criticism from commissioner Bowie Kuhn, but the bats of Johnny Bench, Tony Perez, Joe Morgan, and George Foster buried the Yankees. On Oct. 12, the Reds had won the National League pennant over the Philadelphia Phillies in a three-game sweep and the Yankees had taken the American League pennant from the Kansas City Royals three games to two. The Yankees won their pennant on an unforgettable Chris Chambliss first-pitch shot to the bleachers in the bottom of the ninth to break a 6-6 tie.

Oct. 21 **Julius "Dr. J" Erving,** 26-year-old star forward of the New York Nets, was sold, following a contract dispute, to the Philadelphia 76ers, reportedly for nearly $3,000,000.

Oct. 24 The seventh **New York City Marathon** was won by Bill Rodgers, with a time of 2 hrs., 10 min., 10 sec. The first woman to finish was Miki Gorman of California, with a time of 2 hrs., 39 min., 11 sec. It was New York's first citywide marathon. Previous marathons had been run within the confines of Central Park.

Nov. 4 In major league baseball's **first free agent draft,** 24 players from 13 clubs participated. Reggie Jackson signed the most lucrative contract, calling for $2,900,000 to be paid over five years by the New York Yankees.

Nov. 30 The **Heisman Trophy** for outstanding college football player of 1976 was voted to U. of Pittsburgh tailback Tony Dorsett, who had set a varsity rushing record of 6082 yards.

Dec. 21 The highly publicized retrial of boxer **Rubin "Hurricane" Carter and John Artis** for the 1966 murders of three people in a Paterson, N.J., bar ended with conviction of the de-

fendants despite the fact that two of the key witnesses in the original trial recanted their testimony.

1977

John Naber of the U. of Southern California ended his collegiate swimming career by capturing his tenth individual title in four years, eight of them in backstroke events. He also swam on five winning USC relay teams.

Racquetball was now being played by over 5,000,000 people at more than 600 racquetball clubs.

Jan. 1 In **college football bowl games,** the results were Houston 30, Maryland 21 in the Cotton Bowl; Ohio State 27, Colorado 10 in the Orange Bowl; USC 14, Michigan 6 in the Rose Bowl; and Pittsburgh 27, Georgia 3 in the Sugar Bowl. This season the AP and UPI polls chose Pittsburgh as national college champion of 1976.

Jan. 9 **Super Bowl XI** was won by the Oakland Raiders (AFC), who defeated the Minnesota Vikings (NFC) 32-14. On Dec. 26, 1976, the Raiders had beaten the Pittsburgh Steelers 24-7 for the NFC championship and the Vikings had beaten the Los Angeles Rams 24-13 for the AFC title.

Feb. U.S. **archer Luann Ryon** of Riverside, Calif., set a world's record in the individual women's event with a score of 2515 at the world archery championships, held at Canberra, Australia. This year the three-member U.S. men's and women's teams also set world records of 7,444 and 7,379, respectively. Richard McKinney completed the U.S. sweep of events by winning the men's title.

Feb. 1 Television rights to the **1980 Olympics** in Moscow were secured by the National Broadcasting Company, which agreed to pay $35,000,000 for exclusive rights to the games and an additional $50,000,000 for production and equipment costs.

Feb. 3-5 **U.S. figure skating championships** were won in Hartford, Conn., by Charles Tickner, men's singles; Linda Fratianne, women's singles; Tai Babilonia and Randy

Gardner, pairs; and Judi Genovesi and Kent Weigle, dance.

Feb. 15 At the **Westminster Kennel Club** dog show, Ch. Dersade Bobby's Girl, a Sealyham terrier owned by Dorothy Wimer of Churchtown, Pa., took best-in-show.

Feb. 21-24 The **first national women's curling championships,** sponsored by the USWCA, were held at Wilmette, Ill. In an eight-team round robin tournament, the Westchester County (N.Y.) team won.

Mar. 3 At the **world figure skating championships** in Tokyo, Japan, Linda Fratianne won the women's singles title. She won again in 1979.

Mar. 26 The **AIAW basketball championship** was won for the third consecutive year by Delta State, defeating Louisiana State 68-55.

Mar. 28 The **NCAA basketball championship** was won by Marquette, defeating North Carolina 67-59. Marquette's coach, Al McGuire, retired with a championship after coaching for 20 years, 13 of them with Marquette.

Apr. 10 The **Masters golf tournament** was won by Tom Watson. Tied with Jack Nicklaus with four holes to play, Watson pulled ahead to win by two strokes.

Apr. 18 The 81st **Boston Marathon** was won by Jerome Drayton of Canada, with a time of 2 hrs., 14 min., 46 sec. The first woman to finish was Miki Gorman of California, with a time of 2 hrs., 48 min., 44 sec.

May 7 The 103rd **Kentucky Derby** was won by Seattle Slew, with a time of 2:02⅕. The jockey was Jean Cruguet.

May 7-14 The **NHL Stanley Cup** was won by the Montreal Canadiens, who swept the Boston Bruins in four games.

May 19 The **first man to fly more than 1000 mi. in a glider** was Karl Striedeck. In a flight from near Williamsport, Pa., to near Oak Ridge, Tenn., and back, he covered 1015.8 mi.

May 21 The 102nd **Preakness Stakes** was won by Seattle Slew, with a time of 1:54⅖. The jockey was Jean Cruguet.

May 22-June 5 The **NBA basketball championship** was won by the Portland Trail Blazers, who beat the Philadelphia 76ers four games to two after losing the first two games of the series. Bill Walton of Portland was the dominant player throughout the series.

May 29 The 61st **Indianapolis 500** auto race was won by A. J. Foyt, completing the 500-mi.

course in 3 hrs., 5 min., 57.7 sec., at an average speed of 161.331 mph. Janet Guthrie became the first woman to compete in the racing classic. She was forced to drop out after 27 laps when her car developed mechanical problems.

June 10 A **PGA tournament record for 18 holes** was set by Al Geiberger in the second round of the Danny Thomas Classic. Geiberger shot a 59 on a par-72 course.

June 11 The 109th annual **Belmont Stakes** was won by Seattle Slew, finishing in 2:29⅗ to take the race and become the tenth horse to win racing's Triple Crown. The jockey was Jean Cruguet.

June 12 The **LPGA golf tournament** was won by Chako Higuchi of Japan, with a 279 total.

June 19 The **U.S. Open golf tournament** was won in Tulsa, Okla., by Hubert Green, whose 278 led Lou Graham by one stroke. Following a telephoned death threat, Green was surrounded by police on the last four holes.

July 2 At the **Wimbledon** tennis championships in England, the only U.S. player to win in finals play was Joanne Russell, who teamed with Helen Gourlay Cawley of Australia to win the women's doubles championship. Bjorn Borg of Sweden beat Jimmy Connors in five sets in the men's finals.

July 6 Establishment of a **six-city professional rodeo circuit** was announced in Kansas City, Mo. Each team was to comprise 13 men and three women.

July 19 The **baseball all-star game** was won for the sixth time running by the National League, beating the American League 7-5. Four runs in the first inning off Jim Palmer got things started right for the winners.

July 24 The **U.S. Women's Open golf tournament** was won by Hollis Stacy, a previous nonwinner, who beat Nancy Lopez by two strokes.

Aug. 8 The **Baseball Hall of Fame** inducted six new members: Ernie Banks; Martin Dihigo, pitcher in the old Negro leagues; John Henry "Pop" Lloyd, shortstop in the Negro League; Al Lopez; Amos Rusie; and Joe Sewell.

Aug. 14 The **PGA golf tournament** was won by Lanny Wadkins, who beat Gene Littler on the third hole of a sudden death playoff. Wadkins followed this up with a $100,000 purse for his 13-under-par victory in the World Series of Golf at Firestone Country Club, Akron, Ohio.

Aug. 15 A new U.S. **soccer attendance record** of

77,961 was established in a playoff game between the New York Cosmos, starring Pelé, and the Fort Lauderdale Strikers in East Rutherford, N.J.

Aug. 23 The **first human-powered airplane** to attain sustained flight flew a 1.4-mi. course at Shafter, Calif. The pedal-driven craft, *Gossamer Condor,* was invented by Paul MacCready and flown by Bryan Allen. The feat won them a prize of $85,000 offered by the Royal Aeronautic Society of Great Britain.

Aug. 28 The **North American Soccer League championship** was won by the New York Cosmos, who beat the Seattle Sounders 2-1. This was Pelé's last league game for the Cosmos before retiring.

Sept. 3 The 52nd **Hambletonian Stakes** was won in straight heats by Green Speed. The driver was Billy Haughton. It was the first time a New York-bred horse had won the event.

Sept. 10-11 The **U.S. Open tennis singles championships** were won by Chris Evert, defeating Wendy Turnbull for her third straight win in the women's division, and by Guillermo Vilas of Argentina over Jimmy Connors in the men's division.

Sept. 13-18 The **America's Cup** was successfully defended by the U.S. yacht *Courageous,* which beat the challenger *Australia* in four straight races.

Oct. 1 The soccer superstar **Pelé** played his farewell game, playing the first half with the New York Cosmos and the second half with his former team, the Santos of Brazil. The game drew 75,646 fans to Meadowlands Stadium, East Rutherford, New Jersey.

Oct. 11-18 The **World Series** was won by the New York Yankees (AL), defeating the Los Angeles Dodgers (NL) four games to two. In the final game, Reggie Jackson hit three home runs in successive times at bat to power the Yankees to an 8-4 victory. In the series, "Mr. October" scored ten runs and drove in eight. On Oct. 8, the Dodgers had won the National League pennant over the Philadelphia Phillies, three games to one, and the following day the Yankees had clinched the American League pennant by beating the Kansas City Royals, three games to two.

Oct. 23 The eighth annual **New York City Marathon** was won by Bill Rodgers, with a time of 2 hrs., 11 min., 28.2 sec. The first woman to finish

was Miki Gorman of California, with a time of 2 hrs., 43 min., 10 sec.

Dec. 2 A prominent veterinarian, Mark J. Gerard, was indicted in a **horse-switching scandal.** A purportedly dead 4-year-old champion colt, Cinzano, had apparently won a Sept. 23 race at Belmont Park disguised as Lebon, a 57-1 longshot in the betting.

Dec. 8 The **Heisman Trophy** for outstanding college football player of 1977 was voted to University of Texas running back Earl Campbell.

Dec. 31 **Steve Cauthen** set a new record for purses won in a year by a jockey when he finished 1977 with a total of $6,151,750. The 17-year-old rider had earlier set a record for apprentice jockeys. By June of this year, when his apprenticeship ended, Cauthen's purses totaled $4,300,000.

1978

Kenny Roberts won the **world motorcycling championship** on the 500-cc grand prix circuit. He repeated in 1979 and 1980.

This year the **U.S. Open tennis championships were moved** permanently from Forest Hills, N.Y., to the new National Tennis Center in Flushing Meadow Park, N.Y.

Jan. 2 In **college football bowl games,** the results were Notre Dame 38, Texas 10 in the Cotton Bowl; Arkansas 31, Oklahoma 6 in the Orange Bowl; Washington 27, Michigan 20 in the Rose Bowl; and Alabama 35, Ohio State 6 in the Sugar Bowl. This season the AP and UPI polls chose Notre Dame as national collegiate champion of 1977.

Jan. 9 In a major ruling on **coeducational sports,** a federal judge in Dayton, Ohio, ruled against preventing high school girls from playing on the same sports teams as boys.

Jan. 15 **Super Bowl XII** was won by the Dallas Cowboys (NFC), defeating the Denver Broncos (AFC) 27-10. On Jan. 1, the Cowboys had beaten the Minnesota Vikings 23-6 for the NFC championship and the Broncos had defeated the Oakland Raiders 20-17 to take the AFC title.

Feb. 12 U.S. **figure skating championships**

Baseball
AMERICAN LEAGUE HOME RUN LEADERS

	PLAYER	TEAM	TOTAL
1901	Nap Lajoie	Philadelphia	14
1902	Socks Seybold	Philadelphia	16
1903	Buck Freeman	Boston	13
1904	Harry Davis	Philadelphia	10
1905	Harry Davis	Philadelphia	8
1906	Harry Davis	Philadelphia	12
1907	Harry Davis	Philadelphia	8
1908	Sam Crawford	Detroit	7
1909	Ty Cobb	Detroit	9
1910	Jake Stahl	Boston	10
1911	Home Run Baker	Philadelphia	9
1912	Home Run Baker	Philadelphia	10
1913	Home Run Baker	Philadelphia	12
1914	Home Run Baker	Philadelphia	8
	Sam Crawford	Detroit	8
1915	Braggo Roth	Chicago/Cleveland	7
1916	Wally Pipp	New York	12
1917	Wally Pipp	New York	9
1918	Babe Ruth	Boston	11
	Tilly Walker	Philadelphia	11
1919	Babe Ruth	Boston	29
1920	Babe Ruth	New York	54
1921	Babe Ruth	New York	59
1922	Ken Williams	St. Louis	39
1923	Babe Ruth	New York	41
1924	Babe Ruth	New York	46
1925	Bob Meusel	New York	33
1926	Babe Ruth	New York	47
1927	Babe Ruth	New York	60
1928	Babe Ruth	New York	54
1929	Babe Ruth	New York	46
1930	Babe Ruth	New York	49
1931	Babe Ruth	New York	46
	Lou Gehrig	New York	46
1932	Jimmy Foxx	Philadelphia	58
1933	Jimmy Foxx	Philadelphia	48
1934	Lou Gehrig	New York	49
1935	Jimmy Foxx	Philadelphia	36
	Hank Greenberg	Detroit	36
1936	Lou Gehrig	New York	49
1937	Joe DiMaggio	New York	46
1938	Hank Greenberg	Detroit	58
1939	Jimmy Foxx	Boston	35
1940	Hank Greenberg	Detroit	41
1941	Ted Williams	Boston	37
1942	Ted Williams	Boston	36
1943	Rudy York	Detroit	34
1944	Nick Etten	New York	22
1945	Vern Stephens	St. Louis	24

(continued)

AMERICAN LEAGUE HOME RUN LEADERS (Continued)

	PLAYER	TEAM	TOTAL
1946	Hank Greenberg	Detroit	44
1947	Ted Williams	Boston	32
1948	Joe DiMaggio	New York	39
1949	Ted Williams	Boston	43
1950	Al Rosen	Cleveland	37
1951	Gus Zernial	Chicago/Philadelphia	33
1952	Larry Doby	Cleveland	32
1953	Al Rosen	Cleveland	43
1954	Larry Doby	Cleveland	32
1955	Mickey Mantle	New York	37
1956	Mickey Mantle	New York	52
1957	Roy Sievers	Washington	42
1958	Mickey Mantle	New York	42
1959	Rocky Colavito	Cleveland	42
	Harmon Killebrew	Washington	42
1960	Mickey Mantle	New York	40
1961	Roger Maris	New York	61*
1962	Harmon Killebrew	Minnesota	48
1963	Harmon Killebrew	Minnesota	45
1964	Harmon Killebrew	Minnesota	49
1965	Tony Conigliaro	Boston	32
1966	Frank Robinson	Baltimore	49
1967	Carl Yastrzemski	Boston	44
	Harmon Killebrew	Minnesota	44
1968	Frank Howard	Washington	44
1969	Harmon Killebrew	Minnesota	49
1970	Frank Howard	Washington	44
1971	Bill Melton	Chicago	33
1972	Dick Allen	Chicago	37
1973	Reggie Jackson	Oakland	32
1974	Dick Allen	Chicago	32
1975	Reggie Jackson	Oakland	36
	George Scott	Milwaukee	36
1976	Graig Nettles	New York	32
1977	Jim Rice	Boston	39
1978	Jim Rice	Boston	46
1979	Gorman Thomas	Milwaukee	45
1980	Reggie Jackson	New York	41
	Ben Ogilvie	Milwaukee	41
1981	Tony Armas	Oakland	22
	Dwight Evans	Boston	22
	Bobby Grich	California	22
	Eddie Murray	Baltimore	22
1982	Reggie Jackson	California	39
	Gorman Thomas	Milwaukee	39
1983	Jim Rice	Boston	39
1984	Tony Armas	Boston	43
1985	Darrell Evans	Detroit	40
1986	Jesse Barfield	Toronto	40
1987	Mark McGwire	Oakland	49

*162-game season.

were won in Portland, Oreg., by Charles Tickner, men's singles; Linda Fratianne, women's singles; Tai Babilonia and Randy Gardner, pairs; and Stacey Smith and John Summers, dance.

Feb. 14 At the **Westminster Kennel Club** dog show, Ch. Cede Higgins, a Yorkshire terrier owned by Barbara A. and Charles W. Switzer, took best-in-show.

Feb. 15 The **world heavyweight boxing championship** was won by Leon Spinks in a 15-round decision over Muhammad Ali in Las Vegas, Nev.

Mar. 9 At the **world figure skating championships** in Ottawa, Canada, Charles Tickner won the men's singles title.

Mar. 18 Leon Spinks lost recognition as **heavyweight boxing champion** by action of the World Boxing Council. Spinks had won the title in February, when he defeated Muhammad Ali. The council said its action was taken because Spinks had shown bad faith in negotiations for a title defense against Ken Norton. Spinks was still recognized as champion by the rival World Boxing Association.

Mar. 25 The **AIAW basketball championship** was won by UCLA, defeating the U. of Maryland 90-74.

Mar. 27 The **NCAA basketball championship** was won by the U. of Kentucky, beating Duke 94-88. Jack Givens scored 41 points for Kentucky.

Apr. 9 The **Masters golf tournament** was won for the third time by Gary Player. His final round of 64 brought him home at 277.

Apr. 10 Completion of the formation of the **Major Indoor Soccer League** was announced. The league games would be played between teams of six players each on artificial surfaces of fields roughly the size of a hockey rink.

Apr. 17 The 82nd **Boston Marathon** was won by Bill Rodgers, with a time of 2 hrs., 10 min., 13 sec. The first woman to finish was Gayle Barron of Georgia, with a time of 2 hrs., 44 min., 52 sec.

Football doesn't build character. It eliminates the weak ones.

Darrell Royal

May 5 **Pete Rose** of the Cincinnati Reds (NL) made his 3000th base hit. He was the 13th player in baseball history to do so and, at 37, the youngest.

May 6 The 104th **Kentucky Derby** was won by Affirmed, with a time of 2:01 1/5. The jockey was Steve Cauthen.

May 13-25 The **NHL Stanley Cup** was won by the Montreal Canadiens, defeating the Boston Bruins four games to two.

May 20 The 103rd **Preakness Stakes** was won by Affirmed, with a time of 1:54 2/5. The jockey was Steve Cauthen.

May 21-June 7 The **NBA basketball championship** was won by the Washington Bullets, who beat the Seattle Supersonics four games to three. The 1978 season was the longest in NBA history.

May 28 The 62nd **Indianapolis 500** auto race was won by Al Unser, completing the 500-mi. course in 3 hrs., 5 min., 54.99 sec., at an average speed of 161.363 mph.

June 9 The World Boxing Council **heavyweight boxing championship** was won by Larry Holmes in a 15-round decision over Ken Norton in Las Vegas, Nev.

June 10 The 110th **Belmont Stakes** was won by Affirmed, with a time of 2:26 4/5, to become the 11th horse to win racing's Triple Crown. The jockey once again was Steve Cauthen. As in the Kentucky Derby and Preakness, Alydar finished second. This was the first time there were Triple Crown winners in consecutive years, Seattle Slew having won in 1977.

June 11 The **LPGA golf tournament** was won by Nancy Lopez with a tournament record of 13 under par. During the year she won nine events, five in a row.

June 14 The **National Hockey League** Cleveland Barons and Minnesota North Stars merged. The new team would be located in Minneapolis, play its home games at Bloomington, Minn., and retain the North Stars name.

June 18 The **U.S. Open golf tournament** was won by Andy North, beating J. C. Snead and Dave Stockton on the last hole after seeing a substantial lead vanish.

July 7 At the **Wimbledon** tennis championships in England, Martina Navratilova defeated Chris Evert to win the women's singles title. On the next day, Bjorn Borg of Sweden defeated Jimmy Connors to win the men's singles.

July 11 The **baseball all-star game** was won for the seventh consecutive year by the National League, beating the American League 7-3. This time the National League had to come from behind, scoring four runs off Rich Gossage in the eighth inning.

July 23 The **U.S. Women's Open golf tournament** was won for the second year in a row by Hollis Stacy.

July 28-Aug. 6 The world championship of the **National Horseshoe Pitching Association** was won by Walter Ray Williams, Jr., at Des Moines, Iowa. Williams has been the dominant figure in the sport in the 1980s.

Aug. 6 The **PGA golf tournament** was won by John Mahaffey, who bested Tom Watson and Jerry Pate on the second hole of a sudden death playoff.

Aug. 8 The **Baseball Hall of Fame** inducted three new members: Adrian "Addie" Joss; Larry MacPhail, baseball executive; and Eddie Matthews.

Aug. 11-17 The first successful **transatlantic balloon crossing** was made by Max Anderson, Ben Abruzzo, and Larry Newman, who flew from Presque Isle, Maine, to Paris, France, in 137 hrs., 18 min.

Aug. 27 The **North American Soccer League championship** was won by the New York Cosmos, who beat the Tampa Bay Rowdies 3-1.

Sept. 2 The 53rd **Hambletonian Stakes** was won by Speedy Somolli. The driver was Howard Beissinger. In winning heats, both Speedy Somolli and Florida Pro set a new record for 3-year-olds of 1:55.

Sept. 10 The **U.S. Open tennis singles championships** were won by Chris Evert over 16-year-old Pam Shriver in the women's division and by Jimmy Connors in the men's division.

Sept. 15 The World Boxing Association **heavyweight boxing championship** was won in New Orleans, La., by Muhammad Ali, who beat Leon Spinks in 15 rounds to regain the title for an unprecedented third time.

Oct. 10-17 The **World Series** was won by the New York Yankees (AL), defeating the Los Angeles Dodgers (NL) four games to two. Under manager Bob Lemon, the Yankees ran off four games in a row after dropping the first two. Reggie "Mr. October" Jackson came through again, hitting five home runs in the series, three of them in consecutive times at bat. It was the

Yankees' 21st series victory. Bucky Dent, normally a weak hitter, had a series average of .417 and was named most valuable player in the series. On Oct. 7, the Yankees had won the American League pennant by beating the Kansas City Royals three games to one and the Dodgers had taken the National League title by downing the Philadelphia Phillies three games to one.

Oct. 22 The ninth **New York City Marathon** was won by Bill Rodgers, with a time of 2 hrs., 12 min., 12 sec. The first woman to finish was Grete Waitz of Norway, with a time of 2 hrs., 32 min., 30 sec.

Nov. 28 The **Heisman Trophy** for outstanding college football player of 1978 was voted to U. of Oklahoma running back Billy Sims.

Dec. 8-10 The **Davis Cup** international tennis championship round was won by the U.S., defeating Great Britain four matches to one.

Dec. 15 In the **World Hockey Association,** the Indianapolis Racers folded for financial reasons. The league was now reduced to six teams.

1979

U.S. **speed skater Eric Heiden** foreshadowed his 1980 Olympic triumphs by setting a new world record of 1 min., 14.99 sec. in the 1000-m. event at the U.S. Olympic trials.

Professional tennis had become so successful that both the U.S. Open and the Wimbledon tournaments would pay out prize money in excess of $500,000.

Jan. 1 In **college football bowl games,** the results were Notre Dame 35, Houston 34 in the Cotton Bowl; Oklahoma 31, Nebraska 24 in the Orange Bowl; Southern California 17, Michigan 10 in the Rose Bowl; and Alabama 14, Penn State 7 in the Sugar Bowl. This season the AP poll chose Alabama as national collegiate champion of 1978; the UPI poll picked Southern California.

Jan. 21 **Super Bowl XIII** was won by the Pittsburgh Steelers (AFC), defeating the Dallas Cowboys (NFC) 35-31. On Jan. 7, the Steelers had beaten the Houston Oilers 34-5 for the AFC

Baseball
NATIONAL LEAGUE HOME RUN LEADERS

	PLAYER	TEAM	TOTAL
1901	Sam Crawford	Cincinnati	16
1902	Tom Leach	Pittsburgh	6
1903	Jimmy Sheckard	Brooklyn	9
1904	Harry Lumley	Brooklyn	9
1905	Fred Odwell	Cincinnati	9
1906	Tim Jordan	Brooklyn	12
1907	Dave Brain	Boston	10
1908	Tim Jordan	Brooklyn	12
1909	Red Murray	New York	7
1910	Fred Beck	Boston	10
	Wildfire Schulte	Chicago	10
1911	Wildfire Schulte	Chicago	21
1912	Heine Zimmerman	Chicago	14
1913	Gavvy Cravath	Philadelphia	19
1914	Gavvy Cravath	Philadelphia	19
1915	Gavvy Cravath	Philadelphia	24
1916	Dave Robertson	New York	12
	Cy Williams	Chicago	12
1917	Gavvy Cravath	Philadelphia	12
	Dave Robertson	New York	12
1918	Gavvy Cravath	Philadelphia	8
1919	Gavvy Cravath	Philadelphia	12
1920	Cy Williams	Philadelphia	15
1921	George Kelly	New York	23
1922	Rogers Hornsby	St. Louis	42
1923	Cy Williams	Philadelphia	41
1924	Jack Fournier	Brooklyn	27
1925	Rogers Hornsby	St. Louis	39
1926	Hack Wilson	Chicago	21
1927	Hack Wilson	Chicago	30
	Cy Williams	Philadelphia	30
1928	Hack Wilson	Chicago	31
	Jim Bottomley	St. Louis	31
1929	Chuck Klein	Philadelphia	43
1930	Hack Wilson	Chicago	56
1931	Chuck Klein	Philadelphia	31
1932	Chuck Klein	Philadelphia	38
	Mel Ott	New York	38
1933	Chuck Klein	Philadelphia	28
1934	Ripper Collins	St. Louis	35
	Mel Ott	New York	35
1935	Wally Berger	Boston	34
1936	Mel Ott	New York	33
1937	Mel Ott	New York	31
	Joe Medwick	St. Louis	31
1938	Mel Ott	New York	36
1939	Johnny Mize	St. Louis	28
1940	Johnny Mize	St. Louis	43
1941	Dolph Camilli	Brooklyn	34

(continued)

	PLAYER	TEAM	TOTAL
1942	Mel Ott	New York	30
1943	Bill Nicholson	Chicago	29
1944	Bill Nicholson	Chicago	33
1945	Tommy Holmes	Boston	28
1946	Ralph Kiner	Pittsburgh	23
1947	Ralph Kiner	Pittsburgh	51
	Johnny Mize	New York	51
1948	Ralph Kiner	Pittsburgh	40
	Johnny Mize	New York	40
1949	Ralph Kiner	Pittsburgh	54
1950	Ralph Kiner	Pittsburgh	47
1951	Ralph Kiner	Pittsburgh	42
1952	Ralph Kiner	Pittsburgh	37
	Hank Sauer	Chicago	37
1953	Eddie Mathews	Milwaukee	47
1954	Ted Kluszewski	Cincinnati	49
1955	Willie Mays	New York	51
1956	Duke Snider	Brooklyn	43
1957	Hank Aaron	Milwaukee	44
1958	Ernie Banks	Chicago	47
1959	Eddie Mathews	Milwaukee	46
1960	Ernie Banks	Chicago	41
1961	Orlando Cepeda	San Francisco	46
1962	Willie Mays	San Francisco	49
1963	Hank Aaron	Milwaukee	44
	Willie McCovey	San Francisco	44
1964	Willie Mays	San Francisco	47
1965	Willie Mays	San Francisco	52
1966	Hank Aaron	Atlanta	44
1967	Hank Aaron	Atlanta	39
1968	Willie McCovey	San Francisco	36
1969	Willie McCovey	San Francisco	45
1970	Johnny Bench	Cincinnati	45
1971	Willie Stargell	Pittsburgh	48
1972	Johnny Bench	Cincinnati	40
1973	Willie Stargell	Pittsburgh	44
1974	Mike Schmidt	Philadelphia	36
1975	Mike Schmidt	Philadelphia	38
1976	Mike Schmidt	Philadelphia	38
1977	George Foster	Cincinnati	52
1978	George Foster	Cincinnati	40
1979	Dave Kingman	Chicago	48
1980	Mike Schmidt	Philadelphia	48
1981	Mike Schmidt	Philadelphia	31
1982	Dave Kingman	New York	37
1983	Mike Schmidt	Philadelphia	40
1984	Dale Murphy	Atlanta	36
	Mike Schmidt	Philadelphia	36
1985	Dale Murphy	Atlanta	37
1986	Mike Schmidt	Philadelphia	37
1987	Andre Dawson	Chicago	49

championship and the Cowboys had defeated the Los Angeles Rams 28-0 for the NFC title.

Feb. 2-3 U.S. **figure skating championships** were won in Cincinnati, Ohio, by Charles Tickner, men's singles; Linda Fratianne, women's singles; Tai Babilonia and Randy Gardner, pairs; and Stacey Smith and John Summers, dance.

Feb. 13 At the **Westminster Kennel Club** dog show, Ch. Oak Tree's Irishtocrat, an Irish water spaniel owned by Anne E. Snelling, took best-in-show.

Mar. 17 At the **world figure skating championships** in Vienna, Austria, Linda Fratianne won the women's singles title. On Mar. 14, Tai Babilonia and Randy Gardner had won the pairs title, marking the first pairs victory for the U.S. since 1950.

Mar. 22 The **National Hockey League** voted to accept four World Hockey Association franchises by merger: the New England (later Hartford) Whalers, Quebec Nordiques, Winnipeg Jets, and Edmonton Oilers. The agreement was ratified on Mar. 30.

Mar. 25 The **AIAW basketball championship** was won by Old Dominion, defeating Louisiana Tech 75-65.

Mar. 26 The **NCAA basketball championship** was won by Michigan State, defeating Indiana State 75-64. Each team had a star player in the tournament: Michigan State had Earvin "Magic" Johnson, and Indiana State, Larry Bird.

Apr. 15 The **Masters golf tournament** was won by Fuzzy Zoeller in a sudden death playoff with Tom Watson and Ed Sneed, who lost ground on each of the last three holes of regulation play to fall back into the tie. Zoeller was the first player to win the Masters in his initial appearance.

Apr. 16 The 83rd **Boston Marathon** was won by Bill Rodgers, with a time of 2 hrs., 9 min., 27 sec. The first woman to finish was Joan Benoit, with a time of 2 hrs., 35 min., 15 sec.

May 5 The 105th **Kentucky Derby** was won by Spectacular Bid, with a time of 2:02⅖. The jockey was Ron Franklin.

May 13-21 The **NHL Stanley Cup** was won by the Montreal Canadiens, who defeated the New York Rangers four games to one. This was the 18th Stanley Cup victory for the Flying Frenchmen.

May 19 The 104th **Preakness Stakes** was won by Spectacular Bid, with a time of 1:54⅕. The jockey was Ron Franklin.

May 20-June 1 The **NBA basketball championship** was won by the Seattle Supersonics, who defeated the Washington Bullets four games to one after losing the opening game.

May 27 The 63rd **Indianapolis 500** auto race was won by Rick Mears, completing the 500-mi. course in 3 hrs., 8 min., 27.97 sec., at an average speed of 158.899 mph.

June 9 The 111th **Belmont Stakes** was won by Coastal, with a time of 2:28⅗, foiling Spectacular Bid's attempt at a Triple Crown victory. The jockey was Ruben Hernandez.

June 10 The **LPGA golf tournament** was won by Donna Caponi Young over Jerilyn Britz at Kings Island, Ohio.

June 12 Two Americans made the **first human-powered aircraft flight across the English Channel.** Paul MacCready and Bryan Allen flew their plane, the *Gossamer Albatross,* 23 mi. from England to France in just under 3 hrs. The flight won the pair a prize of £100,000.

June 17 The **U.S. Open golf tournament** was won by Hale Irwin, repeating his 1974 victory. His par 284 was enough at the Inverness Club, Toledo, Ohio.

June 24 Affirmed became the **first racehorse to earn $2,000,000** by winning the $500,000 Hollywood Gold Cup at Inglewood, Calif. The 1978 Triple Crown winner was ridden by Laffit Pincay, Jr. Affirmed's total earnings reached $2,044,218, putting the horse ahead of the previous record holder, Kelso, with earnings of $1,977,896. On Dec. 11, Affirmed was named the winner of the Eclipse award as horse of the year.

June 26 Muhammad Ali formally gave up the **heavyweight boxing title.** Ali's record stood at 56 victories, 37 by knockouts, and only 3 defeats.

July 6 At the **Wimbledon** tennis championships in England, Martina Navratilova defeated Chris Evert Lloyd for the women's singles title. The next day, Bjorn Borg of Sweden defeated Roscoe Tanner in the men's singles, and Billie Jean King and Martina Navratilova won the women's doubles. This marked King's 20th Wimbledon win, breaking Elizabeth Ryan's record of 19. Ryan, 87, had collapsed at Wimbledon the day before and died a short time later. She once had said that she hoped never to see her record broken but that if anyone were to break it, she wanted it to be Billie Jean King.

July 1-15 At the eighth **Pan-American Games** in San Juan, P.R., the U.S. took 127 gold medals and finished first in the unofficial team standings.

July 15 The **U.S. Women's Open golf tournament** was won by Jerilyn Britz, whose score of 284 was the lowest in the tournament's history. It also brought Britz her first victory in her six-year professional career.

July 17 The **baseball all-star game** was won by the National League, defeating the American League 7-6 for the 16th time in 17 games. A walk with bases loaded did the American League in.

Aug. 1 An **open basket balloon altitude record** was set by Chauncey Dunn, who soared 53,000 ft. He wore a pressurized suit.

Aug. 5 The **Baseball Hall of Fame** inducted three new members: Warren G. Giles, club owner and league executive; Willie Mays; and Hack Wilson.

Aug. 6 At Colorado Springs, Colo., the **Prorodeo Hall of Champions** and Museum of the American Cowboy was opened with 82 persons and animals honored as the first inductees. By 1986, a total of 71 performers and 14 animals had been enshrined.

Aug. 6 The **PGA golf tournament** was won at Oakland Hill, Birmingham, Mich., by David Graham of Australia, who beat Ben Crenshaw on the third hole of a playoff. Graham double-bogeyed the 72nd hole to fall into the tie, but recovered strongly.

Aug. 31 A U.S. parachute team set a **new free-fall record** when its members formed a ten-way spread star at the third World Parachute Championships at Chateauroux, France.

Sept. 1 The 54th **Hambletonian Stakes** was won in straight heats by Legend Hanover. The driver was George Sholty.

Sept. 8 The **North American Soccer League championship** was won by the Vancouver Whitecaps, who beat the Tampa Bay Rowdies 2-1.

Sept. 9 The **U.S. Open tennis singles championships** were won by John McEnroe over Vitas Gerulaitis in the men's division and by Tracy Austin over Chris Evert Lloyd in the women's division. Austin, at 16, was the youngest player ever to win the singles title.

Oct. 10-17 The **World Series** was won by the Pittsburgh Pirates (NL), defeating the Baltimore Orioles (AL) four games to three. Down three games to one, the Pirates swept the last three behind exceptional pitching and with the help of Willie Stargell's hot bat. On Oct. 5, the Pirates completed a three-game sweep of the Cincinnati Reds for the National League pennant. The following day, the Orioles took the American League championship from the California Angels, three games to one.

Oct. 20 The World Boxing Association **heavyweight boxing championship** was won in Pretoria, South Africa, by John Tate in a 15-round decision over Gerrie Coetzee.

Oct. 21 The tenth **New York City Marathon** was won by Bill Rodgers, with a time of 2 hrs., 11 min., 42 sec. The first woman to finish was Grete Waitz of Norway, in a new women's world record time of 2 hrs., 27 min., 33 sec.

Dec. 3 The **Heisman Trophy** for outstanding college football player of 1979 was voted to Southern California tailback Charles White.

Dec. 17 A new **record for a wheeled land vehicle** was set by Stan Barrett when he drove the rocket-powered Budweiser Rocket 739.666 mph at Edwards Air Force Base, Calif. In the one-way drive, the vehicle became the first to break the sound barrier on the ground.

1980

The **Johns Hopkins lacrosse team** won the NCAA national championship at Cornell for the third year in a row by defeating Virginia in overtime 9-8. From 1972 to 1985, Johns Hopkins won the title six times and was runner-up six times.

Jan. 1 In **college football bowl games,** the results were Houston 17, Nebraska 14 in the Cotton Bowl; Oklahoma 24, Florida State 7 in the Orange Bowl; Southern California 17, Ohio State 16 in the Rose Bowl; and Alabama 24, Arkansas 9 in the Sugar Bowl. This season the AP and UPI polls chose Alabama as national collegiate champion of 1979.

Jan. 18-20 U.S. **figure skating championships** were won in Atlanta, Ga., by Charles Tickner, men's singles; Linda Fratianne, women's sin-

Baseball
WORLD SERIES CHAMPIONSHIPS

	WINNER	LOSER	GAMES
1903	Boston (AL)	Pittsburgh (NL)	5–3
1904	(not played)		
1905	New York (NL)	Philadelphia (AL)	4–1
1906	Chicago (AL)	Chicago (NL)	4–2
1907	Chicago (NL)	Detroit (AL)	4–0, 1 tie
1908	Chicago (NL)	Detroit (AL)	4–1
1909	Pittsburgh (NL)	Detroit (AL)	4–3
1910	Philadelphia (AL)	Chicago (NL)	4–1
1911	Philadelphia (AL)	New York (NL)	4–2
1912	Boston (AL)	New York (NL)	4–3, 1 tie
1913	Philadelphia (AL)	New York (NL)	4–1
1914	Boston (NL)	Philadelphia (AL)	4–0
1915	Boston (AL)	Philadelphia (NL)	4–1
1916	Boston (AL)	Brooklyn (NL)	4–1
1917	Chicago (AL)	New York (NL)	4–2
1918	Boston (AL)	Chicago (NL)	4–2
1919	Cincinnati (NL)	Chicago (AL)	5–3
1920	Cleveland (AL)	Brooklyn (NL)	5–2
1921	New York (NL)	New York (AL)	5–3
1922	New York (NL)	New York (AL)	4–0, 1 tie
1923	New York (AL)	New York (NL)	4–2
1924	Washington (AL)	New York (NL)	4–3
1925	Pittsburgh (NL)	Washington (AL)	4–3
1926	St. Louis (NL)	New York (AL)	4–3
1927	New York (AL)	Pittsburgh (NL)	4–0
1928	New York (AL)	St. Louis (NL)	4–0
1929	Philadelphia (AL)	Chicago (NL)	4–1
1930	Philadelphia (AL)	St. Louis (NL)	4–2
1931	St. Louis (NL)	Philadelphia (AL)	4–3
1932	New York (AL)	Chicago (NL)	4–0
1933	New York (NL)	Washington (AL)	4–1
1934	St. Louis (NL)	Detroit (AL)	4–3
1935	Detroit (AL)	Chicago (NL)	4–2
1936	New York (AL)	New York (NL)	4–2
1937	New York (AL)	New York (NL)	4–1
1938	New York (AL)	Chicago (NL)	4–0
1939	New York (AL)	Cincinnati (NL)	4–0
1940	Cincinnati (NL)	Detroit (AL)	4–3
1941	New York (AL)	Brooklyn (NL)	4–1
1942	St. Louis (NL)	New York (AL)	4–1
1943	New York (AL)	St. Louis (NL)	4–1
1944	St. Louis (NL)	St. Louis (AL)	4–2
1945	Detroit (AL)	Chicago (NL)	4–3
1946	St. Louis (NL)	Boston (AL)	4–3
1947	New York (AL)	Brooklyn (NL)	4–3
1948	Cleveland (AL)	Boston (NL)	4–2
1949	New York (AL)	Brooklyn (NL)	4–1
1950	New York (AL)	Philadelphia (NL)	4–0

(continued)

WORLD SERIES CHAMPIONSHIPS *(Continued)*

	WINNER	LOSER	GAMES
1951	New York (AL)	New York (NL)	4–2
1952	New York (AL)	Brooklyn (NL)	4–3
1953	New York (AL)	Brooklyn (NL)	4–2
1954	New York (NL)	Cleveland (AL)	4–0
1955	Brooklyn (NL)	New York (AL)	4–3
1956	New York (AL)	Brooklyn (NL)	4–3
1957	Milwaukee (NL)	New York (AL)	4–3
1958	New York (AL)	Milwaukee (NL)	4–3
1959	Los Angeles (NL)	Chicago (AL)	4–2
1960	Pittsburgh (NL)	New York (AL)	4–3
1961	New York (AL)	Cincinnati (NL)	4–1
1962	New York (AL)	San Francisco (NL)	4–3
1963	Los Angeles (NL)	New York (AL)	4–0
1964	St. Louis (NL)	New York (AL)	4–3
1965	Los Angeles (NL)	Minnesota (AL)	4–3
1966	Baltimore (AL)	Los Angeles (NL)	4–0
1967	St. Louis (NL)	Boston (AL)	4–3
1968	Detroit (AL)	St. Louis (NL)	4–3
1969	New York (NL)	Baltimore (AL)	4–1
1970	Baltimore (AL)	Cincinnati (NL)	4–1
1971	Pittsburgh (NL)	Baltimore (AL)	4–3
1972	Oakland (AL)	Cincinnati (NL)	4–3
1973	Oakland (AL)	New York (NL)	4–3
1974	Oakland (AL)	Los Angeles (NL)	4–1
1975	Cincinnati (NL)	Boston (AL)	4–3
1976	Cincinnati (NL)	New York (AL)	4–0
1977	New York (AL)	Los Angeles (NL)	4–2
1978	New York (AL)	Los Angeles (NL)	4–2
1979	Pittsburgh (NL)	Baltimore (AL)	4–3
1980	Philadelphia (NL)	Kansas City (AL)	4–2
1981	Los Angeles (NL)	New York (AL)	4–2
1982	St. Louis (NL)	Milwaukee (AL)	4–3
1983	Baltimore (AL)	Philadelphia (NL)	4–1
1984	Detroit (AL)	San Diego (NL)	4–1
1985	Kansas City (AL)	St. Louis (NL)	4–3
1986	New York (NL)	Boston (AL)	4–3
1987	Minnesota (AL)	St. Louis (NL)	4–3

gles; Tai Babilonia and Randy Gardner, pairs; and Stacey Smith and John Summers, dance.

Jan. 20 Pres. Jimmy Carter announced that the **U.S. would not participate in the summer Olympic Games** in Moscow as a protest against the Soviet invasion of Afghanistan in Dec. 1979. Some 50 nations followed suit, but many athletes who had trained for the games for years were bitterly disappointed.

Jan. 20 **Super Bowl XIV** was won by the Pitts-burgh Steelers (AFC), defeating the Los Angeles Rams (NFC) 31-19. On Jan. 6, the Steelers had beaten the Houston Oilers 27-13 for the AFC title and the Rams had defeated the Tampa Bay Buccaneers 9-0 for the NFC championship.

Feb. 12 At the **Westminster Kennel Club** dog show, Ch. Innisfree's Sierra Cinnar, a Siberian husky owned by Kathleen Kanzler, took best-in-show.

Feb. 12-24 At the **Winter Olympics** in Lake Placid, N.Y., the U.S. won six gold medals and finished third behind the USSR and East Germany. The U.S. hockey team scored a 4-3 major upset over the USSR team, which had been favored to win the gold medal. The team went on to defeat Finland 4-2 and clinch the hockey championship. Eric Heiden swept the speed skating events, becoming the first athlete to win five gold medals in the Winter Olympics.

Mar. 14 Twenty-two members of a **U.S. amateur boxing team died** when the Polish airliner they were traveling on crashed near Warsaw. The crash killed 87.

Mar. 23 The **AIAW basketball championship** was won for the second consecutive year by Old Dominion, defeating Tennessee 68-53.

Mar. 24 The **NCAA basketball championship** was won by the U. of Louisville, beating UCLA 59-54.

Mar. 31 The World Boxing Association **heavyweight boxing championship** was won by Mike "Hercules" Weaver, who knocked out John Tate in the 15th round at Knoxville, Tenn.

Apr. 13 The **Masters golf tournament** was won by Severiano "Seve" Ballesteros of Spain, 23, the youngest player ever to win the tournament. His 275 total gave him a four-stroke winning margin.

Apr. 21 The 84th **Boston Marathon** was won by Bill Rodgers, his third consecutive win, with a time of 2 hrs., 12 min., 11 sec. Rosie Ruiz of New York was the first woman to finish, but on Apr. 29 she was disqualified on grounds that she had not actually run the entire distance. Jacqueline Garreau of Canada, who had finished in 2 hrs., 34 min., 26 sec., was declared the women's winner.

May 3 The 106th **Kentucky Derby** was won by Genuine Risk, the second filly ever to win the race, with a time of 2:02. The jockey was Jacinto Vasquez.

May 4-16 The **NBA basketball championship** was won by the Los Angeles Lakers, who defeated the Philadelphia 76ers four games to two.

May 12 The first nonstop **transcontinental balloon flight** was completed by Max Anderson and his son Kris, who flew 3100 mi. from Fort Baker, Calif., to Matane, Quebec, on the Gaspé Peninsula, in four days aboard the balloon *Kitty Hawk*.

May 13-24 The **NHL Stanley Cup** was won for the first time by the New York Islanders, who beat the Philadelphia Flyers four games to two.

May 17 The 105th **Preakness Stakes** was won by Codex, with a time of 1:54⅕. The jockey was Angel Cordero, Jr.

May 25 The 64th **Indianapolis 500** auto race was won by Johnny Rutherford, who clinched his third Indy victory with a time of 3 hrs., 29 min., 59.56 sec. and an average speed of 142.862 mph.

June 7 The 112th **Belmont Stakes** was won by Temperence Hill, with a time of 2:29⅘. The jockey was Eddie Maple.

June 8 The **LPGA golf tournament** was won by Sally Little. It was her first major win, and she was the only player to finish under par.

June 12-15 The **U.S. Open golf tournament** was won by Jack Nicklaus. It was his fourth U.S. Open win. Nicklaus carded a 272, the lowest 72-hole total in U.S. Open history. The tournament was played at the Baltusrol Golf Club, Springfield, N.J.

June 28 A new **transcontinental bicycle record** was set by John Marino, a 32-year-old physical education teacher from Santa Monica, Calif. He started from there on June 16 and arrived at New York's City Hall after 12 days, 3 hrs., 31 min. Marino had pedaled 2853.9 miles.

Summer **Wayne Gretzky,** 19-year-old center for the Edmonton Oilers, was named the National Hockey League's most valuable player. He was the youngest ever to receive this honor. Gretzky continued to win this award for six consecutive years.

July 5 At the **Wimbledon** tennis championships in England, John McEnroe lost to Bjorn Borg of Sweden in the men's finals, and Chris Evert Lloyd lost to Evonne Goolagong Cawley in the women's finals.

July 8 The **baseball all-star game** was won for the ninth consecutive year by the National League, defeating the American League 4-2. After Fred Lynn hit a two-run homer for the American League, Ken Griffey's bat sparked a rebound against Tommy John to give the National League the win.

July 13 The **U.S. Women's Open golf tournament** was won by Amy Alcott by nine strokes.

July 24-Aug. 3 The **National Horseshoe Pitching Association world championship rules** settled down to a qualifying round followed by round-robin matches among the 32 top scorers.

Walter Ray Williams regained his title with a perfect 31-0 record.

Aug. 3 The **Baseball Hall of Fame** inducted four new members: Al Kaline, Chuck Klein, Duke Snider, and Tom Yawkey, deceased owner of the Boston Red Sox.

Aug. 10 The **PGA golf tournament** was won for the fifth time by Jack Nicklaus, with a record score of 274 at Rochester, N.Y.

Aug. 30 The 55th **Hambletonian Stakes** was won in three heats by Burgomeister. The driver was Billy Haughton. This was the last Hambletonian to be run at Du Quoin, Ill., where the classic had been held since 1957.

Sept. 6-7 The **U.S. Open tennis singles championships** were won by John McEnroe over Bjorn Borg of Sweden in the men's division and by Chris Evert Lloyd over Hana Mandlikova of Czechoslovakia in the women's division.

Sept. 16-25 The **America's Cup** was successfully defended by the U.S. yacht *Freedom,* which beat the challenger *Australia* four races to one.

Sept. 21 The **North American Soccer League championship** was won by the New York Cosmos, who defeated the Fort Lauderdale Strikers 3-0.

Oct. 1 A **new pacer mile record** on a mile track of 1:49⅕ was set by Niatross at Lexington, Ky. The driver was Clint Galbraith.

Oct. 4 Playing the **highest-scoring game in major college football,** Oklahoma defeated Colorado 82-42. Oklahoma also set two NCAA records by rushing for 758 yards and gaining 875 yards in total offense.

Oct. 14-21 The **World Series** was won by the Philadelphia Phillies (NL), defeating the Kansas City Royals (AL) four games to two. The Phillies' third baseman, Mike Schmidt, was named most valuable player. The Philadelphia police deployed police dogs in the final innings of the sixth game because of unruly behavior by spectators that was anticipated after the victory of the Phillies. Philadelphia bats three times pulled games out of the fire, and Tug McGraw slammed the door shut on the Royals in the late innings of the last two games. On Oct. 10, the Royals had completed a three-game sweep of the New York Yankees to win the American League pennant. On Oct. 12, the Phillies had won the National League pennant, beating the Houston Astros three games to two.

Oct. 26 The 11th **New York City Marathon** was won by Alberto Salazar of Wayland, Mass., with a time of 2 hrs., 9 min., 41 sec. The first woman to finish was Grete Waitz of Norway, with a time of 2 hrs., 25 min., 41 sec.

Oct. 31 Julian Nott and Leo Dickinson set a **hot-air balloon altitude record** when they ascended 55,900 ft. in their balloon *Innovation.* They made the ascent near Denver, Colo.

Dec. 1 The **Heisman Trophy** for outstanding college football player of 1980 was voted to U. of South Carolina running back George Rogers.

> *I've found there are three things everybody thinks they can do: star in a movie, write a book, and coach a pro football team.*
>
> Charley Winner

1981

Davis Cup tennis rules were changed this year. The new regulations provided for 16 qualifying nations, divided into four zones, to engage in an elimination tournament, thus reducing the time needed for the competition. This change plus increased prize money brought back top players who had found the previous system burdensome.

Jan. 1 In **college football bowl games,** the results were Alabama 30, Baylor 2 in the Cotton Bowl; Oklahoma 18, Florida State 17 in the Orange Bowl; Michigan 23, Washington 6 in the Rose Bowl; and Georgia 17, Notre Dame 10 in the Sugar Bowl. This season the AP and UPI polls chose Georgia as national collegiate champion of 1980.

Jan. 25 **Super Bowl XV** was won by the Oakland Raiders (AFC), defeating the Philadelphia Eagles (NFC) 27-10. On Jan. 11, the Raiders had beaten the San Diego Chargers 34-27 for the AFC championship and the Eagles had defeated the Dallas Cowboys 20-7 for the NFC title.

Feb. 3-8 **U.S. figure skating championships** were won in San Diego, Calif., by Scott Hamilton, men's singles; Elaine Zayak, women's singles; Kitty and Peter Carruthers, pairs; and Judy Blumberg and Michael Seibert, dance.

Feb. 10 At the **Westminster Kennel Club** dog show, Ch. Dhandy's Favorite Woodchuck, a pug owned by Robert A. Hauslohner, took best-in-show.

Feb. 23 **Equal athletic programs** for men and women do not have to be provided by educational institutions receiving federal funds, a federal judge in Detroit ruled. The decision was praised by the NCAA but was termed "disastrous" by proponents of equal funding.

Mar. 5 At the **world figure skating championships** in Hartford, Conn., Scott Hamilton won the men's singles title.

Mar. 6 A **hot-air balloon distance record** was claimed by Kris Anderson, who landed his *Knight Hawk* at Moundsville, W.Va., after having taken off from Lakeland, Minn. His balloon traveled about 700 mi., exceeding the record of 493 mi. set in the summer of 1980 by Bruce Comstock.

Mar. 29 The New York Arrows won the **Major Indoor Soccer League championship** for the third year in a row by defeating the St. Louis Steamers 6-5.

Mar. 29 The **AIAW basketball championship** was won by Louisiana Tech, defeating Tennessee 79-59.

Mar. 30 The **NCAA basketball championship** was won by North Carolina, which defeated Indiana 63-50.

Apr. 12 The **Masters golf tournament** was won by Tom Watson, whose score of 280 led Jack Nicklaus by two strokes, giving Watson his second Masters championship.

Apr. 20 The 85th **Boston Marathon** was won by Toshihiko Seko of Japan, with a time of 2 hrs., 9 min., 26 sec. The first woman to finish was Allison Roe of New Zealand, with a time of 2 hrs., 26 min., 45 sec., a new course record for women.

Apr. 27 The **first female soccer game official,** Betty Ellis, was hired by the North American Soccer League.

May 2 The 107th **Kentucky Derby** was won by Pleasant Colony, with a time of 2:02. The jockey was Jorge Velasquez.

May 5-14 The **NBA basketball championship** was won by the Boston Celtics, who defeated the Houston Rockets four games to two.

May 12-21 The **NHL Stanley Cup** was won by the New York Islanders, who defeated the Minnesota North Stars four games to one.

May 16 The 106th **Preakness Stakes** was won by Pleasant Colony, with a time of 1:54⅗. The jockey was Jorge Velasquez.

May 24 The 65th **Indianapolis 500** auto race ended in controversy. A day after the race, Mario Andretti, who had finished second, was named winner over Bobby Unser because Unser had broken a rule during a slowdown period near the end of the race. On Oct. 8, the U.S. Auto Club (USAC) reversed the decision and gave the victory to Unser but fined him $40,000 for his infraction. Unser had completed the race in 3 hrs., 35 min., 41.78 sec., at an average speed of 139.085 mph.

June 6 The 113th **Belmont Stakes** was won by Summing, with a time of 2:29, to foil Pleasant Colony's chance at winning the Triple Crown. The jockey was George Martins.

June 12 A **baseball strike,** the first midseason strike ever, began when players walked out in a controversy over compensation of free agents. An agreement was reached between the players' organization and the owners on July 31, but a third of the season had been lost.

June 14 The **LPGA golf tournament** was won by Donna Caponi Young.

June 21 The **U.S. Open golf tournament** was won at Merion Cricket Club, Ardmore, Pa., by David Graham of Australia, the fifth foreign player to win this title. A superb final round of 67 produced a final score of 273.

July 3-4 At the **Wimbledon** tennis championships in England, John McEnroe won the men's singles title over Bjorn Borg of Sweden. Chris Evert Lloyd won the women's singles over Hana Mandlikova of Czechoslovakia. McEnroe teamed with Peter Fleming to win the men's doubles, and Pam Shriver and Martina Navratilova won the women's doubles.

July 26 The **U.S. Women's Open golf tournament** was won by Pat Bradley. Her 72-hole total of 279 was a record for the event.

Aug. 2 The **Baseball Hall of Fame** inducted three new members: Andrew "Rube" Foster, a pitcher and a founder of the National Negro League; Bob Gibson; and Johnny Mize.

Aug. 8 The 56th **Hambletonian Stakes** was won in four heats by Shiaway St. Pat. The driver was Ray Remmen. This was the first Hambletonian run at the Meadowlands in East Rutherford, N.J.

Tennis
DAVIS CUP
Challenge/Final Rounds (through 1986)

NATION	ROUNDS PLAYED	WINS	LOSSES
United States	54	28	26
Australia (Australasia)	41	26	15
Great Britain (British Isles)	17	9	8
France	10	6	4
Italy	6	1	5
Sweden	5	3	2
Rumania	3	0	3
Czechoslovakia	2	1	1
India	2	0	2
Spain	2	0	2
West Germany	2	0	2
Argentina	1	0	1
Belgium	1	0	1
Chile	1	0	1
Japan	1	0	1
Mexico	1	0	1
South Africa*	1	1	0

*Won over India by default.

Aug. 9 The **baseball all-star game** was won for the tenth consecutive time by the National League, defeating the American League 5-4. The largest crowd ever to see an all-star game, 72,086 fans, saw the National League win its 19th game out of the most recent 20 when Mike Schmidt hit a two-run homer off Rollie Fingers.

Aug. 9 The **PGA golf tournament** was won by Larry Nelson, who beat Fuzzy Zoeller by three strokes.

Aug. 19 A new **world record for the 110-m. hurdles,** 12.93 sec., was set by Renaldo Nehemiah at Zurich, Switzerland.

Sept. 9-13 The **U.S. Open Tennis singles championships** were won by John McEnroe over Bjorn Borg of Sweden in the men's division and by Tracy Austin over Martina Navratilova, now a U.S. citizen, in the women's division.

Sept. 26 The **North American Soccer League championship** was won by the Chicago Sting, who shut out the New York Cosmos 1-0.

Oct. 25 The 12th **New York City Marathon** was won by Alberto Salazar, a recent graduate of the U. of Oregon, with a time of 2 hrs., 8 min., 13 sec. The first woman to finish was Allison Roe of New Zealand, with a time of 2 hrs., 25 min., 28 sec. Both times were new records for this event.

Oct. 28 The **World Series** was won by the Los Angeles Dodgers (NL), defeating the New York Yankees (AL) four games to two. Down 0-2, the Dodgers swept the last four games, bringing down criticism on the heads of manager Bob Lemon and catcher Rick Cerrone of the Yankees by owner George Steinbrenner, who also made a public apology for the team's performance. The bat of Pedro Guerrero won games five and six for the Dodgers. On Oct. 15, the Yankees had won the American League pennant over the Oakland Athletics in a three-game sweep. On Oct. 19, the Dodgers had won the National League pennant, defeating the Montreal Expos three games to two.

Nov. 9-12 The **first manned balloon flight across the Pacific Ocean** was achieved by four Americans in the *Double Eagle V.* Ben Abruzzi, Larry M. Newman, Ron Clark, and Rocky Aoki took off from Nagashima, Japan, and landed near Covelo, Oreg. The helium-filled balloon also set a distance record of 5208.68 mi.

Dec. 5 The **Heisman Trophy** for outstanding col-

lege football player of 1981 was voted to USC tailback Marcus Allen.

Dec. 11-13 The **Davis Cup** international tennis competition was won by the U.S., defeating Argentina three matches to one in Cincinnati, Ohio. John McEnroe and Roscoe Tanner were the U.S. singles stars.

1982

The **Field Hockey Association of America** brought Gavin Featherstone, an experienced British field hockey player, to the U.S. to develop the sport among men and to build a team for the 1984 Olympics.

Jan. 1 In **college football bowl games,** the results were Texas 14, Alabama 12 in the Cotton Bowl; Clemson 22, Nebraska 15 in the Orange Bowl; Washington 28, Iowa 0 in the Rose Bowl; and Pittsburgh 24, Georgia 20 in the Sugar Bowl. This season the AP and UPI polls picked Clemson as national collegiate champion of 1981.

Jan. 24 **Super Bowl XVI** was won by the San Francisco 49ers (NFC), defeating the Cincinnati Bengals (AFC) 26-21. On Jan. 10, the 49ers had beaten the Dallas Cowboys 28-27 for the NFC title, and Cincinnati had beaten the San Diego Chargers 27-7 for the AFC championship.

Jan. 28-31 **U.S. figure skating championships** were won in Indianapolis, Ind., by Scott Hamilton, men's singles; Rosalynn Sumners, women's singles; Kitty and Peter Carruthers, pairs; and Judy Blumberg and Michael Seibert, dance.

Feb. 9 At the **Westminster Kennel Club** dog show, Ch. St. Aubrey Dragonora of Elsdon, a Pekingese owned by Ann Snelling, took best-in-show.

Mar. 11-13 At the **world figure skating championships** in Copenhagen, Denmark, Scott Hamilton won the men's singles title and Elaine Zayak won the women's singles title.

Mar. 18-20 The **first NCAA Division I women's swimming and diving championships** were held at the U. of Florida. The host team won the title, with Stanford second. In 1983, Stanford was first in the final standing and Florida took second.

Mar. 18-20 **Megan Neyer** of the U. of Florida women's swimming team began her domination of both 1- and 3-m. diving at the NCAA championships. By the time she graduated, Neyer had won both events four times.

Mar. 28 The **NCAA women's basketball championship** was won by Louisiana Tech, which defeated Cheyney State 76-62. This was the first major NCAA basketball championship for women and marked the virtual end of the annual AIAW championship, which had been held since 1972.

Mar. 29 The **NCAA men's basketball championship** was won by North Carolina, which defeated Georgetown 63-62.

Apr. 11 The **Masters golf tournament** was won by Craig Stadler, who defeated Dan Pohl in a sudden death playoff. Stadler won three other tournaments this year and was 1982's leading money winner, earning $446,462.

Apr. 19 The 86th **Boston Marathon** was won by Alberto Salazar of Eugene, Oreg., with a new record time of 2 hrs., 8 min., 51 sec. The first woman to finish was Charlotte Teske of West Germany, with a time of 2 hrs., 29 min., 33 sec.

May 1 The 108th **Kentucky Derby** was won by Gato del Sol, with a time of 2:02²/₅. The jockey was Eddie Delahoussaye.

May 7 A federal jury said the **NFL had violated antitrust laws** when it unsuccessfully attempted to prevent the Oakland Raiders from moving to Los Angeles. The Los Angeles Coliseum, where the Raiders were to play their games, also benefited from the decision. On Apr. 13, 1983, the court awarded the Raiders and the Coliseum a total of $49,000,000 in triple damages as a result of the 1982 decision.

May 8-16 The **NHL Stanley Cup** was won by the New York Islanders, who swept the Vancouver Canucks in four straight games.

May 12 The **United States Football League** (USFL), a new professional organization, was founded. Planning its season on a March-to-July schedule so as not to compete head-on with the NFL, the USFL played its first games in 1983, with 12 teams competing.

May 15 The 107th **Preakness Stakes** was won by Aloma's Ruler, with a time of 1:55²/₅. The jockey was Jack Kaenel.

May 25-29 The NCAA conducted its **first national collegiate women's lacrosse championships** at Widener U., Chester, Pa. Massachusetts defeated Trenton State 9-6 in the final round.

May 27-June 8 The **NBA basketball championship** was won by the Los Angeles Lakers, who defeated the Philadelphia 76ers four games to two.

May 30 The 66th **Indianapolis 500** auto race was won by Gordon Johncock, completing the 500-mi. course in 3 hrs., 5 min., 9.33 sec., at an average speed of 162.026 mph.

June 5 The 114th **Belmont Stakes** was won by Conquistador Cielo, with a time of 2:28⅕. The jockey was Laffit Pincay, Jr.

June 13 The **LPGA golf tournament** was won by Jan Stephenson of Australia who carded a 279.

June 20 The **U.S. Open golf tournament** was won by Tom Watson, who beat Jack Nicklaus by two strokes. On the 71st hole, Watson sank an almost impossible pitch from the rough. A month later he won his fourth British Open.

July 3-4 At the **Wimbledon** tennis championships in England, Jimmy Connors defeated John McEnroe in a match lasting 4 hrs., 14 min., the longest by time in Wimbledon history. Martina Navratilova defeated Chris Evert Lloyd in the women's finals. Navratilova teamed with Pam Shriver to win the women's doubles, and Anne Smith and Kevin Curran of South Africa won the mixed doubles.

July 13 The **baseball all-star game** was won for the 11th consecutive time by the National League, beating the American League 4 to 1. Shortstop Dave Concepcion was the game's most valuable player on a two-run homer and sparkling play afield.

July 25 The **U.S. Women's Open golf tournament** was won by Janet Alex, her first tournament victory.

Aug. 1 The **Baseball Hall of Fame** inducted Hank Aaron; Happy Chandler, former commissioner of baseball; Travis Jackson; and Frank Robinson.

Aug. 7 The 57th **Hambletonian Stakes** was won in straight heats by Speed Bowl. The driver was Tom Haughton, at 25 the youngest driver ever to win the Hambletonian.

Aug. 8 The **PGA golf tournament** was won by Raymond Floyd, who posted a record opening-round score of 63.

Sept. 11-12 The **U.S. Open tennis singles championships** were won by Jimmy Connors over Ivan Lendl of Czechoslovakia in the men's division and by Chris Evert Lloyd over Hana Mandlikova in the women's division.

Sept. 19 The **North American Soccer League championship** was won by the New York Cosmos, who defeated the Seattle Sounders 1-0.

Sept. 21 The first regular season **pro football strike** began when the NFL players' association and the team owners failed to agree on a basic contract. It continued until Nov. 16 and became the costliest strike in sports up to that time. Half the season's games were canceled, and the season was cut to nine games for each team.

Fall **Martina Navratilova** became the first women's professional tennis player to win more than $1,000,000 in a year. She finished the season with $1,461,055 in purses, having won 90 of 93 singles matches and 15 of 18 tournament championships.

Oct. 12-20 The **World Series** was won by the St. Louis Cardinals (NL), defeating the Milwaukee Brewers four games to three. The Cards crushed Milwaukee in the final two games, 13-1 and 6-3. Dane Iorg, the Cards' designated hitter, batted .519, but the Cards' catcher, Darrell Porter, was named most valuable player. On Oct. 10, the Cardinals had won the National League pennant over the Atlanta Braves in three straight games. The same day, the Brewers had won the American League pennant over the California Angels, three games to two. The Brewers became the first team to win a playoff after losing the first two games.

Oct. 24 The 13th **New York City Marathon** was won for the third year in a row by Alberto Salazar of Eugene, Oreg., with a time of 2 hrs., 19 min., 13 sec. The first woman to finish was Grete Waitz of Norway, scoring her fourth win, with a time of 2 hrs., 27 min., 14 sec.

Nov. In the **NCAA's first soccer playoffs** for the women's collegiate championship, North Carolina defeated Central Florida by a score of 2-0.

Nov. 1 The contract of **Bowie Kuhn,** commissioner of baseball, would not be renewed, the owners of the 26 major league teams announced. Kuhn, a controversial figure, was in the final year of his second seven-year term.

Nov. 26-28 The **Davis Cup** international tennis championship was won in Grenoble, France, by the U.S., led by John McEnroe, defeating France four matches to one.

Dec. 4 The **Heisman Trophy** for outstanding col-

Basketball
TOP TEN PRO ALL-TIME SCORERS
Through 1986–1987 season

PLAYER	YEARS IN NBA	FIELD GOALS	FOUL THROWS	TOTAL POINTS
Kareem Abdul-Jabbar	18*	15,044	6,385	36,474
Wilt Chamberlain	14	12,681	6,057	31,419
Julius Erving	16	11,818	6,256	30,026
Dan Issel	15	10,421	6,591	27,482
Elvin Hayes	16	10,976	5,356	27,313
Oscar Robertson	14	9,508	7,694	26,710
George Gervin	14	11,362	2,737	26,595
John Havlicek	16	10,513	5,369	26,395
Rick Barry	14	9,695	5,713	25,279
Jerry West	14	9,016	7,160	25,192

*Still active.

lege football player of 1982 was voted to U. of Georgia running back Herschel Walker.

Dec. 10 The **WBA heavyweight boxing championship** was won by Michael Dokes, who knocked out Mike Weaver in the first round of a bout at Las Vegas, Nev.

1983

Chip Hanauer set the **Gold Cup record** speed for one lap, 131.387 mph, for unlimited hydroplanes.

Winter Henry Bossett of New Jersey won the **Gold Cup World DN Championship** in ice-boating, becoming the sport's only three-time champion.

Jan. 1 In **college football bowl games,** the results were Southern Methodist 7, Pittsburgh 3 in the Cotton Bowl; Nebraska 21, Louisiana State 17 in the Orange Bowl; UCLA 24, Michigan 14 in the Rose Bowl; and Penn State 27, Georgia 23 in the Sugar Bowl. This season the AP and UPI polls picked Penn State as national collegiate champion of 1982.

Jan. 30 **Super Bowl XVII** was won by the Washington Redskins (NFC), defeating the Miami Dolphins (AFC) 27-17. On Jan. 22, the Redskins had beaten the Dallas Cowboys 31-17 for the NFC championship and the Dolphins had shut out the New York Jets 14-0 for the AFC title.

Feb. 3-4 At the **U.S. figure skating championships** in Pittsburgh, Pa., all 1982 winners repeated their victories: Scott Hamilton, men's singles; Rosalynn Sumners, women's singles; Kitty and Peter Carruthers, pairs; and Judy Blumberg and Michael Seibert, dance.

Feb. 15 At the **Westminster Kennel Club** dog show, Ch. Kabiks The Challenger, an Afghan hound owned by Chris and Marguerite Terrell, took best-in-show.

Mar. 6 The new **United States Football League** (USFL) began its first season, with five games nationwide. The new league had 12 teams and was scheduled to play an 18-game spring schedule.

Mar. 7 Phil Mahre won the **Alpine World Cup overall championship** in skiing for the third consecutive year. He was the third person ever to accomplish this, and in 1981 he had been the first American to take this title. At this 1983 meet, Tamara McKinney became the first American to win the women's overall championship.

Mar. 10-11 At the **world figure skating championships** in Helsinki, Finland, Scott Hamilton won the men's singles title and Rosalynn Sumners won the women's singles title.

Apr. 2 The **NCAA women's basketball championship** was won by Southern California, which defeated Louisiana Tech 69-67.

Apr. 4 The **NCAA men's basketball championship** was won by North Carolina State, defeating the U. of Houston 54-52.

Apr. 11 The **Masters golf tournament** was won by Severiano "Seve" Ballesteros of Spain. His score of 280 led Tom Kite and Ben Crenshaw by four strokes.

Apr. 18 The 87th **Boston Marathon** was won by Greg Meyer of Wellesley, Mass., with a time of 2 hrs., 9 min. The first woman to finish was Joan Benoit of Boston, with a women's record time of 2 hrs., 22 min., 42 sec.

Apr. 25 A new **long-distance soaring record** was set by Tom Knauff. Taking off from near Williamsport, Pa., he soared to a point just north of Knoxville, Tenn., and returned for a total of 1022.4 mi. Knauff made the flight in 10 hrs., 36 min. at an average speed of 96.55 mph.

May 7 The 109th **Kentucky Derby** was won by Sunny's Halo, with a time of 2:02⅕. The jockey was Eddie Delahoussaye.

May 10-17 The **NHL Stanley Cup** was won by the New York Islanders, who defeated the Edmonton Oilers in four straight games.

May 21 The 108th **Preakness Stakes** was won by Deputed Testamony, with a time of 1:55⅖. The jockey was Donald Miller.

May 22-31 The **NBA basketball championship** was won by the Philadelphia 76ers, who swept the Los Angeles Lakers in four straight games.

May 29 The 67th **Indianapolis 500** was won by Tom Sneva in 3 hrs., 5 min., 3.066 sec., at an average speed of 162.117 mph.

June 11 The 115th **Belmont Stakes** was won by Caveat, with a time of 2:27⅘. The jockey was Lafitt Pincay, Jr.

June 12 The **LPGA golf tournament** was won by Patty Sheehan, whose 279 led Sandra Haynie by two strokes.

June 20 The **U.S. Open golf tournament** was won by Larry Nelson, whose 280 beat Tom Watson by one stroke.

You can't even celebrate a victory. If you win today, you must start worrying about tomorrow. If you win a pennant, you start worrying about the World Series. As soon as that's over, you start worrying about next season.

Bill McKechnie, on the life of a baseball manager

July 2-3 At the **Wimbledon** tennis championships in England, John McEnroe defeated Chris Lewis of New Zealand for the men's singles title. Martina Navratilova defeated Andrea Jaeger in the women's singles. McEnroe teamed with Peter Fleming to win the men's doubles, and Navratilova and Pam Shriver won the women's doubles.

July 6 The **baseball all-star game** was won by the American League, routing the National League 13-3 for its first all-star win since 1971. Fred Lynn of the California Angels hit the first grand slam home run in the 50-year history of the all-star game.

July 17 The first **USFL championship** was won by the Michigan Panthers, defeating the Philadelphia Stars 24-22.

July 31 The **Baseball Hall of Fame** inducted four new members: Walter Alston, George Kell, Juan Marichal, and Brooks Robinson.

July 31 The **U.S. Women's Open golf tournament** was won by Jan Stephenson of Australia. Her score of 290 topped JoAnne Carner and Patty Sheehan by one stroke.

Aug. 6 The 58th **Hambletonian Stakes** was won by Duenna in the third heat of a split-field competition. The driver was Stanley Dancer.

Aug. 7 The **PGA golf tournament** was won by second-year pro Hal Sutton, who led Jack Nicklaus by one stroke. Sutton finished the year as the leading money winner, at $426,668.

Aug. 14-18 At the **Pan-American Games** in Caracas, Venezuela, the U.S. won 137 gold medals and finished first in the unofficial team standings.

Sept. 10-11 The **U.S. Open tennis singles championships** were won by Jimmy Connors over Ivan Lendl of Czechoslovakia in the men's division and by Martina Navratilova over Chris Evert Lloyd in the women's division.

Sept. 14-26 The **America's Cup** was lost by the U.S. for the first time in the yachting classic's 132-year history. The Australian challenger *Australia II* defeated the U.S. yacht *Liberty* four races to three.

Sept. 23 The **World Boxing Association heavyweight boxing championship** was won by Gerrie Coetzee of South Africa, who knocked out Michael Dokes in ten rounds at Richfield, Ohio.

Oct. Ricky Henderson became the **all-time leading base stealer.** The Oakland Athletics star stole 130 bases this season, surpassing the previous record of 118, set by Lou Brock in 1974.

Oct. 1 The **North American Soccer League championship** was won by the Tulsa Roughnecks, defeating the Toronto Blizzard 2-0.

Oct. 4 A new **auto speed record** was set by Richard Noble of Great Britain at Black Rock Desert, Gerlach, Nev., when he drove the jet-powered *Thrust 2* at 633.6 mph. This is the official record for a two-way run.

Oct. 11-16 The **World Series** was won by the Baltimore Orioles (AL), defeating the Philadelphia Phillies (NL) four games to one. The Orioles lost the opening game but then took four in a row, with fine pitching and Rick Dempsey's outstanding hitting. Philly pitching held Mike Schmidt to one single in 20 times at bat. On Oct. 8, the Orioles had won the American League pennant over the Chicago White Sox, three games to one, and the Phillies had won the National League pennant from the Los Angeles Dodgers by the same margin.

Oct. 23 The 14th **New York City Marathon** was won by Rod Dixon of New Zealand with a time of 2 hrs., 8 min., 59 sec. The first woman to finish, scoring her fifth victory, was Grete Waitz of Norway, with a time of 2 hrs., 27 min.

Dec. 3 The **Heisman Trophy** for outstanding college football player of 1983 was voted to U. of Nebraska running back Mike Rozier.

Dec. 8 The contract of **Bowie Kuhn** as commissioner of baseball was extended to Mar. 1, 1984, by the major league team owners. They had voted in 1982 not to renew his contract.

1984

Jan. 1 In **college football bowl games,** the results were Georgia 10, Texas 9 in the Cotton Bowl; Miami (Fla.) 31, Nebraska 30 in the Orange Bowl; UCLA 45, Illinois 3 in the Rose Bowl; and Auburn 9, Michigan 7 in the Sugar Bowl. This season the AP and UPI polls picked Miami as national collegiate champion of 1983.

Jan. 20-21 **U.S. figure skating championships** were won at Salt Lake City, Utah, by the same slate of skaters for the third year in a row: Scott

Baseball
TOP TEN
MAJOR LEAGUE BATTERS
Lifetime Home Runs

Hank Aaron	755
Babe Ruth	714
Willie Mays	660
Frank Robinson	586
Harmon Killebrew	573
Reggie Jackson	563
Mickey Mantle	536
Jimmie Foxx	534
Mike Schmidt	530*
Ted Williams	521**
Willie McCovey	521**

*Still active.
**Tied for tenth place.

Hamilton, men's singles; Rosalynn Sumners, women's singles; Kitty and Peter Carruthers, pairs; and Judy Blumberg and Michael Seibert, dance.

Jan. 22 **Super Bowl XVIII** was won by the Los Angeles Raiders (AFC), defeating the Washington Redskins (NFC) 38-9. On Jan. 8, the Raiders had defeated the Seattle Seahawks 30-14 to win the AFC championship and the Redskins had beaten the San Francisco 49ers 24-21 for the NFC title.

Feb. 8-19 At the **Winter Olympics** in Sarajevo, Yugoslavia, the U.S. won four gold medals and finished fifth in the unofficial team standings. For the U.S., twin brothers Phil and Steve Mahre won the gold and silver medals in the slalom, and Bill Johnson became the first U.S. athlete to win a gold medal in the Olympic downhill. The U.S. ice hockey team disappointed American fans by losing its opening game to Canada 4-2. When the team lost to Czechoslovakia 4-1, the U.S. lost its chance for a medal.

Feb. 14 At the **Westminster Kennel Club** dog show, Ch. Seaward's Blackbeard, a Newfoundland owned by Seaward Kennels, took best-in-show.

Mar. 3 **Peter V. Ueberroth,** president of the Los Angeles Olympic Organizing Committee, was elected commissioner of baseball by the major league team owners.

Mar. 9 The World Boxing Council **heavyweight boxing championship** was won by Tim Witherspoon, who outpointed Greg Page in a 12-round bout at Las Vegas, Nev.

Mar. 15-17 At the **NCAA Division I women's swimming championships,** Tracy Caulkins of the U. of Florida won four individual titles, setting new records in all, and helped her team win two record-setting relay races. The U. of Texas won the team title, which it went on to win again in 1985, 1986, and 1987.

Mar. 23 At the **world figure skating championships** in Ottawa, Canada, Scott Hamilton won the men's singles title.

Apr. 1 The **NCAA women's basketball championship** was won by Southern California, defeating Tennessee 72-61.

Apr. 2 The **NCAA men's basketball championship** was won by Georgetown, which defeated Houston 84-75.

Apr. 15 The **Masters golf tournament** was won by Ben Crenshaw. His 277 beat Tom Watson by two strokes.

Apr. 16 The 88th **Boston Marathon** was won by Geoff Smith of Great Britain, with a time of 2 hrs., 10 min., 34 sec. The first woman to finish was Lorraine Moller of New Zealand, with a time of 2 hrs., 29 min., 28 sec.

May 5 The 110th **Kentucky Derby** was won by Swale, with a time of 2:02⅖. The jockey was Laffit Pincay, Jr.

May 8 The **USSR withdrew from the 1984 Olympics.** The USSR Olympic Committee said Soviet athletes could not compete because of "gross flouting" of Olympic ideals by the U.S. The move was seen in some quarters as retaliation for the boycott of the 1980 Games in Moscow

Baseball
TOP TEN
MAJOR LEAGUE BATTERS
Lifetime Base Hits

Pete Rose	4,256
Ty Cobb	4,191
Hank Aaron	3,771
Stan Musial	3,630
Tris Speaker	3,515
Honus Wagner	3,430
Carl Yastrzemski	3,419
Eddie Collins	3,311
Willie Mays	3,283
Nap Lajoie	3,251

by the U.S. and some other Western nations.

May 10-19 The **NHL Stanley Cup** was won by the Edmonton Oilers, who defeated the New York Islanders four games to one.

May 19 The 109th **Preakness Stakes** was won by Gate Dancer, with a time of 1:53⅗. The jockey was Angel Cordero, Jr.

May 27 The 68th **Indianapolis 500** auto race was won by Rick Mears, completing the 500-mi. course in 3 hrs., 3 min., 21 sec., at an average speed of 163.612 mph.

May 27-June 12 The **NBA basketball championship** was won by the Boston Celtics, who beat the Los Angeles Lakers four games to three.

June 3 The **LPGA golf tournament** was won by Patty Sheehan by a record margin of ten strokes. She went on to win the Vare Trophy for the lowest scoring average at 71.40 per round.

June 9 The 116th **Belmont Stakes** was won by Swale, with a time of 2:27⅕. The jockey was Laffit Pincay, Jr. Eight days after the race, Swale suddenly collapsed and died.

June 18 The **U.S. Open golf tournament** was won by Fuzzy Zoeller in an 18-hole playoff with Greg Norman at Winged Foot, Mamaroneck, N.Y.

June 27 In a major decision on the **televising of college football games,** the Supreme Court ruled that the NCAA's exclusive control over TV coverage of college football constituted an "unreasonable restraint of trade" and violated the Sherman Antitrust Act.

July 7-8 At the **Wimbledon** tennis championships in England, John McEnroe won the men's singles title over Jimmy Connors. Martina Navratilova won the women's singles, defeating Chris Evert Lloyd. McEnroe teamed with Peter Fleming to win the men's doubles, and Navratilova and Pam Shriver won the women's doubles.

July 11 The **baseball all-star game** was won by the National League, 3-1. Fernando Valenzuela and Dwight Gooden pitched outstanding baseball for the National Leaguers.

July 15 The **U.S. Women's Open golf tournament** was won for the third time by Hollis Stacy, who beat Rosie Jones by one stroke.

July 15 The second **USFL football championship** was won by the Philadelphia Stars, who routed the Arizona Wranglers 23-3.

July 22 Kathy Whitworth became the winner of the **most professional golf tournaments** in a

Baseball
TOP TEN
MAJOR LEAGUE PITCHERS
Lifetime ERA

Walter Johnson	2.37
Grover Cleveland Alexander	2.56
Whitey Ford	2.74
Jim Palmer	2.83
Tom Seaver	2.86
Stanley Coveleski	2.88
Wilbur Cooper	2.89
Juan Marichal	2.89
Bob Gibson	2.91
Carl Mays	2.92

career when she triumphed in the Rochester Open for her 85th career win. She passed Sam Snead's total of 84 PGA tourney wins.

July 28-Aug. 12 At the **Summer Olympics** in Los Angeles, the U.S. won 83 gold medals and finished first in the unofficial team standings. Carl Lewis won four gold medals as victor in the 100- and 200-m. dashes, the long jump, and as a member of the 400-m. relay team. In the swimming and diving events, Greg Louganis won both the springboard and platform dives, and U.S. women won nine individual gold medals and two in relay races. Tiffany Cohen and Mary Meagher each accounted for two of the U.S. gold medals in swimming events. U.S. cyclists took home nine medals, the first won by Americans since 1912. In the equestrian events, Karen Stives became the first U.S. woman ever to win an individual medal. On Aug. 7, Joan Benoit won the women's marathon in 2 hrs., 24 min., 52 sec. This was the first Olympic marathon for women. By the final day of the Games, U.S. boxers had won 9 of the 12 gold medals. The victories were spread over the weight classes from light flyweight to heavyweight and super heavyweight.

Aug. 4 The 59th **Hambletonian Stakes** was won by Historic Freight in a fourth-heat race-off with Gentle Stroke and Delvin G. Hanover. Ben Webster was the driver.

Aug. 12 The **Baseball Hall of Fame** inducted Luis Aparicio, Don Drysdale, Rick Ferrell, Harmon Killebrew, and Pee Wee Reese.

Aug. 19 The **PGA golf tournament** was won by Lee Trevino, with a 15-under-par 273, to finish

four strokes ahead of Gary Player and Lanny Wadkins at Birmingham, Ala.

Aug. 22 A new **100-m. dash world record for women** of 10.76 sec. was set by Evelyn Ashford at Zurich, Switzerland, in a race with Marlies Gohr of East Germany.

Aug. 22 The USFL voted to **switch to a fall schedule** for 1986, abandoning its spring football season. The move would put it in direct competition with the NFL.

Aug. 31 The World Boxing Conference **heavyweight boxing championship** was won by Pinklon Thomas, who outpointed Tim Witherspoon in a 12-round bout in Las Vegas, Nev.

Sept. 8-9 The **U.S. Open tennis singles championships** were won by John McEnroe in the men's division and Martina Navratilova in the women's division. McEnroe defeated Ivan Lendl of Czechoslovakia, and Navratilova beat Chris Evert Lloyd in the finals.

Sept. 14-18 The **first transatlantic solo balloon flight** was completed by Joe W. Kittinger, who flew 3535 mi. from Caribou, Maine, to near Savona, Italy. He made the flight in the gondola of his ten-story-tall, helium-lifted craft, named *Rosie O'Grady's Balloon of Peace.*

Oct. 3 The **North American Soccer League championship** was won by the Chicago Sting, who beat the Toronto Blizzard 3-2.

Oct. 7 A new **lifetime pro football rushing record** was set by Walter Payton of the Chicago Bears, when he ended a game against the New Orleans Saints with a lifetime total of 12,400 yards. This feat broke the previous mark set by Jim Brown. Payton finished the 1985 season with a lifetime record of 13,309 yards and in the 1986 season increased his total to 14,860 yards.

Oct. 9-14 The **World Series** was won by the Detroit Tigers (AL), defeating the San Diego Padres (NL) four games to one. The story behind the Tiger victory was strong pitching and the outstanding play of Alan Trammell, named most valuable player in the Series. Trammell had nine hits in 20 at bats to help Sparky Anderson, his manager, to become the winner of World Series victories in both leagues. On Oct. 5, the Tigers had won the American League pennant over the Kansas City Royals in a three-game sweep, and two days later the Padres had taken the National League pennant over the Chicago Cubs, three games to two.

Oct. 21 A new **world marathon record** of 2 hrs.,

Baseball
TOP TEN
MAJOR LEAGUE BATTERS
Lifetime Runs Scored

Ty Cobb	2,245
Hank Aaron	2,174
Babe Ruth	2,174
Pete Rose	2,165
Willie Mays	2,062
Stan Musial	1,949
Lou Gehrig	1,888
Tris Speaker	1,881
Mel Ott	1,859
Frank Robinson	1,829

Angeles Rams when he rushed for 215 yards in a game. He went on to finish the season with a total of 2105 yards, breaking O. J. Simpson's record of 2003 yards.

Dec. 16-18 The **Davis Cup** international tennis championship was won by Sweden, defeating the U.S. four matches to one at Göteborg, Sweden.

1985

8 min., 5 sec., was set by Stephen Jones of Great Britain at the America's Marathon-Chicago race in Chicago.

Oct. 28 The 15th **New York City Marathon** was won by Orlando Pizzolato of Italy, with a time of 2 hrs., 14 min., 53 sec. The first woman to finish was Grete Waitz of Norway, with a time of 2 hrs., 29 min., 30 sec., bringing her win total to six.

Nov. 5 In a decision on **football franchise shifts,** the U.S. Supreme Court ruled the NFL could not prevent its teams from moving from one city to another. The Court refused to hear an appeal of a lower court ruling that the NFL's refusal to allow the Oakland Raiders to move to Los Angeles in 1980 constituted a violation of federal antitrust law.

Nov. 9 The first world heavyweight boxing match under the auspices of the **International Boxing Federation** (IBF) was won by Larry Holmes, who knocked out James "Bonecrusher" Smith in the 12th round of a bout in Las Vegas, Nev. Holmes had vacated his WBC title when arrangements to fight Greg Page, the top contender, fell through.

Dec. 1 The **Heisman Trophy** for outstanding college football player of 1984 was voted to Boston College quarterback Doug Flutie.

Dec. 1 The WBA **heavyweight boxing championship** was won by Greg Page, who knocked out Gerrie Coetzee of South Africa in the eighth round of a bout in Sun City, Bophuthatswana (South Africa).

Dec. 9 A new **single-season pro football rushing record** was set by Eric Dickerson of the Los

The **U.S. Water Ski Team** won the World Water Ski Championships for the 19th consecutive time.

Jan. 1 In **college football bowl games,** the results were Boston College 45, Houston 28 in the Cotton Bowl; Washington 28, Oklahoma 17 in the Orange Bowl; USC 20, Ohio State 17 in the Rose Bowl; and Nebraska 28, Louisiana State 10 in the Sugar Bowl. This season the AP and UPI polls chose Brigham Young, which had beaten Michigan 24-17 in the Holiday Bowl, as national collegiate champion of 1984.

Jan. 17 The **New York Cosmos** soccer club announced it needed $2,000,000 to be able to continue operating, and the North American Soccer League began to fall apart. On January 22 the Tampa Bay Rowdies announced that they would not compete in 1985. By mid-March only two league franchises remained.

Jan. 20 **Super Bowl XIX** was won by the San Francisco 49ers (NFC), defeating the Miami Dolphins (AFC) 38-16. On Jan. 6, the 49ers had blanked the Chicago Bears 23-0 for the NFC championship and the Dolphins had beaten the Pittsburgh Steelers 45-28 for the AFC title.

Feb. 1-2 **U.S. figure skating championships** were won in Kansas City, Mo., by Brian Boitano, men's singles; Tiffany Chin, women's singles; Jill Watson and Peter Oppegard, pairs; and, in a fifth consecutive win, Judy Blumberg and Michael Seibert, dance.

Feb. 12 At the **Westminster Kennel Club** dog show, Ch. Braeburn's Close Encounter, a Scottish terrier owned by Sonnie Novick of Plantation Acres, Fla., took best-in-show. During its career the Scottie won a record 186 best-in-show awards.

Horse Racing
TRIPLE CROWN WINNERS
Kentucky Derby, Preakness, Belmont Stakes

	HORSE	TRAINER	JOCKEY
1919	Sir Barton	H. Guy Bedwell	J. Loftus
1930	Gallant Fox	Jim Fitzsimmons	E. Sande
1935	Omaha	Jim Fitzsimmons	W. Saunders
1937	War Admiral	George Conway	C. Kurtsinger
1941	Whirlaway	Ben A. Jones	E. Arcaro
1943	Count Fleet	G. Don Cameron	J. Longden
1946	Assault	Max Hirsch	W. Mehrtens
1948	Citation	Ben A. Jones	E. Arcaro
1973	Secretariat	Lucien Laurin	R. Turcotte
1977	Seattle Slew	Billy Turner	J. Cruguet
1978	Affirmed	Lazaro S. Barrera	S. Cauthen

Mar. 3 The **first jockey to win $100,000,000** in career purses was Willie Shoemaker, who rode Lord at War to victory in the Santa Anita Handicap in Arcadia, Calif. By the time Shoemaker retired in June, his total winnings had reached $101,691,102. He had ridden 8478 winners in 37,044 races.

Mar. 28 The **North American Soccer League,** reduced to two surviving franchises, suspended operations for the 1985 season. Some of the clubs joined the Major Indoor Soccer League.

Mar. 28-30 At the **NCAA men's national swimming championship,** records were broken in profusion: 100-yard and 200-yard freestyle, Matt Biondi of the U. of California; 500-yard freestyle, Mike O'Brien of USC; 100-yard backstroke, Tom Jager, UCLA; 200-yard butterfly, Pablo Morales, Stanford; 400-yard individual medley, Jeff Kostoff, Stanford; and 400-yard medley relay, Stanford.

Mar. 31 The **NCAA women's basketball championship** was won by Old Dominion, defeating Georgia 70-65.

Apr. 1 The **NCAA men's basketball championship** was won by Villanova, which beat Georgetown 66-64.

Apr. 14 The **Masters golf tournament** was won by Bernhard Langer of West Germany, who beat Curtis Strange, Raymond Floyd, and Seve Ballesteros by two strokes.

Apr. 15 The 89th **Boston Marathon** was won by Geoff Smith of Great Britain, who scored his second consecutive win, with a time of 2 hrs., 14 min., 5 sec. The first woman to finish was Lisa Larsen Weidenbach of Battle Creek, Mich., with a time of 2 hrs., 34 min., 6 sec.

Apr. 23 The **Brooklyn College soccer team** was the upset winner of Nepal's sixth annual invitational tournament.

Apr. 29 The WBA **heavyweight boxing championship** was won by Tony Tubbs in a 15-round decision over Greg Page at Buffalo, N.Y.

May 4 The 111th **Kentucky Derby** was won by Spend a Buck, with a time of 2:00⅕. The jockey was Angel Cordero, Jr.

May 18 The 110th **Preakness Stakes** was won by Tank's Prospect, with a time of 1:53⅖. The jockey was Pat Day.

May 21-30 The **NHL Stanley Cup** was won for the second consecutive year by the Edmonton Oilers, who beat the Philadelphia Flyers four games to one.

May 26 The 69th **Indianapolis 500** auto race was won by Danny Sullivan, completing the 500-mi. course in 3 hrs., 16 min., 6.069 sec., at an average speed of 152.982 mph.

May 27-June 9 The **NBA basketball championship** was won by the Los Angeles Lakers, who defeated the Boston Celtics four games to two.

June 2 The **LPGA golf tournament** was won by Nancy Lopez, who beat Alice Miller by eight strokes with a 15-under-par 273.

June 8 The 117th **Belmont Stakes** was won by Creme Fraiche, with a time of 2:27. The jockey was Eddie Maple. Creme Fraiche was the first gelding ever to win the Belmont, and trainer Woody Stephens became the first to win the Belmont four successive times.

June 16 The **U.S. Open golf tournament** was won by Andy North, who came from behind to beat Tze-chung Chen of Taiwan by one stroke.

June 21 The strongest **college sports sanctions** were approved by the NCAA for violations of its rules concerning recruiting, amateur status, academic standards, and ethics. At a special convention called to deal with what some described as an "integrity crisis" in college sports, NCAA delegates approved suspension of teams for as long as two seasons.

July 6-7 At the **Wimbledon** tennis championships in England, Martina Navratilova won the women's singles title over Chris Evert Lloyd. Navratilova teamed with Paul McNamee of Australia to win the mixed doubles, and Kathy Jordan teamed with Elizabeth Smylie of Australia to win the women's doubles. Boris Becker of West Germany, 17, won the men's singles, becoming the youngest player ever to win the men's title.

July 11 **Nolan Ryan** of the Houston Astros (NL) became the first pitcher in major league history to strike out 4000 batters when he fanned Danny Heep of the New York Mets on three pitches in the sixth inning at Houston. The Astros won 4-3.

July 14 The **USFL football championship** was won by the Baltimore Stars, who defeated the Oakland Invaders 28-24.

July 14 The **U.S. Women's Open golf tournament** was won by Kathy Baker, who beat Judy Clark by three strokes.

July 16 The **baseball all-star game** was won easily by the National League, 6-1.

July 21 John Henry, a 10-year-old gelding, the **greatest money winner in the history of horse racing,** was retired. John Henry had won purses totaling $6,597,947 in 83 starts, 39 wins.

July 23 A new **record auction price for a thoroughbred** was set at Lexington, Ky., when a yearling son of Nijinsky II and My Charmer sold for $13,100,000.

July 28 The **Baseball Hall of Fame** inducted Lou Brock, Enos Slaughter, Arky Vaughn, and Hoyt Wilhelm.

Aug. 3 The 60th **Hambletonian Stakes** was won by Prakas in straight heats, running the final

heat in a record 1:54⅗. The driver was Bill O'Donnell.

Aug. 4 **Tom Seaver,** playing for the Chicago White Sox (AL), became the 17th pitcher in major league history to win 300 games with a 4-1 win over the New York Yankees at Yankee Stadium. On Oct. 6, the Yankees' Phil Niekro became the 18th 300-game winner, triumphing by 8-0 over the Toronto Blue Jays.

Aug. 6 A **baseball strike,** the second in five seasons, began after nine months of negotiations failed to produce an agreement between players and team owners on such matters as salary arbitration, free agency, and minimum salary. An agreement was soon reached, and play resumed on Aug. 8.

Aug. 11 The **PGA golf tournament** was won by Hubert Green, who beat defending champion Lee Trevino by two strokes.

Aug. 25 **Dwight Gooden,** the 20-year-old pitching phenomenon with the New York Mets (NL), became the youngest major league pitcher to win 20 games in a season. Dr. K, as he was called by his fans, was less than 21 years old when he won his 20th game, a 9-3 victory over the San Diego Padres.

Aug. 31 A new **trotting mile record** of 1:53⅖ on a mile track was set by Prakas at Du Quoin, Ill. The driver was Bill O'Donnell.

Sept. 7-8 The **U.S. Open tennis singles championships** were won by Ivan Lendl of Czechoslovakia in the men's division and by Hana Mandlikova of Czechoslovakia, defeating Martina Navratilova, in the women's division.

Sept. 11 **Pete Rose** of the Cincinnati Reds (NL) set a new major league baseball record of 4192 career hits in a 2-0 win over the San Diego Padres at Cincinnati. The old record of 4191 hits was set by Ty Cobb in 1928.

Sept. 21 The International Boxing Federation **heavyweight boxing championship** was won by Michael Spinks in a 15-round decision over Larry Holmes in Las Vegas, Nev.

Oct. 5 Eddie Robinson of Louisiana's Grambling State U. became the **winningest college football coach** in history when his team picked up its 324th win. During Robinson's 44-year career, Grambling State lost 106 games and tied 15.

Oct. 19-27 The **World Series** was won by the Kansas City Royals (AL), defeating the St. Louis Cardinals (NL) four games to three. The Royals came roaring back after losing the first two

MEMBERS OF NATIONAL BASEBALL HALL OF FAME

Hank Aaron
Grover Cleveland Alexander
Walt Alston
Cap Anson
Luis Aparicio
Luke Appling
Earl Averill
Home Run Baker
Dave Bancroft
Ernie Banks
Ed Barrow
Jake Beckley
Cool Papa Bell
Chief Bender
Yogi Berra
Jim Bottomley
Lou Boudreau
Roger Bresnahan
Lou Brock
Dan Brouthers
Three Finger Brown
Morgan Bulkeley
Jesse Burkett
Roy Campanella
Max Carey
Alexander Cartwright
Henry Chadwick
Frank Chance
Happy Chandler
Oscar Charleston
John Chesbro
Fred Clarke
John Clarkson
Roberto Clemente
Ty Cobb
Mickey Cochrane
Eddie Collins
James Collins
Earle Combs
Charles Comiskey
Jocko Conlan
Tom Connolly
Roger Connor
Stan Coveleski
Sam Crawford
Joe Cronin
Candy Cummings
Kiki Cuyler
Ray Dandridge
Dizzy Dean
Ed Delahanty
Bill Dickey
Martin Dihigo
Joe DiMaggio
Bobby Doerr

Don Drysdale
Hugh Duffy
Billy Evans
John Evers
Buck Ewing
Urban Faber
Bob Feller
Rick Ferrell
Elmer Flick
Whitey Ford
Rube Foster
Jimmy Foxx
Ford Frick
Frank Frisch
Pud Galvin
Lou Gehrig
Charlie Gehringer
Bob Gibson
Josh Gibson
Warren Giles
Lefty Gomez
Goose Goslin
Curt Gowdy
Hank Greenberg
Clark Griffith
Burleigh Grimes
Lefty Grove
Chick Hafey
Jesse Haines
Bill Hamilton
Will Harridge
Bucky Harris
Gabby Hartnett
Harry Heilmann
Billy Herman
Harry Hooper
Rogers Hornsby
Waite Hoyt
Cal Hubbard
Carl Hubbell
Miller Huggins
Catfish Hunter
Monte Irvin
Travis Jackson
Hugh Jennings
Ban Johnson
Byron Johnson
Walter Johnson
William Johnson
Addie Joss
Al Kaline
Tim Keefe
Willie Keeler
George Kell
Joe Kelley

George Kelly
King Kelly
Harmon Killebrew
Ralph Kiner
Chuck Klein
Bill Klem
Sandy Koufax
Nap Lajoie
Kenesaw Mountain Landis
Bob Lemon
Buck Leonard
Fred Lindstrom
Pop Lloyd
Ernie Lombardi
Al Lopez
Ted Lyons
Joe McCarthy
Tom McCarthy
Willie McCovey
Joe McGinnity
John McGraw
Connie Mack
Bill McKechnie
Larry MacPhail
Mickey Mantle
Heinie Manush
Rabbit Maranville
Juan Marichal
Rube Marquard
Eddie Mathews
Christy Mathewson
Willie Mays
Joe Medwick
Johnny Mize
Stan Musial
Kid Nichols
Jim O'Rourke
Mel Ott
Satchel Paige
Herb Pennock
Ed Plank
Old Hoss Radbourn
Pee Wee Reese
Sam Rice
Branch Rickey
Eppa Rixey
Robin Roberts
Brooks Robinson
Frank Robinson
Jackie Robinson
Wilbert Robinson
Edd Roush
Red Ruffing
Amos Rusie
(continued)

Babe Ruth	Bill Terry	George Weiss
Ray Schalk	Sam Thompson	Mickey Welch
Joe Sewell	Joe Tinker	Zach Wheat
Al Simmons	Pie Traynor	Hoyt Wilhelm
George Sisler	Dazzy Vance	Billy Williams
Enos Slaughter	Arky Vaughan	Ted Williams
Ken Smith	Rube Waddell	Hack Wilson
Duke Snider	Honus Wagner	George Wright
Warren Spahn	Bobby Wallace	Harry Wright
Albert Spalding	Ed Walsh	Early Wynn
Tris Speaker	Lloyd Waner	Tom Yawkey
Willie Stargell	Paul Waner	Cy Young
Casey Stengel	John Ward	Ross Youngs

games at home, and a five-hit shutout by Bret Saberhagen won the finale, 11-0. On Oct. 16, the Royals had won the American League pennant against the Toronto Blue Jays four games to three and the Cardinals had won the National League pennant against the Los Angeles Dodgers four games to two.

Oct. 27 The 16th **New York City Marathon** was won by Orlando Pizzolato of Italy, gaining his second consecutive win with a time of 2 hrs., 11 min., 34 sec. The first woman finisher was Grete Waitz of Norway, who picked up her seventh win with a time of 2 hrs., 28 min., 34 sec.

Nov. In the **NCAA women's soccer title** match, George Mason U. defeated North Carolina 2-0, ending North Carolina's three-year reign.

Dec. 7 The **Heisman Trophy** for outstanding college football player of 1985 was voted to Auburn running back Bo Jackson.

Dec. 14 In the **NCAA soccer title match,** UCLA defeated American U. 1-0, at Seattle, Wash., scoring the only goal of the game in the eighth overtime period. This was the longest college soccer game in U.S. history.

1986

For the first time, the **men's world volleyball championship** was won by a U.S. team. The team also won the World Cup in 1985 and the gold medal at the 1984 Olympics. Together, these events constitute the triple crown of volleyball, and the USSR is the only other country to accomplish this feat.

The U.S. **national racquetball championship** was won by Mike Yellen of Southfield, Mich., for the fourth consecutive time. This tied the record for consecutive wins held by Marty Hogan of St. Louis, Mo.

Every **women's professional racquetball** tournament this year was won by Lynn Adams, of Costa Mesa, Calif. Adams's perfect season was unparalleled in racquetball history.

The **U.S. Handball Association national open singles championship** was won by Naty Alvarado, of Hesperia, Calif. He beat Vern Roberts, Jr., of Tucson, Ariz., 21-15 and 21-4. This was Alvarado's fifth consecutive title, his eighth overall, and one short of Joe Platak's record, set in the 1940s. Peanut Motal repeated her 1985 victory in the women's competition, this time winning out over Rosemary Bellini of New York City.

In the final round of the **President's Cup tennis tournament,** played in England, the U.S. amateur champion, Kevin McCollum, lost to the British amateur champion, Alan Lovell.

The second **World Cup women's lacrosse championship tournament** was held at Swarthmore College, with teams representing England, Scotland, Wales, Canada, Australia, and the U.S. In the final round, the U.S. team lost to Australia 4-3 and 10-7.

Joe Murphy, a Canadian studying at Michigan State U., became the first U.S. college hockey player to be the number one draft choice of an NHL team.

Jan. 1 In **college football bowl games,** the results were Texas A&M 36, Auburn 16 in the Cotton Bowl; Oklahoma 25, Penn State 10 in the Orange Bowl; UCLA 45, Iowa 28 in the Rose Bowl; and Tennessee 35, Miami (Fla.) 7 in the Sugar Bowl. This season both the AP and UPI polls selected Oklahoma as national collegiate champion of 1985.

Jan. 8 The **Baseball Hall of Fame** elected Willie McCovey in his first year of eligibility. On Mar. 10, Bobby Doerr and Ernie "Schnozz" Lombardi were also voted in.

Jan. 17 The **WBA heavyweight boxing championship** was won by Tim Witherspoon in a 15-round decision over Tony Tubbs in Atlanta, Ga.

Jan. 25 Heavyweight Mike Tyson scored his **17th consecutive knockout** when he defeated Mike Jameson in five rounds. For this stage of a boxer's career, Tyson broke the record of 16 set by Rocky Marciano. Tyson was 19 years old and had been a professional only since Mar. 1985. He ran his string of knockouts to 19 before he had to settle for a ten-round decision over James "Quick" Tillie.

Jan. 26 **Super Bowl XX** was won by the Chicago Bears (NFC), who defeated the New England Patriots (AFC) 46-10. The Bears had beaten the Los Angeles Rams 24-0 for the NFC title on Jan. 11. The following day, the Patriots defeated the Miami Dolphins 31-14 for the AFC title.

Feb. 6-8 **U.S. figure skating championships** were won in Uniondale, N.Y., by Brian Boitano, men's singles; Debi Thomas, women's singles; Gillian Wachsman and Todd Waggoner, pairs; and Renee Roca and Donald Adair, dance. Thomas was the first black to win a singles championship.

Feb. 12 Josh Thompson of Colorado became the first American to win a medal in the **world biathlon championships.** He finished second and took the silver medal at Lake Placid, N.Y.

Feb. 12 At the **Westminster Kennel Club** dog show, Ch. Marjetta National Acclaim, a pointer owned by Mike Zollo of Bernardsville, N.J., took best-in-show.

Feb. 28 **Seven baseball players were penalized** by Peter Ueberroth, commissioner of baseball, for past involvement with drugs. The seven were given a choice of a year's suspension or a contribution of 10% of one year's salary to drug-abuse programs plus performance of 100 hrs. of drug-abuse-related community service over two years and submission to random testing for drug use. All chose the latter alternative.

Mar. 17-22 The **women's world figure skating championship** was won by Debi Thomas, of San Jose, Calif. She was the first black to win the title. Thomas beat two-time winner Katarina Witt, of East Germany. Brian Boitano, of Sunnyvale, Calif., won the men's title when he alone of all the contenders brought off a successful triple-axel jump.

Mar. 22 The WBC **heavyweight boxing championship** was won by Trevor Berbick in a 12-round decision over Pinklon Thomas in Las Vegas, Nev.

Mar. 30 The **NCAA women's basketball championship** was won by Texas, defeating USC by a score of 97-81.

Mar. 31 The **NCAA men's basketball championship** was won by Louisville, defeating Duke 72-69. The Cardinals had won in 1980 as well, thus making coach Denny Crum the first to coach teams that won two NCAA titles in the 1980s.

Apr. 2 The **three-point field goal** in men's basketball, made from a minimum distance of 16 ft., 9 in. from the basket, was adopted by the NCAA. The association also approved use of instant TV replays to check scoring and timing decisions.

Apr. 3-5 At the **NCAA men's swimming championships** in Indianapolis, Ind., Matt Biondi of the U. of California men's swimming team lowered the NCAA 50-yard freestyle record to 19.22 sec. Joe Bottom of USC in 1977 had been the first to break the 20-sec. barrier. Pablo Morales of Stanford set a new record of 46.26 sec. for the 100-yard butterfly, and California set a new record of 2:53.02 in the 400-yard freestyle relay.

Apr. 4 **Wayne Gretzky** of the National Hockey League's Edmonton Oilers raised his season's scoring record, set in the 1981-1982 season, from 212 points to 214.

Apr. 11 A new **sailing record** for a solo nonstop circumnavigation of the globe was set by Dodge Morgan, 54, who completed his voyage in St. George, Bermuda, aboard his 60-ft. sloop *American Promise.* Morgan, the first American to accomplish this feat, had left Bermuda on Nov. 12, 1985, sailed 27,000 mi. in 150 days. The previous record had been 292 days.

Apr. 13 The **Masters golf tournament** was won for a record sixth time by Jack Nicklaus, who at 46 thus became the oldest golfer to win the Masters. His sensational closing nine on the last day, caddied by his son, caught Tom Kite and a faltering Greg Norman, for a dramatic match finish.

Apr. 21 The 90th **Boston Marathon** was won by Bob de Castella of Australia, with a time of 2 hrs., 7 min., 51 sec. The winner in the women's division was Ingrid Kristiansen of Norway, with a time of 2 hrs., 24 min., 55 sec.

Apr. 29 **Roger Clemens,** pitcher for the Boston Red Sox, set the major league record for strikeouts when he fanned 20 Seattle Mariners at Fenway Park, Boston.

Apr. 30 A new **world record for somersaulting** was claimed by Ashrita Furman, 31, of Queens, N.Y. In 10 hrs,. 40 min., he somersaulted the 12-mi., 390-yard route of Paul Revere's famous ride in 1775. It took 8800 rolls to accomplish the feat.

May 2 An **expedition to the North Pole** was completed by six U.S. and Canadian adventurers, the first expedition since 1909 to reach the pole assisted only by dogs. They made the 500-mi. trek from Ward Hunt Island, Canada, in 56 days and returned from the pole by airplane.

May 3 The 112th **Kentucky Derby** was won by Ferdinand, with a time of 2:02⅘. The jockey was Willie Shoemaker, 54, who picked up his fourth Derby win and became the oldest jockey to win the classic race.

May 16-24 The **NHL Stanley Cup** championship was won by the Montreal Canadiens, who beat the Calgary Flames four games to one. In the quarterfinals, the Flames had defeated the defending champions, the Edmonton Oilers, led by Wayne Gretzky, in a hard-fought seven-game series.

May 17 Hobart College defeated Washington, Md., in the finals of the **NCAA Division III lacrosse championships** to score the team's seventh straight title in the seven years of the event.

May 17 The 111th **Preakness Stakes** was won by Snow Chief, with a time of 1:54⅘. The jockey was Alex Solis.

May 26-June 8 The **NBA basketball championship** was won by the Boston Celtics, who won the final game 114-97 and brushed aside the Houston Rockets four games to two for the Celtics' 16th NBA title. Larry Bird won his second

Baseball is not the sport of the wealthy, it is the sport of the wage earner.

Bill Veeck

MVP playoff trophy, adding to his MVP trophy for the 1985-1986 season.

May 31 The 70th **Indianapolis 500** auto race was won by Bobby Rahal, completing the 500-mi. course in 2 hrs., 55 min., 43.48 sec., at an average speed of 170.722 mph, a new record. It was the first time the full race was run in under 3 hours. Originally scheduled for May 25, the race had been postponed because of rain. This was the first postponement since 1915.

May 31-June 2 The U.S. national championship in **wild-water canoeing** was won by Jon Lugbill in title events held on the Ocoee R., Tenn. John Fishburn won the wild-water kayaking championship, and Chris Doughty won the men's slalom kayaking event. In the women's division, Cathy Hearn won the slalom and wild-water kayaking titles.

June The **17th Sunfish Worlds** were held on Narragansett Bay, R.I. The largest fleet in the world is claimed for this fiberglass surfboard sailboat—over 230,000 worldwide.

June The **NCAA lacrosse championship** was won by North Carolina, winner over Virginia in overtime 10-9.

June 1 The **LPGA golf tournament** was won by Pat Bradley, who became the first to win all four of the top women's tournaments. She had won the du Maurier classic in 1980 and 1985, the U.S. Open in 1981, and the Nabisco Dinah Shore on Apr. 6, 1986. On May 18 she had become the first woman to surpass $2,000,000 in career earnings.

June 7 The 118th **Belmont Stakes** was won by Danzig Connection with a time of 2:29⅘, the slowest time since 1980. The jockey was Chris McCarron. It was the fifth straight Belmont victory for trainer Woody Stephens.

June 8 In the **longest nine-inning game** in American League baseball history, the Baltimore Orioles beat the New York Yankees 18-9 at Yankee Stadium in 4 hrs., 16 min.

June 15 The **U.S. Open golf tournament** was won by Raymond Floyd, 43, who beat Chip

Beck and Lanny Wadkins by two strokes to become the oldest golfer to win the Open.

June 19 **Len Bias,** star forward for the U. of Maryland's basketball team, died of a heart attack, reported to have been brought on by using cocaine at a party celebrating his signing of a lucrative contract with the Boston Celtics.

June 21 **Roger Clemens,** Boston Red Sox (AL) ace pitcher, became the seventh pitcher in major league history to start a season with 13 straight wins, beating the Baltimore Orioles 7-2 at Boston. On Apr. 29, Clemens had struck out 20, a major league record, in a Boston win over the Seattle Mariners.

Summer **Wayne Gretzky** was named most valuable player in the NHL for the seventh consecutive year. Paul Coffey won the best defenseman award, and Mike Bossy won the Lady Byng Trophy for sportsmanship. John Van Liesbrouck won the Vezina Trophy for best goaltender.

July The **world lacrosse championship,** held every four years, was won by the U.S. team, which successively beat Canada 21-11, Australia 18-12, England 32-8, and Canada in the final round, 18-9.

July 5-6 At the **Wimbledon** tennis championships in England, Martina Navratilova bested Hana Mandlikova of Czechoslovakia to win the women's singles title, her fifth consecutive and seventh career win in this event. Navratilova teamed with Pam Shriver to win the women's doubles. Ken Flach and Kathy Jordan won the mixed doubles.

July 5-20 In the first **Goodwill Games,** held in Moscow, the Soviet Union dominated the games with 118 gold medals and 241 in all. The U.S. was second with 42 gold and a total of 142. The Goodwill Games were the idea of the American entrepreneur and sports promoter Ted Turner.

July 7 The **U.S. Open tennis singles championships** were won by Martina Navratilova over Helena Sukova of Czechoslovakia in the women's division and by Ivan Lendl of Czechoslovakia over his countryman, Miloslav Mecir, in the men's division.

July 14 The **U.S. Women's Open golf tournament** was won by Jane Geddes in an 18-hole playoff with Sally Little.

July 15 The **baseball all-star game** was won by the American League, defeating the National League 3-2 at Houston. Roger Clemens, enjoy-

ing a 14-game winning streak, opened the game with three perfect innings of pitching for the American League. Dwight Gooden was the National League's losing pitcher.

July 27 Greg LeMond became the **first American to win the Tour de France,** the best-known bicycle racing event in the world. LeMond covered the 2500 mi. over-the-road route in 110 hrs., 35 min., 19 sec., beating his nearest competitor by 3 min., 10 sec. The race began on July 4.

July 29 The **United States Football League** lost a suit it had brought against the National Football League in federal court in New York. The jury found that the NFL had violated antitrust laws, as the USFL claimed, but the jury awarded damages of only $1. The USFL had sought as much as $1,690,000,000 on the grounds that the NFL had used monopoly power "to control prices and exclude competition" in the "relevant market" of pro football.

Aug. The U.S. **women's field hockey** team defeated the team representing England at Leicester, England, 2-1 and 3-1. The English team had earlier finished in fifth place in the sixth international World Cup tournament.

Aug. 1-2 A new **world's record for the women's heptathlon** was set by Jackie Joyner, who racked up 7158 points at Houston, Tex.

Aug. 2 The 61st **Hambletonian Stakes** was won by Nuclear Kosmos in straight heats, winning the first by a neck. Ulf Thoresen was the driver.

Aug. 4 The **USFL canceled its 1986 season** following the adverse court decision of July 29 in its suit against the NFL. The league had completed its spring 1985 season and had planned to change to a fall season in 1986 and compete head-on with the NFL.

Aug. 11 The **PGA golf tournament** was won by Bob Tway, who sank a spectacular bunker shot on the final hole to edge out Greg Norman.

Sept. 12-14 The **U.S. Open tennis singles championships** were won by Martina Navratilova over Steffi Graf of West Germany in the women's division and by Ivan Lendl over Mats Wilander of Sweden in the men's division. It was Lendl's third consecutive U.S. Open win. Navratilova, in winning the women's doubles and mixed doubles events as well as the singles, became the first player to top the $1,000,000 mark in career winnings in U.S. Open competition. She also became the first triple winner at

Football
SUPER BOWL GAMES

GAME	YEAR	WINNER	LOSER	SCORE
I	1967	Green Bay Packers (NFL)	Kansas City Chiefs (AFL)	35–10
II	1968	Green Bay Packers (NFL)	Oakland Raiders (AFL)	33–14
III	1969	New York Jets (AFL)	Baltimore Colts (NFL)	16–7
IV	1970	Kansas City Chiefs (AFL)	Minnesota Vikings (NFL)	23–7
V	1971	Baltimore Colts (AFC)	Dallas Cowboys (NFC)	16–13
VI	1972	Dallas Cowboys (NFC)	Miami Dolphins (AFC)	24–3
VII	1973	Miami Dolphins (AFC)	Washington Redskins (NFC)	14–7
VIII	1974	Miami Dolphins (AFC)	Minnesota Vikings (NFC)	24–7
IX	1975	Pittsburgh Steelers (AFC)	Minnesota Vikings (NFC)	16–6
X	1976	Pittsburgh Steelers (AFC)	Dallas Cowboys (NFC)	21–17
XI	1977	Oakland Raiders (AFC)	Minnesota Vikings (NFC)	32–14
XII	1978	Dallas Cowboys (NFC)	Denver Broncos (AFC)	27–10
XIII	1979	Pittsburgh Steelers (AFC)	Dallas Cowboys (NFC)	35–31
XIV	1980	Pittsburgh Steelers (AFC)	Los Angeles Rams (NFC)	31–19
XV	1981	Oakland Raiders (AFC)	Philadelphia Eagles (NFC)	27–10
XVI	1982	San Francisco 49ers (NFC)	Cincinnati Bengals (AFC)	26–21
XVII	1983	Washington Redskins (NFC)	Miami Dolphins (AFC)	27–17
XVIII	1984	Los Angeles Raiders (AFC)	Washington Redskins (NFC)	38–9
XIX	1985	San Francisco 49ers (NFC)	Miami Dolphins (AFC)	38–16
XX	1986	Chicago Bears (NFC)	New England Patriots (AFC)	46–10
XXI	1987	New York Giants (NFC)	Denver Broncos (AFC)	39–20
XXII	1988	Washington Redskins (NFC)	Denver Broncos (AFC)	42–10

a Grand Slam event since Billie Jean King's triple win at Wimbledon in 1973.

Sept. 28 **Jim Kropfeld** in the turbine-powered *Miss Budweiser,* owned by Bernie Little, won the final heat of the season's final event for unlimited hydroplanes sponsored by the American Power Boat Association. He edged out defending champion Chip Hanauer by 31 points, the closest margin since 1958. The race was run at Boulder City, Nev.

Oct. 17 Detroit dedicated a **memorial to Joe Louis,** one of boxing's all-time greats. It was an enormous black fist cast in bronze as a tribute to a fighter who had grown up in Detroit. The memorial, sculpted by Robert Graham, was paid for by a grant from *Sports Illustrated* magazine.

Oct. 18-27 The **World Series** was won by the New York Mets (NL), who defeated the Boston Red Sox (AL) four games to three. New York lost the first two games at home, and the Sox lost the next two in Boston before winning game five to take a 3-2 advantage. The sixth game, played in New York, went to the Mets 6-5 in the tenth,

after Boston had taken a 5-3 lead. New York scored the winning run with two outs in the bottom of the tenth. On Oct. 15, the Mets had beaten the Houston Astros four games to two for the National League pennant and the Red Sox had defeated the California Angels four games to three for the American League championship.

Nov. 2 The 17th **New York City Marathon** was won by Gianni Poli of Italy with a time of 2 hrs., 11 min., 6 sec. Among the women, Grete Waitz of Norway won for the eighth time. Her time was 2 hrs., 28 min., 6 sec. A legless Vietnam veteran, Bob Wieland, using his arms to propel himself, completed the full marathon course in 98 hrs., 48 min., 17 sec.

Nov. 22 The WBC **heavyweight boxing championship** was won by Mike Tyson, who knocked out Trevor Berbick in the second round at Las Vegas, Nev. Tyson, 20 years old, became the youngest heavyweight champion in boxing history.

Nov. 22 George Branham III became the **first black champion in professional bowling**

when he defeated Mark Roth 195-191 in the title game of the Professional Bowlers Association Brunswick Memorial World Open.

Dec. A record for **career rodeo earnings** was set by Tom Ferguson, who reached a total of $1,049,744. He also shared with Larry Mahan the record of six champion world cowboy titles. Ferguson won the title in six consecutive years, 1974-1979; Mahan won in 1966-1970 and 1973.

Dec. 6 The **Heisman Trophy** for outstanding college football player of the year was voted to U. of Miami quarterback Vinny Testaverde.

Dec. 12 The WBA **heavyweight boxing championship** was won by James "Bonecrusher" Smith, who knocked out Tim Witherspoon in the first round of a bout in New York City.

Dec. 14-23 The **first around-the-world flight on one load of fuel** was completed at Edwards Air Force Base, Calif., when the experimental plane *Voyager* landed. The plane, which took off on Dec. 4, covered 25,012 miles in 216 hrs., 3 min., 44 sec. The pilot was Richard G. Rutan, and the copilot was Jeana Yeager. The very light aircraft featured an H-shaped design.

Dec. 31 The end of the year saw **new records set by harness racing drivers.** Michel Lachance set a new mark of most races won in a year, 770. Hervé Filion reached all-time records of 9789 wins and purses totaling $51,542,763.

1987

Jan. 1-2 In **college football bowl games,** the results were Ohio State 28, Texas A&M 12 in the Cotton Bowl; Oklahoma 42, Arkansas 8 in the Orange Bowl; Arizona State 22, Michigan 15 in the Rose Bowl; and Nebraska 30, Louisiana State 15 in the Sugar Bowl. Both the AP and UPI polls chose Penn State as national champion for 1986 after Pennsylvania's Nittany Lions, in a battle of previously undefeated teams, triumphed over Miami (Fla.) 14-10 in the Fiesta Bowl on Jan. 2.

Jan. 25 **Super Bowl XXI** was won by the New York Giants (NFC), defeating the Denver Broncos (AFC) 39-20. On Jan. 11, the Giants had won the NFC title by defeating the Washington Red-

skins 17-0 and Denver had won the AFC championship by defeating the Cleveland Browns 23-20 in overtime.

Jan. 31-Feb. 4 The **America's Cup** was regained by the U.S. when the American challenger *Stars & Stripes,* skippered by Dennis Connor of San Diego, Calif., defeated the Australian yacht *Kookaburra III* in four straight races at Freemantle, Australia. Connor, the losing skipper in 1983, thus became the first American skipper to lose and regain the yachting trophy.

Feb. 5-7 **U.S. figure skating championships** were won in Tacoma, Wash., by Brian Boitano, men's singles; Jill Trenary, women's singles; Jill Watson and Peter Oppegard, pairs; and Suzanne Semanick and Scott Gregory, dance.

Feb. 8 Nancy Lopez earned a place in the **LPGA Hall of Fame** by winning the 35th tournament victory of her career. She won her first pro tournament in 1978 and was the 11th player to qualify for the LPGA Hall of Fame.

Feb. 10 At the **Westminster Kennel Club** dog show, Ch. Covy Tucker Hill's Manhattan, a German shepherd owned by Shirlee Braunstein, took best-in-show.

Feb. 24 A **world record ice-fishing catch** was made by Omer J. Lebel of Van Buren, Maine, when he caught a brook trout weighing 8 lbs., 4 oz.

Feb. 25 The NCAA ruled that **Southern Methodist U.** could not field a football team this year because athletic officials had violated NCAA rules by paying about $61,000 to players. This, the stiffest penalty ever imposed on a football program, also provided that in 1988 SMU could play only seven games, all away from home and thus earning no revenue for SMU.

Feb. 26 Michael Spinks was **stripped of his IBF heavyweight championship.** The action was taken because he failed to defend his title within nine months of winning the crown from Larry Holmes on Apr. 19, 1986, thus failing to live up to IBF rules.

Feb. 27 Michael Conley set a new **world record for the triple jump** at Madison Square Garden, New York City, when he hopped, stepped, and jumped 58 ft., 3¼ in.

Mar. The **Iditarod,** a grueling 1157-mi. dogsled race, was won by Susan Butcher, 31-year-old breeder and trainer of Alaskan huskies, for the second year in a row. The Iditarod is run from Anchorage to Nome, Alaska. One of two women in a field of 63, Butcher lowered the race record by 13 hrs. She completed the course in 11 days, 2 hrs., 5 min., and 13 sec.

Mar. 7 The **combined WBA and WBC heavyweight boxing championship** was won by Mike Tyson, who defeated James "Bonecrusher" Smith by a unanimous decision in a 15-round bout at Las Vegas, Nev.

Mar. 15 Don Pooley made the **most valuable single shot in golf history** when he aced the 192-yard 17th hole at the Hertz Bay Hill Classic in Orlando, Fla. The feat brought a prize of $1,000,000. Half of it went to Pooley and half to the Arnold Palmer Children's Hospital. It was payable over 20 years. The offer had been made for three years by the Hertz Corporation.

Mar. 28 Setting a new **college basketball attendance record** before 64,959 fans, Indiana defeated the U. of Nevada, Las Vegas, 97-93 in the semifinals of the NCAA championship in the New Orleans Superdome.

Mar. 29 The **NCAA women's basketball championship,** held in Austin, Tex., was won by Tennessee over Louisiana Tech 67-44.

Mar. 30 The **NCAA men's basketball championship** was won by Indiana, defeating Syracuse 74-73. Hoosier guard Calvin Smith was voted the outstanding player among the final four teams.

Apr. 12 The **Masters golf tournament** was won by Larry Mize on the second hole of a three-way playoff, when he sank a 50-yard wedge shot to defeat Greg Norman and Seve Ballesteros.

Apr. 17 **Julius Erving** of the Philadelphia 76ers became the third player to score 30,000 points in a pro basketball career. Erving, his retirement announced, scored 38 points while his team was losing to the Indiana Pacers in Philadelphia. Wilt Chamberlain and Kareem Abdul-Jabbar, earlier known as Lew Alcindor, are the others who reached the 30,000 mark.

Apr. 18 An **unconscious sky diver was rescued** by another jumper. Debbie Williams was knocked out by colliding with another sky diver. Noticing her plight, Gregory Robertson dived to reach her and yanked open her ripcord when she was less than 3500 ft. from the ground. Williams was seriously injured, but Robertson resumed sky diving the same day.

Apr. 18 The **Kenduskeag Stream Canoe Race** was won for the sixth straight year by Robert Land, of New Brunswick, Canada, with a time of 2 hrs., 8 min., 37 sec. for the 16.5-mi. stretch through rock-infested waters to Bangor, Maine.

Apr. 20 The 91st **Boston Marathon** was won by Toshihiko Seko of Japan, with a time of 2 hrs., 11 min., 50 sec. The winner in the women's division was Rosa Mota of Portugal, with a time of 2 hrs., 25 min., 21 sec.

May 2 The 113th **Kentucky Derby** was won by Alysheba, with a time of 2:03⅖. The jockey was Chris McCarron.

May 3 The **richest prize in PGA tour history,** $225,000, was won by Paul Azinger when he captured the Panasonic Las Vegas golf tournament. In addition, Scott Hoch received a $118,299 Rolls-Royce for a hole-in-one at the 17th hole.

May 10-18 The **NHL Stanley Cup** championship was won by the Edmonton Oilers, who beat the Philadelphia Flyers four games to three.

May 16 The 112th **Preakness Stakes** was won by Alysheba, with a time of 1:55⅘. The jockey was Chris McCarron.

May 24 The **LPGA championship** was won by Jane Geddes by one stroke.

May 24 A record **10,000th winning harness race** was won by Hervé Filion, a French-Canadian driver, at Yonkers Raceway, N.Y.

May 24 The 71st **Indianapolis 500 auto race** was won by Al Unser, completing the 500-mi. course in 3 hrs., 4 min., 59.147 sec. In winning this race for the fourth time, Unser became the oldest Indy winner, five days short of his 48th birthday.

June 2-14 The **NBA basketball championship** was won by the Los Angeles Lakers over the Boston Celtics four games to two.

June 4 The **longest winning streak in track history** ended when Edwin Moses lost a 400-m. hurdles race in Madrid to Danny Harris, another American. Moses had won 122 consecutive races, his last loss coming on Aug. 26, 1977, when he was beaten by Harald Schmid of West Germany. Moses holds the world record of 47.02 sec. for the 400-m. hurdle event.

June 6 The **119th Belmont Stakes** was won by Bet Twice by 14 lengths, with a time of 2:28⅖. The jockey was Craig Perret. In addition, Bet Twice won $1,000,000 in the first Triple Crown participation bonus. Bet Twice finished second in both the Kentucky Derby and the Preakness Stakes. Alysheba had won those two races but finished fourth in the Belmont. On a 5-3-1 point basis, Bet Twice earned 11 points to Alysheba's 10. Had one horse won all three races, and thereby the Triple Crown, the bonus would have been $5,000,000.

June 11 The gold medal for the **women's World Bowling Championship** was won for the third straight time by the U.S. team in Helsinki, Finland. The American women finished with a record six-game total of 6011 and rolled a record final game of 1063.

June 14 The winning streak of **Juan "Chi Chi" Rodriguez** in senior golf tournaments was ended when Gary Player defeated him by one stroke in the Senior Tournament Players Championship. Rodriguez had already won six tourneys in 1987, including an unprecedented four in succession. In two years on the senior tour, he had won $681,000, more than any other player.

June 15 In a bout promoted as deciding the **heavyweight championship,** Michael Spinks knocked out Gerry Cooney in the fifth round of a scheduled 15-round fight. The WBA and the WBC said they would not recognize the winner as champion, but several state boxing commissions said they would.

June 16 For the first time in a single meet, **three long jumpers cleared 28 ft.** at the USA/Mobil Outdoor Track and Field Championships at San Jose, Calif. The winner, with a jump of 28 ft., 4½ in., was Carl Lewis. He thus extended his winning streak in track and field to 50 in six years. Lewis also won the 200-m. dash.

June 21 The **U.S. Open golf tournament** was won by Scott Simpson, who defeated Tom Watson by one stroke.

June 23 The **oldest living Olympic medalist in the U.S.** celebrated his 95th birthday by jogging along Fifth Ave. in New York City. He was Abel Kiviat, who won the silver medal in the 1500-m. race at the 1912 Olympics. He once held the records for 600 yards, 1000 yards, and the mile, all at the same time.

June 30 Most recommendations of an **NCAA Presidents Commission** were rejected by college sports officials at a meeting in Dallas, Tex. Among the recommendations voted down were reductions in the number of football and basketball scholarships allowed. Even proposals to study sports problems were put off to 1989.

July 13 The 50-year-old **Texas Prison Rodeo** will

not be held anymore, prison officials announced. In the rodeo, cowboy convicts competed for cash prizes. The arena was said to be in need of $800,000 worth of repairs, and the money was not available.

July 14 The **baseball all-star game,** held in Oakland, Calif., was won in extra innings by the National League, defeating the American League 2-0 on a two-run triple by Expos left fielder Tim Raines in the 13th inning. The 3 hr., 39 min. contest was dominated by excellent pitching, which compounded the difficulty hitters had in seeing pitches in the twilight conditions that prevailed in the game time.

July 21 Lady's Secret became the **richest filly or mare in racing history** when she won a race at Monmouth Park, Oceanport, N.J. The victory brought total winnings to $3,015,764, surpassing the record set by All Along. Lady's Secret was sired by Secretariat, the Triple Crown winner in 1973.

July 22 **Television sports fans favored pro football** over baseball, the second most popular sport among watchers, according to a 1986 survey by Simmons Market Research. Pro football was watched frequently by 63,200,000 people, with baseball close behind at 62,700,000. The two leaders were followed by college football, 48,900,000; boxing, 37,200,000; and college basketball, 36,200,000.

July 25 Secretary of Commerce **Malcolm Baldrige,** 64, died as the result of a rodeo accident at Walnut Creek, Calif. An enthusiastic amateur rodeo performer, he was practicing for a steer-roping at the Contra Costa County Fair Grounds when his horse reared and fell on him. Baldrige died in a hospital soon after the accident.

July 26 The **Baseball Hall of Fame** inducted three new members: Jim "Catfish" Hunter, Billy Williams, and Ray Dandridge.

July 28 The **U.S. Women's Open golf tournament** was won by Laura Davies of Great Britain in an 18-hole, three-way playoff with JoAnne Carner and Ayako Okamoto. The tournament was the longest men's or women's Open ever, lasting six days because of the playoff and the cancellation of one day's play due to heavy thunderstorms.

July 29 The Dallas Cowboys became the first NFL team to **test its personnel for AIDS.** The testing was described as voluntary and the results as confidential. All tests administered were reported to be negative.

July 30 Smith College will have the nation's **first competitive collegiate croquet court,** the *New York Times* reported. The court will be arranged for the English version, not the American version, of the game. Colleges are taking up the sport, and the New England Collegiate Croquet Association has been formed with a dozen member schools.

Aug. 1 The unified **heavyweight boxing championship** was won by Mike Tyson, who earned a unanimous 12-round decision over Tony Tucker at Las Vegas, Nev. Tyson held the World Boxing Association and World Boxing Council titles, and Tucker was the champion of the International Boxing Federation. Tyson thus became the first undisputed titleholder since Feb. 1978, when Leon Spinks beat Muhammad Ali.

Aug. 2 In the **fastest race in Indy car history,** Michael Andretti won the Marlboro 500 at Michigan International Speedway in Brooklyn, Mich., with an average speed of 171.490 mph. This bettered the mark of 170.722 mph set by Bobby Rahal when he won the Indianapolis 500 in 1986. One of the drivers who lost to Andretti was his father, Mario.

Aug. 8 The 62nd **Hambletonian Stakes** was won by Mack Lobell in two heats. The horse set a world record for two heats of 3:37⅗. The driver was John Campbell. On Aug. 21, Mark Lobell set a world trotting record for the mile by turning in a time of 1:52⅕ at the Illinois State Fairgrounds in Springfield. The previous record was 1:53⅖, set by Prakas in 1985.

Aug. 8-23 At the tenth **Pan-American games** in Indianapolis, Ind., the U.S. won 369 medals, including 168 gold medals. Cuba was second with 75 gold medals and 175 in all, and Canada was third with 30 and 162. For the U.S., track star Jackie Joyner-Kersee tied the world record for the long jump at 24 ft., 5.5 in., and Jeff Kubiak set a record for the games of 2 min., 17.62 sec. in the 200-m. breaststroke.

Aug. 9 The **PGA championship** was won by Larry Nelson, who defeated Lanny Wadkins on the first hole of a sudden death playoff. The two had tied at 287 for the four rounds, only one under par, the highest winning score since the event became a stroke-play, 72-hole tournament in 1958.

Aug. 29 **Little League baseball** celebrated the 40th anniversary of its world series. It claims 2,500,000 participants in 16,000 chartered programs. THe world championship was won by Hua Lian, the Taiwanese team, beating the Irvine, Calif., team 21-1 at Williamsport, Pa. Teams from the Far East had won 17 Little League championships in the last 21 years. It was Taiwan's seventh win in 11 years. Taiwanese teams had won 12 championships since 1969.

Aug. 31 A new **record for single-season earnings in golf** was set by Curtis Strange when he won the NEC World Series of Golf, bringing his total to $697,385. This surpassed the mark of $635,296 earned by Greg Norman of Australia in 1986.

Sept. 12 The women's division of the **U.S. Open tennis singles championship** was won by Martina Navratilova over Steffi Graf of West Germany. It was Navratilova's fourth victory in this event in five years. After a 24-hour rain delay, Ivan Lendl on Sept. 14 defeated Mats Wilander of Sweden for the men's title.

Sept. 21 Major league baseball clubs were found to have **violated their 1985 agreement with the Major League Players Association** when club owners acted in concert to block free agents from changing teams. Thomas T. Roberts, arbitrator in the case, found that no clubs would sign free-agent players unless the clubs they played for in 1985 indicated lack of interest in retaining the players.

Sept. 29 A new **major league record for grand slam home runs** was set by Don Mattingly of the New York Yankees when he hit his sixth of the season. The opposing pitcher was Bruce Hurst of the Boston Red Sox. In July, Mattingly had tied a major league record by hitting home runs in eight consecutive games.

Oct. 10 A **record-breaking losing streak** for a Division I college football team was set by Columbia when the Lions lost to Princeton 38-8. The loss was Columbia's thirty-fifth consecutive defeat on the gridiron since Oct. 15, 1983, when the Lions beat Yale. After the loss to Princeton, Columbia continued its 1987 losing season until, on Nov. 21, 1987, the team's schedule concluded with a 19-16 defeat by Brown. As a result, Columbia's string of games without a victory stood at forty-one. The previous record for consecutive Division I football games without a victory was held by Northwestern, which lost

It's really impossible for athletes to grow up.

Billie Jean King

thirty-four games between 1979 and 1982. The overall record for most consecutive losses is held by a Division III team, Macalester College, which suffered fifty consecutive defeats between 1974 and 1980.

Oct. 15 The **NFL Players Association ended its 14-day strike,** which commenced on Sept. 22. The union failed to win significant gains. In the first week of the strike, no games were played, but after that clubs were able to field teams of players considered by fans to be below NFL standards. A poll taken by the *New York Times* and CBS after the strike ended showed that 46% of the fans sided with the owners and 26% favored the players. A factor thought to be significant in the poll was the high average pay of NFL team members, about $15,000 a game for a regular season of 16 games.

Oct. 17-25 The **World Series** was won by the Minnesota Twins (AL), who defeated the St. Louis Cardinals four games to three. In every game played, the home team won. Thus, with the Series opening in Minnesota, the Twins jumped out to a two-game lead. The next three games, played in St. Louis, were won by the Cardinals. On the teams' return to the Twins domed stadium, which provides a poor background against which to track high fly balls and with loyal hometown fans in full voice creating a din, the Cardinals folded in games six and seven. On Oct. 12, the Twins had won the American League pennant against the Detroit Tigers four games to one, and two days later the Cardinals won the National League pennant against the San Francisco Giants four games to three.

Nov. 1 The 18th **New York City Marathon** was won by Ibrahim Hussein of Kenya in the men's division with a time of 2 hrs., 11 min., 1 sec. The women's division was won by Priscilla Welch of Great Britain with a time of 2 hrs., 30 min., 17 sec.

Nov. 1 The **richest prize in tournament golf history,** $384,000, was won by Tom Watson at the $3,000,000 Nabisco Championship at San Antonio, Tex. The first place money brought Watson's total PGA tournament earnings to $4,701,629 in 17 years on the PGA tour. Although Curtis Strange finished last in this tournament, he won the title for highest golf earnings in 1987, a record $925,941.

Nov. 8 Ayako Okamoto of Japan became the **LPGA top money winner** for 1987 with a total of $466,034 when she placed second in the Mazda Japan Classic held in Hanno, Japan. She was the first non-American to finish as high as runner-up in this event. She also became the LPGA player of the year.

Nov. 13 The **fastest mile ever recorded by a trotter** on a five-eighths-mile track, 1:54⅕, was registered by Mack Lobell at Pompano Park, Fla., in the Breeders' Cup Trot. The driver was John Campbell. By winning this race, Mack Lobell became the second trotter ever to achieve world records on all three sizes of tracks. The great standardbred had set the mark of 1:52⅕ on a mile track and shares the record of 1:57⅖ on a half-mile track. The first trotter to achieve world records on all three sizes of tracks was French Chef, in 1980.

1988

Jan. 1 In **college football bowl games,** the results were Texas A&M 35, Notre Dame 10 in the Cotton Bowl; Miami 20, Oklahoma 14 in the Orange Bowl; Michigan State 20, USC 17 in the Rose Bowl; and Syracuse 16, Auburn 16 in the Sugar Bowl. The Syracuse-Auburn stalemate was the first tie in Sugar Bowl history. This year the AP and UPI polls selected Miami the national collegiate champion of 1987.

Jan. 7-9 **U.S. figure skating championships** were won in Denver, Colo., by Debi Thomas, women's singles; Brian Boitano, men's singles; Jill Watson and Peter Oppegard, pairs; Suzanne Semanick and Scott Gregory, dance.

Jan. 12 The **Baseball Hall of Fame** elected Willie Stargell, former Pittsburgh Pirate slugger, in his first year of eligibility. In his 21-year career, Stargell had recorded 475 home runs, 2232 hits, and 1540 RBIs. Induction ceremonies at Cooperstown, N.Y., were scheduled to be held on July 31.

Jan. 31 **Super Bowl XXII** was won by the Washington Redskins (NFC), defeating the Denver Broncos (AFC) 42-10. Redskin quarterback Doug Williams starred for the winners, throwing four second-quarter touchdown passes and breaking a Super Bowl record by passing for a total of 340 yards. On Jan. 17 the Broncos had beaten the Cleveland Browns 38 to 33 for the AFC championship, and the Redskins had defeated the Minnesota Vikings 17 to 10 for the NFC title.

How to Use the Index

Most index entries include a full date. The citation

> Amoros, Sandy:
> World Series catch, 1955 Sept. 28-Oct. 4

directs the reader to the year 1955 in the text and the entry under that year dated September 28-October 4.

When an index entry appears with only a year or a span of years, the corresponding text item is undated except for year or years. The citation

> Allen, Ted:
> horseshoe championships, 1937

directs the reader to an undated paragraph in the text under the year 1937. All undated paragraphs for a given year or span of years appear before the first dated entry for that time period.

Short sports biographies and *memorable sports events* are indexed by page number. The citation

> Ali, Muhammad (Cassius Clay):
> *biog.,* p. 164

directs the reader to page 164 in the text. The citation

> Ruth, Babe (George Herman):
> *memorable event,* p. 138

directs the reader to page 138 in the text.

I
n
d
e
x

**I
n
d
e
x**